THIRD EDITION

Doing Social Research

Therese L. Baker
California State University, San Marcos

McGraw-Hill College

Boston   Burr Ridge, IL   Dubuque, IA   Madison, WI   New York   San Francisco   St. Louis
Bangkok   Bogotá   Caracas   Lisbon   London   Madrid
Mexico City   Milan   New Delhi   Seoul   Singapore   Sydney   Taipei   Toronto

McGraw-Hill

A Division of The McGraw-Hill Companies

DOING SOCIAL RESEARCH
International Editions 1999

Exclusive rights by McGraw-Hill Book Co – Singapore, for manufacture and export. This book cannot be re-exported from the country to which it is consigned by McGraw-Hill.

1 2 3 4 5 6 7 8 9 10 KKP UPE 2 0 9

Library of Congress Cataloging-in-Publication Data

Baker, Therese L.
  Doing social research / Therese L. Baker. – 3rd ed.
    p.   cm.
  Includes bibliographical references and index.
  ISBN 0-07-006002-9
  1. Social sciences–Research–Methodology.   I. Title.
H62.B286   1998
300'.72–dc21   98-3563

www.mhhe.com

When ordering this title, use ISBN 0-07-116092-2

Printed in Singapore

Doing Social Research

14
-
14

THERESE L. BAKER is one of the 12 founding faculty members, and professor of sociology at California State University, San Marcos. She currently serves as program director in sociology and in social science. Born and raised in Minneapolis, she received her undergraduate education at Cornell University and graduate education at the University of Chicago. For 18 years, she was a member of the Sociology department at DePaul University in Chicago.

Her principal research interest is in the changing ways gender and ethnic differences affect the educational and career aspirations of American youth. The experience of founding a new university has encouraged an interest in access and opportunity in higher education. She has been an advisory editor for *Contemporary Sociology, The Sociological Quarterly, The American Sociologist,* and *Gender and Society.* Professor Baker has taught social research methods since 1975.

FOR JULIAN AND FAYE

This third edition of *Doing Social Research,* like the first and second, could never have been written had I not taught social research methods for years. It has grown out of my own experiences of delivering the hows and whys of doing social research to college students, first at DePaul University in Chicago and for the last nine years at California State University at San Marcos in North County, San Diego.

We took our first students at CSU, San Marcos in 1990—juniors and seniors—and, in the Spring of 1991, I offered the first Social Research Methods class at CSU, San Marcos. There was a makeshift computer lab on our temporary campus site, and an emerging library facility; I had 17 eager students, many of whom had been out of college for years. Drawing on *Doing Social Research,* the class designed for its final project a survey of the attitudes of the residents of San Marcos to the development of a new state university in their community. Since that time students in Social Research Methods have benefited from the social science research lab we have developed on campus, the Social and Behavioral Research Institute *(SBRI).* For the past three years in each semester, research methods students design a survey that is then carried out by telephone interviews in the SBRI. Once the data are collected, students use the data to carry out analyses. In this text, we will describe one of these student-led surveys.

In writing the book, I have been guided by several principles. I am convinced that the way to get students interested in social research, and to recognize what it involves, is to think seriously about some of the exciting social research studies that have already been done. To consider carefully what researchers did in carrying out their studies, and what they found out, is to begin to understand not only the techniques of social research, but also the motivation for doing it. In other words, by trying to share the experience of doing social research with previous researchers, a student can come to know why people are committed to this enterprise. For this reason, interviews with three of the prominent researchers whose studies are detailed in Chapter 1 are presented.

This doesn't mean that every research methods student has to do a study. But I would like every student who reads this book to know what it would feel like to do social research and to move in the direction of wanting to do it. So I have also tried to encourage students to ask themselves, "Couldn't I do a study? What would I have to do to be able to take a question that I find tantalizing and turn it into a research project?"

I have also aimed to make this book eclectic in the wide range of methods discussed. Of course, most individual social researchers tend to specialize, using a relatively small range of methods almost exclusively. And many instructors may prefer to emphasize some methods rather than others. But a text should give broad options and encourage students to explore the rich universe of social research. Although research styles and preferences may differ, each of the methods described in this text has in the hands of some researchers produced studies of real fascination and value. In considering how they might generate a study of their own, students are invited to decide if one type of method or another would be appropriate to their interests.

Finally, I wanted the tone of this book to encourage a sense of commitment to doing social research. Other texts adopt a more humorous tone, or remain neutral and technical. Neither of these has seemed right to me. Naturally, working on a research project has its humorous moments, and nothing can be accomplished without appropriate techniques. But these do not capture the essence of social research. Students need to see—and will be more generally engaged by—the choices, the challenges, and the excitement of trying to study some piece of social action. And since the object of this book is to welcome students into the social research enterprise, students are encouraged to think that they *can* become social researchers, and that this is an activity, a way of thinking and working, that requires and is worthy of commitment.

In this third edition, several earlier sections have been substantially revised. Six new studies are presented in chapter 1 with a seventh from the earlier editions. Interviews with three of the authors of studies described in Chapter 1 are presented as a way to personalize the experiences of doing social research. Chapter 2 includes new discussions of feminist and postmodern theory.

Chapter 5 presents a new section on sampling distribution means and how to calculate a standard error.

Chapter 7 has an extensive section on designing and conducting focus groups. Offering a broad purview of different types of qualitative research, Chapter 8 explores the research techniques of the participant observer and the qualitative interviewer.

There are descriptions of currently available datasets, such as the General Social Survey (the National Longitudinal Surveys (NLS), the Panel Study of Income Dynamics (PSID), the National Health Interview Survey (NHIS), and the American National Election Study (all described in Chapter 9).

Qualitative analysis skills as well as quantitative are reviewed in Chapter 11. A quantitative survey of attitudes toward recycling, how the survey data were analyzed, and statistics were generated and interpreted form the bases of Chapters 12 and 13.

Appendix A offers an updated guide to the use of libraries for social research purposes highlighting the use of computer searches using CD-ROM or online databases, as well as the most recent bibliographical materials, handbooks, and encyclopedias available for social research topics.

In response to users' suggestions, there is a greater emphasis on qualitative research, focus groups, evaluation and action research. There is also an expanded glossary at the end of the book in which all of the Key Terms which appear at the end of chapters are defined.

The book in both its editions has been the outgrowth of suggestions from reviewers from other universities and colleges who have told me how they teach research methods, what they think should be covered, and what they aim to accomplish in their own courses. For the third edition. I want to thank the following reviewers: James G. Ahler, University of St. Thomas; Robert A. Bylund, Morehead State University; Simon Gottschalk, University of Nevada at Las Vegas; Ronald J. McAllister, Northeastern University; James R. Reynolds, Winona State University; and Ira M. Wasserman of Eastern Michigan University. Keith Baker lent assistance on the postmodern discussion.

Jacqueline M. Borin, librarian at California State University, San Marcos, did a splendid job of revising and updating Appendix A on the use of libraries for social research. Allen Risley, Assistant Director of our social science lab helped prepare the computer tables and the sampling histograms. Three of the scholars whose research studies are highlighted in the first chapter—Professors Barrie Thorne, Larry Sherman and Travis Hirschi—were interviewed about their experiences in doing field research at grade schools (Thorne), on the effects of arrest on domestic violence suspects (Sherman), and in the landmark study of the causes of juvenile delinquency (Hirschi). I am very appreciative to them for their insights.

This edition would never have appeared without the help and advice of Phillip Butcher, the Sociology editor at McGraw-Hill, who has been supportive of this project from its earliest planning stages. In preparing the third edition, I was assisted by Jill Gordon and Amy Smetzley. Their support has made working on this project easier and much more pleasant. Finally I wish to thank Paula Buschman who has done a marvelous job at supervising the editing of the book.

This third edition has benefited from the support I have received from my colleagues at Cal State, San Marcos: my dean and associate dean Victor Rocha and Patricia Worden, my close colleague friends Isabel Schon and Trini Melcher, my sociology colleagues Richard Serpe, Sheldon Zhang, Bob Roberts, Darlene Piña, and Linda Shaw as well as from close friends Muriel Bell, Marian Adams, Mariella Evans, and Bettina Huber. My sister, Judy Mandel and my cousin Linda Michels have always encouraged my efforts. My two sons, Julian and Felix, are my closest and dearest friends who with Faye Jacob and Heather Bogdanoff, have helped and supported me in innumerable ways enabling me to complete this revision. In this year of Julian's marriage, I dedicate this third edition to Julian and Faye.

Therese L. Baker

CONTENTS IN BRIEF

CONTENTS

4. Operationalization and Measurement: From Concepts to Variables   101

8. Qualitative Research   239

9. Methods of Analyzing Available Data   266

PART ONE

The Foundations of Social Research

What are the foundations of social research? What types of subjects have social researchers addressed? What problems and issues have motivated individuals to carry out social research? The first part of this textbook examines the context of social research. In the Introduction we consider ways in which topics for social research may emerge from our everyday ideas and thoughts. Subjects for social research may arise from what C. Wright Mills defined as *the sociological imagination*, that is, the effort to understand the relationship between an individual's experiences and the complex flow of actions of others in our social environment. Or an originating question for social research may stem from curiosity about a *social fact*, as Robert Merton suggested.

Since subjects for new social research projects often grow from earlier efforts to study similar problems, reading well-crafted research studies can be useful in formulating new subjects for study. Methods of social research also have evolved from the earlier efforts of researchers to develop ways to study different subjects. Chapter 1 examines a number of classic social research projects done in the past, employing three of the primary social research methods: survey research, experiments, and qualitative research using observational and interviewing methods.

Chapter 2 asks what it is that makes social research scientific and discusses the role of theory in social research. We will examine the empirical and logical-rational character of social research; the role of observation, measurement, and theory building and testing. We will review current theories influencing social research, including postmodernism and feminism. We will examine the conditions under which causality can be established and the degree to which social research follows a causal model. Lastly, we will consider what it really means to do science, that is, to carry out scientific research as a human activity. We will see that science emerges from the unsolved problems of earlier research and is subject to more or less agreed-upon sets of values.

The Foundations
of Social Research

Subjects for Social Research

Why do social research? Most of you reading this textbook probably would answer, "To fulfill a course requirement for my major." But let's ask more broadly, "Why have people set out to systematically study human society and behavior?" We need to subdivide this question into two parts. First, we should ask what *subjects*, what aspects of human society, have motivated individuals to want to study them. Second, we need to know what *methods* have been developed to carry out systematic studies of human society.

This book is really about the second part of our question: the methods of social research. However, it is essential to ask as well about the subjects of social research, for after all, if you don't have a subject for research, knowing about methods of research will not be useful. Hence, let's begin by considering what types of subjects have motivated people to carry out social research. The aim of this book is both to understand research that has been carried out by others and to help you design and carry out research of your own.

YOUR TROUBLES AS SOURCES FOR SOCIAL RESEARCH SUBJECTS: THE EXAMPLE OF C. WRIGHT MILLS

Subjects for social research often grow out of things that trouble people in their own lives. We want to know how these troubles take shape in the society around us and in the organized social systems that coordinate and affect our actions. The effort to understand the tension between our individual lives as we experience them and the complex flow of the experiences of others whom we deal with both directly and indirectly lies at the heart of the *sociological imagination* as it was defined by C. Wright Mills (1959). At the base of the sociological imagination lies a need to understand how one's individual life mingles with that of the wider society while at the same time one tries to distinguish oneself within that society. Mills wanted to remind us that we all live out our lives in a particular society and during a specific period

of history. Thus, the features of that society and the character of that period of history naturally affect how each individual acts and reasons. Mills was concerned with the interrelatedness and interdependence of the components of society, such as social classes, basic forms of work, major socializing forces (the structure of families, education, social organizations), and rules and forms of social control that organize a society.

Mills liked to call a problem that is defined in individual terms a *personal trouble*. Once a problem involves a large number of individuals, however, it can no longer be considered only a personal trouble and becomes a *social issue*. Take the example of unemployment, which Mills uses to show how public issues are more than merely the aggregate of personal, individual troubles. One person unable to find a job is an unemployed person. However, when one-third of a nation's inhabitants are unemployed (as was true in the Great Depression of the 1930's), that is an issue, and we may not hope to find its solution within the range of opportunities open to any one individual. . . . Both the correct statement of the problem and the range of possible solutions require us to consider the economic and political institutions of the society, and not merely the personal situation and character of a scatter of individuals (*1959, p. 9*).

But what about a 5 percent level of unemployment, the level which roughly characterizes the United States in the late 1990s? Is that the basis of a social issue? Everyone would agree that for the individual unemployed person, whatever the overall unemployment rate, being unemployed is a personal trouble.

But at what point do these aggregate personal troubles become a social issue? Politicians often disagree about the meaning of the unemployment rate; that disagreement makes unemployment a public issue.

DEVELOPING AN APPRECIATION FOR SOCIAL COMPLEXITY

The sociological imagination grows best in minds that are open to complexity, minds that are able to examine an issue from various points of view, some of which may seem less familiar and "natural" than others. We all know that everyone else does not see the world exactly as we do, but the sociologically imaginative person must ask, "Am I not able to view a problem from totally contradictory vantage points?" This does not mean that you must forget or disregard your values but rather that you can place your values in a framework where they compete with contrary values. Learning to appreciate the complexity of social situations can be enjoyable and profitable, for it can add to your repertory of understanding; it can enable you to deal with future events more effectively.

Most jobs require you to deal with people and changing circumstances with understanding and flexibility. Although only a few students may end up as professional researchers, everyone can profit from developing a sociological imagination which

can be applied both to work and to personal life. You must cultivate your natural interest first, in your own troubles; second, in social settings and organizations with which you are familiar; and third, in events beyond your life's setting that strike you as intriguing, puzzling, and edifying.

The tone of social research is that of genuine concern for the subject under study, This is easy if you study what genuinely concerns you. Such an attitude is not incompatible with the style of research we call scientific. Science does not mean that creative, spontaneous interest in a subject must be squeezed out of the researcher. On the contrary, a committed interest in social issues can be expressed in—indeed, is indispensable to—a scientific and disciplined style of investigation.

PROGRESSIVELY FORMULATING A SOCIAL RESEARCH SUBJECT: THE EXAMPLE OF ROBERT MERTON

In an article on problem finding in sociology, Merton suggested "three principal components in the progressive formulation of a problem" (1959, p. xiii): (1) an originating question, (2) a rationale, and (3) the specifying questions. Chapter 3 discusses developing the rationale for a study. Much of the rest of this textbook addresses various ways to specify research questions by developing concepts, types of measurement, research designs, samples of subjects to study, and procedures for data collection—all of which make explicit what the research will in fact be.

The originating question, in Merton's view, often stems from a social fact, that is, some observation of a condition in society that can be measured and is subject to change. He gave as an example increasing rates of mental illness in the United States (1959, p. xiv). A current social fact is that people are changing their beliefs about how a society should treat those with AIDS or those who are homeless. Factual evidence can be ascertained about these issues, and then a question can be posed in relation to these facts. Merton also suggested that originating questions can grow from a consideration of the relationship between a certain social act and the society as a whole, for example, asking what it is about a certain type of society that determines the types of crime that occur there (1959, p. xv). For Merton, problems for social research do not come "out of the blue" but are grounded in factual evidence.

Mills placed the sociological imagination at the intersection of an investigator's biography and the historical context in which that investigator is living. Merton also recognized the centrality of the individual in defining research problems. Noting that a prominent historian once stated that while everyone might like to be his or her own historian, few feel they have sufficient knowledge of the past to do so, Merton argued that this is not the case with sociologists: Everyone in the society feels confident that he or she understands it well, and we all develop firm opinions about how it works. Of course, our assumptions about society may be wrong, and "getting the facts" may force the social researcher to reconceptualize a research problem.

LEARNING ABOUT SUBJECTS AND METHODS FROM EARLIER RESEARCH STUDIES

An essential characteristic of scientific research is that it is interactive. From study to study, research methods and strategies are progressively refined, research subjects are redefined and transformed, and new ideas are sparked by earlier findings and changing concerns. The methods you choose to carry out a research project will be driven to some degree by the questions you pose and the problems that intrigue you. But these components will also be affected by your choice of a research style. For this reason, Chapter 1 will introduce you to seven classic research studies that utilized quite different styles of research to explore a varied array of sub-

jects. Consideration of these exemplary studies will give you some sense of the range, depth, and texture of the sociological imagination.

RECOMMENDED READINGS

1. Berger, Peter L.: *Invitation to Sociology: A Humanistic Perspective*, Anchor Books, Garden City, N.Y., 1963. Berger's stress on sociology as a pastime and a form of consciousness offers many ideas for subjects of social research. A very readable book.
2. Frost, Peter J., and Ralph E. Stablein (eds.): *Doing Exemplary Research*, Sage, Newbury Park, Calif., 1992. In this collection, senior and junior scholars reflect on their research experiences, emphasizing the research process.
3. Hunt, Morton: *Profiles of Social Research: The Scientific Study of Human Interaction*, Russell Sage, New York, 1986. Written by a nonsociologist, this book attempts very successfully to explain social research to those both inside and outside the social sciences. Includes detailed discussions of five social research studies.
4. Merton, Robert K.: "Notes on Problem-Finding in Sociology," in Robert K. Merton, Leonard Broom, and Leonard S. Cottrell, Jr. (eds.), *Sociology Today*, Basic Books, New York, 1959. In this short essay, Merton suggests which ingredients are necessary to the makeup of a sociological problem. He also discusses the conditions that are likely to lead to the discovery of new sociological problems that require research.
5. Mills, C. Wright: *The Sociological Imagination,* Oxford, New York, 1959. Mills's vibrant work includes marvelous chapters on grand theory and empirical work in sociology. However, the part of the book that will probably be the most helpful in your efforts to initiate a research project is the appendix on "intellectual craftsmanship."

CHAPTER 1

Varieties of Social Research

INTRODUCTION

*T*o do good research, you need to know what good research is. To whet your sociological appetite, you need delicious sociological studies to chew on—studies with exciting, vivid, memorable designs. This chapter will describe seven such studies, which are characteristic of many of the most interesting carried out in the last 30 years. These studies will be described in enough detail that you will develop some level of familiarity with them. In later chapters, examples from these studies will be used to explain various aspects of research design and analysis.

These seven studies were selected because they represent a broad array of social research methods. The researchers in each of these studies maintained a certain intensity of engagement in their research projects, and so the studies have a liveliness and a sense of personal commitment that make them memorable. I should add that some of these studies are particular favorites of mine.

The studies discussed here are examples of three of the major methods currently used in social research: survey research, experiments, and qualitative field studies. These are not the only three social research methods, as this text will clearly show. They are, however, three central types of social research, which represent very different styles of research methods. Beginning by contrasting these types will help you appreciate the range of ways in which a social researcher can choose to study a subject. Let me offer a brief and summary description of these three types.

Survey research can *describe* the attitudes and behaviors of a population of people by selecting in a representative way a sample of individuals and soliciting their responses to a set of questions. Such descriptive surveys are familiar to you in the form of polls. Social researchers, however, often use survey research to attempt to *explain* phenomena, not merely to describe them. In such cases, hypotheses (that is, problems that an explanation suggests) are set up to be tested by relating the responses to different questions to one another.

Experimental research attempts to *explain* how a specific part of a social unit operates when it is stimulated by an experimental device. This method involves setting up controlled conditions in which the individuals being studied, the experimental group, are subjected to the experimental stimulus. Their reaction is compared to that of the control group, another set of individuals not subject to the experimental conditions. By randomly assigning subjects to the experimental or control groups, the experimenter controls differences between the subjects in the two groups that might affect the outcome of the experiment. Both survey research and experiments are examples of *quantitative* research, since their findings can be reduced to numerical summaries.

Qualitative field research attempts to *understand* how an entire social unit such as a group, organization, or community operates in its own terms. While some facets of qualitative research may produce data which can be quantified, this is not a goal of qualitative research. Researchers using qualitative methods often immerse themselves in the day-to-day life of the social unit, trying not to alter the environment by their presence. Then they carefully observe what is going on, interview participants, take notes on their observations, and try to develop an understanding of the meaning of the social environment and the individuals within it.

You can see from these brief descriptions that each of these methods of research involves very different activities and requires different skills and sensitivities. Qualitative research, for example, is often carried out to explore some important issues located in some segment of the human scene. The scene to be studied may be very unfamiliar to the researcher, as is often the case with anthropologists studying exotic cultures, or it may be a very familiar environment where the researcher hopes to gain a new perspective.

Qualitative research often begins with open-ended questions, with a wide-eyed eagerness to take in all that can be observed. The researcher must be very observant but not intrusive, very open to understanding other and unfamiliar situations but not easily misled.

In contrast, experimental designs are quite different; in such studies the researcher starts by trying to understand a small piece of behavior, a reaction, by constructing a carefully planned situation (or stimulus) which should produce the reaction. The "if . . . then" proposition which states how the stimulus will lead to the reaction is a *hypothesis* (for example, "If teachers praise their students, then the students will have higher self-esteem."). In other words, in an experiment the focus is narrowed to the testing of specific hypotheses. Here the researcher as an experimenter is very much in charge; he or she creates the experiment and tries to keep it under control so that what the researcher thinks is being tested in the experiment actually is what is being studied. Because of the greater level of control (and hence the greater precision of the outcomes), experimental findings can more easily be translated into numbers.

Survey research may also test specific hypotheses, but it usually has other aims as well, such as describing the characteristics of a select sample and evaluating the presence and effects of various factors. A survey researcher has a carefully designed set of questions (a questionnaire), a specific group of individuals to be studied, and a plan for how these questions will be studied to accomplish the researcher's purpose. The survey researcher must be highly organized, matter-of-fact, and impersonal when collecting the answers, combining (or aggregating) the answers from the entire sample, and analyzing the findings. This again signifies how survey research is a quantitative research method.

How, you may wonder, do you pick a method to use? Your choice may depend on your particular stage in formulating and conceptualizing the problem. One or another method may be more appropriate at a particular stage of a project, or one or another method may be appropriate to the particular theoretical assumptions on which the project is based. If you are at an early stage in thinking about a problem and are trying to "generate concepts" about a social environment, becoming a participant observer in the social environment may enable you to clarify what seem to be the important issues, the significant types of social action which characterize the setting. In other words, at this early stage of conceptualizing a problem, qualitative field research may be the best choice.

In fact, qualitative research may produce concepts which can then be tested more specifically in a laboratory experiment. To design an experiment, you must already be at a point where you can be very precise about exactly what you want to study. This demands a narrowing of focus to a small number of testable questions. A particular research question, however, may seem to require a broadening of focus, a testing of how far what has been observed in one social setting can be generalized to a wider social environment. At this stage, a survey may be called for.

Your choice of method may also depend on your particular theoretical commitments. One researcher may believe that certain methods are preferable to others because of an underlying outlook on how to explain things social. Another may look askance at certain methods as being largely useless. While this is a rather subtle point and I don't want to confuse you, let me offer a few examples.

Some social researchers believe that participant observation, the method of qualitative field research, is *the* method of choice because it puts the researcher where the action is. An example of social researchers in sociology who generally hold this view would be those who call themselves *symbolic interactionists,* those who think that the meaning of social behavior can best be captured through careful observation of the ways in which individuals interact one with another. Such researchers think that if you want to understand the social world around you, you must look at it directly, unimpeded by a variety of research contraptions (such as experiments and questionnaires).

Other social researchers have very different beliefs about what is needed to explain social situations. For some social scientists, the point of social research is to look at broad patterns of social life; in their view, observing children in a playground and studying slowly the changes in a community will never give you the best picture of things. For such individuals—Nicholas Mullins (1973) described them as Standard American Sociologists—survey research is *the* method; qualitative research may be *suggestive* of concepts and hypotheses, but they would not consider it a complete method in itself.

Another set of social researchers find both qualitative field and quantitative survey research too casual, uncontrolled, and messy. They demand the precision that can be better achieved in an experimental study. An experimentalist will argue that it is only when you can control (block out) all the extraneous occurrences going on in a social environment that you are able to focus on the behavior relevant to the idea you are testing. Naturally, qualitative researchers may find experiments much too contrived and artificial; survey researchers may find experiments too narrow and unrepresentative.

Assuming that you do not have a commitment to a theoretical point of view, your selection of a method will depend both on the type of problem you want to study and the stage of your thinking about it. Let me add one other criterion that I think helps determine what type of method a researcher may select: the type of research which actually seems to appeal to the researcher personally. Some may think it would be great fun to go somewhere and submerge oneself in a *real* social environment, that is, to do a qualitative field study. Others may consider it exciting to design a questionnaire and go out and interview different people on the same set of questions. Still others may think it more challenging to develop a clever experiment to test an idea in a very careful way. As you read through these studies, try to envision what it must have been like to *do* each piece of research, what was the stage of conceptualization of each problem. Naturally you can't ask the researchers whether they were totally committed to a particular theoretical form of studying society, but reading these studies may help you see that different methods enable researchers to reach different types of explanations.

Finally, note that many social researchers do not collect their own data. Instead, they design studies to reanalyze data that already have been collected. This kind of research is referred to as *secondary analysis* and is one of the most common forms of social research undertaken today in the social sciences. Its methods will be discussed in depth in Chapter 9. We will here concentrate on three very different types of study designs where the data were being collected by (or for) the researcher in order to show you the complete process of doing social research. Keep in mind, however, that many of the study questions you might pose could be addressed as effectively (or often more effectively) by utilizing a set of already collected data.

The first studies to be described are surveys, the most popular form of social research in sociology.

SURVEY RESEARCH

A survey often begins by identifying a number of individuals considered representative of the group to be studied (what is referred to as a sample) and deciding what questions they should be asked. Let me add here that individuals need not be the focus of study (what is often called the unit of analysis) in a survey. Instead the focus might be groups, organizations, or even whole societies. In these cases, responses to surveys of members of the larger units would be drawn together (or aggregated) to represent these units. For beginning researchers, however, survey research generally focuses on individuals.

Surveys can be used to test accepted explanations, or *theories,* and develop new ones. They can lend support to a theory by indicating that a relationship that is postulated actually occurs among the group studied, or they can throw doubt on the applicability of a theory by offering little evidence that the relationships suggested by the theory actually exist. If the sample is statistically representative of a larger population, the findings can offer greater support or greater denial of the theory.

Surveys must, however, be limited to the study of questions to which people can in fact give answers. Thus they focus on attitudes, opinions, pieces of information about the conditions of life, and the categories that define and differentiate individuals. The object of a survey is to determine the variation in the responses; each item of information in the survey represents one *variable,* that is, a measure by which the differences in response can be established. For example, surveys generally ascertain the sex of each respondent. In this case the variable, sex, can have only two possible responses: male and female. If a survey were carried out among males only (say, a study of the inmates in a men's prison), sex would not be a variable in the survey but a *constant.*

Surveys may be largely descriptive, for example, to study voting preferences or to determine how people voted in the last election. A survey that asks which candidates individuals plan to vote for is measuring attitudes; one that asks, after an election, for whom the voter voted is measuring behaviors (assuming, of course, that voters tell the truth about how they voted). A survey may measure the variation in attitudes about some issue, for example, support for a nationalized health care system. Or surveys may be designed to determine the relationship between one variable and another, for example, "Are husbands of wives who work outside the home more helpful in the household than are husbands of wives who do not?" Because the causes or results of what is being studied may be so various, surveys often include numerous sets of questions (in other words, questions which will measure many different variables) to explore a number of possible explanations for a specific relationship.

The two surveys to be described here both addressed important social issues. The first, a national survey of sexual behavior, assessed the frequency of, range of practices, and attitudes about sexuality. The second, a study of the causes of juvenile delinquency, focused on three different theories of why delinquency occurs.

A National Survey on Sexual Practices

A subject that has received little academic attention in survey research is sexual behavior. While numerous popular surveys have reported on the sexual practices of Americans, they have gathered their data from individuals who responded to questionnaires in popular magazines. Since these volunteers were not drawn from a defined population, their responses cannot be considered to be representative of Americans as a whole. Even the famous Kinsey Report on sexual behavior which appeared in the 1950s had drawn its findings from volunteers.

Thus by the late 1980s, when many in the United States were becoming alarmed about the rise in the incidence of AIDS, a disease which can be transmitted sexually, a solid statistical base of evidence regarding the incidence and frequency of different types of sexual practices was not available. At the level of public health projections, the issue was how to predict the rise and rates of AIDS; at the level of public health protection, the issue was how to offer sufficient and compelling information to reduce the behaviors that spread the disease. To further both of these goals, it was imperative to gain a more accurate picture of the sexual practices of the American population.

Yet when a group of social scientists, led by the sociologist Edward Laumann at the University of Chicago, tried to get financial support for a nationwide survey on sexual behavior that would be representative of all adult Americans, they ran into many roadblocks. Some opposed the survey, fearing that collecting and disseminating information on sexual practices might encourage certain types of sexual behavior. Others objected to the collecting of such information as an invasion of privacy, especially if the government was to be involved in funding the project. Finally, there were those who believed (as had Kinsey) that it would be impossible to obtain a "random sample" of respondents among all Americans who would be willing to give accurate and honest information about their sexual behavior.

In response, the Laumann team offered its own rationale for why a national random survey on sexual behavior was imperative and in the national interest (Laumann, et al., 1994, p. xxix). The first objective, they argued, must be to create an informed citizenry, especially at a point at which AIDS was potentially threatening to every sexually active adult. The widespread concern for privacy in sexual matters notwithstanding, sexuality is a subject on which many seek advice; it is therefore critically important that those offering such advice (counselors, therapists, religious advisers, teachers) have accurate information about the prevalence of sexual practices. The researchers thus set out their simple goal: to provide accurate information about the sexual behavior of the adult population of the United States.

As social science researchers, they began by considering the theories (or explanations) that might explain why different types of sexual practices are engaged in by individuals who vary in certain ways (by age, education, sex, ethnicity). The theories they drew on will be examined in Chapter 2; it is enough to say here that they recognized that complex factors affect the types of sexual behaviors a person may engage in and with whom. For the purposes of the survey they were to design, it was important to include questions that would enable them to test the various hypotheses they had posed.

To get a sample of respondents truly representative of the U.S. population—that is, a probability sample, in which every member of the known population has a known probability of being selected into the sample—the researchers used the most widely respected procedures for determining the required size of the sample and establishing the best ways to reach that sample. (See Chapter 5 for a more extensive discussion of the design of this sample.) However, they were unable to secure the funding for the sample of 20,000 that they felt was necessary and had to fall back on a much smaller sample of 3,400, which would not allow the study of certain subgroups of interest (such as male homosexuals). Thus, the final sample on which their study is based represented those adults aged 18 to 59 living in households in the United States between February and October 1992 who were conversant in English.

Developing the questions for the survey was also a challenge. It was important to have questions that would minimize error and bias by discouraging both under- and overreporting. In this regard, though, it was difficult to decide on the choice of words since sexual behaviors could be described technically with scientific words which some might not understand or colloquially with slang or other expressions which others might find offensive or unfamiliar. It was also important that the environment of the interview be neutral and nonjudgmental, though respondents would need to feel sufficiently comfortable to confide in the interviewer. It was decided that on some sensitive topics, respondents would not be asked questions verbally but instead would be asked to fill out questionnaires on their own.

But how would the selected respondents be approached by the interviewers? About a week before an individual was contacted by the survey team, he or she received a letter explaining the purpose of the study ("to help doctors, teachers, and counselors better understand and prevent the spread of diseases like AIDS and better understand the nature and extent of harmful and healthy sexual behavior in our country," p. 55). Respondents were also offered a fee as an encouragement to participate.

Now let's briefly consider a few of the researchers' findings. Nothing about sex has been subject to greater speculation than its frequency. Thus, one of the most surprising findings of this survey was that sexual activity occurred less often ("a few times a month" was the most common response) than many had assumed. Let's examine Table 1-1, which reports the frequency of sex in the past year separately for women and men, for different ethnic groups, and for different age groups, marital statuses, and education levels. Note first that only 8 percent of the men and 7 percent of the women reported having sex four or more times per week, while 10 percent of the men and 13.6 percent of the women reported having sex four or more times per week, while 10 percent of the men

TABLE 1-1

FREQUENCY OF SEX IN THE PAST YEAR BY MASTER STATUS VARIABLES (% DISTRIBUTIONS)

Master Status Variables	Not at All	A Few Times per Year	A Few Times per Month	Two to Three Times a Week	Four or More Times a Week	Total N
			Frequency of Sex in the Past Year, %			
Men						
Total population[a]	9.8	17.6	35.5	29.5	7.7	1,330
Age						
18–24	14.7	21.1	23.9	28.0	12.4	218
25–29	6.7	14.8	31.0	36.2	11.4	210
30–34	9.7	16.7	34.7	31.5	7.4	216
35–39	6.8	12.6	40.0	35.3	5.3	190
40–44	6.7	16.9	44.4	26.4	5.6	178
45–49	12.7	19.8	33.3	27.8	6.3	126
50–54	7.8	19.6	45.1	22.5	4.9	102
55–59	15.7	24.7	41.6	16.9	1.1	89
Marital status						
Nev. marr., not coh.	22.0	26.2	25.4	18.8	7.6	382
Nev. marr., coh.	0.0	8.5	35.6	37.3	18.6	59
Married	1.3	12.8	42.5	36.1	7.3	687
Div./sep./wid., not coh.	23.8	22.5	28.5	20.5	4.6	151
Div./sep./wid., coh.	0.0	8.3	36.1	44.4	11.1	36
Education						
Less than HS	14.8	20.2	28.4	29.5	7.1	183
HS grad. or eq.	10.1	15.1	34.4	31.7	8.7	378
Some coll./voc.	8.7	19.9	33.5	28.8	9.1	427
Finished coll.	9.0	15.8	43.9	25.8	5.4	221
Master's/adv. deg.	7.0	15.8	42.1	30.7	4.4	114
Race/ethnicity[b]						
White	9.7	17.3	35.6	29.6	7.8	1,053
Black	8.3	16.5	37.6	30.4	7.2	194
Hispanic	8.5	14.7	34.1	28.7	14.0	129
Women						
Total population[a]	13.6	16.1	37.2	26.3	6.7	1,664
Age						
18–24	11.2	16.1	31.5	28.8	12.4	267
25–29	4.5	10.3	38.1	36.8	10.3	223
30–34	8.1	16.6	34.6	32.9	7.8	283
35–39	10.8	15.7	37.8	32.5	3.2	249
40–44	14.6	15.5	46.1	16.9	6.8	219
45–49	16.1	16.1	41.0	23.6	3.1	161
50–54	19.3	20.7	40.0	17.8	2.2	135
55–59	40.8	22.4	29.6	4.8	2.4	125
Marital status						
Nev. marr., not coh.	30.2	23.5	26.0	13.3	7.0	315
Nev. marr., coh.	1.4	6.9	31.9	43.1	16.7	72
Married	3.0	11.9	46.5	31.9	6.6	905
Div./sep./wid., not coh.	34.3	23.2	21.9	16.8	3.7	297
Div./sep./wid., coh.	0.0	9.4	39.6	39.6	11.3	53

(continued)

Education						
Less than HS	18.7	14.5	36.2	22.6	8.1	235
HS grad. or eq.	10.8	15.9	37.7	29.6	6.0	483
Some coll./voc.	13.5	15.9	37.7	25.2	7.7	571
Finished coll.	12.5	18.3	33.5	29.7	6.1	263
Master's/adv. deg.	17.8	15.8	44.6	17.8	4.0	101
Race/ethnicity[b]						
White	12.8	16.4	38.1	26.2	6.7	1,277
Black	17.0	18.3	32.5	25.1	7.1	323
Hispanic	11.4	10.2	35.2	33.0	10.2	176

[a]Cross section N = 3,159. [b]With over samples, N = 3,432.
Source: Adapted from Laumann, et al., 1994, Table 3.4, pp. 88–89.

and 13.6 percent of the women reported no sexual activity over the past year. Table 1-1 reports very small differences between racial/ethnic groups or between those with varying levels of education.

Marital status and age, however, are strongly related to frequency of sex. Those who were currently married were among the most sexually active, nearly approaching the rate of those who were cohabitating. Not surprisingly, Table 1-1 reports that the frequency of sexual activity decreased with age. Examining the table carefully enables you to see a number of interesting findings. Compare, for example, the frequency rates of the youngest group (ages 18 to 24) to those of the oldest group (ages 55 to 59). Among the youngest men and women, 12.4 percent engaged in sex four or more times per week, while only 1.1 percent of the oldest men and 2.4 percent of the oldest women were that sexually active. However, if we examine the column of those with no sexual activity, we see roughly the same proportions of the youngest and oldest men reporting no activity within the last year (14.9 percent and 15.7 percent), but for the women there is a much greater difference in the abstinence level of the oldest compared to the youngest (11.2 percent of the youngest group compared to 40.8 percent of the oldest group).

Let's stop and think for a minute about what Table 1-1 shows. It reports a range of data on the study's main topic: sexual behavior (in this case, the frequency of sexual behavior) in relation to a set of other characteristics of the respondents: age, education, race/ethnicity, and so on. These characteristics (which the authors call "master statuses")

are criteria we commonly use to differentiate and compare people (by age, educational attainment, race/ethnicity, gender, etc.). Table 1-1 poses the question in exactly these terms: Is the sexual activity of whites, or men, or those with college degrees, or the elderly more or less frequent than that of nonwhites, women, those without college degrees, or the young?

But this survey also needed to examine how respondents thought and felt about sexual practices. We call these thinking-feeling states attitudes and opinions, and survey research is an excellent method for measuring them. Therefore, respondents were asked about their attitudes toward premarital and extramarital sexual behavior, how far religious beliefs had shaped their sexual behavior, and their opinions regarding homosexuality, abortion, and pornography.

Clearly, with so much information the researchers could easily get lost in the details. But the purpose of such research is to clarify ideas, not to muddy the issues. Therefore, Laumann and his colleagues combined attitudinal measures and developed clusters of measures that indicated the overall perspectives of the respondents on sexual behavior. They called these perspectives "normative orientations." Let's stop a moment and ask ourselves how we think about the sexual behavior of Americans. We would probably conclude that some people are very sexually involved and liberated in their beliefs and activities while others may not be engaged at all and that most people fall somewhere between these two extremes. If we

---

HOW TO READ TABLE 1-1

The left-hand column lists master status variables: age, marital status, education, and race/ethnicity. Within each of the variables the range of values presented (from 18 to 24 down to 55 to 59 for age; from Less than HS (high school) to Master's/adv. deg. (master's degree to advanced degree for education) are broken down into categories. Note as well that these are presented separately for men and women.

Reading across the top of the table, you can see the categories under "Frequency of Sex in the Past Year, percent." If we examine the top row, across from Men ages 18–24, we see that 14.7 percent reported "not at all," 21.1 percent reported "a few times per year," 23.9 percent reported "a few times per month," 28 percent reported "two to three times a week," and 12.4 percent reported "four or more times a week." Note that at the end of this row, under Total *N,* 218 is reported. This row indicates the percentages of the men in this youngest group (numbering 218 altogether) who reported having sex in each category of frequency, in other words, the percentage distribution of sex frequency. If you add up these five percentages across the row, you will have 100 percent. See that the percentages rise from the left-most category ("not at all")

to the center category and then fall again as one moves to the right. Looking down the table, we can see that the central category ("A Few Times Per Month") is the most popular category for nearly every value of every variable (except for never-married men and women who are cohabitating, for whom the frequency of two to three times per week is higher).

Let's now compare this youngest group of men to the youngest group of women. Look down the table to find the comparable row (Women, 18–24). Note that the percentages are nearly the same for the two most active categories (12.4 percent for men at 4 or more times per week compared to 12.4 percent for women; 28.0 percent for men at two to three times per week compared to 31.5 percent for women), but for the lower frequency groups such as "a few times a year" and "not at all," the percentages of young men in that group are higher than those of women. How might you account for this? Perhaps young women are more likely to have older sex partners who include those from the more sexually active age groups, while men may be more likely to draw their sexual partners from among slightly younger women who are less likely to be sexually active.

---

asked ourselves what sorts of people would be likely to fall into these categories, we'd probably suggest that a person's religious beliefs, age, and marital status, as well as the region of the country that person lived in and other factors, might affect a person's sexual orientation. This is precisely what Laumann and his colleagues were trying to do: not only to get the "facts" but to try to make sense of them. Thus the facts needed to be fleshed out with interpretations of what they meant.

The researchers turned to earlier studies of sexual behavior and found that most of those studies had concluded that there were three general orientations to sexuality: a *traditional* one shared by those who believe that couples should engage in

sexual activity primarily for the sake of procreation or who feel that sex within marriage is a sacred expression of love; a *relational* one, accepting that sexual activity occurs within a loving long-term relationship; and a *recreational* one, which sees sexual activity as undertaken primarily for pleasure. In the Laumann study, however, the researchers found certain major breaks in attitudes within these three orientations. Among those holding a *traditional* orientation, for example, there was still a split in attitudes toward abortion (between those who were prolife and those who were prochoice). Sexual orientations were also related to other measures of sexuality, such as frequency of sex. In this regard, the researchers found that the frequency of sexual activity among those holding a *relational* orientation was often higher than it was among those holding a *recreational* orientation; this seemed to be explained by the availability of a close partner. In other areas as well, they found that attitudes held were not always indicative of behavior. For instance, 58 percent of those claiming that premarital sex was always wrong had engaged in it (Laumann et al., 1994, p. 543).

We will now examine a much smaller survey that was done in the 1960s to address an equally critical social issue—the causes of juvenile delinquency.

The Causes of Delinquency

One of the most difficult questions in any society is why some of its members break its rules, in other words, why some people commit crimes. In our society, responses to this question often begin with the developmental consideration of how a person becomes delinquent in behavior, For this reason, the study of delinquent behavior among youth becomes a focus for trying to understand the causes of criminal behavior in general. If an understanding of how a youth becomes a delinquent can be achieved, there is some hope that the conditions which bring this about can be altered or ameliorated.

We all have some notions about why young people become delinquents: for example, they come from "bad" families, they are not supervised, they hang about in gangs, or they feel they have no chance to be successful through legitimate avenues. These notions are based on different underlying assumptions about why a person might break laws and how a society is constructed to minimize the number of people who do so. In very simplistic terms, two different views (or theories) of society have been posed to explain the occurrence of delinquency. According to one theory, a society is assumed to be cohesive and unified, with those actions which are beneficial to its optimal running widely supported by most people. From such a perspective, delinquency results from cracks in a unified whole, areas where the cohe-

siveness of the society has been strained. According to this conception, delinquent behavior is aberrant; that is, it goes against the natural and widely held norms of the society as a whole.

The contrary theory on why delinquency develops is based on a different view of the natural state of society, one in which society is assumed to be fragmented and divisive. According to this view, the primary effort of the society must be to control the largely selfish interests of individuals so that the society can function even minimally. From this perspective, delinquency is a natural occurrence which can be precluded only by a rigorous system of social controls. When such restrictions are lax or do not exist, delinquent behavior will naturally break out. Thus delinquent behavior is to be expected, and the society must continually ward it off by reinforcing its systems of social control. These different conceptions of society, along with the different explanations of delinquency they suggest, are *theories*. In other words, they offer tentative explanations why a set of conditions leads to a number of effects.

It was to test such theories that Travis Hirschi, a criminologist, set out to discover the "causes of delinquency." Hirschi's research has a classic survey design. It begins by identifying contradictory theories; it then sets out a research design to test the theories; it then presents the relevant data, analyzes the data, and comes down in support of one of the theories. In this research, the first theory of delinquency (in which society is assumed to be cohesive) was called the *strain theory*. For Hirschi, this theory assumed that humans are moral, that we desire to obey the rules and conform to the norms of society (1969, p. 5). Those who break laws are therefore motivated by their inability to fit into the normal, cohesive order. They are "discontent," "frustrated," "deprived" (Hirschi, 1969, p. 6). These negative tendencies grow "from a discrepancy between aspirations and expectations" (1969, p. 8) for opportunities and success and may explain why delinquency is much more prevalent among the lower classes, where adverse social conditions serve as its source.

Thus the strain theory seeks to answer the question "Why do people *not* obey rules of society?" Its opposite, which Hirschi called *control theory,* tries to answer the question "Why *do* people obey rules of society?" The search for the source of people's motivation to commit crimes is therefore less important in control theories of delinquency. Instead, the sources of control which keep most people—but not all—from delinquency are what need to be carefully examined, for when these controls are lacking, individuals commit crimes.

Hirschi set these two opposing theories against a third way of explaining why individuals commit deviant acts: the *cultural deviance theory.* This theory assumes that deviant behavior does not in fact exist; rather, behavior is called deviant only by those with sufficient power and authority in the society to label it in this way (Hirschi, 1969, pp. 11–12). In short, people may break the standards established by others, but they cannot break their own standards. Such a theory suggests an extreme form of relativism according to which each person operates with his or her own cultural values and learns deviant as well as nondeviant behavior within the natural confines of his or her own cultural milieu. For the cultural deviance theorists, neither the strain theory (with its emphasis on motivation) nor the control theory (with its emphasis on social restraint) has the right focus. Instead, cultural deviance theory stresses a phenomenological explanation which states that perspectives on what is and what is not delinquent behavior vary widely and preclude establishing a precise definition of delinquency.

What Hirschi set out to do was to test these three theories of the causes of delinquency—strain, control, or cultural deviance—on data from a larger survey, the Richmond Youth Project. The sample for this survey was drawn from public junior and senior high school students in western Contra Costa County in the San Francisco–Oakland Bay area in 1964. Approximately 12 percent of the area's population was composed of African-Americans with some Asian and Mexican-Americans as well; the rest were white. Before questionnaires were administered to the students, written permission from par-

ents was required. Questionnaires included items about the student's family situation (characteristics of parents, nature of interaction within the family, attachment to parents) and attitudes and opinions (sense of opportunities for social mobility, positive self-image, attitudes toward minorities). In addition, information from school records (general demographic characteristics used to establish the sample and grade point averages and achievement-test scores) and police records (number and type of offenses, date of most recent offense, age of youth at time of offense) were also collected.

In a survey, the manner in which one asks the question determines how the ideas one is studying will be measured. Hirschi had to decide what would serve as an adequate measure of delinquency: he selected delinquent acts (reported by the respondents) as the factor to be measured. He asked his subjects a series of six questions about whether they had ever taken things that did not belong to them, wrecked property that was not their own, or beaten up anyone (not counting a brother or sister) (1969, p. 54). The responses to these questions were then added up to form an index of delinquency (described in Chapter 2, p. 46).

Who would report more delinquent acts? To answer this question, Hirschi needed to know various characteristics of those studied: their sex, race, social class, and ability levels. The first characteristic—sex—he eliminated after determining that very few girls in the sample had reported delinquent acts. Thus he confined his analysis to boys (sex became a *constant* in this survey). Race differences were much greater than social class differences. But Hirschi also found that lower academic aptitude (revealed in tests on verbal ability) was related to delinquency. Since the minority-race students more often had lower academic aptitude, this factor helped account for the noted differences in delinquency between the races.

Since strain theory and cultural deviance theory both expect large differences between social classes and races in delinquency rates, Hirschi moved in the direction of control theory as the more plausible explanation of his findings. Thus

Hirschi explored the attachment of youth to parents, to school, and to peers. How closely did the parents supervise the son? How much did the son identify with his father? How intimately did the son communicate with his father? Not surprisingly, Hirschi found "that the closer the child's relations with his parents, the more he is attached to and identifies with them, the lower his chances of delinquency" (1969, p. 94). This was the case regardless of the race or class of the father and son. Obviously, this finding did not lend support to the cultural deviance theory, which suggests that some lower-class parents might actually support deviant behavior. On the contrary, it made the strength of attachment to parents, whatever their social class, a positive predictor of nondelinquency.

Having thus considered the link between delinquency and attachment to parents, Hirschi next explored the relationship of delinquency and attachment to school. He found that a general dislike of school, a disdain for what teachers think of students, and the belief that the school had no right to supervise personal behavior (such as smoking) were all related to higher levels of delinquency. In short, the more attached the boy was to the school environment and its norms, the less likely he was to be delinquent. Hirschi found a similar relationship between attachment to peers and nondelinquency.

But what about the case of a boy attached to peers who are themselves delinquent? Both strain theory and cultural deviance theory hold that the influence of peers is central to the development of deviance. Both contend that a youth subculture contrary to the law-abiding adult culture is the seedbed of delinquency. Both therefore suggest that a boy attached to delinquent peers is more likely to be delinquent himself. In fact, Hirschi found that the evidence was more complicated: delinquent boys were more likely to have delinquent peers, but boys attached to their peers (whether or not the peers were delinquent) were less likely to be delinquent. Thus the most delinquent boys had delinquent peers to whom they were not particularly attached; the least delinquent boys had nondelinquent peers to whom they were attached.

Hirschi had found the strongest support for the control theory of delinquency, modified to incorporate some influence of delinquent friends (cultural deviance theory). His findings offered little support for strain theory, in which social class influence is deemed of central importance. However, his study also did not strengthen the notion that delinquency must be learned in a subcultural setting, which is characteristic of cultural deviance theory. Box 1-1 presents an interview with Hirschi on why this study has maintained an important place in delinquency research.

BOX 1-1

INTERVIEW WITH TRAVIS HIRSCHI ON *CAUSES OF DELINQUENCY*

Travis Hirschi, a Regents Professor of Sociology at the University of Arizona, was formerly a professor at the State University of New York, Albany, and at the University of California, Davis. This research project was carried out when he was a graduate student at the University of California, Berkeley.

Was the study of delinquency the primary concern of the researchers who did the Richmond Youth Project (RYP) survey, or was it your
particular interest while other researchers mined the survey for other analyses? That is, was the delinquency analysis a secondary analysis from that dataset, or would you say that it was a primary analysis?

The study of delinquency was not the primary concern of the RYP. The study was, as I recall, funded by the Office of Economic Opportunity, and it reflected concern for the educational and occupational prospects of lower-class youth.

If a delinquency theory could be found in the study proposal, I suspect it was the strain theory of Cloward and Ohlin. My delinquency study was a "tack-on" project, made possible by the generosity of Charles Y. Glock and Alan B. Wilson. Because I was involved in instrument design and data collection, and had major responsibility for the delinquency component, I would certainly describe the analysis as primary, however.

What role would you say that the Causes of Delinquency *book played in establishing control theory in criminology? Why has the theory stood up so well?*

I am not sure of the role played by *Causes of Delinquency* in establishing control theory in criminology. It helped in some ways, but it may have hurt a little as well. Once in a while I think that *Causes* more or less absorbed several excellent theories and left the control tradition less vibrant than it was before. In my view, the theory has stood up as well as it has because its origins are in the kinds of data delinquency research traditionally produces—data on family functioning, school performance, and the like.

Why do you think strain theory and cultural deviance theory have had a continuing impact in the study of crime?

I think strain and cultural deviance theories have deep roots in the social science disciplines and for that matter in American culture. Fortunately, they appear to be especially vulnerable to analyses that focus on the nature of the criminal act, and I am optimistic that in due time they will get their comeuppance.

In your (and Michael Gottfredson's) more recent book, A General Theory of Crime *(1990), you also address economic, psychological, and biological theories of crime. Why didn't you address these theories in* Causes of Delinquency?

Economic, psychological, and biological theories of crime were (or appeared to be) much less important when I wrote *Causes* than they are today. I am not sure, however, that if I were doing *Causes* today I would pay much attention to them.

I selected your analyses from Causes of Delinquency *because they were comprehensible to a beginning undergraduate research methods student, set up to test the theories you had presented, and cogently explained and defended. This is no mean feat. At the time you did the study, did it occur to you that the study might serve as a classic piece of empirical sociological research?*

I don't think it did occur to me. Recall that when I was working on *Causes* I was also finishing a book called *Delinquency Research,* a book critical of the research of others. This was a source of considerable strain. There I was, holding others to standards I was unlikely to be able to attain myself. But there was more to my modesty than this: I assumed that work subsequent to *Causes* would quickly move beyond it—that better data and more sophisticated analysis would quickly reveal its shortcomings. That this may not have happened, at least as clearly as it should have happened, is a sad commentary on the depth of our commitment to the task of understanding crime.

Finally, did you think at the time you were writing Causes of Delinquency *that it would have such a long-term impact? Did it have an impact in areas (and on groups of people) which you hadn't expected?*

My guess is that *Causes* is cited for essentially four reasons: (1) as an example of control theory, (2) as a research report containing particular "findings," (3) as a source of information on the Richmond Youth Project, (4) as an example of how to do, or how not to do, survey research. It is difficult for me to imagine the book having much of an impact with any of these elements missing or radically modified. The theory is crucial, but so are the findings. The widespread, immediate availability of the Richmond data for secondary analysis did not hurt. The least important element would appear to be the data analysis. I much enjoy the use of *Causes* as an example of how to do analysis, but such uses are few and far between. I continue to believe, however, that the mode of tabular analysis I employed was essential to the book's integrity. I was complaining about the new techniques of analysis even before they took over the field. And I am still of the opinion that they often merely muddy the waters.

I have been pleasantly surprised by the book's reception outside sociology.

Some Characteristics of Surveys

Laumann and his associates used the survey technique to describe the range and frequency of sexual practices of Americans so that that information could be used to develop policies for public health safety and for sex education and therapy. Hirschi used a survey to test competing theories of the causes of delinquency. In each case, major social issues were studied by gathering large numbers of responses to a set of questions. In the Hirschi survey, the sample was selected from a single county in California; in the Laumann survey, it was selected from the nation as a whole. The findings from the Laumann survey were representative of a whole society (this is called a national sample) so that the survey could address a national problem.

The small-scale self-report survey Hirschi developed in the 1960s as a way to study and measure delinquency has over time been greatly expanded by other researchers (including Hirschi) into a much more lengthy self-report survey of delinquency, the ISRD (International Self-Report Delinquency survey), which has been tested and retested on various populations in many parts of the world (see Junger-Tas et al., 1994). The evidence from this research has been used to argue for and against a range of theories, including the three Hirschi studied.

The Laumann survey was the first really large-scale probability survey on sexual practices that was collected on a national sample through face-to-face interviews. The development of the questions and the methods of interviewing the respondents required tremendous care. If respondents were uncomfortable answering these questions, that might have encouraged either underreporting or overreporting, in which case the validity of the survey would have been jeopardized. For this reason, the whole success of the study hinged on whether the questions were clearly posed and whether they would measure what they were intended to measure, in other words, their validity as measures of the attitudes, characteristics, and behaviors being studied.

Once the answers to these questions were accumulated, the range of attitudes, characteristics, and behaviors could be established and significant variations could be identified by looking at the proportions of respondents who answered particular questions in different ways. Furthermore, the variables could then be related to one another in a way that would show how a change in one variable (say, marital status) would be associated with a change in another (say, frequency of sexual behavior). Precise analysis of the relationships established between the variables thus made it possible to test hypotheses identified at the very beginning of the study.

EXPERIMENTAL RESEARCH

There is a sharp contrast between the design of large surveys in which many people are asked the same questions and the design of an experimental study. An experimental study involves setting up precisely controlled conditions to which the individuals or groups being studied (usually referred to as the *subjects*) must react. Their reaction then forms the central focus of an experimental study. Experiments that sociologists carry out are more likely to take place in natural (or field) environments than in laboratories; however, laboratories allow experimental researchers to control and manipulate the experimental environment so that they can focus on the reaction being studied.

A second quality which differentiates experiments from other types of social research methods is that the stimulating experimental condition (the independent variable, or IV) may be created by the experimental researcher: this is called a "true" experiment. Experimental designs also can be used to study something that happens naturally, say, a natural disaster such as an earthquake or a strike at a factory. Alternatively, a social program or an intervention set up to alter a problematic condition (say, a drug abuse therapy program) could serve as the independent variable in an experimental design, in which case the object of the experimenter would be to carefully monitor what results (the dependent variable, or DV) from the program. Researchers would ask questions such as: What are the outcomes of the program? What are the program's effects? Does the program work? This type of an experiment is called a natural experiment because the independent variable is not "created" by the researcher but occurs outside the researcher's domain; in other words, it occurs "naturally" before the experimenter moves in to study its effects. To develop our understanding of experiments, let's closely examine two experiments. The first is a true experiment taking place in a laboratory, in which the experimenters create the stimulating experimental condition (IV) and then observe its effects (DV); the second takes place in the field and combines qualities of both a true experiment and a natural experiment in which the experimental condition is an arrest (IV) or an alternative sanction of a suspect of domestic assault and the effects of this arrest on repeat offenses (DV) are measured.

Bystander Intervention: A True Experiment in a Laboratory

An unusual instance of social behavior that caught the interest of many in the 1960s was a case in which a woman (Kitty Genovese) returning to her apartment in Queens, New York, very late at night was stabbed by a stranger. When she called out for help, although a number of residents in the large apartment building opened their windows and looked out and although one man shouted at the attacker to leave her alone, no one actually came to her aid or even called the police during the 35-minute period during which the man returned three times to repeatedly attack (and subsequently kill) her. The newspapers took little note of this murder until it was determined that 38 people had actually seen and heard the attack from the nearby apartment building but had done nothing to help the victim. By the time the police were called (they arrived within two minutes), she was dead. If someone had called the police more quickly, the victim might well have survived the attack. How, one wondered, could so many people have observed an event like this and done nothing about it?

Why, psychologists and sociologists pondered, had no one come to her aid? Were people so indifferent to the fate of their neighbors? Did this event represent a total lack of a sense of responsibility to help one's fellow women and men? Were people so frightened of being drawn into a dangerous situation that they would let their neighbors be stabbed to death rather than "get involved"? Or did each of the observers assume that another observer had surely called the police that he or she need not do so?

The incident inspired the social psychologists John Darley and Bibb Latane to ask whether the magnitude of the group of people who had clearly observed this attack and the awareness of each that others were also observing the event (indicated as the lights went on in the apartments) had weakened the "helping" responses of each of the observers. Under what conditions, the researchers wondered, would a bystander actually intervene to help someone? Would an increase in the number of people observing someone in need of help possibly *diffuse the sense of responsibility* in a way that would lead each observer to conclude that someone else had probably helped or called the police so that he or she need not do so?

How could this matter be studied? Such a question about a behavioral reaction is a perfect candidate for an experimental design. A scenario to determine in which cases a bystander would intervene and how this might vary according to the number of people observing the situation could be created in an experimental setting. An experiment in which the subjects could be led to believe either that they were alone in witnessing another person in an emergency situation or that they were observing this at the same time that varying numbers of others were could approximate the real-life situation that had happened in Queens and explore some possible variables within it. This is exactly the type of experiment that psychologists John Darley and Bibb Latane originally set up to study bystander intervention. Their subjects were undergraduates in New York, and their setting was a psychology laboratory.

Let's run through how this experiment would have felt if you had been the subject. You would have been brought into a room alone and told that you would talk over an intercom system with other students (two to five in number) about personal problems confronted in college. The other students were supposedly in similar private rooms. You would be asked to take turns speaking and would be told that the intercom had been set up to be on for two minutes at a time for each student in turn; when another student's microphone was on, yours would be off. (In reality, each subject was alone and all the other contributions to the "conversation" were taped.) The session would begin with the tape recording of the student "victim," who would tell you, the subject (and, supposedly, the other bystanders if the group was larger than two), that he or she had found it difficult to get adjusted to New York City and work as a student. Then the student "victim" would also mention that he or she was prone to seizures. If there were supposed to be more than two in the group (that is, more than the subject and the "victim"), a tape recording of one of the "bystanders" would be played next in which the "bystander" would describe similar problems of coping, but without the problem of seizures. You as the subject would always be assigned to be the last to speak.

Once you had spoken, the round of conversation would start a second time. Now the victim would begin to stutter, gasp for words, and finally beg for help, stating that he or she might die. At this point, the experimenter would begin to time how long it would take you (the subject) to seek help for the victim (usually by going out of the room and informing the experimenter or someone else that the "victim" needed help). If you did not try to seek help for the "victim," you would be allowed to remain in the room for six minutes before the experiment was terminated and you were told the true nature of the experiment.

This was the basic experiment, but the experimenters also set up a few variations in the experimental design. There was variation in the size of the groups, from just the subject and the "victim" (group size of two), to the subject, the "victim," and one other "bystander" (group size of three), to the subject, the "victim," and four other "bystanders" (group size of six). Furthermore, they varied the sex of the bystander(s), and in one experiment the bystander was also supposedly a medical student. Victims and subjects also varied in gender.

While the "seizure" which the subject heard was in fact a tape recording of a simulated seizure, nearly all the subjects believed it to be real. What the experimenter wanted to measure was how far the *number of bystanders* in the situation (IV) affected the *time to help* of reporting the crisis (DV). In short, this experiment was studying the effect of group size on helping behavior. What the experimenters found was that every one of the subjects in a two-person group reported the emergency, but only 62 percent of the subjects in the three-person groups and 31 percent of the subjects in the six-person groups. Moreover, the speed of the response to the crisis was much higher in the two-person group (mean time of 52 seconds) than in the three-person group (mean time of 93 seconds) and in the six-person group (mean time of 166 seconds). There was no appreciable difference in the response of males or females, and it did not matter whether the victim was male or female; having a "bystander" with medical expertise also did not affect the responses.

The conclusion the experimenters reached was that the speed of helping was affected by the "perceived presence of others" (p. 383), not by apathy or indifference. The evidence supported a *theory of diffusion of responsibility*, which holds that responsibility for helping becomes diffused in a group situation in which individuals sense that others have observed an emergency and may respond more to concerns about how the others might be reacting than to the immediate situation itself.

Does Arrest Deter Domestic Assaults? A Field Experiment

Do you think that people arrested for domestic assault are less likely to commit such an assault again? Or might they be more likely? Criminologists would argue that whether you believe that an arrest has a "deterrent effect" on future deviant behavior depends on how you explain the relationship between the sanction of arrest and subsequent behavior. You might argue that the act of arresting someone suspected of committing a crime may have positive effects on deterring further crime if you assume that being arrested is a punishing event that the individuals will try to avoid (this would be employing a *deterrence theory*), or conversely, you might argue if one effect of an arrest is for those in the suspect's social world to label him or her negatively, an arrest might actually increase subsequent delinquent behavior (this would be employing a *labeling theory*), meaning that once a person's reputation is tarnished, that person might as well live up to this tarnished label.

An interesting experimental design was set up to study the potentially positive or negative effects of arresting men charged with domestic assault. The subjects for the study were real assailants in domestic violence situations to which police had been called. The experiment took place in Minneapolis in two police districts which had the highest rates of domestic violence. The plan of the experiment was as follows: Police called to scenes of domestic violence which met the criterion of being simple domestic assaults (categorized as misdemeanors, not felonies, which involve life-threatening or severe injuries) would take whatever action (an arrest, an advice session, or separation from the victim) was indicated on the top of each form in their pads. Since the three actions had been distributed randomly among the forms, the treatment given to each assailant was randomly dealt out. After the action taken, the police officer filled out a brief report on the incident. The effects of the "treatment" were then assessed within a six-month period by follow-up interviews with the victims to measure the frequency and seriousness of subsequent assaults by the suspect. In addition, reviews of criminal records were carried out to see if the suspect had been involved in any reported criminal activity (Sherman and Berk, 1984).

The researchers found that arrests produced the lowest recidivism rate (a repeated incidence of an assault or other criminal behavior) regardless of whether they used the follow-up interviews with the victims or the criminal record to establish subsequent behavior. This was not due to the incapacitation of the suspect to repeat an assault since very few of the arrested suspects were incarcerated for very long (86 percent were jailed for less than one week, and 43 percent were released within one day). The researchers therefore concluded that arresting domestic violence suspects appeared to have a positive deterrence effect on future assaults.

There are potentially many ways in which an experiment like this could be charged with not actually measuring what it purports to measure (in other words, with not having *validity*), whether because of actions by the victims, the suspects, or the police officers or because of the follow-up efforts. We will examine these issues in Chapter 4 when we address the issue of validity. For the moment, keep in mind how a "real-life situation" can become the basis for a field experiment if there is a "treatment" to be offered, if the subjects can be randomly assigned to experience or not experience the "treatment," and if there is a way to measure the effects of this treatment at some posttreatment time.

Given that the treatments issued were typical responses that police regularly handed out in such cases, the experiment had qualities of a "natural" experiment in which the "independent variable" is a natural phenomenon. Recall that in a true experiment, the independent variable is controlled and manipulated by the experimenter and often has been created to artificially represent a real-life response. Since the handing out of the treatments in the domestic assault experiment was under the control of experimenters who had used principles of random assignment of treatments (in which members assigned to the "experimental group" were arrested and those assigned to the two "control groups" were required to attend an advising session or to undergo a forced separation from the victim for a short period), the experiment followed many of the rules for a "true" experiment. Box 1-2 presents Larry Sherman's current reflections on this experiment.

BOX 1-2

INTERVIEW WITH LAWRENCE SHERMAN ON THE DOMESTIC VIOLENCE ARREST EXPERIMENT

Lawrence W. Sherman is Professor and Chair of the Department of Criminology and Criminal Justice at the University of Maryland. He is also Adjunct Professor of Law at the Research School of Social Sciences, Australian National University, where he is currently directing a long-term experiment in restorative justice alternatives to criminal prosecution. At the time of the Minneapolis experiment, he was the Director of Research of the Police Foundation, based in Washington, D.C.

Why did you pick Minneapolis for this research? (In the New York Times in October there was a long article on how Minneapolis has become much more multi-ethnic in the 1990s.) How might the research findings have been different had you carried out the experiment (when you did) in a city like Los Angeles?

Minneapolis was the site for the original research simply because I had a good relationship with the new police chief there, Anthony Bouza, and he was willing to risk undertaking the first randomized experiment in arrest. The Mayor and City Council were also very interested in the issue, and agreed to endorse the research—just as the Milwaukee City Council did unanimously in 1986 prior to our replication of the experiment there.

The fact that the demographic composition of Minneapolis in 1981 was primarily white middle class no doubt affected the findings, which is why Richard Berk and I called for replications before enacting mandatory arrest laws. As later replications of the Minneapolis experiment in Milwaukee (by me) and Miami, Charlotte, Colorado Springs and Omaha (by others) found, the effect of arrest on misdemeanor domestic violence varies

widely by city. My book, POLICING DOMESTIC VIOLENCE: EXPERIMENTS AND DILEMMAS (Free Press, 1992), discusses these complexities, and shows how the results show arrest causing more domestic violence among unemployed men, but less among employed men. Elizabeth Marciniak's 1994 PhD dissertation at Maryland found that this was an area or neighborhood effect independent of individuals, so that arrest in high unemployment neighborhoods backfires, but it works in areas of high employment. That is what Minneapolis was in 1981–82—a city with almost no areas of high unemployment.

Given that the subjects for the Minneapolis experiment were only misdemeanants, do you think the findings would have been different had you been able to include felons? If so, how?

The effect of arrest or release on domestic violence felons remains unknown. At this time, few felons are released, although that was not true in the early 1980s. Thus the policy-relevance of this question has declined. The question of how felons are prosecuted remains very important, yet prosecutors have refused to cooperate with research in the area.

What do you think is exactly deterring the offenders? Is it the legal consequences? the confrontation with the police officers? the possible loss of reputation, freedom, job security? or something else?

My book POLICING DOMESTIC VIOLENCE suggests that the deterrent effect

of arrest is conditional on having a stake in conformity, or informal social ties that will suffer from further legal punishment. But if your neighborhood or friends give you prestige for standing up to the police, the deterrent effect appears to backfire, creating what I call a "defiance" effect: the more you are punished, the more crimes you will commit.

Why does the social stigma of arrest work for certain types of offenders but not for others? What would be the policy implications of your later findings that arrest mainly deterred domestic violence for employed middle class white males?

The policy implications for these differential effects of arrest are controversial, and depend in part on value judgments. My values place prevention of future violence higher than imposing vengeance on past violence. If we can find alternatives to arrest in high unemployment areas, such as cooling-out centers for offenders where they can stay separated from their victims without confronting the machinery of the criminal law, we might find much better ways of preventing further violence. It is not clear what effect this might have on the GENERAL Deterrence of domestic violence, but there is no evidence that mandatory arrest laws have accomplished that. Domestic homicides of women have remained fairly stable, when the increase in murders of girlfriends is included, over the time period of the expansion of mandatory arrest. Measuring other domestic violence citywide will require data sources independent of the police, such as hospital emergency room records.

Women's organizations were very supportive of your research findings. Given that many police departments have adopted mandatory arrest policies for domestic violence, do you think that this strategy has been successful in deterring domestic violence?

The research suggests that mandatory arrest has deterred domestic violence in neighborhoods of average employment, but increased it in neighborhoods of high unemployment. Since most cases in which police are called occur in high-unemployment areas, the net effect of mandatory arrest has probably been to increase total domestic violence. This conclusion is a sobering thought about the relationship between research, advocacy based on values, politics and public policy. Whether mandatory arrest would have grown without the research we did is an open question, and the research will have long-term benefits in advancing the science of criminal sanctions. I have no regret about doing this research, but I am strongly opposed to state laws mandating arrest. Such a "one-size-fits-all" policy is contrary to the principle of community-based policing, and makes the worst possible use of strong research findings.

What changes did you make in the redesign of the experiment on deterring domestic violence that you carried out in Milwaukee after the Minneapolis experiment? What other changes would you now advocate?

For the Milwaukee experiment, I made the following changes: 1) random assignment by research staff over the phone, so that officers did not know what treatment the offender would receive at the time they declared the case

eligible for the experiment; 2) interviews of offenders in the lockup while they were being processed. This allowed us to learn a lot about how they understood what was happening. Even more research needs to be done now on serious injury cases, in which the focus is on how to protect the victim from being injured again despite the offender having fled the scene. The most important method to test with a new experiment is the personal radio alarm necklace for the victim so she can summon police by the push of a button if the offender approaches her again. This could be especially effective in the first days or weeks after the last incident, which is the period of highest risk.

Some Characteristics of Experimental Studies

These two experiments were selected to illustrate the ingenious ways in which social behavior can be studied through experimentation. The experiment on bystander intervention was motivated by the desire to understand what appeared to be inexplicable group behavior. The researchers felt that while there were theoretical explanations available to explain why bystanders might choose to ignore a person in crisis, none were sufficiently convincing. Their experiment (and others that followed) moved toward developing and sustaining a *theory of diffusion of responsibility*. In the experiments on the deterrent effects of arrest, the researchers began by posing two opposing theories (*deterrence theory* and *labeling theory*) that could be used to explain why arresting a suspect could have positive or negative outcomes on repeated offenses (recidivism); the actual experiment tested which theory best fit the evidence collected.

The settings for these experiments were totally different. Darley and Latane's experiment took place in a psychology lab at a university in a carefully planned, contrived setting of the kind considered to be a "laboratory" environment. Sherman and Berk's experiment, in contrast, had a field setting: two police precincts in Minneapolis. Note that the field setting is in many ways more difficult because of the problems entailed in trying to impose all the conditions required for the experiment in an environment where the experimenter is much less able to control the possible effects of extraneous factors that could undermine the experiment. Thus, some efforts usually are made in a field experiment to try to reduce extraneous factors that may occur in the real-life setting. (For example, efforts taken by the experimental team to supervise the experiment included having an observer occasionally ride around with the police involved in the experiment to check that they were randomly handing out arrests, offering advice, or requiring separation. But this monitoring program was difficult to maintain because it took so many hours of riding along for the monitors to observe actual cases.)

While nearly all the officers in the two districts to be studied initially agreed to participate in the deterrence experiment, many did not fully follow the experimental design. Some would forget their report pads and thus could not follow the randomization procedure. However, the researchers noted that if the officers didn't feel like filling out forms on occasion, such random acts did not invalidate the experiment (Sherman and Berk, 1984, p. 264). The experimenters were particularly worried about whether certain officers might have deliberately excluded certain cases from the randomly prescribed treatment when they were uncomfortable with the assignment. Remember that the random assignment of suspects to the different treatment groups reduces the significance of a whole range of other extraneous factors that could affect the outcome of the experiment since their effects would be diminished by being spread across the groups in a random fashion.

Thus social-research experiments of this type have many similarities to natural scientific experiments, except that the topic to be observed in a social-research study is usually the social behavior of people rather than a phenomenon in the natural world. The two experiments described here studied different human behaviors: helping (or not helping) a stranger in a crisis and repeating (or not repeating) domestic assault after being arrested for it. What is impressive about these two experiments is that fairly simple designs could be employed to study these complex behaviors. This is consistent with the scientific style, in which simplicity and clarity are valued because they foster the understanding and acceptance of the findings.

The precision of an experimental design is intended to make such studies easy to replicate by others who are able to re-create similar conditions. Both of these experiments were subject to extensive efforts to replicate them, often by varying certain conditions of the experimental design and by changing the location or the qualities of the setting. [See, for example, replications and modifications of the bystander intervention experiment in Latane and Darley (1968) which placed subjects in a room gradually filling with smoke as well as Darley and Batson's (1973) other version of the experiment with seminary students. For a few examples of later experiments on arrests as deterrence to domestic violence, see Sherman and Smith (1992) for a deterrence experiment in Milwaukee and Pate and Hamilton (1992) for a modified replication in Dade County, Florida.] This propensity for replication and modification of experiments in the replications is also a characteristic of the natural sciences.

QUALITATIVE SOCIAL RESEARCH STUDIES

While the object of this chapter is to give you summaries of some interesting studies so that you can recognize certain qualities of their designs on your own, it may be more difficult for you to do this as you read about qualitative research projects compared with experiments or surveys. Because such studies are more naturalistic ways of studying a social issue, they may read more like stories. Thus I've included here three quite different qualitative research studies that were carried out in very familiar settings so that you will be exposed to a range of ways in which a qualitative researcher can carry out a study.

A term commonly used to describe many studies in this area is *field research*. It is apt because qualitative research projects often focus on a particular environment or field in order to understand it better. When the primary aim of a study is to understand a whole group of people (a culture, a distinct group of individuals), such research often is referred to as an *ethnography*. Many qualitative research projects use methods, such as interviews, which are employed in other types of research (interviews often are used in both surveys and experiments). But when the interviews are more informal and intensive, when they are carried out in naturalistic settings, they form the basis of qualitative interview research.

Here we will describe three quite different qualitative studies: an ethnography of children at play, a long-range field study of two adjoining urban neighborhoods, and a naturalistic interview study of two-job couples with young children. As you read about these studies, it will be helpful to keep the following issues in mind:

- How did the researcher do the preplanning for the study?
- What were the orienting questions that guided the research?
- How did the researcher observe and interview individuals in the field?
- How involved and immersed in the field did the researcher become?
- Were ethical considerations (for example, issues about privacy or confidentiality) raised in the course of these studies?
- How did the researchers form generalizations from the observations and interviews?

Gender Play: An Ethnography

The setting for an ethnographic study can be very exotic or very familiar. It may focus on an environment that few have seen or one with which everyone is acquainted. Barrie Thorne's (1993) study of the social world of girls and boys in elementary school had as its field a very ordinary setting: the public grade school. She observed two elementary schools: "Oceanside" School in a coastal city in California and "Ashton" School in a large city in Michigan. Skeptical that the meaning and significance of one's "gender" (the social significance of being a male or a female) is learned simply through a process of passive socialization of children by adults, Thorne reckoned that children "create" their gender through play. Thus the researcher needed a field in which she could actually observe children at play. Her object was to understand better the "social construction" of gender as "an active and ongoing process" (p. 4).

At Oceanside School, Thorne observed children in a fourth- and fifth-grade classroom who were approximately age 9 and 10. She was presented to the children as a "note-taking" visitor (p. 11). But she tried to enter the worlds of the children "with open-ended curiosity" (p. 12), which meant that she had to drop typical adult reactions toward children's play: that it was largely "trivial" and must be controlled. Nevertheless, she could not be a "full participant" in the classroom or the schoolyard. Thorne's self-reflectiveness on the process of doing this type of field research is revealing of her feelings. She states that in the classroom she easily identified with the teacher, a mature woman like herself. Moreover, as a mother Thorne found that her own maternal feelings and perspectives were engaged as well. She also relates that the memories of her own grade school days affected her ability to observe these children. Her memories of specific children from the past who exemplified types (the most popular, an unkempt "smelly" child, a loner) helped establish these types in the school setting. Interestingly, in terms of the deeper significance of gender, all the children Thorne remembered most fully from her own grade school days in Utah were, like herself, girls.

At Ashton School in Michigan, Thorne stuck less closely to a single classroom and spent much time in the kindergarten and with a second grade class. When she was in the classroom, she was more clearly separated from the children. Though the teachers did not expect Thorne to help maintain authority, they often shared their amusement or recognition of a child's reaction by meeting her eyes. (Thorne worried that such shared adult responses would be looked on by the children as a form of betrayal.) When Thorne was in the lunchroom she often ate with the children, and in the school playground she sometimes entered the children's games (such as jump rope or statue buyer). But for the most part, she says, "I usually roamed and watched from the margins of ongoing activities" (p. 14).

Thorne carried a spiral notebook and took down descriptions that were later developed into field notes (p. 17). This note taking brought forth many questions from the children—"You spying on us?" "You still takin' notes?" "What you 'sposed to be?" (p. 17)—to which she responded as straightforwardly as she could. She discovered that telling the children that she was studying behavior was looked on dubiously since it sounded like a socially controlling practice. Some of the children feared that she was "taking down names" and that they might get into trouble. The children seemed to prefer the explanation that she was studying "play."

Initially Thorne saw chaos in the children's activity, but over time their rapid movements took on different meanings to her. Instead of seeing "poking, pushing, tripping, grabbing, pinning from behind" as antagonistic, she came to view such activity as imaginative and exploratory. Thorne also clearly observed the "things" the children brought to school, traded, and shared with each other, seeing in this activity a primitive economic system based on principles of exchange. From these close observations Thorne discovered the borderlines between boys and girls and the meaning of the separate cultures that segregated them.

These cultural differences were not represented by the external differences in the behavior of girls and boys but the "symbolic dimensions of experience—patterns of meaning, stereotypes, beliefs, ideologies, metaphor, discourses" that characterize the different spheres of girls and boys. Between these gender boundaries there was "borderwork" in which the distinctions between "the boys" and "the girls" got sharpened and separate collectivities were formed (pp. 64–65). Situations such as competitions between the boys and girls and chasing tended to reaffirm the clear boundaries between the sexes.

But Thorne also found much variation in the cultural worlds boys and girls inhabit. Concerned that the stress created by cultural differences between boys and girls leads to the continual domination of one sex over the other, Thorne concludes that it is important to start with "a sense of the whole rather than with an assumption of gender as separation and difference" (p. 108). To do this, one needs to examine gender in context, looking for which boys tend to dominate and which girls seek out intimacy. Thorne turned to studying children who crossed gender lines in their behaviors and asked whether this type of crossing behavior challenges the boundaries between the sexes (pp. 133–134). She saw that such subversive behavior was partially controlled by teasing and labeling, but she also concluded that "incidents of crossing may chip away at traditional ideologies and hold out new possibilities" (p. 133). When a girl beat up one of the boys, Thorne felt the excitement rise among the girls. When girls played games such as soccer, this seemed to open up more arenas for other girls. However, when a lone girl joined a boy's game, Thorne felt that the gender boundaries remained intact (p. 133).

The uneven transition into adulthood during adolescence, Thorne noted in her observations, heightens gender differentiation. But Thorne's concern is more with the fuzzier boundaries between the sexes which support more complex appraisals of the meaning of gender differences and cross-sex association. She concludes with a chapter advising adults to support a broader range of cross-sexual relationships beyond those of "heterosexual romance," ones based on friendship and collegiality (p. 172). Box 1-3 offers insights into Thorne's research experiences.

BOX 1-3

INTERVIEW WITH BARRIE THORNE ON *GENDER PLAY*

Barrie Thorne, currently a Professor of Sociology at the University of Berkeley, carried out her research on children at play in two elementary schools (one in California in the late 1970s, the other in Michigan in 1980). Dr. Thorne previously was a member of the faculty at the University of Southern California and at Michigan State University.

How did you first decide to study children at play as a way to better understand gender?

I got interested in studying children when we had our first child in 1973; running around with him took me back to spaces of childhood. I was already involved in the study of gender (I had done a book with Nancy Henley: *Language and Sex Difference in Dominance*) and I started thinking about children and the analogy with women in their absence from and marginalization in knowledge. Given that gender was on my mind, and I was wondering about all the feminist prescriptions about trying to raise gender-free children, it just sort of grew on me that I would like to study children and gender. I chose schools to do my observations in, not so much because they were schools, but because that's where one can find "captive populations" of children.

(continued)

What were the major differences between the children in the California school and those in the Michigan school?

The children at the school I studied on the coast of California in the mid-1970s were mostly white. The children's parents had jobs such as working in auto body shops, or in the service sector, or many worked on farms. (Let me add that currently I'm studying a school in Oakland, California, that is incredibly ethnically diverse; the children come from families representing 11 different language groups. Ethnicity modulates and cuts through gender—including the kinds of games kids play.) The Michigan school was also a white working-class school, but in 1980, when I was observing there, many of the children's parents who were autoworkers were unemployed. Because of this, the Michigan school had a much more depressing environment. There was more obvious poverty. And the cold Michigan winter made the poverty all the more visible and harsh. Some of the children, for example, didn't have adequate covering for their legs. That was the major regional difference.

How did the chaos of the children's play finally make sense to you? How were you able to get to the point that you could actually interpret it?

One way is to use the method for counting crowds by using grids. It's a step-by-step process. Or, using the analogy of a microscope, I would focus on one piece of the complex, chaotic field of children at play. So, for example, I might see a jump rope game and zero in on it. Or I might focus on the skateboarding area. Each day I did an inventory of who was doing what on the playground. I also made little maps that I literally would draw in my fieldnotes—Which play groups were where? What activities were going on? How were the groups composed? These strategies helped me fix certain observations, although the scenes changed all the time. Then I would sometimes go to a particular scene of action because it was dramatic or interesting or unusual. And sometimes I would go to a particular scene of action because I hadn't really tapped that one (this is a kind of "theoretical sampling"). Sometimes the real challenge is noticing the less dramatic incidents; you need these so that you can get a more rounded view of the whole social environment.

You found that there were gender boundaries between the boys and girls, and that group gender distinctions got established through borderwork. How important a role did competition between groups of girls and of boys play in making the gender distinctions?

Borderwork has to do with group gender distinctions, so it's not individual competition, but rather clusters of the same gender operating in a gender-defined way so the group gets defined and the boundary is marked by gender. For example, I observed a game in the playground where girls piled on one side and boys on the other. It became clear that gender was the organizing principle for setting up the sides. Many of the incidents on the playground were much more fleeting, like those of chasing—girls chase the boys, boys chase the girls; these actions are more fluid and might be transmuted into another kind of play.

In the classroom, the math and spelling contests were explicitly girls versus boys; that's how the teacher set them up, joking that it was the "beastly boys" against the "gossipy girls." These classroom competitions were more institutionalized than those in the playground, since they were ratified by an adult in an environment that was mixed and usually not separated by gender. The very fact that the teacher helped to set up an antagonistic relationship between the boys and girls helped establish the gender antagonism between them.

You wrote about some children who crossed gender lines. Were there ways in which you felt the school, the teacher, or the structure of the classroom could encourage gender crossing?

I use the term *gender crossing* to describe situations where there are individual children who cross, but the borders between gendered groups remain firm. In cases like that, the girl (or boy) enters the other gender group as an honorary boy or an honorary girl. An honorary gender situation (like the position of Margaret Thatcher) doesn't do much to change the status quo. The kind of mixing that does change things is where group gender boundaries are diminished, it's easier for girls and boys to mix, and the situation is more balanced or fluid and less gender-marked

In the conclusion of the book, I describe moments (although I was sure that this was not the goal in some of these incidents) when specific teacher practices had the effect of encouraging mixing. One example was the game London Bridge Is Falling Down, which an aide introduced on the Michigan playground. Because it was a new game which the kids had never played, she taught it to everyone. It didn't have gendered roles in it: the children just had to get in line and go underneath the bridge. And the boys and girls just mixed in it. It wasn't two teams; it wasn't an oppositional structure. It was a cooperative game.

Teachers sometimes employed principles other than gender in sorting children, like counting off, which has the effect of mixing the genders. In the school that I'm currently studying, there is a poster in the teachers' lunchroom that says something like: "100 Ways to Sort Students without Resorting to Gender." The kindergarten teacher said she had seen it all the time, and it finally sunk in. She was trying some of the ways, like sorting children by the color of shoe laces, what they had for breakfast, whether or not they had on a belt. That's a bit of pedagogy, but it's also an example of shifting away from a gender principle in organizing activities.

There's something so self-revealing and genuine about the way you describe yourself as an ethnographer of children—how you had writing dilemmas and how you tried to solve them. In other words, you seem to share your methods and your worries with the reader. How did you decide to do this? Would you advise other qualitative researchers to delve into how they struggled with their research and make this public?

If I'd written *Gender Play* right after I collected the first wave of data, it would have been a very different book. First of all, theories of gender hadn't reached a point where I could make

the central arguments of the book. And by the time I wrote the book, the new ethnographic trends in anthropology and sociology (that have partially also been enhanced by feminist critiques of knowledge) had moved away from the "fly-on-the-wall" kind of ethnographic stance in which the observations are presented in an objective voice as if the researcher wasn't there. The "new ethnography" approaches a move toward telling what is actually closer to the truth, which is that as an observer you are part of the scene you're observing, and you're the instrument collecting and presenting, and constructing the knowledge of the event. Putting more of the observer into the scene gives a better feel for how the knowledge has been constructed.

I was trying to be less transparent about how knowledge is constructed and trying to reveal more of how one actually goes about doing ethnography. Chapter Five describes the process, trying out one story and then unraveling it, and trying out another with the same data— that was actually the process I went through. That was one of the most thrilling moments in the writing. I had just chipped away at the problem of "separate worlds" depictions of girls' and boys' styles of interacting. But I had not really consolidated an alternative way of understanding and then it consolidated as I wrote it—so I shared those two ways of illuminating the information, partly as a way of arguing for the virtues of the second more complex and less dichotomous interpretation. Of course this kind of reflexivity (reflecting about the observer's relationship to the observed) or the researcher's relationship to those whom she studies can sometimes get confessional, and sort of narcissistic and gooey. I was trying to use a light touch but I also knew that if I had written it back when I was a graduate student in the late 1960s, the self-reflections would have been entirely in an appendix (as in my dissertation on the draft resistance movement). There has been a change over a course of 20-30 years toward a more visible presence of the researcher in some forms of ethnographic writing.

Two Urban Neighborhoods: A Long-Term Community Study

One of the field studies I used in the earlier editions of *Doing Social Research* was the study of a bar called Jelly's on Chicago's South Side (Anderson, 1978). This study had grown out of the doctoral dissertation Elijah Anderson had completed in Chicago. When Anderson moved to Philadelphia to become a faculty member at the University of Pennsylvania, he began a community study. This time he examined two neighborhoods: "the Village," a racially mixed community that was becoming "gentrified," and an adjacent neighborhood, "Northton," populated predominantly by lower-income African-Americans. Whereas his study of Jelly's was based on intensive participant observations of one bar over a fairly short period, this study of two urban neighborhoods drew on a range of data-gathering techniques extending over a 14-year period. In comparison to Thorne's study of primary schools which she visited extensively over a period of months, Anderson's neighborhood study has a broader field and a longer time frame (Anderson, *Streetwise,* 1992).

During this time, Anderson tells us, he "spent hours on the streets, talking and listening to the people of the neighborhood. . . . I photographed the setting, videotaped street corner scenes, recorded interviews . . . got to know all kinds of people from small-time drug dealers to policemen, middle class whites, and outspoken black community activists" (p. ix). Anderson frequented bars, laundromats, and carryouts and attended parties and community gatherings. For two years he served on the board of a community educational committee to improve the quality of the schools. At first he thought he would just study the Village, focusing on its transitional character, but as the problems of the adjacent community of Northton spilled over into the Village, he decided to shift his focus to encompass both neighborhoods.

As Anderson saw the neighborhoods change over this period, he became more involved in the communities. He states:

Much of what I learned came from informal interviews and direct ethnographic observation over an extended period, and it draws on my experiences in the Village-Northton and in nearby communities that share some of the area's more prominent features. In a sense, over time I became my own informant. What emerges, then, is to a certain sense conceptual and abstract, but it reflects my sense of what is true (*p. xi*).

For anyone who has lived in a racially diverse urban community which has undergone urban renewal and gentrification (as I previously did in Chicago) Anderson's description of the Village and how people interact with each other within it rings true. His perspective offers insight into how black men deal with life in both the integrated community of the Village and the poorer neighborhood of Northton. He continually moves between two roles: being a black man in the community of "liberal" whites who are nevertheless both fearful and apprehensive of black males and taking the neutral position of the social researcher trying to understand the range of reactions that residents of such neighborhoods experience.

One of Anderson's research strategies is to look for people who play similar and noted roles in the neighborhood. In Northton he finds elderly black women recognized for having lived "a good life," being involved "in church" or with "the lord" (p. 74). These women, whom he called "female old heads," take upon themselves a sense of responsibility for the younger members of the community, who often lack parental control. As one female "old head" stated that "when you see any child out there doing wrong, you goes to him and you corrects him, just like he is yo' child" (p. 74). Anderson then describes the characterizations of those engaged in taking drugs. He distinguishes "pipers" (who smoke dope from a pipe) from "zombies" (who are seriously addicted). He poignantly portrays how young women, coerced by pimps to "do tricks" and try crack, become hooked. As "coke whores" they must continue to prostitute themselves in order to pay for their addiction (p. 88).

Anderson also wants to explore the meaning of youth culture among urban blacks. He uncovers the sense of "rap" as the verbal element (the conversation) of the young black man's self-presentation, which also includes his "dress, grooming, looks, dancing ability" (p. 114). The success of a young man's rap can be assessed in terms of how much "booty" he claims (that is, how much sex he is getting). Conversely, a sexually unsuccessful young man's rap is termed "tissue paper" (p. 115). Offering these verbal descriptors is a way of letting outsiders (the readers) better understand the deeper meaning of the links that bind social groups.

Determining the fatherhood of new babies is a common community topic (p. 130):

> Casual sex with as many women as possible, impregnating one or more, and getting them to "have your baby" brings a boy the ultimate in esteem from his peers and makes him a man. "Casual" sex is therefore fraught with social significance for the boy who has little or no hope of achieving financial stability and hence cannot see himself taking care of a family (*p. 136*).

For the adolescent girls, early pregnancies and becoming a teenage mother are easily accepted. Anderson relates the astonishment of middle-class observers at this "ready approval" of pregnancies and babies and the very weak sanctions against illegitimate births (p. 136).

The Village is a very different type of urban community, populated with people of culturally different backgrounds, many of whom have come from the suburbs to create some type of urban oasis closer to their work. Over time, the newer middle-class residents in such a community drive out the older poorer residents and the community becomes more homogeneous (pp. 138–139). Many of the developers want to restore the Village to its earlier elegance as they envision it (p. 150). Anderson contrasts these newer middle-class residents to the older Quaker families still living in the neighborhood, who maintain easier and less in-

trusive associations with their less-advantaged neighbors (p. 141). The newer city dwellers demand better schools and community services and feel quite distant from their poorer neighbors.

On the borders of the Village, "the edge," where the neighborhood intersects with Northton, there is pressure from Village residents to "clean up" by changing the stores, the street sounds, and the street action (p. 152). Anderson describes what happens when a store on the edge applies for a liquor license: the full range of Village residents (the older ones, the yuppies, the counterculture types) unites in protest, while residents of Northton approve (p. 153).

Some of Anderson's most sensitive observations focus on how black men and white residents behave toward each other:

> White women are said to plant broad grins on their faces in hope of not being accosted. The smile may appear to be a sign of trust, but it is more likely a show of deference, especially when the woman looks back as soon as she is at a safe distance (*p. 179*).

Anderson also describes a personal situation in which his car was stolen and a white police officer offered to drive him around the Village to see if he could identify it. He relates how another police car meets them and how the officer in his car immediately explains why Anderson is in the backseat, assuming that the other officer would suspect that as a black man, Anderson must have been picked up for some violation. Nevertheless, throughout the officers' conversation, Anderson remains a "nonperson." When his car can't be found, the officer drops him off and he spots one of his university colleagues at a bus stop. The colleague calls out to see if he's all right, but when Anderson tells him why he was in the police car, he doubts that the white colleague believes him (pp. 190–193).

Anderson's field study of these two urban neighborhoods ends up by drawing generalizations from his observations on the street etiquette of the two areas. Anderson recognizes that the concerns of blacks and whites in urban areas truly differ.

Blacks who abide by the law feel quite secure in such areas and are less fearful of black-on-black crime because they are more likely to be able to recognize a mugger. White men are less threatening to both whites and blacks, and this makes whites feel more vulnerable and encourages white men to exaggerate their protectiveness of white women (p. 209). He also senses that while whites in mixed racial areas such as the Village would often like to get to know their black neighbors better, this usually does not happen:

> Many whites may wish to get closer to the black, but for complicated reasons having to do with local history, class etiquette, and lingering racism, they normally maintain their established social distance (*p. 213*).

As Anderson defines it, "street wisdom is really street etiquette wisely enacted" (p. 231). Those who are "street dumb" are unable to differentiate potentially dangerous situations from nondangerous ones. Whites who are newcomers to such neighborhoods are often incapable of handling the meanings of street encounters. Unfamiliar with blacks and black culture, they develop a form of street etiquette based on stereotyping people by race and gender which serves to separate them more fully from their black neighbors (p. 253). Thus although the ethos of the neighborhood calls for "decency and tolerance toward others," the residents must still come to hold a shared perspective on the neighborhood that offers a sense of security and order. It is through this experience that residents in a racially diverse neighborhood "create at least the appearance of an ordered and racially tolerant public space" (p. 253).

The Second Shift: A Naturalistic Interview-Observation Study

Qualitative research very often involves some interviewing, even if observation is the primary mode of data gathering. It is also possible to base a qualitative research project largely on intensive interviewing, with observations making up a smaller proportion of the data-gathering effort. In such studies, interpretations of these interviews serve as the form of analysis. A good example of this strategy can be seen in Arlie Hochschild's study of how far husbands and wives share housework and child care when both partners work. This study became the basis of her well-known book *The Second Shift* (1989).

The "second shift" is the job you have at home caring for your family after you have completed your "first shift" at the workplace. In the book's appendix, "Research on Who Does the Housework and Childcare?" Hochschild describes how, to explore this topic of the second shift, she and Anne Machung interviewed 145 different people (some more than once) including 50 two-job couples and 45 others, including baby-sitters, schoolteachers, and persons supporting the interviewees, as well as some traditional couples with young children (in which the wife did not work) and some former two-job couples who had divorced. After the first set of interviews, Hochschild also carried out more intensive interviews and home observations of 12 of the families, selected as representative of the different types of families studied.

The selected couples were initially chosen from those who had completed a short questionnaire distributed to a systematic sample (every thirteenth name) from the personnel files of a large corporation. Using "snowball" sampling techniques, selected couples were asked to add the names of others who were two-job couples with children under age 6. To estimate initially how the respondents would relate to the subject under study, they were asked, "Can you tell me about your typical day?" What Hochschild was looking for was whether the respondents would mention some type of work at home or attending to children. What she found was that only 3 percent of the wives but 46 percent of the husbands mentioned *nothing* about the home; in terms of children, 3 percent of the mothers but 31 percent of the fathers made no "spontaneous mention of doing something for a child" (p. 281).

The activities of the second shift were sorted into three categories: housework, child care, and managing domestic life (e.g., planning, paying bills, arranging baby-sitters, preparing birthday parties). Then the proportional share of the work undertaken by men in each of the three categories was determined. In addition, on the basis of interview material, Hochschild learned what roles the men expected to play in their families. From this, she defined three ideological types: *traditional men, transitional men,* and *egalitarian men.* Comparing the men's ideological beliefs to their sharing of child care, housework, and the management of domestic life, Hochschild found a strong relationship between the ideology of egalitarian men and the sharing of the *second shift.* The situation was much less clear, however, for transitional men who were beginning to believe in equal roles for men and women in the home but in many cases were not yet contributing much to the work of keeping the home. In fact, larger proportions of traditional men than transitional men (22 percent compared to 3 percent) actually shared equally in the three types of work.

The analysis Hochschild presents is very lively and readable. She uses eight situations of particular families to show major differences in how couples handle the second shift. In the Holt family, for example, Hochschild presents a "transitional" father who takes an active, though circumscribed role in the home and a "do-it-all" mother who believes she is egalitarian. The Holts' compromise is for the mother to do all the "upstairs work" and the father to work in the garage and do other handyman roles.

Hochschild is always looking for the psychological strains and readjustments couples employ. In the Stein family, for example, we are presented with two lawyers who believe in egalitarianism though the father's overriding drive for professional success results in his not participating at all in the second shift. In this family, the mother maintains her part-time career as an attorney by hiring a number of helpers. But again, Hochschild is never content with empirical details. Instead, she searches for the psychological costs of this inegalitarian family life and sees the Stein couple as pulling away from each other emotionally.

Hochschild wants to understand the characteristics of men who share in the second shift. To do this she presents two couples struggling to develop egalitarian family roles in which the fathers are at different stages of adjustment to their roles as fully equal partners in homemaking. "Greg Alston" is somewhat distant from and tentative about his children but is fully engaged in other work in the second shift. "John Livingston" splits the work of the home fifty-fifty with his wife, but the Livingstons' situation is particularly stressful because of the husband's career tensions and the couple's willingness to house and entertain "live-in" relatives and visitors.

Finally, Hochschild presents two men who have accommodated to the second shift. The first, "Michael Sherman," an academic, has realigned his career and life so that his wife, "Adrienne," can finish her doctorate and pursue her career goals while raising twins. Their accommodation requires "Adrienne" to request a half-time academic position and "Michael" to slow down in his scientific career. Lastly, Hochschild offers "Art Winfield," a lab assistant with a high school education whose commitment to his adopted son exemplifies a very strong parental role. Though "Adam," the five-year-old son, goes to an after-school program at a day-care center, "Art" spends intensive time with his son every day: "My son gets only three-and-one-half hours of my time a day, so the time I spend with him is very important to me" (p. 181). Both "Michael Sherman" and "Art Winfield" engage in what Hochschild terms "primary parenting."

Hochschild's study is memorable not only for the wonderfully insightful descriptions of these particular families but also for her ability to draw interpretations from these cases that address the home lives of all families. In searching beneath the ideologies and activities of families in dealing with the second shift, Hochschild finds strategies and strains. For example, she concludes that men's participation with their families developed in response not only to their ideological goals but also to their psychological needs and the degree to which they identified with their own fathers or wished to play a fatherly role they had never experienced as boys. She also notes social class differences: Those in the working classes more often hold traditional ideals of caring, while those in the middle classes more often hold the egalitarian ideal of "sharing" child care. In the working classes, however, lack of money makes getting assistance impossible, while among the more affluent, the problems arise more because of the instability of paid help and the greater pressures of the partners' careers.

As Hochschild shows, women try to change their roles or cope with them by adopting various strategies: being a "supermom" or reducing efforts at work, at housework, at child care, toward one's partner, or toward oneself. Or the woman might seek help outside the family. Men's strategies include trying to cooperate or to resist. Hochschild also examines the impact of the demands of the second shift on marital stability, finding that many marriages cannot withstand the complex pressures of jobs and home life. For some working women, however, a recognition of the weaker position of women in the economy may increase their fear of divorce and hence dissuade them from asking their husbands for more help with the second shift (p. 249–253). Finally, she contrasts men who participate in the second shift with men who don't, looking for the factors that differentiate these two groups. The only common factor which the "helping" men shared was that they themselves had lacked a positive father figure: their fathers had been "detached, absent or overbearing" (p. 217). These men wanted to be the fathers they had never had. In addition, they were comfortable identifying with their mothers or with an emotionally supportive man.

Some Characteristics of Qualitative Research

All three of these qualitative studies have at their core *interpretation*. The point of the studies is not the precise empirical evidence but what the evidence signifies. Each focuses on a very ordinary and familiar aspect of modern life: children at play, urban neighborhoods in transition, juggling the second shift in a two-job family. But each brings these commonplace situations into finer relief by carefully comparing realities to idealized goals, actions to words, and expectations to accommodations. Thorne recognizes that encouraging girls to participate in less stereotypically feminine forms of play conflicts with the belief that little girls need to learn how to become nurturing mothers; Hochschild finds that men in two-job families who accept the egalitarian ideology of sharing the second shift often are not able to take on the tasks and roles this ideology demands; Anderson learns that achieving racial integration in an urban neighborhood does not necessarily alleviate the fears of white residents toward black men or increase the level of trust on the part of blacks that whites will deal with them fairly.

In each case the authors are studying very familiar territory: Anderson, an African-American male sociologist who has lived and worked in urban neighborhoods in transition, is studying such neighborhoods and focusing on the roles of black men within them; Thorne and Hochschild, two white women sociologists who themselves are mothers, are studying children at play and two-career families. This familiarity with the topics may help the authors bring the environments they are analyzing to life for their readers.

How does Hochschild's naturalistic interview study of couples compare to Anderson's community study of two neighborhoods and to Thorne's ethnography of schoolchildren at play? The "locales" are very different. Thorne confined herself to two primary schools, though one was in California and the other was a great distance away in Michigan; Anderson had a broader field of two neighborhoods, but they were adjacent to each other in Philadelphia. Hochschild is largely indifferent to her geography; though the interviews were carried out in California's Bay Area, one might say that Hochschild's locale is the space two-job couples occupy. Note that only Thorne had a "fixed" setting (the schools); Anderson's field had geographic specificity (urban neighborhoods), but it is public space open to anyone.

For Anderson in his urban neighborhoods and for Throne in her elementary schools, the central qualities of these social environments are described and analyzed so that the reader can get a clear picture of the forces that are operating. Individuals are never mere numbers in these studies; instead, their situations exemplify the roles within their social structures. If we consider the couples described in Hochschild's study, their homes, careers, and children are so finely portrayed that her study reads like a novel and many of the characters in the study, such as Art Winfield, seem familiar and recognizable. In comparison, Anderson more often develops types of individuals (female old heads, zombies) to exemplify specific role patterns and distinguish social types within a setting.

As to the conduct of the researchers, the authors did not try to deceive anyone about what they were studying. Recall that Thorne found it challenging to decide how to present herself to the children she was studying, who seemed comfortable thinking of her as studying their "play" rather than their "behavior." In an interview study Hochschild naturally identified her interest in two-job families. Most of those interviewed were reinterviewed, and 12 couples were intensively interviewed in depth. Hochschild describes her approach as "naturalistic." For example, respondents were asked to describe a "typical day." Whether a male respondent included information on his home or his children in his description of a typical day was the indicator Hochschild used to select men whose roles in the second shift varied.

Anderson describes himself as "his own best informant" (p. xi). After years of involvement with community groups, informal interviews, and ethnographic observation, he was able to describe the culture of these neighborhoods in depth. Clearly Anderson was close to various residents of Northton and the Village. Thorne's role in the schools was more formal, though she tried to break down barriers between herself and the children and not ally herself too closely with the teachers. Hochschild's role as an interviewer was also formal, though her shared status as a mother and career woman leveled her experience with the experiences of those being interviewed.

In each case, the researcher tried not to intrude on the scene so that the true nature of the environment and the individuals being studied would emerge. This unobtrusive approach, in which the investigator does not make his or her presence too forceful but blends in with others in the social setting to gain their trust and reduce artificiality, is characteristic of qualitative research. In addition, the researcher must hold a natural sympathy for the environment and issues being studied. It follows that the qualitative researcher must be a very fine informal interviewer, gaining the confidence of those interviewed to elicit introspective considerations and evaluations of their lives.

Furthermore, qualitative studies often have a certain openness in their design. Rather than entering the setting with very specific, fixed questions, many qualitative researchers begin with more general questions and a certain sense of direction and then let the research experience affect the future course of the study. Note that even in Hochschild's interview study the questions evolved from her initial data gathered by having the subjects describe a typical day. Recall that Thorne cautiously moved into the play worlds of the children, trying several settings and personal approaches to gain a closer view of the children's play. The course of a field study may vary with what happens in the field. In Anderson's research, the slow evolution of the study is apparent as his attention shifts from the gentrified neighborhood of the Village to the poorer urban neighborhood of Northton and then to the impact of one neighborhood on the other. These open, evolving designs are very different from the highly contrived and preestablished designs of an experiment and the precision and definiteness of a questionnaire.

The research setting chosen also must represent a case considered typical of a group of other cases. Thorne's elementary school playgrounds could be in any public school; Anderson's urban neighborhoods represent familiar zones in most major American cities; Hochschild's two-job couples have become more and more the typical American family arrangement. Thus, while field studies may center on a unique place, a specific set of people, and a set time frame, their aim is to tell a tale of many settings, many people, and a continuing period of time. To do this, the social researcher must turn the particular into the universal, the personal experience into a role experience. The specific events must be understood as representing regular patterns of happenings.

However, many social researchers would challenge the contention that field studies are representative of the environments and individuals they portray. A critic might ask: "How can we know whether the residents Anderson describes in Northton are representative of poor urban neighborhoods in general?" Since field studies generally focus on specific settings, their typicality often can be questioned. The challenges may be serious, but qualitative researchers claim that their purpose is less to present a common phenomenon that can be replicated than to uncover the deeper meaning of the particular situation being studied to gain an appreciation of a human social setting. Qualitative studies of the kind described here represent research not as a cold, microscopic view of a social question but as a keen, sensitive appreciation of a fragment of the human picture. The reader of a well-done qualitative study usually feels closer to—and warmer about—the topic being studied, more understanding of the situation, and more desirous of gaining additional insight into the world being examined.

CHARACTERISTICS OF SOCIAL RESEARCH STUDIES

Commonalities

This chapter has examined characteristic studies using three general types of research methods as a means of exemplifying the major aims and features of social research. We can now ask what characteristics they have in common. First we can say that they all seek *regularities*. In field research, the confusion of evidence must be sorted out to form patterns that help us understand the interconnectedness of activities in a particular setting. In the Philadelphia communities, residents who played noted roles in the community often protected the young from more dangerous residents. In the experiments, the reactions studied— the diffusion of responsibility and deterrence of domestic assaults—were regular responses to a prearranged stimulus. In such studies, it need only be shown that a large enough number of subjects respond in a certain fashion to support the regularity of the reaction. Finally, the surveys used a large number of respondents to determine regularities in relationships between various factors. Thus regularity is gleaned from particular situations in qualitative field studies, inferred from common responses in experimental studies, and extracted from extensive evidence of similar characteristics and relationships in survey research.

The second common quality of social research studies is that they examine individuals and social units *representative* of wider numbers of individuals and social units. Surveys (such as the sexual behavior survey) do this most clearly by using probability samples to represent statistically the populations on which they are drawn. Experiments assume that the reactions of the individuals serving as subjects are representative of human reactions in general, and in experiments in which subjects are randomly assigned to the experimental and control groups, researchers minimize the possible effects of unique individual characteristics affecting the experimental outcome. Field studies select sites (such as the primary schools study) that represent typical social settings and human situations of wide social interest.

Third, these studies all develop *concepts* or apply existing concepts to express the regularities noted among the representative subjects. Anderson's concept of "street wisdom" characterized experienced residents of the Village who could differentiate dangerous from benign situations. Hirschi studied delinquency by operationalizing it to mean delinquent acts either formally recorded as violations or informally self-reported by the youths. Laumann and his colleagues developed the concepts of six different sexual orientations to represent the range of values and attitudes toward sexuality represented by their respondents. Hochschild used the concept of the second shift to emphasize that work in the home is as demanding, time-consuming, and potentially significant to the quality of life as work outside the home.

Anything that varies or is prone to variation can be studied as a *variable*. Studies single out specific variables for consideration. For Laumann and his colleagues, the major variables in the sexuality survey were measures of sexual practices, attitudes, and "master statuses" such as age, educational attainment, marital status, gender, and religion. In the domestic assault experiment, variation was built into the range of "treatments" offered to suspects (arrest, advice, and separation). Anderson studied variation across two neighborhoods, Thorne studied variation in play behavior between girls and boys, and Hochschild studied variation in the housework roles that men and women assumed. Each study begins, however, with certain *constants*, which are the common features that tend not to vary in a study. Sherman and Berk's subjects were all suspects in domestic assault cases; Hochschild's subjects were all married couples with two jobs and preschool-age children.

Each study either built on or helped test a *theory*, an explanation for a set of coordinated occurrences or relationships. Darley and Latane developed a theory of "diffusion of responsibility" to

account for the failure of bystanders to respond to a crisis if others had observed it as well. The domestic assault experiment had two theories defined initially: deterrence theory and labeling theory. The field researchers developed theories out of their observations; for example, Anderson concluded that the residents of integrated neighborhoods had to develop a shared perspective to promote order, security, and a sense of racial tolerance. Hirschi's delinquency survey tested three possible explanations for delinquency: strain theory, control theory, and cultural deviance theory.

Each study followed a *preconceived design*. A research design is both a plan and a strategy. As a plan, it encompasses a set of steps to follow and a kind of ideal model of what should occur. As a strategy, a research design must search out the potential obstacles to the study and consider ways to avoid or confront these obstacles. The strategy aspect of a research design suggests the "active" quality of developing a project: the need to make things happen, make requests of others, gain support, and possibly intrude on the privacy and work of others to carry out a research objective. The experimental studies had the most precise designs: every step was prearranged, carefully ordered, and controlled. The expected results were considered in the design, and variations were set up in the experimental procedures to elicit differences in response. The surveys were the next most heavily predesigned. Questions were written to represent all phases of the analysis to be carried out. Of the qualitative studies presented, Hochschild's was the most preplanned in that it depended on interviews carried out by assistants as well as by herself. Thorne's and Anderson's studies clearly developed over time as the projects evolved.

Creative Components of the Studies

Each of the studies we have considered bears the mark of its researcher. Of course, the qualitative studies seem to be the most dependent on the qualities of those carrying them out. Because they began with less fully preconceived designs and because the course of the research was altered as the researcher proceeded with the project, the special interests of the researcher guided the course of the study. Clearly, Hochschild's interest in women's changing social roles and their impact on home life gave a direction to her efforts. Her intuitive insight into the meaning of two-job families coping with the second shift gave her study vitality and a sense of relevance.

Anderson uncovered the qualities of urban communities, developing insight about the forms, strengths, and constraints of life in ghetto and gentrifying neighborhoods. Such insight requires taking down the protective covering which insulates the observer from the observed, approaching strangers openly without preconceived notions. Such a process is both shocking and eye-opening. It loosens fixed ideas, shakes up the givenness of beliefs, and makes situations appear to be more susceptible to change. Generally, a person is more open to what is familiar. The danger is that we can be so familiar with a situation that we are unable to see it with "fresh eyes." Recall Thorne's efforts to reduce the barriers between herself and the children she studied. Whether an insider or an outsider is more perceptive in understanding a social environment is debatable. An outsider enters an unfamiliar environment with a desire to understand it in order to account for what appears to be surprising or unusual. In Anderson's earlier study of a ghetto bar in Chicago, he spent many evenings in the bar in order to come to know the patrons so closely that he became a trusted confidant. He was an outsider turned insider.

Both experiments had creative qualities. Darley and Latane's fabricated crisis involving bystanders was created in such a way to be believable to college students. The influence of this created "crisis" stimulus would determine whether the subjects would sense the need to help. The crux of the creativity in this experiment was in the believability of the "victim's" crisis. The domestic assault experiment offered a range of different

sanctions, creatively delivered to be more or less punishing and degrading.

The surveys may seem the least creative. Following the old dictum "If you want to find something out, ask," the survey tries to be explicit and largely unambiguous. Yet the selection of questions, the wording of questions, and the combining of different items to measure more complex concepts (such as Hirschi's set of questions to tap delinquent behavior) suggest areas where creativity has played a part in the design of specific questions and sets of questions.

Field studies allow for greater spontaneity on the part of the researcher to change directions in reaction to some aspect of the study. This spontaneity makes the field study appear more imaginative. In experiments and surveys, however, the creativity must be built into the study design. Neither method depends on spontaneity. Instead, consistency is the hallmark of both good experiments and good surveys.

Scientific Components of the Studies

What is scientific about the studies described? First, the meaning of the term *science* must be clarified. You may think of science as a body of knowledge, as something more or less fixed that can be learned. I would prefer you to think of science in more dynamic terms as an activity, a means of finding things out. To carry out scientific activity means that the scientist must do something. There are two primary characteristics of scientific activity. The first is that what is studied needs to be observed. Science, in other words, is *empirical research*. It is based on observable evidence (what the qualitative researchers saw, answers to questions, reactions to experimental stimuli) which has been carefully recorded and presented to make it as close to the actual observation as possible. This attention to recording and presenting the observations carefully and precisely is part of the effort to make these studies scientific.

Science depends on a *logical and rational* system of rules for thinking and using language; therefore, precision in the measurement of what is being studied and clarity in the presentation of the data are both necessary. Much of this book will be about the different kinds of rules appropriate for the various kinds of research methods that will be described. The cardinal rule is to make the means appropriate to the ends of a study. Thus definition is a critical part of science. What is being studied must be clearly defined to determine whether a finding has been made.

The purpose of each study is to seek to know something better, more deeply, and more clearly by applying rational, logical rules of analysis to the empirical evidence gathered through observation. In some cases, these rules were already defined in the *hypotheses* set prior to carrying out the study. In the domestic assault experiment, for instance, deterrence theory led to a hypothesis that those arrested would be deterred from subsequent acts of assault. This study exemplifies the *deductive method,* in which a hypothesis is derived from a theory to test the theory against specific evidence. In other cases, an explanation is built out of the accumulated evidence. In the field study by Anderson, a theory of how "street wisdom" emerges in response to social changes in urban neighborhoods develops slowly out the observations he makes over many years. In Thorne's study, a theory of how gender gets constructed is built on her observations and subsequent interpretations of the meaning of the social action among and between primary-school-age girls and boys at play. This *inductive method* uncovered behavioral patterns (such as gender-crossing behaviors in children) which indicated both the fluidity in the meaning of gender and its conceptual strength, as such crossing was disapproved of by many of the children and adults. Thus the inductive approach is one in which the researcher reasons from particular cases to more general, ideal cases, from a few instances of a class to all members of that class.

Each study zeroed in on specific phenomena which were subject to variation under certain conditions. These selected *variables* became the central focus of the study. How the variables were measured is emphasized in great detail in the studies, for if the variables are inadequately measured, the validity of the study, that is, its ability to represent what it claims to represent, is jeopardized. The ultimate challenge to such studies is to argue that the effect being studied is not really the effect at all. Was Hirschi's operationalization of delinquency as self-reported delinquent acts valid? And if it was, did the set of questions on committing delinquent acts serve as a valid indicator of delinquency?

Finally, the association between variables, how one variable related to another—sometimes approaching a cause-effect model—serves as the primary plan for analyzing the results of the study. This is central to the scientific method. In most cases, there are no cast-iron findings. Because social occurrences are so complex, it is difficult to find single causes which are inalterably necessary to bring about certain effects. In the Laumann survey on sexuality, for example, frequency of sexual activity was related to a range of statuses of individuals, and those which were most strongly related (age and marital status) were then carried over into further analyses.

One of the simplest means of determining whether a study has scientific qualities is to ask whether it could be replicated by another person in the expectation of reaching similar results. How can you know if a study could be replicated? First, it has to be described carefully enough so that someone else could reproduce the design. Second, the conditions of the study must not be so unusual or esoteric that they could not be reestablished. Yet there is a distinction between a study that is actually replicable (that is, that someone else would carry out an exactly similar study, a replica of the first study) and one that can be described as if it were replicable (so that it might be comparable to other studies). This ability to replicate or make comparable is a key to the scientific quality of a study. Once the study is replicated, those findings which support the original findings are then shown to be generalizable. If they can be generalized to a second test, they should then prove to be generalizable to a third, a fourth, or a fifth test. Note that all seven of the studies reviewed could be replicated to some degree. The "bystander intervention" and the "domestic assault arrest" experiments have been repeated, modifying various aspects of the designs to explore and test the strength of the results. Hirschi's classic study of delinquency described here, which measured delinquency by asking youths to offer self-reports of their behavior (though delinquency surveys have been modified and expanded), continues to be the primary method of studying delinquency in youth in many countries.

Having picked out the scientific qualities of studies like those described here, we will turn in Chapter 2 to a more comprehensive consideration of science and theory in social research.

REVIEW NOTES

- Surveys may be used to describe attitudes and behaviors, explain relationships that test hypotheses and challenge theories, or evaluate institutions and programs.
- Survey data are gathered through interviews or questionnaires, carefully designed sets of self-administered questions.
- Social experiments may be set up in laboratories or organized in a natural setting.
- An experiment is based on manipulating a stimulus to produce a response, which is then measured. Generally the subjects who receive the stimulus (the experimental group) are compared to those who do not (the control group). To measure the effects of the stimulus, tests are often taken before the experiment (pretests) and then compared to those taken after the experiment (posttests) to determine the amount of change.
- Field studies attempt to understand an entire social field in its own terms.

- Field researchers must immerse themselves in the field but must remain aware of their particular vantage point. They must try not to have an impact on the field they are studying; that is, they must be unobtrusive.
- Social research studies regularities in social life by examining representative individuals, groups, and institutions.
- The creative aspects of social research can be seen in the imaginative qualities of a research design, a data-gathering instrument, or an analysis.
- The scientific activity of a social researcher includes gathering empirical evidence (what is observed) and applying logical and rational rules to this evidence to test a predicted outcome.

KEY TERMS

constant
deductive method
empirical research
ethnography
experimental research
field research
hypothesis
inductive method
qualitative research
quantitative research
regularities
replication
secondary analysis
survey research
theory
variable

STUDY EXERCISES

1. Consider the following six research questions and select which of the three methods (survey, experiment, or qualitative research) would best be employed to study each of them. Justify your selections.

a. Has the Medicare program (providing financial support for medical care to older Americans) improved the health of the elderly?

b. What is it like to run a marathon, and why do people do it?

c. How are attitudes toward drinking alcohol related to attitudes toward the use of illegal drugs?

d. Do high school athletes more often aspire to go on to college than do nonathletes?

e. How do residents living in a public housing project feel about their living conditions?

f. Are men or women more persuasive?

2. Which of the seven studies described in this chapter do you think would have been the most difficult to carry out? Why? Which would have been the most interesting for you to have worked on? Why did you make this choice?

RECOMMENDED READINGS

1. Burgess, Robert G. *Investigating Society,* New York: Longman, 1989. The contributors, who are British sociologists, relate experiences of doing research on a wide array of social topics to broader issues in sociology.

2. Denzin, Norman *The Research Act,* 3rd ed. Englewood Cliffs, NJ: Prentice Hall, 1989. This theoretical introduction to social research offers a symbolic interactionist perspective on social research methods.

3. Mason, Jennifer, *Qualitative Researching,* Thousand Oaks, CA: Sage, 1996. This is a book that focuses on key issues that must be identified and handled in qualitative studies, including intellectual, philosophical, technical, ethical, and practical issues.

4. Slife, Brent D., and Richard N. Williams: *What's Behind the Research?* Thousand Oaks, CA: Sage, 1995. Discusses key assumptions behind theories by tracing the intellectual history of concepts and presenting contrasting options.

Science and Theory in Social Research

INTRODUCTION

We will begin by considering what is scientific about social research. The scientific character of social research is both empirical (built on observations) and logical-rational (seeks an understanding of patterns, associations, relationships between and among the things observed). The observational activity requires accurate, appropriate, and precise observation and the recording of those observations as measures, using either quantitative or qualitative recording procedures. The recorded measures of observed variation then become the variables of a study. The logical-rational activity directs the search for patterns and associations among variables and the distinctions between dependent and independent variables. Once this has been explained more fully, we will stop to consider just how rational science is.

We then will turn to a consideration of the role of theory in social research. To do this, we will begin by laying out in detail the scientific model covering inductive scientific inquiry (which moves from observations to generalizations as a means of developing theories) and deductive scientific inquiry (in which hypotheses are deduced from theories and tested against observations). We will review the major theories relevant to social research, including current postmodern and feminist theories, and their impact on social research. We will then turn back to some of the studies reviewed in Chapter 1 to consider how theory both grew out of and guided them.

But what about causality? Can it be determined in social research studies? We will examine how far causality can be applied to social research, what conditions are required to establish causality, and how causal models may guide research designs.

Finally, we will consider the values and politics of social research by focusing on how scientific activity continually shifts as new paradigms replaced older ones. Doing social research involves a range of scientific practices, values, and models. We will conclude by considering the values of the scientific ethos, which are composed of rules governing the functioning of scientific activity, and asking to what degree this ethos governs the activity of social research.

THE EMPIRICAL CHARACTER OF SCIENCE AND SOCIAL RESEARCH

At the end of Chapter 1 we examined the scientific aspects of the studies presented. Here we will examine much more carefully the components of scientific research as they apply to the study of social questions.

Science is *empirical* because it is based on the study of observed evidence. This means that science as an activity is an advanced form of *seeing* and of *sensing*. Science is the effort to observe how the real world works. If we could directly *see* and gain sense of how a living cell operates, *see* and *sense* how the force of gravity works, or *see* and *sense* how juveniles become delinquent, scientific

activity would be much simpler. However, since our unaided eyes cannot see all these things, we have devised scientific instruments and scientific methods to enable us to better observe the world.

Empirical Science Is Based on Observation

The primary work of science is careful observation. To observe a cell too small to see with the naked eye, a biologist needs the assistance of an instrument, the microscope. To observe the invisible force of gravity, a physicist must devise tests (such as the pendulum) to prove its existence. To observe delinquent acts when most occur out of public view, a social researcher needs to develop a method for detecting this behavior.

Note that if we ask, "What is delinquency?" no immediate answer is obvious. We might say that delinquency is the committing of actions that are illegal and that a juvenile delinquent is a youth who commits such illegal acts. But how can we know who *is* a juvenile delinquent? This is what Travis Hirschi tried to figure out in his landmark study, *Causes of Delinquency* (1969) and what has been the subject of debate and reformulation of meaning and measurement ever since.

To observe delinquency, first Hirschi had to decide what he would accept as a definition of delinquency, and then he had to come up with a way to measure this quality among a group of youths. Hirschi could have used police records of official acts of delinquency as evidence of delinquency, or he might have disguised himself as a delinquent youth (or hired an assistant to do so) and tried to infiltrate youth groups so that he might be able to directly see delinquent acts being performed. However, he decided to use a set of survey questions to measure delinquency.

Hirschi reasoned that if a large number of youths would truthfully respond to a set of questions by reporting on whether they personally had engaged in delinquent behavior, Hirschi would be able to observe who was (and who was not) delinquent. Note that the method that Hirschi subscribed to was "self-reporting"; that is, youths would be asked to report on their own behavior. A set of six questions (see box below), each describing a delinquent act, which together formed the index of delinquency served as the measure of delinquent behavior. This set of questions could then be asked of a group of youths to find out who was delinquent. Thus the Index of Delinquency was the instrument Hirschi developed to assist him in "observing" delinquency. While later criminological researchers (including Hirschi himself) modified and expanded the type of instrument used to measure delinquency, Hirschi's general strategy of having youth give self-reports of previous delinquent acts continues to be the primary way to measure delinquency.

Observation Must Be Accurate and Precise. A biologist observing a cell must carry out observations accurately and precisely, never haphazardly. Such observations must be made under the best conditions—where the lighting is good, the technician is trained to know what to look for, and the equipment is properly handled and maintained. Then the observations must be carefully recorded. Such care applies to the observation of social phenomena as well. For example, techniques for measuring delinquency attempt to observe and record delinquent acts accurately, and each technique can be evaluated in terms of the credibility of the observations made.

INDEX OF DELINQUENCY QUESTIONS FROM THE RICHMOND YOUTH PROJECT SURVEY

67. Have you ever taken little things (worth less than $2) that did not belong to you?

68. Have you ever taken things of some value (between $2 and $50) that did not belong to you?

69. Have you ever taken things of large value (worth over $50) that did not belong to you?

70. Have you ever taken a car for a ride without the owner's permission?

71. Have you ever banged up something that did not belong to you on purpose?

72. Not counting fights you may have had with a brother or sister, have you ever beaten up on anyone or hurt anyone on purpose?

USE THESE ANSWERS NOW

A. No, never
B. More than a year ago
C. During the last year
D. During the last year and more than a year ago

Source: Travis Hirschi: *Causes of Delinquency,* University of California Press, Berkeley, CA: 1969, p. 256.

Let's consider more fully the observation technique Hirschi used to measure delinquency: the Index of Delinquency. The questions aim to measure acts of thievery, vandalism, and assault. Clearly, if the respondents refuse to answer questions 67 to 72 or if they lie, Hirschi will not have produced an accurate observation. But note that the questions are posed in a nonthreatening way. The researcher does not want to arouse fear in the respondents, which might discourage them from answering truthfully. Furthermore, the survey questions are placed within a wider series of questions on a number of different subjects rather than being singled out as a specific measure of delinquency.

Measures Are Developed to Record Observations

The Index of Delinquency was developed as a way to record the incidence of delinquent behavior. In essence, it was designed as a *measure* of delinquency. As a measure, it could be evaluated in terms of how closely it seemed to assess the concept it was trying to quantify. This need to develop "good" measures raises two issues: does the measure really measure what it purports to measure (is it valid?), and is the measure consistent (is it reliable?) so that the same respondent would answer it in the same way if the question were asked again? Measurement, validity, and reliability are dealt with in greater detail in Chapter 4. Here we want to stress that social science research aims to develop valid and reliable measures of the things it is trying to observe.

Measures Record Variation across Repeated Observations. A natural scientist (a biological researcher or a physicist) makes repeated observations of the natural phenomenon being studied. Each observation is not identical to the previous one; there are variations. Measures such as the Index of Delinquency are set up to indicate the degree of variation in responses. Examine the Index of Delinquency shown in the box. Note that the first three questions ask whether the respondent

has taken things of greater and greater value. This is done both to differentiate more minor from more major delinquent acts and in more general terms to measure variation.

One of the central qualities of scientific observation is the study of variation. Note that the Index of Delinquency offers a range of four possible responses to each question ("no, never" to "during the last year and more than a year ago"). This again will provide variation in response. Variation needs to be observed because it characterizes all things. Human behavior (delinquent acts), gravity, and cell composition all vary.

The aim of scientific observation must be to capture this variation across *repeated observations.* The biologist examines many cells, looking for the same phenomena. Hirschi carried out repeated observations by having his questions included in a large survey which was administered to numerous young people.[1] A central characteristic of scientific research involves taking repeated observations to determine the degree of variation.

Variables Serve as the Recorded Measures of Observed Variation of Specific Phenomena

In Hirschi's study, delinquency is one of the primary variables. This means that it is a measure on which differences in response can be established. Naturally, delinquent behavior varied among the respondents to the study. Even those who answered "no, never" to each of the six questions in the Index of Delinquency could be recorded in terms of the delinquency variable as "not delinquent." Those who answered positively, at a more frequent rate, to a greater number of the items could be considered more delinquent than those who responded negatively or those who responded positively to fewer items, at a less frequent rate.

---

[1][The newer, more comprehensive self-report survey of delinquency, the ISRD (International Self-Report Delinquency) survey, has been administered to youth in many countries (Junger-Tas, 1994)].

Variables such as delinquency become the building blocks of a scientific study. When Hirschi goes on in his study to relate delinquency to social class, attachment to parents, and so forth, what he is doing concretely is associating the variable of delinquency to the variables of social class, parental attachment, and the like. Each of the variables represents a set of observations recorded using some form of measure, which has been classified and named as a variable. When you carry out your study, you will discover that working with your variables is the very heart of your research project. That is why definition and accuracy are so important in the measurement of variables. Once your variables are set up, it becomes much easier to direct and make progress on your project.

Let's summarize what we have said about science being empirical. This means that scientific research is based on observation, that the observation must be accurate and precise, that measures are developed to record observations accurately, that the observations must be measured repeatedly and variations must be recorded, and that the recorded measures are classified into variables which become the building blocks of scientific study.

THE LOGICAL-RATIONAL CHARACTER OF SCIENCE AND SOCIAL RESEARCH

Scientific research is not a method for proving or disproving revealed truths. Hence, science is different from religion, which is based on truths that are believed to have been revealed from divine sources. Science is the effort to understand the natural and social world by applying reason to careful observations. But to move from observation (however precise that observation may be) to understanding requires that the observations be rationally explained. In other words, a scientific researcher is not merely an observer and recorder of phenomena. Instead, a scientist must apply reason and logic to these observations to try to understand their character and significance. We will return to the issue of just how rational science (and, in particular, social science research) is after we have explored the characteristics of science and the scientific model.

Patterns and Associations among Variables

In the scientific quest to understand observed phenomena, we seek to uncover the patterns in the data collected and the associations that exist among variables. Here is where we apply logic to the scientific enterprise. The object is not only to isolate and measure separate observations but to associate—relate—different observations with each other. Furthermore, since we record observations as variables (which vary), we need to examine how a change in one variable may be associated with a degree of change (an increase, a decrease, no change) in another variable.

In Hirschi's study, for example, the aim was not just to measure delinquency (though that was important and not easy to do!) but to determine what other variables were associated with high levels of delinquency. We described in Chapter 1 how Hirschi related delinquency to a number of other factors he had measured in the survey. For example, attachment to parents and social class background were both considered to be variables that might be strongly associated with delinquency. Recall that Hirschi found that delinquency was associated with low levels of attachment to parents but was not strongly associated with social class. In other words, Hirschi found that the likelihood of delinquent behavior depended on the presence and strength of other variables. Thus, in the Hirschi study, delinquency was the dependent variable and attachment to parents and social class were independent variables.

Dependent and Independent Variables

Dependent and independent variables are most easily envisioned in a specific experiment (Chapter 6 describes such experiments in detail). The *in-*

dependent variable in an experiment (sometimes called the *stimulus*) is the variable that brings about the effect or *dependent variable* (sometimes called a *response*). The general model of an experiment is to test whether the independent variable led to (brought about, increased the likelihood or occurrence of, or caused) the dependent variable.

The object of the experiment is to try to block out the influence of (that is, "control for") other factors which might produce change in the dependent variable. In this way we can isolate and examine the effect of the independent variable on the dependent variable. However, in most social research projects experimental designs are not feasible. It is not possible in relating an independent to a dependent variable in a survey (such as Hirschi's delinquency survey) to totally control for the effects of all other variables. Instead, the researcher looks for the strength of association between two variables such that when the independent variable changes (increases or decreases), the dependent variable also changes.

In the delinquency study, Hirschi was able to say that the stronger was the attachment of a boy to his father (an independent variable), the less likely the boy was to be delinquent (the dependent variable). Moreover, he was able to say that the social class background of a youth—whether the youth was from a lower social class or a higher social class—was *not* strongly related to self-reports of delinquency. In this case, social class is the independent variable and delinquency is the dependent variable.

On the face of it, the first association he found seems logical. However, the second seems to go against our notions of what might be related to delinquency (we might well have expected lower-class youths to be more delinquent). To make sense of these potential arguments, we need to develop explanations for possible relationships. In the delinquency study, Hirschi tested a number of potential explanations. This is another quality of the rationality and logic of scientific research—its effort to test or build explanatory theories.

Collecting Facts Is Not the Goal of Social Research

Whatever else social research is, it is not just a matter of collecting facts based on careful observation. This type of fact seeking as an end in itself is called *positivism*. The act of accumulating facts and information as if this material were the sole means of establishing an explanation (what C. Wright Mills called *abstracted empiricism,* 1959, pp. 50–75) is neither possible nor profitable in science. To think otherwise is the error of the positivist, who seeks only empirical evidence unimpeded by prior theoretical notions. We know from everyday life that there can be no facts without interpretation of some kind.

Take, for example, what we call mental illness. What facts would you gather to prove a case of mental illness? Suppose you say being overly suspicious of others (paranoid) is one fact indicating mental illness. But a police officer may be trained to be suspicious of others as a protective stance on the job. What might be used as a fact of mental illness in one case would not be construed in that way in another case. This shows that facts can mean all sorts of things, depending on the interpretation they are given in particular instances.

A *hard positivist* might argue that it is only the present state of our imperfect knowledge which makes it difficult to directly comprehend the facts. The *antipositivist* argues, on the contrary, that empirical evidence (the facts) is always predefined in terms of some theoretical notions. In other words, for the antipositivist, all facts are socially constructed. This is particularly important in social research, where the phenomena studied usually consist of the actions of thinking, interpreting beings. While we will talk about ways to gather facts, one must start with the recognition that the facts themselves are not the ultimate goal of social research. Only by interpreting these facts, recognizing their complex meanings and relationships, and understanding the way they are created in social life do we produce social research. This position does not deny the importance of carefully obtaining empirical evidence, but it stresses the significance of building and testing explicit theories by which to interpret the facts.

How Rational Is Science?

We have stressed that science and scientific social research are rational activities. What is meant by this? For science to be rational, it must have a precise goal: to develop true theories which have high explanatory powers or which are useful for making predictions (Newton-Smith, 1981, p. 4). In addition, there must be some agreed-upon rules which can be used to determine whether one theory is superior to another. The issue of the rationality of science has been of great concern in recent years.

Many sociologists of science have tended to support a view that science is nonrational, at least in some respects. Mulkay argues that since facts cannot be independent of theories, theories cannot be proved by an assessment of the facts. Rather, he stresses the relativism of the understanding of facts, which may mean different things not only to scientists and laypersons but even to members of different sectors of the scientific community (1979, p. 35).

Newton-Smith (1981) has tried to counter the arguments about the nonrationality of science by reminding us of its relatively limited aims. While the ultimate objective of science is the discovery of truth, he has argued, science can be considered rational if its theories only get *nearer to the truth:*

> For a theory to have explanatory power it must latch on to something about the world. In the long run the ultimate test as to whether one theory has more successfully latched on to a facet of the world than another theory is their relative observational success (*Newton-Smith, 1981, p. 223*).

What Newton-Smith means by observational success includes two factors: the ability of the theory to generate "novel predictions" and its ability to "account for known observations" (1981, pp. 223–24). According to these criteria, Newton-Smith contends that science has produced many good theories, and he concludes that science is based on a temperate rationalism which is gradually capturing more truth about the world.

But while Newton-Smith's conclusions about the virtues of "temperate rationalism" may be well suited to the natural sciences, do they square with the present state of the social sciences? Perhaps social scientists, rather than "capturing more truth about the world," are positing numerous social worlds about which there are a great variety of often contradictory truths. For truth is an assessment of the value that an answer gives to a question. As questions are revised in the course of research, what might earlier have been considered a truth may no longer satisfy the new question. In short, different questions will seek out different "truths." The theoretical differences between social scientists will affect the types of research questions they pose and the types of truths they seek to uncover. We have seen that theory is the link between ideas grown from our observations and prior knowledge and that theory drives the design and focus of social research.

The Role of Theory in the Scientific Model

The object of science is to move beyond observation, beyond the development of measures to record observations, and beyond the study of the associations between recorded variables to the task of putting together explanations for associations—in short, to build theories. A *theory* is a proposed explanation for a set of coordinated occurrences, or relationships.

The aim of science is to establish theories and then prove (or disprove) them. In other words, theories are logical arguments that try to make sense of empirical data. Theories are not fixed; rather, they are probable explanations which we formulate and reformulate in an attempt to make sense of a body of evidence. And the work of science is both to *build theories* which will explain relationships noted among variables and to *test existing theories* with new evidence.

The process of science is usually thought to be either inductive or deductive. By *inductive,* we mean that the scientist develops generalizations based on a limited amount of data about a class of events. By *deductive,* we mean that hypotheses are derived from a generalized explanation (that is to say, a theory). In practice, it is difficult to fully separate these two procedures. The researcher usually has a prior logical-rational model, with a set of hypotheses (or propositions about the relationship between two or more factors) guiding the design of the study which has been developed before the data gathering. This model, however, usually undergoes change as the evidence is brought to bear on the problem, and the formal testing of set hypotheses gives way to a reformulation of hypotheses which require a better test. Such a research process often has been viewed as a cycle in which the various phases are interdependent and the beginning point is left indefinite. Walter Wallace's (1971) model of the scientific process has been widely used and adapted to depict the research cycle. An adapted version will be described here to help you to gain a fuller conception of the scientific enterprise. Then some of the studies which were presented in Chapter 1 will be considered in the light of this model.

Figure 2-1 is a version of the Wallace model showing the four components of the scientific process: observations, empirical generalizations, theories, and hypotheses. The arrows indicate the direction of the process. Before describing this model in some detail, let me state that researchers may not go through every stage of this process in a single research project. In one study a researcher may only move from observation to an empirical generalization. Over a series of studies,

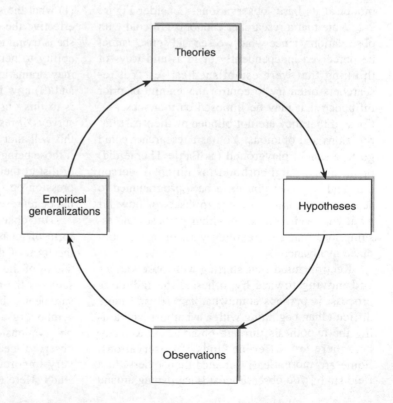

FIGURE 2-1
An adaptation of Wallace's model of science. (From Walter Wallace: *The Logic of Science in Sociology,* Chicago: Aldine, 1971, p. 18.)

a researcher may move through the entire cycle. Given the traditional emphasis on hypothesis testing, most researchers begin on the deductive side, starting with a hypothesis and working out a research plan to test it. The object in taking you through the entire cycle is to see how the scientific process works across time and many projects, not to suggest the steps that each project must go through.

Hirschi's study of delinquency, however, did move through the entire cycle. Recall that Hirschi started with a theory (in fact, three competing theories). Next, he formulated hypotheses from these theories that would be tested with empirical evidence. On the basis of the evidence, Hirschi formed empirical generalizations which enabled him to determine which theories his research most strongly supported.

The Inductive Half of the Research Process. Let's begin the consideration of the research model at its base: observations. Consider Figure 2-1. Note that a researcher cannot begin cold with observations, since what we see and sense cannot be perceived independently of ideas and ways of thinking that were established earlier. Yet researchers often try to control the amount of prior influence that may be imposed on their observations so that they are not blinded by their past impressions and opinions. You as a researcher could go to a school playground (as Barrie Thorne did) or an urban neighborhood (as Elijah Anderson did) and see what you have been programmed to see, or you could go there to discover how far what you see is consistent with hypotheses and assumptions that were explicitly set up and recognized in advance.

Keep in mind that starting with observations and moving toward hypotheses, the inductive process, is perhaps somewhat *messier* and more difficult than beginning with a hypothesis and testing the hypothesis through observation. Remember, there are different kinds of observations. Some are more clearly created than others. In a field study, you observe what is happening around

you. In an experiment or a survey, you create what you observe. In the field, you must be open-minded enough that what you see can modify your views. In an experiment or a survey, you help produce what you observe much more directly.

A great deal of care and clarity of purpose must go into the creation of a questionnaire or the selection of an experimental situation. In the domestic violence experiment with the Minneapolis police and the laboratory bystander intervention experiment, the observations were based on responses to certain stimuli. In the surveys, the observations are the responses to the questionnaires, the data generated from written records. Note that in this case the nature of the questions asked will determine what observations will be produced. Say, for example, the survey researcher forgot to ask the respondents their age; then age would go unreported and therefore be unobserved and unknown.

Thus, what is observed will be determined by (1) what the scientist sets out to observe, (2) how effective the scientist is in observing what he or she is trying to observe (here the scientist's lack of ability to perceive, to see accurately, to discern may dramatically alter what is in fact observed), and (3) how favorable the context being observed is to this observation process. Note here that in surveys, if respondents skip some of the questions, this will alter the observations, or in a field setting, if those being observed deliberately conceal things or distort their environment to make a certain impression on the researcher, the observations will not be representative of the environment.

But observations must be presented in the form of measurements. Here we can distinguish the form of the measurement (its scale) from the taking of the measurement (which is virtually the same as the observation itself). A scale of measurement is based on a system in which different symbols (usually numbers) are given to different observations of the same thing. The way in which observed measurements are summarized is also a very important part of the measurement in any study. Here note that measurements are made in the process of making observations and help in the forming of empirical generalizations. In a survey, each response is in and of itself only a part of the findings to the degree that it represents the sample being studied. It is presented in a summary form representing the aggregation of the responses of the members of the sample. For example, the average age of the respondents to the sample may be 20.6 years, or 62.5 percent of a sample may agree that the president is "doing a good job."

It is necessary to reduce the data to manageable proportions by using summarizations, but the strength of the summarizations will depend on the quality of the scales being used. In addition, these summary measures must be appraised in terms of the plausible limits for that measurement. What range of values could be expected? Against what standard are the measured observations in this study high or low, common or unusual? Statistical tests may be employed in certain cases to help make these determinations. In Chapter 13 we will discuss in more detail how this is done. In certain instances a single observation may serve as an estimate: this would be true in a case study (see Chapter 10 for a discussion of case studies). Clearly, it is more difficult to base a generalization on a single observation; replication is preferable (Wallace, 1971, p. 41).

In this quarter of the cycle, during the inductive effort, the scientist is moving from seeing to knowing, from observing to naming, from taking in the variety and range of sights to sorting them out into the patterns that make the variety comprehensible. The one certain relationship between observations and generalizations is that the scientist is looking for regularities. This was the first commonality which (I suggested in Chapter 1) was shared across all the studies described. In the ethnographic study of children at play by Thorne, it was the regularities she saw in the girls' and boys' behavior on the playground that indicated the gendered nature of their social world. In the experiments, the regularities were the common reactions to stimuli; in the surveys, they were the common responses to questions. However, the process of moving from observation to generaliza-

tion is only part of the inductive process. The next quarter of the cycle moves the scientific process from generalizations to theories.

As Wallace recognizes, it is more difficult to explain how one moves from empirical generalization to theories. He describes two different views of the procedure (Wallace, 1971, p. 50). In the first view, which has been developed by the philosopher Karl Popper, theories do not automatically follow from generalizations. On the contrary, they require a kind of imaginative leap, a creative or irrational element which does not spring from empirical evidence or from the generalizations derived from the evidence (1968).

According to the second view, which is represented by Merton (1968) and Kuhn (1970), the inductive process is much more central to the development of new theories, which spring from anomalies—unanticipated observations and surprising exceptions to generalizations that occasionally occur in the course of scientific research. This confrontation with anomalies has been called the *serendipity factor* and will be discussed below. Suffice it to say for now that coming up with the unexpected, in the process of observation, forces the scientist to bring new ideas to the forming and understanding of theories, in short, to alter and possibly create new theories.

To the degree that generalizations lead to the creation of theories, this is accomplished through the formation of concepts and propositions. Hochschild's generalizations about what she saw happening to urban working women as they struggled to handle the pressures of their jobs and coordinate them with the ever-increasing demands of child care, housework, and home management led her to conceptualize these women as "urbanized peasants." As Hochschild states,

the term *peasant* suggests the humility of a feudal serf. I draw the analogy between modern American women and the modernizing peasantry because women's inferior social, legal, educational, and economic position had until recently been like that of peasants (*1989, p. 243*).

The very meaning of work in the home had changed. In earlier times, "a woman's claim to honor was based primarily on her relation to her husband, her children, her home" (p. 245), but as paid work spread among women, the "unpaid" work of the home lost its value. "The housewife became 'just a housewife'" (p. 245). But for working mothers, while there were various ways to simplify or share the tasks of the home, those ways often required more management (such as preparing meals in advance, securing baby-sitters, or trying to persuade a husband to participate). One women stated that "when I told my husband to share the laundry, he just said, 'Let's take it to a laundry'" (p. 244).

Recall that in the bystander intervention experiment the researchers generalized from their repeated observations that subjects would be much less likely to report a stranger in a crisis if there were other bystanders supposedly observing the event with them. They termed the behavior of helping in emergencies as "bystander intervention" (or "bystander nonintervention"). The larger the number of people who observed the situation, they concluded, the less likely any one person would be to intervene. This finding led Darley and Latane to develop the concept of *diffusion of responsibility* to explain this phenomenon of withholding assistance to a stranger when bystanders are present. This concept served as a theoretical base for making sense of the data collected in their laboratory, but it could also be extended to real-life situations in which individuals may confront strangers in need of help.

After the development of concepts (such as *diffusion of responsibility*), propositions can be set up in the "if . . . then" form, which hypothesizes under what conditions the theory will hold true. Using the "if . . . then" format, the hypothesis derived from the diffusion of responsibility theory would state: If a subject observes a stranger in a crisis but knows that other bystanders are also witnessing this situation, the subject may be less likely to assume the responsibility of reporting this crisis or trying to offer assistance to the stranger in need. This hypothesis sets down conditions under which Darley and Latane's theory of the diffusion of responsibility would operate.

Theoretical propositions are also ordered into a system that follows the rules of logical deduction. Once this is accomplished, theories can be used either to explain empirical observations or to predict future observations (Wallace, 1971, p. 57). For example, the diffusion of responsibility theory was used to explain the behavior of the strangers who had observed the killing of Kitty Genovese as well as to predict the likelihood that similar effects would occur in the future. In addition, a theoretical concept shown to apply in one area of observations may be predicted to be applicable in slightly varying arenas. Darley and Latane and other researchers (1968, 1973) continued to refine their theory by testing it under situations which varied not only in terms of the number of bystanders but also in terms of the type of crisis being observed, the characteristics and training of the subjects (seminarians), the conditions of the subject (whether they were in a hurry, topics they had been considering), and information about who the other bystanders might be (e.g., medical students).

As Wallace stresses, theories have two primary functions. They help isolate the variables to be observed; in other words, they prepare for the observation phase of research. They also structure how the findings will be expressed for the purposes of generalization. Taking the diffusion of responsibility theory as an example, we can see that the theory both set up new variables (such as number of bystanders) and provided a comprehensive explanation of various findings which were already available.

The Deductive Half of the Research Process. This half of the research process starts with theories at the 12:00 position on the research clock and moves through the process of deduction back to observations. This is the phase of the cycle in which already developed theories are used to generate hypotheses that then can be tested with new observations. The first steps Wallace suggests are to (1) scrutinize the theory for its own consistency, (2) compare it to other theories to determine whether it is preferable to them, and (3) analyze the consistency of the empirical generalizations which led up to the development of the theory with hypotheses that seem to flow from the theory (1971, p. 63). Once there is confidence in the theory, the deductive process may begin.

Generating hypotheses is a form of setting predictions. But Wallace argues that hypotheses in social research are more important for determining the precise observations to be made than for predicting the actual outcome of such observations. Consider Darley and Latane as they are making deductions from the implications of the diffusion of responsibility theory. The implications of the theory are such that Darley and Latane can arrive deductively at the following hypothetical chain:

> If an individual is alone when he notices an emergency, he is solely responsible for coping with it. If he believes others are also present, he may feel that his own responsibility for taking action is lessened, making him less likely to help (*Latane and Darley, 1968, p. 215*).

The importance of this hypothesis is not simply that it predicts an outcome but that it specifies the measurements to be carried out to test the theory. The process of developing instruments to make these measurements is not always an easy one. The bystander intervention experiments developed a series of situations in which to test the diffusion of responsibility theory.

The choice of the sample on which the hypothesis will be tested is also a critical part of the methodological procedure. The researcher must first decide on the population to be studied, that is, the group about which one wishes to make generalizations. A sample must then be selected according to procedures that will make it representative of that population. We will consider issues of sampling more fully in Chapter 5.

This process of moving deductively from theory to hypotheses and then operationalizing the

hypotheses for the purposes of research will be illustrated again by going through the steps Hirschi used in his study of delinquency. You will remember that Hirschi began with three contrasting theories of delinquency: strain theory, control theory, and cultural deviance theory.

Next, Hirschi sought to identify the conditions that followed logically from each of these theories and those which were incompatible with them. For example, in considering the logical implications of strain theory, Hirschi noted that the theory had been used to explain the apparently irrational aspects of crime in terms of its relationship to frustration. Desires that cannot be met through legitimate means lead to frustration which can be relieved only by finding other (illegitimate) means to fulfill them. Such a theory can help explain why disadvantaged groups may turn to crime to achieve success goals which other, less disadvantaged groups might be able to accomplish through law-abiding means.

But Hirschi also had to point out what was logically incompatible with this theory: If frustration is the primary source of crime, why does delinquency also occur among those from advantaged classes? Here the more general deduction that it is the discrepancy between aspirations and expectations which leads to delinquency can be used to explain middle-class delinquency as well as lower-class delinquency. The hypothesis that youths with a greater discrepancy between their aspirations and their expectations are more likely to turn to delinquency can be tested by translating the concepts into scalable variables. In doing this, the researcher may only be able to approximate the variable that he or she actually desires to measure. For example, Hirschi could measure the gap between aspirations and expectations but had no way of telling whether the discrepancy between them makes a youth feel deprived (1969, p. 9).

Testing Hypotheses.   The final step in the research cycle is to test the hypotheses to determine whether they should be accepted or rejected and then establish the implications of these tests for the theory on which the hypotheses depend. If the research findings conform with what was expected on the basis of the hypothesis, it is supported. However, as Wallace stresses, some hypotheses are more amenable to testing than others:

> A hypothesis is highly testable in principle when it can be shown to be false by any of a large number of logically possible empirical findings and when only one or a few such findings can confirm it (*1971, p. 78*).

Even when a hypothesis is testable in principle, it must also be testable in practice; that is, the necessary data from observations must be obtainable and thus the methods to collect these data must be known to and feasible for the researcher.

Once the hypothesis has been tested, it must be accepted or rejected by a process of determination in which an assessment of the original theory, how the hypotheses were formulated, and the methods used to test the hypotheses are all scrutinized to decide if the testing of the hypothesis can be considered to be fair. Once a hypothesis is accepted or rejected, the implications of this conclusion must be brought to bear on the theory. There are a number of ways in which the test of the hypothesis may bear on the theory. It can

1. *Lend confirmation to the theory* by not disconfirming it;
2. *Modify the theory* by disconfirming it, but not at a crucial point; or
3. *Overthrow the theory* by disconfirming it at a crucial point in its logical structure, or in its competitive value as compared with rival theories (*Wallace, 1971, p. 82*).

In addition, since any test of a hypothesis has been carried out on some sample, the representativeness of the sample must be considered before one accepts that the test is applicable to the population to which the theory applies.

Finally, this process of appraising the results of testing a hypothesis also may stimulate the creation of new hypotheses (or new theories) which were unanticipated in the study design. As was mentioned prior, Robert Merton called the potentiality for unexpected outcomes of this kind the *serendipity factor* in scientific research:

> Fruitful empirical research not only tests theoretically derived hypotheses; it also originates new hypotheses. This might be termed the "serendipity" component of research, i.e., the discovery, by chance or sagacity, of valid results which were not sought for (Merton, 1968, p. 157).

Such findings may occur in the scientific process as "*unanticipated results,* when the test of one hypothesis yields an unexpected observation which bears upon theories not in question when the research was begun" (Merton, 1968, p. 158). Such an observation is also "anomalous, surprising, either because it seems inconsistent with prevailing theory or with other established facts" (1968, p. 158). Finally, Merton contends that the surprising fact must be *strategic* so that the observer can relate such an observation to some universal explanation. Merton gives the example of Freud, who took the occurrence of "slips of the tongue" as evidence of repressed, subconscious states. In other words, Freud strategically applied the evidence of slips of the tongue to expand a theory he was developing. In short, serendipity explains how tests of hypotheses stemming from one theory can in some cases lead to the development of new and even seemingly quite unrelated theories.

Merton offers an example from his own research on a suburban working-class community called Craftown. Merton and his colleagues discovered that many of the residents belonged to more voluntary associations in Craftown than they had in their previous places of residence. In addition, this increase in membership was especially noteworthy for those with small children. This seemed surprising since having young children would seem to make such participation more difficult. When young parents were asked how they managed this, they claimed that the presence of many teenagers in the community made getting a baby-sitter easier. However, Merton and his colleagues discovered in studying the census data for the community that there were not many teenagers in the community; rather, Craftown was full of young adults and small children. In fact, the proportion of teenagers in Craftown was decidedly lower than it had been in the communities from which most of the residents had come.

How could Merton and his colleagues explain such an anomalous finding? Their conclusion—the "strategic" leap they made—was described in the following way:

> It is not that there are objectively more adolescents in Craftown, but more who are *intimately known* and who, therefore, *exist socially* for parents seeking aid in child supervision (*1968, p. 161*).

Craftown was the kind of community where "reciprocal intimacies" were more easily developed than in the urban settings from which most of the residents had moved. Such a finding then was applied by Merton to the more general theory that "social perception is the product of a social framework" (1968, p. 162). In other words, an unexpected finding (that parents of young children were particularly active in voluntary associations) demanded an explanation. The residents offered an explanation (the availability of teenagers) which could not be substantiated with factual evidence. This created an anomalous finding which needed to be understood by relating it to broader theories of the social process.

CURRENT THEORIES INFLUENCING SOCIAL RESEARCH

Many of you have taken a course in social theory. As you may recall, three main types of theories (or explanatory frameworks) have been very influential in the development of sociology and social research.

Structural-Functionalism, Conflict, and Symbolic Interaction Theories

Structural-functionalism, which grew from the work of the French theorist Emile Durkheim, emphasizes the norms which societies develop and instill to hold themselves together. Durkheim saw the functioning of these norms in many aspects of human cultures, from the division of labor to religious practices. He recognized that those who found themselves outside the bonds of social norms were much more likely to commit suicide and became one of the earliest social scientists to use empirical data to try to show that suicide rates varied across societies and social units that had stronger or weaker normative structures. The concepts that are the strongest in this structural-functionalist framework are those of *socialization* and *norms.*

The second major theoretical framework you have surely encountered is *conflict theory.* This theory grew from the ideas of Karl Marx and those of one of his critics, the German theorist Max Weber. Marx viewed society as a struggle of classes of individuals who differed in their economic positions: Capitalists, for example, owned the means of producing things and could secure others to work for them; proletarians or workers had to sell their labor. For Weber, however, economic advantage was only one form of status. Weber emphasized the differences in status between people whose positions of power and authority conferred on them different levels of prestige. The ensuring struggle between these status groups could break out into conflict or could be contained or repressed through the belief system and values that those with the greatest power and authority used to keep the less advantaged in check. The major concepts in conflict theory are *inequality, social status,* and *social stratification.*

The third major theoretical framework, *symbolic interaction,* shifts its focus from the broader society (the macro level) to the social interaction of individuals (the micro level). Here the work of George Herbert Mead has been very important. Mead was concerned with the everyday interaction of individuals but also recognized that people interact by means of all sorts of symbols (for example, traffic lights, flags or banners, and popular songs) whose meanings influence how the individual may think or act in relation to others. In this theory, the focus is on everyday life and the ways in which individuals derive meaning from their interactions with others.

Two other theoretical frameworks have come to be influential in social research in this decade. We will examine them here in greater detail than the three just discussed in case you have not been exposed to them as fully. We will also consider the implications of these newer theories on the design and purpose of social research.

Postmodern Theory and the Methods of Social Research

Postmodern theories have raised serious questions and concerns about the value of the methods typically used in social research. In the simplest terms, postmodernism challenges the belief in reason and rationality which we earlier stated is a cornerstone of science. One form of postmodernism, *deconstructionism,* derives principally from the ideas of the French philosopher Jacques Derrida. Deconstructionists argue that western thinking has been tied too closely to a tradition Derrida calls "logo-centrism," the notion of some ultimate "presence" or absolute certainty (truth) which language is supposed to express. Derrida argues that language can never express an absolute certainty, because language itself is never stable and unambiguous: it always undermines itself by suggesting something more (or other) than it seems to say. Efforts to define one truth as absolute therefore are always attempts to repress other "truths." Since the "real" world can never be apprehended in and of itself, outside of language, our knowledge of the real world must share in the ambiguity and instability of language. The overriding pursuit of certainty has brought about the discrimination against the "other" which has characterized the forms of totalitarian dogmatism, oppression, and tyranny in the twentieth century.

Another postmodern philosopher-historian, Michel Foucault, also starts from the position that what we take to be reality is produced for us by the language we speak. Foucault has emphasized how different languages—he calls them *discourses*—create different relations of power between and among groups of individuals. To speak of one person as a "doctor" and another as a "patient," for example, is to give the former authority over the latter. To label some people as "deviant" privileges those deemed "normal," turning difference into a form of inequality and above all empowering the "specialist" who decides which persons are "normal" and which are not. To speak of a body of water as a reservoir rather than a lake changes its nature and gives one kind of person (the engineer) greater authority over it than another (the bird-watcher). In Foucault's analysis, then, every "discourse" is also a form of power.

How do postmodern thinkers believe that society, social life, and social artifacts should be studied? For a deconstructionist there is, to use Derrida's phrase, "nothing outside the text." This implies that the natural and social worlds experienced by individuals and groups in society are already interpreted worlds, worlds that are never experienced directly and immediately as an external, objective reality. A researcher with a postmodern sensibility will therefore want to tease out (deconstruct) the ways in which the social world is constructed for us (and by us) through sets of interpretative meanings rather than operating upon us externally as an objective order of social facts and to see the extent to which it is rendered unstable by competing or contradictory meanings. At the same time, in accepting that there is "nothing outside the text," a postmodern researcher has to admit that he or she cannot stand apart as an external, objective observer from the particular social world he or she studies (or makes into his or her text). Because the observer can never be neutral, he or she must always try to make explicit the interpretative stance, or values, he or she brings to the study of that world and the way he or she interacts with it.

Thus postmodernism in general advocates "introspective, anti-objectivist interpretation" (Rosenau, p. 118–19), which rejects observation from the outside in favor of "vision" (p. 120), in which the observer and the observed, the self and the other, are not clearly distinguished. There is no absolutely superior interpretation, no interpretation that can be shown to be preferable to any other, irrespective of the values of the observer. Critics of postmodernism have argued, however, that in order to tease out what is contradictory, inconsistent, or unstable in the text of social life, there must still be some standards of consistency, contradiction, and noncontradiction. Since postmodernists don't allow for this, the critics argue, their position is itself contradictory and quite opposed to the scientific method.

Looked at in terms of the social sciences, postmodernism rejects attempts to generalize from a set of empirical observations, develop hypotheses, and test them against the evidence. Instead it wants to focus on individual cases and interpret them by discerning and deconstructing the often contradictory narratives that shape their meaning. Postmodernism "announces the end of all paradigms. . . . Only an absence of knowledge claims, an affirmation of multiple realities, and an acceptance of divergent interpretations is left" (Rosenau, p. 137). Many would say that postmodernists don't even have the desire to convince others that their view is best.

If you are confused by this, it is not surprising. The point to be considered here is that the postmodern attack on social sciences and on its typical methods for doing social research is very extreme. Most postmodernists in academic life are found in the humanities; however, the social sciences and the methods that guide them have been challenged by this new form of thinking and appraising things. The postmodern rejection of social research methods has some similarities to the challenges to social research methods made by feminists. However, many feminists propose ways of "doing" social research that they accept as legitimate.

Feminist Theory and the Forms of Social Research

As all of you are aware, the effort to improve the place of women in society has been a major char-

acteristic of the past 30 years. This repositioning of women has raised a number of important questions for the practice of social research. What have women contributed to the development and practice of social research methods? Are there methods which are typically used by social researchers that are biased or prejudicial against women? Are certain methods preferable for studying women or for women as researchers to use?

These are very important concerns, and many books and studies have been written on this subject (Belenky et al., 1986; Harding, 1987; Reinharz, 1992). This brief discussion of feminism and social research should help you decide if this is an area in which you need to seek additional information. To address the first question about women's contributions to the development and practice of social research, there is much evidence that both from a historical point of view and in our own time women have contributed to the development and practice of social research. Lynn McDonald (1994) has shown in her study of pre-twentieth-century women social scientists that women have made extensive contributions to many types of methods for carrying out research:

> Contrary to the feminist critique of the social sciences, that empiricism necessarily supports the powers-that-be, advocates of women's equality for three hundred years used empiricism to expose bias and prejudice and argue for equality (*McDonald, 1994, p. 2*).

While some feminist researchers today challenge the use of quantitative data, there were women who collected and analyzed such data from the earliest periods, such as the Englishwoman Mary Astell (1668–1731), whose writings included an article advocating smallpox inoculation that was based on comparative quantitative data showing the relationship between inoculation and mortality from smallpox (Astell, *The Plain Dealer,* cited in McDonald, 1994, p. 53). Perhaps the best known nineteenth-century woman methodologist was Harriet Martineau

(1802–1876). Her early methodological efforts were done in relation to her voyage to America, when she wrote on "How to Observe Morals and Manners" (1838) and "Essays on the Art of Thinking" (published in a collection in 1836). These works are perhaps the earliest writings on how to carry out research.

In the United States, nineteenth- and early twentieth-century feminists also used social research methods to study issues relevant to women. Jane Addams (1860–1935), the developer of the first settlement house, Hull House in Chicago, and the founder of social work, was also a social researcher. As Mary Jo Deegan (1988) has argued, Addams's contributions to research methodology have been erased from the early history of the social sciences; however, Deegan found much evidence of Addams's research in the evaluative study of the work of Hull House which included a survey with radical interpretations and suggested recommendations for dealing with problems (McDonald, 1994, p. 231).

There is also extensive evidence that in our own time women have made major contributions to every kind of social research methodology. Reinharz's text (1992) provides an overview of the ways women have participated in and helped form interview research, ethnography, survey research, experimental design, cross-cultural research, oral history, content analysis, case studies, action research, and the use of multiple methods in research. Box 2-1 reports on differences between men and women in regard to the types of methods employed in their research from studies published in 10 sociological journals between 1974 and 1983.

In addressing the issue of potential bias against women in social research, feminist research nearly always employs a critical analysis of whether women's unequal social status has affected the subject under study. Feminists also carry out reviews of the literature, mindful of the possibility that earlier research on their subjects may be distorted or incomplete in terms of its analysis of women. Feminist researchers do not want women's points of view overlooked or ignored in research. They also argue that qualitative research should not be considered "less solid" than quantitative research. Here feminists share common ground with postmodern approaches.

On the question of whether feminist research sometimes employs unique methods, we need to appreciate the fact that while women have contributed to all types of social research methods, feminist researchers have altered and refined ways of "doing" social research that affect what they focus on and how they analyze and interpret their results. Box 2-2 includes the 10 themes that Rein-

BOX 2-1

DO WOMEN AND MEN TEND TO USE DIFFERENT RESEARCH METHODS?

To address the questions of whether women prefer to use *qualitative* in contrast to *quantitative* methods in their research and whether in studying the topic of gender qualitative research is even more often their method of choice, Grant, Ward, and Rong (1987) carried out an analysis of a sample of 214 research studies published in 10 sociological journals between 1974 and 1983. (This is an example of content analysis, which will be described more fully in Chapter 9.) They found that women, like men, more often published research based on quantitative methods; surprisingly, this was especially true when the topic of an article was gender issues. They also found that male-authored studies on gender were largely quantitative secondary analyses of large-scale datasets. However, women were more likely to employ qualitative methods than men were. The authors considered that the scarcity of qualitative publications could be due to the hesitancy of journal editors to publish research of this type, and this reluctance to publish qualitative research could even be stronger when the topic of the study is gender-related.

harz (1992) determined covered the full range of feminist methodological themes. As we examine these various forms of research in subsequent chapters, we will at points consider what special contributions women have made to these fields and what concerns raised by feminist scholarship you should bear in mind in designing a research project.

The Role of Theory in Social Research Designs

As we saw in Chapter 1, theories may play a central role, either explicitly or implicitly, in nearly all social research. The arguments put forth to explain or defend a theory need to have some rational basis, generally stemming from widely accepted

BOX 2-2

FEMINIST THEMES FOR SOCIAL RESEARCH

1. **Feminism is a perspective, not a method.** Reinharz's (1992) compendium of the efforts feminists have made in terms of social research methodology convinced her that because "there are multiple definitions of feminism . . . there are multiple feminist perspectives on social research methods" (1992, p. 241). However, one idea that all feminist researchers hold is that "women's lives are important" (ibid.). This commitment to the study of women's lives in a whole range of ways convinced Reinharz that feminism is more a perspective than a method.

2. **Feminists use a wide range of research methods.** Feminists may use the traditional methods of their discipline but try to turn the interpretations toward a greater understanding of women, or they may alter methods or refine them to fit their goals.

3. **Feminists carry out critiques of nonfeminist scholarship.** In some cases facts are distorted or the methods used are prejudicial to a fair understanding of women; in other cases data on women are not gathered or are ignored. Feminists try to point this out when necessary.

4. **Feminist research needs to be guided by feminist theory.** In mainstream sociological research gender may be downplayed in favor of the study of social class. For example, in trying to understand why the study of incest or divorce has been ignored or slanted, feminist re-

searchers have argued that only the inequality in power relations between the sexes can explain these circumstances.

5. **Feminist research is open to crossing disciplines (being transdisciplinary).** There are many examples of feminist sociologists using historical evidence, psychoanalytic theory, or legal studies (to name just a few disciplines in their work).

6. **Feminist research attempts to bring about social change.** This means that the object of feminist research is often to affect policies or raise consciousness. The legal scholar Catherine MacKinnon believes that consciousness-raising (the practice that characterized the women's movement from its reemergence in the 1960s and 1970s) is the most important contribution of feminist scholarship (cited in Reinharz, 1992, p. 220).

7. **Feminist research both recognizes and asserts the importance of diversity.** The women's movement has often been criticized as being too representative of middle-class white women, but feminists have tried to emphasize cross-cultural themes. In their study of women's cognitive styles, Mary Belenky and her colleagues (1986) brought together women from very diverse geographic areas and organizational connections to study the development of women's self, voice, and mind.

8. **Feminist social research involves the researcher as a person.** Feminist researchers care about personal experience

and often focus on such experience in their projects. Thus they challenge the "passion-less objectivity" of much social research (Reinharz, 1992, p. 259). There is often a link between the research project and the researcher's own experience which makes the work more informal and personal. There are feminist researchers who support "value-free" objective research as a surer way for women to have their research taken seriously, those who believe that "objectivity is itself the biased stance of privileged white males," and still others who recognize the tension in social research between these two positions (Reinharz, 1992, p. 262).

9. **Feminist research involves the persons who are the subjects of study**. In observational and interview methods (such as the studies by Thorne and Hochschild) feminist researchers often try to develop a rapport with those being studied to avoid exploiting the subjects they study.

10. **Feminist research engages the potential reader**. Feminist researchers want to draw readers into their projects by directly addressing them. For this reason, the use of direct quotations is often employed, and in some cases researchers offer self-disclosure as a means of reducing the distance between themselves and their readers.

Feminist research is concerned not to exploit, misrepresent, or be irrelevant. For these reasons, it is deeply concerned that all involved in the research process be carefully considered and appreciated so that research can serve those it studies and those who learn from it.

Source: Adapted from Reinharz (1992), pp. 240–69.

commonsense notions or from empirical evidence that has been accumulated and tested. In short, theories must follow the rules of logic so that they are convincing and cannot be easily refuted.

We have noted that scientific studies need to be formal and explicit. Many critics of the social sciences argue that these qualities do not sufficiently characterize theory development in the social sciences. Instead, they argue, theoretical ideas remain inexplicit or somewhat vague and underdeveloped in many studies. Many social research projects, however, do not have explanation as an explicit goal; instead, they are exploratory. Let's return to some of the examples from Chapter 1 and consider how far theory directed, informed, or was generated by these studies.

The Role of Theory in Laumann and Colleagues' Research on Sexual Behavior. We can see how theory guides research by considering how Laumann and his colleagues used a number of different theoretical models to guide the design of their national survey on sexuality. Choosing to follow a so-cial-scientific approach to sexuality, Laumann and his colleagues recognized that most research on sexuality had seen it as "individual" behavior. However, these sociological researchers recognized that a person's sexual behavior is only partly determined at the "individual" level and that "a person's socialization into a particular culture, his or her interaction with sex partners, and the constraints imposed on him or her become extremely important in determining his or her sexual activities" (Laumann et al., 1994 pp. 3–4). Recognizing that persuasive theories had been developed to explain other types of social behaviors, the authors turned to three of these theories as possible bases for their study.

The first was *scripting theory,* which is based on the idea that people's social behaviors follow scripts which are culturally derived, though individuals may deviate in some ways from those scripts (p. 6). The scripting model suggests that there are patterns most people follow in engaging in sexual activity. This theory is most useful in identifying the range of behaviors that an individual may engage in sexually.

Choice theory, the second theory the researchers considered, suggests how an individual may choose among various possible types of sexual behavior, depending on the type of partner and the type of situation that individual is in. Choice theory requires a consideration of what the possible goals of sexual behavior might be: pleasure, emotional satisfaction, procreation, acquiring a reputation among one's friends (p. 8). However, choices often are made under conditions of uncertainty, and risks may be undertaken. In this way, a person making choices about his or her sexual behavior may be not only trying to maximize the attainment of goals that are deemed important but also managing the risks that could be encountered. In the market for sexual partners, various factors make certain individuals potentially more attractive and more able to secure partners. This theory is taken from economics and seems to help explain many aspects of sexual behavior, though many might find it too "rational" to actually explain sexual behavior.

Finally, Laumann and his colleagues were persuaded that to understand sexual behavior it was important to understand the bases of partnerships, especially two-person dyads, among which most sexual behavior take place. For this they turned to *network theory.* Most "couples" share a broad range of social and cultural characteristics. In other words, individuals are likely to form friendships and marriages with persons equal in status to themselves. However, certain types of sexual alliances may be undertaken with persons less similar in status (such as an extramarital affair in which the ability to keep the affair quiet might be enhanced if the partner does not share the same social or cultural turf). Then the authors try to combine these theories to see how far they do and do not work together.

Recognizing that it would be difficult with a national survey to get detailed information on cultural scripts or to determine specific networks of respondents, they decided to use measures of "master statuses" (age, marital status, education, religion, race/ethnicity) and relate them to various sexual behaviors and practices. For example, dif-

ferences in status affect the different types of scripts to which a person may be exposed (scripting theory), both the types of choices available to that person and a sense of the costs and benefits associated with those choices (choice theory), and affect, in the area of network theory, the "structure of the social networks in which people are embedded" (p. 31). Hence, Laumann and his colleagues were able to consider the relevance of these three theoretical frameworks by relating sexual behaviors and attitudes to the master statuses.

The Role of Theory in Hirschi's Research on Delinquency. Hirschi's study had a classic deductive style: Hirschi posed theories and deduced hypotheses from those theories; then he tested the hypotheses to see which received the most support. Where did the theories come from? Most came directly from earlier research on juvenile delinquency. For example, strain theory and cultural deviance theory were widely used in the study of juvenile delinquency in the 1960s, when Hirschi carried out his study. But before trying to develop and test his own control theory, Hirschi needed to understand the underpinnings of all theories. Let's consider the steps Hirschi took to make sense of and substantiate the theories he would be testing.

First, he looked for the underlying assumptions and presuppositions on which these various theories rested. He recognized, for example, that strain theory—the view that the social order is whole and beneficent and that delinquency is a result of "strain" in a cohesive system—is based on assumptions very different from those underlying control theory—the view that society is fragmented and conflicted and that delinquency is a natural occurrence which must be regularly precluded through control. However, as the interview with Travis Hirschi made clear (see Box 1-1), in the decades after the publication of *Causes of Delinquency,* criminologists and other investigators began to focus on psychological and economic motivations for criminal behavior in addition to the factors Hirschi had examined. Thus,

Hirschi also examines these theories in his and Michael Gottfredson's *A General Theory of Crime* (1990). In other words, theories about the causes of delinquent behavior changed over time; scholars used different assumptions and presuppositions, which led to a shift in disciplinary trends. (We will discuss change in scientific perspectives when we describe Thomas Kuhn's work on scientific paradigms.)

Second, Hirschi noted that the theories accounting for delinquent behavior also stemmed from commonsense notions ordinary people hold about why young people break laws and misbehave. A delinquent act such as stealing is commonly thought to be the result of a lack of discipline (in short, a lack of "control"), the result of a response to unfairness (a "strain" which demands to be righted), or the result of "hanging out with the wrong crowd" (mixing with a "culturally deviant" group). Note that these different commonsense notions are not compatible with one another. However, each can serve as the basis for an explanation, a theory, from which hypotheses can be deduced and then empirically tested.

Third, Hirschi noted that each of the proposed theories offered a logical explanation in that if A were true, then B would follow. For example, if a particular youth lacked strong ties to his or her society (in other words, had weak attachments to family and other institutions), then he or she would not have sufficiently incorporated the norms to be law-abiding; therefore, given the chance, the youth would break laws. Furthermore, given that the outcome of the lawbreaking might benefit the youth (give him or her material benefits), a delinquent act such as stealing would be a rational behavior. Thus each theory presented a *rational* explanation as well. Hirschi developed each of the three theories with precision in order to test them accurately in his study. In other words, he offered a formal and explicit presentation of the three theories. By making clear their presuppositions, considering commonplace notions about them, and developing the theories in clear and unambiguous terms, Hirschi was able to develop means for measuring the underlying concepts of the theories by creating variables to represent them. Once this operationalization was completed, Hirschi could test the hypotheses he had posed.

The Role of Theory in Thorne's Ethnographic Research on the Gender Relations of Children at Play.   In her first chapter, Barrie Thorne placed her study in its feminist framework as a study in the social construction of gender. But hers would *not* be a study of how children are passively socialized to play the roles of girls or boys but would focus on active play. One definition of *play* that intrigued Thorne was "opportunity for action," in other words, situations full of possibilities in which the outcomes were not at all clear. She recognizes that such a perspective has postmodern ties:

> Those versed in current feminist theory will recognize the influences of postmodern and deconstructive ideas in the approach I develop, although I am intent on understanding discourses in the context of social practices (*1994, p. 5*).

In examining gender separation in play, Thorne also considers the implications of feminist psychoanalytic theory, which has argued that boys separate from girls and devalue what is associated with girls as a way to break away from their mothers (p. 59; also see N. Chodorow, *The Reproduction of Mothering,* 1978). Play would become the central concept of this study, and Barrie Thorne considered the broad range of associations which define this concept, including action and activity, dramatic performance, and opportunity for action. But when it is specifically associated with children, that is, "child's play," the concept of play also suggests triviality (p. 5). Thorne took issue with this final meaning, though, in that she found in her study of children at play that the "social relations . . . document[ed] entail consequential structures of *power*"(p. 6). Even in this exploratory study, in which hypotheses were not laid out to be tested, the exploration of concepts and theories preceded the development of the research design and was referred to again in the interpretation of the evidence.

CAUSALITY: THE NEATEST WAY TO LINK THEORIES TO EVIDENCE

The careful observation and logical explanation characteristic of scientific research are necessary for the purpose of determining causality. This is one of the primary goals of science. But is it one of the primary goals of social research?

Recall that in Hirschi's delinquency study strain theory, control theory, and cultural deviance theory all postulated that qualities of the social order produced, or caused, delinquency. This is the kind of rational, logical explanation with which we are all familiar. "Smoking causes cancer," "Gravity causes the pen to fall to the ground," "Hanging around with the wrong crowd causes delinquency"—these are all causal statements which state that variable A (smoking, gravity, or hanging around with the wrong crowd) causes variable B to occur (cancer, objects falling, delinquent behavior). In scientific terms, this means that the presence of an independent variable (smoking, gravity, hanging around with the wrong crowd) is associated with the occurrence of a dependent variable (cancer, objects falling, delinquent behavior).

Conditions Required to Establish Causality

To establish causality, three conditions must be satisfied. *The first condition is that a change in the independent variable must precede (in time) a change in the dependent variable.* This makes sense if we consider the association between smoking and cancer. If a person had cancer before he or she began smoking, it would be illogical to argue that smoking caused the cancer. This simple logic is generally more difficult to apply to social phenomena. It seems logical to argue that hanging around with the wrong crowd may cause a youth to become delinquent, but it also seems logical to argue that a youth who is delinquent may be more likely to hang around with a "bad" crowd. In other words, it is often difficult to decide which variable is really the dependent variable in terms of the issue of time. Thus the first challenge for a social

researcher who wants to establish causality is to try to ascertain the temporal order of the variables he or she is measuring.

In some cases, this is easier because one can simply determine that the influence of one factor must have preceded another. For example, in testing the strain theory, Hirschi selected social class membership as the independent variable predictive of delinquency. Here he could assume that the influence of family social class (in terms of the financial and cultural resources more available to a youth from a higher-class family compared with one from a lower-class family) had an impact prior to the time when the youth committed a delinquent act. Thus, while he could not precisely date the onset of "social class" influence (as you could the onset of smoking), he could assume that it preceded the occurrence of the delinquent behavior.

The second condition for establishing causality is that there must be a high correlation between the independent and dependent variables. This means that a change in the independent variable corresponds to a change in the dependent variable so that an increase in the independent variable is related to an increase (or decrease) in the dependent variable. This related change (the correlation) can be measured statistically, as we will describe in Chapter 13.

Let's return to the smoking example. This second condition for establishing causality requires that among a large group of people, there must be a relationship between which people smoke and which ones get cancer. In addition, higher levels of smoking should be more likely to cause cancer than lower levels of smoking, and people who have smoked for longer periods of time should be more likely to develop cancer than those who have smoked for shorter periods.

The relationship between delinquency and mixing with the wrong crowd is more difficult to think through. Young people who mix with members of the wrong crowd should be more likely to exhibit delinquent behavior. We also expect that those who are more frequently involved with members of the wrong crowd, those who have a greater number of "wrong crowd" friends, and those who hang out for longer periods of time with such friends would be more likely to be delinquent (and to have committed more delinquent acts) than would those who had hung out with "wrong crowd" friends less frequently, who had fewer such friends, and whose association with these friends had been shorter in duration. In sum, there should be a high correlation between measures of associating with the wrong crowd and performing delinquent acts.

Finally, the third condition for establishing causality is that other, competing variables (other independent variables) must be shown to have little influence on the dependent variable. For example, perhaps people who smoke are more likely to be anxious. If so, it could logically be argued that anxiety, not smoking, causes cancer. But we can control the effect of anxiety on the original relationship ("Smoking leads to cancer") so that we can examine this relationship without being influenced by the factor of anxiety. First, we need to measure anxiety, which is much more difficult to measure than smoking. Once it was measured, we could determine in the group of people being studied which ones had high levels of anxiety, which ones had moderate levels of anxiety, and which ones had low levels of anxiety. Then we could look at the association between smoking and cancer *within* these "anxiety" groups. In this way we have controlled for the influence of anxiety, and so we can examine whether there is a causal relationship between smoking and cancer.

In the delinquency study, Hirschi found that attachment is strongly related to delinquency; he needed to control for that factor when he examined other potential independent variables. Thus, in testing the cultural deviance theory, Hirschi controlled for the attachment of the youth to his peers and found that only when a youth was weakly attached to members of the wrong crowd was this affiliation related to delinquency. In fact, youths who were strongly attached to their peers, even if those peers were themselves delinquent, were less likely to be delinquent. This suggested to Hirschi that the "wrong crowd" variable was a much weaker causal factor in influencing delin-

quency than was attachment. This goal of trying to establish causality is not the aim of all types of social research. However, the strategy of moving back and forth between the observational, empirical side of science to the explanatory, theoretical side is generally the way science is carried out.

Causal Models in Social Research

Many social research studies start with causal models to represent the theoretical contentions of the study. Such models identify the variables in the theory, establish the time precedence between those variables, and set up the grounds for testing the model. Hirschi set up causal models for the three theories in this study:

> *Strain theory:* a person is forced into delinquency because of legitimate desires that cannot be met otherwise;
>
> *Control theory:* a person is free to commit delinquent acts because of the weakness of ties to the sources of conventional social support which would discourage delinquency;
>
> *Cultural deviance theory:* a person who commits delinquent acts is merely conforming to a different set of rules supported by a subculture within the society (*Hirschi, 1969, p. 3*).

One of the major tenets of strain theory is that lower-class youths are more likely to commit delinquent acts than are higher-class youths. Social class is the independent variable, and number of delinquent acts is the dependent variable. This relationship is depicted in Figure 2-2. Very simply, the figure shows that a person's social class is related to (may cause) the likelihood of that person engaging in delinquent acts. It also implies that variations in social class are related to variations in delinquent activities. To study this relationship, Hirschi compared the rates of delinquent acts of boys from lower-class families with those of boys from higher-class families. In other words, he moved from stating a theory, to setting up an analytic model of how to test the theory, to testing the theory with empirical evidence.

FIGURE 2-2
Hypothesized relation between social class and delinquent acts.

FIGURE 2-3
Hypothesized relation between attachment to father and delinquent acts.

One of the major contentions of control theory is that youths who are attached to their families, schools, or peers (the independent variables) will be less delinquent (the dependent variable) than will those who are less attached. Recall that this would be the case if delinquency were the result of a divisive society, where conflict would naturally occur unless individuals were firmly attached to social institutions and relationships. Figure 2-3 shows a model of how attachment to a father relates to delinquency. To study this relationship, Hirschi compared the rates of delinquent acts by boys with stronger and weaker levels of attachment to their fathers.

The cultural deviance theory sought to explain delinquency as the result of differences in values among different subcultural groups. Thus, it predicts that youths who are members of delinquent subcultural groups (the independent variable) are more likely to be delinquent (the dependent variable) themselves. Another factor, however, is how important it is for the youth to conform to the general (or conventional) values of the society. Hirschi hypothesized that those in a delinquent subcultural group who had a "high stake in conformity" to the general values of the society at large would have difficulty deciding whose values to follow: those of the delinquent subgroup or those of the wider society.

The model Hirschi offered for this relationship is depicted in Figure 2-4. To study this relationship, Hirschi needed to compare the rates of delinquent acts for boys who had many delinquent friends *and* were low in conformity to the general norms of the society with boys who had many delinquent friends but were high in conformity. In this instance, the number of delinquent friends is

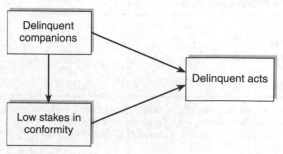

FIGURE 2-4
Hypothesized relations among stakes in conformity, delinquency of companions, and delinquent acts. (From Travis Hirschi, *Causes of Delinquency*, University of California Press, Berkeley, p. 153.)

the independent variable, the rate of delinquent acts is the dependent variable, and the level of conformity is a control (or test) variable. (Chapter 12 explains the role of control variables and shows how three-variable relationships can be examined.)

For each of these theories the first condition for establishing causality holds: the occurrence of the independent variable precedes (in time) the occurrence of the dependent variable. For the strain theory, social class is determined before the youth commits any delinquent acts. For the control theory, attachment to a parent precedes delinquent acts. And for the cultural deviance theory, the number of delinquent friends can be empirically observed before determining the number of delinquent acts.

The object of Hirschi's analyses was to determine whether the second and third conditions for causality could be met. First, he needed to know whether there was a correlation between the independent variables from each theory and the dependent variable, delinquent acts. Hirschi prepared

TABLE 2-1

**SELF-REPORTED DELINQUENCY BY FATHER'S OCCUPATION—
WHITE BOYS ONLY**
(in Percent)

| Self-Reported Acts | Father's Occupation[a] | | | | |
	Low 1	2	3	4	High 5
None	62	53	56	49	61
One	16	26	25	28	25
Two or more	23	21	19	23	14
Totals	101	100	100	100	100
Number of cases	(151)	(156)	(390)	(142)	(282)

[a]1 = unskilled labor; 2 = semiskilled labor; 3 = skilled labor, foreman, merchant;
4 = white collar; 5 = professional and executive.
Source: Travis Hirschi, *Causes of Delinquency*, University of California Press, Berkeley,
1969, p. 69.

cross-tabular analyses in which reported data on each respondent's delinquent acts were matched with reported data on social class background, attachment to the father, and the like. Let's examine a few of these relationships for two of the theories Hirschi was testing.

For the strain theory, Table 2-1 cross-classifies delinquent acts (measured by self-report) and father's occupation (the social class measure that was used). This table presents the percentage of boys from families in which the father had different levels of occupation who had committed "none," "one," or "two or more" delinquent acts. Thus, 62 percent of boys from the lowest-class families had not committed any delinquent acts, compared to 61 percent of boys from the highest-class families. When we examine the columns from lowest-class occupation to highest, we do not see that higher-class boys report fewer delinquent acts. The only difference between these distributions is that among those reporting delinquent acts, a larger proportion of the highest-class boys report a single act, while a larger proportion of the lowest-class boys report more than one delinquent act. In short, Table 2-1 does not offer strong evidence that increases in delinquent activity are strongly related to social class.

Table 2-2 offers evidence to test the control theory. It cross-classifies self-reported delinquent acts (the dependent variable) and intimacy of communication with the father (the independent variable representing parental attachment). Table 2-2 shows a pattern of steady increase in reported delinquent acts among boys with weaker levels of attachment to their fathers; conversely, boys who are closer to their fathers tend to avoid delinquency. Comparing the boys who have the lowest and highest levels of attachment to their father, we note a very large difference in terms of reporting no acts (39 percent vs. 73 percent).

Comparatively, Table 2-2 offers much stronger support that lack of attachment to fathers is related to delinquency than Table 2-1 offers for the relationship between lower social class and delinquency. This means that Hirschi found more convincing evidence to support the control theory than the strain theory for explaining delinquency. Because this study examined one independent variable at a time, it is more difficult to make the case that influence from other explanatory variables that might have affected the original relationship has been blocked—in other words, to make the case that the third condition for causality has been met. Instead, Hirschi successively exam-

TABLE 2-2

**SELF-REPORTED DELINQUENCY BY INTIMACY OF COMMUNICATION
WITH FATHER**
(in Percent)

Self-Reported Acts	Little Intimate Communication		Much Intimate Communication		
	0	1	2	3	4
None	39	55	55	63	73
One	18	25	28	23	22
Two or more	43	20	17	15	5
Totals	100	100	100	101	100
Number of cases	(97)	(182)	(436)	(287)	(121)

Source: Travis Hirschi, *Causes of Delinquency,* University of California Press, Berkeley, 1969, p. 91.

ined the effects of one independent variable after another and compared them in terms of which had the greatest influence on the number of delinquent acts. The Hirschi example has been presented here to show you how one investigator attempted to show causality in a social research project.

THE VALUES AND POLITICS OF SOCIAL RESEARCH

In this chapter we have examined both science and theory in relation to social research. These are the most contentious topics in the study of social research methods. The argument about the extent to which social research is scientific goes to the core question of what social research tries to accomplish and whether it can meet its objectives. Of course, some social researchers have no interest in claiming any scientific basis for their studies because they ground their research in a type of theoretical framework in which scientific principles are not relevant. Thus the differences in theoretical orientations and commitments between social researchers establish the range of perspectives which social researchers hold about what is important in social research, what types of social research are worth doing, and what impact researchers expect their research to have on the wider society.

All this may seem confusing to you as a student, and you may wonder why we should consider studies that aren't scientific or should bother with the scientific model if it can't fully fit all social research designs and why researchers don't agree on a theoretical model so that the whole field could be more fully advanced. This is the case because science, social research, and the societies and social actions and processes that social research studies are all continually changing, and with them the ways in which it seems best to study social issues. Social research is affected by the changing values of researchers who may be university professors or government workers and who over time include broader ranges of people (more women and more members of minority groups).

Moreover, the topics of social research grow out of the political arena, in which ideas during some periods seem more important, more transformative, and more vital for the social interest. Note that some topics hold interest over time. Concern about the causes of delinquency—which motivated Hirschi in the 1960s—has not waned through the subsequent decades. In studying urban neighborhoods and the interactions of the races within them, Anderson has been followed by a continuing stream of urban researchers. In contrast, Laumann and his colleagues' concern with sexual behavior was certainly not new, but the AIDS crisis made it politically more critical in the 1990s. Hochschild's examination of how couples handle the second shift was clearly of greater interest in a society in which the majority of members of couples both hold jobs, and surely her concern with the sharing of this shift was influenced by the greater concern brought forth by the women's movement for the equality and betterment of women's (and men's) lives.

We will conclude this chapter by examining two factors that will help us appreciate this continual change in the values and direction of social research. The first is the fact that science as a human endeavor reaches no fixed and permanent ends but continually shifts as new models, new ways of thinking, and new paradigms gain sway. The second is the way in which the norms and values which supposedly guide science and research activity are continually challenged by political expediencies, economic pressures, and changing beliefs about what is effective and what is socially useful.

Paradigm Shifts and the Changing Nature of Research Activity

The research activity of a scientist or a social researcher never starts from scratch. The researcher has been educated and trained in institutions by more senior researchers who have encouraged a commitment to certain ways of doing things while rejecting other ways. The researcher will also be deeply affected by the types of research that are being published and talked about in his or her field. This means that the very work that is done by researchers rests on *already developed assumptions* which are widely shared (though possibly contested) as well as on established ways of studying certain subjects and presenting the findings both orally and in writing. These shared assumptions and ways of knowing form what the philosopher-historian of science Thomas S. Kuhn (1970) has called a scientific *paradigm*. In general terms, paradigms are "universally recognized scientific achievements that for a time provide model prob-

lems and solutions for a community of practitioners" (1970, p. viii).

In a sociological sense, a paradigm includes the habits of thought and practice which researchers in a given field take for granted, the things that newcomers to a field have to learn. These would include the language, the terms, the mathematical symbols that an individual researcher uses, which are already largely established within the particular discipline. While the outcome of the research could challenge, refute, or redefine these generalizations, they are already present and taken for granted at the start of any research endeavor. There is usually also an agreed-upon model which guides the design and execution of any new research project. Moreover, researchers share certain values as to what makes a specific theory "good." These values include the requirement that a theory or explanation be (as far as possible) accurate, consistent, broad in its scope, simple, and fruitful. Individuals entering a particular field learn what kinds of problems established researchers in that field regard as the most difficult and important. Further, they learn how to proceed appropriately in carrying out their own work and presenting their theories and results to their colleagues.

The Practice of Research and the Scientific Ethos

How far is scientific research as it is practiced guided by a set of rules based on deeply held values? Robert Merton, the eminent sociologist of science, has specified a set of norms or *institutional imperatives* which form a *scientific ethos* protecting the integrity of the scientific enterprise (1973, pp. 270–278). While many would argue that the four principles that make up the scientific ethos as defined by Merton are ideals that researchers may aspire to rather than rules that are normally applied, it is useful to consider them in regard to social research. Let us examine these four norms and how they should ideally operate among scientific researchers.

Universalism, in contrast to particularism, refers to the principle that ideas and knowledge in science must be evaluated on the basis of their merit, not on the basis of the status of the persons who establish them. Similarly, scientists should be evaluated solely on the basis of meritorious achievement, and any other factors should be considered wholly irrelevant. Scientific findings must be tested on a purely impersonal basis; no sets of findings are favored or above refutation.

Communalism indicates that knowledge is not knowledge unless it is shared by a relevant community. Creating knowledge is therefore a *public* act; knowledge cannot simply be the property of one person. However, people claim a right to their ideas in terms not of property but of priority. This would explain the claim of a scientist to recognition as the first to make a particular discovery or formulate a particular idea. Thus communalism in science implies the common availability of scientific work on the condition of recognition of individual contributions.

Disinterestedness refers to the principle that scientific activity must proceed with a sense of neutrality: the scientist must be able to be impartial and receptive to any unexpected observations which might occur and be open-minded in considering the work of others.

Finally, unlike religion, science fosters the norm of *organized skepticism:* what has been accomplished is not the goal of science but only a way station to be left behind when new findings supersede old ones. Everyone's work must be scrutinized and challenged. Scientific authority must be reappraised regularly.

While most scientists believe that these values are important to protect the integrity of scientific investigation, careful studies of scientific activity have shown, as was mentioned above, that scientists often operate quite differently. For example, Ian Mitroff (1974), in a study of the Apollo moon scientists who were the first to examine the materials brought back from the moon landings, found that the principles guiding the behavior of the scientists were often counter to those which Merton

had described as normative. Mitroff found that rather than being *disinterested,* neutral seekers of the truth, none of the scientists interviewed over a 3½-year period changed their positions; instead, most became even more committed to their "pet" hypotheses (1974, pp. 586–587). Furthermore, there was great secrecy among the scientists, counter to the norms of communalism (according to which ideas should be shared) and universalism (according to which ideas are independent of the status of those who have developed them). Mitroff concluded that these counternorms to those prescribed by Merton were most evident in areas of science where the problems being studied were "ill-structured" and therefore open to challenge. However, in areas where the research was better defined, the classic norms were more often practiced (1974, p. 594).

In comparison to scientific research, social research may not be as strongly affected by paradigms or by the norms that ideally operate to protect the integrity of science. However, as we proceed with learning how to do social research, it will be well to keep in mind how scientific research is conditioned by the paradigms under which it operates and the deeply held values and norms that make it socially meaningful.

REVIEW NOTES

- Science is empirical: it is based on the study of accurate and precise observations, which are recorded as measures classified as variables.
- Science is logical and rational. Its aim is to look for patterns and associations among variables, to determine independent and dependent variables.
- The ultimate goal of social research is not to seek empirical evidence (facts) alone, as the positivist would do, but to interpret the facts.
- The building and testing of theories (logical sets of propositions based on empirical evidence developed to explain the meaning and significance of the evidence) are the goals of science and social research.

- The scientific model includes an inductive half, moving from observation to empirical generalizations to theories, and a deductive half, moving from theories to hypotheses to observations.
- The serendipity factor in scientific research explains how tests of hypotheses from one theory sometimes can lead to the development of quite unrelated theories.
- Postmodern and feminist theories challenge many accepted ways of doing social research.
- Causality can be established if a temporal order can be determined in the relationship of the independent variable to the dependent variable, if there is a high correlation between the variables, and if no other variable causes the association between the two variables.
- Merton's scientific ethos is based on four principles of scientific behavior: universalism, communalism, disinterestedness, and organized skepticism. There is much evidence that these principles serve more as ideals than as established practice.

KEY TERMS

conflict theory
empirical generalizations
feminist theory
hypotheses
observation
paradigm
positivist
postmodern theory
scientific ethos
scientific model
serendipity factor
structural-functionalism
symbolic interaction theory
theories

STUDY EXERCISES

1. Look through three issues of the *American Sociological Review* or the *American Journal of Sociology* and find (1) an article that closely links empirical research with theory, (2) an article that presents the findings from an empirical research study with little reference to theory, and (3) an article that is solely theoretical (and presents no empirical data). Which type of article was the most difficult to find? Which was the easiest to find?
2. What cautions would postmodern or feminist researchers recommend in designing a study?
3. Take one of the studies discussed in Chapter 1 and try to give examples of how each of the four components of the scientific model (Figure 2-1) occurred. For example, you might start with observations or theories.

RECOMMENDED READINGS

1. Barnes, Barry, *Scientific Knowledge and Sociological Theory,* London: Routledge & Kegan Paul, 1974. The influence of scientific thinking and models on sociology and social research is examined in this work.
2. Coleman, James S., *Foundations of Social Theory,* Cambridge, MA: Harvard University Press, 1990. This ambitious volume of social theory presents a theory of social action. It is a good source for examing choice theory.
3. Collins, Randall, *Four Sociological Traditions,* Oxford: Oxford University Press, 1994. This volume presents the conflict, rational/utilitarian (economic), Durkheimian, and microinteractionist traditions.
4. Craib, Ian, *Modern Social Theory: From Parsons to Habermas,* 2nd ed. New York: St. Martin's Press, 1992. This excellent small text describes a range of modern theories up through postmodernism.
5. Gidden, Anthony: *Social Theory and Modern Sociology,* Stanford, CA: Stanford University Press, 1987. An essay by a prominent British sociologist on the significance of social theory in our times.
6. Kuhn, Thomas S.: *The Structure of Scientific Revolutions,* 2d ed., Chicago: University of Chicago Press, 1970. This influential work on the human activity of science focused great attention on the role of paradigms in the development of science.
7. Ritzer, George: *Sociology: A Multiple Paradigm Science,* Boston: Allyn and Bacon, 1975. Ritzer examines how far and in what ways paradigms can be applied to sociological research.

The Design
of Social Research

*T*he first section of this text was intended to provide you with a broad understanding of the foundations for the social research enterprise. In Part Two the components of a research design will be laid out. Chapter 3 will examine how a topic can be turned into a problem for social research and will outline a plan covering all the components of a research project. Chapter 4 is concerned with concepts, measurement, and operationalization. Once a topic has been selected and the research plan has been proposed, a careful consideration of precisely what concepts will be studied and how they will be measured is necessary. When the major concepts in the study have been determined, the research project must conceive of a way to make these concepts observable, in other words, to *operationalize* the concepts. Once the concepts have been operationalized, the issue of concern becomes finding an appropriate set of subjects (people, events, institutions, or whatever) to observe or question. The selection of these subjects requires a knowledge of the principles of sampling, which will be the subject of Chapter 5.

Defining, Designing, and Developing a Research Project

INTRODUCTION

*T*o start a research project, you first need to develop a clearly defined research topic. Before launching a project, you must set out the necessary steps you will follow to produce the final research report; that is, you need a detailed research plan which may form the basis of a written *research proposal*. However, between defining the topic and producing a research plan, you need to design and develop the necessary components of the study. The first objective of the chapter is to help suggest ways of finding topics and turning them into researchable problems. It will suggest sources of topics, offer criteria to be used in selecting a topic, indicate ways to intensify knowledge about a topic, and delineate how a topic of interest can become a researchable problem. The second objective will be to consider the rationale for doing the study: What purpose will be served by doing the study? Are there actual or potential uses for the findings from this research? The third objective will be to develop the components of the study design: the units of analysis and the time dimension.

The final objective of this chapter is to propose a plan to follow in doing your research project. Once a research problem has been formulated and the subjects for a study have been determined, the actual means for carrying out the research project must be delineated. This is the proposal-writing stage of the research process, when the overall plan for the project must be set out in logical order.

SOURCES TO USE IN SELECTING A TOPIC

In the Introduction, I emphasized that what is going on in your own life and in the social world around you, what troubles you, what interests you, what your life experiences are—all these areas of concern are full of possibilities for social research projects. Following C. Wright Mills's notion that for a social research project to be sociologically imaginative, you need to draw on your personal resources to relate issues in the society to your own experience. What Mills was stressing is that social research is not just a matter of dry numbers and charts or even of careful descriptions or intricate theories; instead, social research should have a relevance, a depth of concern that raises it above what is mundane and uninteresting to a level of intellectual commitment. However, you cannot begin to get committed to a project until you have selected a topic for study. Besides your own experiences and ideas, there are many sources to which you may turn in trying to identify a research topic. Social research topics need not derive from your own experiences and interests; they can come from more formal efforts at finding a topic. To find a topic, you must expose yourself to some potential sources for ideas. These sources may be already published materials, other people, or research projects which are in progress.

Printed Sources

The studies described in Chapter 1 were examples from the vast literature on social research that is already published. Such studies can provide many ideas for projects, but where can you find these published sources? The results of many research projects have been published in book form. For example. the Laumann survey on sexuality became the basis of two books: *The Social Organization of Sexuality* (1994) and *Sex in America* (for which R. T. Michael was the first author) (1994). Laumann and his colleagues also disseminated their findings in a number of articles in academic journals, and their results were noted in popular magazines and newspaper articles.

A large study reported in a book holds many ideas for smaller projects. Consider the Laumann study. You might want to consider a few of their findings. Let's say you were interested in people who share a "recreational" orientation to sexuality. In that case, you would want to glean from the Laumann study how they had defined and measured that "normative orientation" and what other factors it had been related to (other attitudes and statuses of the respondents). You might note that they had further separated those with this orientation into two smaller groups: (1) the *prolife recreational,* who at the same time held liberal views on extramarital sex and pornography and more conservative views on homosexuality and abortion, and (2) the *libertarian recreational,* whose views on all aspects of sexuality were liberal. If this recreational orientation toward sexuality interests you as a topic for study, you may want to conceptualize it as Laumann and his colleagues did or reformulate and reconceptualize it. You would want to look carefully at all the factors that Laumann and his colleagues found to be related to this orientation. The important point is that reading the work of other researchers and figuring out how they designed their study and measured their concepts should help you formulate your project.

In the Hochschild (1989) study, you might find the topic of how couples share the work of the family and home (the "second shift") of interest. Which parts of the work in the home are the most fully shared (e.g., cooking)? Does the father do more if the mother has a higher-paying job than he has? How do the mother's reactions to the father's efforts seem to affect what he does? How does the age of the children affect the sharing of the second shift? In "blended families," which include children born from earlier unions of the couple, is there more sharing of the second shift? You might read Hochschild's study with your question in mind and try to find out (1) if she speaks directly to your interest or (2) her findings suggest a slightly different topic. Take the issue of the relative wages of the couple: Would the husband participate more in the second shift if he earned less than his wife? Hochschild found the following in her interview study:

Of the men who earned more than their wives, 21 percent shared housework. Of the men who earned about the same, 30 percent shared. But among men who earned *less* than their wives, *none* shared *(1989, p. 221).*

Your study might produce different results, and you would want to consider how Hochschild had conceptualized and measured both income and the sharing of housework.

There are so many published studies that for any idea you might think of, numerous other researchers will have already been at work on it. Don't feel discouraged by this. No two researchers ever produce the same study. An area in which there has been a lot of research is by definition an important area. Juvenile delinquency is a good example of a heavily studied area. New approaches and new points of view, however, can generate valuable new findings, and new findings will be more valuable if they have been informed by earlier studies (such as Hirschi's 1969 classic study on delinquency carried out more than 25 years ago).

Appendix A offers a detailed description of how to use a library to look for a topic or to intensify knowledge about a topic once it has been selected. We will now turn to a different source for finding a topic: connecting your efforts to an ongoing project.

Ongoing Social Research Projects and Available Data

One way to discover a topic is to find a project that is currently under way. Talk to the people doing the project and see if they can suggest some aspect of the project that you might study further or from which you might develop a researchable idea. Alternatively, you might look for already collected data which you can use for your purposes.

Finding an Ongoing Project.   How can you find ongoing projects? First you might find out what kind of research your professors are conducting or what graduate students are studying. Another good way to hear about current research is to attend a scholarly meeting in sociology, education, political science, psychology, or whatever discipline you think most likely would address your interests. Such meetings have printed schedules giving the titles of all the papers, their authors, and the times and places they will be given. Remember that you need not attend a national meeting. Many regional associations have conferences, and there are special interest groups that hold meetings (the Law and Society Association, the Women's Studies Association, etc.). Individual universities and research centers often sponsor meetings where papers are delivered or where roundtable discussions are held, which may be directly of interest to you.

Never assume that you would be unwelcome. While there are a few exclusive conferences which only invited participants may attend, they are very rare. Generally, students are welcome at professional meetings, and usually there are special registration fees for students, allowing them to participate at reduced rates. Don't feel shy about asking a question either during the discussion following the presentation of the paper or after the session has formally ended. Nothing makes a researcher happier than finding other people interested in his or her project. Many professional meetings make available photocopies of papers which have been delivered. These copies may be purchased at the meeting, or you may write directly to the author to request a copy.

Finding Available Data. A topic for a social research project may stem from an available dataset. You may be surprised that a topic for a study could grow from a set of data that has already been produced. But national surveys (like the one on sexuality) are usually so broad and may include so many items that a multitude of projects could be produced from a single dataset. Don't think that simply because a book has already been written which was based on a national survey, all the data must have been analyzed. Most survey datasets are vastly underutilized. Even the same sets of questions may be analyzed in so many different ways

that no two researchers are likely to produce identical analyses. (It is, of course, legitimate to replicate an earlier study with different data, but most replications add new twists to the earlier design.) Many social research projects rely on data that were collected for other purposes. Chapter 9 specifically examines studies that use already collected data sources and suggests where to find such sources.

HOW TO INTENSIFY KNOWLEDGE ABOUT A TOPIC

Once you have selected a topic, you will need to get more information about it. There are many ways to do this.

Using the Library: Print and Electronic Resources

Both the above discussion and Appendix A address how to use a library to find a topic. Very similar methods are used to intensify knowledge about a topic once you have chosen it. The major difference is that in this stage of the project you must be more selective. You cannot look at everything that has been written on this topic. Instead, you must continually make choices about what to look up, what to scan, and what to read in detail.

Let me describe how, in preparation for designing a study, I "reviewed the literature" on the topic of how attending a predominantly white college affects black students. The studies on African-Americans in predominantly white America were numerous. Since my subject concerned black students in predominantly white educational institutions, I needed to look at studies of African-Americans in mixed racial environments, in educational settings, and in institutions that people had entered to enhance their opportunities. Some of the earliest works I found were studies done early in this century on the experiences of individual black students at particular institutions. Since I planned to study two universities in a large northern city which had always had some black students, I would not really be looking at institutions where enforced integration had taken place. Nevertheless, I decided that studies on the effects of integration might suggest how black students reacted to an environment in which their sensitivities to the meaning of entering a predominantly white environment were heightened. What I was doing at this stage was to look at other studies that addressed similar research topics.

At this point in the project I did not know what type of effect I would be looking for. I began by looking up studies, books, articles, and data related to a few subtopics of the project; with the vast expansion of colleges and universities in the 1960s, the subject "College Effects" had been very popular. Such research came under the general disciplines of social psychology (the effects of college usually were measured in terms of an attitude change) or of education (in this instance the subfield might be higher education or the sociology of education). I needed to consider two things: which effect I would study and which potential causes of the effect I might be interested in studying. The causes include such things as the influence of significant others, the types of activities and behaviors of the students, the background characteristics of the students, and their abilities and aspirations for being at college. The effect to be studied would be the dependent variable; the causes, the independent variables. In this stage I was determining the dependent and independent variables in the study.

In the course of my reading I found in a number of studies a scale which had been used to measure the effects of college on students, often in conjunction with a number of other scales. The scale which appealed to me was called the *Autonomy Scale* (Heist and Yonge, 1968). I thought the items which made up the scale were measures of the types of attitudes I wanted to study in black students. My adviser was more suspicious of this scale. He wanted to know more about it. This took me on a very interesting search for the origins of this scale. It turned out that the Autonomy Scale was a greatgranddaughter of the famous *F-Scale of authoritar-*

ianism (Adorno et al., 1950), though it was a measure of its converse, nonauthoritarianism. Finding out about the concept of authoritarianism and how it was measured by the F-Scale (which will be described more fully in Chapter 4) led me back through a fascinating history of how this concept had developed and how it had been operationalized. With a much firmer grasp of what the Autonomy Scale was actually measuring, I felt more confident in using it. At the third stage I selected a means for measuring the dependent variable.

For the search I have described, I used a university library to look up books and articles. I also used a collection of different types of tests, available in a research library, to select the Autonomy Scale and look at its earlier versions. I also ordered a few earlier dissertations on topics similar to my own, which were available on microfilm from University Microfilms at Ann Arbor, Michigan.

This search I have described was done solely with printed sources, which were all that were available at that time. Today modern university and college libraries have become electronic. While the printed resources mentioned above are still vital to a thorough search for a topic, emphasis would now be placed on electronic catalogues and databases. So let's alter the topic I posed above slightly to be "Retention of African-Americans in Higher Education" and consider ways in which we would intensify our knowledge about this topic by using electronic resources.

For an electronic search on this topic, the easiest place to start is with a library's on-line catalogue to see what books are available in the collection (and possibly in other local collections). From there one would move to searching CD ROM databases such as Sociofile (sociology), ERIC (education), and PsychLit (psychology). Each of these databases has an on-line (as well as printed) thesaurus in which you can check for appropriate search terms.

Many libraries also have available full text databases such as Lexis, Nexis, and Ethnic Newswatch. From Lexis you can print or download full text, up-to-date newspaper articles highlighting recent changes and trends relevant to your topic. For the topic of African-American retention in higher education, Ethnic Newswatch might be helpful, as it provides the full text of publications from the African-American press in the United States. Finally, check with your library to see what access it has to full text journals that are on-line; this means that entire articles appear on-line. Academic libraries are beginning to acquire access to databases such as Project Muse (full text of Johns Hopkins University Press journals) and Ideal (full text of Academic Press journals), which are available over the Internet.

The box below gives some examples of the way you might search for this topic in different kinds of databases. Different databases require different vocabulary or search terms. For a more detailed discussion of this subject, see Appendix A: Using an Electronic Library for Social Research.

ON-LINE CATALOGUE SEARCH* (USING LIBRARY OF CONGRESS SUBJECT HEADINGS): AFRO-AMERICAN** COLLEGE STUDENTS

ERIC

African-American** and (college-students or higher-education) and (retention or school-holding-power)

SOCIOFILE

(college-students or higher-education) and (african-american** or black-americans) and (attrition or educational-opportunities)

LEXIS

African w/l American and (college or university) w/l student! and retention

ETHNIC NEWSWATCH

Ethnic Group: African/Caribbean and Article Keyword: retention and (college or university) and student

*Thanks to Jacqueline Borin for assistance.
**Note difference in search term.

Using Integrative Research Reviews

In many areas of interest in the social sciences, reviews of current and past research in specific fields have been prepared. Such *integrative research reviews* offer excellent groundwork for beginning researchers. For example, Maccoby and Jacklin's (1974) two-volume review of studies on sex differences both provided a foundation for the rapid rise in research in that area and helped researchers push beyond questions of sex differences to a consideration of other gender-relevant concerns in the social sciences. Academic journals often offer review articles.

These integrative articles, referred to as meta-analyses, may simply compare the findings of research on similar topics, or they may assess the theoretical contributions of comparable studies (Cooper, 1989). Integrative reviews help beginning researchers by scanning the literature, noting the most common directions taken by research on a particular topic, and summarizing the cumulative knowledge gained. Finally, reviews often delineate which areas of a field remain to be explored.

Carrying out an integrative research review is itself a form of social research. Cooper's book *Integrating Research: A Guide for Literature Reviews* (1989) overviews the methods for carrying out such literature reviews and offers numerous examples of effective reviews.

Using Written Records and Documents

You can investigate many topics by examining the records or documents prepared by an organization for its own purposes. Suppose you plan to study an organization. Let's say it is a neighborhood community organization. Such an organization will probably have minutes of its meetings; it may have a founding charter under which it was organized; it is also likely to have a clipping file of articles that appeared in the local newspapers; it may well have a newsletter describing its activities; it will have files of memos sent between different members of the organization. There may also be copies of studies that the organization or others have done about some aspect of the organization's work. Can you get access to these materials? The best way to find out is to ask. Minutes from meetings may be considered public or private. Records from the past probably will be more available than current records.

Many researchers need to gather information from government documents. Specific laws may need to be examined, along with proceedings of Congress and the policies of government agencies. Various bodies of the government collect data and analyze them for many reasons. Some of these will be suggested in Chapter 9 on government data. If your subject touches a professional field— say, medicine, law, or teaching—you may want to look at materials from the professional associations of these organizations, such as the American Medical Association, the American Bar Association, and the National Education Association. These organizations tend to have research departments which carry out various studies; they often have newsletters or other informational publications which mention the ongoing research.

Talking to Informed Others

One of the best ways to intensify your knowledge about a topic is to talk to "people in the know." But who are these people? There are three categories to consider. The first group are relevant researchers, those who have studied topics similar to your own. The second are insiders, participants in the very field you are studying. The third are intellectual comrades, people with whom you talk easily and fruitfully about your ideas.

Relevant Researchers.   Many students move into areas of research similar to those of the professors with whom they study. This is a logical thing to do. In graduate school, students generally choose to work with faculty members whose ideas interest them. As an undergraduate, you may select courses, attend lectures, and try to get to know professors whose ideas you find exciting and stim-

ulating. If you know a professor who has done research in the area of your topic for study, go speak to her or him. (Let me repeat how receptive most faculty members are to talking to students interested in their research.) If you can read an article by the faculty member or hear a lecture about the research before speaking to the person, you will be a better conversationalist. Remember, researchers may get ideas from students. Don't feel shy about trying out your ideas on the faculty member. Does the topic sound plausible? What problems might you run into? Are there particularly important studies that you should look up? If the conversation goes well, you might ask the professor whether you could show him or her your proposal for the project once you have it drafted.

Insiders.   If you will be investigating a topic that may require a field study or if you plan to study an organization, institution, neighborhood, special event, or ethnic group, you should seek out members of your subject group to see if they are willing to give you the "inside scoop." These informants can provide you with a basic knowledge about the nature of life in that institution, or wherever. Now, as you know, insiders do not necessarily have an accurate picture of things, but they do have a picture, however slanted or biased. You will want to consider what they tell you in terms of who they are and what their role is in the social environment.

Recall from Chapter 1 how Anderson (1990) got some of his most salient information from a range of people who lived in the neighborhood. Whatever the setting, you will need to be very discreet with the information an insider offers to you. In short, you must generate trust in others is order for them to want to talk to you, and for insiders to continue to talk to you, they must see you as trustworthy.

Intellectual Comrades.   All of us know people with whom we talk easily, people with whom we can discuss our ideas and our work. You should select one such person, pour out all your ideas about what you are planning to study and why, and let that person react however he or she might. Often such a discussion is best held in a casual environment, over a cup of coffee (or whatever). Tell this person your major worry—why you think the study might fail. Then see if the person tries to reconvince you that your topic is a sound one. He or she should know you well enough to sense whether the topic sounds feasible given your abilities, motivation, and other commitments. The very process of talking your ideas through with someone you are close to, someone who is creative and whose judgment you respect, will help you formulate your ideas better. Because social research almost always involves *doing* something in the real world, the very processes of thinking about it are often enhanced through interaction, that is, talking it through with others rather than simply thinking it through on your own. Remember, talking about it is not a waste of time; it is the beginning of doing the research. And the most valuable talking you can do is with those with whom you talk most effectively.

REASONS FOR STUDYING THE TOPIC

Once your topic is selected, you should consider your rationale for the study. You might want to think over what purpose will be served by the topic of the study, what will be accomplished by carrying out this study. The aims of social research are generally of three types: exploration, description, and explanation. If you are helping to clarify a largely undefined area, your aim is exploratory. Your observations and analyses of these data should add to earlier, related efforts of study. If your study is descriptive, it may expand the body of work in this area. Your study may repeat an older study, in which case it is referred to as a *replication study*. This is a very honorable practice in all the sciences and one you might consider. Replication studies also can test hypotheses. If your study is based on a hypothesis, the object of your study is to test that hypothesis. Thus, studies based on hypotheses have as their aim explanation. Since a hypothesis is based on a theory, or explanation of some relationship, hypothesis test-

ing can add to a theory or challenge it. Explanatory studies may develop or alter theories. Descriptive and exploratory studies also may add to or detract from theories. While the evidence from an exploratory field study may not be able to fully refute a theory, it may offer data that could seriously challenge a theoretical explanation. Finally, social research projects may lead to the forming of new theories. In such a case, if the study can account for why a relationship occurs, then this explanatory study is building theory.

Uses for Social Research

A number of broad criteria may be used to determine the rationale of a study, that is, whether the study has a valid purpose. Seeking to understand the purpose of a study is in itself a valuable effort, for it pushes you to explain your interest, to clarify why you are curious about something. In seeking an explanation of your purpose, you are already beginning to think of ways to address your question, to establish a research design to get at the evidence. Or, alternatively, you may conclude that your research topic lacks sufficient purpose and value to make it worth your time and effort.

Robert Merton (1959), in writing about how to start a research project (discussed in the Introduction), stated that the development of a *rationale* is second only to posing the originating question. Since the sociological imagination is so broad, research topics can be based on any aspect of human affairs. Your reason for doing a particular study may be that you wish to know the answer to a question for its own sake [this is a purpose which Merton recognized (1959, p. xx)]. Yet the knowledge generated may be relevant to other aspects of the social sciences. Merton states that

> The scientist may regard his deep interest in a question as reason enough for pursuing it. But sooner or later, if the question and its answers are to become part of the science rather than remaining a personal hobby, they must be shown to be relevant to other ideas and facts in the discipline (*1959, p. xx*).

Here Merton's rationale for research is that it contributes to systematic knowledge in the discipline. This type of research is referred to as *basic research.*

Merton presents a second rationale, which is that the study may have some practical use (1959, p. xxi). He stresses that many social research topics have double relevance; they have import to both systematic knowledge and practical use. Where practical use is an outcome of a research project, it would be an example of *applied research.* An example Merton gives is studies of people in particular professions (teachers, physicians, the clergy). Preparing individuals to fulfill roles to serve social objectives is a practical necessity in any society; at the same time the study of this process—that is, the study of adult socialization—is of theoretical import in the social science disciplines (Merton, 1959, pp. xxi–xxii). Many social scientists claim that the purpose of their research is to accomplish both ends—their work will add to the body of knowledge in the discipline, and it has practical aims as well. Most social research has some practical import.

For social research to be held in esteem, its social value should be made clear in any research project. Here are four broad questions that may be used in considering whether a proposed study has a useful function in the continuing development of the social sciences and/or in the society. Clearly, they do not suggest the *only* possible reasons for deciding whether a project may be useful, but they will serve as a good start. You can then add to the list some reasons of your own.

1. Does the study offer evidence about the changing nature of society?

Most social research studies focus on the present time, leaving to historians the study of the past. Yet what is current today is, by tomorrow, history. Thus the social researcher is always trying to grasp the present in order to understand the contributions of the past and speak to the probable conditions of the future. It is this dynamic aspect of social existence which is critical to an understanding of the social mechanism. Sociologists refer to this as the study of social change. Subjects that lend themselves to the study of the changing nature of society include social processes undergoing revision (e.g., race relations, cross-sex relations), social institutions which appear to be undergoing radical change (families through divorce, small businesses through consolidation and bankruptcy) and the effects of new political and social rules on social structure (e.g., affirmative action, legalization of abortion or pressure to rescind it, desegregation, gun control legislation).

The study of change always highlights the timeliness of the subject: a study should be grounded in a clear time frame, and the researcher must heed the significance of this time frame. The present time is not necessarily typical; rather, it both expresses the results of earlier years and foreshadows new problems and new ways of living which in prior years were of less concern. For example, the current concern about AIDS sprang forth only in the late 1980s, though the disease had been diagnosed in 1981. Public attention to AIDS was magnified when public figures such as the basketball star Magic Johnson announced that they had HIV, the viral precursor to AIDS. Social researchers as well have turned their focus to the study of the social implications of this epidemic. It is by addressing issues which are timely in the ever-changing pattern of social existence that social research attains a clear relevance.

2. Does the study address a subject on which social policies are (or may be) developed or on which decisions must be based?

Social organizations and institutions devise policies to order and control social events. These policies usually aim to bring about specific objectives of the organization. Often social organizations formally require and establish research procedures to evaluate the effectiveness of a new policy or social program. For example, publicly funded programs often have an evaluation component so that the "results" of spending tax money for a specific purpose can be determined. (Chapter 10 will describe how evaluation research is carried out.) A lot of privately funded research also appraises the effects of social policies and procedures.

Furthermore, social research may address some aspect of the social structure or social behavior on which judgments will be formed (legislation enacted, referendum supported). Whether your state will build additional prison facilities may depend on how far the voters are convinced that overcrowding in prisons fosters further crime. Suppose you, as a social researcher, are hired by your community government to carry out a study to determine whether an environmental protection organization is having a positive effect in your community. You would need to consider the objectives and strategies of the organization. You would also try to determine who was being influenced by the organization and what changes in policies and practices in protecting the environment occurred as a result of the activities of the organization. In short, you would have to develop some way to measure the group's effectiveness. This second purpose signifies research which may alter policies and judgments.

3. Does the study seek to develop a better and fuller understanding of an unusual social event or social practice, a less familiar group, or a group whose characteristics and activities have undergone change?

Studies that bring into view aspects of one's own society which are unfamiliar in the dominant consciousness, studies that analyze groups which are in a marginal position, and studies that delve into the makeup of foreign societies enable the researcher and the readers of the research to gain a fuller understanding of human society and social practices. In American society, because of the wide diversity of ethnic and racial groups, there has been an emphasis on ethnic studies and minority relations. Cross-national research has offered an opportunity to compare more familiar (often American) beliefs and practices to those of less familiar cultures. Single case studies of specific foreign or less familiar American cultural groups have also served to uncover aspects of other cultures which shed light on our practices and beliefs.

Sociologists have been fascinated by social groups that break with conventional norms (nudists, members of communes) or impose on their members requirements which appear to be punitive or restrictive (religious cults). There are difficulties in studying unfamiliar groups, because those groups may resist being studied. However, the study of groups without their knowledge through covert means is open to charges of unethical practices, which will be discussed in Chapter 14. However, many less familiar aspects of our culture are easy to observe and study: the rationale and practices of vegetarians, the role relations of parents who are employed by their grown children, the social status of a male nurse. Subjects such as these would pose little threat to anyone.

4. Does the study make use of experience you have had or particular knowledge you have gained so that it capitalizes on your potential for making unique contributions to social research?

Here you may think that as a novice you have nothing original or special to bring to a research project. You are wrong! Each of you has a wealth of knowledge about family life, your ethnic or religious group, your city or neighborhood, or your job that can be used as a starting point for a research subject. If you are able to develop the subject for the study so that you can relate your depth of experience to a specific research question, you may be able to generate unique and valuable perspectives on this topic. Here the ability to reflect on your own experience, view your life from different perspectives, or step outside yourself and look at your affiliations or beliefs from a distance will enable you to extract the significance of your experience from your memories and perspectives.

This potential for the inclusion of self-analysis differentiates the social sciences from the natural sciences. Those who can focus on what they know best with both insight and disinterested objectivity can make special contributions to the overall understanding of human society.

Criteria to Use in Making the Final Selection of a Topic

There are three major criteria to keep in mind when you are selecting a topic.

The Topic Should Be Feasible to Study. If you can't carry out the project to study the topic, then however fine the topic, it is not the right choice. Some people approach research projects pessimistically. They may feel that no one will give them permission to study what interests them, that no one will agree to be interviewed, or that they could never get the money or the help they need to carry out a project. Others are overly optimistic. They may be sure that everyone will be fascinated with the project, that people will rush to participate, or that support will be easy to obtain. The truth about most research projects is probably somewhere in between: you can generate the interest of others and get their help in your project, but you will not be able to get the support of all. Some resources you may want may not be available. Some individuals may refuse to help you or may not be able to provide you with the help you need. The bottom line for most research projects is that you must be inventive; you must adapt your methods if certain plans do not work out. Feasibility must therefore be considered in terms of time, cost, efforts, and skill. Each of these must be available in sufficient amounts to make the research project achievable.

The Topic Should Be of Genuine Interest to You. So many things can be studied effectively that unless you are doing a commissioned study or working on someone else's project, you should carry out a study on a topic which really interests

you. I have argued that this sense of involvement in a research project is what differentiates social research from plain fact-finding or routine, lifeless studies. The Introduction to this text was written to encourage you to explore your own interests and get in touch with what excites you as a way to begin thinking about a social research project.

Your Research Should Enhance Our Understanding of Society. While this may sound overly ambitious to some, your study should be designed to offer new insights or perspectives on the topic which may positively contribute to the body of social research. While you may feel embarrassed to state that your study will enrich our understanding of society, you should keep this in mind in designing your study, for it will tend to push you toward the more relevant aspects of the topic, to ground your study in the "real world" of social realities, social problems, and the search for solutions.

TURNING A TOPIC INTO A RESEARCHABLE PROBLEM

Social research topics don't come neatly packaged as clearly defined subjects. Your very interest in the topic may lie in its complexity, in the myriad ways in which you can think about it. The best way to begin exploring a topic more systematically is to narrow it down to a researchable question or group of questions. This process of turning ideas into questions and then refining these questions until you have a research problem involves a lot of trial and error. I will suggest the course you might follow in doing this.

First: Consider the Most Problematic Aspects of the Topic

Think of all the most troubling aspects of your topic. Where do the roadblocks seem to lie? Don't be afraid to immerse yourself in the problems of the topic until you think the topic seems the most "undoable" you could imagine. Then try to pull out the central problem that underlies the whole issue. In the study I carried out on the effect of college on black students, I had felt beaten down by a whole variety of concerns. For example, could I study this if I were not black? What was I really trying to find out?

The central issue that came forth was: What in fact were black students getting from their efforts to achieve a higher education? I felt convinced (perhaps naively) that the real goal of a college education was more than a credential, more than a lot of information which one learned. It was the development of a kind of self-consciousness, an ability to reflect on yourself and your world so that you could think, read, talk about ideas with a freshness, an openness, a sophistication not characteristic of those who have not been asked to consider ideas carefully. I found this an interesting question to pose about African-American students in college, because there seemed to be several possible outcomes of that experience. On the one hand, they might feel like outsiders in a predominantly white college and thus not able to fully partake of their college environment. On the other hand, the potential culture shock which a predominantly white college might create for them could have a powerful impact on them and help them develop the kind of self-consciousness and propensity to see things from a multiplicity of viewpoints which is the essence of autonomy.

Second: Define the Aim of the Project

Recall that the aims of a research project (the reasons for doing it) can vary. Babbie (1995, pp. 84–86) suggests three general purposes of any research project. Many field studies map largely unknown territories. There may be very few guidelines in pursuit of such a problem, though there is usually a lot of advice. When a project addresses largely uncharted areas, its aim is to *explore*. A good exploration of a topic may provide a wealth of material for others to think about. When a project seeks to carefully detail evidence so that a clearer picture can be seen and therefore a firmer understanding of its topic can be gained, its aim is

to *describe*. When a project set out to test a specific idea—to see under what conditions a phenomenon will increase or decrease, whether it will matter more or matter less—its aim is to *explain*.

One way to tell what your aim is in studying a topic is to think about what you would like to be able to report on once the project is complete. Do you want to say why something occurs (to explain)? Do you want to carefully and thoroughly show the state of the situation you are studying (to describe)? Do you want to uncover new knowledge or a new idea which may excite or surprise others (to explore)?

Third: State the Topic as a Series of Questions

Jot down all the questions your topic poses. It is best to express these concerns in the form of questions, because questions demand answers. And thinking of your study as a question (or a set of questions) to be answered will propel you to the next stage of thinking, namely, how you will go about answering your questions. Once the questions have been set down, try to write an answer to each one. This is, in a way, both the beginning and the end of a research project. The methods apply to the middle. For each question posed, indicate what would need to be known (what data would need to be collected and analyzed) to try to answer the question.

Now look at the different questions. Which one do you think the study you envision would be best able to address? Is there a second question which the study might also pose? Could it be combined with the first question to strengthen the focus of the study?

Fourth: Set Up a Hypothesis Based on One Alternative Answer

If the aim of the study is explanation, a research question usually can be the basis for establishing a number of hypotheses. Each hypothesis sets out one possible answer to the research question as the stated expectation to be studied. For example, the research question

Do commuter students participate less in extracurricular activities on campus?

could be the basis for this hypothesis:

If commuter students spend less time on campus than residential students, then commuters will have lower rates of participation in campus extracurricular activities than students living on campus.

The hypothesis sets up a prediction to be tested which is logically derived from the research question. The research question merely poses the subject of interest.

Note that once a hypothesis is formulated, the agenda for the study is determined: the researcher has clarified what data will be needed and how the variables will have to be related. In short, the direction of the study is established by posing a hypothesis. It should be added that studies are often guided by many different hypotheses or by alternative hypotheses. Recall that Hirschi's study of delinquency compared three alternative theories of delinquency by testing different hypotheses derived from the theories.

WHOM OR WHAT TO STUDY— THE UNITS OF ANALYSIS

Generally, before a topic is fully clarified, the researcher has in mind the types of subjects he or she will need to study. Most commonly, social researchers take individuals as their subjects. Remember, however, that people are not the only subjects of study in social research. You may study groups, programs, organizations, larger communities (states, nations), and artifacts as well as individuals. These social entities whose social characteristics are the focus of the study would be the units of analysis. They are the collection of "things" that will be studied. Box 3-1 gives examples of studies that would be based on each type of unit of analysis.

Depending on the research question posed, a more or less specific set of subjects may be suggested. Some research questions can be answered only with a probability sample representative of the population of subjects to whom the findings refer. For example, if your research question is to ask whether auto accident deaths in the United States are largely caused by drunken drivers, your data must represent those auto accidents nationwide. A study of the auto accidents in your community would not answer this question, nor would the driving patterns of teenage youths in a local high school. Note that data from these two examples might be able to address interesting research questions but would not provide evidence bearing on the question as it was posed above.

Often there needs to be a balancing of the kinds of subjects you can feasibly study against the research question you wish to address. In some cases the question may need to be restated. However, don't restrict your scope too much in considering a set of subjects for study. Start by defining the very best set of subjects you could imagine in the best of all possible worlds (that's the world in which everything is possible!). That way, you will have the characteristics of the sample which are both desirable and necessary fully laid out. Now ask yourself which of these characteristics are absolutely essential to you in answering your research question. Are there some qualities which would be a bonus to your study but would not be absolutely vital to its success? In short, separate the clearly essential from the advantageous but nonessential qualities.

Remember that if you use already collected data (census data or survey data), you should read the materials that explain how those samples were formed to be sure that they represent the populations you want to address. (Chapter 5 will address sampling techniques and strategies in detail.) Even if you plan to carry out a field study of a single case, you will in effect be studying some sample of some population. The problem here is that the definitions of the sample and the population may never be fully clear. You must ask yourself who

BOX 3-1

EXAMPLES OF DIFFERENT UNITS OF ANALYSIS

INDIVIDUALS

Most studies in the social sciences address individuals. Hirschi's study of delinquency took as its primary units of analysis delinquent and non-delinquent boys. Even when individual measures are aggregated to form group scores, the units of analysis will be individuals.

GROUPS

Social researchers are often interested in studying groups such as gangs. A study comparing the type of leader-member interaction or the degree of centralization of leadership would use a measure of a group process as a characteristic of the group. These would be different from Hirschi's effort, where individual delinquency acts were the primary unit under analysis.

PROGRAMS

Evaluation research (to be discussed in Chapter 10) generally has programs serving as the units to be analyzed. A study comparing Head Start or drug rehabilitation programs would use programs as the units of analysis when the programs were being compared.

When these programs are compared on variables measured at the program level (program funding, type of administration, type of curricula) then the units of analysis are the programs.

ORGANIZATIONS OR INSTITUTIONS

When comparisons are made of qualities of institutions, such as schools and churches, or organizations such as businesses and nonprofit agencies, the units are organizations. The important thing to remember here is that if the variables being analyzed from the organization are based on aggregated data of individuals, the units of analysis may be individuals. It is when the variables are based on measures of the organization or institution that are not reducible to individuals (such as resources, finances, or physical and structural characteristics of the organization) that the units of analysis will be the organization.

COMMUNITIES, STATES, NATIONS

Political scientists are likely to use communities, states, or nations as their units of analysis. In their classic cross-national study of political participation and attitudes, Almond and Verba (1963) compared Italians, Britons, Germans, Mexicans, and Americans in terms of factors such as their levels of political information, membership in voluntary associations, and a subjective sense of "competence" (when an individual believes that he or she can have political influence, p. 181). Using nation-states as the units of analysis, Almond and Verba were able to show the distinctiveness of the American and British sense of political competence.

ARTIFACTS

Content analysis, to be described in Chapter 9, often takes artifacts as its units of analysis. Artifacts may be analyzed at the individual or aggregate level. What this generally refers to is that cultural items (such as paintings, newspaper articles, songs, television advertisements, short stories) are selected and their contents are compared using a set of criteria.

the people you observe represent. In Thorne's study of two grade schools, the pupils represented primary school children from two different communities in Michigan and California. However, they might well have been characteristic of similar-aged children in other communities and other states.

My study of African-American college students in predominantly white colleges included only two colleges (ones to which I had access). I clearly could not assume that my findings would be generalizable to the nation as a whole. I had to recognize the particular qualities of the colleges studied. They were both in an urban area. One was largely a commuter college; the other, residential. One was a state institution; the other, private. I also needed to consider the proportion of black students in each college: Was it higher or lower than the national average for black students in colleges? Did it differ appreciably from the proportion of black residents in the areas studied? In the nation as a whole?

It was also important to assess how representative the particular black students I studied were of black students at the colleges studied (in terms of social background, academic aptitude, earlier educational experience, and especially whether their prior education had taken place in segregated or integrated schools). Then I could also see where the black students I studied fit among black students nationwide. Were they unique in some ways? Were they quite typical of black students attending colleges with few black students? This kind of thinking, which tries to place the subjects you plan to study in a larger framework in order to understand who they represent, must be done in the early stages of the project design.

The Twin Traps: The Ecological Fallacy and Reductionism

Although data representing individual units of analysis can be aggregated into group units if this is desired, once the units of analysis have been determined for a particular analysis, it is important to fix them clearly in mind as the analysis progresses. Often there is a tendency to move from one unit of analysis to another. This is a particular problem in the analysis stage, when the findings of the study are discussed. Nevertheless, it is essential to consider these potential traps when you are designing your study so that you can select a unit of analysis which will meet your later analytic requirements.

The Ecological Fallacy. Studies done on aggregate units of analysis such as states often present quantitative statistical data on those aggregate units, such as the birthrate or homicide rate or the percentage of the population which is unemployed

or the percentage which is Hispanic. In addition, such studies usually offer comparative aggregate data so that you can see if the birthrate or the homicide rate is higher in Delaware or Arizona. It is also common for such studies to present correlations between these percentages or rates, for example, the correlation between the percentage unemployed and the percentage Hispanic in each state. These are called *ecological correlations* because the measures are based on group (aggregate) units, not on individual units.

In a particular state there may be a high correlation between the percentage unemployed and the percentage Hispanic. What you might be led to conclude from this finding is that in this state many Hispanics are unemployed and that a higher proportion of Hispanics are unemployed than non-Hispanics. These conclusions would be examples of the *ecological fallacy*. What you have done is form conclusions about individuals from data that were based on aggregate units. Note that if you have the aggregate percentages from that state only for unemployment and for ethnicity, you can't ascertain from these data the ethnic backgrounds of the unemployed, which is what you would have needed to reach the conclusion about Hispanics being unemployed more often.

The data you would need to determine whether Hispanics are more often unemployed than non-Hispanics are data measured on individual units indicating an individual's unemployment (or employment) and ethnicity. You could then do *individual correlations* between individual measures of unemployment and the individual's ethnicity. It could be the case that in states with high ecological correlations between unemployment and percentage Hispanic there are low individual correlations between unemployment and being Hispanic. What this would mean is that the unemployment rate is high among the non-Hispanic residents in this state. Note that it could also be the case that ecological and individual correlations could be similar. But you will know this only if you have examined data measured both on an individual unit and on an aggregate (or group) unit of analysis.

(To read the classic study that made this case against the ecological fallacy, look up in the library W. S. Robinson, "Ecological Correlations and the Behavior of Individuals," *American Sociological Review,* **15:** 351–357, 1950.)

Let's take another example. Suppose you are studying high school dropout rates. You find that dropout rates are higher in school districts where there are lower proportions of intact families. Can you conclude that children from single-parent families are more likely to be high school dropouts? No, not on the evidence you have. Doing so would be another example of the ecological fallacy, because it could be that in areas that have fewer intact families, it is the students from homes with both parents who drop out. You cannot reach conclusions about individuals (in this case, dropouts) by using evidence from a group level (in this case family patterns in communities). In short, data based on group-level units of analysis should never be used to reach conclusions about individuals, because such a practice may lead to incorrect conclusions.

Reductionism. The tendency to reduce complex social phenomena to a single cause is in some cases the reverse of the ecological fallacy, since it may involve drawing conclusions about the behavior of groups on the basis of evidence regarding individuals. A common example of reductionism is to use individual personality measures to explain the behavior of groups. Consider these conclusions: (1) Nazism took over Germany because German boys hated their fathers. (2) The stock market crashed in 1929 because of the sexual looseness of people in the 1920s. (3) American women have attained so few elected offices because they have lower self-esteem than men do. In each case, a group-level occurrence is being reduced to an explanation at the individual level. Complex phenomena such as the rise of Nazism, the stock market crash, and the election of officials in the United States probably cannot be reduced to the effect of an individual attribute (hating fathers, sexual behavior, or women's self-esteem), even though such an attribute might

be a factor in explaining them. There are surely other factors that need to be considered.

Explaining social phenomena solely in terms of individual psychological characteristics is a kind of *psychological reductionism.* Another common form of reductionism is *economic reductionism,* or the tendency to explain social phenomena purely in economic terms. In this case, Nazism might be explained as the result of inflation in post–World War I Germany, the stock market crash as the result of capitalist accumulation without reinvestment, and the scarcity of female elected officials as the result of the economic dependency of women. While these may or may not be important factors in explaining the particular phenomena, it is overly simplistic to reduce such phenomena to a single cause or to try to account for all phenomena in terms of a single kind of explanation.

TIME DIMENSION OF THE STUDY

Once a research topic is defined, you need to determine the time frame in which the study will be carried out. The first set of questions to be considered are: What period of time does the study question address? Will a present time frame be sufficient? Does the study need to make projections into the future? Does it need to take into account material from the past? The second set of questions concern the time period over which you will do the study: Will all the observations be carried out during roughly the same period? Or will you plan to make observations at different points in time?

Period of Time Addressed by the Study

Almost all social research projects take into account some elements of the past. What you are now studying was probably not established the first day you showed up on the project. Thus there is a general need to get some background information about the setting (the group, the organization, the neighborhood) you are studying. All social researchers must also in some ways be historians. As such, they must abide by the norms of historians which require that they respect the past and try to interpret it accurately. (Chapter 9 will describe historical research methods.)

If you are studying an organization, there are records, as was mentioned earlier, which can be used to offer evidence about the past. Of course, informants may be interviewed, but generally speaking, written records made at the time under consideration are more accurate than the memories of those who were there. (This, of course, is not always the case; records may have been written to be deliberately misleading, and some individuals have very good memories.) It must be kept in mind that any source of information regarding the past will have some biases. An individual's memories will tend to revolve around his or her participation in the event, and as a result, the person may see that area as more central. Written records may be biased by the views of the recorder or by those of the person in power who may have gone over the minutes (or the newsletter copy) to edit out materials that were considered harmful to the purposes of the organization. Thus it is important to keep in mind that materials from the past must not be taken as pure facts; they are also interpretations made at the time, and they may include some distortions and half-truths. One of the best ways to get a fuller understanding of the past is to see different types of records or interview several persons who played different roles in the organization you are studying. This diverse data gathering may help build up some elements of a picture about which there is a lot of agreement.

If your subjects are individuals, they have pasts as well. Almost all surveys elicit information about some aspects of the respondents' pasts. The information sought is usually about the family of origin (its socioeconomic status, the number of siblings in the family, the region of the country in which the individual grew up, its religious affiliation, etc.) but may also include evidence about schooling, peers, or activities engaged in during childhood and youth.

A content analysis study (to be described in Chapter 9) may have as its dataset a collection of magazines (or other materials) from different periods of time, from which the researcher hopes to extract patterns of meaning. Such studies have clear historical time frames. A study of current television commercials, however, would have a present time frame. For the study to have lasting relevance, the researcher should offer an introductory general description both of the time in which it was carried out and of what was happening in the society during this time which might help explain this content.

Time Frame in Which the Study Is Carried Out: Cross-Sectional or Longitudinal

There are two major ways to set a study in time. From one point of view, the study may be considered as occurring in a single period of time (though it rarely is completed in a day or even a week). Such one-time studies are referred to as cross-sectional studies. The other possibility is that the study has two or more data collection periods which are set at different times for the specific purposes of studying changes that may or may not have occurred between those points in time. Such multiple-time studies are referred to as longitudinal studies. Box 3-2 presents evidence on how time dimensions and units of analysis can affect a study's outcomes.

Cross-Sectional Studies. In a *cross-sectional study,* whatever is being studied is being observed at a single point in time, as if a section of time were being cut out for observation. Perhaps a good comparison would be with a medical procedure such as a biopsy or x-ray. These diagnostic procedures are done at a specific point in time to discover the state of the body at that moment (from which it is possible to infer what happened to the body previously to bring it to its current state). It is possible, of course, that they may detect signs that help predict what may happen in the future.

A cross-sectional study can accomplish the aim of exploration or description. It can also be used for explanatory studies since background information and retrospective data can be related to current statuses, and current statuses to future expectations

BOX 3-2

HOW DIFFERENT TIME DIMENSIONS AND UNITS OF ANALYSIS CAN PRODUCE DIFFERENT RESULTS

In looking at studies on the same topic, would you find different results if a study had been carried out at one point in time (cross-sectional) or over time (longitudinal)? Moreover, if the units of analysis in these studies were at the individual level or were based on aggregated group-level data, would there be systematic differences? To see if this is the case, Stephen Platt carried out a meta-analysis (a type of analysis which combines the results from earlier studies on the same topic) on relationship of unemployment to suicides and parasuicides (attempted suicides). He examined whether the *time dimension* of each study—*cross-sectional* or *longitudinal*—and whether the *units of analysis* of the study—*individual* or *aggregate*—strengthened or weakened the relationship between unemployment and suicidal behavior.

What he found was that in studies with

- *Cross-sectional* time dimensions and *individual* units of analysis, suicides and parasuicides were more prevalent among the unemployed.
- *Cross-sectional* time dimensions and *aggregate* units of analysis, parasuicides were

more prevalent among the unemployed but suicides were not.

- *Longitudinal* time dimensions and *individual* units of analysis, suicides had had greater job instability or unemployment than did nonsuicides.
- *Longitudinal* time dimensions and *aggregate* units of analysis, a strong association existed between suicide and unemployment in the United States and in certain European countries but not in all countries.

Platt cautioned that while there is clearly some association between suicides or parasuicides and unemployment and while both factors may be influenced by mental illness, the direct relationship between suicide and unemployment remains problematic. He concluded that large-scale societal economic conditions could also be important antecedent factors but that they could be captured only with longitudinal designs.

Source: Stephen Platt, "Unemployment and Suicidal Behavior: A Review of the Literature," *Social Science Medicine,* 19: 93–115, 1984.

---

and aspirations. Studies that aim to describe the current state of something—the reading abilities of eighth-graders in a city, for example—usually have a cross-sectional time frame. (However, it is characteristic of such studies to compare these scores with those of the previous year, which then gives them a longitudinal time frame.)

Longitudinal Studies. In a *longitudinal study*, data are collected at more than one point in time. There are three primary types of longitudinal study designs: *trend studies*, which compare data across time intervals on different subjects; *cohort studies*, which compare data on subjects across time whose age differences parallel the time inter-

vals (so that 15- to 19-year-olds in 1960 are compared to 25- to 29-year-olds in 1970); and *panel studies*, which compare changes in the same subjects as they occur across time. Let's consider as an example a national survey of drug use. The simplest design would be to survey people once and report on these findings; this would be cross-sectional. The three longitudinal designs would be characterized by the qualities described below.

Trend study. The data from this year's national survey of drug usage could be set against data from the last 5, 10, or more years. In this way, comparisons could be made across time. This is the basis of a *trend study*, in which similar data collected in different years (and on different subjects) are compared. However, the national sample selected for study this year would not be the same as that selected last year, 5 years ago, or whenever. Thus if there were a reporting of higher drug use this year, we could not say for certain that this was due to an increase in drug usage, because it might only mean that our sample this year tended to draw disproportionately on drug users. Such changes may come about because of the effects of factors such as migration and mortality, which produce differences in samples across time. Nevertheless, data from more than one point can, across time, offer strong evidence of changing trends.

Cohort study.   A cohort is a group of persons who were born within the same time period. A *cohort study* is one in which the subjects are grouped by their ages for comparative purposes. Sometimes we refer to such groups as generations. We would refer to those born in the 1930s as Depression-era babies. We also often refer to groups that participated in a historical event; those who were young men and women during World War I are part of the war generation. Note that in this example, such war generation individuals would have been born approximately 20 years before the war.

We are also familiar with referring to the 1960s as a special era. But *who* was the generation of the 1960s? Those born in the 1950s, who were growing up in the 1960s; those born in the 1940s, who were young adults in the 1960s; or those born during the 1960s, who are the 1960s cohort? Probably we consider those born in the late 1940s and early 1950s, who were young adults and teenagers in the 1960s, as being most characteristic of the 1960s generation.

Cohorts usually are studied not in the time period in which they are formed, during their birth years, but at a future time. Furthermore, they usually are studied comparatively with an earlier or later cohort. But what should form the confines of a cohort? Often instead of specifying the birth years to form a cohort, age groups are used.

Returning to the example of a study on drug users, the data for such a study would probably be given within age groups. Let's say it was reported in terms of age groups: 15–19, 20–24, 25–29, 30–34, 35–39, and so on. Assume that a similar study was done five years ago: those who were in the 15–19 age group five years ago would now be in the 20–24 age group, those in the 24–29 age group five years ago would now be in the 25–29 age group, and so on. If comparisons were made within these age cohorts, there should be somewhat greater evidence on which to base conclusions about change. Remember, however, that the 20–24 age group cohort is *not* made up of the same individuals as the 15–19 age group studied five years ago.

Assume that five years ago, 10 percent of the 15–19 age group reported using cocaine, but now 15 percent of the 20–24 age group report such usage: this suggests that among that age cohort of the population there has been an increase. (Now, there could still be various explanations for this. Perhaps the older group has more access to the finances needed to buy this expensive commodity. However, you still could not be sure whether the earlier users were continuing their habit and being joined by others or whether the earlier users had dropped it and the current group consisted of earlier nonusers.) Cohort studies emphasize qualities of age groups over time.

Panel study.   One of the best ways to measure change is to study the same people over time. You first sample a group at one point in time and then return at a later time to ask the same questions again. Then, by bringing together the responses of the subjects, you can see whether a characteristic or attitude continues or whether it is taken up and then dropped over time. This is a *panel study,* one in which the same group of respondents is followed up over time. You are in a much stronger position to try to relate this pattern (a change or a continuation) to other qualities of the individual. Panel studies lend themselves to much more rigorous forms of analysis than do other types of studies.

BOX 3-3

PANEL DATASETS ON AMERICAN SCHOOL-AGED YOUTH

Because of the great interest of social researchers in social status, opportunity, and inequality in American society, there has been a long-standing need to have nationally representative data on school-aged youth to use as a baseline and then follow those same youths into adulthood. This is the meaning of a panel study: Subjects are followed up over time so that information collected from them at an earlier point can be compared to information from a later point.

The first quality panel survey based on a national sample of school-aged American youth was the *National Longitudinal Study of the High School Class of 1972*, which was followed up five times during the decade of the 1970s and then again in 1986 (when they were approximately age 32). Given the widespread use of this dataset, another nationally based dataset representative of all American school-aged youth was started in 1980. This dataset, *High School and Beyond*, began with national samples of both high school seniors and high school sophomores and was followed up biannually across the decade of the 1980s. These datasets are available from the National Center for Education Statistics (NCES), which is a part of the U.S. Department of Education in Washington, D.C.

By the later 1980s, increasing interest in less advantaged youth encouraged the NCES to launch a new panel survey of American students this time starting with a sufficiently young group of students that allowed them to detect early "dropouts" and follow these youths to understand their patterns of work, educational reentry, and so on. This dataset, NELS: 88 (the National Education Longitudinal Study of the Eighth Graders of 1988) began with a national sample of eighth-graders in 1988, following them up as tenth-graders in 1990, twelfth-graders in 1992, two years beyond high school in 1994 (when some would be sophomores in college), and six years beyond high school in 1998 (when some would have college degrees and some would be in or have completed graduate school). Note that this dataset would track not only those who proceeded in lockstep through the educational system but also those who dropped out at various stages, reentered, followed careers, married, had children, and so forth.

In considering a panel study on drug use, data from a sample of junior high school students might be collected, and then the respondents to this sample might be followed up both during and after high school. Following such a sample of respondents would not be easy. You might need access to school information to find out if the junior high school students you were looking for were currently in a particular high school. You would also want to ask the respondents themselves to provide their home addresses during the first survey so that you could locate them for later surveys.

Panel surveys have been widely used in educational research. Box 3-3 overviews the panel datasets available on American school-aged youth.

As was stated above, such linked data on individuals provide excellent material for the study of change. One can study changes in attitudes and aspirations for the same persons over time as those individuals are exposed to different experiences and statuses across the course of life. In fact, a whole new interest in sociological research in the "life course" often depends on the analysis of panel datasets (a few of which have followed the same individuals from childhood to old age). Box 3-4 describes a longitudinal study of families across four generations. Individual researchers rarely collect their own panel data, because it is time-consuming, expensive, and difficult to do. However, many fine panel datasets have been made available to researchers at a modest cost.

BOX 3-4

THE USC LONGITUDINAL STUDY OF GENERATIONS

The University of Southern California Longitudinal Study of Generations combines qualities of both cohort and panel designs. The datasets are based on six surveys carried out between 1971 and 1997 on four generations of families in southern California. In 1971, the study began with the members of approximately 300 three-generation families drawn randomly from the membership list of a health maintenance organization (HMO). The average age of the G1 grandparents in 1971 was 67, that of the G2 parents was 44, and that of the G3 children was 19. By 1991, the G4 great-grandchildren of the G1s were added (approximately aged 16) to the G3s, who were now about 40; the G2s, who were in their sixties; and the remaining G1s, who were nearing 80. The birth dates of these four generations range from 1900 to 1978. The purpose of this design was to enable comparisons of older birth cohort members across time with members of younger birth cohorts across time; this meant that the effects of the aging of the cohort on the future cohorts (their younger family members) could be measured.

This dataset has both the qualities of a panel study in that the same family members are resurveyed time after time and the qualities of a cohort study in that comparisons can be made across the different generations representing different birth cohorts and the historical time periods through which they have lived. For example, the G3 generation represents the "baby boomers" (born 1945 to 1955), and the G4s represent Generation X (born 1973 to 1978). This enables the researchers to match age groups at different measurement times and to see what influence parents have on their children's outcomes (such as occupational aspirations, value orientations, and self-esteem) in different generations. Chapter 9 will offer an example of how this fascinating dataset has been the basis of many secondary analyses.

Source: R. E. L. Roberts and V. Bengston, 1993.

PROPOSING A RESEARCH PLAN

Once a research problem has been formulated and the subjects for a study have been determined, the actual means for carrying out the research project must be established. This is the proposal-writing stage of research, when the overall plan for the project must be set out in logical order to see if it makes sense. For many researchers, the object of proposal writing is to obtain a grant to cover the expenses of the study. Whether or not you are applying for a grant, writing a *research proposal* should be useful. Using a method similar to one developed by Julian Simon (1969), I will lay out a series of steps that you must move through to complete a project. In describing how you will carry out each step to meet the objectives of the research project, you write the research plan or proposal.

THE ELEVEN STEPS IN A RESEARCH PROJECT

Step 1: Define the Topic

In your proposal the research topic should be posed in such a way that it is clearly grounded in the general social field relevant to it. If you are studying alcoholism, you need to put your research question into a framework which suggests that you know something about alcohol consumption and abuse. If you are studying the effects of using computers in elementary schools, you should offer some preliminary information about the prevalence of such equipment in the schools and what it is used for. In short, topics must be grounded in some already known factual information which is used to introduce the topic and from which the research question will stem.

Step 2: Find Out What Is Known about the Topic

The beginning of this chapter suggested ways for you to immerse yourself in material relevant to the topic you want to study. Social research topics usually are embedded in so many different kinds of materials that the researcher must be careful to select the best materials to examine. While everyone goes down some blind alleys, you need to keep the central meaning of your topic in mind to guide you through your search of the literature in the field. It is also important to examine different types of materials where relevant—quantitative data interpretations, studies using various methods.

For the research proposal, you should refer to the most salient findings you have uncovered which seem to raise significant questions or which offer suggestions for avenues for you to follow for your project. You must be able to draw out these findings from the studies in which they are embedded and summarize them succinctly so that someone unfamiliar with the study can easily grasp their meaning and importance. To help you do this, you should look at the background literature review sections which generally come at the beginning of published research articles. Most of these reviews are very condensed; they extract a few salient points from numerous studies, summarizing them in a way that is relevant to the study in question.

Step 3: Clarify Concepts and Their Measurement

This will be the subject of Chapter 4. The discussion of the language of science in Chapter 2 and the conceptual stage of the research model developed in that chapter are relevant to this step. Precision in conceptualization is very important in social research and is not easy to achieve. Concepts such as alcoholism, autonomy, and juvenile delinquency may all seem to be familiar terms. However, the precise meanings you attach to these concepts must be defined, and then an appropriate way to measure concepts must be found or devised.

In the proposal, a clear definition of the main concept or concepts must be given. The general question of measurement should be discussed so that it is clear that the potential problems in measuring the concepts have been thoroughly thought out. These include two critical issues: *validity,* that is, whether the measurement of a concept in fact produces a result that truly represents what the concept is supposed to mean, and *reliability,* that is, whether the measurement would lead to consistent enough outcomes, were it to be repeated, that one could have some confidence in the results. Validity and reliability will be discussed in Chapter 4.

Step 4: Establish an Appropriate Data Collection Method

Chapter 1 considered a number of fine studies representing three primary means of data collection in the social sciences. Chapters 6 to 8 are devoted to explaining these methods in detail so that you can use them to design and carry out experiments in laboratory or natural settings (Chapter 6), a survey based on questionnaires or interviews (Chapter 7), and qualitative methods using different types of observation and interview techniques (Chapter 8). Chapter 9 describes different forms of what might be called data selection procedures for using data that have already been collected. In reading these chapters, remember that the same topic may be studied with a variety of methods and that the use of multiple methods is desirable in social research.

Anderson's study of the two Philadelphia neighborhoods was an example of a research project that used more than one method (interviews as well as participant observation) in its design. In addition he made videotapes, attended community meetings, and collected census data on the two neighborhoods.

For the proposal, you must describe how you will collect data and which source of available data you will actually use. Issues of access to the data are important to discuss. After all, you must be able to get the data you propose. If you anticipate problems in securing the desired data, these problems should be discussed and possible alternative sources of data might be suggested. Most studies have one central type of method to be used (a survey, an experiment), though they also may draw on a few other data sources to widen their scope.

You must also plan how you are going to analyze the data. Do you intend to compare women with men, contrast one drug rehabilitation program with another, explore the length of time spent in a shopping mall by the average shopper in terms of whether there is a difference between covered and outdoor malls? Such intentions require that the planned contrast be set into the sampling design. Will you have comparable samples of women and men? Which drug programs will you study? What shopping malls should be selected?

In addition, you need to consider which variables you plan to relate to one another. In Hirschi's study, he knew that he would need to measure sets of variables to test each of the theories he posed, and so he had to select a data collection method that could get the data he needed.

Step 5: Operationalize Concepts and Design the Research Instruments

This refers to the "nuts and bolts" of the study. In a survey, the questionnaire or interview schedule is the operationalized survey. In an experiment, the operationalization of the independent variable is the actual stimulus. In field studies, this process of operationalizing occurs rather differently. It often must wait until the field notes have been gathered. Then the researcher may find evidence that suggests certain meanings, at which time conceptualizations are formed to describe and explain observations. To test whether the researcher is accurate, he or she may go back to the field to see if another instance of this operationalized concept occurs. Chapter 4 will address this subject.

A concept is sometimes better measured by using more than one indicator of that concept. Chapter 4 will describe how measuring multiple

indicators of a concept can strengthen a study. Using indexes and scales to measure complex concepts, a topic to be addressed in Chapter 4, can help accomplish this goal.

In a survey, how the concepts are operationalized in the questionnaire will determine what will be produced from the survey. If the concepts are poorly operationalized, the best national sample and the fanciest statistical routines will not make something useful of the data. In the proposal, the actual way in which the concepts will be operationalized should be spelled out. If a survey is to be carried out, it is usually appended to the proposal. In addition, the critical questions that measure the most important concepts in the study should be discussed and their level of adequacy should be addressed.

Step 6: Select a Sample of Subjects to Study

The selection process for deciding what or whom to study rests on a large body of thought about the nature of sampling. This subject will be addressed in Chapter 5. Remember that even if you study your parents, the residents of your block, or the dog next door, all these represent elements in some type of sample. Many researchers want to be able to generalize their findings to subjects beyond those studied. When probability samples are used, it is possible to determine how representative your sample is of all the others out there (the population) who might have gotten into your study. Sampling plans may be very complex or quite straightforward. When the rules of probability are not followed and you merely select a sample of subjects who seem to fulfill the needs of your study, you have a nonprobability sample. For many studies, such a sample is sufficient, and for some, it is the best that can be achieved. Whatever the design of your sample, it needs to be explained in detail in your proposal. It should be so precise that someone else could generate a similar sample by following your procedures.

Step 7: Consider the Purpose, Value, and Ethics of the Study

Once the topic, the background, the clarification of concepts, and the major methods of data collection have been presented, it is time to address the purpose, value, and ethics of the study. We have discussed the purpose and values of research in this chapter. Chapter 14 will consider the ethics and politics of social research. But in a proposal the study design must be presented before the rationale and ethical issues involved can be discussed. Remember that the rationale for doing the project will be accomplished only if the study is done well. By showing that you have devised a plan to study your topic that looks plausible and seems feasible, you reinforce the sense that the purpose will be achieved. The value of the project lies not only in what it alone will produce but also in how it may add to or challenge other research in the area.

The ethical issues are often confronted in data collection, for example, in maintaining the confidentiality of the data, gaining access to the field, and avoiding deception as to the role of the researcher. If these will be major issues in your study, they should be addressed. Many universities and colleges require students to have their projects reviewed by a human subjects review committee. In any proposal seeking public funding, potential ethical issues are of great importance, and researchers who ignore such issues may be penalized. Often it is necessary to complete special forms concerned with the protection of human subjects. (This may be true for already collected data that you plan to use as well as for data you will collect.)

Step 8: Collect the Data

The separate chapters on the different methods (Chapters 6 to 10) will give many different types of procedures that might be followed. Each form of data collection has its special concerns which need to be considered fully before you do the study. This is why pretesting is so valuable: it helps you find and address potential problems before they enter the study and cause bigger problems.

For the proposal, the plans for collecting data should be described carefully. In a field project, it is always more difficult to be precise, and you may need to make changes once the field is entered. Nevertheless, it is better to have a clear plan that can be altered as you go along than to have only some vague ideas that subsequently you cannot be sure you have followed. For an experiment, data collection procedures usually can be described very precisely. This is also true of a survey. Mail surveys tend to have multiple stages in the data collection procedure to increase the response rate. If you are using already available data, you need to describe at this stage how you will obtain the data.

Step 9: Process the Data

Once the data are collected, they must be put into a form which will enable them to be analyzed. If they are quantifiable data, you usually have to prepare them for the computer. If they are field notes, they must be organized and categorized. There are computer programs that can help systematize qualitative data. The chapters on the different methods each describe preliminary forms of data handling. Chapter 11 will examine some ways in which quantifiable data are processed and qualitative data are interpreted.

In the proposal, a concise statement may be included to address this subject. It may describe what type of computer facilities are at the disposal of the researcher, what software programs will be used, what possible sources of assistance are available, and what efforts are being made to increase accuracy in the handling of the data. There are now some technological advances in data gathering which speed the process from data gathering to data entry. An example is the CATI (computer-assisted telephone interviewing) method—to be described in Chapter 7—now becoming quite common in telephone surveys. Interviewers call from a computer terminal, and answers to the questions are entered directly into the computer by the interviewer as they are given.

Phase
A 7

10: Analyze the Data

you plan to analyze the data must be thought
gh carefully while the study is being de-
d. It is true that once the data are collected,
may be some changes in these plans. Never-
ss, it is better to have a strategy that can be
adapted than to end up with piles of data for which
you have no organized plan. There are numerous
analytic tools for studying quantifiable data. A
number of these will be described in Part Four of
this book.

The proposal should indicate the analyses
planned; it may suggest that some analytic strategies will depend on how earlier ones turn out. In a
field study, only very preliminary plans will probably be possible.

Step 11: Present the Results

The data for an entire study may be collected, but
the research is not complete until the results of the
study have been written up. For research projects
which are funded, final reports must be written.
Most social research projects become the basis for
articles, books, chapters in books, or unpublished
papers offered at professional meetings. A single
study may lead to many and varied types of publications and presentations. Chapter 15 will review
how the results of a research project are assembled
for presentation.

REVIEW NOTES

- Sources for finding research topics include
  printed sources (books, journals, magazines,
  newspapers), ongoing research projects, and already available datasets.
- To intensify knowledge about a topic, consult a
  library, use other written records or documents,
  and talk to informed others.
- Other persons who may help intensify knowledge about a research project are relevant researchers, who have worked on such projects;
  insiders, who are familiar with a field or subject;
  and intellectual comrades, who are the persons

with whom the researcher can most easily and
profitably talk.
- The possible reasons for studying a topic are to
  explore a largely undefined area, to describe a
  social phenomenon, or to explain a hypothesized
  relationship. A study may be a replication of an
  earlier study to see whether the findings can be
  verified.
- A rationale for a research project is a sound reason for selecting the particular subject and
  method for carrying out the research based on
  some value or purpose.
- Merton's two rationales for research are that the
  study will contribute to systematic knowledge
  in a discipline (that is, basic research) or that it
  will be of some practical use (that is, applied
  research).
- Four criteria that may guide you in developing a
  rationale are whether the study offers evidence
  about the changing nature of society, whether
  the study addresses a social policy topic,
  whether the study will broaden knowledge of an
  unusual or unfamiliar topic, and whether the researcher has particular knowledge or expertise
  which may enable him or her to make unique
  contributions in the research effort.
- Three criteria to use in making a final selection
  of a research topic are that it should be feasible
  to study, should be of general interest to the researcher, and should contribute in some way to a
  greater understanding of society.
- The four steps for turning a topic into a researchable problem are (1) consider its most
  problematic aspects, (2) define the aim of the
  project, (3) state the topic as a question (or series of questions), (4) develop a hypothesis as
  one (among many possible) alternative, hypothesized answer to the research question.
- The units of analysis in a study are the subjects
  to be studied. They include individuals, groups,
  programs, organizations and institutions, larger
  communities (states and nations), and cultural
  artifacts.
- Studies in which the data are gathered at a single
  point in time are called cross-sectional studies;

those which gather data at multiple points are longitudinal studies.

- The three types of longitudinal studies are trend studies, in which data are compared across time points on different subjects; cohort studies, in which data on subjects from one age cohort (that is, individuals born within a certain period of time) are compared at different points in time; and panel studies, in which the same subjects are compared across time.
- The 11 steps of a research project are:
  1. Define a topic.
  2. Intensify knowledge about the topic.
  3. Clarify concepts and their measurements.
  4. Select a data collection method.
  5. Operationalize concepts and design the data collection instruments.
  6. Select a sample.
  7. Consider the purpose, value, and ethics of the study.
  8. Collect the data.
  9. Process the data.
  10. Analyze the data.
  11. Write up the results.

KEY TERMS

cohort studies
cross-sectional studies
ecological fallacy
longitudinal studies
panel studies
reductionism
research proposal
trend studies

STUDY EXERCISES

1. Select two of the studies described in Chapter 1 and decide which of the uses is best exemplified in each study.
2. How might you turn the topic of college varsity athletes not graduating from college into a researchable problem for study? Go through the four steps: (1) list problematic aspects,

(2) define your aim, (3) state your problem as a researchable question, and (4) develop a hypothesis.
3. Assume that you have defined a researchable topic to be that urban police are less satisfied with their jobs than are police working in the suburbs. Briefly write out how you might carry out the next six steps (steps 2 to 8) of the research project.
4. What would be the best time dimension to use in designing (1) the college athletes study and (2) the police study?

RECOMMENDED READINGS

1. Bouma, Gary D., and G. B. J. Atkinson: *A Handbook of Social Science Research,* 2d ed., New York: Oxford University Press, 1995. Offers very helpful advice on selecting a research problem and designing a study to address it.
2. Cooper, Harris M.: *Integrating Research: A Guide for Literature Reviews,* 2d ed., Thousand Oaks, CA: Sage, 1989. This volume defines integrative research, lays out the methods for carrying it out, and offers current examples of integrative reviews of research projects on varying topics.
3. Girden, Ellen R.: *Evaluating Research Articles from Start to Finish,* Thousand Oaks, CA: Sage, 1996. Provides help in pulling out important aspects of research articles and deciding if the conclusions are justified.
4. Locke, Lawrence F., et al.: *Proposals That Work,* Thousand Oaks, CA: Sage, 1993. Provides updated, easy-to-follow advice for preparing academic and grant proposals.
5. Menard, Scott: *Longitudinal Research,* Thousand Oaks, CA: Sage, 1991. Presenting longitudinal research designs in a nontechnical manner, this volume addresses common problems in data collection. Comparisons with cross-sectional designs are offered.
6. Roberts, Robert E. L., and Vern L. Bengston: "Relationships with Parents, Self-Esteem, and Psychological Well-Being in Young Adulthood," *Social Psychology Quarterly,* 56: 263–277, 1993.

CHAPTER 4

Operationalization and Measurement: From Concepts to Variables

*T*he object of this chapter is to introduce you to the central intellectual effort required by social research: how to move from abstract concepts to operational definitions and from operational definitions to the specification and measurement of variables. Once this process has been described in general terms, it will be illustrated and elaborated in detail through an examination of how two very different abstract concepts came to be measured by social researchers. The reason for concentrating on a history of the development of the two measures is to help you see what kinds of strategies may be employed in trying to develop operationally defined measures for abstract concepts. The two concepts were selected because (1) they represent different starting points in conceptualization (one, happiness, is a simple everyday term; the other, authoritarianism, is a constructed term) and (2) the types of instruments developed to measure these two concepts represent contrasting solutions to the measurement problem.

We will then move from this specific discussion to a more general consideration of measurement, describing the central ways to assess the quality of measurement: validity and reliability. In the course of the discussion on reliability, brief attention will be paid to classical test theory, which underlies its meaning. Subsequently, the four different levels of measurement will be compared and explained. Finally, the measurement characteristics of six commonly used social research variables will be presented.

CONCEPTS

We use concepts all the time in everyday life. They are the abstract terms we employ to explain or make sense of our experience. Take a term such as *happiness*. We learn at a relatively early age that happiness means the state of being happy. We also learn to use this term in evaluating experiences and phenomena which we perceive as making us happy (or unhappy). Thus, the term *happiness* represents a concept, or abstract idea, which we apply to particular situations.

But wait a minute. What is happiness? When did you last see it? Who has it? Where do you get it from? Can you get rid of it? How can you use a concept all the time that seems so vague and difficult to define that it is not easy to think about it carefully? What would be a satisfying definition of this concept? John Stuart Mill, the English philosopher, suggested this kind of problem when he remarked that in asking ourselves whether we are happy, we immediately cease to be so. In fact, the happiness we refer to all the time is not a concept which we could easily define.

In everyday life, of course, we rarely need to ask ourselves exactly what a concept such as happiness means in general terms. It is usually enough for us to say (with Snoopy), "Happiness is . . . [a particular thing]"; in short, we don't often ask what happiness is apart from the things that make us happy. We simply use the term to describe or evaluate particular situations. While happiness is a psychological term related to a state of being or feeling, it generally is used to describe the results of social relationships among individuals or between individuals and groups of organizations.

This means that happiness is often the result of sociological occurrences. Our understanding of the concept develops as we improve our ability to relate it to particular phenomena. To say "I am happy" or "This makes me happy" refers to a specific piece of experience. It makes sense, however, to describe particular experiences in this way only because the idea of happiness logically implies the possibility of its opposite: unhappiness. At the same time that we apply the concept to particular, concrete experiences, we are also relating it in an abstract way to other concepts. If happiness were not defined logically in relation to other concepts, it would make no sense for us to use it. In other words, a concept involves logical relations.

Now let's consider a more unusual concept, that of *authoritarianism*. This is not a term we use in everyday life. Instead, it is a concept that was developed by social scientists to explain a phenomenon which came to be recognized after World War II: the state of mind that disposed individuals to accept the kind of authoritarian regime that appeared most dramatically in Nazi Germany. In this case, a number of beliefs and opinions which appeared to be logically connected to one another and to the kind of behavior the social scientists were trying to explain, were drawn together to form a single concept: authoritarianism.

The effort to make sense of things by deliberately constructing general concepts (which seems to be the correct way to describe the development of the concept of authoritarianism) may seem in some respects to be the converse of the way in which the concept of happiness is used. Happiness may seem to be part of our basic repertory of ideas, which can be singled out and applied in specific instances where appropriate, while authoritarianism may seem to be a much more technical and artificial invention. Remember, however, that in developing the concept of authoritarianism, social scientists were not drawing their ideas out of thin air. They were reflecting on other related concepts and on the applicability of those concepts to particular phenomena in everyday life in order to develop a new concept which would more accurately capture the complex nature of the appeal of anti-democratic ideology.

OPERATIONALIZING DEFINITIONS

Our concern about whether we could define happiness occurred because happiness is a concept which refers not to a specific thing that can be seen or heard but to an abstract idea that is not easy to put into general terms. In the philosophical study of the meaning and use of definitions, three types of definitions have been isolated: real definitions, nominal definitions, and operational definitions.

The aim of a *real definition* is to capture the ultimate or essential nature of the actual phenomenon in question. One example of a real definition would be the mathematical definition of a triangle as a three-sided figure. Outside the abstract realm of mathematics, however, philosophically real definitions may be sought after but rarely achieved. We could, for example, define happiness as a feeling of well-being, but that would tell us very little about its ultimate nature or essence. From this perspective, Snoopy's definition of happiness is an ironic commentary on the fact that a real definition of *happiness,* taken in the abstract, always seems to elude us.

When the nineteenth-century English philosopher John Stuart Mill said, "By happiness is intended pleasure, and the absence of pain; by unhappiness, pain, and the privation of pleasure," he was providing not a real definition but a *nominal definition,* one that specified the meaning and components of the term for the purposes of rigorous philosophical inquiry. In practice we often think of happiness in positive terms, on the one hand, as the pleasure resulting from some form of good fortune and in negative terms, on the other hand, as an absence of problems (or pain). Both aspects could be embraced in a definition of happiness as a feeling of well-being. If we decided to use Mill's definition, we would have established a nominal definition of happiness. Note that we would have established a nominal definition of happiness. Note that we would not have defined the essence of what happiness is, but we would have moved toward a working definition which is reasonably clear and precise.

As social researchers, however, we would not only want to develop a nominal definition of happiness, we would also want to develop a way of studying it. In other words, we would want to "operationalize" our definition; that is, we would want to develop an operational definition. How could we do this? One thing we could do would be to go back to our observation that there might be two qualities of happiness: the pleasurable feeling resulting from good fortune and the absence of problems (note that these are not the converse of each other but two separate qualities). We would call these two different qualities the *dimensions* of the concept of happiness. How could we then explore these dimensions more fully? What empirical observations could we make in order to study the experience of happiness? In answering these questions, we would be trying to develop an *operational definition* of happiness, a definition that specifies ways of measuring the concept.

Let's take an example of a situation illustrating the positive dimension of pleasure resulting from the presence of good fortune. We might assume that someone who won a lot of money in a state lottery was presented with "good fortune." Suppose we see on television a group of people who have shared a large lottery prize. They are smiling and throwing their arms around each other, and they seem to be quite elated. Naturally, we assume that these winners are happy. But what if we wanted to measure *how* happy they are? What could we look for that would indicate their degree of happiness? We might observe the degree of their smiling, hugging, or other behavior indicating the *depth* of their happiness. Or we might question them and find out just how much they think their winnings will matter in changing their economic situations (in altering their fortunes). From efforts like these we might conclude that the winners were very happy, or quite happy, or not so happy. Of course, in making this judgment, we would in effect be comparing their behavior with the behavior we would expect from similar winners in similar situations.

Note that in observing these winners, we have identified a number of actions or behaviors that we are prepared to accept as *indicators* (that is, measurable evidence) of how happy the winners are. In social research terms, we have operationalized the good fortune *dimension* of our definition of happiness by identifying indicators of it. We have used variations in these indicators, such as the degree of smiling, as measures of the winners' degree of happiness, and we have done so by implicitly comparing what we have seen in this case with what we would expect to see in others. Of course, there might be some variation among the winners in their degree of happiness, and if we observed other winners of big lotteries, we might find more or less similar reactions, which we would then label as indicators of happiness.

If some winners are ill or have other personal problems, for example, they might be unable to respond to winning the lottery with as much happiness as would winners without such problems. To appreciate more fully how happy the lottery winners are, we might also want to ask them about the absence or presence of problems in their lives. These indicators of the second dimension of happiness (the absence of pain or problems) would reinforce our sense that what we were labeling as happiness *really* was happiness. In such cases, if we had evidence on both the presence of good fortune and the absence of problems, we would have *multiple indicators* of happiness. (Later in this chapter, when we discuss reliability of measures, we will see that multiple indicators make the measurement instrument more likely to have higher reliability or consistency.) The more complex a concept is, the more desirable it is to have multiple indicators, since they are more likely to cover all the dimensions of the concept.

Let's recapitulate our discussion of the concept of happiness. We started with John Stuart Mill's definition of happiness as the presence of pleasure and the absence of pain (a nominal definition). Then we recognized that this definition distinguished two separate dimensions of the concept of happiness. Next we operationalized the definition by taking each of the dimensions of the concept of the concept—the feeling of pleasure deriving from good fortune and the absence of pain or problems—and looked for actions or behaviors to serve as indicators of them. (Of course, concepts do not necessarily have two dimensions. They may be unidimensional—they may have only one dimension—or they may be multidimensional—they may have a number of dimensions.)

Finally, we observed variation in the measurement of the indicators which suggested that happiness occurs in varying degrees. In social research terms, this means that we moved from happiness as a concept to happiness as a *variable*. Let's say that we wanted to go one step further and ask what other differences there were between winners who appeared to be "very happy" (as measured by our indicators) and those who appeared to be "pretty happy." In that case we would be using happiness as a measured variable and would be asking how variation in this variable might be related to variation in another variable (which would have to be defined and measured by the same process of *operationalization*).

OPERATIONALIZATION AND MEASUREMENT

In considering how one might operationalize the concept of happiness, we have talked about the example of a group of people winning a lottery. We suggested that if one were to do a study of lottery winners like this, one might try to measure such indicators as the expression of their joy and the absence of overriding problems. This would be a pretty good way of measuring happiness if one were interested only in studying lottery winners. Social researchers, however, probably would want to look for a more general way of operationalizing the concept of happiness, one that could apply to a wide range of particular circumstances. For this reason, I would now like to turn from the hypothetical example we have been using to a real attempt to operationalize happiness in a social research study.

Measuring Happiness

When Norman Bradburn and the late David Caplovitz at the National Opinion Research Center (NORC) undertook a project in the mid-1960s to measure the concept of happiness in a survey, their efforts were met with some ridicule. At some level, the idea that social scientists can measure a concept such as happiness seems ludicrous. How could one possibly measure so "personal and subjective a phenomenon"? Bradburn and Caplovitz decided to adopt a very straightforward approach of asking people directly how happy they were.

They did not join the scores of philosophers who have pondered the true meaning of the concept of happiness. Instead, avoiding the potential hang-up of trying to think through precisely what happiness is, they took a shortcut through the philosophical discussion to find a way of getting at a measure of happiness. In the language we have used so far, Bradburn and Caplovitz first decided to use a respondent's self-report as an indicator of happiness. Then they had to work out a way of measuring variation in that indicator. They did this by devising a series of categorical responses to the question "Are you happy?" (Actually, they dressed the question up a little bit by asking, "Taking all things together, how would you say things are these days?"). Then they simply gave the respondents the option of replying that they were "very happy," "pretty happy," or "not too happy."

Once they had happiness measured, the researchers could examine the other qualities of those who were more or less happy. In other words, Bradburn and Caplovitz were able to relate the response to the happiness question, their dependent variable, to a host of other factors. In the discussion of validity later in this chapter, the efforts of Bradburn and Caplovitz to validate their measure of happiness will be considered.

Measuring Authoritarianism

Earlier in this chapter I talked about authoritarianism as a concept developed by social scientists to try to make sense of the appeal of antidemocratic ideas. The concept was formulated by members of the Institute for Social Research established in Frankfurt, Germany, in 1923. Forced into exile by the rise of Hitler in 1933, the researchers came to the United States and continued their work, first at Columbia University in New York and later at the University of California at

Berkeley. Their efforts led to a series of studies of prejudice (anti-Semitism and ethnocentrism) conducted by T. W. Adorno in collaboration with a team of psychologists and social scientists at Berkeley. This research culminated in the well-known work *The Authoritarian Personality* (1969; originally published in 1950).

In thinking about prejudiced attitudes such as anti-Semitism and ethnocentrism (the dogmatic tendency to glorify one's own group and cast aspersions on other groups), the authors thought they saw a common feature in all the different types of prejudice they studied: a more general, unquestioning belief in authority, to which they gave the name *authoritarianism.*

What were the dimensions of this new concept? The researchers came to define nine attitudes as the *dimensions* of authoritarianism. Defining these dimensions involved thinking about a whole series of attitudes that might be associated with the concept and examining their relationship to one another. This process would enable the researchers to establish a comprehensive operational definition of authoritarianism which logically seemed to fit the abstract concept of authoritarianism.

Having identified the dimensions of their new concept, the researchers next had to develop ways of measuring them. A group led by Daniel J. Levinson, a psychologist on the research team, prepared a series of statements expressing the attitudes in each dimension so that respondents could be asked to express their level of agreement or disagreement. Different groups of statements therefore served as the *indicators* of each dimension. Take the statement "Young people sometimes get rebellious ideas, but as they grow up, they ought to get over them and settle down." Under which dimension do you think it would fall? Since it refers to the giving up of rebellious or unpopular ideas as the proper thing for a mature person to do, it suggests approval of giving in to those in control. Thus agreement with this statement was considered an indicator of *authoritarian submission.*

Similarly, agreement with the statement "A person who has bad manners, habits, and breeding can hardly expect to get along with decent people" was seen as an indicator of *conventionalism.* Note that the statement was written in a way that placed a high value on getting along with other people and gave this desire for conformity a moralistic quality

---

THE DIMENSIONS OF AUTHORITARIANISM AS MEASURED BY THE F-SCALE

The nine dimensions include

1. *Conventionalism*: rigid adherence to conventional, middle-class values.
2. *Authoritarian submission*: submissive, uncritical attitude toward idealized moral authorities of the group.
3. *Authoritarian aggression*: tendency to be on the lookout for, and to condemn, reject, and punish people who violate conventional values.
4. *Anti-intraception*: opposition to the subjective, the imaginative, the tender-minded.
5. *Superstition and stereotype*: the belief in mystical determinants of the individual's fate; the disposition to think in rigid categories.
6. *Power and toughness*: preoccupation with dominance-submission, strong-weak, leader-follower dimension; identification with power figures; overemphasis on the conventionalized attributes of the ego; exaggerated assertion of strength and toughness.
7. *Destructiveness and cynicism*: generalized hostility, vilification of the human.
8. *Projectivity*: the disposition to believe that wild and dangerous things go on in the world: the projection outward of unconscious emotional impulses.
9. *Sex*: exaggerated concern with sexual "goings-on."

Source: T. W. Adorno et al.: *The Authoritarian Personality*, Harper & Row, New York, 1950 (Norton, 1969), pp. 255–257.

by using such loaded terms as *bad* and *decent*. (It may seem a little humorous to you, because attitudes such as good breeding are no longer taken as seriously as they were in the 1950s, but think about how brilliantly the statement was devised in order to tap underlying attitudes without making them too explicit. I will say more later on about the art of devising good items like this.)

Working in this way and testing the effectiveness of different statements as they went along, the researchers eventually agreed on a set of statements for each dimension to represent the overall concept of authoritarianism. The respondent's level of agreement or disagreement with each statement was measured on a seven-point scale from +3 (strongly agree) to -3 (strongly disagree). The total score, based on averaging the scores for all the statements, then became the measure of the respondent's degree of authoritarianism.

This way of operationalizing and the measuring authoritarianism was called the *F-Scale* (Fascism Scale) by its inventors. It became one of the most widely used and influential attitudinal measures ever developed. One of the fascinating things about the F-Scale is that it played such a large role in the development of other measures of complex concepts in social psychology. Unsatisfied with certain aspects of how the concept of authoritarianism had been operationally defined, a stream of other researchers developed new measures that reflected variations from or refutations of the original concept. In this continuing process of operationalization, the concept itself was refined and redefined.

Comparing the Measurement of Authoritarianism to the Measurement of Happiness

If we compare the efforts to measure authoritarianism with those to measure happiness, we see a very interesting contrast. Happiness is a commonplace concept that everyone uses all the time and no one bothers to define. In fact, happiness is such an abstract concept that it would be extremely hard to define it in any satisfactory way. What did

Bradburn and Caplovitz do with this abstract concept? They merely took the concept as largely given and operationalized an indicator by asking persons to report how happy they were. In other words, they greatly simplified the concept-to-operationalization phase and moved swiftly to the operationalization-to-measurement phase.

In comparison, the operationalization of the concept of authoritarianism was a much more complex matter. Adorno and his colleagues virtually invented the concept of authoritarianism (which was not used in everyday life) as a means of measuring the underlying dynamics of prejudice. They then defined the concept operationally by developing a set of indicators to represent what they had defined as the various dimensions of authoritarianism. This operationalized concept, which was developed first as a measure of the potential for antidemocratic ideology, came to be applied more widely and diversely to different types of social situations and experiences. Thus, for Adorno and his colleagues, the concept-to-operationalization phase was central to their efforts. The operationalization-to-measurement phase was a secondary, though very important, effort.

This contrast is also representative of two of the most important trends in the development of measurement in the social sciences. The efforts of Bradburn and Caplovitz to measure happiness are characteristic of the relatively simple and straightforward (and somewhat nonphilosophical) means that survey researchers have developed for measuring concepts, by devising simple questions that require self-reports. The efforts of Adorno and his colleagues are highly characteristic of the more ambitious (if never fully satisfactory) efforts by social psychologists to operationalize complex psychological concepts by developing scales.

THE MEASUREMENT OF VARIABLES

Measurement is the central concern of all sciences. If we think back to Wallace's model of science in Chapter 2, measurement occurs in between observations and empirical generalizations in the inductive half of the model and between hypotheses and observations in the deductive half of the model. This formulation suggests that measurement is not so much the end, or goal, of science but rather the means to that end. Without good measurement, the goals of scientific research are unattainable. In social research, the researcher must use variation to make comparisons and test hypotheses, two of the central tasks of social research. For a social researcher, the art of good measurement is to capture variation in an operationally defined variable. This section will discuss what is at stake in trying to do this.

As was shown in the previous section, measurement requires the identification of variables. *Variable* is a term used to describe something that varies. One result of this definition of a variable is that the term can be applied to anything that is measured in a social research study. For example, in the happiness study, the question "Taking all things together, how would you say things are these days?" produces measurable variation by offering the response categories "very happy," "pretty happy," and "not too happy." The question (with its set of possible responses) is therefore thought of as a variable. In the authoritarianism study, each of the separate statements also might be considered a variable, since they too are capable of capturing the measurable variation in the responses to them. However, the whole authoritarianism scale (the F-Scale) also can be considered a variable because the measured responses can be combined into a single measure of variation.

DEFINING MEASUREMENT

The most common definition of measurement presented in the literature is one first offered by S. S. Stevens:

> Measurement is the assignment of numbers to objects or events according to certain rules (*1951, p. 22*).

Let's look at this definition carefully. It contains two parts. First, it indicates that measurement is a *doing* activity—assigning numbers—which involves performing operations sequentially. Second, it specifies that what you are doing must follow certain rules or a model which lays out the principles of the measurement system (Borgatta and Bohrnstedt, 1980, p. 151).

There is also a third quality of this activity which is implied in this definition: the rules that guide measurement have to do with establishing a correspondence between what is observed and the number it is given. In other words, measurement is carried out according to *rules of correspondence* in which certain phenomena (or types of phenomena) are designated by a particular number (Bohrnstedt, 1983, p. 70).

Here's an example. Suppose you are measuring the variable educational attainment. You decide to use "number of years of education completed" to represent that variable. A person finishing elementary school would be assigned an 8 (for eight years of schooling); a person who dropped out of high school in the tenth grade would be assigned a 9; a graduate of a two-year college would be assigned a 14; a holder of a master's degree would be assigned an 18.

Now let's go over the steps in this measurement process:

1. You define a phenomenon—educational attainment—as a variable which includes different levels at which education is terminated to which you assign corresponding numbers according to the number of years of education completed.
2. You observe that a particular subject has a particular educational attainment level.
3. You select the number representing the educational termination point which corresponds to the educational attainment level. That is a measurement!

However, in the social and behavioral sciences, many of the variables that interest us (as we saw with happiness and authoritarianism) are not as readily convertible to a numerical scale as is educational attainment. In fact, many are not at all the "objects and events" Stevens spoke of. Carmines and Zeller state the problem with Stevens's formulation clearly:

> Phenomena such as political efficacy, alienation, gross national product, and cognitive dissonance are too abstract to be considered "things that can be seen or touched" (the definition of an object) or merely as a "result, consequence, or outcome" (the definition of an event). In other words, Stevens's classical definition of measurement is much more appropriate for the physical than [for] the social sciences (*1979, p. 10*).

In place of this definition, they offer another definition of measurement as an "explicit, organized plan for classifying (and often quantifying) the particular sense data at hand—the indicants— in terms of the general concept in the researcher's mind" (Carmines and Zeller, 1979, p. 10). What has changed here is that "objects and events" have been replaced by "the general concept in the researcher's mind," and "numbers" have been replaced by "indicants." In other words, measurement is the process by which empirical data are organized in some systematic relationship to the concept being studied. This definition of measurement fits better with the kind of activity in which social researchers engage when they study phenomena that are not directly observable.

Let's give an example here of trying to measure an abstract concept which has no clear observable indicator. Suppose we are carrying out a door-to-door survey and are required to determine the happiness of the families being interviewed. Now, how will we link our concept of family happiness to some empirical evidence in these households? It could be the case that when you go to the Jones's door, Junior Jones has just thrown a frying pan at his sister and Mrs. Jones is shouting at Mr. Jones, who is crying. In this instance our ability to link the behavior we observe to our abstract concept of family happiness would be quite straightforward. But this is not what we could expect to find at most households.

What indicators could we use that would fairly measure happiness from one household to the next, and would those indicators be truly linked to our concept of family happiness? Suppose we had decided to adopt Bradburn and Caplovitz's measure of happiness and change it slightly to refer to *how* happy a family was. Now what if we went to the Jones's house (with the frying pans flying) to interview Mrs. Jones, and she claimed that the family was "pretty happy"? Would you believe her? Wouldn't this response introduce error into our careful measuring process?

All measurement leads to some error. Measurement theory contends that however precise our instruments for measuring (and in social research our instruments are generally quite crude) and however careful our efforts at observation, there will always be some error introduced into our measurement. In fact, the central formulation of measurement theory states that an observed measure (or score) is equal to the true score plus the error—above or below the true score—necessarily occurring in the process of observing the phenomenon. In short, all measurement contains some degree of error, called *measurement error*. Even though it is impossible to abolish all error, the aim is to reduce it as much as possible. Box 4-1 describes possible measurement error in a study on lynching.

The most important criterion of the goodness of a measure is its validity, that is, whether the measure is measuring what it intends to measure. It is also important that a measure be consistent so that when it is repeatedly used, it will lead to the same results. This consistency in measurement is referred to as reliability.

VALIDITY

Put most simply, *validity* addresses the question "Am I measuring what I think I am measuring?" The validity of the previously discussed F-Scale of authoritarianism has been challenged repeatedly. In developing instruments to measure abstract concepts, the issue of validity is critical.

BOX 4-1

MEASUREMENT ERRORS IN A STUDY OF NEWSPAPER REPORTS OF LYNCHINGS

An interesting example of measurement error was offered to me by Ira Wasserman of Eastern Michigan University. He has been studying how the *Chicago Tribune* and the *Los Angeles Times* covered lynchings in the late nineteenth century and early twentieth century. Since these newspapers did not have indexes classifying their topics, Wasserman selected five specific years to study and then hired assistants to carefully examine the articles covered in those two papers on the day after specific lynchings occurred to see if the papers reported the incidents.

He notes two types of measurement errors that might have occurred in his data collection efforts. In the first place, the reports of the lynchings may have been published more than one day after the event so that his specific method of having the observations taken only on the day after the lynching might have introduced measurement error into his study. Now Professor Wasserman notes that he could probably ad-

dress this problem (and thus reduce this type of measurement error) by hiring more assistants to read papers up to four days after each incident.

In the second place, the assistants need to be able to locate reports of the lynchings, which might have been difficult to find since these reports might have been included in the context of discussions of other crimes or events. In 1886, the earliest year he selected to study, the *Los Angeles Times* was only four pages in length; thus it would probably be unlikely for an assistant to miss the discussion of a lynching, no matter how far it was buried within an article. However, by 1907, the *Times* had expanded to two sections. In this case, it might be more likely that a research assistant would fail to uncover the report of a lynching in a specific day's paper. This would be another example of a measurement error.

Source: Personal Correspondence from Ira Wasserman, 1995.

The questions that are designed to tap an abstract concept must do precisely that.

The validity of a measure depends on the correspondence between a concept and the empirical indicators that supposedly measure it. In short, validity is a property of a measuring instrument that you want to test for. While reliability addresses the consistency in measurement, validity addresses the even more critical issue of the "crucial relationship between concept and indicator" (Carmines and Zeller, 1979, p. 12). It should also be recognized that validity is not synonymous with reliability. It is possible for a scale to be reliable (i.e., it repeatedly produces similar responses in similar situations) and still not be valid. As was mentioned above, a reliable but invalid measure is worthless. There are a number of methods to test for validity by determining the association between a concept and the empirical indicator(s)

chosen to measure it. The three methods described here test for content validity, criterion-related validity, and construct validity (see American Psychological Association, 1974).

Content Validity

The most basic method of testing for validity is to carefully examine the measure of a concept in light of its meaning and ask yourself seriously whether the measurement instrument really seems to be measuring the underlying concept. This form of careful consideration and examination is a method of establishing *face validity* (or what is sometimes called "armchair" validity). In some instances, an instrument may need to appear to be measuring what it purports to measure even if another instrument which looks less relevant—but actually was valid—could be used. For example,

Allen and Yen (1979, p. 96) suggest that in a test used to screen applicants for a job, it may be essential (for purposes of public relations) to have questions that seem to be relevant to the job even if other types of questions would be just as good for selecting the best applicants. However, face validity is not an adequate test of the content validity of a measure.

Another method of testing for *content validity* asks whether the empirical indicators (tests, scales, questions, or whatever) fully represent the *domain of meaning* of the underlying concept being studied (Bohrnstedt, 1983, p. 98). In this sense, "content validity concerns the extent to which a set of items taps the content of some domain of interest. To the degree that the items reflect the full domain of content, they can be said to be content-valid" (Zeller and Carmines, 1980, p. 78). A simple way to understand this type of content validity is to consider the example of an achievement test. Suppose we are developing a college board achievement test in American history. The issue is whether the test items fairly represent the range of topics and ideas that should be covered in American history courses throughout the country. A test that has content validity would be one that samples fairly (selects without bias) from each of the different parts of the domain of meaning covered by the study of American history or that is truly representative of the full content of this subject taught in high schools and presented in high school textbooks. This form of content validity is often called *sampling validity* because the object is to sample accurately from the various domains. It is used widely by educational psychologists and test developers. Carmines and Zeller stress (1979, p. 21) that for purposes of establishing sampling validity, it is always preferable, in test development, to create a greater number of items for each part of the content domain, since it is easier to discard items than to add new ones once the test has been formed.

When the concept to be measured is more abstract (as in the example of authoritarianism), it is much more difficult to establish content validity.

This is true because the full domain of content of such concepts has usually not been as fully agreed upon. In addition, even when the domain is fully laid out, it is much more difficult to develop a pool of items large enough to represent each part of the content domain. Without a sufficient number of items in each stratum, sampling from each stratum cannot take place. For these reasons, sampling validity is rarely tested for in validating measures of abstract social science concepts.

The ultimate problem with testing for content validity is whether there is acceptance of the universe of content defined by the variable being measured (Cronbach and Meehl, 1955, p. 282, as discussed in Zeller and Carmines, 1980, p. 79). For a test of American history as presented in our example, it might seem at first glance to be fairly easy to establish some "acceptance" for the universe of content. However, educators do not agree about what *is* the appropriate and important content of American history. This is the case for many social-scientific concepts (alienation, self-esteem, etc.), for which the acceptance of what constitutes the universe of content is usually exceedingly difficult to establish. For this reason, content validity is not very useful in trying to validate social-scientific concepts.

Criterion-Related Validity

Why are college board examinations given? One reason is so that admissions offices can select entering students. But how does the admissions staff know that the college board exams are measuring anything relevant to a student's success in college? The answer is that college boards have been shown to be highly related to students' academic success in college. This is an example of *criterion-related validity*. In other words, the validity of the college board examinations can be established by showing that their results are highly associated with a particular outcome—academic success in college—which serves as the criterion of their validity.

In such cases, two measures need to be taken: the measure of the test itself (the set of empirical indicators) and the criterion to which the test is supposedly related. The usual procedure is to use a correlation (to be described in Chapter 13) between the measure and the criterion to determine the criterion-related validity. In the example given, the criterion—academic success in college, usually measured by college grade-point average (GPA)—would be measured subsequent to the original measure of college academic potential (the college board examination). In such an instance, the criterion-related validity is referred to as *predictive validity,* for the test scores purport to predict future academic performance.[1]

In other cases, a criterion may be measured at the same time as the concept. Bohrnstedt offers the example of measuring religiousness in terms of the seriousness of commitment to religious beliefs and relating it to the frequency of attendance at church (or another place of worship). In this case, a measure of the attitudes expressing a person's religious commitment is related to a piece of evidence about a person's religious behavior (attending church). Because these are measured at the same time, they are said to have *concurrent validity*.

Another example offered by Bohrnstedt uses a technique for testing for validity based on membership or affiliation with a *known group,* that is, a group known to support certain values, beliefs, and practices (1983, p. 98). Suppose you develop a set of questions to measure antiabortion attitudes. The validity of these questions might be established by relating the responses to membership in pro-life organizations or fundamentalist religious groups.

The problem with criterion-related validity for much social research is that it is often not possible to determine a relevant criterion. Remember that the criterion must represent not just some outcome

that might logically be related to the concept but also evidence that can serve as proof that the measured concept (or test) represents what it claims to represent. It is because of the difficulty in determining criteria for theoretical variables that construct validity has been developed to address this need.

Construct Validity

Criterion-related validity is based on getting some empirical evidence (such as college grades) to serve as the basis for judging that what is being measured (college board exams) really measures what it is supposed to measure (ability to succeed in college). This is an empirically based form of validity, in which some observable evidence can be used to confirm the validity of a measure. However, when there is neither a criterion nor an accepted universe of content that defines the quality being measured, criterion-related and content validity cannot be used to test for validity. With more theoretical concepts, the form of validity testing itself must become more theoretical. This is what characterizes *construct validity*.

Construct validity is based on forming hypotheses about the concepts that are being measured and then testing those hypotheses and correlating the results with the initial measure. Zeller and Carmines clarify the purpose of construct validity as

> the assessment of whether a particular measure relates to other measures consistent with theoretically derived hypotheses concerning the concepts (or constructs) that are being measured . . . (*1980, p. 81*).

Then they describe the steps required to test the construct validity of measures:

> First, the theoretical relationship between the concepts themselves must be specified. Second, the empirical relationship between the measures of the concepts must be examined. Finally, the empirical evidence must be interpreted in terms of how it clarifies the construct validity of the particular measures (*1980, p. 81*).

---

[1]Carmines and Zeller warn that since the sole reason for accepting the criterion-related validity of a concept is the strength of the correlation between the test and the criterion, even a nonsensical criterion (if it could be shown to be related to the test) would be proof of criterion-related validity (1979, p. 18).

VALIDATING THE MEASURE OF HAPPINESS

To strengthen the evidence that their measure of happiness was valid, Bradburn and Caplovitz related it to statements designed to be "more detailed measures of well-being." One set of statements was devised to measure "subjective feeling states which were conceptualized as having positive and negative poles" (Bradburn and Caplovitz, 1965, p. 15). Simply put, this means that Bradburn and Caplovitz developed a series of statements, the responses to which would serve as indicators for feeling good about something on the one hand and feeling bad about something on the other hand. The following categorical responses (Bradburn and Caplovitz 1965, pp. 16–17) were offered in answer to the question "How are you feeling?"

FOR THE POSITIVE SET:

Pleased about having accomplished something
Proud because someone complimented you on something you had done
On top of the world
Particularly excited or interested in something
That you had more things to do than you could get done

FOR THE NEGATIVE SET:

Vaguely uneasy about something without knowing why

So restless you couldn't sit long in a chair
Bored
Very lonely or remote from other people
Depressed or very unhappy

Responses to the items in each set were combined to form an index (a form of measurement in which several indicators are added together). This produced a *positive feelings index* and a *negative feelings index*. Bradburn and Caplovitz were then in a position to compare respondents' scores on each of these indexes with their responses to the happiness question. They found that it was the balance of these positive and negative feeling indexes that was related to the responses to the happiness question. When the positive feelings index was higher than the negative feelings index, more of the respondents claimed to be "very happy." When the negative feelings index was higher than the positive, more respondents stated that they were "not too happy." When there was a balance between the two indexes so that there were roughly equal levels of positive and negative feelings, the respondents were more likely to report being "pretty happy." They believed that the importance of the balance in positive and negative feeling states in determining one's general level of happiness could help explain why some people who seemed to have many problems were nevertheless generally "pretty happy," while others who seemed to have very few problems reported being "not happy."

Source: Norman M. Bradburn and David Capolvitz: *Reports on Happiness*, Aldine, Chicago, 1965, p. 21.

Clearly, according to Zeller and Carmines, construct validity is "theory-laden," though this does not mean that only concepts linked to fully developed theories can be tested with construct validity:

What is required is only that one be able to state several theoretically derived hypotheses involving the particular concept (*1980, p. 82*).

Carmines and Zeller offer a fairly easy example to describe this. Suppose you have a measure of self-esteem which you want to validate. You might begin by developing hypotheses that set up expectations about what self-esteem might be likely to vary with. If you hypothesized that self-esteem would more likely be high among students who participated in extracurricular activities at school than among those who did not, you might correlate the self-esteem scale with participation rates in school activities as a means of gathering one kind of evidence that the self-esteem scale was measuring what you believed to be a part of the theoretical construct of the meaning of self-esteem (Carmines and Zeller, 1979, p. 23).

Bradburn and Caplovitz tried to validate their measure of happiness. Their efforts to relate responses to *feeling states* (feeling bad and feeling good) to their measure of happiness is an example of aiming for construct validity. By hypothesizing how their happiness measure should relate to another measure and subsequently by seeing how far this turned out to be the case, Bradburn and Caplovitz were able to strengthen confidence in their own measure of happiness and offer evidence of construct validity for the measure. In the course of trying to establish the validity of their measure of happiness in this way, they came to better understand the meaning of the concept (or construct) of happiness itself.

Naturally, you could offer greater support for construct validity if you tested a greater number of measures that you hypothesized to be related to the concept in question. Construct validity increases as numerous researchers correlate different measures based on hypotheses about the probable relations of a concept. In some cases, of course, these correlations may turn out to be negative. Over time, such negative evidence (if it is based on theoretically sound hypotheses and carefully developed measures to test the hypotheses) may challenge the construct validity of a concept.

Construct validity also can be strengthened if more than one empirical indicator is used to measure the underlying concept. When this is the case, each of the indicators can be correlated with the external variable being used to test for construct validity. If the two indicators relate in different ways to the external measure, this suggests that the two indicators are not in fact measuring the same underlying concept (Carmines and Zeller, 1979, p. 26). In summarizing the various types of

validity testing for their effectiveness in social research, Zeller and Carmines concluded that construct validity is the most useful and applicable to the social sciences:

> It not only has generalized applicability for assessing the validity of social science measures, but it can also be used to differentiate theoretically relevant and theoretically meaningless empirical factors (*1980, p. 100*).

RELIABILITY

Put simply, *reliability* is defined as the degree to which a procedure for measuring produces similar outcomes when it is repeated. If a measuring procedure produces roughly similar results when it is repeated, we can then state that the measuring instrument is reliable. We would expect that certain measures, no matter how long the time interval between the measurements, would produce the same results. For example, if we measured gender, birthplace, or mother's maiden name, we would expect that the repeated responses to such measures would be identical to the ones collected previously. Why might a carefully constructed question measuring a variable not produce the same measured response each time it is given to a particular respondent? Let's say you had a very short questionnaire which asked people only two questions: "What is your age?" (for which a specific number of years was to be given) and "What is your opinion about the effectiveness of the president?" (to which the measured responses were "very effective," "somewhat effective," "not too effective," and "not at all effective"). If you worked for a polling organization and went door to door on a particular street to ask individuals their age and their opinions about the effectiveness of the president and then returned at intervals over the next six months to ask the same questions, how likely would it be that each person you surveyed would give the same response to the two questions over and over again?

Consider first the variable of age. This is a factual question for which the only expected change might be that a person's birthday might have occurred and therefore the person would be a year older. This would not of course be an example of unreliability. However, you might find that some individuals gave quite varying responses each time you asked. Some elderly individuals might be unsure of their ages as a result of confusion or forgetfulness. Other individuals might be struggling between the "socially desirable" urge to sound younger (or, if young, older) and the realistic urge to state a fact as one knows it. These examples suggest that respondents' feelings may change their answers in ways that affect the reliability of the responses.

For the question about presidential effectiveness, one would expect greater variation over time because the question measures an attitude (which is often subject to change) in comparison to a fact (which should be less subject to change). For staunch supporters of the president or, conversely, staunch opponents of the president, responses would be expected to be at the extreme level and changes would be less likely to occur with changing events. In other words, those with stronger attitudes toward a subject should be less susceptible to change. However, for those with less strong commitments for or against the president, changing political events might alter attitudes over time. This would reflect actual changes in respondents' attitudes and would not be evidence of unreliability in the measuring instrument. If attitudes shifted from one day to the next, this would be greater evidence of unreliability than would be the case if they shifted over a month's or over six months' time.

What if the question had been about attitudes toward the effectiveness of the secretary of the interior? Such a question would raise greater worries about unreliability. Many individuals would not know who this secretary was or what he or she was responsible for, let alone whether the secretary was performing adequately. A question such as this would lead to unreliable responses because many respondents would not want to admit lack of

information to answer the question and would just offer some answer. Because the answer was not based on any factual knowledge or on any developed opinion, it would be unlikely to remain stable over time.

If a question is irrelevant to a respondent or is too complicated or likely to be misinterpreted by the respondent, it is likely to produce highly unreliable responses. Thus, the aim of developing measured variables is to produce ones that present material understandable to the respondent on topics which should be familiar to the respondent, not too complicated, and easy to interpret. The researcher should be careful on questions that may encourage a respondent to respond in what might seem a socially desirable manner.

As was stated above, there will always be some error no matter how carefully the measurement procedures are carried out. Nevertheless, there are ways to reduce measurement error. In assessing reliability, the problem is to determine the degree of random error rather than systematic error. Because the effects of random error tend to cancel each other out if a greater number of indicators are being measured, it is preferable to have a composite measure (one with numerous indicators) than a single measure in developing reliable measures for social science concepts (Zeller and Carmines, 1980, p. 75). For example, as was mentioned in the section on authoritarianism, if you use more than one indicator for each concept, that is, if you collect data on *multiple indicators* for each abstract concept, you can develop more reliable measures of the concept. (Note that for the F-Scale of authoritarianism, numerous questions were developed to measure each of the scale's nine dimensions. It was the combined score on the set of items that determined the level of each dimension.)

Why should multiple indicators produce greater reliability than do single indicators? Any observed (or measured) score is equal to the "true score"—the "hypothetical, unobservable quantities that cannot be directly measured" (Carmines and Zeller, 1979, p. 29)—plus the error. Since we can never be sure that our observed score is equal to the true score, the best that can be achieved is to retest the measures over and over (an "infinite number of repeated measurements," 1979, p. 30) and use the response given most often as the true score. The assumption made about measurement error is that in repeated measures of the same phenomenon, the errors will sometimes be higher (more positive) than the true score and sometimes be lower (or more negative) but over time will cancel each other out and thus produce an average error score of 0. For this reason, the measurement error is referred to as *random measurement error,* or simply *random error.* The theory of random error forms a central part of what is called *classical test theory.* As Zeller and Carmines (1980, p. 7) explain, the

> main body of statistical theory . . . that has been used to estimate the reliability (and indirectly, the validity) of empirical measurements is classical test theory . . . which begins with the basic formulation that an observed score, *X,* is equal to the true score, *T,* plus a measurement error, *e.* To state this idea as a formula:

$$X = T + e$$

However, they later go on to say that "in classical test theory, it is assumed that all measurement error is random." While this idea may be justified in strict experimental designs in the social sciences, it is not justified in sample surveys, observational studies based in the field, or more structured environments (1980, p. 11). In surveys, for example, respondents' tendencies toward yea-saying and nay-saying and in responding in a socially desirable fashion may produce systematic error (p. 11).

In addition, classical test theory is not very good at determining the validity of a measure or clarifying the relationship between validity and reliability (Zeller and Carmines, 1980, pp. 11–12). In a reformulation of classical test theory, Zeller and Carmines show that "the difference between reliability and validity is entirely dependent upon systematic error" (p. 14). If there were no systematic error, validity would be equal to reliability; conversely, if there were a fair degree of systematic error, validity would be less than reliability (p. 14).

The preceding discussion has described repeated measurements of the same phenomenon on single individuals. It could also apply to repeated measurements across different individuals on the same measure. In this case, you would need to look at the range of scores in relation to the overall mean from all the scores. This is called *variance* (to be described more fully in Chapter 5). Two general procedures can be used to reduce the amount of random error and improve the reliability of a measure: measuring for stability and measuring for equivalence.

Measures of Stability

Reliability tests that determine how much change will occur in the responses of individuals from one testing time to the next are measuring the stability of the measurement instrument. This is often called *test-retest reliability.* There are different possible explanations for unreliability from one testing time to the next. As was described in the above examples, unreliability may be due to the varying states individuals are in when the measure is taken: They may be more or less alert, healthy, concentrating, and so on. Or unreliability may be due to weaknesses in the measuring instrument: respondents may be uncertain about what is being asked yet offer an answer to avoid appearing unintelligent. Under such conditions reliability may be weak from one test to the retest. Also, changes could occur during the period between the tests: then the different answers given at each test do not signify lack of reliability but instead indicate true change. An example of such true change can be found in achievement tests, where the individual actually learns more between the testing times.

Measures of Equivalence

Another way to test for reliability, instead of comparing scores on tests given at different times, is to compare parallel items at the same point in time.

This provides an on-the-spot form of test-retest. If one has two indicators of the same concept, comparisons of these items can help determine the reliability of the measure. For example, let's assume you are trying to measure the concept of *anomie* (normlessness). You decide to select two items from Srole's Anomia Scale (1956) (a scale to be discussed at greater length in the final section of this chapter) which are two of the five indicators of anomie Srole defined (see Miller, 1977, pp. 375–377, for the scale). The two items are (1) "In spite of what some people say, the lot of the average man is getting worse," and (2) "These days a person does not know who he can count on." You test those items on a sample of respondents. The responses to the two items are equal to the same *true* score; the differences are the result of random error. Therefore, the correlation (a statistical procedure to be described in Chapter 13) between the two items measured at the same time offers an estimate of the reliability of the scale. It also follows that since the random errors will cancel each other out, the more items tested, the better the estimates of reliability.

TYPES OF VARIABLES

One essential feature of measurement is that it depends on the possibility of variation. Another way of saying this is that measurement requires the identification of *variables,* a term that we have defined before as something that varies. One result of this definition of a variable is that the term can be applied to anything that is measured in a social research study. Variables can be measured in two general ways: they are either categorical or numerical.

Categorical Variables

A *categorical variable* is made up of a set of attributes that form a category but do not represent a numerical measure or scale. Many of the most significant variables defining our social existence can be described only as sets of attributes belonging to a category. For instance, a teacher, a Catholic, a man, and a Republican are all primary defining characteristics of a person. Each represents one attribute within the categorical variables of *occupation* (teacher, plumber, salesperson, etc.), *religion* (Catholic, Jew, Protestant, Muslim, etc.), *gender* (man, woman), and *voting preference* (Republican, Democrat, independent). These variables are made up of sets of categories (or attributes) which must follow two rules. In the first place, the categories must be distinct from one another; that is, they must be *mutually exclusive.* This means that no respondent should be able to place himself or herself into more than one category. Let's say that for the variable of religion you included the following categories: "Catholic," "Protestant," "Christian," and "Jewish." In this case, your categories would not be mutually exclusive, because "Christian" would subsume both "Catholic" and "Protestant," and a choice among them would be meaningless.

In the second place, the categories of a variable must be *exhaustive.* This means that they should cover all the potential range of variation in a variable. In other words, even respondents with a very extreme position on one variable should be able to place themselves comfortably within one of the categories. In the religion example, you would need to add the categories of "other" and "none" to Catholic, Protestant, and Jewish in order to have an exhaustive list appropriate to an American sample. When a variable has a potentially different or extreme response, there should be a catchall category at the end to pick up extreme cases (for example, "favor none of the above candidates" might be the final choice in a candidate preference variable).

To incorporate categorical variables into a quantitative study and computerize the data, it is customary to assign numbers to the categories. For example, for gender, males may be designated by a 1 and females by a 2. This use of numbers, however does not imply that the categories represent numerical quantities that can be manipulated mathematically. The numbers are merely used as a way to code the categories for analysis on a computer. (Chapter 11 will describe coding.) For analyzing categorical variables, the primary forms of arithmetic that can be used are simple counting and percentages.

Numerical Variables

Numerical variables, as distinct from categorical variables, are broken down into units in which the numbers used to represent each unit of the variable carry mathematical meaning. For example, achievement test scores, personality scale scores, age and labor force participation rates are all variables in which the numbers represent not merely category labels but mathematical measurement of the variable. In other words, they represent a scale.

The numbers represented by a numerical variable may be either *discrete* or *continuous*. If the variable is number of children, its range of numbers are discrete (1, 2, 3, etc.), which is to say that they cannot be broken down continuously into smaller and smaller fractional quantities. For example, consider the discrete variable number of children. While no family has 2.35 children, average family sizes are often presented in this manner. In many statistical reports, discrete variables such as average family size are treated as if they were continuous. However, if the variable is weight, the measurement it represents is unambiguously continuous. The weight may be 2.35 or 2.36 pounds. To better conceptualize the differences in the measurement of variables, let us here consider the types of graphs which are used to depict the range of responses to different types of variables. This should help you visualize the differences between categorical and numerical variables.

Bar Graphs, Histograms, and Frequency Polygons. A *bar graph* is a graph on which categories of a variable are presented on the horizontal axis and the frequency of this category is presented on the vertical axis. Then a bar and the height of each frequency is drawn. These bars have gaps between them on the scale. Figure 4-1 gives a bar graph of the religious affiliations of students at a hypothetical college.

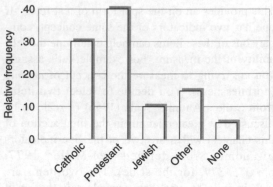

FIGURE 4-1
Bar graph of religious affiliations.

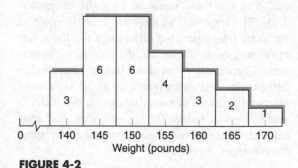

FIGURE 4-2
Histogram of weights, using a continuous variable.
(From T. W. Anderson and Stanley L. Sclove: *Introductory Statistical Analysis*, 2d ed., Houghton Mifflin, Boston, 1986, p. 45.)

A *histogram*, sometimes mistakenly called a bar graph, is used to depict the frequency distribution of a numerical (preferably a continuous) variable, such that the bars have at their centermost point the value being presented. The edge of each bar is halfway to the next centermost value, and therefore it touches the edge of the bar next to it. A histogram of the weights of students in a class could be made. Histograms are often used to represent discrete numerical variables as well. For example, if the discrete variable number of children is used, the bar representing one child would actually depict 0.5 to 1.5 children, the bar for two children would cite from 1.5 to 2.5 children and so forth. Figure 4-2 shows a histogram for a continuous

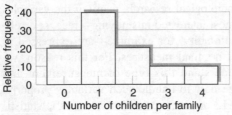

FIGURE 4-3
Histogram of number of children per family, using a discrete variable. (From T. W. Anderson and Stanley L. Sclove: *Introductory Statistical Analysis*, 2d ed., Houghton Mifflin, Boston, 1986, p. 39.)

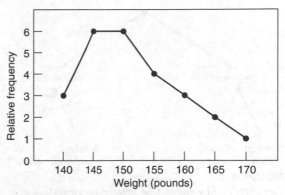

FIGURE 4-4
Frequency polygon of weights in Figure 4-2.

variable, weight, and Figure 4-3 shows a histogram for a discrete variable, number of children per family.

Consider the histogram of weights. To form a graph from these weights, you would first need to group the weights into classes: 137.5–142.5, 142.5–147.5, 147.5–152.5, and so on, as you can see in Figure 4-2. Then you would find the midpoints of these groups (140 and 145, etc.) and build a graph with those midpoints. In each class of weights you would count the students who fell into that class and register them on the vertical axis.

A *frequency polygon* is another type of graph that can represent the same thing as a histogram. However, instead of presenting bars with the centermost point for each value on the horizontal axis, the centermost point is where the top of the bar would be, and the bar is not drawn in. Such a dot graph makes it easier to draw lines connecting the points that indicate the shape of the distribution. Figure 4-4 presents a frequency polygon for the weights in Figure 4-2.

The distribution of continuous variables can be described by a fuller range of statistical measures such as the mean and the standard deviation, which will be described more fully in Chapter 5 on sampling and Chapter 13. Discrete variables can be described by a narrower range of statistics, such as the median and mode, although many analysts employ the mean as well in describing the distribution of a discrete variable.

LEVELS OF MEASUREMENT

In the social sciences, four types of scales for measuring a variable (two types for categorical variables and two types for numerical variables) have been delineated. These scale types (or *levels of measurement,* as they are usually called) are useful in helping to classify and catalog variables in a study as well as in designing questions to measure variables.

It is often possible for a variable to be measured at different levels. In deciding how to set up the variable (that is, how to "operationalize the variable"), you are also making the relationship between your measured variable and the underlying concept more precise. Of course, your choice of measurement categories will also determine the quality of the response data you get. Both the reliability of a variable and its validity will depend on the operational decisions made in the design of the variable. If the measurement of the variable is not a good fit with the underlying concept you are trying to measure, the data gathered on this variable will be invalid. If the variable is imprecise or unclear, it will not produce reliable responses. In short, poorly measured variables will produce meaningless data, which will in turn make your analysis a waste of effort. Once your data have been produced, it will be too late to decide that your measurement categories should have been

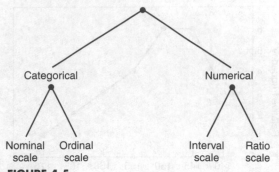

FIGURE 4-5
Classification of variables: the four measurement levels.
(From T. W. Anderson and Stanley L. Sclove: *Introductory Statistical Analysis,* 2d ed., Houghton Mifflin, Boston, 1986, p. 29.)

quite different. Therefore, you should apply the principles of measurement in designing your data-gathering instruments.

Figure 4-5 is a diagram of the four scales or levels that constitute the classification of variables. Two of the levels (nominal and ordinal) are used for categorical variables; two (interval and ratio) are used for numerical variables.

Nominal Measurement

A variable with a *nominal level of measurement* consists of a set of distinctive categories that imply no specific order. Consider the variable of gender (or sex). This variable can take only two forms: male and female. There is no real order between the categories; respondents must simply be one or the other. Or take the variable of religion. Here in the United States there are three major categories. But note that it would make no sense to place them on a scale from high to low, because they are different choices with no particular rank order among them. (For religion, not only would the major religious groups be given, but a catchall category for other religions would need to be included, along with a category for none.) In summary, a nominal variable must have at least two categories (but may have as many as are needed), and these categories must be characterized as having no prescribed order.

In sociological research, many of the variables we are most interested in studying—race, sex, religion, nationality, for example—are expressed in terms of nominal measures. For this reason, we must understand this type of measurement and recognize how to handle such variables properly. Chapter 13 on statistics will offer specific statistical tests that can be used in studying relationships between nominal variables.

Ordinal Measurement

Variables that have two or more categories with an inherent order among them are measured at an *ordinal level* of measurement. Consider the variable of social class. However many categories are used, they suggest an order. Even a two-category breakdown of "high class" and "low class" implies an order from high to low. For most purposes, of course, two categories seem too few for the variable of social class. The simplest form of ordinal scale generally used to measure social class has three points: "upper class," "middle class," and "lower class." But more complicated nine-point scales have been created by identifying three categories within each of the initial three groups ("upper-upper," "middle-upper," "lower-upper," "upper-middle," "middle-middle," "lower-middle," "upper-lower," "middle-lower," "lower-lower").

How many categories you use in setting up your variable will depend on how much variation you expect to find out there among your respondents and how far these differences interest you in terms of your research. If you wanted to study the fine differences between the upper-upper classes (those with "old money") and the middle-upper classes (those with "new money"), these categories might be very important. If, however, you were planning to use the variable of social class only in fairly broad terms in your study, the three-category variable might be preferable.

Although many variables cannot be converted into ordinal scales, a great many can. In some cases ordinal measures can be joined together with nominal measures to intensify the understanding of a concept. Take the concept of religion. To find out someone's religious affiliation, a nominal variable is needed. To find out how religiously observant a person is, however, an ordinal measure should be used, such as "Do you attend religious services daily, weekly, a few times a month, monthly, a few times a year, yearly, less often than once a year, never?"

The most common forms of ordinal variables are attitudinal items to which level of agreement is assessed. For example, an index (that is, a combined set of variables added together) of job satisfaction might include this item: "I consider my job rather unpleasant," to which the respondent must select one of the following: "strongly agree," "agree," "undecided," "disagree," "strongly disagree" (from Brayfield and Rothe, 1951, in Miller, 1977, pp. 368–370). These categories generally are given code numbers of 1 to 5. These numbers imply order of agreement but suggest nothing about the distance between the number (is "strongly agree" further from "agree" than "agree" is from "undecided"?)

Attitude scales such as the one described above are ordinal scales. However, they are often treated as continuous variables such that the *average* score of all respondents to the item might be given as 2.3. Or, as in the case of the Job Satisfaction Index, a set of items is summed and then the average scores and measures of variation among the scores are computed. In this way a variable with an ordinal scale of measurement is actually treated like an interval scale. This practice has raised some questions about the meaning and utility of ordinal measurement.[2]

Interval Measurement

To picture an interval scale, think of a thermometer. It has lines marking off points on the scale to register the changing temperatures. However, there is no true zero point—no point at which there would be *no temperature*. If it is a Fahrenheit thermometer, the zero on the scale will be at 32 degrees below the freezing point of water; if it is a centigrade thermometer, the zero on the scale will be at the freezing point of water. In neither case, however, will the zero refer to a point where there is no temperature. An interval scale is a created scale that has clearly defined intervals between the points on the scale and has order, but it has no true zero point.

An example of an interval scale would be a scale of test scores, such as an IQ score. The SAT examination has scores ranging from 200 to 800 (again no true zero point); the ACT is also an interval scale, but with a very different number range of scores. What happens with these tests is that the raw score achieved by an individual on a test is converted into a test score based on test norms developed from knowledge about how others have scored. In some cases, parts of a test are weighted more highly than others are.

Because the scores from social-psychological scales, such as the F-Scale of authoritarianism, are generally treated as continuous measures, such scales are often considered interval scales. Some methodologists would disagree and classify scales of this type as ordinal scales, since they are based on an accumulation of ordinal items—items to which the respondent usually offers a level of agreement.[3] Scores for the F-Scale are computed by cumulating the levels

---

[2]Borgatta and Bohrnstedt have argued that ordinal measures are really weak forms of interval measures in which the information on the distance between the intervals has been "lost." Since ordinal variables are generally described with statistical measures that assume continuous numerical scales, Borgatta and Bohrnstedt think it makes much more sense to treat ordinal variables as imperfect interval variables (1980, pp. 153–160) than as separate levels of measurement.

[3]Some methodologists would not consider psychological scales of this type as true interval-level measures, because they are based on an aggregated set of ordinal measures. However, as footnote 2 states, other methodologists consider all ordinal scales to be weak forms of interval scales. Suffice it to say that there is controversy in interpreting the meaning of ordinal and interval measures.

of agreement (+3 to –3) for the 38 items. Since it is not possible to have a zero on the F-Scale, ratios cannot be established. Thus it is inappropriate to describe one person as twice as authoritarian as another because the first person's score is twice as great.

In summary, interval scales are created devices which assist us in ordering things quite precisely. An *interval level of measurement* has separate categories, like nominal scales, and also has ordered categories, like ordinal scales; in addition, the distance between the points on an interval scale can be determined mathematically and precisely. Interval scales are used for continuous variables that can register very small differences between categories. Most mathematical operations that are carried out in statistics (see Chapter 13) can be done with interval-level measures. The lack of a true zero point usually is not regarded as a critical deterrent to carrying out many statistical tests.

Ratio Measurement

A ratio scale encompasses all the qualities of the earlier forms of scales: it must have more than one category, it must have an implicit order, and it must be able to determine the exact distance between the intervals. In addition, however, it must have a true zero point. Think of variables such as income, age, number of children, and cost of housing. Note that the *ratio level of measurement* can be applied to either continuous or discrete variables. However, strictly speaking, in the examples given and in most other social research variables with ratio levels of measurement, the variables would be discrete. Income cannot be broken down further than to cents; age is usually given in years. Questions about these variables could be answered on a scale with a true zero point. Your income could be nothing; your age before your were born was zero; you might not have children; your rent could be free. For these kinds of questions, a ratio scale is appropriate.

While there are advantages to using a ratio scale, in fact variables (like income) which could be expressed by a ratio scale are often converted into ordinal scales by grouping possible categories of income, e.g., "0 to $4,999," "$5,000 to $9,999," "$10,000 to $14,999." Ratio scales are most commonly used in converting ratio-level variables into *rates*. Examples of these will be given in the following section.

Comparing the Measurement Levels

Box 4-2 describes how information about viewing soap operas and attitudes toward such programs can be collected by using variables measured at different levels. Box 4-2 has used the different levels of measurement and presented different types of questions.

If your analyses were to be based largely on two-variable, or bivariate, tables for cross-tabular analyses (to be described in detail in Chapter 12), it

BOX 4-2

SOAP OPERA VARIABLES: EXAMPLES OF MEASUREMENT LEVELS

RATIO
How many television soap operas did you watch last week?

INTERVAL
Estimate the IQ score of the hero or heroine of your favorite soap opera

ORDINAL
How true to life are the soap operas you watched last week? Very true, somewhat true, not too true, not at all true.

NOMINAL
Which of the following types of soap operas do you watch?
Medical themes, household dilemmas, etc.

would be better to have a ratio variable converted into a categorical variable (either at the nominal or the ordinal level). For a multivariate analysis where you planned to use a form of analysis such as multiple regression (where variables need to be at least at the interval level), it would be preferable to have interval or ratio-level variables.[4]

Some variables can be converted into different types of levels of measurement which might be selected in accordance with the type of analysis you hoped to do. An example might be educational attainment. For cross-tabular analyses, it would be better to present the variable in ordered categories (less than high school, high school graduate, some college, college graduate, etc.). For other types of analyses, it might be preferable to convert this variable into number of years of schooling completed, which would be a ratio variable.

MEASURING SIX COMMONLY USED SOCIAL RESEARCH VARIABLES

As a social researcher, you need to learn how to select, work with, and develop variables for the studies you are doing. Because so much social research has already been carried out, you rarely need to start from scratch. Generally you can find ways of measuring concepts that have been tried out by others. Always remember, however, to determine carefully whether your measure is actually measuring what you want it to measure (the validity issue), whether your measure is sufficiently clear that it is likely to produce consistent results (the reliability issue), and whether the scale of measuring the variable is appropriate and best suited for your needs.

In the next section we will examine six commonly used variables in social research which represent different levels of measurement. You will find that there are a number of different ways to measure some variables, and you must choose the one that best serves your particular research purpose. In the case of other variables, there may be only one agreed-upon way to measure them. When, for example, a variable measures a phenomenon defined by law (say, crime rates), it must meet the specific criteria laid down in the law. In other cases, social researchers have over the years developed certain ways of measuring social indicators that have become widely accepted. For example, the unemployment rate is determined in a precise way, and you could not just come up with what seemed to you to be a good way to determine an unemployment rate and use yours instead.

Two Nominal Variables

Marital Status.   This is a nominal variable which generally includes five categories: "single," "married," "widowed," "divorced," and "separated." Often the last three categories are grouped together, creating a three-category variable measuring "never married" (single), "currently married" (married), and "previously married" (widowed, divorced, or separated). Even in this latter case, there is no clear order among the categories.

Type of Housing.   Housing types are designated by the United States Census Bureau as (1) public housing, which refers to housing units owned by a local housing authority or any other public agency and operated as public housing, (2) private housing, which refers to all other housing units, and (3) subsidized housing, which refers to private

---

[4]One thing that you should keep in mind about nominal variables is that any concept that can be operationally defined into a variable can be measured by a two-category nominal level of measurement. The first category would represent the presence (or possession) of the quality. The second category would represent the absence (or lack of possession) of the concept. In research analysis, setting up a variable in this either-or method is referred to as creating a dummy variable. In the case of religion, this variable would usually be measured in terms of a series of categories representing different religions. However, for some purposes, it might make sense to have a variable for religion that had only two categories, for example, "Catholic" and "non-Catholic." Or you might take the variable on voting preference for a specific candidate and have either-or categories: "favor Republican candidate," "not favor Republican candidate."

housing in which the occupant pays a lower rent because a federal, state, or local government program pays part of the cost of construction, building mortgage, or operating expenses (U.S. Department of Commerce, *Social Indicators III,* 1980, p. 574). One might see these three categories as characterized by some order from "wholly private," to "partially private/partially subsidized" to "wholly public." However, such a variable would best be categorized as a nominal variable.

One Ordinal Variable

Occupational Status.　Identifying the job a person holds is the main way to determine that person's social status. If someone tells you that she or he is a bank president, a garbage collector, or a shoe salesperson, you fit this person into some sense of the overall social hierarchy of the society. Without ever having taken a course in sociology, you probably thought that bank presidents had more status than garbage collectors and that shoe salespeople had less status than bank presidents but more than garbage collectors. How did you arrive at these conclusions? Probably because you connected a number of other factors to the meaning of a specific occupation: that it suggested a certain level of education and that it carried with it different rewards in terms of income, prestige, and benefits. In short, the measure of occupations— which could consist merely of a set of job titles (a nominal variable)—also suggests more complex, ordered measures.

In the first place, using the simple nominal level of job titles leads to numerous problems. There are so many job titles that you would need to use a system to group people with the same types of jobs in the same categories. A usual source for job titles is that used by the Census Bureau, which lists numerous job categories under six major occupational groups:

　　Managerial and professional specialty
　　Technical, sales, and administrative support

Service occupations
Precision production, craft, and repair
Operators, fabricators and laborers
Farming, forestry and fishing (*U.S. Department of Commerce, 1992*)

These categories and the job titles encompassed by them have an inherent order; those in the top categories imply higher levels of education, and higher rewards than do those in the lower categories, though the final group does not clearly belong at the bottom of the order. Therefore, if you subdivide occupations into these six groups, you have an ordinal scale. However, greater differentiation often is preferred so that actual job titles can be given a rating to distinguish them as either higher or lower than another job title within the same category.

Fortunately for social researchers, few variables have received more attention, in terms of developing measures and scales, than occupation. Occupational prestige scales (based on the relative ratings of occupations) and socioeconomic indexes (based on income and education data as well as in some cases on prestige ratings) have been developed to "measure" occupation. These occupational scales will be described in greater detail in the next section of this chapter. Scales and indexes enable the researcher to collect job titles from a study and score the jobs on a selected scale or index (an interval measure). This scale or index can be used to determine the mean and range of occupations, etc. If you use an occupational prestige scale or a socioeconomic index, the variable of occupational status will be measured at the interval level.

One Interval Variable

Srole's Anomia Scale.　This scale, which was referred to earlier, is presented here as an example of the many social-psychological scales available in the literature. (Refer to footnote 3, which discusses the reservations which some methodologists have about considering this a true interval scale.) Srole defined this scale as representing "the individual's generalized pervasive sense of self-to-others belongingness at one extreme compared with self-to-others distance and self-to-others alienation at the other pole of the continuum" (Miller, 1977, p. 375). We have already suggested that the F-Scale of authoritarianism and occupational prestige scales are treated as interval-level measures. Srole's Anomia Scale, which is also as interval scale, consists of five items (see Miller, 1977, p. 376):

1. In spite of what some people say, the lot of the average man is getting worse.
2. It's hardly fair to bring children into the world with the way things look for the future.
3. Nowadays a person has to live pretty much for today and let tomorrow take care of itself.
4. These days a person doesn't really know who he can count on.
5. There's little use writing to public officials, because often they aren't really interested in the problems of the average man.

The respondent either agrees or disagrees with these five items; the responses are cumulated. Validation studies have shown that this scale correlates quite highly with the F-Scale of authoritarianism ($r = .47$) and with measures of socioeconomic status ($r = .30$). (See Chapter 13 for an explanation of the correlation coefficient, Pearson's r.)

Two Ratio Variables

Income. If the first variable requested specific yearly income, it would be a ratio measure, since an income could be zero. Note that income might be grouped to set up ordinal-level variables of this type: less than 10,000, 10,000–19,999, 20,000–29,999, 30,000–39,999 . . . 100,000 or more. But when it is based on an actual dollar figure of the income, it is a ratio variable. Again, the type of measurement level a researcher would choose to use would depend on various factors: the types of analyses planned, how important it was to be able to make fine discrimina-

tions between respondents in terms of the sizes of their incomes, and so on.

Labor Force Participation Rate. This is a measure determined from the work status of individuals. It is a ratio measure with a precise, agreed-upon definition of how it must be measured. The labor force participation rate is based on the number of persons in the civilian labor force per 1,000 persons (16 years old and over) in the civilian noninstitutional population (*Social Indicators III,* 1980, p. 576). It is often reported separately for men and women, for different ethnic groups, and for those from different regions of the country or different cities.

Variables: The Tools of Social Research

Note that for all these six variables, as for all others, it is important that definitions be established and used consistently throughout a study. If you are doing your own study and gathering your own data, your measures may be your own. Even in this case, you need to follow common procedures for defining variables (though there are often choices that can be made). If, however, you want to use an established rate or a population figure, you must get that information from the appropriate source and be certain you are using the official definitions. A study that uses established variables in a way that does not conform to accepted definitions of those variables will not be taken seriously.

Many of the six variables offered could be transposed into different levels of measurement. Take employment. If it is set up in terms of a rate (labor force participation rate), it is at the ratio level; if it refers to an ordered set of work involvement ("work full time," "work part time," "not work"), it is an ordinal variable. This work of measuring variables is one of the primary tasks of the social researcher. You need not start from scratch, for there are many good examples to use. However, you must be certain that the variables you choose and measure follow the accepted procedures and serve your needs.

SELECTING ALREADY DEVELOPED INDEXES AND SCALES

Many of the most commonly measured variables in social research (for example, socioeconomic status) already have corresponding indexes or scales which you might use. In this section, I want to suggest the types of variables likely to have already available scales and discuss how you might find these instruments. But we need to begin with a few definitions.

Definitions: Index, Scale

An *index* is a composite measure developed to represent different components of a concept. It is composed of a set of indicators that have simply been added together. Recall that Hirschi's Index of Delinquency (Chapter 2) was based on six indicators of delinquent acts that were combined into a single measure.

An index is much like a test score that you might receive on a multiple-choice test. Your score (the number of answers you got right) would be easily constructed by adding up your correct answers. This would be your index score. In some cases, your instructor might then average the grades (by adding up all the scores and dividing by the number of students who took the test): this would be the average index score for your class. If the instructor then ordered all the scores from the highest to the lowest, he or she could determine the *median* score (by picking out the score received by the student who was exactly in the middle between highest and lowest). Or the instructor might group scores into grade categories by breaking down the distribution into the highest group (perhaps the top quintile, or 20 percent) who are given A's, the second highest group (the second quintile, from 21 to 40 percent) who are given B's, and so on. These procedures are very similar to the manner in which an index would be constructed and the results would be analyzed.

The difference between an index and a *scale* is that a scale takes into consideration not only how

each item is answered (right or wrong, true or false, liberally or conservatively) but also patterns which the answers present. As an example, let's return to the multiple-choice test. Suppose your instructor wanted to know which question on the test was most often answered correctly (this would be the easiest item) and which question was least often answered correctly (this would be the hardest item). One logical assumption that could be made is that those individuals who answered the hardest question correctly would be more likely to have higher scores on the test as a whole. In other words, answering the hardest question correctly should be an indicator that the person had understood the material better (and possibly studied more) than whether she or he had answered the easiest item correctly.

Assume that the instructor selected five items from the test which had been answered correctly by the following proportions of students: for the first item, 95 percent of the class; for the second, 75 percent of the class; for the third, 50 percent of the class; for the fourth, 25 percent of the class; and for the fifth, 5 percent of the class. (Note that the instructor would not want to pick an item on which everyone answered correctly or incorrectly, because such an item would not be a good differentiating item for any purpose since it would not record any variation.) From these five items, your instructor might want to determine the patterns of answers of those who correctly answered the hardest item, the second hardest item, and so on.

If the material examined on the test represented a cumulative body of knowledge, those who answered the hardest item correctly should have answered the other four easier items correctly; those who answered the hardest item incorrectly but answered the second-hardest item correctly should have the next three correct, and so on. Thus, a comparison of the actual pattern of responses with the expected pattern would tell you whether this was true in this particular case. In such a scale with a cumulative unidimensional structure, knowing the toughest question subsumes knowing the next toughest one. A scale like this is an example of a Guttman Scale. Srole's Anomia

Scale has been shown to be unidimensional and meets the requirements for a Guttman-type scale (refer to Miller, 1991, p. 471). Naturally, not all the respondents would answer questions in the assumed patterned order; the Guttman scaling technique offers a number of tests for determining how far the items you are looking at form an expected pattern.

Your instructor might also decide that the 50-item test was too long and wish to reduce the number of items in the test. This is one of the functions of scales; they enable you to reduce the amount of material asked while retaining the conceptual components of the scale and the ability of the test instrument to differentiate. One way to reduce the number of items would be to get a group of judges to assign level-of-difficulty scores to each of the questions. Suppose the judges were told to assign a 10 to the questions considered to be the hardest, a 9 to the next hardest questions, down to a 1 for the easiest questions. The instructor could then take all the items and see how the judges had rated them. Those items receiving 10s or mostly 10s and 9s would be considered difficult questions. A few of these could then be selected for the shorter test. Then the instructor could look for items assigned 6, 7, or 8; those with the most scores in these categories might be selected as moderately difficult questions. Items scored as 5s might be considered neither difficult nor easy; those scored 3 or 4, moderately easy; those scored 1 or 2, the easiest. Remember that the instructor would select items on the basis of those on which the judges had indicated the most agreement. This procedure is a form of *Thurstone scaling.* A test that selected several questions from each of the five levels of difficulty should provide as good an indicator of the range of students' abilities as the longer test does.

What these two types of scales have in common is that a comparison of the items is made in terms of some factor (their difficulty, for example). This attempt to figure out the patterns which make the best sense of the multiple items and their interrelations—what is referred to as the *intensity structure* of the scale—distinguishes scales from

indexes, which are merely cumulative measures. However, both indexes and scales aim to reduce the number of items needed to represent the full meaning of the underlying abstract variable. This is the rule of *parsimony.*

Scales are very popular in both psychology and sociology. To measure complex psychological qualities, such as authoritarianism, anomie, and alienation, self-report statements cannot often be used (you can't really ask someone, "Do you feel alienated?"). Rather, sets of questions that tap various aspects of these complex measures must be developed. Most complex psychological concepts have been the basis for scales. Using the bibliographical resources discussed in Chapter 3 and looking for the concept name itself (authoritarianism, for example) would lead you to a vast number of references to articles in which this concept was studied. Delbert Miller's *Handbook of Research Design and Social Measurement,* (1991) first published in 1964, has many references to published scales and indexes and examples of these composite measures.

The earliest articles and the titles of articles would tell you where the scale might first have been published. Remember that most scales, if they are popularly used, undergo revisions over time. The revised versions may shorten the scale, may make it more applicable for different types of audiences (for example, children or non-Americans), and may revise anachronistic items. For this reason, a revised version of a scale may serve your purposes better than the original. It is a good rule of thumb not to grab the first scale you find that you think might measure what you want. Instead, use this first scale as a reference point for finding earlier or later versions or for finding scales to which it has been correlated. You will want to examine quite a few scales before making a final decision. Above all, remember that the wording of the items must be appropriate for your population.

Excellent reference sources are available to help you find the right scale or index. Perhaps the most comprehensive is O. K. Buros (ed.), *Eighth Mental Measurements Yearbook* (1978). This reference work has six different types of indexes for finding scales (by name, by scale title, etc.). It briefly describes each scale, outlining its length and the types of factors involved; it suggests appropriate audiences for the scale and gives references to where it can be found. As stated above, another excellent resource is D. C. Miller, *Handbook Research Design and Social Measurement* (1991). There are other reference works that are more specialized, for example, O. G. Johnson (ed.), *Tests and Measurements in Child Development: Handbook II* (1976).

Some volumes offer copies of the scales themselves. These include collections of attitudinal scales, such as Robinson and Shaver, *Measures of Social Psychological Attitudes* (1973), and M. E. Shaw and J. M. Wright, *Scales for the Measurement of Attitudes* (1967). For special types of scales and indexes, you might turn to Robinson et. al., *Measures of Occupational Attitudes and Occupational Characteristics* (1969); Robinson et. al., *Measures of Political Attitudes* (1968); and C. A. Beere, *Women and Women's Issues: A Handbook of Tests and Measures* (1979). Usually you need permission to use a scale, and sometimes there is a charge. It is normally acceptable to shorten a longer scale to meet your purposes, but if you do so, the validation and replication evidence that its authors developed will not apply to your shortened version.

Occupational and Socioeconomic Scales

Occupation is one of the central characteristics of individuals in modern society and it is the primary factor in identifying the social status of individuals. Thus a measure of occupational status is needed in many social research projects. Other factors, such as geographic region, ethnicity, and age, may also be important differentiating factors, but "What do you do?" is the one question in the United States which is most readily asked and is considered the primary measure of one's status. For this reason, the use of occupation as a primary social indicator is widespread. The problem with measuring occupation is that it is a nominal variable with numerous categories which have no inherent order. To be able

to use it to rank individuals, you must place the occupations on a scale in some fashion to denote differences in their qualities.

Two different types of scales or indexes are generally used for this purpose. The first is an *occupational prestige scale,* such as the one developed at the National Opinion Research Center (NORC) by Paul Hatt and Cecil North in 1947 and revised by Robert Hodge, Paul Siegel, and Peter Rossi (1964) or the newer cross-nationally validated occupational prestige scale developed by Donald Treiman, the *Standard Scale* (1977). The other type is a *socioeconomic index* (SEI) based on indicators other than occupational prestige (such as income and educational attainment). The best-known example here is the Duncan Socioeconomic Index (described in detail in Reiss, 1961). We will consider the NORC Prestige Scale, the Treiman Standard Scale, and the Duncan SEI.

Occupational Prestige Scales. The rationale for developing an occupational prestige scale is that individuals conceive of occupations as forming a ranked set of job categories; therefore, to establish such a scale only requires asking a large enough number of individuals to rank occupational titles and forming the composite scores these occupations receive into a scale. The original procedure used by NORC was to give the following statement to the subjects (Reiss, 1961, p. 19):

For each job mentioned, please pick out the statement that best gives *your own personal opinion* of the *general standing* that such a job has.

1. *Excellent* standing.
2. *Good* standing.
3. *Average* standing.
4. *Somewhat below* average standing.
5. *Poor* standing.
X. I don't know where to place that one.

Many subjects were asked to rank the occupations. The ratings from each subject were converted into scores of 5 for "excellent," 4 for "good," and so on. The "don't know" responses were excluded. For

BOX 4-3

RANK-ORDER SCORING FOR THE ORIGINAL NORC OCCUPATIONAL PRESTIGE SCALE

Suppose the title "carpenter" received the following percentages from respondents:

    Excellent = 20%
    Good = 30%
    Average = 20%
    Below average = 15%
    Poor = 15%

Each percentage would be multiplied by the assigned weighted scores, summed together, and then divided by 5:

$$\frac{(20 \times 5) + (30 \times 4) + (20 \times 3) + (15 \times 2) + (15 \times 1)}{5} = 65$$

Thus the occupational prestige score for "carpenter" would be 65. Note that if everyone ranked an occupation as "excellent," the score would be 100 [(100 × 5)/5 = 100]; if everyone rated it "poor," the score would be 20 [(100 × 1)/5 = 20].

each occupational title, the percentage of responses in each of the five categories was multiplied by the assigned score ("excellent" = 5, "good" = 4, etc.). these products were then summed and divided by 5 to yield an average score for each occupation. Box 4-3 shows how this was done.

There was also the issue of which job titles to give respondents to rate. Occupational titles are not easy to select; there are a number of problems. First, there are so many titles it is difficult to make the selection; second, titles may by ambiguous ("engineer" or "supervisor" can refer to a vast array of actual jobs); third, individuals in the society may not use the same terms for each occupation; fourth, the use of titles changes over time. The revised versions of the original NORC Pres-

tige Scales have had to readdress the issue of job titles. When the NORC Prestige Scale was revised in 1963 by Hodge, Siegel, and Rossi, a national sample was asked to rank 90 occupations (1964).

One of the surprising findings of these prestige studies was the degree of agreement among the respondents on the ranking of occupations. Evidence was accumulated over time that people throughout the world rated occupations similarly. Donald J. Treiman (1977) developed an international scale by taking scores from 509 occupational titles (which naturally varied among different languages and within languages between different cultures) in 60 countries where occupational prestige studies had been carried out and converted them into a standard score. This required using a somewhat complicated formula which compared the differences in means and standard deviations (see Chapter 13) of scores for occupations in each country to those in the United States. The result was that each occupational title was given a score between 0 and 100 (Treiman, 1977, pp. 166–167). One quality of Treiman's *Standard Scale* is that unit group categories (those used by the Census Bureau to categorize sets of job titles) are also given scores. This means that if you wanted to score only large categories ("manager" compared to "clerical workers"), you would have a numerical scale to use. Table 4-1 gives these group categories and their corresponding scores.

Duncan SEI. An alternative to an occupational prestige scale is a composite measure based on variables other than the level of prestige attributed to occupations. The most widely used of these scales is the Duncan Socioeconomic Index. This was developed to extend the effort begun in the Hatt-North Occupational Prestige Scale, which had rated only a relatively small number of occupations on the basis of prestige. Otis Dudley Duncan and his associates wanted to scale a much larger number of occupations on the basis of income derived from the occupation and educational attainment normally held by those in the occupational group. The SEI ranges from 1 to 100.

TABLE 4-1

TREIMAN'S STANDARD SCALE[a]

Unit Group Categories	Standard Scale Score
Professional, technical	59
Managers, administrators (except farm)	53
Sales	39
Clerical	42
Craftsmen	39
Operatives (except transport)	32
Transport equipment operatives	30
Laborers (except farm)	21
Farmers and farm managers	41
Farm laborers and farm foremen	24
Service workers (except private household)	29
Private household workers	20

[a]Scores for unit group categories for the 1970 census, detailed occupational classification.
Source: Condensed from Donald J. Treiman, *Occupational Prestige in Comparative Perspective,* Academic Press, New York, 1977, pp. 306–314.

In developing the SEI, stronger weights were given to occupations (measured by income and educational attainment) that had higher prestige scores. In short, the SEI was created in such a way that it would be highly correlated to the NORC Occupational Prestige Scale. The SEI was applied to a very wide range of occupational titles. (For a detailed discussion of how the SEI was developed and how it compares with the North-Hatt Occupational Prestige Scale, see Reiss, 1961.)

Whether you should choose an occupational prestige scale or a socioeconomic index "is not at all obvious," as Treiman states (1977, p. 211). He suggests that a socioeconomic index should be a better measure of occupation if you are using occupation as an indicator of *resources* that might be transmitted intergenerationally or that might be considered beneficial for some other end. Therefore, if you are doing a study of intergenerational mobility (let's say, how sons' careers compare to

their fathers'), the SEI might be preferable. By contrast, occupational prestige seems to be a better indicator of career attainment, since it implies the subjective "rewards" gained by holding an occupation (1977, p. 212). Furthermore, Treiman argues that his scale is useful in the study of employed women, black workers, and other minority groups whereas income differences between these groups and white men makes the SEI a less reliable measure for the former groups (1977, p. 212). Naturally, if you are using cross-national data, Treiman's Standard Scale is preferable, since it was built from a large set of studies from 60 different nations.

How useful a scale or index might be for your project will naturally depend on what you are planning to do. Social researchers vary in terms of the types of scales they are likely to use. Some of the differences in usage have to do with which branch of the social sciences one is working in—social psychologists are particularly fond of personality scales; sociological survey researchers almost always use occupational status scales. You should carefully consider what you are trying to measure in your study and decide whether a composite instrument would help you achieve your goals. Remember that if you use an already constructed scale or index, evidence will be available concerning the validity and reliability of the scale. If you develop your own index or scale, you will have the creative experience of developing a measuring instrument of your own.

REVIEW NOTES

- The measurement of concepts is a major challenge in social research. It proceeds from defining terms, to developing operational definitions, to preparing instruments which can measure the variation in the concept.
- Social research concepts can be commonplace or very abstract. They can have one or many dimensions. Single or multiple indictors of these dimensions need to be isolated in order to de-

velop an effective instrument to measure the full domain of the concept.

- Measurement involves assigning numbers according to rules of correspondence between definitions and observations.
- The validity of a measure is determined by tests of correspondence between the concepts underlying the measure and the empirical indicators. Content validity, criterion-related validity, and construct validity offer different means for assessing this correspondence.
- The reliability of a measure is determined by whether repeated measuring procedures produce similar results.
- The measurement of categorical variables assigns numbers to distinct categories that must be mutually exclusive of one another and exhaustive of the range of possible meaning. The numbers assigned carry no mathematical significance.
- Numerical variables assign numbers to units which have mathematical meaning. These numerical scales may represent discrete data based on whole numbers (e.g., number of children) or continuous data which have a continuous range of values (e.g., weight).
- Variables are classified according to four commonly defined levels of measurement: nominal, for distinct categories with no order; ordinal, for ordered categories; interval, for numerical scales with mathematically defined intervals between points on the scale but no true zero point; and ratio, for numerical scales with mathematically defined intervals and a true zero point.
- An index is a composite of indicators to measure a complex concept. The cumulative score on the indicators serves as the index score.
- A scale is a measurement instrument based on a set of indicators which have certain interrelationships to one another. These internal interrelationships are referred to as the intensity structure of the scale.

KEY TERMS

bar graph
categorical variables
classical test theory
concurrent validity
construct validity
content validity
continuous variables
criterion-related validity
dimensions
discrete variables
exhaustive categories
face validity
frequency polygon
histogram
index
indicators
interval level of measurement
measurement error
mutually exclusive categories
nominal definition
nominal level of measurement
numerical variables
operational definition
operationalization
ordinal level of measurement
predictive validity
random measurement error
ratio level of measurement
real definition
reliability
sampling validity
scale
validity

STUDY EXERCISES

1. Consider the concept of educational aspirations (which is different from educational attainment).
   a. Give a nominal definition of this concept.
   b. Now develop an operational definition of this concept.
      (1) Determine how many dimensions it has and what they are.

(2) Develop an indicator for each dimension.

(3) Turn the indicators into a variable which can measure the concept.

2. Consider the educational aspirations variable.

   a. How could you determine its criterion-related validity?

   b. How might you set up a test of predictive validity?

3. Give one example of a variable common in social research that would be measured at the nominal, ordinal, interval, and ratio levels. (You might consider the variables presented in the surveys or the experiments described in Chapter 1.)

4. Find one already created scale in the research literature. Briefly describe it and present evidence of its validity. In what kind of study might you want to include this scale?

RECOMMENDED READINGS

1. Allen, Mary J., and Wendy M. Yen: *Introduction to Measurement Theory,* Belmont, CA: Wadsworth, 1979. The authors describe this textbook as an attempt to bridge the gap between a "cookbook" on measurement and a mathematically rigorous discussion of measurement theory. It can be quite easily followed by readers with some mathematical background.

2. Burgess, Robert G. (ed.): *Key Variables in Social Investigation,* London: Routledge & Kegan Paul, 1986. Essays on 10 commonly used variables, reviewing their underlying concepts and how they have been operationalized.

3. Carmines, E., and R. Zeller: *Reliability and Validity Assessment,* Beverly Hills, CA: Sage, 1979. A brief and clear presentation of the meaning of and tests of reliability and validity; an explanation of classical test theory.

4. Hoover, Kenneth R.: *The Elements of Social Scientific Thinking,* 5th ed., New York: St. Martin's, 1992. This highly readable book has an excellent discussion of levels of measurement.

5. Miller, Delbert C.: *Handbook of Research Design and Social Measurement,* 5th ed., Thousand Oaks, CA: Sage, 1991. This work is a good introduction to modern research scales with reference lists and information on where to obtain scales.

CHAPTER 5

Sampling

INTRODUCTION

S ampling refers to planned ways of selecting subjects. Since most social research is based on studies of people, sampling generally refers to the simple question, Which people are going to be studied? Thus, to draw a sample of individuals is to determine *who* will be studied. Of course, many social research projects focus on organizations, programs, or other aggregates of individuals in formal or informal groups. In the study of groups, the question becomes not who but *which*. Social research also may have as its subjects things, that is, cultural artifacts (such as films and diaries). In the study of things, the question posed is, *what* things will be studied? But whatever the unit of analysis, the focus in sampling is on the selection of the "units" to be studied. As you will see throughout the next set of chapters on different methods of social research, some research methods utilize certain types of sampling while other methods more commonly use other forms.

In this chapter we will first address the general question of why social researchers need to sample by considering how sampling helps achieve representativeness and reduce bias. Next we will examine how probability samples enable a researcher to make inferences about the broader population from which a sample is drawn and will show how accurate the preelection polls of 1996 were in predicting the actual voting results in November 1996. Then we will consider how a researcher can determine the necessity and feasibility of sampling by estimating the level of potential resources available, the homogeneity of the subjects being studied, and the types of analyses that are being planned. These considerations help determine whether a researcher decides to carry out a probability sample or a nonprobability sample.

We will first describe different types of nonprobability samples. Hochschild's study of two-job couples (see Chapter 1) will be offered as an example of a purposive nonprobability sample. Our discussion of probability samples will begin with a careful consideration of how probability sampling works: (1) how increases in sample size affect the representativeness of measures from a sample, (2) how a sampling distribution mean (the average mean from a series of samples drawn from the same population) comes to approximate the normal curve, and (3) how the normal curve enables researchers to make inferences from a measure based on one sample (e.g., mean age of the sample) to the same measure from the broader population from which the sample was drawn.

Next we will address the issue faced by all researchers: How large does a sample need to be? After considering how probability sampling depends on the ability to establish an enumeration of the population (a sampling frame), we will present the steps required in carrying out different types of probability sample designs. Examples of actual probability samples designs, such as the one used for the sexual survey described in Chapter 1, will be presented. This chapter will close with a review of the considerations you will need to recognize in designing a sample to meet the needs of the study you may be carrying out.

WHY SAMPLE?

There are two major goals that sampling can achieve: The first is to establish the *representativeness* of what we are studying and, conversely, to *reduce bias;* the second is to be able to *make inferences* from findings based on a sample to the larger population from which that sample was drawn.

Achieving Representativeness and Reducing Bias

One of the major principles of sampling—that choice be based on *representativeness*—goes to the heart of the issue of why to sample at all. The purpose of social research, as well as its general value as an activity, is that it helps bring about a stronger understanding of the social world in which we live. To do this, it is important that what is studied represent something greater than itself. We are interested in the findings of the survey on sexual behavior precisely because they purportedly represent the behaviors of nearly all adult Americans. By contrast, Arlie Hochschild's interview study was based on a nonprobability sample of 50 couples in California's Bay Area who were selected so that they represented the experiences of a broad range of two-job couples with preschool-age children.

In different types of survey research, sampling takes on different forms. Probability samples select subjects from a larger universe of possible subjects (the population), and this allows the evidence from the sample to be representative of the whole population. In content analysis (see Chapter 9), the researcher needs a method for selecting materials to analyze that will fairly represent the range of content that is being examined. In field research (see Chapter 8), the subjects to be studied are selected on the grounds that they should be representative of a greater whole which is of interest to the researcher.

Consider Barrie Thorne's selection of two elementary schools (from two different parts of the country) and of a range of children within those schools to study (from different grades, of different sexes, of different types). Clearly these children were selected as representative of a range of American children of grade school age. Consider Elijah Anderson's study of two Philadelphia neighborhoods. Those particular neighborhoods were representative of two types of neighborhoods common in many American cities: one a poor neighborhood with few resources and the other an adjacent neighborhood which was more socially and racially integrated and had been undergoing a process of renewal and gentrification. Similar neighborhoods could have been chosen in Chicago, Atlanta, Los Angeles, or Boston.

The converse of maximizing representativeness is reducing or *avoiding bias*. What this means is that the researcher must select subjects and observe them in a way that will not bias the findings. Recall that in the observational studies of Thorne and Anderson, a range of subjects were observed and the researchers stressed that there were variations in the ways in which individuals in those settings responded to their social conditions. In psychological experiments, a researcher can assume that as human beings, all human subjects have potentially the same range of behavioral reactions. Thus, probability sampling is not a major concern to an experimenter. However, to see if the experimental stimulus leads to an effect, the experiment usually needs a control group that is not subject to the experiment. Also, the experimenter needs to make sure that there is no bias in the distribution of subjects between the groups, and so randomization is used in assigning subjects to either the experimental group or the control group (this is referred to as the *random assignment* of subjects to groups). Recall Sherman and Berk's efforts in the Minneapolis domestic violence experiment in which police officers were to randomly administer a "treatment" (an arrest or another response) to suspects. In this way, the suspects were being assigned randomly to an experimental group (those getting arrested) or to a control group. Random assignment, which will be discussed in Chapter 6 on experiments, is the method used in experimental design to *avoid bias*.

Making Inferences

If the sample selected has been drawn according to rules of probability (which means that every member of the population has a known probability of being selected into the sample), the researcher can make *inferences* from the findings on the sample to the broader population from which the sample was drawn. Drawing inferences to a broader population is the primary goal of *probability sampling*. In fact, the main reason for doing probability sampling is to be able to make inferences on the basis of evidence from one sample to the whole population from which the sample was drawn. This ability to make inferences from a sample to a much broader population means that the findings from a sample of a limited size (which therefore costs less in terms of both time and money to carry out) can be used to predict what the findings would have been for the whole population. From the measures of a probability sample (the sample statistics), the probable measures from the population (the population parameters) from which the sample was drawn can be inferred. This is what makes probability sampling so powerful a method.

The clearest evidence we have of how accurately probability sample statistics can predict measures from a broader population are the election polls which precede elections. Box 5-1 describes how effectively the preelection polls of different samples of likely American voters predicted the actual presidential election in November 1996. As you can see from this example, the craft of drawing probability samples has been so finely developed that evidence from these samples can be used to predict future outcomes very precisely.

Determining the Necessity and Feasibility of Sampling

There are three major considerations in making decisions about sampling:

1. *What are your limitations in terms of resources?* Clearly costs will affect the type of sample one can design. Note that studying everyone in a population would reduce the need to develop a sample but would expand the effort at data collection. Thus one of the main reasons for sampling is to serve as a way to contain costs. Since complex sample designs are costly to plan and implement, a researcher sometimes may have to go ahead with a sample design that is somewhat less favorable than would be desired because of limitations in funding. (This was exactly the case for the Laumann team when it was unable to get federal government support for its sexuality survey.)

BOX 5-1

THE 1996 PREELECTION PRESIDENTIAL POLLS

Polling before American presidential elections has gained momentum in the 50 years since early polling organizations wrongly predicted that Thomas Dewey would defeat Harry Truman in 1948. In the few days preceding the presidential election of November 1996, two polling organizations, Gallup (for CNN and USA Today) and ABC News, which had tracked "likely voters" every day for the month preceding the election, came up with the following results on the two days (Sunday and Monday) before the Tuesday election:

	Clinton, %	Dole, %	Perot, %	Undecided, %	Error Margin, %
Gallup	48	40	6	6	±2.5
ABC	51	39	7	3	±4.5
Actual vote	**49**	**41**	**8**	**2 (other candidates)**	

The Gallup poll included 1,448 likely voters. Its findings with a 2.5 percent error margin meant it was within range of the final outcome. This is also true of the ABC poll, which had surveyed 703 likely voters (a smaller sample) and thus had a larger error margin. It too was within range of the final outcome, though note that ABC predicted a 12-point spread between Clinton and Dole whereas the actual spread was only 8 percentage points. Nevertheless, these polls of relatively small numbers of likely voters generated very accurate estimates of the actual vote.

2. How similar or different are the subjects you will be studying? If the subjects in a study are very similar to each other (*homogeneous* in background), they may tend to be more representative of each other in a number of other ways so that a smaller and less complex sample design may serve you well. However, if the subjects are *heterogeneous,* you may need to have a sample design that captures representatives from the different types of subjects in the population. Note that in terms of analyzing the data, you may need sufficient numbers in a subgroup to carry out the types of analyses you desire (recall that the sexuality survey oversampled Hispanics and African-Americans to enable researchers to analyze evidence from those subgroups).

3. *What types of analyses are you planning to carry out once the data have been collected?* If you plan to study many different variables in your analysis, you may need a larger sample that is designed to get sufficient variation within those variables. If you plan to focus on a particular group in your analysis, you will need to be sure that your sample includes enough representatives from that group. Recall that one of the types of analyses that the sexuality survey team envisioned was a study of the sexual behavior of homosexual men. However, the sample design they ultimately had to settle for did not allow them to focus specifically on that group. If you want to be able to make inferences to a larger population, you must employ a probability design for your sample, because a nonprobability sample will not allow you to make statistically valid inferences to a broader population.

Probability or Nonprobability Samples

For the rest of this chapter we will consider the characteristics and designs of these two classes of samples. As we have said, only a probability sample allows a researcher to make statistical inferences to a broader population. However, many

very fine studies do not require that this be an aim of the research. Recall the Hochschild study of two-career couples. Her sample was a purposive nonprobability sample. This meant that the findings of her study could *not* be used with powerful statistical tests and that the results of her study could *not* be inferred as representative of evidence from other two-job couples. However, her sample did include couples from a range of backgrounds, and so it is likely that the evidence from her study was characteristic of many couples beyond her sample. Naturally, the costs of the Hochschild study were far lower and required much less formal funding than did the sample design used in the national study of sexuality.

The National Health and Social Life Survey (NHSLS) carried out for the sexuality study was based on a probability sample in that every member of the defined population had a known probability of being selected into the sample. In this way the researchers could infer that their evidence represented the behaviors and attitudes of the other members of the broader population who had not been surveyed. This allowed the use of very advanced forms of statistical tests to indicate relationships within the study. We will turn first to a careful consideration of the designs of nonprobability samples and then to probability samples.

NONPROBABILITY SAMPLING DESIGNS

In many instances probability sampling is simply not feasible. A sample that does not follow the rules of probability sampling is a *nonprobability sample*. Although many statistical tests require probability sampling, in certain cases nonprobability samples are the best that can be achieved. It is important that you understand whether you can select a probability sample and that if you cannot, you consider the best means for developing and explaining a nonprobability sample. Many groups may be interesting to study, but for various reasons no sampling frame can ever be developed for them. Imagine that you want to do a study of pros- titutes. Certainly there is no list available (or un- available) of individuals who engage in prostitu- tion. However, you might be able to draw together a sample useful for your purposes by using a form of nonprobability sampling.

The rationale for using nonprobability sam- pling is that it is the best form of sampling that can be used for the study you are designing. While a study based on a nonprobability sample has disad- vantages (especially the fact that its findings can- not be generalized to a definable wider popula- tion), it nevertheless can be an excellent way to study a particular sample of interest. Nonprobabil- ity samples often are used for pretests of large sur- veys where the cost and effort of selecting a prob- ability sample may be considered unnecessary for the purposes of the pretest.

Nonprobability sampling also may be used ef- fectively in studies that seek to explore ideas that are still undeveloped. In such exploratory studies, the object may be to generate theories or hypothe- ses that might then be studied using a probability sample. Here a few commonly employed types of nonprobability samples will be described.

Convenience Sampling

Assuming that you have little access to a sample of prostitutes, you might change your design and try to study attitudes toward prostitution. Now it would seem to be easy to find a sample of respon- dents prepared to give you answers to such a study. (You could, of course, design a probability sample and include in your survey a question on attitudes toward prostitution.)

But let's assume that you need your informa- tion quickly, so that designing a probability sam- ple is out of the question. In other words, you need "warm bodies" willing to answer your questions without too much hassle. However, you don't want to build a sample from your friends who are likely to share similar views to yours. It is impor- tant to gather opinions that will be representative

of the range of people being sampled. If you de- cide to sample students on your campus, select a spot where many students are likely to pass by. On my campus, this would be the central plaza area that all students cross from the parking lots to the classroom buildings. Then if you interview a range of students who pass by (possibly at different hours to increase the representativeness of stu- dents with diverse schedules), you will have a *convenience sample.* A college instructor who asks a college class to complete a survey for his or her research is using a convenience sample. A *convenience sample* is merely an available sample which appears able to offer answers of interest to your study.

Naturally, a convenience sample cannot be composed of just anyone. It would probably not be a good idea to stand on a street corner, stop people walking down the street, and survey them on their attitudes toward prostitution. Many would feel that the answers to such questions are too sensitive to be given to a stranger on a street corner. In other words, it is always better to con- sider carefully whether the people you plan to use as respondents are likely to comply with your request and give careful consideration to your questions.

Purposive or Judgmental Sampling

Assuming that you are still trying to do the study on prostitutes, you might decide to go to a certain street or a particular bar and try to interview per- sons who seemed to you to exemplify the typical prostitute. This form of sampling generally con- siders the most common characteristics of the type it is desired to sample, tries to figure out where such individuals can be found, and then tries to study them. Another method is to look for untypi- cal, or deviant, individuals. Responses from un- typical respondents allow a comparison with typi- cal cases. A *purposive sample* is a form of nonprobability sample in which the subjects se- lected seem to meet the study's needs.

A student of mine once wanted to study the characteristics of Beatles fans. Although many individuals fit this description, the problem is to know where to find them. The student came up with a good strategy. A national Beatles fan conference was going to be held. He went off to this conference armed with 250 questionnaires and found a ready set of respondents. Although this sample would not represent the *average* Beatle fan, it would be a group highly motivated to respond to this survey.

Box 5-2 describes the purposive sample Arlie Hochschild designed for the study of two-career couples.

Quota Sampling

Quota sampling is a form of nonprobability sampling that often is mistaken for stratified probability sampling. This occurs because there is an attempt to select certain-sized subsamples from clearly defined groups. The difference is that in quota sampling, sampling frames from which to select the sample are not set up. Rather, the groups are defined and the sizes are specified, and then individuals who fit those descriptions are selected to fill the quotas wherever they can be found. Hence, *quota samples* are nonprobability samples in which subsamples are selected from clearly defined groups.

Quota sampling generally begins by setting up a matrix of the characteristics desired: sex, age, race, and so on. Let's say you want to do a survey of the student body at your university to find out whether students would prefer to change to a trimester system (or, if you are already on one, to a semester system). You recognize that such opinions might vary for those in different colleges, for those in different years in college, for those with (or without) jobs off campus, and so forth. You would begin by trying to get from the administration the percentages of students (1) in each college, (2) in each year, (3) who work off campus. Let's say that you find out that 65 percent of the students are in arts and sciences and 35 percent are in business. Considering the next

variable, you find out that 30 percent are first-year students, 20 percent are sophomores, 25 percent are juniors, and 25 percent are seniors. Considering the third variable, you discover that 40 percent work off campus and 60 percent do not. Now you decide to get a sample of 100 students. Of these 100, 65 should be from arts and sciences and 35 from business; there should be 30 first-year students, 20 sophomores, 25 juniors, and 25 seniors; 40 should work off campus. Be sure to remember that these divisions overlap. Thus, of the 65 arts and sciences students selected, 35 percent should be first-year students, 20 percent sophomores, etc., and 40 percent should be employed off campus. By setting up a matrix, as seen in Table 5-1, you can set out all the various subgroups you need.

The procedure for quota sampling, once the quota sizes have been determined, is simply to go out and fill the quotas. Since you see in the matrix that you need 5.2 (5) sophomores who are arts and sciences students and work off campus, you merely seek out 5 such students. You do the same for the 7.8 (8) sophomores who are arts and sciences students and do not work off campus. Note that you figured the first-mentioned quota by multiplying the 65 arts and sciences students by .40 (40 percent work off campus), which equals 26, then multiplying these 26 off-campus workers by .20 (20 percent sophomores), which equals 5.2, and rounding to 5.

Don't be fooled into thinking that this will get you a probability sample. We have mentioned the famous polling error made at the time of the 1948 election by the Gallup organization, which predicted a victory for Thomas Dewey over Harry Truman. That poll was based on quota sampling. Because the subgroups are not selected from sampling frames representing the population of all members of the subgroup, the selected subgroups do not establish a known probability of every member in the subgroups being included in the sample. This means that the selection of cases within the quota groups can be biased. As a result, you cannot make valid inferences to a wider population from a quota sample.

BOX 5-2

THE SAMPLING DESIGN FOR *THE SECOND SHIFT*

Arlie Hochschild's study of two-career couples was based on a set of interviews she and Anne Machung (with the help of a few others) carried out in the Bay Area in California. The final sample included 50 two-job couples (that is, 100 individuals) and 45 others, including "babysitters, daycare workers, school teachers, traditional couples with small children (in which the wife was not working), and divorcees who had been in two-job couples" (*The Second Shift*, 1989, p. 280). In addition, Hochschild selected 12 of the 50 couples to be interviewed and observed more intensively by visiting their homes and having meals with them and by accompanying them to outings, shopping, or day care centers to gain a more in-depth understanding of how they handled their daily lives.

How were these people selected? Hochschild explains that she and her associates began to interview two-job couples in the 1970s in Berkeley, California, who were mostly professors, artisans, or university students. On the basis of those early interviews, Hochschild decided that for a larger study it would be preferable to get a sample more representative of "mainstream" America, and so in 1980 she acquired a personnel roster from a large manufacturing company in the Bay Area. From this list, she selected every thirteenth name and sent a brief questionnaire about home and work. Fifty-three percent of those who were sent the questionnaires returned them. At the end of the questionnaire, requests for more intensive interviews were made to those who were members of a two-job couple with one or more children under age 6. To expand the sample of two-job couples, additional names of similar couples among the friends and neighbors of those who were interviewed were added to the sample. The 12 couples chosen for the more intensive interviews represented the range of gender ideologies (traditional, transitional, and egalitarian) that Hochschild had de-

lineated from her analyses as well as differences in ethnicity and family income.

This *purposive* sample was designed to meet the criteria which the researchers believed were necessary to carry out the study. It did not try to be representative of all two-job couples with young children in the United States or even in California or the Bay Area (this would have required a probability sampling design). Nevertheless, Hochschild was seeking *representativeness* by using a random method to select names from among the employees of a large manufacturing company. She knew that the jobs of these employees would include blue-collar and white-collar jobs and unskilled, semiskilled, professional, and managerial jobs. She also expanded her first sample by requesting names of other two-job couples from those who had been selected (that is, she used *snowball sampling* techniques, which will be discussed below), in which the sample is increased by asking those with specific characteristics if they can offer the names of others with the same characteristics). Moreover, she selected from the first sample studied a subsample of subjects to be considered more intensively.

To gain a better appreciation of the qualities of her sample, Hochschild presented aggregate data on the characteristics of her sample in the appendix (1989, pp. 280–281). She also offered evidence from other studies on two-job couples which were based on different sample designs (including probability samples). Thus Hochschild makes a case for the representativeness of her sample by explaining her sampling methods, describing the characteristics of her sample members, and comparing her findings from a relatively small purposive sample to those of studies based on larger and, in some cases, probability samples representative of specifically defined populations.

Source: Hochschild, 1989, pp. 4–6, 277–284.

TABLE 5-1

MATRIX FOR A QUOTA SAMPLE OF COLLEGE STUDENTS

Year in College		College of Arts and Sciences Students (65%: N = 65)		College of Business Students (35%: N = 35)		Total N
		Work (40%)	Do Not Work (60%)	Work (40%)	Do Not Work (60%)	
First year	30%	7.8 (8)[a]	11.7 (12)	4.2 (4)	6.3 (6)	30
Sophomore	20%	5.2 (5)	7.8 (8)	2.8 (3)	4.2 (4)	20
Junior	25%	6.5 (7)	9.75 (9)	3.5 (4)	5.25 (5)	25
Senior	25%	6.5 (6)	9.75 (10)	3.5 (3)	5.25 (6)	25
Total N	100%	26	39	14	21	100

[a]Rounded numbers in parentheses designate the actual numbers to be sampled. They must sometimes be rounded up or down to produce the needed row and column totals.

Snowball Sampling

In snowball sampling, you first find a few subjects who are characterized by the qualities you seek, interview them, and then ask them for names of other people whom they know who have the same qualities or other qualities that interest you. In this manner, you accumulate more and more respondents by using each respondent you get as a source of new names for your sample. A *snowball sample* is built from the subjects suggested by previous subjects.

This approach might be a way to select subjects for the prostitution study. If you were able to find a few prostitutes willing to talk to you, you might ask them for the names and locations of others they know who also might be willing to be interviewed. Sampling of this type has often been done in studies of elite groups, either those in power in a community or members of the upper classes. In community studies, there has often been the sense that only those in power really know who else has power. Because there is no sampling frame listing all those who are powerful (as there would be a listing of all those who hold office), a snowball sampling technique might lead you from one power holder to another.

HOW PROBABILITY SAMPLING WORKS

To show why it is the case that probability sampling leads to samples that are representative of the population from which they are drawn, I've developed an example from an actual study. In the fall of 1996, before the 1996 presidential election, my research methods class (SOC360) at California State University at San Marcos designed a survey of registered voters in North County San Diego, the area in which the town of San Marcos is located. The survey would be carried out at our social research center [the Social and Behavioral Research Institute (SBRI)], which has a computer-assisted telephone interviewing (CATI) system (to be explained in greater detail in Chapter 7).

First, we got a computerized list of registered voters from a particular supervisory district in North County San Diego, which for this example will serve as our population. It included 4,819 names and telephone numbers of registered voters. In addition, the "list" included two other pieces of information: the voters' political party affiliations and the voters' birth dates.

For the purposes of this example, we will call this "list" of 4,819 names our *sampling frame*. A *sampling frame* is a list of all units or elements in a population. The names on the list will represent our *population* composed of 4,819 units. Thus a *population* is the collection of all the units or elements (either known or unknown) from which a sample is drawn. Because we had the age data of all the members of the population, we could compute a mean age for the population. This population mean age serves as a *population parameter,* which is the value of a *sample statistic* which has been computed for a whole population. This means that a *population parameter* represents the true values of a population's characteristics, which often may be inferred only from the descriptions of those values (that is, the statistics) in a sample. If the sample drawn is a probability sample the statistics (which are summary descriptions of data from the sample) can be used to estimate the corresponding population parameters. In this case, the statistics are inferential statistics. The population parameter (that is, the mean age of the population of North County registered voters)

equaled 47.06 years, the variance was 347.06, and the standard deviation equaled 18.63.

If you would like to refresh your memory of how means, variances and standard deviations are computed, refer to Box 5-3. The age values in the population ranged from 18 (the minimum age for voting) to 100 years of age (the age of the oldest member of the population). This meant that the range was 82 years.

Probability sampling uses a "random" system of selection so that every person in the sampling frame list has a known probability of being selected into the sample. Probability sampling in which every unit in the population has an equal chance of being selected is called EPSEM (equal probability of selection method). This is the kind of probability sampling that will be used in these examples. Since this exercise was being done on a computer, the computer would make the "random" selections from the computerized file of telephone numbers of the registered voters.

BOX 5-3

COMPUTING A MEAN, VARIANCE, AND STANDARD DEVIATION

Let's suppose that we were computing a mean age of 10 registered voters whose ages are 18, 27, 28, 36, 45, 54, 63, 64, 72, and 81. We would add up the 10 ages and divide by 10 to get the mean age:

$$18 + 27 + 28 + 36 + 45 + 54$$
$$+ 63 + 64 + 72 + 81 = 488$$
$$488/10 = 28.8$$
Mean age of sample = 48.8 years

To compute the variance, you need to subtract each of the 10 ages in the sample from the mean age, square the differences, and add up the squared differences and then divide by 10 (the sample size):

$$[(18 - 48.8)^2 + (27 - 48.8)^2 + (28 - 48.8)^2$$
$$+ (36 - 48.8)^2 + (45 - 48.8)^2 + (54 - 48.8)^2$$

$$+ (63 - 48.8)^2 + 64 - 48.8)^2 + (72 - 48.8)^2$$
$$+ (81 - 48.8)^2]/10 = 40.696$$
Variance = 40.696
Standard deviation = square root of variance
Standard deviation (SD) = 6.379
SD = 6.4

So what we know is that the average (or mean) age of the voters in this sample of 10 was 48.8 years and that the standard deviation was 6.4. What the standard deviation describes is the degree of dispersion (or distance) of all the values from the mean value. Thus the larger the SD, the more spread out the range of values is from the mean value, and the smaller the SD, the closer the range of values is to the mean value. Thus the SD tells you how representative your mean is of the range of values in your sample.

What we want to do in this example is explore three issues:

1. Is the mean age of voters from a probability sample randomly drawn from the population similar to the mean age of the population? This question asks whether the summary information based on a probability sample is representative of the information which would have been gathered from the whole population. We will address the question: How close is a sample mean to its population mean?

2. If we increase (or decrease) the size of the probability sample, would the mean age from the sample get closer (or farther from) the mean age of the population? If differences in sample size affect sampling error, large samples should have smaller sampling errors (which are based on the difference between a sampling statistic and a population parameter). This question asks whether larger samples are more representative of the populations from which they are drawn than are smaller samples. We will address the question: How do differences in sample size affect sampling error?

3. The principles of probability are based on the logic of repeated measures: If repeated samples are drawn from a population and the means from each sample are averaged across all the samples drawn (so that you create a *mean of the sampling distribution means*) will this mean of means get closer to the population mean? This question asks whether combining statistics from repeated probability samples will produce a sampling distribution mean closer to the population mean. We will address the question: Would a sampling distribution mean be closer to the population mean than a mean from a single sample?

How Close Is a Sample Mean (a Statistic) to Its Population Mean (a Parameter)?

What we are doing here is seeing how close the mean age of a probability sample of a particular size drawn from this population of 4,819 will be to

the actual mean age of the population. The first sample drawn included 50 voters. When the mean of the ages of those 50 voters was determined, it turned out to be 49.46 (turn to Table 5.2). Recall that the mean age of the population was 47.06; thus, this mean age from the sample of 50 was 2.4 years older than the population mean. The minimum age of a person drawn into this sample of 50 was 20 years, and the maximum age was 88 years, giving a range of 68 years, and the standard deviation for the sample of 50 was 20.97.

This difference of 2.4 years in mean age between the sample mean (the *sample statistic*) and the population mean (or the *population parameter*) is called the *sampling error*. The *sampling error* represents the variability of a mean in a probability sample from the mean of the population. This sampling error is *not* the result of mistakes made in the sampling procedures; instead, it represents the variability of the sample from the population. As a result, all samples will have some sampling error (though it is conceivable that a sample could produce exactly the same mean as the population).

Sampling errors must be distinguished from *nonsampling errors,* which are due to other types of mistakes that may be made in a sampling procedure. If in the study described the ages of the voters had been given falsely or entered incorrectly or if there had been other mistakes in the way the sample was drawn or the data were gathered, these would be nonsampling errors. Often in survey research, nonresponse is a major source of nonsampling error which can introduce bias into the results of a study. Nonsampling errors are ones that the researcher might cause, and therefore they are errors which a researcher must try to eliminate. Conversely, sampling errors are errors that naturally occur as a result of the variability of any sample from the population from which it has been drawn.

How Differences in Sample Size Affect Sampling Error

If a sample of 50 would produce a sampling error of 2.4, what would happen if we doubled the size of the sample? Would the sampling error get even smaller? A new sample of 100 was drawn, and the average age of this sample was determined. This turned out to be 45.99, which was 1.07 years below the population mean age, indicating a somewhat smaller sampling error than occurred in the sample of 50. Note as well that for this sample of 100, the minimum age dropped to 19 but the maximum age dropped to 86, giving a range of 67 years. The standard deviation fell slightly to 18.81.

Maybe it was the case that the larger the sample size, the smaller the sampling error. To test this more fully, I drew a very large sample of 500, which in a population of 4,816 would represent one sample member for (roughly) every nine population members. This time the sample mean equaled 45.89 (which gave a slightly larger sampling error of 1.17 than we had produced from a sample of 100 in size). Clearly the very large sample of 500 had not reduced the sampling error. However, the maximum age came to equal the population maximum of 100, though the minimum age was 20, giving a range of 80 years. The standard deviation dropped a little (from 18.81 for the sample of 100 to 18.55 for the sample of 500).

If the sampling error had not dropped for a large sample of 500 workers, would it make much difference if I had drawn a very small sample, say, of only 5 voters? To test this notion, I drew a sample of only five people from the population. When I determined the mean age of the sample of five, it equaled 59.20 (which was 12.14 years above the population mean). Here we see that with such a small sample size, ($N = 5$), the sampling error increased substantially. Moreover the minimum age drawn into the sample was 29 and the maximum age was only 81, giving a much smaller range of 52 years. The standard deviation was 22.12, slightly larger than any of the standard deviations in the earlier samples. Clearly this sample of five did not produce a very representative mean age. But we must note that it was possible that a very small sample of five could have produced a very tiny sampling error if, by chance, the five voters selected had been of ages very close to the population mean age. However, the odds of selecting voters close to the population mean age would be lower if we only selected five voters than it would be if we selected 50 or 100 or 500. Table 5-2 presents all the statistics from the four different-sized single samples drawn. Let's briefly go over what these numbers represent. In the top row, which refers to the sample size of 50, the mean age for this sample is 49.46 and the standard deviation is 20.97. (Please refer back to Box 5-3 if you need to refresh your memory on how means and standard deviations are computed.) The minimum refers to the youngest age (20 years old) of any of those in the sample of 50, the maximum refers to the oldest age (88 years old) of any of those in the sample of 50, and the range refers to the difference between the maximum and minimum ($88 - 20 = 68$). You can see how the standard deviations decreased as the sample sizes increased, and you can see that the range of values increased as the sample size increased.

Keep in mind that the examples shown here only illustrate how sampling size affects sampling error

TABLE 5-2

DESCRIPTIVE STATISTICS (MEAN AGE) FROM FOUR SAMPLES
(of Different Sizes: $N = 50$, $N = 100$, $N = 500$, $N = 5$)

Sampling Size, N	Mean Age	Standard Deviation	Minimum	Maximum	Range
50	49.46	20.97	20	88	68
100	45.99	18.81	19	86	67
500	45.89	18.55	20	100	80
5	59.20	22.12	29	81	52

using single samples of different sizes. Figure 5-1 depicts how the statistic of the mean age from the four probability samples varied from the population parameter (the mean age of the population). Clearly, the smallest sample ($N = 5$) had a substantial sampling error and both of the large samples ($N = 100$ and $N = 500$) produced quite small sampling errors. Therefore, it seems to be the case that larger samples tend to produce statistics (such as the mean) that are closer to the parameters of the population from which they are drawn than do smaller samples. However, very large samples may not be much more representative than fairly large samples.

Would a Sampling Distribution Mean Be Closer to the Population Mean than a Mean from a Single Sample?

This leads me to the third question, What would I learn from drawing repeated samples? Note that in actual practice the researcher generally draws only one sample. However, if I were to draw 50 samples of the same size and determine the mean age from each of those samples and then average those means (that is, take the mean of the means, which is called the mean of the sampling distribution or the *sampling distribution mean*) would I get a mean that was closer to the population mean? This sampling distribution mean is the mean of the means from repeated probability samples drawn from the same population. It seems logical that if probability sampling operates on a random principle, the more random samples you would draw to estimate their sample means, the closer the aver-

age of those sample means (the sampling distribution statistic) would become to the actual mean of the population (the population parameter) from which all the samples were drawn. Let's see if this is the case and whether the case becomes stronger if the samples drawn are larger in size.

I started by having the computer draw 50 samples, each with 50 voters. Figure 5-2 presents a histogram of the mean ages from each of the 50 samples of 50. (You may want to refer back to Chapter 4 for the presentation and discussion of histograms.) Note that the horizontal axis represents the mean ages and the vertical axis represents the number of samples that produced different-sized means. Figure 5-2 reports a sampling distribution mean of 46.82 with a standard deviation of 2.55 (presented at the top of the histogram), and this can be compared to the population mean of 47.06 (presented at the bottom of the histogram).

What we see in Figure 5-2 is that many of the samples had means that were close to the population mean but that a few had means that were quite far from the population mean. The minimum mean (that is, the "lowest" mean) was 41.68 years, and the maximum mean (the "highest" mean) was 53.38 years, which gave a range of 11.7 years. Clearly, the effects of repeatedly drawing samples was to produce more samples whose mean age (the statistic) was closer to the population mean age (the parameter).

Now let's explore how the sample means would be distributed if the sample size were doubled, that is, $N = 100$. Figure 5-3 shows a histogram for 50 samples drawn with a sample size

47.06 (population mean)

FIGURE 5-1
Comparing mean ages from single samples of different sizes to population mean age.

45.99 (sample size = 100, sampling error = 1.07)
45.89 (sample size = 500, sampling error = 1.17)
49.46 (sampling size = 50,
sampling error = 2.4)

59.2 (sampling
size = 5, sampling
error = 12.14)

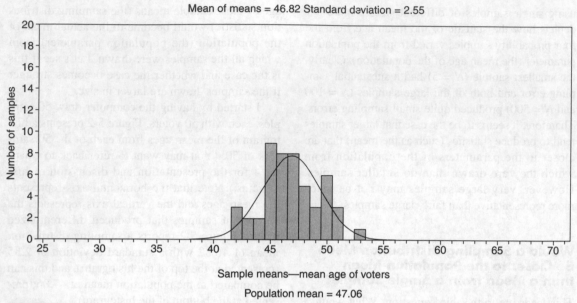

FIGURE 5-2
Distribution of sample means: 50 samples of N = 50 (mean of means = 46.82, standard deviation = 2.55).

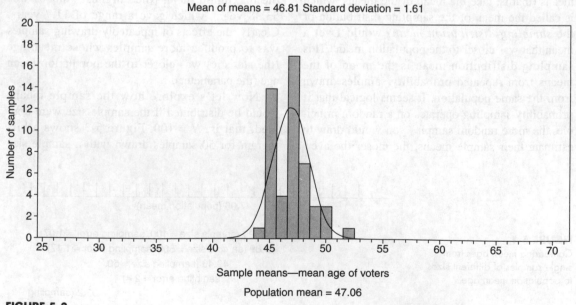

FIGURE 5-3
Distribution of sample means: 50 samples of N = 100 (mean of means = 46.81, standard deviation = 1.61).

of 100. We see here that the sampling distribution of means was 46.81 (almost identical to the sampling distribution mean when the sample size was 50). However, note that the standard deviation of 1.61 is much smaller. The minimum mean age for these 50 samples of $N = 100$ was 44.32, and the maximum mean age was 51.82, giving a range of 7.5 years. Thus when the sample size was increased, the range of the mean ages from the different samples to the mean of the sampling distribution means narrowed (and this was captured by the smaller size of the standard deviation). We can visually see this by comparing the shapes of the histograms in Figure 5-2 to those in Figure 5-3.

Would these same trends occur if the sample sizes were increased even more? A sampling distribution mean based on very large samples should be much closer to the population mean. Moreover, the standard deviation (representing the spread of the various means around the mean of the means) from a sampling distribution of means from large samples should, conversely, be much smaller. This

would crowd the means from the various samples around the average mean, and therefore the shape of the histogram (the sampling distribution of means) should be even higher in the center near the mean of means and should trail off more sharply on the sides.

Let's examine a sampling distribution of mean ages from 50 samples of sample size 500. Figure 5-4 presents a histogram which looks like a skyscraper, with 20 of the sample means coming near age 47 (recall that the population mean is 47.06 years), 12 samples producing means of about 48 years, and another 12 producing means of nearly 46 years. In this case, the minimum mean age was 44.86 and the maximum mean age was 48.83, giving a very narrow range of 3.97 years. Recall that the mean of the sampling distribution means was 47.06, rounded to be *identical* to the population mean, with a very small standard deviation of .93 (that is, less than 1 year). Note that if we plotted a line through this histogram, it would form a very steep bell-shaped curve.

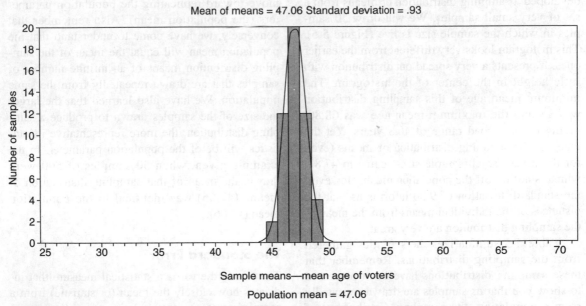

Mean of means = 47.06 Standard deviation = .93

Sample means—mean age of voters

Population mean = 47.06

FIGURE 5-4
Distribution of sample means: 50 samples of $N = 500$ (mean of means = 47.06, standard deviation = .93).

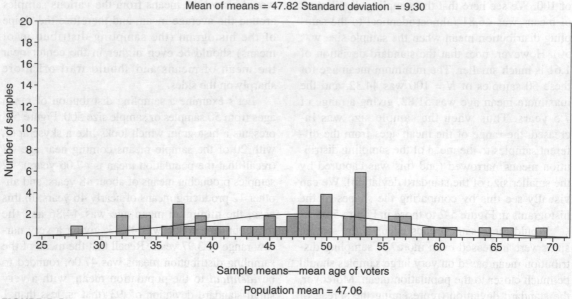

Mean of means = 47.82 Standard deviation = 9.30

FIGURE 5-5
Distribution of sample means: 50 samples of N = 5 (mean of means = 47.82, standard deviation = 9.30).

Finally, let's examine what would happen if we developed a sampling distribution of means from a set of very small samples. We will draw 50 samples in which the sample size is five (Figure 5-5). This histogram looks very different from the earlier ones. It presents a very spread out distribution with little height in the center of the histogram. The minimum mean age of this sampling distribution was 28 and the maximum mean age was 68.80, giving a very broad range of 40.8 years. Yet the mean of the sampling distribution of means (even for these very small sample sizes) came to 47.82, which is not far off the population mean. However, the standard deviation of 9.30 informs us that the distances of the individual means from the mean of the sampling distribution are very great.

Table 5-3 summarizes the statistics gathered from the sampling distributions. Remember that these sampling distributions have been presented to show you that as samples are drawn repeatedly from a population, the sampling distributions of

statistics (such as a mean) from these samples will move toward replicating the population parameters (the population mean). Also remember that conversely, we have come to understand that the population mean will equal the mean of the sampling distribution means of an infinite number of samples that are drawn repeatedly from the same population. We have also learned that the larger the size of the samples drawn to produce a sampling distribution, the more representative its statistics will be of the population parameter. In the example given, when 50 samples of 500 were drawn, the mean of that sampling distribution of means (47.06) was identical to the population mean (47.06).

The Standard Error

The standard error is a statistical measure that indicates how closely the mean (or statistic) from a sample represents its population mean (or popula-

TABLE 5-3

DESCRIPTIVE STATISTICS FROM FOUR SAMPLING DISTRIBUTIONS OF FIFTY SAMPLES DRAWN
(Different Sample Sizes of 50, 100, 500, 5)

N for Each Sample in Distribution	Sampling Distribution Mean	Standard Deviation	Minimum	Maximum	Range
50	46.82	2.55	41.68	53.38	11.7
100	46.81	1.61	44.32	51.82	7.5
500	47.06	.93	44.86	48.83	3.97
5	47.82	9.30	28.00	68.80	40.80

tion parameter). It is calculated from the distance of all the means of the sampling distribution of means from the population mean. In other words, it is the standard deviation of the sampling distribution of means. However, in actual research studies we rarely know what the population parameters are (that is, in our example, what the mean age of the population would be) and are rarely able to draw repeated samples from a population (we only select a single sample). However, with the mean of one sample and the standard deviation we can calculate a *standard error* which can be used to represent the distance of the sample mean from the hypothetical mean of the sampling distribution mean. The standard error is a statistical measure showing how closely a sample statistic represents its population parameter. It is calculated from the distribution of all the sample means from the mean of means of the sampling distribution (the standard deviation of the sampling distribution).

Box 5-4 explains how to calculate a standard error for the four single samples we drew. Look carefully at this presentation. Given that the standard error is created by dividing the standard deviation of the sample mean for the variable under study by the square root of the sample size (n), this means that the larger the sample size, the smaller the standard error (SE). (The SE for the sample of 500 was .83; the SE for the sample of 5 was 9.84.) Once you have calculated the standard error, you are able to move toward an understanding of *confidence intervals* and *the normal curve*.

The Normal Curve and Confidence Intervals

Understanding the sampling distribution of the means from repeated samples from the same population is "the fundamental concept in sampling theory" (Williams, 1978, p. 57). It is this repeated activity of sampling and then plotting how the sample means vary from one sample to the next (as we have done in our examples) which begins to form the shape of a bell curve (or what is called the *normal curve*) as more and more samples are drawn and as the sizes of the samples get larger. It is the principle drawn from the type of activity we have just engaged in (drawing repeated samples and drawing samples of larger and larger sizes) that form the basis for understanding probability samples. When we drew 50 samples of 50 and then 50 samples of 100 and then 50 samples of 500, our histograms took on more of a bell shape with one hump in the center trailing off on each side. When we drew 50 samples of five, the curve was much flatter and more spread out.

The *central limit theorem* from mathematical statistics informs us that if we had drawn an infinite number of samples from the same population, the shape of the curve would have rounded out more and more as the sampling distribution means spread gradually above and below the population mean in roughly equal numbers. But the central limit theorem also indicates that when the sample size is sufficient the mean of the sampling distribution of means will equal the mean of the

BOX 5-4

CALCULATING THE STANDARD ERROR

The formula for estimating a standard error requires dividing the sample's standard deviation by the square root of the sample size:

$$SE = \frac{s}{\sqrt{n}}$$

in which s = standard deviation of the variable under study and n = sample size

So, returning to our single samples reported in Table 5-2 for the sample of 50, where the standard deviation was 20.97 and the sample size was 50:

$$SE = \frac{20.97}{\sqrt{50}} = \frac{20.97}{7.07} = 2.97$$

Or, for the sample of 100, where the standard deviation was 18.81 and the sample size was 100:

$$SE = \frac{18.81}{\sqrt{100}} = \frac{18.81}{10} = 1.88$$

Or, for the sample of 500, where the standard deviation was 18.55 and the sample size was 500:

$$SE = \frac{18.55}{\sqrt{500}} = \frac{18.55}{22.36} = .83$$

However, when the sample is very small, a correction needs to be added to the formula for the standard error. The formula for the small sample is

$$SE = \sqrt{\frac{s^2}{n}\left(1 - \frac{n}{N}\right)}$$

where s^2 = sample variance, n = sample size, and N = population size

So for our small sample of five in Table 5-2, where the standard deviation was 22.12, the sample variance was 489.29, the sample size was five, and the population size was 4,819. Thus, SE =

$$\sqrt{\frac{489.29}{5}\left(1 - \frac{5}{4,819}\right)} = \sqrt{97.89(.999)} = \sqrt{96.8} = 9.84.$$

population. Moreover the central limit theorem tells us that the sampling distribution will be normal even when the population distribution is skewed. It is the knowledge of this theoretical bell-shaped sampling distribution, which statisticians call the *normal curve,* that makes it possible to infer from a single sample how confident you can be that the statistics from that sample are representative of the population from which it was drawn.

The normal curve as presented in Figure 5-6 shows how with confidence intervals above and below the mean based on the size of the standard error you are able to determine the confidence level for any sample statistic. These *confidence intervals* are measures that indicate the range of values within which a given percentage of the sample

means will fall. However, for a single sample, these intervals can be used to estimate the percentage of confidence that a sample mean would fall within a specified distance from the population mean.

No matter what the sample size, if one calculates two standard errors above and below the mean, one will encompass the parameter 95 times out of 100 samples. To test this, let's go back to our example of the first single sample we drew of 50. For that sample, as we determined in Box 5-4, the standard error equaled 2.97. Since the mean was 49.46, this means that if we went above and below the mean by two standard errors (49.46 + 2.97 + 2.97 = 55.34 for above the mean and 49.46 − 2.97 − 2.97 = 43.52 for below the mean), we could expect with 95.44 percent confidence that the population mean would lie

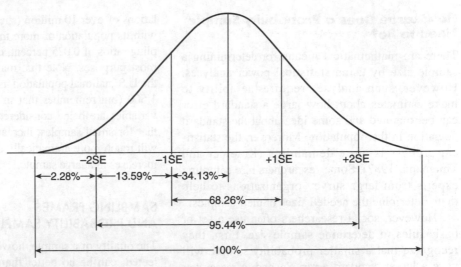

FIGURE 5-6
Normal curve: percent areas from the mean to specified standard error distances. (*Adapted from C. Frankfort and D. Nachmias: Research Methods in the Social Sciences, 5th ed., St. Martin's Press, New York, 1996, p. 198.*)

within those confidence intervals. Since we "know" that the actual population mean in this case is 47.06, we can illustrate that this is true.

Now let's examine our largest single sample, $N = 500$. In that case the standard error was much smaller (SE = .83). Thus, taking that sample mean which equaled 45.89, if we add two standard errors above and below the mean (45.89 + .83 + .83 = 47.55 and 45.89 − .83 − .83 = 44.23) so that our interval is from 44.23 years to 47.55 years, we can be 95.44 percent certain that the population mean will lie within this range. And we can confirm this to be true. Note that for this large sample, if we were content to have a 68 percent confidence level, which would require only one standard error above and below the mean (45.89 + .83 = 46.72 and 45.89 − .83 = 45.06); we would *not* have encompassed the area in which the population mean of 47.06 occurred.

Now let's consider the very small single sample of five which we selected. Recall that the mean for that sample was 59.20 and SE = 9.84. In this case if we chose the 95 percent confidence interval (59.20 + 9.84 + 9.84 = 78.88 above the mean and 59.20 − 9.84 − 9.84 = 39.52), we would again have se-

lected an interval within which the actual population mean fell. However, if we had been content to accept a confidence level of 68 percent in which we would have set the interval at one standard error above and below the mean (59.20 + 9.84 = 69.04 and 59.20 − 9.84 = 49.8), this interval from 49.8 to 69.04 would *not* contain the actual population mean of 47.06. However, within the two standard errors above and below the mean, the population parameter *was* encompassed. This shows that with a small sample, it is more difficult to infer with a high degree of confidence that the statistical evidence from that sample will be representative of the population from which it was drawn. What does change with differences in sample size is the *spread* (in units of the variable considered—here it is years) encompassed by the confidence interval. The 68% confidence of neither the smallest ($n = 5$) nor the largest ($n = 500$) sample size distribution encompassed the population mean. What is important is that in the smallest sampling distribution ($n = 5$), the 95% confidence interval has a spread of 39.4 years; while in the largest sampling distribution ($n = 500$), the same 95% confidence interval has only a spread of 3.3 years.

How Large Does a Probability Sample Need to Be?

There are mathematical means for determining a sample size by using statistical power analyses. However, such analyses require the ability to make estimates about how large a standard error can be tolerated and some idea about the standard deviation in the population. Moreover, the statistical process is quite demanding (Kraemer and Thiemann, 1987). Some researchers hire sampling experts from large survey organizations to help them determine the needed sizes of their samples.

However, social researchers often use a set of basic rules to determine sample size. First, they recognize that a smaller probability sample will have a larger standard error. Second, a researcher needs to think carefully about the makeup of the population being sampled. If the population is made up of people who have many similarities—that is, a homogeneous population—a smaller sample size may be adequate. However, if the population is very heterogeneous, you may need a larger sample to capture the variations in the population. Third, a researcher should think about the types of analyses he or she plans to carry out. If only a few variables will be used and the planned analyses are quite simple, a smaller sample size may work. However, if more variables will be studied and the researcher plans to use complex multivariate (many variables) analyses, the sample may need to be larger. Fourth, and this may seem strange, if the population is very large, a smaller sample (relative to the size of the population), may work better than it would if the population were small.

This fourth rule means that you need to think about the *sampling ratio,* that is, the proportion of the members of the population that will be selected. The sampling ratio is equal to the sample size divided by the population size. If a population is under 1,000, it is generally thought that a sampling ratio of 30 percent is good. For populations of 10,000 or more, a sampling ratio of 10 percent may be adequate. For very large populations of over 150,000, a 1 percent ratio may suffice, and for very large popu-

lations of over 10 million (such as the United States with its population of more than 260 million), sampling ratios of 0.025 percent, or 2,500 may work for most purposes. Note that many voting samples of the U.S. national population use samples of less than 1,500 (but remember that in these cases very few variables are being considered). Keep in mind also that for small samples, increases in the sample size will much more dramatically reduce errors than will increases in a large sample.[1]

SAMPLING FRAMES AND PROBABILITY SAMPLES

The quality of a sample, however carefully it is selected, can be no better than the sampling frame from which it is drawn. If the sampling frame is not truly representative of the population it supposedly enumerates, the sample cannot be representative of the population. In fact, samples are really representative only of sampling frames. Therefore, in designing a sample, you should consider the possible mismatches of sampling frames to populations.

As I will discuss in Chapter 7 on surveys, telephone directories, which may seem to be good sampling frames, are notoriously weak sampling frames for city residents. Poorer people are much less likely to have telephones, and many people in large cities have unlisted numbers for reasons of security. In rural areas, telephone directories are considered to be much more representative of households and therefore can be used more effectively as sampling frames. Today the increasing use of random digit dialing (RDD) which is a technique to be described in Chapter 7 has made selecting a sample for telephone surveys much easier.

---

[1]As Seymour Sudman (1976) explained, increasing a sample size from 50 to 100 can decrease errors from 7.1 percent to 2.1 percent, while increasing a sample size from 1,000 to 2,000 will decrease errors only from 1.6 percent to 1.1 percent. This illustrates that in large samples, there must be a disproportionate increase in sample size to realize a lowering of error as compared to smaller sized samples.

Any list that is used as a sampling frame should be given careful scrutiny. Suppose you want a list of all the students at your college. That seems unproblematic. But what should be the criteria used to determine the list? Is the student population at your college based on all students registered for courses in a particular term? Do these students need to be degree-seeking, or would nondegree students be included as well? Are students who have not paid their tuition for that term excluded from the list? Most colleges can generate different lists of their students, depending on the criteria requested. In drawing your sample and in discussing your findings, you need to keep these criteria in mind.

A sampling frame of students at a college is like a membership list. It represents an association which is of fairly long duration. Membership lists of this type often make the easiest and best sampling frames. Let's consider the characteristics of some other lists prepared to record the participation of individuals, which may lead to better or worse sampling frames.

For example, a sampling frame could be based on a list of persons who came to a particular type of institution in one state (say, a blood bank in Texas), who ordered a certain product (tulip bulbs from Holland), or who participated in a single event. Let's consider the problems inherent in each of these lists, which would need to be considered in deciding if such lists could be used effectively as sampling frames.

For the blood donors, we would first need to get a list of all blood banks in Texas so that we could select at random a number of blood banks that would be representative of the whole group (the technique for doing this will be discussed later). Then we would need to get from these blood banks the names and addresses of all persons who had donated blood during a particular period. We would need to consider the possibility that these blood donor lists might not include all the persons who donated blood at the selected banks during that period of time (in other words, we would want to know the match between the sampling frame and the population). Since blood

banks would be unlikely to let persons give blood without recording this information, you might expect that blood bank lists would be composed of an accurate compilation of donors.

A list of those who order tulip bulbs would also probably be a good one, since such orders would require paying for them, and this would generate names and addresses. Marketing firms use such lists to generate more customers for other products. The issue with these lists would be whether these buyers represented a definable larger population. Would it be appropriate to assume that such a list constituted a representative sample of tulip lovers? Were orders for these bulbs a response to an advertisement? Where did the advertisement appear? (Was it in a regional publication? Did it appear in a special-interest magazine?) In other words, were certain types of people more likely to have been exposed to this ad compared with others? In this case, the list of tulip bulb customers might be an accurate list of those who ordered bulbs, but it is not apparent who, exactly, these customers might represent.

Finally, let's consider the population attending a single event. What type of list might be available? It is unlikely that the names of those who attended would have been written down and registered in any manner.

Much of the issue of the relationship between a population and a sampling frame is that the frame must be truthfully described, but in many sampling situations no sampling frame can be established. Here's an example. Suppose you want to sample people who have gone to Disney World. You fly down to Orlando and interview people there for a few days. Clearly you have not drawn their names from any sampling frame, for a list of all the people who go to Disney World does not exist. This is not to say that there is no population of Disney World attenders; it only means that there has been no effort to keep records of their names. There are some types of records of who goes to Disney World maintained by marketing companies, and this may give you some ideas about what types of people (by age, sex, race,) they are. You might then be able to use this information to select a quota sample (explained above) representing these different types of persons. However, since this sample has no sampling frame, it is not a probability sample but a form of nonprobability sampling.

PROBABILITY SAMPLING DESIGNS

Probability sample designs all are characterized by the requirement that each unit in the sampling frame have a known probability of being selected into the sample. Thus, the designs of probability samples can vary with

1. The random method used to select the units into the sample [**simple random sampling (SRS) or systematic sampling**].
2. Whether the sampling frame has been stratified by characteristics (such as sex) which form homogeneous subgroups which are called strata **(stratified sampling).**
3. Whether the sample will be weighted to bring it more into line with the population or to alter the proportions of certain strata for purposes of analysis once the sample is selected and the data are collected **(weighting for disproportionate sampling).**
4. Whether the sample is drawn in a series of stages with the primary stage being one in which larger, heterogeneous clusters (such as organizations and institutions) or areas based on geographic-political regions (such as cities and nonmetropolitan areas) are drawn first and the secondary (or later) stage being one in which members within the selected larger clusters are then drawn into the sample **(multistage probability sampling).**
5. Whether every member of the sampling frame has an equal probability of being selected or whether the sample is deliberately designed to select proportionately to the size (of the strata or cluster or area) [**probability proportionate to size (PPS)**].

These are the topics we will cover.

Simple Random Sampling

Simple random sampling (SRS) is a method of sampling in which the units in a sampling frame are numbered and then drawn into the sample if they match the random numbers which have been selected. Suppose you are able to get a list of 5,000 students registered for the spring term at your college. You might number the students on the list from 0001 to 5,000 and then use a *random number* series to randomly choose numbers between 0001 and 5,000 to match to your numbered list. Those students whose numbers were drawn would be selected for the sample. This would be *simple random sampling*. Today there are numerous computer programs that will generate random numbers for you (after you have specified the range within which these numbers should be drawn) and select a sample based on these random numbers.

The more traditional method of selecting random numbers has been to use a random number list. There are books printed with as many as a million random numbers (Rand Corporation, 1955). A single page from such a book is included in Appendix B. Table 5-4 describes how I selected a sample using SRS from a list of college students in a college course.

Table 5-4 offers an example of how a simple random sample and a systematic sample were drawn from a class of 48 students. After it was decided to draw a sample of 12, the activities required to draw an SRS were as follows:

1. Develop a numbered list of the members of the population. Note here that the list is alphabetical and is numbered from 01 to 48.
2. Turn to a random number list (the section of the random number list that was used is presented in Table 5-4) and select a two-digit column. In this example, the selections began in the upper left of the table using the two-digit columns on the far right that begin with 33, 05, 53.
3. Select the names matching the numbers that appear in the random number list. Thus 33 appears first, and so Sam Peters, number 33 on

TABLE 5-4

SELECTING A SIMPLE RANDOM SAMPLE AND A SYSTEMATIC SAMPLE: BREAKDOWN ON GENDER, ETHNICITY, AND CLASS IN COLLEGE

# Name	SRS	Systematic	Gender	Hispanic	Jr/Sr
01. Augustine, Steven		11	M		
02. Bachelor, David	5		M		Senior
03. Burke, Kristen	10				Senior
04. Castillo, Lily				Yes	
05. Coleman, Michael	2	12	M		
06. Copeman, Shelly					Senior
07. Dane, Christopher			M		
08. Duke, Darlene					
09. Ellis, Vicki	RSª 1				Senior
10. Farmer, Tammy					
11. Fortune, Russell			M		Senior
12. Fox, Teresa					
13. Garcia, Pam		2		Yes	
14. Gilles, Carol					
15. Gonzales, Ben			M	Yes	
16. Hernandez, Maria				Yes	Senior
17. Hines, Stacy	4	3			
18. Hodges, Kim					
19. Host, Gina					
20. Hill, James			M		Senior
21. Jacobson, Patricia		4			Senior
22. Jones, Jeffrey			M		
23. Kains, Shelly	11				
24. LaGrange, Quincy					
25. McCune, Nicole		5			Senior
26. Mendez, Marco			M	Yes	
27. Melville, Deborah					
28. Miller, Charles					Senior
29. Morales, Wayne	3	6	M	Yes	
30. Nordquist, Sandra					
31. Painter, Robert	7		M		Senior
32. Pattison, Jenny					
33. Peters, Sam	1	7			
34. Pollock, Janet	8				
35. Pyle, Beth	6				
36. Ricardez, Pedro			M	Yes	Senior
37. Rodriguez, Barbara		8		Yes	
38. Sandel, Stephanie					
39. Sher, Margaret					
40. Silver, Martin			M		
41. Solano, Juan		9	M	Yes	
42. Temple, David	12		M		Senior
43. Wallace, Joann					
44. Welk, Louise					Senior
45. Williams, Lorraine		10			
46. Winters, Brenda					
47. Zamora, Luz				Yes	
48. Zapata, Geraldo	9			Yes	
Total: Sample	n = 12	n = 12			
Total: Population	N = 48	N = 48	18 males = 37.5%	11 Hispanics = 22.9%	16 Seniors = 33.3%
Males in sample	7 = 58.3%	5 = 41.7%			
Hispanics in sample	2 = 16.8%	4 = 33.3%			
Seniors in sample	6 = 50%	3 = 25%			

ªRS = random start.

RANDOM NUMBER TABLE

10	09	73	25	33ᵃ		65	48	11	76	76
37	54	20	48	05		80	12	43	56	35
08	42	26	89	53		74	35	09ᵇ	98	17
99	01	90	25	29		69	91	62	68	03
12	80	79	99	70		09	89	32	05	05
66	06	57	47	17		91	49	91	45	23
31	06	01	08	05		80	33	69	45	98
85	26	97	76	02		44	10	48	19	49
63	57	33	21	35		12	55	07	37	42
73	79	64	57	53		63	60	64	93	29
98	52	01	77	67						
11	80	50	54	31						
83	45	29	96	34						
88	68	54	02	00						
99	59	46	73	48						

ᵃUnderlined numbers led to selections.
ᵇNumber in box is random start number.

the list, was the first member of the sample selected. Next was 05, Michael Coleman. The next number was 53, but since no one on the list had number 53, that number was skipped over and we moved on to 29, which matched with Wayne Morales. The next number, 70, exceeded our list numbers, and so it was passed over. Then came 17, Stacy Hines. Then 05 appears again; since 05 had already been selected, that number was also skipped.[2] Numbers from the random number list were matched to numbers of the students until 12 matches were secured. In this case, the twelfth match selected for the sample was number 42, David Temple.

Systematic Sampling

The feasibility of carrying out a simple random sample may depend on the type of sampling frame that can be provided (a consecutively numbered

[2]This example describes random selection *without replacement.* Many statisticians consider random sampling *with replacement* to be purer.

one is most helpful). For this reason, it is less commonly used than systematic sampling. The more common form of selection for a probability sample is to select every *n*th person once you have made a random start—this is *systematic sampling.* This method is simpler if you are working by hand. Let's say you want the sample of 100 from a population of 5,000. You need to define a *sampling interval* by dividing the population (or sampling frame) size by the desired size of the sample. In the example, 5,000 divided by 100 equals 50. In this case, you simply pick every fiftieth name after beginning with a random start. How do you select where to begin with your list of names? Since you want one-fiftieth of the names to appear in your sample, you should make a random start somewhere among the first 50 names and then consider the list continuous, so that when you reach the bottom, you will go back to the top of the list to include the names on the list that came before the random start number. In this way, every element on the list will have an equal chance of being selected.

You might select a number randomly between 1 and 50. Let's say it's 23. You will take the 23rd name on the list, then count down 50 more and take the 73rd name, the 123rd name, the 173rd name, etc., until you have selected 100 names.

Remember that the sampling frame list must not be ordered in a way that sets up systematic intervals. If there is some fixed, repeated interval in the list (such as a sergeant always listed prior to every 100 privates), then such a list will not produce an unbiased sample. Usually lists are alphabetical and present no problems.

Considering Table 5-4 again, examine the third column, which is labeled "Systematic." These are the strategies followed in selecting a systematic sample:

1. Begin with a random start. One way to do this is to blindly point at the random number table and select the closest number (which must be within the range of 01 to 48). I landed on 09 and therefore selected the student numbered 9, Vicki Ellis.

2. Note that for systematic sampling, we treat our list as if it were on a circular wheel. Wherever we start, we continue through the entire list until we get back to our random start position.

3. Determine the sampling interval by dividing the population size ($N = 48$) by the desired sample size ($n = 12$). Since this equals 4, we will select every fourth name following 09, which selects Pam Garcia, Stacy Hines, Patricia Jacobson, Nicole McCune, Wayne Morales, Sam Peters, Barbara Rodriguez, Juan Solano, and Lorraine Williams. Then we move back to the top of the list, taking Steven Augustine and finally Michael Coleman.

4. Let me add that if you had set your sampling interval first (4), you could have made a random start between 01 and 04 and then just carried through the list without treating the list as a circular wheel. This would have had the same effect of giving every person on the list an equal chance of being drawn into the sample. In this case, you might have thrown a die to see which number between 1 and 4 would come up first and make that your random start.

Stratified Sampling

Stratified sampling is a variation on the forms of sampling discussed above. In *stratified sampling*, the sampling frame is divided into one or more *strata* based on sex, region, grade, and the like. Then the sample is drawn from each of the stratum. The reason researchers often want samples stratified on demographic or social characteristics, such as sex and region, is that such factors may influence responses.

Stratified sampling sets up *homogeneous groups* and then selects within those groups to the proportions in which these groups are represented within the sample. Stratified sampling can be used in conjunction with either simple random sampling or systematic sampling (the more usual choice).

Table 5-5 is based on the same list (sampling frame) of 48 students we examined in Table 5-4, but in this case the list has been subdivided by specific characteristics (strata) of the students. We have separated the students into homogeneous groups of males or females, Hispanics or non-Hispanics, and juniors or seniors. Now we determine what proportions of the population of 48 students share these characteristics (see the population percentages at the bottom of the three right-hand columns in Table 5-5).

There are 37.5 percent males in the population. Looking back to Table 5-4, we see that in the SRS sample, there were 58.3 percent males while the systematic sample got much closer to the proportion of males in the population with 41.7 percent males. If we consider Hispanics, we see that the population contained 22.9 percent Hispanic students; however, in Table 5-4 we see that by SRS we had selected only 17 percent Hispanics, while the systematic random sample selected 33 percent of Hispanic students. Finally, if we consider class status, we see in Table 5-4 that the population was one-third seniors (33.3%) and two-thirds juniors. But the SRS selected 50 percent seniors and 50 percent juniors, while the systematic random sample selected only 25 percent juniors and 75 percent seniors.

We would have drawn proportions of these subgroups that were closer to the population proportions by employing the techniques of stratified sampling. In this strategy, the names in the list are sorted into separate groups representing every combination of the three strata: male Hispanic juniors, male Hispanic seniors, male non-Hispanic juniors, male non-Hispanic seniors, female Hispanic juniors, female Hispanic seniors, female non-Hispanic juniors, and female non-Hispanic seniors. Table 5-5 shows how this stratified sampling frame would look. Then, with the use of either SRS or systematic sampling within each group, a stratified sample can be achieved.

Simple random sampling would first require determining the proportion of the population characterized by each of the eight strata types (how many are needed from each of the eight strata). Since the sampling ratio is .25 (sample size divided by sampling frame size), we need 25 percent

TABLE 5-5

SETTING UP A SAMPLING FRAME FOR A STRATIFIED SAMPLE WITH THREE STRATA: GENDER (MALE, FEMALE), ETHNICITY (HISPANIC, NON-HISPANIC), AND CLASS IN COLLEGE (SENIOR, JUNIOR)

# Name	Strat + SRS	Strat + Systematic	Gender	Hispanic	Jr./Sr.
Male Hispanic Juniors	Need 1	Land on 1	MALE	HISPANIC	JUNIOR
01. Gonzales, Ben			M	Yes	
02. Mendez, Marco		4	M	Yes	
03. Morales, Wayne			M	Yes	
04. Solano, Juan	1		M	Yes	
Male Hispanic Seniors	Need 0	Land on 1	MALE	HISPANIC	SENIOR
05. Ricardez, Pedro			M	Yes	Senior
06. Vapata, Geraldo		5	M	Yes	Senior
Male Non-Hisp Juniors	Need 2	Land on 1			
07. Augustine, Steven			M		
08. Coleman, Michael			M		
09. Dane, Christopher			M		
10. Jones, Jeffrey		6	M		
11. Peters, Sam	2		M		
12. Silver, Martin	1		M		
Male Non-Hisp Seniors	Need 2	Land on 2			
13. Bachelor, David			M		Senior
14. Fortune, Russell	1	7	M		Senior
15. Hill, James			M		Senior
16. Miller, Charles			M		Senior
17. Painter, Robert	2		M		Senior
18. Temple, David		8	M		Senior
Female Hisp Juniors	Need 1	Land on 1			
19. Castillo, Lily				Yes	
20. Garcia, Pam				Yes	
21. Rodriguez, Barbara				Yes	
22. Zamora, Luz	1	9		Yes	
Female Hisp Seniors	Need 0	Land on 0			
23. Hernandez, Maria				Yes	Senior
Female Non-Hisp Jrs	Need 4	Land on 4			
24. Duke, Darlene					
25. Farmer, Tammy					
26. Fox, Teresa		10			
27. Giles, Carol					
28. Hines, Stacy					
29. Hodges, Kim	3				
30. Host, Gina		11			
31. Kains, Shelly					
32. LaGrange, Quincy					
33. Melville, Deborah					
34. Nordquist, Sandra		12			
35. Pattison, Jenny	2				
36. Pyle, Beth					
37. Sandel, Stephanie					
38. Sher, Margaret		RSᵃ 1			
39. Wallace, Joann	1				
40. Williams, Lorraine	4				
41. Winters, Brenda					
Female Non-Hisp Srs	Need 2	Land on 2			
42. Burke, Kristen	1	2			Senior
43. Copeman, Shelly	2				Senior
44. Ellfs, Vicki					Senior
45. Jacobson, Patricia					Senior
46. McCune, Nicole		3			Senior
47. Pollock, Janet					Senior
48. Welk, Louise					Senior
Total: Sample	12	12			
Total: Population	48	48			
			18 males	11 Hispanics	16 Seniors
			= 37.5%	= 22.9 %	= 33.3%
Males in Sample	5 = 41.7%	5 = 41.7%			
Hispanics in Sample	2 = 16.8%	3 = 25%			
Seniors in Sample	4 = 33.3%	5 = 41.7%			
ᵃRS = random start.		Start # 38			

RANDOM NUMBER TABLE

<u>39</u>[a]	29	27	49	45	<u>40</u>	21	81	65	44
00	82	29	16	65	<u>14</u>	38	55	37	63
<u>35</u>	08	03	36	06	96	28	60	26	55
<u>04</u>	<u>43</u>	62	76	59	94	40	05	64	18
<u>12</u>	<u>17</u>	17	68	33	54	38	21	45	98
<u>11</u>	19	92	91	70	37	08	92	00	48
23	40	30	97	32	<u>42</u>	05	08	23	41
<u>18</u>	62	38[b]	85	79	<u>22</u>	22	20	64	13
83	49	12	56	24	28	70	72	58	15
35	27	38	84	35	07	20	73	17	90
50	50	07	39	98					
52	77	56	78	51					
68	71	17	78	17					
<u>29</u>	60	91	10	62					
23	47	83	41	13					

[a] Underlined numbers led to selections.
[b]Number in box is random start number.

of each stratum. (In some cases, this produces fractional requirements, but since we can't select half a person into our sample, we round either up or down to get the required sample size.)

Then we use a random number list to select numbered names until we get the required number for that subgroup stratum. Looking at the random number list that was used for this selection (to the left of the table), we see that the first number was 39, matching Joann Wallace, and so she is the first member of the stratum female non-Hispanic juniors drawn into the sample. The next number drawn is 35, Jenny Pattison, the second female non-Hispanic junior selected. The third number is 04, Juan Solano, the first (and only) member needed in the stratum: male Hispanic juniors. We continue in this manner until all our needs are met.

An easier method to use for a stratified sample is systematic sampling. Here all we need do is to determine the sampling interval (sampling frame (or population) size divided by sample size = 4), make a random start, and then select every fourth name to get the sample of 12. Note that our random start was 38, Margaret Sher, and she was

taken into the sample. We just continue with every fourth name on the list, and this gives us the proportions of each stratum roughly proportionate to the size of that stratum within the population.

Note that the systematic method and SRS each produced nearly the same number of selected members from each stratum (the only difference was that we landed on 06 in the systematic sample, representing the stratum of male Hispanic seniors, and that we had not required a member of that stratum for the SRS). If we examine the proportions of each stratum that came into the stratified sample using the two methods (reported at the bottom of the two left-hand columns in Table 5-5) and compare these to the proportions of the strata in the population (at the bottom of the three right-hand columns), we see that the proportions are quite close. For percent male, the sampling frame proportion of 37.5 percent applied to a sample of 12 would have been 4.5 males, and each of the sampling selection procedures produced 5 males. For percent Hispanic, the sampling frame proportion of 22.9 percent applied to a sample of 12 would have been 2.7 Hispanics; with SRS we selected 2 Hispanics, and with systematic sampling, 3 Hispanics. For percent seniors, the sampling frame percent was a third, SRS produced exactly four, and the systematic sampling produced five seniors. In short, the stratified sampling procedures produced a sample that had percentages of each stratum that were more representative of the proportions in the sampling frame.

Weighting for Disproportionate Sampling

Many probability samples employ a *weighting* technique to give subgroups their fair share of weight in the analyses. (In mathematical terms, all samples are weighted: if the sample sizes are used directly, they are weighted by 1.) Suppose you are doing a study comparing the academic performance of foreign students and American students at American colleges. Naturally there are many fewer foreign students than American students.

Let's say you plan to select 50 American students per campus. You may decide for purposes of comparison to select 50 foreign students as well. However, at a college of 1,000 students, where 100 are foreign students, you would give the foreign students a 50 percent chance of being selected for the sample but give the American students a 5.5 percent chance of being selected. In this case, a subgroup would have been "oversampled" to get a large enough number to study from an underrepresented group in the population. This method might be a good strategy if you compensated in the analysis stage of the study by weighting the findings.

The foreign students in this example are just over nine times as likely to be selected for the sample as are the American students. Since the Americans make up nine-tenths of the students and the foreign students account for one-tenth, you could determine the weights by multiplying this fractional proportion by the number selected from each group. Thus at the college described, the findings from the 50 foreign students would be multiplied by one-tenth, and those from the 50 American students by nine-tenths. This means that in weighted terms 5 foreign students were equivalent to 45 American students. This would be the same as simply weighting the American sample by 9. Most computer package programs allow for simple procedures to weight a sample or parts of a sample. Or you might compose tables separately for the foreign students and the American students and then multiply the American data by 9.

Hirschi's (1969) sample for the delinquency study used a form of disproportionate sampling (see Box 5-5) for the different race and sex subgroups in the study. Each black girl in the sample represented about 8.0 other black girls, whereas each black boy represented only 1.2 other black boys (Hirschi, 1969, p. 37). (You may recall that the delinquency rates for the girls in the sample were so low that they were ultimately excluded from the analysis even though they had been a part of the sample design.)

Weighting also may be used to cancel out the effects of differential response rates from different subgroups. Considering the response rates of he various subgroups—recall that this refers to the proportion of those sampled who responded—Hirschi used the following weighting procedure. If white girls had an overall average response rate of 65 percent in all the schools and in a particular junior high school responded at a rate of 70 percent, the excess responses from the particular junior high school would be selected randomly and discarded from the analysis (Hirschi, 1969, p. 38). In schools with lower response rates from white girls, the responses would be weighted to become the equivalent of a 65 percent rate.

Multistage Probability Sampling

Multistage probability sampling uses designs that select the final units for the sample at the last stage, after one or more earlier stages have selected larger units. One of the most common forms of multistage sampling is *multistage cluster sampling*. Clusters refer to groups or organizations composed of heterogeneous units (such as schools and businesses) which can be selected at the first stage—these are the *primary sampling units (PSUs)*—and then the members of those clusters (the students or the employees) can be selected at the second stage—these are the *secondary sampling units.*

The advantage of this type of probability sampling is that the sampling frame need be composed only of all the large clusters. For example, suppose you want a national probability sample of all American high school seniors. The sampling frame for such a sample might consist of a list of all high school seniors in the United States. This would be extremely difficult to generate. However, it would be much easier to get a list of all American high schools and first draw a sample of high schools. Then, once the much smaller number of high schools is drawn, seniors within these high schools can be sampled.

BOX 5-5

HIRSCHI'S DISPROPORTIONATE SAMPLE IN THE DELINQUENCY STUDY

In Hirschi's (1969) study of juvenile delinquency, described in Chapter 1, the sample was drawn from the population of 17,500 students entering the public junior and senior high schools in western Contra Costa County (across the bay from San Francisco) in 1964. This population was stratified according to race, sex, school, and grade. Certain subgroups were sampled more heavily than others (85 percent of black boys, 60 percent of black girls, 30 percent of non black boys, 12 percent of non black girls). This form of *disproportionate sampling* (described below) was carried out to ensure that sufficiently large numbers of key subgroups would be available for analysis. This procedure produced a sample size of 5,545 students.

Let me mention at this juncture that Hirschi's actual (or realized) sample ended up only three-quarters the size of the intended sample. This reduction was due to losses of members in the selected sample, which is termed *attrition*. The attrition occurred for several reasons. The school system required parental permission for a student's participation in the survey. Letters seeking approval were sent to parents, and if there was no response, a follow-up letter was sent. Finally, a field worker would visit the parents who still had not responded. Despite these efforts, 6.5 percent of the parents refused permission and 5.5 percent could not be contacted.

Another cause of attrition was the time lag between when the sampling frame for the survey was put together in the fall of 1964 and when the survey was administered in the spring of 1965. During this period, 6.2 percent of the students chosen for the sample had transferred out of the county or had dropped out of school. Another 7.1 percent were absent during the administration (and follow-up administrations) of the survey. Once the surveys were completed, a screening indicated that 1.2 percent had to be excluded because of invalid responses on the answer sheet. All in all, 26.5 percent of the original sample was "lost" through these various forms of attrition.

Source: Travis Hirschi: *Causes of Delinquency,* University of California Press, Berkeley, Calif., 1969, pp. 35–37.

For national samples of the United States, the method commonly used is *multistage area probability sampling*. In this case, use is made of the ways in which the U.S. Census Bureau has set up the geographic regions of the United States into Standard Metropolitan Statistical Areas (SMSAs) and nonmetropolitan counties. Let's take, for example, the multistage probability sample design that the National Opinion Research Center (NORC) devised to carry out its annual *General Social Survey (GSS)*, which is the best known social indicators survey in the United States. The GSS is an annual survey of attitudes and opinions in a probability sample of Americans that was begun in 1972 and has continued ever since. The sample design for the GSS (described in Box 5-6) is the 1980 sampling design, which is still employed. Note that the selection methods at each stage were based on the principles of probability proportional to size, which is the topic we will describe in the next section.

The sampling design for the *National Health and Social Life Survey (NHSLS)* on which the sexuality study in Chapter 1 was based used the sampling frame and basic sampling design which NORC had developed for the *General Social Survey* (Davis and Smith, 1991, pp. 700–706). Special features of the NHSLS sample design included a disproportionate oversample of African-Americans and Hispanics to create sufficient-sized subgroups

BOX 5-6

MULTISTAGE PROBABILITY AREA SAMPLING DESIGN FOR THE *GENERAL SOCIAL SURVEY:* 1980

The *General Social Survey* (GSS) modified its 1970 sampling design and followed these principles to establish a multistage probability area sample:

- *Selecting the PSUs.* First, the United States was divided into primary sampling units which consisted of counties, Standard Metropolitan Statistical Areas (SMSAs), independent cities, and, in New England, parts of counties. After the grouping of metropolitan and nonmetropolitan PSUs within each of the four census regions, the PSUs were divided into 84 strata. Other variables were used to define these strata, including the geography and size of a region (as measured by the 1980 census). Because strata are homogeneous groups, each of the 84 strata contained PSUs that shared similar characteristics. Then one PSU was selected from each of the 84 strata. (Sixteen of the 84 strata had only one PSU, and so it was selected; in the other 68 strata, PSUs were selected with probability proportional to size (see the next section).

- *Selecting the Blocks or Enumeration Districts.* At the second stage, blocks or enumeration districts (EDs) were selected. The number of secondary selections varied with the size of the PSU. Before the EDs were selected, the PSUs were sorted by factors such as size and income, and then a geographic ordering was carried out so that systematic selection of zones could be undertaken. At this stage 562 blocks or EDs were selected. Again the probability of selection was proportion to the size of the ED (measured in terms of number of housing units). Each selection included at least 50 housing units.

- *Selecting Specific Housing Units.* At the third stage, if the block or ED had a very large number of housing units, field staff went out to the site and made a rough count of the housing units. On this basis, only a part of a block or ED with many housing units was considered at this final stage. This final selection of 50 housing units in the selected blocks or EDs was made on the basis of probability proportional to size.

James A. Davis and Tom W. Smith: *General Social Surveys, 1972–1990: Cumulative Codebook,* National Opinion Research Center, Chicago, 1990, pp. 632–633.

---

for the analysis. However, in the effort to control costs, certain categories of people were deliberately excluded from the NHSLS: those under 18 and over 59 years in age, non-English speakers and individuals living in group quarters. After considering the sizes of the various groups that were excluded, the authors concluded that their sample was representative of 95 percent of the adult population of the United States between the ages of 18 and 59 (Laumann et al., 1994, pp. 553–554).

If you wanted to carry out a multistage probability area sample of your city, town, or suburb, this is what you could do:

1. Get a list of all the census tracts in the city. (Census tracts are the subdivisions the Census Bureau develops to collect the census.)
2. Using either SRS or the systematic method, select census tracts.
3. Get a list of all blocks in each census tract selected.
4. Select the same number of blocks from each tract.
5. Get a list of each household on the selected blocks. (This may require going out to the blocks.)
6. Select households within each block.

7. Get a list of the members of each household. (This would probably be done during the interview itself.)

8. Select a member of that household to interview, using some random method. (Usually there will be definitions of what types of household members can be selected for the final sampling units. For example, they may have to be age 18 or older.)

When there are so many selection stages, errors are likely to increase. Since the members of an area or cluster tend to be more like one another than like members of other areas or clusters, it usually is better to sample a greater number of areas or clusters and a smaller number of units within each area. However, this is a more time-consuming and costly method of sampling, since each different cluster requires a new sampling procedure within it.

PPS: Probability Proportionate to Size Sampling

When the clusters to be selected for a sample contain greatly varying strata within them, the *PPS sampling method* can be employed to select strata proportionate to their size within clusters. If you want to sample households in a city, you might first draw a sample of city blocks. If the city has 5,000 blocks and you select a sample of 100, you will have given every block a 2 percent chance of being selected.[3] However, there may be great diversity within the blocks in terms of the number of households. Some blocks may be made up of high-rises with hundreds of families in a building, and others of large single-family homes with only one family per building. Let's assume that there are 200,000 households in this city and that you want to select 10 households per block.

To enable every household to have an equal chance of being drawn into the sample, a block should have a probability of being selected into the sample that is proportionate to the number of households on that block. This means that a block with 500 households should have a five times higher chance of being selected into the sample than one with 100 households. PPS is a sampling method that will first select clusters proportionate to size and then give the strata within the clusters a chance of selection proportionate to their number.

This is a two-stage process. Returning to our example, let's say that in a city with 5,000 blocks and 200,000 households we want to select 1,000 households (100 blocks selected at the first stage and 10 households per block selected at the second stage). Here is how we can assure that every household will have an equal chance of being selected.

First we need to select the 100 clusters (blocks). To determine the probability of any particular block being selected, divide the number of households on that block by the number of households in the city and multiply this by the number of blocks to be selected (100). If Block X has 50 households, the following formula would determine its probability of being selected from the 200,000 households in the city:

$$100 \times \frac{50}{200,000} = .025$$

In this equation, 100 represents the number of blocks to be selected, 50 the number of households on Block X, and 200,000 the number of households in the city.

If Block X is drawn into the sample, each of its 50 households will have the following probability of being selected:

$$\frac{10 \text{ (selected from each block)}}{50 \text{ (households on Block X)}} = .2$$

If you multiply the probabilities for the block being selected (.025) by the probability of a household on the block being selected (.2), you get

[3]The example here is similar to one used by Babbie (1992, pp. 223–225).

the overall probability of each household on Block X being selected ($.025 \times .2 = .005$) as 5 in 1,000.

It turns out to be the case that whatever the number of households on a block, the PPS method will produce the same probability of each being selected. For example, on Block Y there are 200 households. Here the probability of Block Y being selected for the sample would be

$$100 \times \frac{200}{200,000} = .1$$

In this equation, 100 is the number of blocks to be selected, 200 the number of households on Block Y, and 200,000 the number of households in the city. The probability of any particular household on Block Y being selected would be

$$\frac{10}{200} = .05$$

In this equation, 10 is the number of households to be selected from each block and 200 is the number of households on Block Y. Hence, if Block Y is selected, every household on it has a 5 percent chance of being drawn into the sample.

Thus the overall probability of the two-stage process ($.1 \times .05 = .005$) leads to the same result. In short, the overall probability of any one house being selected from the larger Block Y (the block with more households) is just as good as that of any one house being selected from the smaller Block X (the block with fewer households). This is the case because the larger block has a higher probability of getting into the sample but a lower probability of any one household being selected on the block. However, the smaller block has a lower probability of being selected in the sample, but if it is selected, the households on it would have a higher probability of being selected at the second stage.

Mathematically, this occurs because the number of households on each block serves as the numerator in the first equation and the denominator in the second equation. Therefore, the differential number of households per block is canceled out. Thus, the overall probability for a household being selected in a city of 200,000 households, where 100 blocks and 10 households per block would be selected, would be

$$100 \times \frac{10}{200,000} = .005$$

Because blocks tend to have similar-type housing on them, they tend to include homogeneous households. For this reason, it is not necessary to sample too many households on any one block. Instead, it is preferable to sample a greater number of blocks.

DESIGNING A SAMPLE TO MEET YOUR RESEARCH NEEDS

The object of this chapter has been to give you some help in understanding the meaning of probability and nonprobability samples, the proper terms to use to describe your sample, and the methods of drawing a decent sample. As was mentioned earlier, the design and objectives of your study will determine the type of sample you need. Perhaps the best way to begin to design a sample to serve your purposes is to draw up a design of the ideal sample you would like to get if you had all the resources possible. Of course, you will be unlikely to be able to actually draw that sample, but at least you will understand the ideal characteristics of a sample that would meet your highest purposes. You can then think about which parts of the sample design might be most feasible (and least feasible) to achieve. Finally, you can begin to redesign a sampling model that can meet your most critical needs, even if it abandons some characteristics of your ideal design. Remember that another strategy is to consider using an already collected dataset, which may be based on a very fine and very ambitious sample that you would not be able to carry out yourself. This is the approach of the secondary analyst, which will be discussed in detail in Chapter 9.

However, if you do carry out your own sample, whatever the design you ultimately implement, remember to keep careful records of exactly what you do. It is essential to your final research report that you be able to explain exactly how your sample was drawn. This commitment to careful explanation of your sample design and of the problems you may have in implementing it is a crucial part of the sampling process.

REVIEW NOTES

- The purpose of sampling is to increase representativeness and reduce bias.
- Data gathered from a probability sample make possible accurate inferences to the larger population from which the sample was drawn.
- Deciding what type of sample to design depends on limitations in resources, the similarity of the subjects being studied, and the types of analyses that are planned.
- Nonprobability sampling does not follow the principles of probability theory. The various types of nonprobability samples include convenience samples, purposive or judgmental samples, quota samples (not to be confused with stratified sampling), and snowball samples.
- Sampling errors are errors that naturally occur as a result of the variability of any probability sample from the population from which it is drawn. These errors must be distinguished from nonsampling errors, which are mistakes that may have been caused by the researcher.
- Understanding the sampling distribution of means from repeated samples from the same population forms the basis for understanding probability theory, probability sampling, and the development and uses of the normal curve.
- The determination of the required size for a probability sample can be based on a statistical power analysis or on a less mathematical consideration of a number of issues: the degree of accuracy (how large a standard error can be tolerated) you need to be able to achieve in making inferences to the population, the homogeneity of

the units making up the sample, the number of variables and types of analyses that are planned, and the size of the population and hence the sampling ratio you desire.
- Probability samples are based on the rules of probability theory, which allow a determination of how likely a particular sample is to be representative of its population.
- Simple random sampling (SRS) is a form of probability sampling in which selected random numbers are used as the criteria for selecting sample members from a numbered list.
- Systematic sampling is a form of probability sampling in which every *n*th member on a sampling frame is drawn into the sample, assuming that the list has no biased order and the first selection is based on a random start.
- Stratified sampling involves stratifying the sampling frame into separate homogeneous subgroups based on characteristics of interest (such as gender) prior to selecting a sample within the subgroups using SRS or systematic sampling selection procedures.
- Multistage probability sampling selects heterogeneous area clusters at primary sampling units and then selects secondary sampling units at the next (or later) stages. The advantage of multistage sampling is that the sampling frame need be composed only of the larger clusters or areas.

KEY TERMS

attrition
confidence intervals
convenience sampling
disproportionate sampling
EPSEM (equal probability of selection method)
inferences (inferential statistics)
judgmental sampling
mean
multistage area sampling
multistage cluster sampling
multistage probability sampling
nonprobability sampling
nonsampling error

normal curve
parameter (population parameter)
population
primary sampling units (PSUs)
probability sampling
probability proportionate to size (PPS) sampling
purposive sampling
quota sampling
random numbers
sample
sampling distribution of the sample means
sampling distribution mean
sampling error
sampling frame
sampling interval
sampling ratio
secondary sampling units
simple random sampling (SRS)
snowball sampling
standard deviation
standard error (SE)
statistics (sample statistics)
strata
stratified sampling
systematic sampling
unit
variance
weighting

STUDY EXERCISES

1. Consider the kinds of samples you might use to carry out the evaluation of the basic writing course (or any other first-year program) in your college. If you decide to use a probability sample of all sophomores in your college representative of every major field within the college who began at this college and never attended any other college:
   a. What is the population of this sample?
   b. Describe the sampling frame you would need to select this sample.
   c. What would the primary and secondary sampling units be for this sample?
   d. Describe the elements of this sample.
2. Let's say that for the above sample you decide to carry out a stratified sample, using the principles of systematic sampling to select each element. Describe carefully and fully what you would need to do to accomplish this.
3. Now reconsider this sampling design for the first-year writing program and set up a nonprobability sample. If you decide to use a quota sample, describe what you would need to do to get a sample of sophomores as defined in question 1.

RECOMMENDED READINGS

1. Fink, Arlene: *How To Sample in Surveys,* Thousand Oaks, CA: Sage, 1995. This book is a guide for selecting the most appropriate sampling method for your survey design, with helpful sections on calculating response rates, estimating standard errors, and determining sample sizes.
2. Kish, Leslie: *Survey Sampling,* New York: Wiley, 1965. The most widely referenced work on sampling in the social sciences. Includes all the mathematical formulas for the sampling principles described in this chapter as well as comprehensible discussions of the relative advantages and appropriateness of different types of sampling.
3. Henry, Gary T.: *Practical Sampling,* Newbury Park, CA: Sage, 1990. A very readable guide to developing samples, with four practical sample designs included.
4. Stephan, Frederick F., and Philip J. McCarthy: *Sampling Opinions: An Analysis of Survey Procedures,* New York: Wiley, 1963. A classic on the principles of designing samples for surveys. Includes a discussion of how sampling and measurement are interdependent.
5. Williams, Bill: *A Sampler on Sampling,* New York: Wiley, 1978. A readable but serious discussion of the principles of sampling. Beginning with examples of "bad samples," Williams goes on to give very lucid explanations of the normal curve, types of probability sample designs, common types of bias in sampling, and a final how-to chapter.

PART THREE

The Methods
of Social Research

*T*his section of the text will introduce you to the major methods used in social research. Chapter 6 presents experimental methods. Because these methods follow scientific rules, a careful examination of the criteria needed to perform social experiments and challenges to the validity of experiments is given. Since social research questions often cannot be studied using a true experimental design, preexperimental and quasi-experimental designs widely used in social research will be examined. In Chapter 7 we will examine survey research, the most widely used method in social research, and explore the range of ways in which surveys can be designed and delivered. Chapter 7 will also address interviewing and focus groups. Chapter 8 raises issues in the designing and carrying out of qualitative research projects, with special emphasis on field research based on observations.

Studies based on a range of methods that utilize already collected data are the subject of Chapter 9. Examples of studies and ways of doing secondary analyses, content analyses, analyses of unobtrusive measures, historical research, and analyses of existing statistics are given. Finally, Chapter 10 addresses evaluation research and case studies. Evaluation research is not a method but a purpose for doing research. Both experimental and nonexperimental evaluation projects are described. A description of case studies—how they are designed and how they can be used for evaluation—is included. The use of social indicators for large-scale evaluations of national trends is presented.

The Methods
of Social Research

Experimental Research

INTRODUCTION

*A*n experiment based on social phenomena is not unlike an experiment based on natural phenomena. For this reason, experiments in the social sciences most closely parallel the methods of the natural sciences. We will begin our discussion by considering the creative and scientific aspects of experimental methods, including an examination of causality in experimentation. Because experimentation is a difficult form of social research, its methods are perhaps best described by laying out precisely the characteristics and procedures of actual experiments. For this reason, two contrasting experiments on the effects of mass-media violence on aggressive behavior will be described in detail. One of these experiments was carried out in a social psychologist's laboratory, and the other was based on an analysis of statistics reporting real-life occurrences.

The greatest challenges to experimentation in the social sciences (as in the natural sciences) are the obstacles that threaten the validity of experimentation; such obstacles will be closely examined. Then a simpler example of an experiment which a student might devise will be offered. This example will be used to consider the general components of an experiment and to contrast the major types of experimental designs: true experiments, preexperiments, and quasi-experiments. Finally, the grounds for choosing to do a particular experiment will be considered.

THE ART AND SCIENCE OF EXPERIMENTS

Creative Aspects of Experiments

The choice of an experiment as the method to use for your research will depend on whether the study's primary goal is to examine a specific reaction or effect. Experimental design must focus on that occurrence, that happening, that moment when a cause supposedly brings forth an effect. It is this production (or observation) of an effect which is the experiment, and this production must be created or observationally selected out of ongoing occurrences by the experimenter. As the two experiments described in Chapter 1 indicated, designing an experiment requires manipulating situations (often artificial copies of real situations) to try to bring forth an effect.

In the natural sciences, this situation or experience is called a *stimulus* and the reaction to it is called a *response*. In the social and behavioral sciences, the causal condition generally is referred to as the *independent variable* (IV) and what is supposedly affected is referred to as the *dependent variable* (DV). The area of experimental design

which must be most creative is that part which addresses the design of the independent variable. Thus the types of topics which can be successfully studied with an experimental design are those where the cause-occurrence (IV) and the effect-result (DV) are of primary concern.

This focusing gives experiments a narrow, highly specified quality. The researcher must zero in on the central meaning of the subject of study. In contrast to survey research, where variables tend to be numerous, experimental research generally has only two primary variables. With so much concentration on these two variables, their qualities become highly significant. As was stated above, the independent variable is the one that requires the most creative effort. This is a variable that not only is measured but is productive of something else.

In certain experiments—more often those in real-life settings—the independent variable may be a particular educational program, a social welfare benefit, a criminal justice procedure, a medical treatment, or another event which is occurring in the real world; the object of the experiment is to see if this independent variable is having its supposed effect. In other experiments—more often taking place in laboratories—the independent variable must be created so that it will resemble the supposed cause of what the researcher is studying. This creation or isolation of an independent variable which may lead to the effect to be studied is the central problem in the design of experiments.

The designers of experiments also may create or use a stimulating situation into which they introduce the independent variable and then see what effects occur. Darley and Latane in their experiment on bystander intervention (1968) reported in Chapter 1, introduced their independent variable (number of bystanders) into a crisis situation (a student having a seizure) to see how far the subjects would assume the responsibility for trying to help. Darley and Latane created other crisis situations (such as having the room in which the subject was located fill with smoke; Latane and Darley, 1968) to see under what circumstances the number of bystanders would affect a subject's willingness to assume responsibility for a crisis situation to try to help a person in need. Note that in these examples, which were creative experimental situations, there was an element of deception. Thus, while the researcher needs to be free enough to try to cook up a stimulating event which can cause the desired effect, the subjects must remain somewhat unaware of the experimenter's strategy or their reaction may not be a genuine response to the independent variable. For this reason, experimental designs may raise difficult ethical issues.

Scientific Aspects of Experiments

The experiment is the quintessential scientific method. Our stereotyped image of a scientist is a person dressed in a white coat working in a laboratory. He or she is pouring some mixture into a test tube, setting it over a fire, watching it change (color or whatever), and recording these observations. And we have it essentially right. The social-scientific experiment, however far from this chemist's laboratory it seems to be, essentially follows the same scientific model. It sets up (or isolates for observation) a condition in order to be able to observe how one factor identified as the stimulus, or independent variable (the heat of the fire), will bring about a change in another factor, identified as the response, or the dependent variable (the composition or other characteristics of the mixture in the test tube). Of course, the scientist still has some of the original mixture in another test tube which was not heated so that he or she can compare the qualities of the heated mixture to those of the unheated mixture.

This little experiment possesses the three primary qualities of a classical scientific experiment:

Independent and dependent variables
Pretest and posttest
Experimental group and control group

The object of the experiment is to determine what (if any) effect can be identified in the dependent variable as being due to the treatment of the independent variable. The reason for having measures taken before the experiment (*pretest*) and compared with measures taken after the introduction of the independent variable (*posttest*) is to try to isolate the specific effects of the stimulus. The reason for making observations on part of the sample which has not undergone the experimental treatment (the *control group*) and comparing it with the part of the sample which has undergone the experimental treatment (the *experimental group*) is to see how different the experimental group is from a group which was not exposed to the experimental treatment. Again, this distinction between experimental and control groups helps isolate the experimental effects.

One of the major differences between the experiments of natural scientists and those of social scientists is that social scientists must interact with their subjects while natural scientists need not do so. There is a major problem in experiments where the experimenter must talk to the subjects. What should he or she tell the subjects about the purpose of the experiment? If the full intention of the experiment is described, the subjects may try to bring forth the experimental effect or possibly abort it. This means that experimenters are rarely frank with their subjects: some type of deception is a common element of most laboratory procedures in social experiments. This problem of the need of the experimenter to interact with subjects is one of the major confounding issues in social experimentation. This will be discussed at greater length when we discuss obstacles to validity.

The Rules of Causality

The experimental method, more than any other type of social research method, forces a consideration of causality, which was addressed in Chapter 2. Let's return to the chemistry lab example. How does that simple experiment exemplify general principles of causality which would be likely to apply in any kind of experiment? Recall that in the experiment, the experimenter poured a mixture into a test tube, heated it, and then observed the changes that had occurred in the mixture.

One characteristic of this experiment is that it followed a known *time-ordered sequence*. First, the experimenter had a mixture in a tube (and naturally observed the characteristics of it); second, the experimenter placed the tube over a flame to heat it; third, the experimenter observed the mixture after the heating and noted the changes that had occurred. The object of the experiment was to look for changes that occurred as a result of a second factor being introduced after observation of the first factor.

A second characteristic of the experiment is that it tried to establish a *association between the stimulus and the response*. The chemist would correlate the occurrence of this change in the quality of the mixture with the temperature change in the mixture caused by the heat of the fire, and he or she would be likely to carry out the experiment again and again to show that the association between those factors occurred repeatedly. The chemist would also observe that the unheated mixture did not change, which would also support the selection of heat as the causal factor in bringing about the change (heat is correlated with a change in the mixture; lack of heat is correlated with no change in the mixture). It is the evidence of a constant correlation (though not always the exact same level of correlation) between two factors that strengthens the contention that there is a causal relation between them.

However, an event that precedes a change does not necessarily have to be the cause of that change. It could be that another, unobserved factor is bringing about the change. When this can be shown, the correlation between the two initially observed factors is considered spurious. Thus, a third characteristic of an experiment is its *search for possible additional (spurious) factors that could explain the observed experimental effect*.

These characteristics of an experimental design follow the rules for determining causality. A causal relationship between two variables means that one variable (the independent variable) brings about a second variable (the dependent variable). Such a relationship is held to exist if (1) there is a time-ordered sequence between the variables so that the independent variables precedes the dependent variable in time, (2) there is a correlation between the two variables so that a change in one variable is related to a change in the other variable, and (3) there is no evidence that the relationship between the independent and dependent variables is spurious such that when the influence of a third variable is examined, the original relationship disappears.

To apply these rules to a social research experiment, let's consider the deterrent effects of the arrest experiment described in Chapter 1. The independent variable (or stimulus) in that experiment was the arresting of certain suspects (the experimental group). The dependent variable (or response) was a measure of subsequent assaults occurring after those arrests. Recall as well that there were two comparison groups of suspects; the first control group was given the treatment of "advice," and the second was ordered to leave the residence for a period of time ("separation" treatment).

How were the rules for determining causality followed in this experiment? First, there was a known time-ordered sequence (the arrest preceded the observation of subsequent assaults). Second, the associations between the arrest (the IV)—or the other two treatments—and the rate of repeated assaults (the DV), measured from police records and victims' reports, served as the correlations between the independent and dependent variables. These correlations for the experimental group subjects could then be compared with the correlations for control group suspects who had received either advice or ordered separation.

Third, there was a search for spurious factors that might account for the positive relationship between arrests and reduced rates of recidivisim. An example was the consideration of incapacitation: If the suspect was jailed, he was not capable of repeated violence during the period of incarceration. However, the experimenters found that this was not important, since most couples were reunited quickly.

The experiments were also concerned that the arrest itself (the IV) might have been considered by the victim to be undesirable and thus might have dissuaded the victim from calling for police assistance again. This would be an example of an *interaction effect* between the first arrest and the propensity of the victim to call for help again. Thus an interaction effect occurs when the independent variable's impact varies because of interaction with another independent variable. This means that the effect of the arrest (the IV) interacts with the future responses of the victim and thus could alter the likelihood of reporting repeated acts of violence (the DV). If the relationship between being arrested and reduced rates of recidivism had disappeared when the original relationship was considered under each condition of a third variable, the original relationship would have been considered spurious.

Thus, all three rules for determining causality were followed in this social experiment: the time-ordered sequence, the study of correlations between the independent and dependent variables,

and the search for the effects of other variables which might explain the observed original relationship between the independent and dependent variables.

The rules for establishing causality do not apply only in experimental designs, though experiments usually are intended to demonstrate causality and therefore most often follow these rules. Surveys also frequently seek to show causal relationships. This is especially common when survey researchers use panel data in which measures have been taken on the same subjects over a period of time. It is then possible to determine the time order between different observations.

Finally, it should be noted that social researchers are often uncomfortable with the concept of causality because they recognize that observations and measurement of human behavior and attitudes are frequently imprecise and subject to a lot of variation. This means that the correlations between variables may be quite unstable. In addition, it is very difficult to determine, let alone control for, all the possible factors that may influence a correlation between two variables. The time order between variables also may be difficult to establish. However, when an experiment is being designed, a researcher should carefully consider whether the experimental design will meet the criteria for determining causality.

SETTINGS FOR EXPERIMENTS

As we stated before, experimental research may take place in a laboratory, where extraneous factors can be controlled effectively, or in the real world, where some phenomenon not controlled by the experimenter can be examined in relation to its possible effects. Note that in the natural sciences certain types of scientific subjects (for example, chemistry) lend themselves to being studied in a laboratory, while other subjects (for example, astronomy) require real-life settings to be studied. In some cases, a subject can be studied either in the laboratory or in the field. Geology would be an example. One may study the effects of erosion on certain types of rocks in a field setting, or one may take rocks into a laboratory for experimental research. In the laboratory, approximate conditions of erosion may be created to replicate those which happen in nature (falling water, different levels of acidity), and their effects on the rocks may help explain how erosion occurs. Note that the primary goal here is to be able to generalize the findings noted in the laboratory to those one would expect in the real world.

A Laboratory Experiment

Darley and Latane's experiment (Chapter 1) brought undergraduate students into a psychology laboratory to participate in a research project. This enabled the researchers to *control* a broad range of extraneous factors that might have affected the results of their experiment. This need for control is one of the most defining characteristics of an experiment, and by holding experiments in laboratories researchers maximize their opportunities to exercise control. Note that a laboratory is by design a setting which can be very neutral in its environment to avoid diverting the attention of the subjects from whatever the experimental stimuli might be or can be reconfigured or rearranged to facilitate the design of the experiment.

In the Darley and Latane experiment each undergraduate was brought into "an individual room from which a communication system would enable him to talk to the other participants" (1968, p. 378). This experiment did not require much from the setting except the individualized space the subject was in. However, in another version of the "bystander intervention" research, Latane and Darley (1968) had undergraduate subjects seated in a "waiting room" facing "an ambiguous but potentially dangerous situation as a stream of smoke began to puff into the room through a wall vent" (1968, p. 217). This experiment varied the "crisis" situation from one which was dangerous to an unknown victim and was supposedly being observed by some number of bystanders who were not visible to the subject to a "crisis" situation in which the subject was also confronting the danger (smoke

pouring in) and was in the same room with the other bystanders, who as confederates of the experimenters were ignoring the smoke. Thus the setup of the laboratory defined the physical situation to the subjects and enabled the researchers to both create meaning and control factors that might have confused or confounded the experimental test.

The "waiting room" in the "smoke pouring in" experiment had a window which was actually a one-way viewing glass, enabling the experimenters to observe the subject. Note here that another feature of a laboratory setting is that the experimenter can be an observer of the effect that is being studied or can be nearby to alter or shore up the experimental apparatus so that the experiment stays on course.

A Field Experiment

Think about how different the environment was for Sherman and Berk (1984) in organizing their experiment with the Minneapolis police department. While two precincts were selected for the experiment that constituted definable physical space, this setting was hardly a laboratory. There were virtually no controls that the experimenters could exercise in terms of the physical setting. They could not make it appear neutral or threatening; they could not add elements to the scene or remove distracting features. Generally, in a field experiment, the setting is by its nature "whatever it is." The experimental design must work around what the experimenters expect will be the conditions in the field.

Furthermore, in a field experiment the researcher often cannot be present to view what is happening. Sherman and Berk were sufficiently concerned about whether the police officers were carrying out the prescribed procedures of randomly giving out arrests or other "treatments" that they had monitors ride with the officers. However, this proved too costly in terms of time because of the infrequent occurrence of domestic assault cases that met the criteria for inclusion in the experiment. Then they tried a "chase along" method in which the monitors rode in their own cars with radio connections to the police cars, but this also broke down over time. Thus the experimenters' ability to "view" the setting as a means of controlling the experiment was ineffective. (In the later section on validity, we will discuss some of the validity problems this field experiment confronted.)

TYPES OF EXPERIMENTS

True and Natural Experiments

In a *true experiment,* the experimenter produces a set of conditions (the independent variable) and then measures its effects (the dependent variable). The variations in the independent variable are expected to lead to differences in the dependent variable. On this point Anderson states that "the defining characteristic of a true experiment is the presence of an IV (independent variable), that an IV is a variable manipulated by the experimenter, and that manipulation of a variable involves both establishing the experimental conditions and assigning the Ss (subjects) to these conditions" (1971, p. 39).

In the experiment designed by Darley and Latane, recall that those researchers varied the number of bystanders (the IV) who overheard the victim's seizure. They also "cooked up" the student's seizure, the bystander's responses, and virtually every other aspect of the experiment except for the subject's reactions. This is often the case in a true experiment: the experimental researcher has created all the conditions by which the subject is confronted and has manipulated the subject in such a way that the subject is ready to be "affected" by the experimental stimulus. Note that in the seizure experiment, the reactions of the bystanders were actually only tape recordings which the subject heard. This strategy kept the bystanders' reactions under the sure control of the experimenter. However, in the "smoke pouring into the room" version of their next experiment, Latane and Darley (1968) placed the bystanders in the same room with the subject. Here the bystanders had to be "actors," displaying no reaction to the smoke in the room. In this situation, how far the bystanders actually convinced the subject that they were indifferent to the smoke and were not confederates of the experimenter was less under the control of the researchers.

A *natural experiment,* on the contrary, would involve no manipulation on the part of the experimenter. Instead, the experimenter would *observe* one condition (the predictor variable) and relate it to another condition (the criterion variable). The major difference between these two forms of experimentation (true and natural) lies in the area of controls.

In a true experiment, the experimenter tries to control as many other factors as possible to eliminate the factors that might have a possible influence on the dependent variable. The usual procedure introduces changes in one control condition at a time to see how this alters the experimental effect. In contrast to this, "the natural experiment begins with a situation in which all variables are free to vary and allows controls to be introduced one at a time" (Anderson, 1971, p. 40). The adequacy of controls in an experiment and the problems addressed in trying to establish sufficient controls without making the experiment hopelessly artificial are the major challenges to experimentation as a method.

One of the primary differences between true and natural experiments lies in the problems they confront, that is, the types of errors that are likely to occur in these experiments. In a natural experiment, where little is controlled during the experiment itself, certain constant errors may occur and affect the whole experiment. In a true experiment, the experimenter tries to control all potential sources of error. This is done by setting up different conditions of the IV and assigning subjects to the various IV treatments according to a system of randomization (to be described later) designed to ensure that any special characteristics of subjects which might affect the outcome are randomly distributed across all the groups.

True experiments have been characteristically used by social psychologists to study specific types of social behavior in a highly focused manner. Sociologists and other social scientists have more frequently used real-life situations and occurrences as the bases for *natural experiments*. The Minneapolis police experiment is an example of a "real" environment in which the experimental stimulus is a real social occurrence (an arrest) and the experimenter comes in to study the specific effects of this occurrence. Recall that experiments like these, which take place in real settings, are often referred to as *field experiments*.

In other cases, some occurrence in social life (such as a regularly scheduled television program) may be isolated and related to other occurrences (perhaps changes in attitudes). In this case, the experimenter is singling out specific parts of social action to see if there is a causal relationship between the observed social phenomenon and a subsequent event or condition. This type of experimentation is also natural. Note that a natural experiment generally is based on real-life occurrences, but it need not take place in a field setting.

Different types of experimental methods can be used to study similar research questions. A true experiment often is used to reduce, as much as possible, extraneous factors that might alter the relationship between the experimental independent variable and specific consequences, the dependent variable. However, the laboratory setting in which true experiments are generally staged always has a somewhat artificial quality that challenges the applicability of the findings to wider social spheres. The natural experiment, by contrast, may be affected by other factors in the real world which cannot be sufficiently controlled. Thus it may be more difficult in a field experiment to be convinced that it was the independent variable that brought about the change in the dependent variable, in other words, that there was a causal relationship between the two.

Here we will once again carefully examine a true experiment which has a quality of a classical experiment, the pretest, which the Darley and Latane experiment did not employ. We will then compare it to a natural experiment. Each tries to address a question of great social significance: Can violence portrayed in the mass media lead to actual increases in aggressive behavior?

TWO CONTRASTING EXPERIMENTS

A True Experiment with a Classical Design

Can Aggression Be Aroused by a Film? In a series of laboratory experiments, the social psychologist Leonard Berkowitz and his colleagues (1963, 1966, 1967, 1973) used the presentation of a prizefight film as the independent variable to try to arouse aggressive behavior in the subjects being studied. In one of these experiments, Berkowitz and Geen (1967, pp. 365–366) had 90 male subjects (University of Wisconsin undergraduates who volunteered to participate) follow the experimental procedure outlined in Box 6-1.

Note that a pretest measure of the subject's mood was taken, to be compared with the posttest mood measure. Each step of the procedure was engineered to produce the desired effect which the researchers were studying. As you can see, Berkowitz and Geen were trying to study how far aggressive acts seen in a film might translate into aggressive acts in real behavior. The primary independent variable was the prizefight film; the primary dependent variable was the number of shocks administered to another subject after viewing the film. As was mentioned above, a prefilm mood questionnaire determined the aggressive levels of the subject before seeing the film. This could then be compared to the postfilm mood questionnaire (posttest) to determine how much the film had altered the subject's moods. Thus the mood questionnaire served as a control in the experiment.

This experiment attempted to show not only that moods may change after exposure to a film but also that aggressive behaviors themselves can be aroused and turned into action as a result of viewing violence. The full experimental treatment

BOX 6-1

THE BERKOWITZ-GEEN EXPERIMENT ON THE EFFECTS OF MASS-MEDIA VIOLENCE

INSTRUCTING THE SUBJECTS ABOUT THE EXPERIMENT

1. Each subject was met by the experimenter and another subject (who was in fact a confederate of the experimenter).
2. The experimenter stated that the experiment was about "problem solving and stress."
3. The subject was told that stress would be produced by receiving mild electric shocks from the other subject in response to how well or how poorly he was able to solve a set of problems (1 shock for a good solution, 10 for a very poor solution).

THE EXPERIMENT

1. The subject was separated from the confederate. He was given a problem to solve (designing a contest for an advertising campaign for a store) while his partner (the confederate) was supposedly watching a film.
2. The solution he gave was then (supposedly) taken to the other subject for appraisal.
3. A shock bracelet was strapped on the subject, and he received seven shocks from the other subject (actually from the experimenter).
4. Then the subject filled out a questionnaire to determine his mood.
5. Now it was the subject's turn to see the film.
   a. Two-thirds of the subjects saw a prize-fight scene from a film.
      (1) Half of these were told that the hero (who would be beaten up in the fight) was a bad person. This was the *justified aggression* condition.
      (2) The other half were told that the hero was a good person. This was the *less justified aggression* condition.
   b. The other third saw a nonaggressive film about a track race. This was the *nonaggression* condition.
6. After the film, each subject's mood was measured by a second mood questionnaire.
7. The confederate came into the subject's room saying he had finished his problem.
8. The experimenter asked the two men their names, implying that both were strangers. In some cases, the confederate said that his name was "Kirk Anderson", in others, "Bob Anderson."
9. For those subjects who had seen the prize-fight film and had a confederate named Kirk, the experimenter mentioned that it was coincidental that the hero who took the beating in the film was the film actor Kirk Douglas.
10. The confederate then returned to his room.
11. The subject was given the confederate's solution (developing a promotion campaign for a laundry powder) and reminded that he was to deliver the appropriate number of shocks depending on the quality of the solution.
12. The subject was left alone to administer the shocks.
13. A final questionnaire was given to evaluate how the subject felt about the confederate's solution.
14. The experiment was over; the experimenter described the deceptions and asked the subject not to discuss the experiment with anyone else.

Source: Leonard Berkowitz and Russell G. Geen, "Stimulus Qualities of the Target of Aggression," *Journal of Personality and Social Psychology,* **5**:364–368, 1967.

was seeing the prizefight film with the "justified" aggression version of the story and learning that the name of the confederate subject in the experiment was "Kirk." The full control treatment was experienced by the group that saw the track race (nonviolent) film. There were also other intermediate control groups (those who heard the "less justified" aggression version of the plot and those who were told that the confederate they were working with was "Bob").

Berkowitz and Geen found that there was a definite correlation between viewing violence in a film and greater aggressive behavior in the viewers. First they say, by comparing the pre- and post-film mood questionnaires, that the prizefight film had had little effect on increasing the anxiety, anger, or worry of the subjects. However, those who had seen the prizefight film administered more shocks to their fellow subjects than did those who had seen the track race film. This was especially true for those who had been in the strongest experimental conditions (those who had heard the justified aggression version and had been told that

their fellow subject was Kirk). From this the authors concluded that a film showing aggressive behavior can trigger aggressive behavior, particularly against those who appear to be similar to the victims portrayed in the film.

Table 6-1 offers the primary results of this experiment. Examine the top row of numbers, which reports the average (mean) number of shocks administered to the confederate after viewing the film. (The subscripts refer to the number of subjects in each treatment group.) Note that the table presents separate figures for the treatment group that was told that the confederate was named Kirk and the treatment group that was told that he was called Bob. In the lower half of the table, mean numbers are given for each of the treatment groups after the five most anxious subjects (determined on the basis of the mood questionnaire) have been excluded. The top row shows that the experimental group members who saw the justified aggression version and were told that the fellow subject was named Kirk gave the greatest number of shocks. Note that the name Kirk was

TABLE 6-1

BERKOWITZ-GEEN, EXPERIMENTAL FINDINGS
(Mean Number of Shocks to Confederate)

Confederate's Name	Justified Film Aggression	Less Justified Film Aggression	Track Race Film
Total sample[a]			
Kirk	5.87_a	5.13_{ab}	4.13_b
Bob	5.00_{ab}	4.67_{ab}	4.60_{ab}
Omitting 5 most anxious men in each group[b]			
Kirk	6.4_a	5.0_b	4.4_b
Bob	5.8_b	4.3_b	4.7_b

[a]$N=15$ in each group
[b]$N=10$ in each group
Note: Cells having a subscript in common are not significantly different at the .05 level.

Source: Data from Leonard Berkowitz and Russell G. Geen, "Stimulus Qualities of the Target of Aggression," *Journal of Personality and Social Psychology,* 5: p. 367, 1967.

more strongly related to increased shocks when the justified version was shown. In the bottom half of the table, which excludes the most anxious subjects—they were excluded on the assumption that the most anxious subjects might inhibit their aggression (Berkowitz and Geen, 1967, p. 366)—the results become even more vivid. In this case, a substantially greater number of shocks were given by those in the experimental group (justified condition and Kirk confederate) than by those whose confederate was called Bob or who saw the less justified prizefight film or the track race film.

Berkowitz, a social psychologist, had been primarily interested in studying aggressive behavior and had used a mass-media form (a film) to try to elicit aggressive reactions. He and his colleague concluded that "available target persons who are associated with the victim of observed violence receive more attacks from angered individuals than do other possible targets lacking this association" (Berkowitz and Geen, 1967, pp. 367–368).

A more sociological concern is to determine how far violence reported or presented in the mass media may lead to actual violent crimes, the most socially deleterious types of aggression. David Phillips (1983) addressed this issue in his study of the potential effects of heavyweight prizefights on homicide rates in the United States. Let us carefully examine the very different experimental design he used.

A Natural Experiment with a Quasi-Experimental Time-Series Design

Can Mass Media Trigger Violent Behavior? To study the widespread social effect of violence experienced through the mass media on violent behavior in society at large, Phillips selected a particular type of violence depicted in the mass media, namely, heavyweight prizefights—the same type of violent stimulus Berkowitz and Geen had used—and then related the timing of those fights to changing homicide rates in the United States as a whole. Instead of bringing subjects into a laboratory, he used available information on the dates of prizefights and aggregate crime statistics to do his study. Box 6-2 lays out the steps in this experiment.

Phillips found that there was an unexpected rise in homicides three days after prizefights. Table 6-2 gives the actual number (called the observed number in the table) of homicides occurring three days after each of the 18 fights and then the expected

BOX 6-2

THE PHILLIPS EXPERIMENT ON THE EFFECTS OF VIOLENCE IN THE MASS MEDIA ON HOMICIDE RATES

1. Using the standard reference work that records prizefights, Phillips selected heavyweight prizefights which took place between 1973 and 1978.
2. He determined the date and day of the week of each fight.
3. He then examined the homicide rate for each of the 10 days after each fight.
4. He used a time-series regression analysis (described below) to see whether there was an unexpected rise in homicides after the prizefights, and if so, on which day after the fight it occurred.

5. In this analysis, he established controls for days of the week, holidays, and months of the year (using statistical techniques) because of the known variation in the frequencies of homicides by day, holidays, and months.
6. He also compared fights held within the United States to those held in other countries and those fights which had been discussed on television news to those which had not.

Data from David Phillips, "The Impact of Mass Media Violence on U.S. Homicides," *American Sociological Review*, **48**:560–568, 1983.

TABLE 6-2

PHILLIPS'S EXPERIMENTAL FINDINGS
(Fluctuation of U.S. Homicides Three Days after Each Heavyweight Prizefight, 1973–1978)

Name of Fight	Observed No. Homicides	Expected No. Homicides	Observed Minus Expected	Fight Held Outside U.S.?	On Network Evening News?
Foreman/Frazier	55	42.10	12.90	Yes	Yes
Foreman/Roman	46	49.43	–3.43	Yes	No
Foreman/Norton	55	54.33	.67	Yes	No
Ali/Foreman	102	82.01	19.99	Yes	Yes
Ali/Wepner	44	46.78	–2.78	No	Yes
Ali/Lyle	54	47.03	6.97	No	Yes
Ali/Bugner	106	82.93	23.07	Yes	No
Ali/Frazier	108	81.69	26.31	Yes	Yes
Ali/Coopman	54	45.02	8.98	Yes	No
Ali/Young	41	43.62	–2.62	No	No
Ali/Dunn	50	41.47	8.53	Yes	Yes
Ali/Norton	64	52.57	11.43	No	Yes
Ali/Evangelista	36	42.11	–6.11	No	No
Ali/Shavers	66	66.86	–.86	No	No
Spinks/Ali	89	78.96	10.04	No	Yes
Holmes/Norton[a]	53	48.97	4.03	No	No
Ali/Spinks	59	52.25	6.75	No	Yes
Holmes/Evangelista[a]	52	50.24	1.76	No	No

[a]Sponsored by World Boxing Council; all other fights sponsored by the World Boxing Association.

Source: David Phillips, "The Impact of Mass Media Violence on U.S. Homicides," *American Sociological Review,* **48**:560–568, 1983.

number (based on a statistical prediction of the number of homicides likely to happen on that day). The difference between the observed number of homicides and the expected number is then determined. You can see in Table 6-2 that for 13 of the 18 fights, the observed number of homicides three days after the fight exceeds the expected number. In other words, more murders usually took place three days after a major heavyweight prizefight than would be expected on those days.

Checking the "personal experience" hypothesis that actual attendance at a prizefight might trigger violence more than exposure through the mass media would, Phillips compared homicide rates three days after a fight held in the United States with those three days after a fight that was held in a foreign country (which Americans were unlikely to have attended). The comparison showed that homicide rates were even higher when the fight took place outside the United States. Testing the "modeling" hypothesis that the greater the publicity for a fight, the higher the rise in the homicide rate, he found that fights covered on network television news were related to much higher postfight homicide rates than were those receiving less television coverage.

Another test of the modeling hypothesis is similar to one Berkowitz and Geen employed in their laboratory experiment when they matched the name Kirk, the actor playing the prizefighter who lost in the film, to the confederate researcher. Phillips compared the race (white or black) of the loser of the prizefight to the race (white or black) of young male homicide victims and hypothesized that if modeling occurred, homicide victims would more often match the racial characteristics of the prizefight losers (victims). This turned out to be the case. When the prizefight loser was white, there was an increase in *white* male homicide victims; conversely, when the loser was black, there was an increase in *black* homicide deaths (Phillips, 1983, pp. 564–566)

Note that in this type of experimental design (which will be described below as one form of quasi-experimental design), pretests and posttests and experimental and control groups are not set up. Phillips was able to enter a series of controls regarding the fight (for factors such as the day of the week, the month, whether it occurred on or near a holiday, its location, and the race of the loser). However, he had no control over the fight itself or how the public might be exposed to it.

Is the Prizefight/Homicide Experiment Valid?
In his experimental research, Phillips attempted to show that homicide rates in the United States were affected by the recent occurrence of and publicity about heavyweight prizefights. In other words, did public sports violence have an effect on the incidence of violent crimes? In the terminology of an experiment, the stimulus was the prizefight (televised, broadcast, and/or reported in the print media) and the response was homicides measured in the aggregate.

Baron and Reiss (1985) challenged Phillips's findings (and other similarly conceived experiments) by arguing that such research lacked a testable theory of imitation which could (1) clarify the qualities of media stimuli that affect the magnitude and duration of the imitation effect, (2) lay out those behaviors which could be considered as imitation responses, and (3) define the process that brings forth the imitation. Examining the average number (and variance of) homicides occurring on specific days of the week during the years covered by the Phillips study, Baron and Reiss found that homicides were more common on weekend days and less common on midweek days: "of the seven fights that apparently induced substantial amounts

of imitative violence, five occurred on a Tuesday or a Wednesday" (1985, p. 357). Thus the three-day lag effect (from prizefights to homicides) may have appeared because Friday and Saturday are the two heaviest days for homicides.

To further challenge Phillips's findings, Baron and Reiss replicated Phillips's analysis of which days, months, and holiday were the highest predictors of high homicide rates for each year in which a major fight took place and for the following year (when no major fight was held). Their design employed this logic: If the imitative effect were an artifact—if the effect appeared because there are more homicides on specific days of the week, holidays, etc.—then homicide rates should remain as high when there had been *no* prizefight three days before. (The only correction they made to the "following year" data was to make the day of the week equivalent from the actual year to the next year). They found that in the year after the prizefight occurred, a similar (though slightly weakened) lag effect on homicide rates appeared. Thus Baron and Reiss contend that Phillips's results were merely an artifact of his research design.

Our interest here has been to consider the research methods of a natural experiment using a quasi-experimental design. Controversial experimental designs are always open to challenge. Phillips and his colleague Bollen (1985) carried out further experiments to try to reconfirm their findings, while Baron and Reiss continued to refute the evidence. Researchers commonly replicate other's experiments, with some variations in the design, to test the reliability and validity of experimental findings.

Another challenge to the validity of natural experiments such as the one described by Phillips is that they use aggregate-level data (in this case on homicides) to explain the behavior of actors at the individual level (a type of *ecological fallacy* problem, as was discussed in Chapter 3). In such a case, it is impossible to tell whether a subject actually experiences the experimental stimulus (knows about and attends to the prizefight) and, even if he or she knows about or has paid a lot of attention to the prizefight, what the process would be that makes this experience actually affect his or her aggressive behavior. One way in which a researcher might address this concern is to determine how much publicity the event received (note that Phillips's experiment did this to some degree by noting if the fight was reported on television news and was held in the United States). But even this evidence does not mean that one has been able to show convincingly how the subsequent behavior of individuals might have been affected by this exposure.

OBSTACLES TO AN EXPERIMENT'S VALIDITY

Any errors in experiments are a serious concern. Any time the dependent variable (or *criterion variable*) in an experiment is affected by anything other than the independent variable (or *predictor variable*) under study, there is experimental error. Naturally, no experimental design can completely eliminate all error. Nevertheless, the object of a good experimental design is to reduce error as much as possible by recognizing how it may occur and choosing a design that will minimize it. The primary obstacles to scientific validity in experiments have been laid out in very influential works by the psychologists Donald Campbell and Julian Stanley (1963) and by Campbell and Thomas Cook (1979). Drawing on their discussions, we will consider how these obstacles were handled in the two experiments just described.

Internal Validity

According to Campbell and his associates, internal validity must be the most central concern of an experimenter. To consider internal validity is to ask whether the investigator can be confident that the experiment actually caused what it appeared to cause or whether there were other factors in the conduct of the experiment that distorted the true experimental purpose.

Cook and Campbell isolated numerous types of problems that may occur to challenge the internal validity of an experiment and suggested means of reducing or controlling for their potential effects. (In a broader sense, the internal validity of any type of research design can be challenged, and many of the problems that will be considered below would also be problems in other types of research designs.)

The problems to be countered may be grouped in the following ways: obstacles stemming from who is in the experiment, what happens during the experimental procedure (from the pretest, through the experimental treatment, to the postest), and what problems arise from time changes or statistical laws (1979, pp. 51–55).

Problems concerning who is in the study:

1. *Selection.* Are there differences between the two groups being compared? In the Berkowitz study, we might ask whether the subjects who saw the prizefight film were somehow different from those who saw the track race film. In a real-life experiment on the effectiveness of a social program (such as a remedial reading program) where the experimental group subjects getting the treatment (the IV) are the ones who need the program and the control group are the ones who do not need it, problems of selection are necessarily present. Recall that in the domestic assault experiment, described in Chapter 1, this potential obstacle was avoided by assigning subjects (the suspects) randomly to groups which either received or did not receive arrests. In such a design, selection effects can be reduced. (Examine Box 6-3, which tested a selection effect in a domestic assault replication experiment in Dade County, Florida.)

2. *Mortality or loss of subjects.* Will all subjects remain in the study? If the experiment occurs over an extended period, some of the subjects may no longer be a part of the study. In the domestic assault experiment follow-up

BOX 6-3

INTERACTIONS WITH SELECTION: THE DADE COUNTY DOMESTIC ASSAULT EXPERIMENT

Pate and Hamilton (1992) carried out an experiment similar to Sherman and Berk's in Minneapolis as one of the replication studies that were funded to address the problems that critics had raised about how far arresting suspects of domestic assault would reduce future incidents of domestic violence. They wanted to test whether the informal sanctions brought about through employment status and marital status would alter the effects of arrest (a formal sanction) on repeated assaults. At first their data indicated no deterrent effects of arrest on domestic violence. However, when they examined certain characteristics of the men, they found some significant deterrent effects of arrest for men who were employed. Conversely, for men who were unemployed, arrest was actually related to an increase in subsequent assaults. This indicated an interaction effect between the treatment (the arrest) and the attributes of the subjects (whether they were employed). There was no interaction between arrest and marital status, though they found that the deterrent effect was weakest for unemployed men who were also unmarried. This lent support to the theory that the effect of an arrest as a deterrent to future deviant behavior—that is, the formal sanctioning power of an arrest—is effective only through the informal sanctioning that occurs in the subject's social world. This informal sanctioning operates only among those who have commitment costs (the possible loss of a job)(1992, p. 692).

Source: Anthony Pate, and Edwin E. Hamilton, "Formal and Informal Deterrents to Domestic Violence: The Dade County Spouse Assault Experiment," *American Sociological Review,* 57:691–708, 1992.

interviews with the victims (one measure of reoccurring domestic assaults) could be carried out in only 62 percent of the cases. Often the victims could not be found. If the victims who were lost were fundamentally different from those who remained, then the victim responses may not be truly representative (Sherman and Berk, 1984, p. 265).

Another example of how such experimental mortality might affect a study might be the case of an experiment intended to cover an entire academic year: the pretest would be given in the fall, the students would then be exposed to some program, and the postest would be given in the spring. In such a study, students who dropped out of college during the year would not be available for the postest. This would be a case of the *experimental mortality* of subjects. Note that if there were more dropouts from the experimental than from the control group, the comparability of the two groups would be affected.

3. *Rivalry between subjects in experimental and control groups.* If members of the control recognize that their performance is to be compared with that of an experimental group, they may outdo themselves in trying to show that they can perform as effectively.

4. *Demoralization of subjects receiving less desirable treatment.* When some control groups receive no treatment or an undesirable treatment, they may become resentful and perform differently from the experimental group, not because they lack the effects of the treatment but because of the negative feelings generated by not being given a treatment or by being treated in a less desirable manner.

Another problem with the assignment of individuals to control groups is that subtle and unintended cues may be given to those in the control group that could weaken their potential reaction. Of course, subjects usually do not know which group they are in. However, if those assigned to the control group perceive that they are not supposed to change less than the other group, they may actually fulfill the prophecy. This phenomenon may work in reverse for the experimental group, where individuals who are expected to react may help bring about this expectation. (The latter phenomenon, which is referred to as the *demand characteristics* of an experiment, will be discussed in a later section.)

Problems concerning the experimental procedure:

5. *Testing.* The effect of what subjects learn on the pretest on their performance on the posttest tends to be a problem in experiments where ability or achievement tests are to be used as the dependent variable. If a pretest is given, some subjects may become overly familiar with the test itself and perform better on the posttest. The effects of testing also show up when attitudinal scales or personality tests are used as pre- or posttests.

6. *Instrumentation.* Validity problems that are due to changes in measurement or to imprecision of the measurement instruments or of the person measuring (or observing or scoring) can result in a false indication of an experimental effect. In other words, an effect may appear to be present when what has actually occurred is a shift in the instrument itself. For example, in the Phillips experiment, if the government were to change its method of reporting homicides (basing the figures on a different type of indicator, such as arrest rates rather than victimization rates), an increase in errors could occur since variables based on different types of rates were being compared.

7. *Imitation of treatment.* In a situation where the control group might be exposed to a treatment or condition similar to the independent variable, it might be impossible to isolate the effect of the independent variable. Cook and Campbell give an example of a study of the effects of

legalizing abortion in one state where residents of a neighboring state were to be used as a control group. If residents of the neighboring state could easily go for abortions to the state being studied, they would not make a satisfactory control group (1979, p. 54).

8. *Compensation to the control group.* In experiments where the experimental group is benefiting from assets of which the control group is being deprived, there may be a tendency to try to equalize the benefits to the control group. Social programs, which usually are set up to increase equity, often distort the efforts of experimenters who are trying to study how effective the benefits actually are by providing forms of compensatory equalization to the control group.

Problems concerning time:

9. *Maturation.* Between the pre- and posttests, the subjects may grow older or more experienced or may change in terms of intelligence and physical strength. This is more often a problem in an experiment that spans a number of years.

10. *History.* Between the pre- and posttests, events occur beyond the experiment that may alter the experimental effect. (Take, for example, a study of attitudes toward airplane safety in which the stimulus is to be a film on causes of airplane crashes. If a major plane crash actually occurred between the pretest and the posttest, it would be very difficult to determine whether attitudes toward safety were due to the film or the the actual event.)

Problems of interaction of selection with other factors:

11. *Interactions with selection.* These obstacles occur in situations where the selection of subjects affects maturation (a selection-maturation interaction), history (a selection-history interaction), or instrumentation (a selection-instrumentation interaction). Selection-maturation interaction occurs when the experimental and control groups are maturing at

different rates. Selection-history interaction occurs when different groups come from different settings and thus are exposed to different historical changes. Selection-instrumental effects may take place if the experimental and control groups have sufficiently different means on the test being used as the pretest. A *ceiling* effect may occur when members of one group score so high that it is not possible for them to raise their scores sufficiently in the posttest. A *floor* effect occurs when a greater proportion of the scores in one of the groups are at the lower end of the scale than is true of the other group (Cook and Campbell, 1979, p. 53).

Problems of statistical regression:

12. *Statistical regression.* There is a tendency for the scores of high scorers and low scorers on a pretest to be more subject to errors than the scores of those in the middle range (which are more likely to be balanced by errors that inflate scores as well as errors that deflate them). Thus, when posttests are given, there is a greater tendency for high scorers (whose earlier scores were increased by error) to move lower and for low scorers (whose earlier scores were decreased by error) to move higher. This regression to the mean of the group by scorers at the extremes will be falsely registered as an effect of the experimental treatment.

Consider an experiment in a social research methods class. Let's say that the instructor decides to regive the midterm exam and offers special preparation sessions to half the class (the experimental group) to see if this will improve their performance. The comparability between the experimental group which gets the special preparation sessions and the control group which does not may be affected by the average scores the two groups had on the first midterm exam (the pretest).

Let's say that although the students are assigned to groups randomly, the experimental group has more high scorers from the first test; it is therefore more likely that these subjects' scores were subject to errors that inflated their scores. Therefore, in a second testing, the scores of the experimental group members might be expected to fall. If the control group had more middle-range scores on the first testing, these scores would represent a better balance of scores affected by inflation and deflation errors, and in a second testing their scores might change less. In such a case, the results of the posttest may lead to a lowering in the scores of the experimental group with initially high scores (regardless of the effects of the special preparation program) and a slight increase in the middle group. Thus the experimental effect of the preparation session appears weaker because of the tendency of those with more extreme scores to regress to more average scores regardless of the experimental treatment.

External Validity

Obstacles to the external validity of an experiment raise the question of how far an experiment can be generalized to other settings, other treatments, or other subjects. In laboratory experiments, there is always a conflict between trying to maximize control over the possibly confounding factors that would distort the treatment effect and trying to minimize the artificiality necessarily imposed in exercising so much control over subjects, the experimental setting, and the treatment itself. Problems of external validity arise because of the unintended effects of aspects of the experiment, the time frame within which it occurs, and the treatment (or independent variable) itself. These cross-effects are referred to as *interactions*. The three types of interactions which Cook and Campbell (1979, pp. 73–74) define as possibly reducing the "generalizability" of an experiment are interactions of (1) the selection of subjects, (2) the setting of the experiment, and (3) the period of history over which the experiment is carried out with the treatment effect.

One problem is that subjects in an experiment usually are aware of the highly controlled experimental environment and may attend very closely to what the experimenter is trying to prove. In this way they may try to be *cooperative* subjects, that is, to "validate the experimental hypothesis" (Orne, 1975, p. 187). Subjects often seem to invest themselves in the experiments they participate in. For this reason, deception of subjects is widespread in experiments. Yet the very deception on the part of the experimenter may encourage the subjects even more to try to figure out what the experiment is meant to study.

Orne describes the subject's behavior as "problem-solving" (p. 187) and defines *the sum total of cues that may "convey an experimental hypothesis to the subject" as the demand characteristics of the experimental situation* (emphasis added; pp. 187–188). Naturally, such a predisposition on the part of the subjects invalidates the experiment itself. Orne argues, in sum, that the subject's behavior in an experiment is determined not only by the experimental variables but also by the "perceived demand characteristics of the experimental situation" (p. 188). One way to try to figure out how far demand characteristics have affected an experiment is through "postexperimental inquiry," but Orne warns that experimenters must be careful not to encourage subjects to deny that they knew what was going on in the experiment (p. 190).

Experiments done on volunteer college students (such as the Berkowitz experiment) suffer from possible interactions caused by the selection of subjects and treatment. Are the students who volunteered characterized by qualities that make their reactions unrepresentative of what the reactions of nonvolunteers might be? Cook and Campbell (1979, p. 73) suggest that one way to reduce the interaction effect of treatment and selection is to make the experiment as convenient (short in time, easy to get to) as possible so that the inconvenient aspects of the experiment do not selectively keep out certain types of subjects and draw other types in.

In the case of the laboratory experiment using the prizefight film, the study might be challenged by asking what the effect of this film would be in a different setting (say, a standard movie theater instead of a laboratory). This challenge to external validity questions an interaction between the setting and the treatment. In the Phillips experiment, the researcher tried to reduce the interaction of history and treatment (by carefully controlling for the day of the week, the month of the year, and holidays) because he knew that homicides were more prevalent on certain days. However, Baron and Reiss challenged Phillips's findings by controlling for the year of the experimental effect.

A FILM'S EFFECTS ON ATTITUDES: A HYPOTHETICAL EXPERIMENT ON ATTITUDES TOWARD DRUNK DRIVING

In order to consider carefully all the components of an experiment and the different types of experimental designs, let's set up a fairly simple hypothetical experiment (one that a student might easily design) as a model. Suppose you are concerned about the incidence of drunk driving and automobile accident fatalities and wonder how you might generate greater concern among teenagers. You see an excellent documentary film on television, showing fatal car crashes, which examines the drinking behavior of the drivers. The film also supports strategies to reduce drunk driving. You expect that the film might serve as a stimulus that could change students' attitudes toward drinking and driving (the effect).

Doing the experiment would require the following steps:

1. Define the independent variable as the movie and the dependent variable as the change in attitude toward drinking and driving from that held before viewing the film.
2. Select a sample of individuals, some of whom would watch the film (the experimental group) and others of whom would not (the control group).

3. Measure the attitudes about drinking and driving before showing the film (the pretest) and after the film (the posttest) among the experimental and control groups.

What are the critical factors which will determine whether this is a meaningful experiment? First, the independent variable, the film, must be considered to be potentially arousing enough that viewers might be subject to a change in attitude. Second, the questions asked before and after the film must be relevant to the nature of the film itself and must be phrased carefully enough to measure attitudes that are potentially alterable by the film. Third, the selection of the groups should not be biased; the groups can be compared only if they are equivalent. Fourth, the administration of the questions to all subjects before and after the film should be done in as similar a fashion as possible (for example, the length of time from the viewing of the film until the posttest should be equivalent). Fifth, the extraneous factors which might interfere between the showing of the film and the response to it should be minimized.

Careful attention to these questions will help validate the experiment. Recall that the central scientific concern in experiments is whether what is discovered is in fact the result of the experiment (whether the experiment has *internal validity*) and whether the experiment itself is representative enough of the real world that what occurs in the laboratory (or even in a natural setting) can form the basis for understanding how this process might occur in the real world (whether the experiment has *external validity*). Remember that the obstacles to internal validity concern the internal qualities of the experiment itself and whether other processes can be occurring at the same time as the experiment which might alter the effects. The obstacles to external validity concern whether the experiment creates conditions that necessarily make it unrepresentative of the actual situation which it is trying to study.

Once potential problems of this kind are recognized, they can in some cases be controlled. In so-

cial research, however, where so many factors—people, organizations, institutions, states—are being studied, it is often difficult to control conditions sufficiently. For example, in presenting the film it would be important to control for the manner in which it was viewed. The experimenter could try to control factors that could alter the impact of the film. The physical condition of the room, the quality of the film and the projection equipment, and the statement made by the experimenter at the outset of the film can all affect how the audience will react to the presentation of the film. If one gets all the members of the experimental group to view the film in a single place, the conditions can be held more constant.

Similarly, the selection of the sample for this study would have many potential problems. What if those with strict attitudes toward drinking and driving watched the film and those with lax attitudes did not? However, if the experimenter used volunteer subjects and assigned them to groups randomly to either view or not view the film, any potential differences between the groups that might have distorted the findings should be randomly distributed and thus made insignificant.

These issues are raised to suggest the variety of ways in which experimenters must try to eliminate or reduce the conditions which might change the relationship between the independent and dependent variables. The most important way is to fix (or control) as many of the possibly confounding conditions as possible so that the true experiment has a chance to produce an effect. This kind of control is achieved by careful, thoughtful design, anticipating all the possibly contaminating problems before the experiment is carried out. In the next two sections we will examine, step by step, the components of a true experiment and the range of types of designs for social experiments, those which meet the qualifications of a true experiment and those which do not meet the qualifications for a true experiment but represent what are referred to as preexperiments and quasi-experiments.

GENERAL COMPONENTS OF AN EXPERIMENT

Independent and Dependent Variables

As I have stated already, the heart of an experiment is to understand a cause-effect relationship. The independent variable must be defined, isolated, and operationalized so that it can be measured. This independent variable is a kind of stimulus which will supposedly trigger a change. Note that if the independent variable brings forth no change, the experiment will be useless; therefore, it is important to select an independent variable that seems likely to lead to a change.

The dependent variable, which is the central focus of the study, is the condition that should be brought about (at least in part) by the independent variable. This dependent variable should show some change in condition from before the experiment and between subjects who experience it and those who do not. The experimenter must isolate the dependent variable as a natural occurrence which can be observed or must create a measure to call it forth (such as answers to specific questions).

Experimental and Control Groups

To experience the experiment is to be subject to its influence. If the experiment works, the subjects who go through it will all be affected in some way. However, what if those who do not go through the experiment show the same effects? This would suggest that the observed effect was not caused, or at least was not solely caused, by the experiment. To control for this possibility, experiments nearly always include a control group which does not experience the experimental conditions. For the control group to be comparable to the experimental group, the two must be equivalent. The primary means for creating equivalence between control groups in a true experiment is the process of *randomization in assignment to groups*.

Randomization.   As you recall from Chapter 5 on sampling methods, the rules of probability en-

---

ORENSTEIN AND PHILLIPS ON HOW NOT TO CONFUSE RANDOM ASSIGNMENT WITH RANDOM SAMPLING

RANDOM ASSIGNMENT AND RANDOM SAMPLING
Warning: Do not confuse *random assignment* and *random sampling*. When we randomly assign subjects to the treatment groups in an experiment, we are trying to create treatment groups that have a high probability of being similar on all variables. If this is the case, then we can infer that something about the treatments, rather than differences in the people or groups exposed to each treatment, led to differences on the dependent variable. The random assignment of subjects does not insure that the results of an experiment can be applied to any larger group of subjects. When we randomly select or sample respondents from a larger population of respondents, we are trying to create a sample of respondents that has a high probability of being similar to the population on all variables. If this is the case, then we can generalize from the results based on the sample to what would have been obtained if our survey had questioned all members of the population from which the sample was drawn. The random sampling of respondents does not insure that the independent variable of the study, rather than other variables associated with the independent variable, led to differences on the dependent variable.

Source: Alan Orenstein and William R. F. Phillips, *Understanding Social Research: An Introduction*, Allyn and Bacon, Boston, 1978.

---

sure that bias can be reduced in the selection of subjects for any study if random procedures are used which place people in a sample (or, in the case of an experiment, in the experimental or control group) according to the laws of chance. Such methods might employ techniques such as flipping coins, pulling names from a hat, throwing dice, using a set of random numbers, and using a computerized means to select random numbers. All these methods give each subject an equal chance of being drawn into the sample (or into the experimental or control group). The box describes how assignment to experimental groups by randomization differs from random sampling for surveys.

In sampling for an experiment, the subjects are usually volunteers. In fact, in social experiments, the vast majority of subjects are college students. Thus, they are not randomly selected from the general population, but they can be randomly assigned to either the experimental group or the control group. This is done by first drawing together a list of all subjects. Then, through the use of a system for randomly placing students in the experimental or control groups, the biases that might have occurred if placement had been done in some other way should be controlled. What this means is that the errors that might occur because of assignment to groups should be randomly distributed between the groups by having randomly assigned subjects to either of the groups. It is this process which makes it justifiable to use statistical tests to compare the results of the experimental and control groups.

Matching.   In this method, which is rarely employed on its own in experimental research the characteristics of subjects are matched; then, one of the subjects is placed in the experimental group and the other is placed in the control group. According to this procedure, if half the subjects are women, half the women should be assigned to the experimental group and half to the control group. This is similar to the principles for the nonprobability sampling called quota sampling, which was described in Chapter 5. If the fifth-grade class under study is in a lower-middle-class suburb, the control classroom should be a fifth-grade one in a like suburb. However, simple reliance on matching cannot address all the potential differences that these two groups may have. This is the case because the important characteristics of the subjects that might affect the experiment may not be recognized by the researcher. However, if the groups are assigned on the basis of randomization, these unknown (but significant) factors should be randomly distributed between the two groups.

This is why matching generally is not used alone, though some forms of matching (having equal numbers of male and female subjects) may be paired with the system of randomization to make the two groups comparable. (This is similar to stratified sampling, where the sample is divided into homogeneous groups before selecting the sample randomly.) Another important reason for using randomization rather than matching is that the statistical tests likely to be used in an experiment depend on the groups being randomized.

Double-Blind Experiments.   In nearly all true experiments, members of experimental and control groups are not told which group they are in. Furthermore, if the investigator knows which subjects are in the experimental group and which are in the control group, the results may be interpreted differently. To avoid this occurrence, experiments are often set up to be *double-blind* so that neither the subjects not the experimenter knows which subjects are in which group. (Clearly the information must be known ultimately by the experimenter, but it may be possible to conceal this information during the experiment and analysis stages by using a coding system for each subject which leaves out information about group placement. Group placement identification can be stored elsewhere and recovered once the initial results of the experiment have been established.)

Problems Caused by Using Volunteer Subjects. Problems are generated by using volunteer subjects, the most common type of subjects used in experiments. Studies by Rosenthal and Rosnow (1975) of volunteers in experiments show that certain types of people are more likely to volunteer for an experiment. Usually, people who volunteer are better-educated, come from higher social classes, are more in need of social approval, and are more intelligent than those who do not volunteer. The fact that particular types of subjects are attracted could affect the generalizability of the findings.

The Hawthorne Effect.   This is a problem generated in many experiments that may require an additional type of control group (that is why we will consider it in this context). In a famous study carried out in the 1930s, it was found that being in an experiment may have an effect whether or not the supposed stimulus is presented. In this study of the Hawthorne plant at Western Electric in Chicago, the conditions of the working environment of those in the wiring room were altered to see if work productivity would increase. While it was found that improving these conditions (for example, by increasing the lighting) improved productivity, it was also discovered that altering the conditions in what would seem to be a negative fashion (such as making the lighting dimmer) also increased productivity. What this suggested was not that workers do better in both bright and dull light but that workers do better in experimental conditions—whatever those conditions might be—than in nonexperimental conditions (see Roethlisberger and Dickson, 1939). Thus the *Hawthorne effect* refers to the tendency of subjects in an experiment to respond in the predicted manner regardless of the experimental treatment.

To control for this effect, some experiments use two control groups: one of the control groups does not experience the experiment at all; the other is subject to experimental conditions, but not the actual ones being studied (this is the Hawthorne control group). The most common examples of these two types of controls are the ones used in testing new drugs. In this type of medical research, there are nearly always three groups of subjects: the experimental group that receives the actual drug, a control group that receives a placebo (a sugar pill), and a control group that receives nothing. What is usually found is that those receiving the placebo tend to show some of the same effects as those receiving the actual drug (though usually not as strongly), while those receiving nothing at all show no effect. In the Berkowitz and Geen experiment, those who saw the track race film were a Hawthorne type of control group: they experienced an experimental treatment, but not with an independent variable that was expected to affect them.

In that experiment, there was no true full control group, that is, one not subject to any form of the independent variable.

Pretest and Posttest

Since the focus of any experiment is on the *effect* of the experimental stimulus (independent variable), it is crucial to prove that the stimulus actually brought about the effect. It is this need to prove the centrality of the stimulus in bringing about the effect that has made the pretest-posttest design so important in experimentation. Thus, what the researcher is looking for is not the after-stimulus effect but the change in the dependent variable from a point in time before the stimulus was presented to a point in time afterward.

Certain problems are generated by giving a *pretest* (as suggested above in the discussion of internal validity) as well as a *posttest*. Subjects may become familiar with the types of questions and interests of the study and may, between the first and second tests, alter their responses to accommodate what they have come to believe is the investigator's interest. Furthermore, a subject may become bored with the test on the second administration and feel less motivated to respond. In addition, a two-test design requires more time on the part of the subject, and there may be a greater number of dropouts in the experiment (mortality) than would be the case if the test were given only once. Finally, between the times of the two tests other factors might have changed either in the subject's own life or in the environment around the subject that would make the subject react differently (history effects). As a result, the differences between the first and second tests could be due to nonexperimental causes.

EXPERIMENTAL DESIGNS

True Experimental Designs

True experimental designs are those organized so that they meet the criterion for an experiment—that an independent variable be related to a change in a

TABLE 6-3

THE CLASSICAL EXPERIMENT

	Time 1	Time 2	Time 3
Experimental group	Pretest	Independent variable	Posttest
Control group	Pretest		Posttest

dependent variable—and at the same time successfully address the potential problems of invalidity. Such designs tend to be more complete than either the preexperimental or the quasi-experimental designs that will be discussed next. The standard true experiment, which is termed the *classical experiment*, follows the pattern shown in Table 6-3.

Let us return to the viewing of the film on the effects of drinking on driving. A classical experiment would have

1. Randomly assigned the subjects into experimental and control groups
2. Given a test (pretest) of attitudes toward drinking and driving to both groups
3. Shown the film (the independent variable) to the experimental group and not to the control group
4. Given another test (posttest) of attitudes toward drinking and driving (virtually a repeat of the first test) after the film

To control for obstacles to validity, the experimenter must be concerned about the period of time covering the testing itself and the time between the tests; these times should be equivalent for both the experimental and control groups and for different members within the groups. If a serious, widely publicized accident involving a drunk driver occurred between two testing times, this incident could affect the responses to the second test. If the tests are given in groups, different administrations of the tests may vary in quality depending on what the administrator of the test said and what times of day the test was given. Campbell and Stanley suggest that these intrasession problems can be allevi-

ated by testing individuals separately (as to avoid group demonstration differences) and by randomly carrying out the tests at different times for the experimental and control groups (1963, p. 14).

In an experiment where observation or interviewing is the mode of testing, there may be biases. These biases can be overcome by assigning observers (or interviewers) randomly to subjects. Randomization of subjects to the experimental and control groups will also alleviate the potential problems of statistical regression (those with extreme scores would be randomly distributed between groups). To address the mortality problem of losing subjects between the two testing periods, Campbell and Stanley suggest keeping those who fail to take the posttest in the analyses to see if they differ systematically from those who do complete the experiment. (If the groups are comparable, the loss of some subjects should not alter the experiment; if the groups differ in some definable way—for example, if the dropouts from the drunk driving film sessions all favor strict antidrinking policies—a distortion is present and the experiment may need to be repeated) (1963, pp. 15–16).

The biases created by retaking the test—due to both the effects of the pretest (on how the subject responds to the stimulus) and the effects of the posttest—can be eliminated with the *Solomon Four-Group Design,* the most comprehensive type of true experiment, which is depicted in Table 6-4. In this more complex design, the problems of the interaction between the pretest and the posttest and between the pretest and the IV can be controlled by comparing the two experimental groups (Groups 1 and 3) and the two control groups (Groups 2 and 4), where one group has had the pretest and one has not.

Applying the experiment of the drinking and driving film to this design would require the following steps:

1. Assigning the subjects among four groups on the basis of randomization
2. Giving the pretest to Groups 1 and 2
3. Showing the film to Groups 1 and 3
4. Giving the posttest to each group

TABLE 6-4

THE SOLOMON FOUR-GROUP EXPERIMENT

		Time 1	Time 2	Time 3
Group 1:	first experimental group	Pretest	IV	Posttest
Group 2:	first control group	Pretest		Posttest
Group 3:	second experimental group		IV	Posttest
Group 4:	second control group			Posttest

Comparisons forming the basis of the experimental effect would use Groups 1 and 2. Control for the pretest bias could be seen by comparing Groups 1 and 3 and by noting the differences in change between Groups 1 and 2 compared with Groups 3 and 4.

Campbell and Stanley argue that pretests are in fact not essential to a true experiment, provided that the groups have been randomly assigned (1963, pp. 25–26). The *posttest-only control group design* is all that is actually needed to have a true experiment. Thus, the posttest-only design is one of the most favored forms of true experiments. It is depicted in Table 6-5. In this design, the pretest is not given to any group. The design includes Groups 3 and 4 of the Solomon Four-Group Design. This simplified design can be fully effective only where there has been assignment of the subjects by randomization and there is no basis for believing that the two groups are not equivalent. It avoids all the problems of the effects of the pretest on the posttest and the problems of how the pretest may alter the way the subject reacts to the stimulus itself.

In the example of the drinking and driving film, the posttest-only design would require these steps:

TABLE 6-5

POSTTEST-ONLY CONTROL GROUP DESIGN

	Time 1	Time 2
Experimental group	IV	Posttest
Control group		Posttest

1. Assigning subjects to the experimental and control groups randomly
2. Showing the film to the experimental group
3. Administering the posttest to the two groups

In this case only one comparison is available (but it is the crucial one): Did those who experienced the stimulus have a posttest effect different from that of those who did not?

Finally, experimental designs which meet the criteria for being *true* may have more than one stimulus, which means that different types of the treatment may be presented to different experimental groups. These *factorial designs* can be extended versions of the three earlier designs presented, where additional stimuli require the same set of experimental and control groups that the design demands (Campbell and Stanley, 1963, pp. 27–31). For example, in the Berkowitz and Geen experiment, there were three different film conditions (the prizefight film with the justified aggression synopsis of the story, the prizefight film with the less justified aggression synopsis, and the track race film) and two different names given to the confederate. Thus, this study had a 3×2 factorial design.

Preexperimental Designs

Many experiments are carried out without the qualifications for true experiments, and many situations which social researchers might wish to study do not allow for the factors required for a true experiment. In such experimental designs, there are even more threats to internal and external

TABLE 6-6

ONE-SHOT CASE STUDY

	Time 1	Time 2
Experimental group	IV	Posttest

TABLE 6-7

ONE-GROUP PRETEST-POSTTEST DESIGN

	Time 1	Time 2	Time 3
Experimental group	Pretest	IV	Posttest

validity. In the simplest cases, a stimulus may be presented to one group and its reaction measured. Campbell and Stanley refer to this type of *preexperimental design* as a *one-shot case study* (1963, pp. 6–7). Using the film example again, group members would see the film and then answer a survey about their attitudes on drinking and driving. If their attitudes support strict enforcement of laws against drunk driving, we might want to conclude that they were affected by the film. However, we not know what their attitudes were before the film, and we do not know how their attitudes would differ from those of others who never saw this film. Thus it is difficult to assess in this case whether the experimental effect occurred. Table 6-6 depicts this design.

A slightly more elaborate preexperiment would add a pretest. This *one-group pretest-posttest design* addresses the problem (in the case of the film experiment) of the level of attitudes before exposure to the film, but it cannot control other factors that might have occurred between the two tests which, other than the film, might have influenced a change in attitudes. Table 6-7 diagrams this design.

Finally, the *static-group comparison*, diagrammed in Table 6-8, is a preexperimental design with a control group but no pretest. In this design, as applied to the film showing, one group would

TABLE 6-8

STATIC-GROUP COMPARISON

	Time 1	Time 2
Experimental group[a]	IV	Posttest
Control group[a]		Posttest

[a]Groups are not randomly assigned.

see the film and answer questions after it, and another group would simply answer questions without seeing the film. In this design, there is a control for possible sources of stimulation beyond the film but no measure of attitudes before viewing the film.

The difference between this design and the posttest-only control group design shown in Table 6–5 is that in the static-group comparison design there is no random assignment to groups. It is therefore not possible to assume that the groups are equivalent in attitudes. These preexperiments are generally less desirable ways of carrying out a research study, though in some cases they may be the only choice. But Campbell and Stanley strongly favor quasi-experimental designs over preexperiment designs when these designs can be arranged.

Quasi-Experimental Designs

Quasi-experimental designs should be employed in situations where the basic elements of a true experiment cannot be set up. For example, in certain cases the experimental and control groups cannot be made to be equivalent through randomized assignment to groups because their natural situation precludes this possibility. In many educational studies, where classes (or classrooms) are being studied, the comparison group can only be a similar class or classroom (but not a randomly assigned one). Nevertheless, this *nonequivalent control group design* can be effectively used in an experimental design where random assignment to groups is not feasible. In a case where the experimental group represents volunteers (such as blood donors), a comparison group may be selected whose members are similar to the experimentals. In this design, characteristics of the experimental and control groups can be compared before the experiment; such comparisons may help explain the results of the experiment.

Regression-Descontinuity Experiment. In most treatment situations, the group receiving the treatment is the group that needs the treatment. Let's take, for example, a remedial math program which a college offers to first-year students to enable them to succeed in fulfilling the natural science and mathematics requirements of that college. Those taking the remedial course will be those who *need* the course, as indicated through a placement or preadmission examination. In this case, the remedial math course is the independent variable. It is offered to the experimental group. Normally, however, it would not be practical to have another group (that did not appear to need the course) take it in order to serve as a control group. It also would not be feasible to refuse the course to half the students who needed it in order to have them serve as a control group. This is a situation in which a *regression-discontinuity design* might be best. In this design, the researcher is looking for differences that occur at the point of the treatment which would differentiate the post-

treatment scores of those receiving the treatment from those of the control group not receiving it. Figure 6-1 shows a diagram of this design for the math remediation program.

In this regression-discontinuity design, students with similar preprogram scores are considered a group. In other words, the groups are ordered in relation to the selection factor. Those below the cutoff line on the pretest are placed in the remedial course; those above it are not. It would therefore be expected that those receiving the treatment (the remedial course) would have a sharper increase in their scores than those not receiving the treatment, but it would also be expected that the scores of the experimental group might remain lower than those of the control group (because they were lower to begin with).

The exposure to the remedial math program (the treatment) serves as the independent variable. The difference between the postprogram math score and the preprogram score serves as the dependent variable. A comparison of the average change in score of groups of individuals who began with similar scores is used to determine whether the treatment had its intended effect. In Figure 6–1, you can see that those who took the remedial course had a sharper increase in their math scores than those who did not; though the math scores of the others did advance, they did so at a more gradual level.

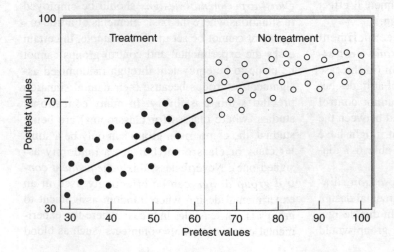

FIGURE 6-1
Hypothetical outcome of a pretest-posttest regression-discontinuity quasi-experiment on the effects of a remedial math program. Preprogram math scores were used to select program entrants (those with scores of 60 and below were selected for the program).

Time-Series Experiment.   When there is a large set of already collected data which indicate rates over time, another form of quasi-experimental design may be used. This is the *time-series experiment*. The Phillips (1983) experiment had such a design. Recall that Phillips was trying to see whether there was an unexpected rise in homicides after a heavyweight prizefight. This required setting up a type of statistical analysis called a regression analysis to see if and when there was an increased homicide rate. Time-series designs generally use already collected aggregate data (which will be discussed in Chapter 9) published regularly over standard intervals of time as the basis for determining the dependent variable. Then another event (a law or a social occurrence) is superimposed on this time line data to see whether there is a change at the point (or somewhat after the point) where the independent variable occurred.

For example, certain states have adopted breathalyzer tests to deter drunk driving and reduce serious traffic accidents. In this case, there would already be data measuring the incidence of serious traffic accidents (e.g., those causing serious injury or fatality), perhaps on a yearly basis. The introduction of the breathalyzer test could therefore be treated as a stimulus, or independent variable, the effects of which could be examined in terms of later measures of yearly rates of serious traffic accidents. Figure 6-2 depicts this design for the serious traffic accidents of a state.

As in the regression-discontinuity design, the interrupted time-series analysis looks for sharp changes occurring after the introduction of a new procedure or program (the treatment). In this case the time frame is *longitudinal,* which means that data are collected at more than one point in time, and the experimenter is looking for changes in a particular measurement over time that occur after the introduction of a treatment. (In contrast, observations in the regression-discontinuity design were taken at one point in time.) Box 6-4 presents a time-series experiment testing the impact of historical events (war and Prohibition) on suicide rates.

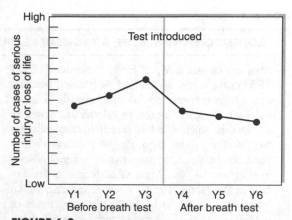

FIGURE 6-2
Serious traffic accidents for years 1 to 6 in State X before and after the breathalyzer test was introduced (Y1=year 1).

The quasi-experimental designs described here may need to be used in cases where the conditions for a true experiment cannot be met. Regression-discontinuity designs are widely used to assess the effectiveness of new programs and treatments, and the time-series regression design is utilized in studies of how specific social policies (laws) or practices can affect patterns of social behavior across time.

DECIDING IF AN EXPERIMENT IS APPROPRIATE FOR YOUR TOPIC

If the object of your research project is to explain some type of behavior, an experiment might be your choice of method. Remember that an experiment requires very careful preparation. The experimenter may need to contrive a situation in order to study it. For some researchers, this makes experiments too artificial. Nevertheless, a very carefully organized experiment has the advantage of producing rather specific findings. Further, if you observe a condition in the social environment (a new law or social program), you might design a natural experiment in which you relate this independent variable to changes in some pattern of events. Such studies often depend on aggregated datasets (such as crime rates). In Chapters 9 and 10, we will look again at experimental designs using aggregated data.

BOX 6-4

PROHIBITION AND SUICIDE: A TIME-SERIES EXPERIMENT

After the classic study of Emile Durkheim ([1897] 1951) on suicide, which had maintained that factors which increase social integration in a country, such as wars, should be related to decreases in rates of suicide, other researchers questioned this relationship by suggesting that an intervening variable (such as a decrease in unemployment during war) is the factor that leads to the decrease (Marshall, 1981). Another variable which had been shown to be lowered during times of war and also was related to reduced rates of suicide was alcohol consumption. Though both Durkheim and his student Halbwachs ([1930] 1978) had argued that alcohol consumption was not strongly related to suicide, there was substantial evidence from medical research of a strong link between alcohol consumption and suicide (though it was not clear whether alcohol consumption directly affected suicide rates or whether it was psychological depression that either brought about or resulted from alcoholism that increased the incidence of suicide).

Wasserman (1989) decided that the era of Prohibition in the United States set the stage for a fascinating natural experiment with a time-series design. Prohibition, which drastically reduced the amount and availability of alcohol by law and closed down the types of institutions (bars) which sold such beverages, could serve as a naturally occurring experimental stimulus in a quasi-experimental design, enabling a researcher to study its effects on changes in suicide rates. The time-series experiment Wasserman designed would relate alcohol consumption patterns as well as war and economic conditions to suicide rates by using aggregate data on the United States between the years 1910 and 1933—the years in which World War I occurred (the United States was engaged in this war only from 1917 to 1918—and the years of Prohibition in the United States (1920–1933). With this time frame, he set out two hypotheses: that World War I would lower suicide rates because of its increase in economic activity and decreasing levels of availability of alcohol and that the drop in al-

cohol consumption that initially came with Prohibition would also reduce the suicide rate.

There were a number of problems with the available data which Wasserman needed to test these hypotheses (this is often the case when one uses data from the past). First, increasing numbers of states contributed to the mortality data over this time period; thus the database enlarged and shifted over the time period. Second, the increase in states included greater numbers of southern states, which were more rural and tended to have poorer-quality mortality statistics (which usually meant that fewer deaths were reported). Third, there are no clear unemployment figures for these years, though Wasserman was able to find a monthly measure of "business activity" during this time period to use as a surrogate for the employment rate. Note that if one is hypothesizing that alcohol consumption should increase suicide rates, there will be a "lag time" between the periods of consumption and the times of suicide; this factor of "lag" also had to be taken account of in the research model.

What did Wasserman find? The war had no real effect on suicide rates, though he cautioned that since there were only two years to study its effects, it was not really possible to see the effects over a long enough period of time. However, he found a significant decrease in suicide rates during the early years of Prohibition. This was explained as a result of the strong effect on high-risk groups, such as skid-row men, whose access to alcohol was reduced greatly after the closing of saloons. Over the years of Prohibition, the alcohol consumption rate of Americans as a whole actually increased. But the early impact of Prohibition "reduced the supply for a high-risk population on skid row, and for some time after the enactment of prohibition this population was unable to obtain a substitute product" (1989, p. 527). This may have explained the downward trend in suicides.

Source: Ira M. Wasserman, "The Effects of War and Alcohol Consumption Patterns on Suicide: United States, 1910–1933," *Social Forces* **68**:513–530, 1989.

Could you develop conditions which would create the behavior you want to study in a laboratory setting? Or would a natural experiment be a better design? Developing the independent variable is one of the most critical parts of an experiment. In some cases, the stimulus is available (such as a strike at a factory) and needs only be utilized by the investigator in an experimental design which incorporates the presentation of the stimulus. In other cases, an investigator may use an independent variable that another experimenter has developed. (Social-psychological literature is full of experimental ideas you may be able to use for your purposes.) Once you have designed the experimental situation, you need to consider the subjects to be studied. Would you be able to randomly assign them to experimental and control groups? This is the major requirement of a true experiment, and it allows the use of statistical tests to compare the groups. The primary advantage of an experiment is that it is a tightly controlled research method which may be small in scope. Furthermore, once all the planning is done, the experiment itself may not take very long to carry out.

REVIEW NOTES

- In a true experiment, the experimenter manipulates the independent variable and assigns subjects to the experimental condition. In a natural experiment, the experimenter does not manipulate the independent variable but instead observes it and relates it to other conditions.
- The primary challenge to experimentation is to establish sufficient controls without making the experiment too artificial and thus invalid.
- A field experiment differs from a laboratory experiment in that the former takes place in a real environment. A field experiment may be based on real-life occurrences (a natural experiment) or manipulated ones (a true experiment).
- Internal validity addresses whether the experimental conditions actually brought forth the intended effect.
- Problems in the internal validity of an experiment can be caused by lack of comparability between the groups; loss of subjects; rivalry between the subjects in the experimental and control groups; demoralization of subjects; testing; problems with instrumentation; imitation of treatment; compensation to the control group; maturation of subjects between the pre- and posttests; historical events that intervene; effects from the interaction of selection factors of the subjects with maturation, history, or instrumentation; and the effects of statistical regression.
- How far the findings from an experiment can be generalized to other settings constitutes the issue of external validity. External validity may be challenged because of the interactions of the experimental treatment with other aspects of the experiment (selection of subjects, experimental setting, and period of history).
- Demand characteristics are the cues that convey the expected hypothesis to the subjects and make the subjects cooperate with the experimenter to bring forth the experimental effect. Such demand characteristics challenge the external validity of an experiment.
- Assignment of subjects to experimental and control groups by randomization is the primary means in experiments of controlling for biases in how the two groups may respond to the independent variable. When the groups have been randomly assigned, statistical comparisons of the outcomes of the experiment can be made.
- In a double-blind experiment, neither the subjects nor the experimenter knows which group is the experimental group and which is the control group. This is done to reduce the possible biases the experimenter might inadvertently introduce if the identity of the groups were known.
- A Hawthorne effect in an experiment occurs when subjects produce the expected experimental effect without being exposed to the experimental independent variable (they are affected merely by being in the experiment). To control for this, an experimental design may have a second control group, a Hawthorne control group. This group is exposed to a supposedly meaningless independent variable (such as a placebo, or sugar pill, in a drug experiment); the regular

control group is exposed to no independent variable (that is, it is given no pill). It is expected that the Hawthorne control group will have a stronger experimental effect than the regular control group, but not so strong an effect as the experimental group.

• True experimental designs include the classical experiment, the Solomon Four-Group experiment, and the posttest-only control group design.

• Preexperimental designs include the one-shot case study, the one-group pretest-posttest design, and static-group comparisons. In all cases of preexperimental designs, there is no random assignment to experimental and control groups.

• Quasi-experimental designs are for experiments with nonequivalent control groups. Comparisons between experimental and nonequivalent control groups can be made using regression-discontinuity or interrupted times-series analyses.

KEY TERMS

classical experiment
control group
criterion variable
demand characteristics
dependent variable
double-blind experiment
experimental group
experimental mortality
external validity
factorial design
field experiment
Hawthorne effect
independent variable
interaction effect
internal validity
laboratory experiment
matching
maturation
natural experiment
posttest
posttest-only control group design
predictor variable

preexperimental designs
pretest
quasi-experimental designs
randomization in assignment to groups
regression-discontinuity design
response
Solomon Four-Group Design
statistical regression
stimulus
time-series experiment
true experimental designs

STUDY EXERCISES

1. Select either the bystander intervention experiment or the deterrent effects of arrest on domestic assault experiment from Chapter 1.
   a. Describe the experimental designs of each of these experiments.
   b. Discuss the validity issues raised by this experiment.
2. Explain why an experimenter must be concerned about demand characteristics. How might such characteristics affect, for example, the outcome of the drinking and driving film experiment?
3. Why is it so important for an experimenter to use randomization in assigning subjects to experimental and control groups?

RECOMMENDED READINGS

1. Boruch, Robert F.:*Randomized Experiments for Planning and Evaluation*, Sage, Thousand Oaks, CA, 1996. A researcher can use experimental designs to tell whether a social program has been effective. This book is a practical guide for designing such experiments.
2. Cook, Thomas D., and Donald T. Campbell: *Quasi-Experimentation: Design and Analysis Issues for Field Settings,* Houghton Mifflin, Boston, 1979. This book includes Campbell's classic work on types of validity problems in experimental designs and detailed discussions of different types of quasi-experimental designs.

3. Fairweather, George W., and William S. Davidson: *An Introduction to Community Experimentation: Theory, Methods, and Practice,* McGraw-Hill, New York, 1986. This small text describes the reasons for and methods of carrying out and analyzing experimental research in community settings.

4. Lipsey, Mark W.: *Design Sensitivity: Statistical Power for Experimental Research,* Sage, Newbury Park, CA, 1989. Very helpful to those with a limited statistical background; points out the potential problems in an experimental design.

Survey Research, Interviewing Techniques, and Focus Groups

INTRODUCTION

*S*urvey research is a method of collecting data in which a specifically defined group of individuals are asked to answer a number of identical questions. Those answers form the dataset of the study. Survey research is the most common type of social research, probably for both the right and the wrong reasons. As the old dictum states, "If you want to find something out, ask!" There is something simple and straightforward about seeking information through questions, yet we all know that to many questions there are no answers, that answers to questions may be wrong, and that a question may be incorrectly asked so that it cannot elicit the desired information. All these possible problems, which frequently confuse everyday forms of communication, also confront surveys. Furthermore, many topics cannot be properly studied simply by asking questions. Many researchers also may find it difficult or impossible to set up a survey which will meet the basic requirements for a respectable survey.

In Chapter 1, we looked carefully at two surveys to give you some idea of what a good survey can accomplish. In Chapter 4, we considered how to operationalize variables, which are the building blocks of a survey. Selecting the group of individuals to be questioned was the subject of Chapter 5, in which sampling techniques were discussed. In this chapter, we will first consider the creative and scientific dimensions of a survey. Next, the components of a survey will be laid out. The major types of survey research will then be presented and compared. This will include an extensive discussion of interviewing techniques and telephone surveys. Focus groups are presented as a way to generate ideas and questions for surveys. Finally, we will consider various ways of determining whether a survey is the best means to study your intended topic.

THE ART AND SCIENCE OF SURVEYS

Creative Aspects of Surveys

On the face of it, a survey may not seem terribly creative. After all, you may think, anybody can put together a set of questions. That may be true, but not just anybody can put together a set of questions which (1) get as precisely as possible the information the researcher wants, (2) are clearly understood by all the respondents to mean the same thing, and (3) constitute a unified whole (that is, a questionnaire or an interview schedule) that is pleasing enough to the respondents that they are willing to spend the time to complete it and sufficiently engaging that they will not give superficial or misleading answers. To be able to produce a survey that meets these criteria is, first of all, an art.

The most vivid and direct forms of communication are produced by artists. Great art is art that touches and moves many people deeply; it is a presentation which forces one to react. Now don't think me strange if I argue that a superb questionnaire should also be irresistible to the respondent. He or she should feel that these questions must be answered. If the questions are given by an interviewer, the presentation of the questions should be so inviting that the respondent again feels fully engaged in the process of answering. In interviewing, the relationship between the questions as written for the interviewer and the questions as presented to the respondent resembles the relationship between the score of a symphony and the symphony as it is played. The score (or the set of questions) must be wonderful if the symphony (or the survey) is to be wonderful. But a wonderful symphony can be massacred by a poorly rehearsed, badly trained orchestra, and a wonderful survey can be destroyed by bad interviewing.

Let's first consider the questions themselves. They must be worded so carefully and unambiguously that they measure the concepts the researcher intends them to measure. If they do, they are valid measurements of the concepts being studied. If they do not, they are useless. Thus, the designing of questions is a critical phase of the survey. This design of questions requires creativity so that the gap between what the researcher wants to measure and what the questions produce for measurement is as narrow as possible. [See the box that presents Hirschi's (1969) survey questions to measure self-reported acts of juvenile delinquency.]

This ability to create questions to tap ideas that may be on the surface undesirable to answer or lacking in interest requires an artistic touch. But this touch can be fostered by carefully re-creating the best types of questions which one has used in everyday life. We don't often ask people outright, "Are you a car thief?" Instead, we pose questions in a way that generates the information we desire without unduly upsetting or annoying the persons asked. So too in a survey. While we don't know the people we are surveying, we must in many ways design our survey as if we did.

Finally, the way in which the survey is presented, either in spoken form as an interview or in written form as a questionnaire to be answered by the respondent, must be creative. Interviewers must be engaging, but not to the point where they strongly affect the responses given. Note that I haven't said to the point where they would have no effect. This is because it is impossible for an interviewer not to have some effect on the types of responses generated. We will discuss the style of the interviewer below. For the moment, it is enough to remember that an interviewer will always affect in some ways the meaning and interpretation of the questions being asked through his or her personal style.

A questionnaire also expresses a certain style. It may look crowded and wordy or uncluttered and inviting. The type of printing may look official and precise, or it may look more like the work of an amateur. Remember that a questionnaire which

---

QUESTIONS TO MEASURE SELF-REPORTED DELINQUENT ACTS

When Hirschi (1969) wanted to measure delinquency, he created a set of questions which together formed an Index of Delinquency. These six items were as follows:

1. Have you ever taken little things (worth less than $2) that did not belong to you?
2. Have you ever taken things of some value (between $2 and $50) that did not belong to you?
3. Have you ever taken things of large value (worth over $50) that did not belong to you?
4. Have you ever taken a car for a ride without the owner's permission?
5. Have you ever banged up something on purpose that did not belong to you?
6. Not counting fights you may have had with a brother or sister, have you ever beaten up on anyone or hurt anyone on purpose?

Hirschi was actually trying to determine whether youths had committed crimes. Since many people would be reluctant to tell the researcher whether they had committed any crimes, the questions describe the acts without any intimation that the writer of the question disapproves of these acts or regards them as very serious. Note how stealing a car is described as "taking a car for a ride without permission." This is a euphemism for "stealing a car." Furthermore, it may more closely represent the way in which the delinquent teenager considers the act: as an essentially harmless activity in which the youth was merely having a bit of fun.

---

appears to have been prepared by an amateur may arouse less suspicion and more cooperation than a study which seems more formal and authoritative. Further, because a questionnaire is an object, its appearance will determine how it is treated.

Scientific Aspects of Surveys

In the research model considered in Chapter 2, the design of a survey would fall into the phase of the research process after hypotheses have been formulated. Wallace refers to it as *instrumentation* (1971, pp. 68–69). The two forms of instrumentation which he defines are those based solely on "human sensory organs" (such as "seeing" things) and those based on "technologically augmented sensory organs." The first type would be best represented by participant observation, in which the researcher's primary instruments are his or her eyes and ears. The second type would be best represented by a survey in which a questionnaire or an interview schedule supports the basic sensory data collectors.

Matilda White Riley explains the differences between the data generated from participant observation (which we will consider in Chapter 8) and that from questionnaires in the following way:

> Data from observation reflect the network of actions and reactions among group members—the objective properties of the system. Data from questioning reflect the subjective network of orientations and interpersonal relationships—the underlying ideas and feelings of the members, their dispositions to act toward the others and to define and evaluate these others in various ways (*1963, p. 184*).

For example, while observing the behavior of people on a city street corner, an observer may see someone ask another person a question. Judging by the behavior of the two people, the observer might decide that the questions concerned soliciting a geographic direction. But the field researcher would not know what question was asked or why it was asked. Questions in a questionnaire or an interview try to get at the underlying attitudes and dispositions (the orientations) surrounding a piece of information. Surveys generally go beyond merely asking people *who* they voted for or *what* their religion is to asking *why* they voted for a particular candidate and *how* religiously observant they are.

Does this make survey data more or less scientific than data based solely on observation? Surveys are more focused and planned. They go after very specific pieces of information, or, in an interview situation, they may probe around an issue—but always with the intent of embellishing a specific piece of information. However, surveys may be so badly designed that they are ambiguous and produce misleading data. When this is the case, the scientific value of the study is undermined.

Surveys also may be based on much more precise samples than an observation study. As we saw in Chapter 5, probability samples enable a researcher to relate findings based on a specific sample to a much wider population. Much of the popularity of surveys and polls rests on the ability to generalize the findings so widely. Finally, survey questions can be developed so that their reliability levels are quite high. This means that questions will tap the same responses from people if they are repeated again and again.

The analysis of survey data rests on a form of scientific logic based on relationships and changes in relationships associated with the introduction of new factors. In certain types of surveys—those based on panel data, where the same respondents have been surveyed at more than one point in time—a clear time dimension can be established, and certain types of casual analyses may be carried out. Chapters 12 and 13 will describe how survey data may form the basis of scientific analyses.

GENERAL COMPONENTS OF SURVEY RESEARCH

Modes of Eliciting Information

There are two primary modes of doing a survey: using questionnaires and giving interviews. Both methods are based on a set of questions. In the *questionnaire*, these questions are written down and the respondent reads them and gives written answers. In an interview, the interviewer asks the questions as they are written in an *interview schedule* and then records the respondent's answers either by writing them down or by recording them electronically. Interviews may be face to face or may be carried out on the telephone.

Modes of Selecting Respondents

In Chapter 5 we discussed the various types of samples that may be used for a survey. The first consideration in choosing among them is whether a potential set of respondents will be able to give answers to the types of questions that will be asked. The relevant issue here is, What is the appropriate population to which your questions apply? If you are doing a study of farm abandonment, you will probably want to survey farmers, ex-farmers, and others who live in rural areas. If you want to survey college students about attitudes toward the Reserve Officers Training Corps (ROTC), you will want only students, probably more male students than female, and may want to concentrate on students who have been in ROTC.

Second, it will be important to design a survey which will be appropriate for this sample. It should include questions which such a group could and would answer. That is, the questions must be presented in language familiar to the sample and phrased so that members of the group will understand them. The questions also must be acceptable to the sample; they cannot probe into subjects which the respondents would refuse to consider because the questions make them look socially undesirable or stupid. If the questionnaire will be received in the mail, it must have an appropriate cover letter designed to encourage the respondents to participate. If an interview is to be given, the opening remarks must encourage participation and mollify any concerns a potential respondent may have. In short, the mode of eliciting information must support the selection of respondents.

Modes of Returning Information

Once a questionnaire is completed, there must be clear instructions about how it is to be returned. In most mail surveys, return self-addressed envelopes—which usually are stamped—are included with the questionnaires. In this case, the questionnaire need contain very few instructions about its return. Interviews, once terminated, need to be fully converted into information which may be processed as a part of the study. Usually, the interviewer completes an interview schedule which is basically like a questionnaire. In certain cases, interviews may be taped. When this occurs, the information on the tape must be transcribed. The sooner this is done after the interview, the more accurately the interviewer will recall the exact details of the interview.

This brief review of the general components of surveys is set up to make you aware of the whole scope of surveys. Before we take them apart and examine them carefully in detail, let me go over the general issues in administering surveys by using examples from four surveys which used different types of data-gathering procedures.

ADMINISTERING SURVEYS: FOUR EXAMPLES

Actually administering the survey is the fourth stage in the process of conducting survey research. The first stage, defining the problem, was discussed in the Introduction and in Chapters 3 and 4. The second stage, selecting an appropriate sample, was addressed in Chapter 5. The third stage, designing the questionnaire or interview schedule, will be the subject of this chapter. The fourth stage, survey administration, will also be described here; the fifth stage, analyzing the data from the survey, will be presented in Chapters 11, 12, and 13.

There are two primary ways of administering a survey: using questionnaires and giving interviews. Questionnaires may be administered to a group or sent to individuals to be filled out on their own; interviews may be carried out in a face-to-face exchange between the interviewer and the interviewee or may be conducted on the telephone. Whether to use a questionnaire or an interview and how to carry it out will depend very much on the circumstances of the particular project you are designing. Four actual surveys, each using a different type of data collection technique, will be presented here for purposes of comparison.

Example 1: A Questionnaire Administered to a Group

To study the effects of ability grouping on the social status of high school students, I gained the cooperation of two large suburban high schools which had different types of ability grouping practices. In North High, students were rigidly placed into ability groups on the basis of test scores, with little chance to select a different group or to change groups if they thought they had been misplaced. Furthermore, ability grouping was practiced in almost all academic subjects. In South High, grouping was much less rigid. Students could select different classes with advice from teachers, and certain academic subjects had no ability grouping at all.

With the support of the school administration, I administered the questionnaire to the entire senior class of South High during a senior assembly, a regular gathering held weekly at that school. In North High, where senior assemblies were not held, questionnaires were distributed in senior homerooms by the homeroom teachers, using the same instructions I had used for the group administration.

Example 2: A Mail Survey

To determine whether attending a predominantly white college increased the autonomy of black students compared to white students, I surveyed black students and white students attending two different predominantly white colleges. The questionnaire included a set of questions from an autonomy scale which was used as an indicator of autonomy. The survey was a panel study in that the respondents answered more than one questionnaire over a period of time, and the data from the questionnaires were linked to each respondent. This study had two questionnaires which formed

the "two waves" of the data collection procedure: The first questionnaire was sent out at the beginning of the first year of college, before the effects of college could have occurred; the second, at the end of the first year. Information at more than one point in time was needed so that any changes in level of autonomy (the hypothetical result of being at college) could be measured.

Selected first-year students were sent questionnaires through the mail shortly after the fall term began. The first mailing included a letter explaining the survey, the questionnaire itself, and a stamped return envelope. Those who did not send the questionnaire back within two weeks received a postcard reminder requesting them to complete the form and return it. A third mailing, to those who had not returned the questionnaire within a month's time, included a different cover letter urging the person to complete the survey, another copy of the questionnaire, and another return envelope. A second questionnaire, which included the same measure of autonomy, was sent at the end of the spring term to every person who had completed the fall survey. Again, two follow-up requests were sent to those who did not return the initial questionnaire.

Example 3: A Face-to-Face Interview

A civic organization, hoping to address some of the causes of youth unemployment in a major city, acquired the services of the Northern Illinois University Public Opinion Laboratory, then headed by political scientist Jon Miller. Miller and his colleagues were to gather information on this subject from face-to-face interviews with youths aged 17 to 24, who were representative of those with the greatest degree of unemployment. Interview schedules were prepared that included questions about the youths' education and skills, aspirations and plans, job searches, and work experiences.

The public opinion laboratory drew a sample of 50 blocks in the city, representing the lower half of the income distribution of the city. Interviewers were selected, hired, and trained from among college students on summer vacation who were roughly similar to those being interviewed in age and race. Teams consisting of a few interviewers and a supervisor went to the selected blocks to interview every youth between the ages of 17 and 24 residing there. They also tried to secure appointments with youths on the block who were away at the time of their visit. Blocks were revisited three and four times over a one-month period of interviewing. The material from the interview was recorded on a schedule by the interviewer during the course of the interview.

Example 4: A Telephone Survey

On my new campus at San Marcos in San Diego County, we developed a social research laboratory [the Social and Behavioral Research Institute (SBRI)] which has a computer-assisted telephone interviewing (CATI) system which will be described in detail later in this chapter. Each term the students in our social research methods classes carry out a small survey using the CATI system. In the fall of 1996, my two research methods classes were joined by our political science research methods class in designing a survey to measure political attitudes and some community concerns in North County San Diego. The assistant director of the SBRI, Allen Risley, secured a voter registration file which served as our population. Then the students signed up for a four-hour session to call residents and interview them on the telephone. The random-digit-dialing function of the CATI system randomly selected the registered voters, and their telephone numbers were dialed. Because of the large number of answering machines, incorrect numbers, and residents who were not available, students often needed to make numerous calls to complete one successful interview. Nevertheless, in the course of three weeks, calling primarily in the early evenings, the students in the three classes were able to successfully interview 567 residents, who became the basis of our sample.

In each of these four surveys, the collected data were entered into a computer, and analyses of the aggregate findings were prepared. Thus, in each of these surveys the researcher ended up with sets of answers to the same questions. The differences in these surveys lay in how the data had been collected. These brief descriptions of surveys that vary in their style of administration have been offered as an overview of the primary forms of surveys.

How to choose the appropriate form of administration for your survey will depend on the type of problem you are studying, your access to a sample to study, your resources, and your personal preferences. We will now carefully go over how to design and prepare questionnaire surveys for in-person and self-administration questionnaires, and we will then describe interview surveys for face-to-face and telephone situations. You will need this information if you decide to do a survey; it will help you select the most appropriate type of survey for your particular circumstances.

SELF-ADMINISTERED SURVEYS

General Rules of Questionnaire Construction

1. Include only questions which will address your research concerns and which you plan to analyze.
2. Make the questionnaire as appealing as possible to the respondents.
3. Keep the questionnaire as short as will suffice to elicit the information necessary to analyze the primary research concerns. Be sure, however, to include questions on all the aspects of the research problem that you will need to address.
4. If the questionnaire is self-administered, keep the instructions brief but make sure they contain all the information required to complete and send back the questionnaire.
5. Consider in advance all the issues a respondent might raise when he or she receives this instrument. Be sure that the questionnaire addresses those issues.

General Format of a Questionnaire

A questionnaire should include a cover letter, brief instructions on how to complete the questionnaire, the questions, a clearly defined space and method for the respondent to register answers to the questions, possibly codes for transcribing the data onto a computer once they are collected, instructions on how to return the questionnaire (as well as a stamped, addressed return envelope), and a final thank you to the respondent for the time and effort expended.

Cover Letter. The primary objective of a cover letter is to tell the respondents the purpose of the questionnaire and to request that they participate. The purpose of the study should be stated clearly and simply. There are often two different purposes in a study: the first is the more general purpose of collecting information to address specific research questions or hypotheses; the second is to accomplish the objectives of the researcher, who may be a student carrying out a study in a methods course, a graduate student seeking data for thesis research, a government researcher collecting data for reporting, a marketing researcher who is exploring the tastes of potential clients, or an academic researcher who is collecting data on some topic.

Whoever is doing the study wants those who receive the questionnaire to complete it. Will the potential respondents be more likely to complete the instrument if the cover letter stresses the importance of the research project itself (its contribution to scientific understanding) or if it stresses the importance of the needs of the researcher as a person? In the first case, you are trying to convince the respondents that valuable information can be gained through survey research and that by participating in this study they may be helping science. This has been called an egoistical approach because it assumes that a respondent who consents to participate has been convinced that participation will better society as a whole, the state of scholarship, and thus, indirectly, the respondent also. In the other case, where you are stressing your needs as a researcher, you are banking on the altruism of the respondents to motivate their participation. If the respondents are convinced that their help is really vital to the study, then out of a sense of generosity they may volunteer the time needed to complete the survey. Usually the significance of the study is also stressed. Further, if the researcher is a student and makes an earnest request for help with the study, the respondents may be encouraged to assist.

Whatever the pitch of the covering letter, the researcher must decide how it will sound to potential respondents. Sometimes a very matter-of-fact letter succeeds. If respondents have very little time (for example, if they have high-pressure jobs), it may be wise to stress both how important the data are for studying the subject and how short a period of time it will take to complete the form. It is important that the suggested time of completion be reasonably accurate. Ethical issues also should be considered. The letter should describe how the protection of human subjects will be accomplished (whether anonymity or confidentiality will be offered).

Instructions. In a self-administered questionnaire all the information necessary to complete the form accurately and completely must be given. The following issues may need to be addressed in the instructions:

1. How and where does the respondent give his or her answers? (Check the box, circle the correct response, etc.) In this case, the questionnaire should be consistent so that all the answers can be given in the same way.
2. If there is a separate answer sheet which is machine-readable, clear instructions must be given about how to move from reading questions on the questionnaire to providing responses on the answer sheet. If a special kind of pencil is required, this must be made absolutely clear. Generally, separate answer sheets are not desirable for a self-administered survey because of the possible problems of confusion and error in using them. Questionnaires themselves may

be printed on machine-readable forms; this simplifies the processing of the data without sacrificing the ease of having respondents place their responses next to the questions. (Of course, some groups, such as college students, probably have had extensive experience taking tests where the responses must be filled in on machine-readable forms, but other groups may not have had much experience filling out such materials.) The most appropriate way to administer a survey using machine-readable forms is to a group. Then not only may the use of correct pencils be clearly stated by the administrator, the pencils themselves may be made available.

3. Clear instructions for contingency questions, where respondents are allowed to skip certain questions or specifically answer certain questions, must be given throughout the instrument as they are needed.

4. Clear instructions for returning the questionnaire are also necessary. They may be given in three different places: in the cover letter, at the end of the survey, or at the beginning of the survey. The best policy is to have the instructions on the survey itself. If the cover letter is in fact the top sheet of the survey, the method of returning the questionnaire may be mentioned in the letter. If the letter is on a separate sheet of paper, however, it may accidentally be disposed of before the respondent finishes the survey. Thus the return instructions are best printed on the survey form itself.

Developing Appropriate Wording for Questions

As Shakespeare knew, the word's the thing! In a written questionnaire, the words that make up the questions form the basis for the study. Hence, the survey designer must develop unambiguous, clear, and simple questions which serve the purposes of the research study. Here are a set of rules developed from suggestions offered by de Vaus (1986, pp. 71–74), which you should go through for every question you prepare for a survey:

1. *Are the words that make up this question and the meaning of the question simple and clear?* Avoid words that are known only by experts in an area (i.e., jargon) and avoid overly complex and unfamiliar words. Carefully consider the sample who will be answering the questionnaire and ask yourself whether the questions will be fully understood by the likely respondents. This means, of course, that if the respondents have particular expertise—for example, if they are pharmacists—you could include words experts in that field would know. Remember that on certain questions respondents may honestly not have a response; therefore, ask yourself whether a "don't know" or "not relevant" category should be offered as an option.

2. *Could the question have an alternative meaning to some respondents?* This addresses the issues of ambiguity and possible group differences in interpretation. You may not see the question or the words within it as ambiguous; however, others may. Sometimes members of particular ethnic groups or occupational groups use words differently from the conventional way. The best assistance you can get on this problem is to show your questions to others and pretest the questions on a broad range of individuals who share the characteristics your sample will have.

3. *Word questions so that the respondents are not likely to give false information to make themselves look more socially desirable or prestigious.* People want to make themselves look good. Your questions must discourage this bias toward *social desirability* by trying to elicit honest answers on years of education, income, number of friends. Ask yourself whether the question easily lets the respondent report, for example, a low income, a low level of education, or a few friends while experiencing as little shame as possible about revealing this information. One method used is to not ask people to give an exact income or education level but to place themselves within grouped categories, which are more neutral.

4. *Avoid negative questions.* The use of negatives in questions—for example, "AIDS cannot be prevented through safe sex practices: Agree or Disagree?"—is confusing. It is always better to word questions positively and then give the respondents a chance to respond positively or negatively.

5. *Avoid double-barreled questions.* Any question that subsumes more than one response is ambiguous. For example, "Do you like San Diego and San Francisco? Yes/No" cannot be easily answered by a respondent who likes one of those cities but not the other.

6. *Check for bias in your questions.* Leading questions encourage respondents to answer in a certain way. Questions such as "Do you agree with Chief Justice . . ." and "If the X welfare program is bankrupting the state, what do you think the state should do with the program?" are biased in favor of one answer.

7. *Should the question be posed directly or indirectly?* Questions that touch on more personal matters are often best posed, or moved toward, indirectly ("Many people have tried marijuana . . ." or "Do you know other people who have tried marijuana?"). Then it is easier to ask whether the respondent has tried it. However, you must be careful that indirect questions do not seem coy or contrived.

Types of Questions

Chapter 4 gave some examples of how variables were operationalized in terms of developing questions. Here we want to consider the different types of questions a questionnaire might contain.

Closed-Ended and Open-Ended Questions.

Closed-ended questions force the respondent to select a single response from a list (for this reason they are often called *forced-choice questions*). Such lists of responses must cover the entire range of possible answers; that is, they must be exhaustive. A question that includes a broad enough range of responses so that every possible answer to the question can fit into a given response has *exhaustive cat-*

egories. For example (as was noted in Chapter 4), if you ask about religion, you might offer as possible responses "Catholic," "Protestant," "Jewish," "other," and "none." This would determine the major religious groups in the United States. Or you might want to include specific smaller religious groups in the United States such as "Hindu" and "Moslem." Even in this case, however, you would still want to keep the "other" category for people who did not feel that they could comfortably place themselves in any specific category. For an attitudinal item such as "How good a job do you think the secretary of state is doing?" where the range of choices is "excellent," "very good," "good," "fair," and "poor," you also would want to include "don't know" or "no opinion" for those who are unsure.

One other condition which must be met in a closed-ended set of responses is that those responses must not overlap one another in such a way that a respondent may think he or she should select more than one category. This requirement means that responses must be *mutually exclusive.* Using the example of food, if the categorical choices offered were "meat," "fruit," "vegetables," "bananas," "dairy products," and "grains," "bananas" and "fruit" would overlap. In other words, since a banana is a subcategory of fruit, it is being measured twice in this list. Be sure that the terminology you use clearly distinguishes one category from another. (Of course, in certain instances multiple answers may be allowed; e.g., "What are your favorite sports?")

Open-ended questions state a question and leave room for the respondent to write out an answer. If a specific number of lines are left, a suggested length for a response is more precise than it would be if only an amorphous space were left. It is also possible that handwritten responses may be clearer if lines are printed on the questionnaire. However, if in the opinion of the respondent too many or too few lines are left, he or she may be more likely to skip the item.

Closed-ended questions with forced-choice responses are more likely to be completed by respondents than are open-ended questions. Questionnaires with numerous open-ended questions often

---

CLOSED- AND OPEN-ENDED FORMS OF THE SAME QUESTION

OPEN-ENDED QUESTION

How much does your job as a program manager *challenge you* in the sense of demanding your skills and abilities?

CLOSED-ENDED QUESTION

How much does your job as a program manager *challenge you* in the sense of demanding your skills and abilities?

    [ ] Completely demands my abilities
    [ ] Demands most of them
    [ ] Demands about half
    [ ] Demands some of my abilities
    [ ] Demands very few of them

Source: Donald P. Warwick and Charles A. Lininger: *The Sample Survey: Theory and Practice,* McGraw-Hill, New York, 1975, pp. 135–136.

---

are returned with many questions left blank. Remember, it takes much more time and thought for the respondent to generate a written response than to merely check an offered response (see the box that contrasts closed- and open-ended questions). Furthermore, open-ended questions are much more difficult to code (see Chapter 11 on this subject). However, there may be certain questions to which only an open-ended response seems reasonable.

Contingency Questions. Questions which depend on the responses to earlier questions are referred to as *contingency questions.* If you want to ask a person how many cigarettes he or she smokes a day, such a question should be contingent on an earlier question ("Do you smoke cigarettes?"). The box shows how such a series of questions might be set up.

Matrix Questions. *Matrix questions* allow for the answering of sets of questions with similar

types of responses. Usually the questions are similar, for example, a set of attitudes with which the respondent is asked to "strongly agree," "agree," "disagree," "strongly disagree," or "have no opinion." Matrix questions help conserve space in the questionnaire and make it easier and quicker for the respondent to give answers. The fear with matrix questions is that the respondent will start to answer questions in a pattern, for example, checking "strongly agree" to every item. This problem, which is called *response set,* can be minimized by clearly reversing the meaning of some questions so that consistency in response requires agreeing with some questions and disagreeing with others. See the box that presents a matrix question.

Ordering of Questions. Here there are two simple rules to remember. In a self-administered questionnaire the first questions should be interesting so that the respondent is encouraged to begin (and, it is hoped, complete) the questionnaire. (In an interview, the early questions often ask for simple, nonthreatening demographic information such as "How many adults over the age of 18 live here?") The other rule is that questions which the respondent may be reluctant to answer (on income or race, for example) should come near the end of the questionnaire. This discourages respondents from refusing to complete the form.

Questions on the same subject generally are grouped together to keep the respondent thinking about the same material. In some cases, a set of questions on a specific topic (say, educational background) may be set off in a separate section.

Pretesting the Questionnaire

Once you have a draft of the questionnaire, you should *pretest* it to determine its effectiveness and problems. This preliminary pretest might be done with friends or acquaintances who agree to take the questionnaire. The questionnaire form may be typed with large margins and spaces between questions. Ask the respondents to go through and answer the questionnaire as if they had received it

EXAMPLE OF A CONTINGENCY QUESTION

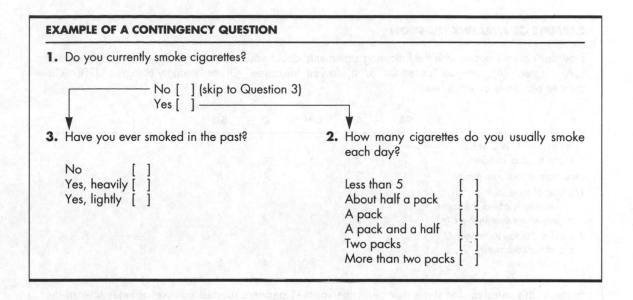

1. Do you currently smoke cigarettes?

             No [   ] (skip to Question 3)
             Yes [   ]

3. Have you ever smoked in the past?

No   [   ]
Yes, heavily [   ]
Yes, lightly   [   ]

2. How many cigarettes do you usually smoke each day?

Less than 5   [   ]
About half a pack   [   ]
A pack   [   ]
A pack and a half   [   ]
Two packs   [   ]
More than two packs [   ]

from someone they did not know. Then ask them to go through the questionnaire again and point out (possibly by writing comments adjacent to the questions) any problems they noted with the questions. Were there some questions that they did not understand? Did some of the questions seem particularly stupid?

After going over the responses of the preliminary pretest and making the changes that seem advisable, it is time to have your formal pretest. For this pretest you should try to have a trial administration that is as similar as possible to the actual survey administration. If you are planning to mail out your surveys, you should mail your pretest to a small sample of individuals who might have been selected for your actual study (but were not). If you plan to administer it to a group, find a similar group and see if you can administer it to them. This pretest questionnaire should look precisely the same as your actual questionnaire will look. In a group administration you might ask them after the completion of the questionnaire to write comments on it or to discuss with you any problems they found with it. In this formal pretest, be sure not to tell the respondents that this is a pretest until it is over.

The main purpose of the formal pretest, however, is to examine patterns of response. For this reason, you will want to have a sufficiently large pretest sample. Look for the following types of responses: (1) questions that many people have skipped (Were they parts of contingency questions? Should they have been skipped?), (2) questions that everyone seems to answer alike (if there is no variation in the responses to an item, it will not prove to be very useful in the analysis), (3) open-ended questions that have been answered ambiguously (for example, the answer to "What is your occupation?" may be very imprecise), and (4) "response set" to matrix-type questions where the respondent seems to have merely circled all the same numbers without seeming to have read the items carefully.

Revise your questionnaire on the basis of the preliminary pretest and the formal pretest. The revised form might be given again to a few friends to make sure you haven't inserted new questions that have problems. It is worth spending the extra time to carry out the pretests and consider the comments and patterns of response. Remember that once you send out the final questionnaire, it is too late to fix any problems in the questionnaire design.

EXAMPLE OF A MATRIX QUESTION

How far do you agree with the following statements about your community? So you "strongly agree" (SA), "agree" (A), are you "uncertain" (UN), do you "disagree" (D), or "strongly disagree" (SD)? (Circle one response on each line.)

	SA	A	UN	D	SD
This community is a good place to raise children.	1	2	3	4	5
I feel safe in this community.	1	2	3	4	5
The cost of food in this community is about the same as anywhere else in the city.	1	2	3	4	5
If I had a chance to move out of my community, I would move.	1	2	3	4	5

Note: In this question for some statements the "agree" answers suggest positive attitudes toward the community; in other cases they suggest negative attitudes. Any person reading the items carefully would be unlikely to circle, for example, all the 1s.

Questionnaire Distribution

On-Site Administration. There are various precautions to consider in administering a questionnaire to a group. The atmosphere of the session must be sufficiently serious that the respondents complete the questionnaires objectively. Sometimes, with a student audience, an amusing question or a joke by the administrator may touch off a mood of frivolity. The light mood can have serious effects on the results of the questionnaire. A researcher must always consider whether an instrument has been filled out in jest. Thus the manner of the person administering the questionnaire should be matter-of-fact and serious.

An explanation of the purpose of the survey must be given. This should be brief and neutral: "Today you will be participating in a survey about college students' attitudes and interests." Again, the researcher must decide what pitch to use. When the sample group is already present, it may not be as necessary to try to sell the benefits of participating. It is much more difficult in a group environment for a respondent to throw out the questionnaire or refuse to participate.

The instructions for completing the surveys also must be given. If the survey researcher will not be giving the instructions, she or he must be certain that the person(s) administering the questionnaire is (are) properly trained.

Mail Questionnaires. Most *mail surveys* contain the survey itself, a cover letter (which may form the top page of the survey), and a return envelope which is addressed and stamped. If the survey is to be printed, the return envelopes may be printed as well. The return envelope should be large enough to hold the completed questionnaire. The envelope in which the survey is sent may be stamped and sent first-class or printed with a bulk-rate permit. Bulk-rate mail must be ordered by Zip codes and must include at least 200 pieces. You should check with the local post office for changes in mailing regulations.

Getting an Adequate Response Rate

Various conditions affect the number of respondents who complete and return a questionnaire. The *response rate* is the percentage of returned questionnaires [the proportion of those sent (or given) out that are returned].

Appearance of the Questionnaire. The appearance of a questionnaire will have an effect on the respondent. A potential respondent will react to a questionnaire initially in terms of its overall appearance. Crowded questionnaires, which look wordy and squeezed together, generally draw fewer responses than will a slightly longer questionnaire which appears more spacious. This does not mean that all mailed questionnaires must be professionally printed. In fact, a questionnaire that looks less official may serve certain purposes better. What is important is that the audience for the questionnaire be carefully considered.

A sloppy-looking survey will turn off most respondents. ("If the researcher can't prepare a better-looking survey than this, why should I bother to fill it out?") However, a clear, accurate, but amateur-looking survey may encourage certain respondents to complete the survey, thinking that the data will be used primarily to help a student complete an educational project. Now that word processors are widely available, you may be able to use one to prepare your survey. With different print formats and other features, a questionnaire prepared on a word processor may incorporate many of the features characteristic of printing. With a laser printer, the copy can hardly be differentiated from actual printing.

In some cases a more professional-looking printed survey may seem preferable. When the survey is quite long, a printed form will conserve space, making the survey seem shorter. Separate sections of a questionnaire may be printed on different-colored paper for emphasis. As was discussed above, printing will make the form appear more official. The reason to do it one way or the other will be based both on cost and on a consideration of whether printing will enhance the response rate. However it is produced, neatness and spaciousness are important.

Nature of the Request to Respond. Encouraging a potential respondent to respond is a critical aspect of survey design. The best-looking questionnaire which does not lead to a strong response rate may have been harmed by a lack of careful consideration of how to request cooperation from the respondents. As was described earlier, the cover letter generally is used to ask the respondent to answer the instrument. You might decide to keep your explanation very simple, expressed without social-scientific jargon. Here are a few examples:

• This survey is being carried out to try to discover what the residents in your community think are the most serious local problems.
• College students need adequate financial support to complete their studies. This survey asks how students get this support.
• What are the attitudes of parents to various child-rearing practices? The purpose of this survey is to ask parents their views.

Personal appeals. As was stated before, the survey researcher may appeal to the potential respondents for assistance so that the study will be a success. Such an appeal is probably more effective when the researcher is a student and the audience receiving the questionnaire can be assumed to be familiar with and sympathetic to the needs of students. If they are not, appeals of this type can backfire.

Sponsorship. If the study is being *sponsored* (paid for) by an organization, a funding agency, or another group, this should be told to the respondent. An alumni association of a university, a marketing research firm, and a government sponsor for research all suggest different objectives for the study. The stationery used for the cover letter may indicate the source of sponsorship. Researchers should always consider what the title of

EXAMPLES OF SPONSORSHIP DESCRIPTIONS

• The Center for Public Broadcasting is interested in finding out whether American college students regularly watch television news discussion shows.

• The Alumni Association of Happiness College wants to know to what degree graduates of Happiness have found their education beneficial to their careers and personal lives.

• This study is being supported by the National Institute of Child Health and Development in the interest of furthering an understanding of the effects of family size on the careers and personal lives of parents.

the sponsor may mean to the respondents. If the respondents are unlikely to know or understand who the sponsor is and why the sponsor is supporting the project, an explanation should be given. The box presents some brief examples of how such explanations might be presented.

Other inducements to participate. The purpose of a study should never be stated falsely. Every objective of the study need not be mentioned. The major aim, however, should be stated clearly, and respondents may be told that if they would like more information about the survey, they may contact the researcher "at the following address or telephone number." In relation to the full-disclosure aspect of surveys, respondents often are told that they will be sent (automatically or on request) a summary of the survey's results. Such promises should be given only if the researcher fully plans to make good on them.

Financial inducements sometimes are sent with a questionnaire to encourage a respondent to reply. The argument for such a plan is that many respondents will feel more compelled to complete

a questionnaire if it comes with such an inducement. In some cases, $1 has been enclosed and the respondent has been told that $5 will be sent once the questionnaire is returned. In other cases, a larger sum has been sent initially. Of course, some respondents may merely keep the money and discard the survey. However, the position favoring financial inducements is that respondents who are disinclined to complete the questionnaire may feel guilty keeping the money and will therefore complete the questionnaire in order to reduce this feeling. By contrast, some respondents may be angered at the small amount of the inducement, feeling that their time is worth more than the token amount of money sent. Financial inducements must therefore be considered in relation to the type of people being surveyed. Young people may be more likely to appreciate a small fee than are older people. People with higher incomes may be more annoyed with a small fee than are those with lower incomes.

Anonymity and Confidentiality. Surveys usually ask some questions which are personal in nature. They almost always ask about attitudes which a respondent may not want to make public. Respondents therefore may not want to divulge their identities. If the survey asks for no identification and includes no code number, when it is returned, it will be completely anonymous. A survey can offer *anonymity* to potential respondents if the researcher is not able to identify the respondents. Naturally, this means that the researcher would not be able to determine which respondents had completed the questionnaire and which had not. In such a study, no follow-up materials could be sent to the nonrespondents and no study of nonrespondents could be made.

For this reason, most researchers do not want to leave respondents completely anonymous. They prefer to have the questionnaires coded so that returned forms can be checked off against a list of names and follow-up efforts can be directed toward the nonrespondents. Also, if the survey is a panel study, where it will be necessary to get back to the respondents and the questionnaires from the different surveys will need to be linked, the researcher must know which questionnaire belongs to which respondent.

In such a case, a researcher can promise the respondents that the data from the questionnaire will be confidential. In this instance, *confidentiality* can be offered to the respondent if no one other than the researcher will be able to associate the respondent's questionnaire and name and if once the follow-up efforts are complete the list of names will be destroyed. Whatever the respondent is told should represent what the researcher actually plans to do.

Studies have shown that respondents usually are not worried about confidential handling of the questionnaires. In some cases, questionnaire forms request that the respondent sign the form. Many respondents do not object to this. In other cases, a detachable postcard is attached to the questionnaire. Respondents are asked to detach it, fill in their names and addresses, and send the postcard back separately from the questionnaire. This enables the researcher to know who has responded without being able to associate the respondent with a particular questionnaire.

Attempts to hide the coded number (for example, with invisible ink or as a phony room number on the return envelope) raise ethical issues if they are accompanied by a promise of anonymity. I once knew a student researcher, desperate to increase her response rate, who wrote the code number in invisible ink under the stamp on the return envelope with the intention of steaming off the stamps of the returned questionnaires. One respondent discovered this method and wrote back furiously to object. Such deception is inadvisable.

Type of Enclosed Material for Return Mailing.

A return envelope which is addressed and stamped should accompany every survey. These envelopes may be printed with business-reply postage which will be charged only if the respondent sends it back. Some believe that stamped envelopes are preferable to business-reply envelopes, possibly because the respondent may be less likely to discard an envelope with an actual stamp (especially if it is an attractive commemorative one). It is not a good idea to use a metered postage marking because it is dated and if a survey is not returned quickly, the post office may refuse to deliver it.

Type of Mailing Procedure.

The type of mail delivery and the timing of the mailing may affect the response rate. Many researchers have found that surveys mailed special delivery are more likely to be answered. First-class postage seems to improve the response rate over bulk-rate mail (possibly because some people are likely to throw away nearly all material sent bulk rate). Here the relative costs must be weighed against the relative benefits. As with a return envelope, a prestigious-looking stamp on the outgoing envelope may stimulate the interest of respondents and discourage them from throwing away the survey without opening it.

When to send out a survey should vary with the intended audience. General rules would suggest not sending them near major holidays, especially Christmas, when people are often inundated with mail. Beginning of school and end of school periods may be undesirable if the respondents are students or teachers. As for the day of the week, the respondents should be taken into account. Studies have found that surveys to organizations are better received early in the week but that those to home addresses may be better received nearer the weekend, when there may be more free time to fill them out.

Follow-up Procedures.

Nearly all surveys which are serious in nature *follow up* the initial questionnaires with two or three additional mailings as well as telephone calls to increase the overall response rate. Generally, the second follow-up occurs two to three weeks after the initial survey was sent out; sufficient numbers of surveys have usually been returned by then to allow the researcher to make up lists of nonrespondents. Second follow-ups generally do not include another copy of the questionnaire. In some cases, a post-card is used to remind the person to complete the questionnaire and return it. In other cases, a letter is sent reexplaining the purpose of the study and reiterating the importance of having every respondent reply to the survey to make it a representative study.

Third follow-ups often include another request letter and a copy of the questionnaire, which may be assumed by then to have been discarded or misplaced. Third follow-ups are sent out a month to six weeks after the original survey. Telephone reminders may come before or after the third follow-up, and these calls may be used to find out why the survey was not returned (it was misplaced or thrown out, the respondent refuses to answer it, the respondent would be happy to answer it as soon as time is available, etc.). Some surveys have had as many as six follow-ups. Generally, it is found that the first follow-up will increase the response rate by one-fifth to one-fourth. Each additional follow-up brings in proportionately fewer respondents (even though the pool is narrowing as the follow-ups continue).

Assessing the Response Rate.   What is a respectable response rate for a survey? There is disagreement on this point. With a carefully selected sample, a researcher would hope to have 70 percent respond in order to feel confident that the respondents were largely representative of the sample (though the researcher might try to determine whether respondents are representative of the sample by gathering some information on the nonrespondents and comparing them to the respondents). Even a 70 percent response rate could produce an unrepresentative sample if the 30 percent nonrespondents included a large proportion of the types of respondents desired for the study. (For example, a survey of delinquency could get a much lower response rate from delinquent youths than from nondelinquent youths.) Surveys without follow-ups are unlikely to surpass 50 percent response rates. Of course, different types of surveys and, more particularly, certain types of individuals

sampled will yield different response rates. A survey sent to a group of people who are professionally concerned about the results may yield a high rate. For example, a survey in a university to study the effectiveness of graduate programs yielded a much higher response rate from the faculty in the program than from the graduate students. Possibly the questions addressed issues the students did not think they could judge yet. And probably the faculty more than the graduate students perceived administrative pressure to provide evaluations of the graduate program.

The best response rate is the largest one you can produce given your time, finances, and persistence. Many researchers have been able to get response rates in excess of 90 percent. In such cases, the analyses are greatly strengthened because the researcher can rest assured that the responses are truly representative of the people sampled.

INTERVIEWING TECHNIQUES

The data for a survey research project can be collected through written questionnaire or through interviewing, but interviewing is not a data collection procedure used only in survey research. We begin by discussing face-to-face interviews carried out for a survey. We then introduce an increasingly popular form of social research, focus groups, which are a group interviewing technique. However, focus groups are not really a survey research method because they do not produce the kind of quantitative aggregate data that result from asking a large number of individuals the same questions. We have included focus groups in this chapter because interviewing is the major data-gathering skill that must be practiced. However, keep in mind that focus groups also have qualities of experiments in that they generally are held in laboratory-type settings and also share qualities of qualitative research in that they are more free-form in style and more natural and unobtrusive in terms of the way the conversations take place. Then we turn back to the most widely practiced form of survey research today, telephone surveys.

BOX 7-1

HIRED-HAND INTERVIEWERS

Roth (1966) warned of the possible effects of hiring interviewers to collect data. Roth gives his own experience doing *hired-hand research* as a case in point:

> One of the questions on the interview schedule asked for five reasons why parents had put their child in an institution. I found most people can't think of five reasons. One or two—sometimes three. At first I tried pumping them for more reasons, but I never got any of them up to five. I didn't want (the director) to think I was goofing off on the probing, so I always filled in all five (1966, p. 191).

Cheating of this type occurs, Roth argues, because the persons hired to carry out interviews rarely hold the "dedicated-scientist" (p. 191)

norms that the original researcher holds. Instead, a hired interviewer would tend to do his or her work much like workers in most other settings [by shaving down the job bit by bit to "just enough to get by" (p. 192)]. Roth also cautions that this type of slacking off is not a moral issue; "rather, it is expected behavior of workers in a production organization . . . [and] there is no reason to believe that a hired hand in the scientific research business will behave any different" (p. 192).

The best safeguard against this, Roth contends, is to tie hired hands as firmly into the research project as is feasible. If those working on a project feel committed to its execution, they are less likely to behave like ordinary hired help.

Source: Julius Roth: "Hired Hand Research," *The American Sociologist*, 1: 190–196, 1966.

DESIGN OF FACE-TO-FACE INTERVIEWS

The difference between *face-to-face interviews* and paper-and-pencil questionnaires is simply that conducting an interview involves having one person address questions to another. The spoken responses are then recorded by the interviewer. In the self-administered questionnaire procedure, the respondent first reads the questions and then writes responses. This difference must be kept in mind in designing an *interview schedule* for an interview. Because the interview involves two people, the nature of the relationship developed between these two people before and during the interview will have a great effect on the success of the interview obtained. As a group interview technique, the *focus group* is an excellent preparatory method for developing a survey. Whether the interviewer is the actual researcher or someone else may affect the outcome of the interview. Box 7-1, which discusses the effects of hired-hand interviewers, should be kept in mind in considering seeking assistance with interviewing.

Preparing the Interview Schedule

A structured interview schedule is very similar to a questionnaire. A questionnaire may be converted into an interview schedule and vice versa. An interview schedule should be prepared in accordance with these rules:

1. Instructions for the interviewer to follow must be clearly given.
2. Questions should be worded so that they can be easily read out by the interviewer without distorting the response which will be given. (They should offer no threat and should be totally neutral.) Furthermore, the response categories should be carefully considered so that they offer a meaningful range of possibilities but are not so vague that the respondent cannot easily select a category.
3. Questions ought to be ordered so that the respondent is quickly engaged in the interview and interest is maintained throughout.

Instructions. An interviewer needs clear and precise instructions about how to give the interview. While many instructions may be spelled out during practice sessions, the interview schedule should include all the basic rules the interviewer needs to follow to carry out the interview successfully. (If you plan to do your own interviewing, you should apply these suggestions to the instructions you write for yourself.) The form should ask for information regarding the time when the interview began, how long it took, where it occurred (if this varies), and on what day of the week it was held. Early questions may serve as the basis for including or excluding individuals from the survey: these questions may request information on residence, age, membership, or other factors. Interviewers should be informed about how to end an interview quickly with a person who does not meet the requirements for the study.

Instructions on how the interviewer should proceed through the instrument must be given. When there are contingency questions which do not apply to the respondent, the interviewer should be able to see at a glance where to move for the next question. The form should include places for responses such as "don't know," "no opinion," and "no answer." Naturally, the interviewer should encourage respondents to give an opinion or a response when they seem to have one that would apply. Usually the interviewer does not offer "don't know" as a selection category to the respondent; rather, it is recorded only when the respondent cannot pick a response from those given.

Wording. Questionnaires and interview schedules often read somewhat differently. Interview schedules may include short transitional expressions to make the interview proceed smoothly: "Now, I wonder if you could tell me . . . ," "We would like to know what you consider . . . ," "Please tell me . . . ," "We are interested in how . . ." This last expression could be used to introduce an assessment of financial security: "We are interested in how people are getting along fi-

---

EXAMPLES OF QUESTIONS ON INCOME

FORM 1

Please tell me approximately where your annual household income fell in ____, before taxes, that is, the income for all members of the household. Stop me when I reach the category that includes your household income. *(The interviewer then slowly reads the various income categories, beginning with the low end).*

FORM 2

For the purposes of our survey, we need to have a rough indication of the income of your family. In which of these groups . . . *(The interviewer hands the respondent a card with the various categories of income delineated in a column, each preceded with a letter)* . . . did your total family income, from all sources, fall last year, in ____, before taxes? Just tell me the letter of the group.

---

nancially these days." This could then be followed by the question: "Compared to your financial situation five years ago, are you (better off, worse off, or about the same?)"

Types of Closed-Ended Questions. To have respondents select from a group of possible responses, choices must be made available. There are a number of different techniques for doing this: rating scales, rank ordering, paired comparisons, and semantic differentials. The card sorting method can be used only in a face-to-face interview situation. In this case, numerous cards with different statements (measuring attitudes) are given to the respondent, who is asked to sort them into piles which signify different levels of agreement or disagreement. A variation on this method may be used to get respondents to select a category from a list printed on a card, which the interviewer hands to the respondent after a question is asked. Consider the income question asked in two forms in the box.

Each of the ways of asking the respondent about income avoids the personal question "Tell me how much?" In the first method, the interviewer reads off income categories and the respondent tells the interviewer when to stop. In the second, the respondent selects an income category from a card. This second method, developed by the National Opinion Research Center (NORC), is probably less intrusive and easier for an inexperienced interviewer to handle (Bradburn and Sudman, 1979, p. 182).

Social Desirability. Questions that address potentially threatening topics or raise the possibility that the respondent is being asked to divulge something personal and derogatory may be answered by the respondent in a way that makes the individual look better. Such responses often tend toward offering the normative response. Sudman and Bradburn found that this was more often the case when the respondent did not relate strongly to the topic being addressed, that is when the respondent knew less about it and was less affected by it (1974, pp. 36–39).

If your interview will include potentially threatening questions about criminal activity, sexual behavior, or personal habits which may seem negative, it will be important to prepare such questions carefully to make them as nonthreatening as possible to the respondents. If you do not do this, your respondents may answer in ways that appear to make themselves look socially acceptable. Techniques have been developed for asking very sensitive questions in interviews (see for example, the Random Response Model of Bradburn and Sudman, 1979).

Minimize the Use of Open-Ended Questions. When open-ended questions are asked, the interviewer should write down the answers. Obviously, there is a potential for shifts in meaning and emphasis between what the respondent says and what the interviewer writes down. Open-ended questions should be worded to encourage brief responses and a greater degree of precision. Interviewers are not psychoanalysts who know how to interpret the deep thoughts of respondents.

Use of Quantifying Words for the Responses. The response categories often contain quantifying adverbs which may be vague. Bradburn and his colleagues found that choices such as "very often," "pretty often," and "not too often" may mean quite different things to different individuals (Bradburn and Sudman, 1979, p. 159). When the events referred to occur more frequently on the average, the responses are higher for everyone; when the responses refer to a more positive event, they also tend to be higher than those for a negative event. You should try to see in pretest interviews whether the responses seem to be skewed in this way. You may want to add one or more quantifying categories or possibly delete one.

Ordering Questions in an Interview Schedule. An interview should try to capture the initial interest of the respondent; therefore, the interview should begin with a question which engages the interviewee. Demographic questions, especially those of a personal nature, should come at the end of the interview. Many interviews start with a question or two to determine whether the person being addressed meets the criteria for being interviewed in terms of age; voter registration; residence in a community, city, or household; or whatever. Actual questioning sometimes commences with an open-ended question which seeks a global response to the major issue of the study: "What would you say is the major problem confronting people in your community?"

One advantage to an interview compared with a self-administered questionnaire is that the interviewer can lead the respondent through the questions in exactly the order in which they are presented, whereas in a self-administered questionnaire the respondent may jump around the survey or skip sections completely. Interviewers should be encouraged to present the interview exactly as it is ordered. This will help standardize the interview situation from one interview to the next and among different interviewers.

The Interview Experience

An interview is a piece of social interaction with one person asking another a number of questions and the other person giving answers. Everyone has, in a number of different situations, been an interviewer. Small children are always interviewing adults: "Mom, why do I have to go to bed?" "Why do you have to go out tonight?" "Why does Mary get a new toy and not me?" As we mature, we tend to become more leery of asking people too many questions and may consider people who seem too inquisitive nosy, intrusive, and certainly not cool. However, our world would come to a standstill if we were unable to ask anyone anything. We must ask people questions in order to carry on with our lives.

Now, this general type of questioning is different from a formal interview, but not entirely different. We have all learned that finding out what we need to know requires *asking the right question.* This means that we need to think through what our question will mean to the other person in order to be able to phrase the question so that we can expect the respondent to give us the answer we need. Furthermore, we must ask it in a way that will not confuse or turn off the person to whom we are speaking and therefore produce an invalid answer.

This is not so different from the situation in a formal interview, a situation you probably all have encountered. Many of you have had job interviews, interviews with college admissions people, or other interviews. In such cases we are generally trying to put our best foot forward and look good so that the person interviewing us will be impressed. Yet we all know that if we brag about ourselves too much, if we try to make ourselves sound too wonderful, we may not seem believable and the interviewer may conclude that we are insincere and shallow. Thus we have all developed some techniques for answering other people's questions about ourselves, our interests, our attitudes, and our characteristics so that we appear to be honest and forthright.

Some of you may have been interviewed in a survey. The major difference between interviews for a job, for admission to a college, and for a survey is that the interviewer in the survey has nothing to offer to, or withhold from, the respondent. If the respondent thinks that the interviewer cannot affect his or her situation, cannot do something for him or her, he or she may conclude that giving all these answers is a waste of time. The reason why so many individuals agree to being interviewed is that the interviewer *sells* the interview effectively (Downs, Smeyak, and Martin, 1980, p. 364). The interviewer must convince the respondent that it is in her or his personal interest to participate. As Downs and his colleagues state (1980, p. 364), the tactics offered to motivate interest include telling respondents that

(a) A neighbor or friend has participated,
(b) A person's opinion is really sought,
(c) The report is important enough to be published or to be used in making important decisions,
(d) You really need the person's help.

Stressing the usefulness of the answers in the aggregate for the study of some subject may ease the respondent's fears of exposure, but the interview situation itself may bring back unpleasant memories of earlier interviews. Such interview experiences, possibly for a job, may have been threatening and anxiety-producing; it is this situation that the prospective respondent may recall when considering whether to let the interviewer proceed. Thus, the interviewer needs to fully consider how to make the request for an interview nonthreatening and the experience of being interviewed as enjoyable (and even enriching) as possible.

The Desirable Interviewer. The sociologist David Riesman once described the ideal interviewer as the person who could adapt the standardized questionnaire to the unstandardized respondent (1958, p. 305). This ability to handle a two-way conversation under varying conditions without losing the central meaning of the survey in any of these conditions is *the art of interviewing*. There seems to be a certain schizophrenic quality about the advice given in regard to being a good interviewer. Interviewers are technical specialists but ordinary persons; they must be prudent in widely varying situations, but they may also need to be persistent to the point of being annoying to get the responses they need; they must probe but remain neutral; they must be interested in what the respondent says but seem oblivious to the implications of what it may mean.

This ability of the interviewer to respond to the answers given with a kind of "friendly obliviousness" (Converse and Schuman, 1974, p. 32) sets up a mood of nonchalance in which the interviewer seems not to be shocked, surprised, or amused or to react in any strong way to the respondent's answers. The cardinal tenet of interviewing, state Converse and Schuman, is to restrain prejudice, to suppress one's own opinions (p. 12). If the answer is incomplete, the interviewer must probe for greater depth and clarity in the response, but without seeming to be personally concerned. Interviewers must veer away from becoming too emotionally involved with the respondent; this is what Converse and Schuman refer to as "overrapport" (p. 54). Box 7-2 gives an example of a situation where an interviewer found it very difficult to remain impersonal.

Converse and Schuman offer four reasons why many people are happy to be interviewed. The first is that most people enjoy telling their opinions to a good listener. Interviewers are terribly good listeners (they even take notes). Second, interviews tend to be about a person's personal experiences and attitudes (career, family, political attitudes)—all topics about which most people spend a lot of time thinking to themselves and talking to those to whom they are close. Third, an interview costs the respondent nothing. Whether the respondent thinks he or she is doing a favor for the interviewer or gives the information to conform to the interviewer's request, the interview is free: the only cost is the time spent. Finally, interviews can offer fresh insights and can be stimulating (Converse and Schuman, 1974, pp. 55–56).

BOX 7-2

INTERVIEWERS SHOULD NOT REACT

This account of an interviewer's experience, offered by Converse and Schuman, is an example of how interviewing may require much self-restraint on the part of the interviewer:

> When the respondent said, "Women shouldn't go past the first grade; then they couldn't take jobs away from men," I [the interviewer] failed utterly to subdue my feminist spirit. I said "What if she never marries or what if her husband dies or deserts her and she has children?" I lapsed instantly into silence. I had biased the interview, in that I had revealed myself even more thoroughly to be the kind of female the respondent most objected to: not only was I working—I was in favor of women working!

Source: Jean M. Converse and Howard Schuman. *Conversations at Random: Survey Research as Interviewers See It,* Wiley, New York, 1974, pp. 12–13.

Most people do not normally converse with strangers about their attitudes, but then, strangers are rarely interested in one's attitudes! In the interview situation, these attitudes may be explored in ways that open up new ideas to the respondent.

As the Survey Research Center (SRC) at the University of Michigan tells its interviewers, interviewers must be both diplomats and boors. They must be able to make the most difficult situation seem comfortable. However, they may not let the respondent feel so comfortable that he or she is allowed to skip pertinent questions. Rather, a good interviewer must be ready to elbow his or her way into whatever questions must be asked (Converse and Schuman, 1974, p. 31). The SRC manual states that the interviewer must be both a human being who "builds a permissive and warm relationship with each respondent" and a "technician who applies standard techniques and uses the same instrument for each interview" (reported in Converse and Schuman, 1974, p. 30).

Whatever the situation, the interviewer must get his or her questions answered by everyone. This may in some cases lead to what Converse and Schuman refer to as "the comedy of questions." Consider this example:

> You sit in a lady's living room, look through cracked, broken-out windows at blocks and blocks of gutted "has-been" homes. You walk across a sagging creaking floor, and look into narrow eyes peering at you from beneath a dresser. Not a dot, nor a cat—no, a child. Now you ask the big question in the neighborhood problem section: "Have you had any trouble because of neighbors not keeping up their property?" (*1974, p. 27*)

The very rationality which is sought in interviews may, Converse and Schuman think, lead to its own biases. Because the interview asks for *opinion,* it denies feelings. Questions tend to be worked up in such a way that they filter out emotion. The one-to-one experience denies the more normal effects of others beyond this dyad. There is a stripping away of spontaneity by the formality in the wording of the questions. The very ultrareasonableness of the interview makes it a little artificial (Converse and Schuman, 1974, pp. 73–74). This distortion seems to be the price that must be paid to accomplish the social survey interview. However, recent concerns about the cognitive meaning of survey data have led to suggestions for input from the respondent about the design of questions. Box 7-3 offers an interesting strategy.

How to Become a Good Interviewer

Five basic rules must be followed in order for a person to become a good interviewer: (1) understand the interview material, (2) make a commitment to complete the interview, (3) practice enough to feel confident and comfortable with the interview, (4) try to reduce the effects your personal qualities may have on the interview situation, and (5) use common sense in dealing with potentially difficult situations.

BOX 7-3

PROBLEMS WITH VALIDITY IN THE FACE-TO-FACE INTERVIEW

Suchman and Jordan (1992) raised the following concern stemming from the need to have an interview both be neutral (so that it can be replicated from one interview to the next and hence provide reliability) and include enough of the "interactional resources" that typify ordinary conversation that the uncertainties occurring in the interview can be cleared up and tangential topics that arise can be pursued. They argue that the validity of survey data from an interview may be weakened by the rules of neutrality and replicability which have been imposed to ensure the data's reliability.

What they suggest is that the structure of the interview be developed collaboratively by the interviewer and the respondent over the course of the interview so that both have a joint sense of the meaning of the questions. In practice, what would this mean? They suggest having the respondent see the interview schedule with the interviewer (possibly on the computer screen) and then having the interviewer talk about the questions with the respondent, offering elaborations and clarifications, allowing a small degree of influence by the respondent on the design of questions. How far would this bias the data? The authors stress that this danger might be offset by the clarification in meaning and hence the greater validity of the data gathered. In this strategy, the respondent's "interactional expertise" is considered a resource, not a problem (p. 266).

Source: Lucy Suchman, and Brigitte Jordan: "Validity and the Collaborative Construction of Meaning in Face-to-Face Surveys" in Judith M. Tanur (ed.), *Questions about Questions: Inquiries into the Cognitive Bases of Surveys,* Russell Sage Foundation, New York: 1992, pp. 241–67.

Rule 1: Understand the Interview. Naturally, the interviewer needs to know what the interview is about. If you are to be doing the interviewing, you should know why the questions being asked are included. Knowing this means that you have a solid understanding of the purposes of the research. If you designed the study, you will be more likely to know why questions are included than you would if you were working on someone else's project. However, there is a tendency to throw in questions which may seem obvious to include, but even you, the designer of the project, are not sure why they have been included.

An interview should not seem to be a fishing expedition where any material that might possibly appear interesting is included on the chance that it might be used. If the study is seeking alternative explanations of a phenomenon, you should understand why one set of questions—very different from an earlier set—has been included. The reason why the interviewer needs this self-understanding is that if the respondent asks why a specific question is being asked, the interviewer can quickly explain its importance to the overall survey. It is not acceptable to say that the question may prove useful or is interesting. Every aspect of the interview must be considered vital to the study.

Rule 2: Make a Commitment to Complete the Interview. Interviews may occur at inconvenient times. In some cases an interviewer may try to reschedule a session. However, whatever the nature of the situation in which the interview occurs, whether there is a baby crying in the background, a dinner burning on the stove, or a person about to go out, once the interview has begun, the interviewer must persist and try to complete it. This can be more easily accomplished if the interviewer remains comfortable. Clearly, short interruptions may need to take place. The interviewer should be gracious but should stress the importance of completing the interview.

One problem in trying to complete interviews is that respondents may give incomplete answers. In this case the interviewer needs to probe for more information and clarification so that the re-

sponse is fully understandable and useful. This tendency to give less than fully developed answers parallels everyday speech. Nevertheless, it is also very common in everyday conversation to try to get the person with whom one is talking to flesh out what he or she is saying.

Converse and Schuman (1974, p. 50) suggest the following types of responses to incomplete answers, which appear exactly as they might in everyday conversation:

Could you tell me a little more about that?

This question is requesting additional information, an expansion of the material that has been given.

How do you mean, exactly?

This is a request for clarification, for a better explanation of what was said.

Why would you say you feel that way?

This is a way to seek out an elaboration of the answer given.

In examples like these, the technique of the interviewer is not to be satisfied with incomplete answers. If you don't think you fully understand what the respondent means, if there may be multiple meanings, if the answer is confusing at the time of the interview, it will mean even less at a later point, when you are trying to code and analyze the data. That is why the interviewer must get full and complete information that will be clear and fully interpretable later on.

Rule 3: Practice the Interview. Interviewers must practice by reading the interview and administering it to others. In the first step, the reading should identify any areas of misunderstanding the interviewer has. Here the adequacy of the instructions for the interviewer will be made evident. The first practice might involve interviewing yourself, as Converse and Schuman (1974, p. 18) suggest. This should help sensitize you to how you might react to the interview. This is a way to explore your own personal attitudes and see whether you have biases that might be aroused if the respondents reply in certain ways.

The second practice might be with a friend or fellow workers with whom you feel completely comfortable. Genuine pretesting of the interview with the types of respondents to be studied should also be carried out. Depending on the size and complexity of the interview, you should pretest the interview on a few people and in a few situations representative of the prospective respondents and situations. These practice interviews (which should not be announced as practice sessions) will inform you about what problems are likely to confront you in the interviews.

Rule 4: Minimize the Effects of Your Personal Characteristics. Your sex, age, race, accent, dress—all your personal characteristics and styles—will in some way affect the interview situation. Although you cannot change your sex, age, and race, you should be aware of the possible effects they may have on respondents. (For example, studies have shown that black respondents often give different answers to black and to white interviewers.) You should consider your appearance and grooming. Different types of interview situations may make certain types of attire desirable. In a formal door-to-door interview, a businesslike appearance may be best; however, college-student attire (jeans) may be fully acceptable for many types of interview settings.

Rule 5: Always Use Common Sense. This is a quality that everyone needs to be ready to use when difficult situations arise. It is especially important for interviewers. If the interviewer realizes that the situation is becoming dangerous, perhaps because the respondent is making menacing remarks, the interviewer must use good judgment about whether to discontinue the interview. No one wants to endanger herself or himself simply to get an interview. However, common sense can often tell you when a situation is a little doubtful and when it is truly ominous. Moreover, the

friendly neutrality of the interviewer often may serve to defuse a difficult situation. A household in which a family fight is in progress may calm down when the interviewer arrives. Whatever the event, the interviewer must always rely on common sense as the ultimate factor in deciding what to do.

This brings us to the point of stating how to end an interview. Naturally, the respondent should be thanked for the time and effort put into the interview. If results are to be sent out, this should be explained to the respondent. Try to end the interview in a positive, upbeat fashion so that the respondent doesn't end up with negative feelings about the experience. Remember, another researcher may want to interview this respondent in some future survey.

FOCUS GROUPS

The focus group method of interviewing has become popular as a fairly inexpensive but effective way to get the reactions of a small group of people to a focused issue. It is widely used in political polling, market research, and the early design of large-scale surveys. It also is useful when a researcher wants to draw together background information on an issue. This is not really a new method of social research. An early form of focus group interviewing was developed during World War II at Columbia University by two prominent social scientists, Paul Lazarsfeld and Robert Merton, to get audience reactions to radio programs. In their method, which they called *focused interviews,* a small audience listened to radio programs and indicated their reactions by pressing a red button when they had negative responses and a green button when they had positive responses. After the program, the audience members were asked to discuss their positive and negative reactions. This method continued to be used to study the influence of the mass media. Merton and his colleagues recognized the potential of this type of interviewing as a form of data collection for social research (see Merton, 1946, and Merton et al., 1990, which be-

gins with a foreword comparing these early focused interviews to focus groups). New interest in
using small groups of people to discuss a focused
topic emerged in the 1980s.

Reasons for Setting Up a Focus Group

There are a broad range of reasons why a researcher may want to set up a focus group as a
means of collecting data. These groups have been
most widely used in the area of market research to
obtain views of products and by political pollsters
and advisers to learn how to manage a campaign
and effectively present a candidate. We need to
consider the types of information one can generate
from interviewing a small group on a focused
topic. At the least focused end of the spectrum,
focus groups can be used to get the *general impressions* of a small group about a product, a film,
what alumni feel about their college, and how positive clients are about a service provided. Such im-
pressionistic reactions often cannot be gained from
questionnaires or even from set face-to-face interviews. The balance and stimuli of the other members in the focus group may facilitate each member's ability and motivation to form and verbalize
his or her impressions. Moving beyond impressions, a focus group can dig more deeply into an
interest area. For developing products and marketing special events or activities, researchers may
want to gain a sense of how people who are very
interested or exposed to this product, event, or activity pursue and maintain their interest and the
terms they use to talk about that interest. Discussions that generate impressions and focus on interests may lead to the creation and suggestion of
new and *innovative ideas.* Taking a more negative
cast, a focus group can be used to *explore the
problems* of a product, program, or social condition. From the perspective of research design, one
of the uses of focus groups is to help *generate research hypotheses* or *interpret the meaning of data*
that have already been collected.

Considering the advantages of focus groups
over individual interviewing both for individual

respondents and for the researcher or sponsor,
Stewart and Shamdasani (1990) summarized 10
advantages which they adapted from Hess (1968).
For the respondent:

- *Security:* Individuals may feel less exposed and
more comfortable in expressing views that may
be shared; they also need not defend or elaborate
their ideas.
- *Snowballing:* Comments from one person elicit
comments from others.
- *Spontaneity:* Since each person is not asked to
answer a specific question, respondents may
"jump in" with ideas and pick up on what interests them. They are not required to answer a
question they have no interest in.
- *Synergism:* More ideas and information will flow
out of this combined interview environment.

For the researcher:

- *Scientific scrutiny:* A range of researchers can
observe the group and/or tape recordings or
videotapes of the discussion. This helps foster
consistent interpretations.
- *Serendipity:* Focus groups may bring forth unexpected "out of the blue" ideas.
- *Specialization:* Since a number of people can be
interviewed together, this reduces the cost of
having a highly specialized interviewer serve as
the moderator.
- *Speed:* Interviewing groups of people reduces
the time that would be required to interview
these respondents individually.
- *Structure:* The moderator can control the order
and time spent on various topics and return to
topics.

How Focus Groups Can Assist Survey Research.
In the early stages of a survey research design, a
focus group can assist in formulating questions for
a survey, relating other topics to the primary research issue, and generating research hypotheses.
Later, when the survey data have been collected
and analyzed, a focus group can help a survey

researcher better understand the results by facilitating a fuller interpretation of the survey data.

How to Design a Focus Group

Recruiting the Participants. A focus group is generally composed of 6 to 12 people, selected by a researcher, who are knowledgeable about or have an interest in the subject of focus because of their experiences. They also may be chosen as representatives of certain demographic groups (African-Americans, North Dakotans, people over age 65) or as members of particular interest groups (vegetarians, owners of sailboats, opera lovers) or because they share certain attitudes (dislike a particular political candidate, like a set of products, combine an unusual set of attitudes such as being prolife Democrats) or have special knowledge about a subject. In terms of specific size, a smaller group may be dominated by one or more persons more easily, while a larger group may make it more difficult for all to participate. A group size of eight generally is believed to be very favorable.

In selecting members of the group, it is important to consider not only the qualities of individuals but how those individuals will interact as a group. The physical appearance, types of personalities, gender, and socioeconomic class distinctions may affect the interaction of the group and thus have to be considered. It generally is believed that it is better if the group participants are strangers to each other since studies of group dynamics show that acquaintances may feel more inhibited about speaking if they know other members of the group. However, the evidence on this is mixed, and since most focus groups begin with a "get acquainted" session, the respondents may get a sense of the views of others during this time. Moreover, the moderator of the group is usually a stranger as well. It is important to develop group compatibility, but it is unclear how much homogeneity in the characteristics of the members aids or abets this effort.

Participating in a focus group is also a voluntary effort. However, there are better and worse ways to encourage potential participants to join, and incentives are often offered. The initial contact may be by telephone, by mail, or in person. Often a few questions must be posed to determine the appropriateness of the person for the topic of the focus group. Group members are then informed about the time and place of the group meeting and are asked to come 15 to 30 minutes before the session. Written or spoken confirmation of a participant's willingness to join a focus group should occur shortly after the initial contact.

Many commercial research groups regularly offer $25 for participation, and some offer much more. Food and snacks are often available. In some cases, transportation and lodging may be required. A location for the focus group which is easy for the participants to reach facilitates the process.

The Task of the Moderator. The moderator of the focus group is its leader. Therefore, who this person is, how this person leads the group, and how this person asks questions and responds to the answers of the group members will determine how the group progresses. Thus, the choice of the moderator is very important, as are the instructions given to that person and the interview set of questions. Recommendations for being an effective moderator include the following: the person should be a good facilitator with unobtrusive qualities, be able to gently draw people out, encourage interaction, listen well, be comfortable with silences, distill participants' ideas so that they can be offered back for more elaboration, and not be too authoritative or judgmental. Thus, the leadership style which tends to work best with focus groups is a supportive one in which the moderator is friendly and caring to the group members and is concerned not to offend their feelings. It is a style in which equality among the group members needs to be fostered (Stewart and Shamdasani, 1990, p. 73).

Moderators need preparation. They must be well versed in the problem of the research and the type of group that is being drawn together. It is important that they understand group dynamics. Moderators also need to understand the major types of bias that may affect a focus group. They need to avoid personal bias in which they are more supportive of ideas that match their own. If the research is being carried out for a client, moderators must take care not to reinforce ideas that please the client. Finally, there may be a tendency for moderators to be more supportive of points of view that seem to have more internal consistency (Stewart and Shamdasani, 1990, p. 84). Since the object of a focus group session is to elicit a range of truly held views, the issue of whether these views are presented in a consistent and well-argued manner is not relevant. The moderator needs to be able to enforce the rule that a member's personal feelings, when expressed, cannot be discounted or rejected by other members (people have a right to their own feelings).

Types of Questions and Their Purposes. As in a survey, questions may be open-ended or closed-ended. They may be primary questions which introduce topics or secondary questions that are designed to follow up on topics. Questions can be designed as directed questions, which means that they force the respondents to answer in a particular manner ("loaded" questions), or they may be neutral questions. The purposes for questions are laid out in Box 7-4.

There is also the issue of the order or sequence of questions in a focus group interview. The funnel approach begins with broad questions and moves to narrower ones; the inverted funnel approach moves in the opposite direction. The quintamensional approach developed by the Gallup polling organization (1947) is aimed at measuring the intensity of a respondent's opinions and attitudes by using questions that cover five steps: (1) degree of awareness, (2) uninfluenced attitudes, (3) specific attitudes, (4) reasons given for holding attitudes, and (5) intensity of attitudes. This technique calls for a high degree of probing. There is also a tunnel approach in which more specific attitudes are asked for throughout. This can be a good method to follow if the intention is to develop quantifiable results. In the tunnel method, there is little probing and the focus group operates more like a set of structured interviews.

BOX 7-4

THE PURPOSES AND USES OF QUESTIONS IN A FOCUS GROUP

1. *Primary research questions:* These questions cover the central issues on which the group is to focus. Such questions generally are developed before the session.
2. *Leading questions:* These questions are often a restating of a group member's words, beginning with "Why?"
3. *Testing questions:* These questions feed back ideas in a more extreme but tentative form, as if the moderator were unclear about the position stated.
4. *Steering questions:* These questions are used to move the group back to the central issues.
5. *Obtuse questions:* These questions serve as ways to encourage group members to consider each other's responses: "Why would X feel this way?"
6. *Factual questions:* These questions are less risky and may help diffuse difficult situations.
7. *"Feel" questions:* These questions ask the group members to express their feelings. They are risky but may produce the most interesting responses.
8. *Anonymous questions:* These questions help get a group comfortable with each other. One strategy is to have the group members write down the first idea that the issue being addressed brings to mind.
9. *No question—keeping quiet:* It is often wise for a moderator to let the group be silent at times. This may encourage certain members to speak up.

Source: Adapted from Stewart and Shamdasani (from Wheatley and Flexner, 1988), 1990, p. 83.

Conducting a Focus Group

The environment of a focus group should be non-threatening and as pleasing as possible. Most groups meet around tables. In many cases the participants wear name tags so that they can easily address each other. The interviewing style described above probably should include some directiveness on the part of the moderator but also should encourage spontaneity and free-form discussion. The level of intimacy of the group may vary. If a moderator offers personal information about himself or herself, this may set the mood for more intimate revelations. Whether the group will be observed or the proceedings will be tape-recorded depends on the purpose of the research. Group members should be informed of these practices. If the observers are present in the room with the group, they should be introduced but seated at a distance from the group.

Focus groups often begin with an effort to have the members introduce themselves to each other and tell the group a bit about themselves (e.g., what type of work they do). If by design there are both experts and nonexperts on a topic in the same group, it may be better not to have the members state their occupations at the beginning to avoid intimidating the nonexperts and keeping them from speaking. Some focus groups use aids such as presentations (possibly with overhead displays) and demonstrations. Other discussion aids include storytelling and the use of illustrations, photographs, and cartoons. Sentence completion and word association exercises sometimes are used, as are projective techniques in situations in which the participants have difficulty recognizing or expressing deep-seated values and feelings.

Usually the aims and purpose of the research are presented at the end of a focus group session. This serves as a form of debriefing.

Interpreting the Data Gathered in a Focus Group

There are two types of data a social research project may hope to gather: *emic data,* which arise from natural settings, and *etic data,* which represent the intended needs and interests of the researcher. The data gathered from focus groups can have both of these qualities, but given the less-structured format and the group nature of a focus group, the data drawn may be more emic in form. This means that they will need to be analyzed with methods sensitive to this type of natural and free-formed material. (See Chapter 9 on content analysis techniques for ideas on how to analyze the content from focus groups)

DESIGN OF TELEPHONE SURVEYS

There are two primary tasks in organizing a *telephone survey.* One is to design the survey instrument itself; the other is to select a set of respondents.

Telephone Interview Schedules

Telephone interview schedules are not so different from in-person interview schedules. In both cases, the schedule must include instructions to the interviewer on how to proceed with the interview and questions which the interviewer is to read off to the respondent. The language of the telephone interview schedule may need to be a little different from that of the in-person interview schedule. It may require a few more verbal clarification statements, such as "OK?" "Did you understand?" "Is that clear?" or "Can we continue?" interspersed throughout the conversation; these are less necessary in the face-to-face situation because the interviewer can see the respondent's reactions.

Questions that depend on visual cues presented on cards, as was described above, can be adapted to a telephone format. Groves and Kahn offer two primary ways to accomplish this: the unfolding method and the numbered-scale method. The boxes that follow give examples of these methods.

In the unfolding method, the respondent is led along to more specific questions on the basis of responses to earlier questions. This makes it less necessary for the respondent to remember too much at one time and reduces the presentation of irrelevant material to the respondent.

In the numbered-scale method the respondent is asked to think of a scale of numbers and register where on the scale his or her response would

THE UNFOLDING METHOD

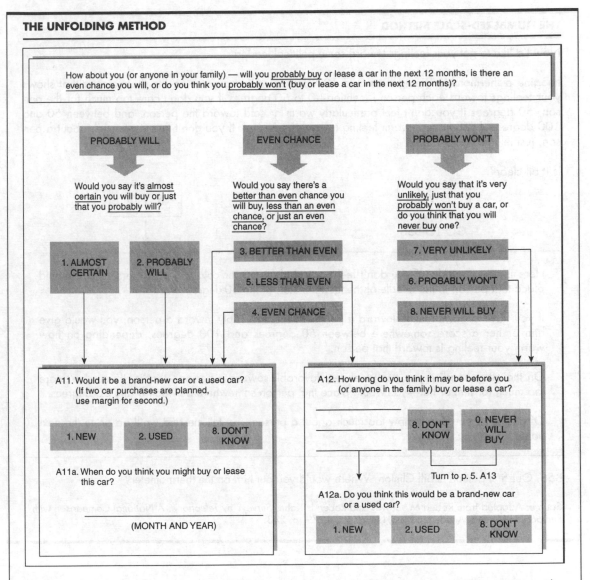

How about you (or anyone in your family) — will you <u>probably buy</u> or lease a car in the next 12 months, is there an <u>even chance</u> you will, or do you think you <u>probably won't</u> (buy or lease a car in the next 12 months)?

PROBABLY WILL

Would you say it's <u>almost certain</u> you will buy or just that you <u>probably will</u>?

| 1. ALMOST CERTAIN | 2. PROBABLY WILL |

EVEN CHANCE

Would you say there's a <u>better than even</u> chance you will buy, <u>less than an even</u> chance, or <u>just an even</u> chance?

3. BETTER THAN EVEN

5. LESS THAN EVEN

4. EVEN CHANCE

PROBABLY WON'T

Would you say that it's very <u>unlikely</u>, just that you probably won't buy a car, or do you think that you will <u>never buy</u> one?

7. VERY UNLIKELY

6. PROBABLY WON'T

8. NEVER WILL BUY

A11. Would it be a brand-new car or a used car? (If two car purchases are planned, use margin for second.)

| 1. NEW | 2. USED | 8. DON'T KNOW |

A11a. When do you think you might buy or lease this car?

_____

(MONTH AND YEAR)

A12. How long do you think it may be before you (or anyone in the family) buy or lease a car?

_____

| 8. DON'T KNOW | 0. NEVER WILL BUY |

Turn to p. 5, A13

A12a. Do you think this would be a brand-new car or a used car?

| 1. NEW | 2. USED | 8. DON'T KNOW |

Source: Adapted from Robert M. Groves and Robert L. Kahn: *Surveys by Telephone: A National Comparison with Personal Interviews,* Academic Press, New York: 1979, p. 233.

fall. In Groves and Kahn's "thermometer" scale to rate various political figures, they found that responses to those scales on the telephone tend to be numbers divisible by 10, whereas in an in-person interview, respondents tend to select numbers that are actually given on a thermometer pre-sented on the show card (1979, p. 122). These examples suggest that when visual material is given, the respondent will attend to its cues. Without such material, a respondent on the telephone must utilize other ways to simplify his or her responses.

THE NUMBERED-SCALE METHOD

Now I'd like to get your feelings toward some political leaders.

Imagine a thermometer going from 0 to 100 degrees. Give a score on the thermometer that shows your feelings toward each person I mention—0 to 50 degrees if you don't care too much for the person, 50 degrees if you don't feel particularly warm or cold toward the person, and between 50 and 100 degrees if you have a warm feeling toward the person. If you don't know too much about a person, just tell me.

Is it all clear?

| 1. YES | | 5. NO |

GO TO B5a

Here is how it works. If you don't feel particularly warm or cold toward a person, you should place that person in the middle of the thermometer, at the 50-degree mark.

If you have a warm feeling toward a person or feel favorably toward a person, you would give him or her a score somewhere between 50 degrees and 100 degrees, depending on how warm your feeling is toward that person.

On the other hand, if you don't feel very favorably toward a person—that is, if you don't care too much for him or her—you would place that person somewhere between 0 and 50 degrees.

Of course, if you don't know too much about a person, just tell me and we'll go on to the next name.

B5a. Our first person is Bill Clinton. Where would you put him on the thermometer?

Source: Adapted from Robert M. Groves and Robert L. Kahn: *Surveys by Telephone: A National Comparison with Personal Interviews,* Academic Press, New York, 1979, p. 243.

Open-ended questions tend to be answered more perfunctorily on the telephone. If the interviewer wants multiple answers to a question ("What are the most important problems in your community?"), it will be difficult to get more than two responses on the telephone (Groves and Kahn, 1979, p. 138). Probing in a face-to-face situation may produce more responses.

Selecting a Sample

Getting a Sample of Telephone Numbers.   There are numerous ways to select a set of telephone numbers to represent the population that will be sampled. The method you choose will depend on the size of the area you are sampling as well as the size of the survey.

Using telephone directories. In the early days of telephone interviewing, telephone directories were largely used. In rural and nonmetropolitan areas, where most households are listed in the directory, this list may still serve as an effective sampling frame. In large cities, however, directories may exclude (because of unlisted numbers) more than one-third of the residential telephone numbers. To get around this problem, Sudman (1973) suggested a method according to which only the last three digits of numbers selected from the directory are replaced by randomly selected numbers. This is a two-stage project: First numbers are selected from the directory, and then the last three digits in each one are replaced with random numbers. In this way, unlisted numbers will have a chance of being selected.

Most localities also have cross-indexed telephone directories (which are usually available in public libraries). These directories list phone numbers by address or by numerical ordering. Such directories may be especially useful if you are studying a particular neighborhood. They also may distinguish between residential and commercial numbers by, for example, printing commercial numbers in bold type.

If directories are used, a means for randomizing the selection numbers should be employed. There are computer programs which will select a page number (once you have given the maximum limits), a column number, and a selection number within the column (once you have specified the number of telephone numbers given in each column).

Random-digit dialing. The newer way to select a telephone sample does not use telephone directories at all. Instead, the use of *random-digit dialing* (RDD) obviates the need to use the telephone book. RDD uses a computer to select the numbers to be called. If the sample is to represent a regional area of the United States or of the country as a whole, there will usually be a desire to get responses from across the area in a random fashion. This can be done by stratifying the computer's choices, first on the basis of the area codes (the three-digit numbers that must be used first to call

long distance) and second on the basis of the three-digit local exchanges or prefixes which preceded the last four suffix numbers. The area codes are given in most telephone directories; the exchanges may be selected from telephone directories or obtained from the local telephone company.

If you want to be exact in your sampling design, Groves and Kahn suggest that you also secure the vertical and horizontal (V & H) coordinates, the phone company uses to determine long-distance charges. Through stratifying the choices of area codes, then the exchanges within the area code, and then the V & H coordinates in a rotated fashion so that people with the same exchanges are selected randomly from across their locale, a representative sample of telephone numbers can be drawn (see Groves and Kahn, 1979, pp. 21–30, for a more comprehensive discussion of this method). Once this ordering is done, a systematic sample of every nth six-digit number (area code and exchange) is drawn. Of course, for a regional study, many fewer area codes (possibly only one) are needed. The number of exchanges varies greatly within an area code. The final four numbers are selected randomly by using a random number generation program or a list of random numbers as described in Chapter 5. If the numbers dialed are unacceptable (businesses, out-of-service, etc.), they are replaced by the next random numbers.

Selecting a Respondent from a Household. A telephone survey will not be random if any person who answers the phone is interviewed. Rather, a selection within the household of individuals who meet certain criteria (usually age) is used, and then among those members of the household, a random choice is made. The model followed is one developed by Kish (1949). Box 7-5 describes how Steven Klineberg in his Houston Area Survey used the Kish table to randomly select one person from each household to be interviewed. To put it more formally, it is a method of randomizing selection within households of varying sizes. The first thing the interviewer does is ask how many people there are in the household, listing them in the summary box by age. Then, considering the last digit in the telephone number, the interviewer turns to the selection table and selects the appropriate number of the person listed in the summary box to interview. Note that in the selection table the numbers change depending on the number of persons in the sampling unit.

Let's again go over how the selection of the person to be interviewed in the household is made. Say that it was a household of three and that the telephone number was 123-4567. You would go to row 3 and across until you got to column 7. Here you see the number 3. That means you will interview the third person on the list. Now, let's try another one (you would, of course, need a different summary box for each household). Say you interview a household of two whose telephone number was 123-1234. You would go down to row 2 (because there are two persons in the household) and then move across to column 4 (to correspond with

BOX 7-5

SELECTING AN INTERVIEWEE AT A TELEPHONE RESIDENCE

Now, how many people living in this household are over the age of 18? Who's the oldest member of the household? (Write in summary box.) How old (was that person/were you) on (his/her/your) last birthday? Who's the next oldest person in the household? Etc. (List names in order of age beginning with the oldest, down to age 18).

Summary Box			Selection Table									
Line No.	**Name**	**Age**	1	2	3	4	5	6	7	8	9	0
1			1	1	1	1	1	1	1	1	1	1
2			1	1	2	2	2	1	1	2	1	2
3			3	2	2	1	2	2	3	1	1	3
4			1	4	2	3	3	2	1	4	2	4
5			5	2	1	1	3	2	4	3	5	4
6			1	6	2	6	4	5	3	2	4	5

Now, let's see: That's *(read names listed)*. Is that everybody over the age of 18 who usually live here? (Have I missed anyone?)

Number over age 18:   1:25%
2:58%
3–6:17%

Now let me see whom I'm supposed to interview next . . .

(From the last number listed in the Summary Box, go to the corresponding row on the selection table. Then go to the column corresponding to the last digit of the telephone number and draw a line straight down to the row associated with the last person listed. The respondent's number is the one that intersects both lines.)

According to my selection table, the person I need to interview next is (Respondent's Name). [Is (he/she) there? Could I speak to (him/her), please? When do you expect (him/her) to be in? Etc. . . .]

Source: Steven Klineberg, Houston Area Survey, 1983.

the last digit in the telephone number). Here you see the number 2. Thus, you would interview the second person listed in the summary table.

Once the person is selected, that person is the only one to whom the interviewer will speak. In many cases this requires calling back at a time when the person on the telephone thinks the respondent will be available. If the desired person cannot be reached, he or she is not replaced by someone else in the household.

Telephone and Face-to-Face Interviewing

Advantages of the Telephone Survey.   Interviewing respondents over the telephone has become increasingly popular in recent years. It is easier to call individuals on the telephone than to go out to interview them in their homes or on the street. This form of survey has been revolutionized by the more sophisticated means for drawing a sample representative of a specific area that have become available and by computer-assisted telephone interviewing (CATI, to be described below) for carrying out the whole interview over the telephone.

The advantages of telephone interviewing compared with face-to-face interviewing are primarily three: (1) Telephone surveys are cheaper to carry out, (2) telephone surveys take less time and effort, and (3) telephone surveys are more impersonal than face-to-face interviews. When these conditions are deemed advantageous, telephone interviewing may be preferable.

Cost.   Estimates of the comparative costs of in-person and telephone interviewing all lead to the conclusion that telephone interviews are less expensive than face-to-face interviews. In a careful comparative study in the 1970s, Groves and Kahn of the University of Michigan's Survey Research Center found that a survey of approximately 1,500 individuals cost more than $84,000 for in-person interviews and nearly $38,000 for telephone interviews. This meant the in-person interview cost about $55 per interview, while the telephone interview cost $23 (Groves and Kahn, 1979, p. 188).

By keeping careful track of the costs in each area, Groves and Kahn found that the costs of selecting the sample were only 2.5 percent of the total budget of the telephone survey, while the costs were 10 percent of the in-person survey. Training and prestudy work for the field staff in the in-person study was twice the cost of the telephone survey (11.2 compared to 5.4 percent). The cost of field staff travel made up nearly 20 percent of the in-person study, while there were no travel costs in the telephone survey. However, the telephone charges made up 41 percent of the costs of the telephone survey, whereas various communication charges (telephone and postage) made up only 7 percent of the cost of the in-person interviews. These figures might well vary today, but telephone interviewing would still be more economical in most cases than face-to-face interviewing.

Time and effort.   Sitting in an office calling respondents saves time and expends less energy than going out to interview in person. Groves and Kahn (1979) estimated that the total hours spent in the telephone survey of 1,500 by all participants equaled 5,419 compared with 13,522 in the in-person survey. This averaged out to 3.3 hours per interview for the telephone survey and 8.7 hours per interview in the in-person study. Clearly, less time is necessary to contact people by phone than to go out and talk to them, even though it may take many telephone calls to make a contact.

The impersonal quality of a telephone survey. Because the interviewer cannot see the respondent, the respondent may feel more willing to divulge personal information than he or she would in a face-to-face encounter. Bradburn and Sudman (1979) found that in a metropolitan survey containing threatening questions (regarding arrests for drunken driving or bankruptcy experience), the respondents were more likely to cooperate by telephone than in the face-to-face situation. However, there is a two-edged problem, as Bradburn and Sudman see it: "overreporting of socially desirable acts [being a registered voter, having a library card] might be highest for the more personal methods, whereas underreporting of socially undesirable acts might be highest for the more anonymous methods" (1979, p. 9). In other words, it seems to be easier to deny to someone on the telephone that an undesirable act occurred than to deny it to someone facing you, but there is less temptation to try to enhance your image to a telephone interviewer.

Disadvantages of Telephone Surveys. There are three disadvantages to telephone interviewing: (1) Selecting telephone numbers that actually lead to completed interviews involves a large number of tries to achieve a small number of successes. (2) There is less motivation generated among respondents in a telephone interview because of the reduced stimulation from not seeing the interviewer in person. (3) Facilitating certain questions by giving the respondent a list with the choices, cards to sort, or some other cue or form of visual assistance cannot be done in the same manner in a telephone survey.

Getting working household numbers. In the past, telephone surveys usually selected numbers on a random basis from telephone directories. As was related above, for many reasons the use of telephone directories for selecting samples is undesirable. Yet the use of RDD, as described above, produces many telephone numbers that are not residential households. This creates what has been called the *dross rate*. *Dross numbers* are those which for one reason or another do not lead to households. The ratio of good numbers to dross numbers is about 1:5 (Groves and Kahn, 1979, p. 46). If the first digit of the suffix (the final four numbers in a telephone number) is selected from directory listings as a "used" digit, it can be assumed that numbers in that set are being assigned. Using only a random choice for the last three digits has led to a ratio of good to dross numbers nearer to 1:2.

Lack of motivation on the telephone. Once an interview has begun, it is much easier for respondents to hang up than it is to discontinue an interview with the interviewer standing (or sitting) right across from them. Because there is no eye contact in a telephone interview, it is more difficult for the interviewer to assess the interest level of the respondent. Therefore, it is necessary for the interviewer to try to keep the telephone conversation flowing so that the respondent doesn't have time to consider whether he or she is bored or too busy. This means that it is more difficult to obtain in-depth information from an open-ended question in a telephone survey.

Questions which depend on visual cues. As was described earlier, some questions are well asked by presenting the possible answers to the respondent on a card (for example, income). In a telephone interview, possible responses must be read off to the respondent for a selection. In some cases, where reactions to pictures or other visual cues are desired, the telephone is not appropriate. Most questions, however, can be adapted for a telephone interview (recall the unfolding and numbered-scale methods described above). The advent of the video telephone would probably alter the receptivity of respondents to being interviewed on the telephone. Whether individuals will be more receptive or less receptive to being interviewed on video, however, will have to be seen.

COMPUTER-ASSISTED TELEPHONE INTERVIEWING (CATI)

The telephone survey, described earlier in this chapter, which we carried out at California State University at San Marcos (CSUSM) used the technology of computer-assisted telephone interviewing (CATI). Let me briefly describe here how a CATI system works; in Chapter 11 we will look more closely at how data can be collected in this manner. In a CATI laboratory such as the one we have at CSUSM there are a number of computer workstations each of which contains a computer keyboard, a monitor, and telephone headsets. These computers are all networked to the main computer in the lab.

If you were a student about to do some telephone interviewing in our lab, you would sit down at the computer workstation, put the telephone headset on, and then read the computer monitor screen. The first thing that happens is that the computer dials a number and a telephone rings at a residence. If you are calling names from a population of some sort that has been entered into the main computer, the screen will tell you exactly who you want to interview at each residence. "Hello, I'm Susan Jones calling from Cal State San Marcos. Our sociology class is carrying out a survey of . . . Could I please speak to *Robert Owens?*"

The computer screen is split. The top of the screen is the question screen: All the words that you as the caller are speaking are written out against one background color (say, red). All the questions are written in uppercase and lowercase regular writing. The bottom of the screen is the answer screen: It contains the possible answers you might receive against a different background color (say, blue). All the answers are written in uppercase to differentiate them from the questions.

If Robert Owens is not at home, is not available to speak, or doesn't live at that number, the bottom of the screen shows the interviewer what number to enter to represent these optional conditions. If he is available, the interview begins. Each question comes up on the top screen, and when the respondent answers, all the interviewer has to do is to enter into the computer the number corresponding to the answer.

The good features of the CATI system are the following: (1) The CATI system selects the numbers to call randomly and dials them automatically, (2) it tells the interviewer who to ask for (by name if the population has been entered into the computer), or the computer is set up to employ a system (much as Box 7-5 shows) in which the members of the household are listed by age or by

sex and age and then one is randomly selected to be interviewed, (3) it allows the interviewer to read the questions off a question screen (the top half of the computer screen), (4) all the interviewer has to do is enter the responses into the computer by pressing the number corresponding to the answer presented on the answer screen at the bottom half of the computer monitor, and (5) the computer begins to aggregate the responses and keep track of the sample being called so that the researchers can monitor the progress of the data collection as it is being carried out. The CATI system is actually computerizing the dataset, readying it for the analysis stage once the data have all been collected.

DECIDING IF A SURVEY, AN INTERVIEW, OR A FOCUS GROUP IS APPROPRIATE FOR YOUR TOPIC

Surveys are undoubtedly the most common research method in the social sciences. Surveys generate data useful for a great range of study topics and lend themselves to wide-ranging forms of analyses. They provide the researcher with a set of responses, often to fixed-choice questions, which in the aggregate can be used to measure the characteristics and attitudes of a definable social group. The substance of the material collected in survey research includes responses to questions, aggregated across many respondents. These responses tend to tap subjective attitudes and orientations as well as more external indicators of the respondents' personal and social situation. As I suggested in Chapter 1, survey research tends to be the method of choice for those who want to look at the broad patterns of social life or describe widespread social reactions (to candidates or social policies). If these are your goals in a study, a survey may be your best choice.

Remember, however, that there are disadvantages as well as advantages to the survey method. As I said in Chapter 1, surveys focus on attitudes, opinions, pieces of information about the conditions of life, and the categories that define and differentiate individuals. But there are other phenomena to study in the social sciences and other ways to study those phenomena. It is not as easy to get a sense of a whole cultural group by interviewing them as it is by living among them. Consider the people of a foreign country. Suppose you decided to do a survey of the Balinese (the people who live in Bali). Would that be a good way to find out all about them? Possibly not. You probably would not know what questions to ask them, what is important to them, or how to question them properly. For such a study, a qualitative field study would be preferable, though once you understood more about the Balinese, you might be able to use more formal interview techniques.

Let's say you wanted to understand under what conditions individuals may become very aggressive toward a stranger. It would be very difficult to get such information from a questionnaire (though you might develop scenarios of aggression-producing situations and ask respondents what they would do); in this case an experimental design might be preferable.

This is not to caution you too much on the use of surveys. They can be used in a myriad of ways to study many subjects. While surveys may be done very poorly, a well-constructed survey that is administered effectively is a powerful means for gaining knowledge about the social world around you.

We have also focused in this chapter on the techniques of interviewing. Interviewing may well be a technique for data collection that you as a social researcher will use. Note that interviewing often is used to collect survey data, either face to face or by telephone. Computer-assisted telephone interviewing as a way to collect survey data is becoming a widely used method for both social research and market research. Interviewing also is used in qualitative research studies, such as Hochschild's naturalistic interview study of two-job couples (see Chapters 1 and 8). Her interviews differed from the typical interview survey in that they did not follow a precise interview schedule but ranged beyond it to obtain more in-depth responses. This means that the types of social re-

search studies in which interviewing may be employed are very broad. We will see in both Chapter 8 on qualitative research and Chapter 10 on evaluation research and case studies that interviewing is widely employed across many social research methods.

We also have suggested that focus groups may be a fine way to gather data as the basis of a research project or as an adjunct method to support a survey or another data collection method. Because focus groups are relatively easy to set up and are not costly or time-consuming, they may be an excellent choice for gaining impressions, reactions, and evaluations from the targeted respondents. They are widely used in both market research and political polling and are likely to become more popular among social researchers.

REVIEW NOTES

- Survey research is a method of data collection in which a defined group of individuals are asked to answer a number of identical questions.
- The components of a survey include selecting a sample of respondents and presenting the survey questions to the sample either in an interview or in a self-administered questionnaire.
- Rules for questionnaire design include the following (1) Include only questions pertinent to the research, (2) make the questions appealing, (3) keep the questionnaire short, (4) have brief but clear instructions, (5) preconsider all the issues a respondent receiving the questionnaire might have.
- The format of a mail questionnaire should include a cover letter, instructions on how to complete and return the questionnaire, the questionnaire itself, and a stamped and preaddressed return envelope.
- There are two strategies for soliciting cooperation in a survey: stressing the importance of the research project as a contribution to science and stressing the needs of the researcher.
- Pretesting of questionnaires should be carried out to determine problems before the actual data collection begins. In reviewing a pretest, look

for widely skipped questions, questions that produce little variation in response, open-ended questions that are ambiguously answered, and response set.

- The following factors may increase the response rate to a mailed questionnaire: (1) its appearance, (2) the request to participate, (3) personal appeals, (4) sponsorship, (5) other inducements (possibly financial) in the survey, (6) promises of anonymity or confidentiality, (7) type of return mailing enclosures, (8) type of mailing procedure and (9) follow-up procedures.
- What is considered a respectable response rate for a mail survey varies, but rates below 50 percent are undesirable. Since few surveys reach a 50 percent response rate on the first mailing, follow-up mailings are advisable.
- Successful interviews are highly dependent on the nature of the relationship developed between the interviewer and the interviewee.
- Focus groups draw a small group of relevant people together to discuss a specific issue. Focus groups can help in developing the concepts and questions for a survey, generating hypotheses, or understanding findings. They also are used to measure impressions, explore problems, or generate creative ideas.
- Interview schedules should have simple instructions for the interviewer to follow, the questions should be worded so that they can be easily read, and the order of questions should quickly attract the respondent and keep her or him interested in completing the survey.
- The cardinal rule of interviewing is to suppress one's own opinions.
- An interviewer must build a warm relationship with each respondent at the same time he or she applies standard techniques of asking each respondent the same questions in the same way.
- The four rules for becoming a good interviewer are (1) understand the interview, (2) commit yourself to completing each and every interview, (3) practice giving the interview, and (4) use common sense in difficult situations.
- Interviewers may need to probe for deeper and fuller responses.

- Selecting a telephone survey sample from a telephone directory to represent an area is not a very desirable method because so many individuals are unlisted or do not have telephones.
- Telephone surveys have three advantages over face-to-face interviews: Telephone surveys are cheaper, take less time and effort, and are more impersonal. The three disadvantages are that they often require many calls to complete a single interview, there is less motivation to comply or complete a telephone interview, and fewer facilitation techniques can be used in gathering sensitive or complicated data in a telephone survey.
- CATI (computer-assisted telephone interviewing) is becoming one of the major means for collecting survey data. CATI systems select respondents randomly, facilitate interviewers by delivering questions and immediately computerizing the responses, and aggregate the responses and track the sample as the data are being gathered.

KEY TERMS

anonymity
closed-ended question (forced choice)
computer-assisted telephone interviewing (CATI)
confidentiality
contingency question
dross numbers
exhaustive categories
face-to-face interview
focus groups
follow-up procedures
hired-hand research
interview schedule
mail survey
matrix question
open-ended question
pretesting
questionnaire
random-digit dialing (RDD)
response rate
response set
social desirability
sponsorship
telephone survey

STUDY EXERCISES

1. Using the hypothesis "Students who commute to campus will participate less in extracurricular activities than will those who live on campus," write a short questionnaire to gather the data to test it. Design two *closed-ended questions* to measure the variable mentioned in the hypothesis. In addition to these, include questions to measure sex, means of commuting to campus, time required to commute to campus, and work status of a student. Try to set up the three questions concerning commuting as *contingency questions.*

2. If you were administering the above questionnaire to students in a college classroom, you will need a brief set of instructions at the top of the questionnaire to inform the respondents how to fill it out. Write out such instructions.

3. Now assume that you are planning to mail this questionnaire to students. You will need to enclose a cover letter. Compose a cover letter for this questionnaire encouraging students to participate (assume that your reason for doing this survey is to fulfill course requirements for a research methods course).

RECOMMENDED READINGS

1. De Vaus, D.A.: *Surveys in Social Research,* Allen & Unwin, Boston, 1986. This short text on survey research includes a lot of useful designs and hints for constructing questionnaires and building scales. Includes exercises.

2. Edwards, Jack E. *et al.: How to Conduct Organizational Surveys,* Sage, Thousand Oaks, Calif., 1996. Shows technological and methodological advances of last decade in designing surveys on organizations.

3. Fowler, Floyd J., Jr.: *Improving Survey Questions: Design and Evaluation,* Sage, Thousand Oaks, CA, 1995. Shows how to word and format questions, produce questions that get the desired responses, and evaluate questions.

4. Frey, James H., and Sabine Mertens Oishi: *How to Conduct Interviews by Telephone and In Person,* Sage, Thousand Oaks, CA., 1995. The book focuses on writing interview questions, scripts for precalls, ordering questions, and designing eligibility screens.

5. Krueger, Richard A.: *Focus Groups: A Practical Guide for Applied Research,* 2d ed., Sage, Thousand Oaks, CA., 1994. A step-by-step guide to planning a successful focus group.

6. Schuman, Howard, and Stanley Presser: *Questions and Answers in Attitude Surveys: Experiments on Question Form, Wording, and Context,* Sage, Thousand Oaks, CA., 1996. The authors are experts on survey development. Subjects addressed here include question order, open and closed questions, "no opinion" options, acquiescence, and tone of wording.

7. Stewart, David W., and Prem N. Shamdasani: *Focus Groups: Theory and Practice,* Sage, Newbury Park, CA., 1990. The potential role of focus groups in survey research and other research methods is discussed. The design and conduct of a focus group, as well as means for analyzing data from focus group interviews, are described.

8. Tanur, Judith M. (ed.): *Questions about Questions: Inquiries into the Cognitive Bases of Surveys,* Russell Sage, New York, 1992. This volume grew out of the Social Science Research Council (SSRC) Committee on Cognition and Survey Research. It includes essays on how questions can influence answers; comprehension, recall and memory, self-reporting, and attitude measurement in interviews; and strategies for collaboration between interviews and respondents.

9. Turner, Charles F., and Elizabeth Martin (eds.): *Surveying Subjective Phenomena,* 2 vols., Russell Sage, New York, 1986. These volumes discuss the central methodological worries which concern leaders in the survey research enterprise. An excellent reference on issues of measuring attitudes, conceptual ambiguity in surveys, interviewer-respondent relations, and the social use (and misuse) of surveys.

Qualitative Research

INTRODUCTION

Qualitative research covers a wide range of different types of research methods. Thus, it may be easiest to clarify what *qualitative* research is by establishing the ways in which it differs from *quantitative* research. Experiments and survey research, as described in Chapters 6 and 7, are the most characteristic forms of quantitative research methods that are carried out within social research. The findings of both experiments and surveys can be presented in numerical terms, though the meaning of those numbers still needs to be interpreted in words. The simplest definition of qualitative research involves the fact that the findings of a qualitative study are presented not in numbers but solely in words.

Many terms are currently in use for various types of qualitative research. We will begin this chapter by considering these different forms of qualitative research. Three major types of data collecting are most typical in qualitative research: observing, interviewing, and reading various types of written documents. We described interviewing in Chapter 7 on survey research, since this is a data collection method which is also widely used for collecting survey data; in this chapter we will consider particular ways in which interviewing is employed in qualitative research designs. In Chapter 9 we will focus on studies that use the data (such as written documents of various types) which are already available. In Chapter 10, when we examine evaluation research and case studies, we will see that qualitative research methods often form the basis of these types of social research (especially case studies). In Chapter 11 ways of analyzing qualitative data will be presented, and in Chapter 14 ethical issues raised in qualitative research studies will be discussed.

Thus, as the first chapter on qualitative research, this chapter will lay the groundwork for you to think more fully about what constitutes this activity by describing a number of different types of qualitative research, examining in depth the data collection method of *observation* which is central to many forms of qualitative research, and considering how interviewing is employed in qualitative research studies. We will utilize as examples of qualitative research Thorne's ethnographic study of school playgrounds, Anderson's long-term community study, and Hochschild's interview study, which were described in some detail in Chapter 1.

FORMS OF QUALITATIVE RESEARCH

Because qualitative research methods are employed in such a wide range of social research designs, we begin by offering brief descriptions of the various types of research that use qualitative methods. These forms of research include *field studies* and *ethnography,* which employ observation as a primary form of data collection; *action research,* which focuses on the purpose of the research and the role of the researcher; *grounded theory research,* which aims to build theory; and finally the many types of *phenomenological sociological research* efforts, which aim to describe the social world as it is. We will see over the course of this chapter and those which follow which aspects of these qualitative methods come into play in different types of research designs.

Field Studies and Ethnographies

Field studies are simply a form of research in which the researcher gathers data directly in real social environments through observation, interviewing, or whatever other type of data gathering makes sense in that field. The findings from field studies usually are presented in words, though quantitative data may be gathered and presented. For this reason, field studies (or field research, as it is also called) generally is seen as a qualitative research method.

Ethnography is a form of field research. As the primary research method of anthropologists, ethnography refers to efforts to describe whole cultures through observation. The work of an ethnographer also takes place in a field, that is, at a site where the researcher can observe and come to understand the culture of the peoples being studied. This is why *ethnography* and *field studies* are often linked terms. In ethnography, the processes of observing and collecting the data are integral parts of the product of this type of research. Hence, fieldwork, the writing of field notes, and the transcription of those notes into writing are the stages of an ethnographic study.

Action Research

Action research is directed toward social change; that means that its purpose is to try to involve the actors being studied in a manner that can lead to improvement in their social situation. Hence, action research is focused on the outcome that might result from the research being done. Its purpose is both to engage the subjects being studied as participants and to lead to practical outcomes. This type of research is common in studies of schools and other organizations. A form of action research, *participatory action research* (PAR), is often carried out with communities or groups that are trying to overcome negative or oppressive conditions (Schwandt, 1997, pp. 112–113). PAR uses a collaborative approach in its effort to foster cooperative and democratic means for doing the research and has as its objective not only the production of knowledge and understanding that may be useful to the organization but also consciousness-raising among group members. In Chapter 10, when we examine case studies, we will look carefully at a study carried out by Darlene Pina which exemplifies action research.

Grounded Theory Research

Grounded theory research has as its purpose the building of theories, theoretical models, and con-cepts through an inductive process which begins with the data. It moves from collecting data (through observation, interviews, or written records) toward generating insights from the data, to the forming of generalizations, theoretical concepts, hypotheses, and then back to collecting more data to test or verify those concepts. Because of this circular process of deriving theoretical ideas inductively from data and then returning to the data to verify those ideas, the theories are considered to be grounded in the data. What is most characteristic of this type of qualitative research is the continual back-and-forth effort of going from data to theory building and then back to collecting more data to verify and test theoretical ideas. Grounded theory research is most closely associated with the sociologist Anselm Strauss (Strauss and Corbin, 1990). As theories emerge, they are tested by evidence from "theoretical samplings" of incidents, actions, and groups of people. The process of returning to the data to get confirmation of theoretical insights continues until theoretical saturation is reached. It should be added that the term *grounded theory* is often used more loosely to refer to any type of effort to build theoretical ideas from data (Schwandt, 1997, pp. 60–61).

Phenomenological Sociological Research

Phenomenological sociological research covers a range of different types of research efforts aimed at describing the social world more validly; if attempts "to describe the structures of experience of the 'life-world' (the common sense world as experienced, the everyday world)" (Schwandt, 1997, pp. 83, 113). Such efforts often are associated with the German term *verstehen,* which means "understanding" or establishing meaning from the point of view of the participants in a social environment. Such efforts at *verstehen* were developed by the nineteenth-century German philosopher Dilthey, who wanted to show how the social sciences differed from the natural sciences.

In America, the theory of *symbolic interactionism* emphasized the importance of communication (interaction) between individuals as the primary generator of meaning. It was these socially developed meanings for people and objects in an individual's world that affected the actions of that individual. Thus, symbolic interactionist research requires the researcher to try to gain an understanding of how individuals interpret their worlds. This means that the researcher must carefully attend to the communication, actions, and social environments in which social interaction occurs. Hence, this type of research requires careful observation by the researcher, who must be a participant in the social setting being observed.

One other type of inquiry that is linked to these phenomenological forms of qualitative research is *ethnomethodology,* which attempts to uncover the rules which govern the process of human interaction. Ethnomethodologists concentrate on small-scale exchanges between individuals in a setting, transcribing this communication and then carefully analyzing the data as a way to understand the world of those being studied. Ethnomethodologists attempt to separate the interpretations of the researcher from the ways in which the actors themselves build shared understandings. All these pheonomenological forms of qualitative research study the real world, focus on human communication, and try to delve into its meaning so that the human experience can be appreciated more richly and fully.

Shared and Distinct Approaches of Qualitative Methodologies

Qualitative research of all types assumes a more naturalistic approach than does quantitative research. Its aim is to construct meaning from social environments. The naturalism of qualitative research means that gaining information about the social setting should be done in ways that will not alter the environment and are natural ways regularly used by individuals to understand their worlds. Thus in qualitative research *observation* is

a central method of gathering data, along with talking to people (that is, interviewing) and looking at written and visual materials about a social setting (reading documents). There are some differences in the various forms of qualitative research in terms of the most desired role for the researcher, but generally the researcher should not intrude on the environment and distort what is being studied.

There are also differences in the goals of qualitative research, though gaining a greater understanding and appreciation of the meaning of social existence is always present. When qualitative research is commissioned by an agency or organization to study what it is doing and/or evaluate its effectiveness, the study will produce recommendations and suggestions for action. What we will do now is look at various aspects of the qualitative approach which should help you see how to generate a study of this type.

THE ART AND SCIENCE OF QUALITATIVE RESEARCH

Creative Aspects of Qualitative Research

The object of most qualitative research, however it is done, is *verstehen,* to understand social action. We have all been in situations—enjoying the festivities at a wedding, overhearing negotiations in a used car lot, listening to the cheers at a pep rally, watching a couple in a restaurant argue over dinner—where we say to ourselves, "I know what's going on here" or "I have it figured out." What we mean is that the situation or event epitomizes some quality of the culture which we have always recognized but taken for granted. Let's take a high school football pep rally (as I remember it from the deep dark past) as an example. The cheerleaders are on the stage, the band is blasting away in the pit, the football team comes on stage, and everyone goes crazy. Then the coach comes out and makes a few remarks about the importance of the upcoming game, and everyone screams again. But let's stop for a moment. What is everyone screaming about? What is really at stake here? Does it really matter who wins the game? What is school spirit anyway?

The sense of blending in with the euphoria of group excitement is one of the great joys of human experience. There is a losing of the sense of self and with it the sense of worry about problems and responsibilities that are difficult to face. How is this all achieved at a pep rally? Well, what do the cheerleaders represent? Usually they are attractive young women and men who are "peppy," which means that they are exuberant, outgoing, and inviting. They draw you out of yourself into the group spirit. In a sense, they are rather like primitive rain dancers. They jump around, shouting common calls and focusing the emotions of the group on the common wish—the wish to succeed, to overcome, to defeat another.

In some ways, this wish to succeed (even if only at a football game) is the universal wish of all humans about life: to make it a successful endeavor. Perhaps the big football players represent human force, a factor which may be less vital in modern life in helping people obtain basic needs but which is still the impulse that makes people sense that they can get where they want to go by pushing ahead. Maybe this is the meaning of football. To want to enter into the spirit of this drive for success is to want to live, to push oneself physically, to strive against odds, and to have the emotional support of others in one's endeavor.

You may be thinking that I've ignored the sexual aspects: the big male players, the petite females jumping, the padded shoulders, the short skirts. These aspects are also present and may be central to some understandings of the pep rally. A good field study of a football rally would try to come to terms with the sense of the event, to make it come alive to the reader, to build meaning out of what seems to be an ordinary event. Remember that what may seem to be ordinary to you and me could seem very exotic (or at least very strange) to a foreign-born person. The reaction would be even stranger to a person living in the future (imagine someone in 2099 reading your field study of a football rally) or someone from outer space! What you must keep in mind is that good-quality field work should convey meaning to anyone who might read it.

I have tried to suggest the various meanings a pep rally may symbolize. Whatever the meanings you seek, you need some methods to know how to see what you are watching, understand what you are hearing, and figure out what is really happening. The techniques for studying a field must be creative; they must be right for the field being studied. The researcher must remain *open* to the field; he or she must be able to absorb what is happening in the environment without being overwhelmed by it. Thus, the creative steps needed to carry out a field study include (1) choosing the field, (2) selecting the methods to be used in the field, (3) observing in the field, and (4) turning observations into meaning. These steps will be described more fully in the section on design. Here it is important to emphasize that at each step, being creative means possessing the following qualities:

Insightfulness: Seeing with understanding
Receptivity: Openness and eagerness to enter into the field
Self-understanding: Ability to understand one's own reactions and distinguish them from reactions that others might experience

To achieve self-understanding, a field researcher with divorced parents might (for example) need to recognize that he or she could have quite a different reaction to watching a couple argue in a restaurant than would one who did not. Knowing how you are personally affected by what you see and how your reactions might differ from those of others is the kind of sensibility field researchers need to develop. The social class background of an observer (race, religion, region of upbringing, etc.) is bound to affect personal perspectives. An observer must be cautious not to intrude on the scene in such a way that the environment being observed is altered. However, a field researcher should not be totally detached. The researcher must experience other situations deeply, as if actually involved, to enter into the world of others and see their world from their viewpoint. Yet the qualitative researcher must at the same time be careful not to get so intensely involved that he or she "goes native" and is no longer objective. There must be a middle ground of "involved detachment."

This ability to become engaged in the human achievements of others (for example, their writings, art, music, acting) is the kind of talent in which those who study the humanities excel. In the social sciences the material which needs to be appreciated may appear to be simpler—the meaning of a meal, the culture of a gas station, the relationship between a teacher and his or her pupils. However, each of these is also a "human production" expressing the values and cultural traditions and customs of a people, and the more closely we study them, the more complex they appear to become.

Recognizing the importance of insightfulness, receptivity, and self-understanding should give you a good start in field research. To set up a good initial design and guide yourself along the way, you also need to carefully consider the scientific aspects of a field project.

The Science of Qualitative Research

Walking into a scene unprepared is not the way to do qualitative field research. Remember Barrie Thorne's (1993) study of two grade schools (Chapter 1). Thorne did not just happen upon these two schools. Having decided to study the difference in girls' and boys' play, she needed access to children's social environments in order to observe them at play. Her objective was to gather information relevant to her subject by submerging herself in the social worlds of girls and boys. This meant that she had to act in a particular way. She had to tone down her role as an adult researcher and build a rapport with the children to gather the kinds of materials she needed to address her research interests. While she was observing at the

two schools, she had to keep her research purpose foremost in her mind in order to focus on relevant activities. Field studies never seek to alter what is happening in the environment being studied. Nevertheless, more or less systematic means for observing what is happening need to be utilized. Thus, the role of the researcher in a qualitative study is deliberative, thoughtful, and always mindful not to distort the environment or organization being studied; this purposefulness is of course characteristic of a scientist.

What varies from the usual role of a scientist is that nowadays in most qualitative research, the researcher does not claim to be value-free in her or his attitudes or claim that she or he has no impact on the environment being studied. It used to be argued, based on the work of Gold (1969), that qualitative researchers in the field could take one of four roles: The researcher might act as a *full observer* or a partial observer—an *observer-as-participant*—or conversely, the researcher might become a *full participant* in a field or a partial participant—a *participant-as-observer*. This last type, which is now most commonly called a *participant observer,* is the most typical role now assumed by qualitative researchers doing field studies. In fact, many qualitative researchers would argue that the role of the detached full observer trying to remain objective so that she or he can report on others has been extensively challenged if not altogether abandoned, and in fact, the politics and subjectivity of the researcher have become of paramount importance in qualitative research. Moreover, in many types of qualitative studies, such as PAR, the researcher tries to empower those being studied, not to stand aside as a detached observer (correspondence from Simon Gottschalk, 1995).

As a scientific activity, qualitative research often is aimed at generating theories. This, as was stated above, is especially the case for grounded theory research. Nearly all qualitative research is based on models, exemplars, or paradigms which lay the groundwork for carrying out the study and help focus the researcher on specific aspects. Many of the procedures used in collecting qualitative data and writing up field notes, such as the practice of *auditing,* in which a third party goes over the way in which the collected materials have been organized by means of an *audit trail* (the organized effort at making sense of the qualitative data collected to see if the procedures appear to be dependable), suggest the desire to make the research follow correct and desired practices.

Another procedure, a *member check* (in which others in the field are asked to corroborate the findings of a study), is supported by some as a way to confirm the findings of a study. However, other qualitative researchers would reject this effort as a form of verifying the study, especially if the qualitative researcher has been engaged in a great deal of participation in the field; then member checking could produce bias in the study. Thus, for many qualitative researchers, member checking would be considered merely another form of data collection.

Validity and Reliability in Qualitative Research

Some would argue that validity and reliability are not the goals of qualitative approaches to social research. In terms of reliability, there is concern about the trustworthiness of the data being gathered, which can become more dependable if the researcher has kept careful notes and an audit trail. In terms of validity, some would argue that qualitative research has higher validity (because it stays closer to the real meaning of social existence) than does research that produces numerical findings. Nevertheless, many qualitative researchers with pragmatic goals reject validity as a goal of qualitative research because direct knowledge of the social world (which is not socially constructed) is impossible to produce. However, efforts such as the member check (described above) and the attempt to gather different types of evidence by using different research methods from the same field—*triangulation* (which will be discussed later)—operate as efforts to further establish that what has been found is what the researcher claims to have found, in other words, to establish validity.

In terms of actual efforts to repeat (replicate) field studies, the anthropological literature has a few fascinating cases. Take, for example, the efforts to replicate the findings of the late renowned anthropologist Margaret Mead in her fieldwork in Samoa in the 1920s.

A Case of Replicating a Field Study.   Derek Freeman (1983) charged that Mead misunderstood Samoan life because she had been sent out by her faculty adviser to find differences from western patterns in adolescent behavior (and had therefore found them). Mead's most prominent findings in the Samoan study were that there was a lack of constraint in adolescent sexuality, that jealousy was rare, and that fidelity in marriage was not highly valued. Freeman argued that these findings were in error: for example, he insisted that Samoans revere virginity and that rape is prevalent.

Freeman's book caused a strong reaction among social scientists. Should his challenges be taken seriously? The debate that ensued (Marshall, 1983) raised many of the issues of concern that a field researcher should consider. Can fieldwork be replicated? Anthropologist Lowell Holmes also had tried to replicate Mead's fieldwork in the 1950s. Although critical of some of Mead's findings, Holmes largely supported her conclusions about the gentle, submissive quality of the Samoans (Marshall, 1983). Fieldwork done by different people at different times might well turn up different perspectives. For one thing, Mead was a woman and therefore was excluded from the all-male councils of the Samoan villages. (Nevertheless, as a young woman she may have had access to communication with adolescent girls, which would have eluded Freeman.)

To what extent is fieldwork affected by the general overview of human behavior that is held by the field researcher? (In other words, to what extent does reliability depend not only on shared field strategies but on shared theoretical predispositions?) Freeman charged that Mead's anthropology ignored evolutionary biology and that she was an extreme cultural determinist. Critics of

Freeman have insisted that his critique of Mead is merely a sociobiological diatribe (Marshall, 1983). In other words, Freeman and Mead believe in different theories for explaining human behavior, and therefore their field work necessarily reflects what they believe.

If theories and preconceptions dictate (or even shape) what a researcher sees as the facts, perhaps selective perception is inevitable. Perhaps qualitative researchers should sensitize themselves to the way in which theories shape perceptions. In practical terms, this may require sharing initial findings with colleagues, especially with those who operate from different assumptions.

OBSERVATION IN QUALITATIVE RESEARCH

In every form of qualitative research, nearly all qualitative researchers use observation as one of their central data-gathering methods. What we shall examine here are the aspects of the activity of observing that you will need to think through carefully before launching a qualitative research project.

Schwandt defines observation in qualitative research as "direct firsthand eye-witness accounts of everyday social action" that answer the question, What's going on? (1997, p. 106). He stresses five qualities of observation as it is carried out in field studies: (1) What happens is viewed in terms of the people being observed in a social setting, (2) great attention must be paid to detail, (3) what is observed must be placed in a historical and social context, (4) the processual and dynamic quality of social action needs to be recognized, not precise discrete events, (5) researchers should not impose premature theoretical ideas on the actions of participants (Schwandt, 1997, p. 106). Marshall and Rossman (1995, pp. 79–80) also stress the idea that researchers observing in the field should not be too predetermined in their behavior (with checklists and defined categories) but that the observation should be natural so that the researcher initially can take in the scene (the "big picture");

then, over time, ways of focusing on subcontexts (body language, less obvious features of the scene) will emerge. This means that the art of observing is not an easy one.

Observation serves most directly the research purpose of description, which is a primary goal of most ethnographic research. It can address research questions in regard to what are the most important events, beliefs, behaviors, and attitudes in a social environment (Marshall and Rossman, 1995, p. 41). Carefully done observations can bring greater clarity to the ambiguities of a particular social setting. Note how when you first go to a new college class, a new job, or new town, you aren't quite sure what it will be like. Let's take a new college class. You go to the first session and check out the instructor, the other students, what the room looks like, what the course will require, what the instructor initially says, the sound of her or his voice, who speaks up in the class, the temperature in the room, and so forth. You are in fact observing this social setting (to understand what you've gotten yourself into). Note that if you have taken many college courses (and thus have had many "first days" in class), you know how to observe and participate in a college class. Hence, you may well be a participant observer.

Participant Observation

Participant observation is a form of observation in which the observer must be somewhat socialized into the social setting in which the observation is being done. As Schwandt notes, "the participant observer is advised to always maintain something like dual citizenship" (1997, p. 111). This role was the typical one of the anthropologist observing a primitive culture. She or he was to be involved in aspects of the daily lives of the people over a prolonged period of time but was not to "go native" and become a full member of the group being studied.

This somewhat ambiguous role raised the issue of who exactly the participant observer represents. How much does the researcher inform those being studied of his or her purposes or how interpretations are made? Feminist researchers often hold that the participant observer should be closer, friendlier, and more clearly aligned with those being studied, and participatory action researchers make the case that the people being observed should be a part of the research team; studies should not be about others but *with* others (Schwandt, 1997, p. 111). If we return to the new college class example, as a student in this class you are in a good position to be a participant observer. Note the duality that would be needed in this role; you would be a student in the course playing that role of seeking to learn a body of material and indicate mastery of it (through exams, papers, etc.), and you would also be an observer researching what exactly was happening in the class.

INTERVIEWING IN QUALITATIVE RESEARCH

In Chapter 7 we described interviewing techniques in some depth as they relate to survey research and focus groups. Here we will describe some of the central ways in which interviewing can serve the needs of qualitative research. In qualitative interviewing, the researcher considers a framework for the interview which differs from the typical survey interview schedule. In a survey interview, the interviewer asks questions and the respondent answers. In a qualitative interview, the interview is constructed more as a discourse between two or more people which is not so fully controlled by the interviewer's questions but is in fact constructed by both the interviewer and the respondent over the course of the discussion (Schwandt, 1997, pp. 74–75).

Clearly, in qualitative research, the interview is perceived as being closer to a conversation than to a question-and-answer session. Steiner Kvale (1996) explores what he calls the "semistructured life-world interview," which aims "to obtain descriptions of the life world of the interviewee" (pp. 5–6). He notes, however, that in such an interview, the interviewee is not an equal partner with the interviewer, who introduces topics and defines

and controls the interview situation. By probing beyond given answers, the interviewer can get multiple responses which may be contradictory. However, for Kvale this is not a problem, because the object of a qualitative interview is to "capture the multitude of subjects' views of a theme" so that the researcher comes to see the respondent's complex social world (1996, p. 7).

Kvale offers 12 factors which make up the "mode of understanding" of the qualitative interview (1996, pp. 29–36):

1. The topic of the interview centers on important themes in the *life world* of the interviewee. The analysis of the interview can focus on the theme or themes or on the total meaning of the life world of the person.
2. The aim of the interview is to understand the *meaning* of these themes and of the subject's life world. In qualitative interviewing, the researcher aims to get not only factual content but also the subjective and often emotional meaning the respondent attaches to an idea. Hence, the researcher needs to observe facial gestures and body language as well as spoken words.
3. The interviewer seeks *qualitative* descriptions which are loaded with meaning. They should be precise but do not require the kind of exactness that a quantitative interview seeking to present its findings in numbers requires.
4. The qualitative interview is *descriptive;* it should seek complex descriptions and not be circumscribed by fixed categories. The type of description sought is similar to the situation in which a doctor interviews a patient to find out what is wrong. Rather than getting down to specific questions about why the patient is ill, the doctor asks about various symptoms, about how the patient sees the situation, about what is wrong. From these less focused questions, a diagnosis is formed.
5. The qualitative interview develops *specificity* about particular situations and actions that have occurred in the respondent's life world.

Exploring specific incidents in detail rather than seeking general opinions is the object of such interviews.

6. The interviewer must maintain a certain *naivete* so that the respondent feels the need to explain and describe more; if the interviewer is too well informed, is too knowledgeable about a theme, the interviewee may actually say less. This curious, emotionally sensitive interviewer needs to be aware of and try to challenge his or her own preconceptions. As Kvale urges, the interviewer needs to be naive in order to gather the richest and most "pre-suppositionless" descriptions of the life world of the interviewee (Kvale, 1996, p. 33).

7. The interview must be *focused* on the themes of the research topic.

8. Qualitative interviews often produce *ambiguity,* and it is then the challenge of the researcher to determine whether the ambiguous qualities are due to objective contradictions in the situations being described or to problems of communication during the interview.

9. Real *change* in the ideas of interviewees may occur during the interview. In therapeutic interviews this is often considered favorable. In qualitative interviewing it may indicate a true reevaluation or a better understanding of a situation.

10. While an interviewer needs to be naive, she or he must be *sensitive* to the comments of the interviewee.

11. Because the research interview actually constitutes a true social interaction between two people, it may have emotional and anxiety-producing qualities as well as cognitive ones. This means that the qualitative interview is an *interpersonal situation* in which the interviewer is the instrument seeking to gain subjective knowledge (Kvale, 1996, p. 35). The knowledge gained from the interpersonal situation itself becomes part of the product of the interview.

12. Finally, a qualitative interview needs to be a *positive experience.* A situation in which one person shows as much interest in and sympathy for another person as occurs in a well-carried-out qualitative interview is a gratifying experience for most people. Thus, the conditions are ripe for a qualitative interview to be a good experience.

Kvale's 12 points indicate the commonplace qualities of a qualitative interview: It should be roughly like a conversation in which the interviewer can gather the richest and most complex and meaningful information possible In the terms of Rubin and Rubin (1995), a qualitative interview should be considered a *guided conversation* (pp. 122–139). They state that in normal conversation people often give perfunctory answers: "How are you?" "Fine." Thus, one of the goals of a good interviewer is to develop conversational depth, to encourage the interviewee to respond in more elaborate ways. The interviewer needs to create a "natural involvement" (p. 129) for the interview, matching the tone of the conversation to the qualities of the social setting.

Interviews often begin with small talk, perhaps a joke, but the interviewer should make known her or his interest in the person and the topic of the interview. One way to show an interviewee that you have understood a response is to ask a follow-up question that indicates this understanding. It is important that the interviewee be empathetic and a very good listener. Rubin and Rubin (1995, p. 132) suggest that a good way to show emotional camaraderie is by responding to an interviewee's statements with comparable examples from one's own life, but they warn that such examples must not diminish the experiences of the interviewee. The examples should be truly comparable and briefly presented so that they do not take up too much of the conversation. Interviewers often need to show support even when they may not feel real approval. An interviewer can show support for a general type of effort without actually feeling positive about a specific case; the Rubins call this "showing support without unqualified approval" (1995, p. 133).

GENERAL COMPONENTS OF A QUALITATIVE STUDY

What we need to do now is describe the various parts of a qualitative study that must be assembled so that you can carry one out. We will use the three qualitative studies from Chapter 1 as examples, since they represent a good range of the types of qualitative studies we have been describing. Recall that Thorne's study of girls and boys at play in two elementary schools was a field study (an ethnography) in which Thorne observed the behaviors and activities of the children. Anderson's study of two Philadelphia neighborhoods was a long-term study of two communities. He was clearly a participant observer in the communities and played various roles in those communities over the course of the study. In his study there is a quality of action research, since Anderson had an interest in strengthening those communities and worked with others toward that end. Hochschild's study of two-career couples was based on in-depth interviewing, generally in the interviewees' homes. All these studies were naturalistic in orientation; the researcher was entering the lives and worlds of those being studied—they were not coming to the researcher's lab or completing a set questionnaire. To do these studies each researcher needed to select a setting, a general topic, a time frame, and the types of things to observe or gather information about.

The Setting

The qualitative studies described in Chapter 1 took place in specific locales. Thorne's study of boys and girls at play was set in two public grade schools (one in Michigan and the other in California). Anderson's study focused on two Philadelphia neighborhoods, and Hochschild's interviews were carried out with couples in San Francisco's Bay Area. Of the three studies, the one that has the strongest focus on a physical and spatial locale is Anderson's. His Philadelphia neighborhoods were true geographic places which are probably identifiable to those familiar with that city, but his choice of this particular city was based on the fact that he lived there and knew a lot about those neighborhoods. Having lived for many years in another large city (Chicago), he could recognize that the two neighborhoods represented typical examples of an "inner-city" neighborhood. Anderson's neighborhoods had clear geographic boundaries. He was also interested in the border area between the two neighborhoods. More importantly, those neighborhoods represented different social and cultural environments.

Note that Thorne's main focus was not specifically on the settings of the two schools but on the actions of the children within them. As I have noted, Hochschild had no particular interest in the fact that the couples she studied were in California's Bay Area but was interested in the social spaces the couples arranged for themselves. Clearly, the lives and lifestyles of the couples interviewed would be more characteristic of "urban" America, but since most Americans live in greater urban areas, she could assume that the lives of these couples were not unique.

Thorne's schools had defined spaces which she studied—the school itself with its walls and specific classrooms—but her primary focus was on the playgrounds of the schools, which have less fixed boundaries. (Note that one of her primary concerns was the social-psychological boundaries boys and girls created between themselves.) The setting of Hochschild's study was less physically defined and more social. She was interested in the social space and existence of two-career couples with preschool age children. Thus the settings were the homes of those families, the day care centers some of their children attended, and the like—the social environments and organizations the couples moved through to carry out their lives. Note that since Hochschild had more concern about how the subjects managed their personal lives and balanced them with their careers, the setting of the study was more the home and personal life space, not the work environment (though details of those environments in some cases slip into the study if they are relevant to how the balancing occurs).

How did the researchers fit into the settings of the studies? In Thorne's study, the two primary schools had their regular members: the teacher, the pupils, and a few administrators and staff members. These "members" were present at the school on a continuous basis; they belonged there. But schools often have visitors as well, and that was Thorne's position at school. The neighborhoods Anderson studied had permanent residents (Anderson himself was a resident of one of the neighborhoods), but the investments of different individuals in those neighborhoods, their identified roles vis-à-vis other neighborhood residents, varied considerably. Hochschild and her assistants tended to interview her subjects in their homes; for the 12 families on which intensive interviewing was done, not only were their homes visited, but Hochschild often followed subjects on their daily rounds to playgrounds and shopping and other task activities. There was no doubt that Hochschild and her assistants were not regular members of the settings in which those families lived (their homes), but a stronger sense of the settings of the lives of the subjects could be gained through seeing and being with subjects in the places (homes) and spaces in which they carried out their lives.

Though public schools in the United States are public in their constituency, they are not open places that anyone can enter, given the security issues and legal responsibilities that are imposed on schools. Thorne needed formal permission from each school and from the teachers whose classrooms she observed to be able to enter those schools to pursue her research objectives. Anderson's setting was not closed and did not require permission to enter; one did not have to live in the area or be a "member" to get in. However, he noted that strangers to the neighborhoods were easy to spot. As a resident of one of the neighborhoods being studied, Anderson actually "belonged" to the place being studied. Hochschild's settings were more private, and so was her subject matter. Therefore, Hochschild needed to get permission and support from her subjects to be able to study them as she did.

In summary, settings have various qualities which need to be considered in a qualitative study:

1. Are the settings public or private? Can anyone walk in? Are there guards checking who can enter (which is true of many buildings which corporations occupy)? Do you need to get formal permission? If so, you will need to be able to justify your request for entry.
2. Are there regular, permanent members in the setting, or do the people in the setting usually vary? Do some members come more regularly than do others? What are the purposes for which people in the setting come? Are they formal or informal?
3. What are the important objects in the setting? Do they seem to belong there? What do they tell you about other characteristics of the people who live and work there?

A General Subject

Field researchers usually have a general or specific subject in mind when they enter the field. At the primary schools, Thorne wanted to understand how gender roles developed out of children's play. Anderson was trying to understand how race and class affected social change in urban neighborhoods. Hochschild wanted to learn how two-career parents of preschool-age children managed their lives.

According to Lofland (1971), an analysis of a social field can pose only three major questions:

1. What are the *characteristics* of a social phenomenon, the forms it assumes, the variations it displays?
2. What are the *causes* of a social phenomenon, the forms it assumes, the variations it displays?
3. What are the *consequences* of a social phenomenon, the forms it assumes, the variations it displays? (1971, p. 13)

Thus, suppose we decide to do a study of a hot line for teenagers with problems. In terms of characteristics, we would want to know both the structure and the characteristics of the hot-line organization itself and the characteristics of the people involved: who works for it (and answers the calls) and who calls in. Furthermore, we would want to know something about the history of the hot line—who started it and why. Such a subject could form the basis of a field study and would require going to the organization itself, talking to its director and workers, and observing the hot line in action. The researcher might even want to take (or listen in on) a few calls to understand exactly what occurs during a hot-line telephone conversation (though ethical objections would arise if a researcher posed as a hot-line receiver).

If our study were focused on why young persons call hot lines, we would have a study concerned with causes. For such a study, we might need to concentrate on a specific period to see what types of requests were received. Or we might want to examine the records of the hot line to study the nature of the calls during a previous period. Such a casual study might well require data from sources other than observation (such as records). Finally, if our primary intent were to study what effect calling a hot line had on the teenager—that is, its consequences—we would need to develop some form of evaluation research design (see Chapter 10) to follow up on the youth who had called and received advice from the hot line. We might also measure results in terms of what the staff thought had been accomplished.

Whatever the subject, it is best, as I stated above, to have it very clearly in mind at the beginning of the study. It will serve as a guide to what you look for in the setting. While it is true that qualitative studies tend to evolve over the course of the research, it is still better to enter the field with a clear understanding of what you would like to discover. Then if what you see and hear leads you toward a different course, at least you will know where you began and how you have altered your plan.

A Theoretical Framework

Qualitative research must be based on a theoretical framework. This means that the researcher design-

ing the project needs to have an integrated set of ideas about how she or he will operate within the social environment to be studied and how the evidence that is gathered will be interpreted. Because in most qualitative research the researcher is the instrument for data collection, the positions, interests, and biases of the researcher necessarily become part of the study. Hence, it is preferable to systemize and set out those positions at the beginning rather than pretend that the researcher is a value-free, impartial vessel open to all experience.

While there are many theoretical positions a researcher might take, the one that will be developed here is *standpoint theory*. From this theoretical perspective, one must not begin with the belief that a social researcher can stand outside a subject and study it from an unbiased and value-free stance. Such a value-free stance assumes a universalistic point of view in which there is a reality every person can experience. Instead, researchers must construct their own standpoints through their actual lived social experience. Thus, different researchers begin at different standpoints. Feminists theorists have argued that women often don't perceive in their own lives the separation between public and private realms in the way men do, and so these spheres may not serve as distinct entities in their thinking. The importance of this lived experience often requires a researcher to begin with autobiographical material to dredge up the basis for his or her own standpoint. (Note that Barrie Thorne in her study of girls and boys at play began by recalling her own childhood experiences.)

Standpoint theory tries to uncover the meaning of the social world as it is experienced by people who may have been defined (or held back) by their race, gender, or nationality, and it attempts to retrieve and place value on the meaning of this lived experience. By starting with actual experience, standpoint theory argues that individuals know their world only as it has been constructed by "unconscious desire" and by the ideologies and cultural influences that have affected them. Thus, researchers cannot study a social issue from a value-free position, cannot understand a social reality outside the constructions of meaning that have developed through their own lived experience (see Clough, 1994, p. 74, as elaborated in Denzin, 1997, p. 59).

In more general terms, qualitative researchers need to recognize and develop a conceptual framework to guide their data-gathering and interpreting activities. Sometimes these conceptions are driven by the demands of those who are supporting the research efforts (as we will discuss in Chapter 10 on evaluation research). But always the perspectives of the researcher, how the researcher puts together her or his own models for understanding social experience, will be carried into qualitative study. Hence, it is always preferable to reveal and clarify these conceptions at the beginning of a study so that they can deliberately guide the research.

A Time Frame

A field research project may occur in one continuous period (such as a structured observational study of interaction) or over a long period of time. Thorne spent 8 months observing at the primary school in California, and then 3 years later she spent 3 months observing at the Michigan school. Anderson's urban communities were studied over a 14-year period (from 1975 to 1989), during which he lived in one of the neighborhoods and served for a few years on an active educational community support group.

The order of the visits may be sequential or nonsequential. In a sequential time frame the visits have a regular order, one regularly following the next, perhaps at a specific time, interval, or daily event (dinnertime). Visits over longer periods are usually nonsequential, but they may be timed to coincide with specific occurrences, occasions which bring together the important characters in the setting, or specific times of the day.

The timing of your project will depend on the nature of the project. Some studies must have a short duration because the event takes place over a short period of time (a Fourth of July parade, for example, though there could be pre- and postpa-

rade activities which might extend the study time). Other subjects have no clear time frame. Clearly a very short period of time for field study might not have given Anderson the depth of information he needed to understand social change in the two urban communities. Timing should also be considered in terms of the researcher. If a limited time frame is necessary, the researcher should try to identify and design a type of study in which it is appropriate to gather data over a short period.

Types of Things to Observe

Once you have a setting and a subject, you must still decide what you will observe on the scene. The following are the types you should consider.

The Environment.   Any field, be it a street corner or a corporation, has a general environment with a social temperature, a smell, a look, and a feel about it. Being in Times Square in New York City gives one a certain sense of the environment of the place. The weather may be cold, hot, or even pleasant; the odors may include chestnuts, car fumes, or nothing in particular; the look may seem exciting, lively, lucid, seedy, or depressing. But clearly Times Square has a certain *feel*. This feel is often what you seek out when you travel somewhere. The Golden Gate Bridge in San Francisco, the River Walk in San Antonio, Palm Beach, Harlem, the Rockies—all have a certain *feel,* but so do less famous places such as Filene's Basement (a department store in Boston), Wrigley Field (the home of the Chicago Cubs), and Felix's Oyster Bar in New Orleans. Specific places like these have a particular ambiance about them that settles in on you when you're there.

Most field studies take place in more ordinary places where people work, study, live, and relax. In the studies we read about in Chapter 1, the primary schools in Thorne's study were familiar places to anyone who has attended a public grade school in the United States. The urban neighborhoods in Philadelphia are places that are familiar to many of us but not to those who have lived mainly in rural or suburban areas. Whatever the environment of the field you study, try to take it all in and capture the feel of it.

The environment, or setting, is the widest angle that can be taken for a field study. All field studies take place in some setting, but the environment itself need not be the primary subject of study.

People and Their Relationships. We tend to notice people more than anything else (probably because we are interested in our own types). Generally, field studies are concerned with studying people. In any field, there are people in it who belong to that field and others who are only visiting or are outsiders to it. The most socially interesting phenomenon about people is the complex type of relationships they have with one another. When these relationships are very specific and formal (and governed by quite precise norms), we describe the people as "playing roles." In *role playing,* a father and son are not equivalent to an older man and a boy. Rather, a father and son are assumed to have a value-based relationship, an economic interdependency, strong affective ties, and long-term commitments to each other, though these assumptions may be wrong.

People not only relate to others as situations evolve but also set fairly regular relationships with organizations and institutions. In short, they become participants as workers, family members, club members, church members, and so on. Some persons come to participate in more unusual and specific groups (war game players, rock climbers), or they may participate with "deviant" groups in special settings for these members (nudest camps, gay bars).

These forms of participation are characterized by power differences in the relationships between persons. Anderson noted such differences among the inhabitants of the two communities. It might also be interesting to contrast people who are non-members in a field with the members. Since their relationships with others will be different, the types of interaction that occur between members and nonmembers should differ.

Behavior, Actions, and Activities. The subject of a field study may be specific examples of behavior. This is the narrowest angle for a study. If the actions become routinized so that they occur over and over again, they become an activity. An example of this would be going to church. To go to church once is an action; to go regularly is an activity because it has a regularity to it that suggests greater commitment and involvement on the part of the churchgoer.

Let's consider a classroom. Here the observer may note who raises a hand to answer questions. (Girls more than boys? Tall students more than short? Hispanic students more than African-American students? Students sitting in the front of the class rather than those at the back?) Or a study which observes the teacher's behavior may consider where the teacher stands. (In front of the desk, in back of the room, in front of the board? Does the teacher move about or remain stationary?) Or a study on attentiveness in a primary school classroom might try to determine which children are attentive by zeroing in on those who are preoccupied with other things. (Which ones are daydreaming or whispering?) These types of behaviors, which are somewhat secretive, can be detected by all of us, though sometimes we may be wrong. The child who seems to be daydreaming could be concentrating on the teacher's instructions, and the student who seems very attentive could in fact be daydreaming.

Clearly a field researcher needs to be very knowledgeable about the scene under study so that behavior can be accurately understood. This is not a new method for any of us; we all interpret the behavior of others regularly. What may be important in field research is that we understand the field we are viewing well enough that we are able to comprehend what we see. This can be done by trying to put yourself into the environment and, in this case, to experience what it would be like to be a child in that classroom. In this way, you may be better able to appreciate the meaning of the scene you are observing.

Verbal behavior. What people say both describes and tries to explain what is happening in a social environment. Thus verbal behavior addresses the meaning of a social field. What is said may be misleading or inaccurate, but it is someone's interpretation. If that someone is important to the social setting, that person's evaluation or description is a critical source for understanding that field. Naturally, a field researcher generally will not want to depend on the comments of only one person. Instead, the more people whose perspective can be gathered, the more comprehensive an understanding can be gained. (Naturally, what different persons say may be contradictory, but the researcher must try to pick out the dominant patterns while not overlooking the deviant perspectives in drawing together an overview.)

Verbal behavior can be "observed" in two primary ways. You can listen for the content of the conversation and record it in terms of the types of language presentations: questions, answers, statements, affirmations, praise, and so on. Or you can view conversation as social interaction and note who talks to whom, who asks questions of whom, who answers questions from whom, and who supports whom. In the first form the conversation is more salient than the speakers; in the second form the speakers are more salient than the content. Of course, the two types of observations may be combined. Since verbal behavior is so complex and full of meaning, it is sometimes helpful to use a system for categorizing the conversational data which may capture the full extent of the meaning.

In the 1950s there was a great interest in the careful study of interpersonal behavior. A number of schemes to measure verbal behavior, such as Bales' Interaction Process Analysis (IPA), were developed at that time (1951). Bales' IPA divides all verbal behavior into 12 categories. The observer follows the pattern of verbal interaction by designating every member of the observed group with a letter and taking down the category number of each verbal utterance, associated with each speaker, over a specific period of time. While such techniques are used less frequently today, they still offer comprehensive means for studying small-group verbal interaction in laboratories and natural settings (see Bales, 1980, for a more recent, three-dimensional coding scheme). One typical environment in which interaction had been closely studied is the classroom. An example of an observational method for coding classroom interaction is Withall's (1952) socioemotional climate index, which evaluates the qualities of teachers' verbal interaction with their pupils.

Psychological Stances. Psychologists often observe the psychological postures of subjects. Certain stances can be readily observed; others are very difficult to detect. For example, an observer can observe amusement, laughter, or contentment quite easily. It may be more difficult to observe discontent and anger because individuals more often conceal such emotions. In children there is usually less concealment; it is more common to see a nursery school child who has been rebuffed cry than to see similar behavior in a company meeting. Observers should know very clearly what they are looking for in terms of psychological reactions.

Histories. Anthropologists and historians often seek to find out the background of their field through historical informants. In many cases, for example, the immigrant history of a specific family resides only in the memories of a grandparent. Certain stories will have been told about great-grandfather so-and-so back in the old country, about how great-great-grandmother got her passage to America, about how the early settlers chose a region of the country and a specific type of work, and about reactions to unusual events such as freak accidents and unexpected successes. Often only fragments of histories remain, but they have been carried down because they reflect the attitude toward important conditions or beliefs of this family both as it was in the past and as it has evolved into the present. These family stories are not just old tales but genuine sources of insight into the nature of a family's life. Accuracy may be gone, but the symbolic meaning of the stories remains.

One story I remember being told repeatedly by my mother was about how she would come home from high school every Friday afternoon to help her mother clean the house (especially to wash the kitchen floor) before going off with her friends to have fun. She did this because she felt guilty about the amount of work my grandmother was expected to do as a Eastern European immigrant woman, the mother of five and the wife of a very traditional man who expected much of her. Why did my mother stress this story so much? It seems to me that it represented the essence of her life situation as she grew up—an American-born child of immigrant parents trying to mix socially with her American friends and enjoy the ease of American social life but at the same time recognizing the difficulty of her mother's role and the distance at which she was placed from her mother by her American birth. Washing the kitchen floor was in one sense the price of her freedom, but it was also an acknowledgment of her origins. Of course, she may also have stressed this story to me so that I would also feel some guilt (and wash some floors for my freedom) because of what I owed to those (especially my mother) who had raised me.

Anderson sought out the history of the two neighborhoods and how they had changed economically and socially over time. Social researchers may consider themselves students of the present, but the present is continually becoming the past, and to understand it requires a consideration of the past.

Physical Objects. People and human interaction are not the only materials in a field. There are also inanimate objects. In a classroom there is the regular equipment—desks, chairs, blackboard, maps, students' work, etc. How have these objects been arranged? If the teacher's desk is in the front of the class, this suggests a leadership position for the teacher in the role of presenter to the class. Sometimes the teacher sits in the back, facing the front, as the children do. Such a desk position alters the meaning of the teacher's role. It might suggest that the teacher is only being a participant

in the class with the students, or it might suggest that the teacher is determined to detect qualities of the students which are better observable from the back of the classroom than from the front (e.g., note passing).

Observing in a person's home (as, in some cases, Hochschild did) offers many chances to consider the types of objects present: plants, art objects, furniture, reading material, musical instruments, basic decorations (paint or wallpaper, carpets or rugs, lighting fixtures or lamps). In addition, the arrangement of objects tells a story. For example, a television centered in the living room suggests the primary purpose of the room. Are there computers? If so, for what are they used (E-mail, word processing, games, the Web)?

The Need for Triangulation

In field research, there is a special need for multiple types of evidence gathered from different sources, often using different data collection methods. Unlike the experimenter, the qualitative field researcher casts her or his net widely to gather in a lot of different fish so that the richness and complexity of human environments can be captured and understood. In *triangulation,* the researcher gathers evidence from multiple sources to address the questions at hand from different points of view. Ultimately a researcher needs to narrow down and focus on the subject, but qualitative field researchers begin more broadly, deliberately exploring the whole mosaic of a situation so that the research subject is not trivialized. Triangulation is the strategy of casting out broadly for diverse evidence to more effectively focus on the study at hand.

As Fetterman contends (1989, p. 89), this bringing together of different types of evidence in order to test sources of information against each other is a way to determine which explanations are accurate and which ones should be rejected. By triangulating evidence, the researcher can prove or disprove her or his hypothesis. In any field study the researcher can gather comparable pieces of evidence to test whether the conclusions initially reached remain valid as additional pieces of evidence are accumulated.

Triangulation can bring together quantitative and qualitative data drawn from distinctly different research methods. These methods could include combining qualitative observation techniques with quantitative ones (counting specific things or people in the setting). Survey research which is quantitative can be combined with intensive in-depth qualitative interviewing, and experimental studies have been combined with ethnographies (see Grant and Fine, 1992, for some examples). While triangulation is one of the primary reasons for combining different types of methods in a study, there are also other good reasons, such as to broaden the study, to develop the research in a sequential manner in which later steps can help inform earlier ones, to address possible contradictions in the evidence, and to search for convergence and complementarity in the results (Cresswell, 1994, pp. 174–175). Triangulation often is employed to strengthen the validity of a study. This is a topic we shall examine again when we consider in Chapter 11 how qualitative data are analyzed.

THE DESIGN OF A QUALITATIVE FIELD STUDY

In the following sections, we will go through a series of steps that you would need to follow to carry out a qualitative field study in which observation would be one of the main types of data collection. We will consider the role of the researcher, how to prepare for fieldwork, what needs to be done before entering a field for research, and ideas for collecting and organizing data. We will not discuss ways of analyzing qualitative data in this chapter but leave that topic for Chapter 11.

The Role of the Field Researcher

As Barrie Thorne describes her role at the public school in California, "I was clearly not a full participant; I didn't have a regular desk, and I watched and took notes" (1994, p. 13). Clearly Thorne was a participant observer in the California primary school, spending most of her time in a single classroom of fourth- and fifth-graders and following them to lunch, the playground, the library, and the music room. In the Michigan school she moved between classes, sticking less closely to a single class. One thing she clearly recognized was that she had a level of free access in the school which the pupils lacked.

Thorne felt more like an observer in the more formal settings of the classroom and the auditorium, but in the playground she was able to move more into the role of a participant observer. One of her major challenges was that while she had depended on adults for entry to the field and it was imperative that the teachers and administrators continue to support her presence, in relation to the children, it was important that she not appear to be an authority figure. Hence, when a teacher's eyes met hers in a classroom to share an adult reaction to a child's behavior, Thorne was concerned that no child take that in and feel she was collaborating with the adult authorities.

Thus, Thorne was trying to move beyond all the adult roles she was familiar with vis-à-vis children, including her experience of being a mother. She also linked with the children by recalling qualities of her own experiences as a girl. (Recall that standpoint theory supports exactly this kind of personal reflection.) This deep concern with a researcher's own perspectives—who she or he is, what she or he believes, how she or he is perceived—is critical in a field study of this type because the researcher is the actual instrument of the study. There is no experiment to be held and no questionnaire to be filled out. What the study will be depends totally on what the qualitative researcher can bring forth from the research experience. This means that the first rule for a qualitative researcher is to "know thyself" and let that knowledge guide the preparations for the study.

Preparing for the Field

Whatever role is planned, the researcher also needs to better understand the field before entering it to do the research. This preparation is of two types. On the one hand, information about the field must be sought from external sources. These sources can include books and other printed materials about contexts like the one to be studied (or, if they exist, about the specific field itself). On the other hand, information should be gathered, if possible, from internal sources, through informants who can advise the beginning field researcher about how best to accomplish research aims.

The type of reading materials you peruse should include (1) field studies of similar fields, if such studies exist, (2) studies of persons similar to those you plan to observe in the field, (3) studies using methods such as those you plan to use, regardless of the type of field they were used in, (4) general information material (statistical, historical, geographic, and evaluative) which may give you greater knowledge about what you are studying before you enter the field, (5) literary or journalistic works describing aspects of the field which may help put you in the proper frame of mind so that you can function effectively in the field. In addition to reading outside source material, it is good to talk to individuals who may be familiar with any aspect of your subject (the types of people to be studied, the type of method to be used, etc.)

You should try to get some perspective on the field from insiders who may be able to help you prepare for your entry and decide how to carry out your project. The prefield entry period—the period before you begin to make your actual observations, collect notes, and go regularly to the field—will not be the same in every study. In a highly unstructured field, the prefield period may seem disorganized and disjointed. You may not know exactly where to go or whom to talk to.

When William Whyte (1943) set out to study his "street corner," he found little help until he met Doc, the leader of the street corner gang, who became the central character in Whyte's classic field study. In a more structured environment, such as a corporation or a school, you would need some insiders (employees) to tell you about the organization and about the people who lead it. Certain individuals who are in key positions in an organization hold a broad view of the organization (secretaries or central figures or employees who have worked for the organization for a long time), but the most valuable informant is one who has insight into his or her surroundings. It is the person who has a sociological imagination.

Entry into the Field

Once the field is selected and the researcher is ready to begin, an initial entry period is begun. Suelzle and Borzak (1981) describe the entry situation as putting the researcher into the role of a stranger. If your field of study is an organization which serves clients (a day care center, a hospital, or a welfare office), your entry phase will not be dissimilar to that of a client initially coming to the agency. Perhaps you can remember your first day in school (kindergarten?) or going to a new school after a move; these impressions often stay very strong. You remember the climate of the place, whether the teacher was warm, whether she (or he) was like your mother (or father), whether you felt you could belong to this environment. Clearly, as we get older, we learn how to belong to all kinds of places. We also learn that even if we are in a place where we would not like to belong, we can act in a nonchalant and casual manner. This is very much the style of entering a new field. Inside you may feel as you did on your first day at school, but outwardly you should act as if the place were "old hat" to you.

Suelzle and Borzak point out that "there may be many subjective responses to the first impressions, both negative and positive" (1981, p. 138), but they warn the field worker that in an organizational setting open-mindedness and a nonjudgmental attitude are essential. Opinions of what is being noted should not be given. If you remain open and innocent, it is much easier to ask questions, ask for advice, and seek assistance. If you sound opinionated or even too informed, you may compromise your position to gain more knowledge about the field.

A newcomer to the field wants to move rather quickly to the role of a guest:

> As a guest you are gradually admitted into interpersonal relationships on a regular basis. You are still a newcomer and are accorded certain privileges: People do not expect you to assume a full share of responsibility. You are still learning the roles, and mistakes are expected and tolerated. Others may be solicitous of your welfare and protective of you (*Suelzle and Borzak, 1981, p.139*).

Rosalie Wax describes field workers as often awkward and insecure in the first stage of field work. To move beyond this stage requires learning and relearning, socialization and resocialization. Success is measured by the point at which *reciprocal relations* have been established between the field worker and the members of the field.

The researcher's involvement in the field is "circular" and "cumulative," according to Wax. With a growing awareness that the research is going well, the field researcher becomes less anxious. Wax contends that it is through the support and help of the hosts in the field that the researcher comes to understand what is happening in the field environment under study (Wax, 1971, p. 20). Of course, Wax is describing field environments which are difficult, where people are uncomfortable and aggrieved about their situation, where suspicion about a field worker can be high.

Her own experience was as a field researcher in the Japanese relocation centers set up to confine Japanese-Americans during World War II. This was a difficult-to-study environment because of the low level of trust the Japanese-Americans had in others. The Japanese-Americans were forced to label themselves either "loyal" or "disloyal" to the United States. Wax naturally thought it would be easier to get to know those who were loyal to the United States, but this turned out not to be the case. Rather, it was the disloyal Japanese who had less to lose by confiding in her and explaining their point of view. Many fields may be more accommodating to you as a field worker, but it is always better to be prepared for a difficult situation which may turn out to be easy than to be unprepared (remember the Boy Scouts' motto!)

Numerous terms have been applied to define how a researcher should set up an entry to the field. Marshall and Rossman (1995, pp. 61–62) developed the concept of "negotiating entry," in which researchers need to identify who they are and clarify how they may be useful (or at least not disruptive) to the social environment. Marshall and Rossman (1995) suggest that the very energy of interest in the social setting generated by a committed researcher may help in the gaining of access. If the researcher is going to observe a complex environment with many settings, the process of entry may be continuous and the researcher may need to negotiate over and over again. Researchers need to recognize and be sensitive to the reluctance that some people might have about becoming part of a study about being observed or interviewed.

In Rossman's study of three high schools, it was necessary to be very persistent to gain entry. In considering entry to one of the high schools, Rossman began by writing a letter to the principal; this was followed by a telephone conversation. Then, with a few other researchers, there was a meeting with the principal, which did not go well since the principal expressed doubt about the usefulness of the concept of "culture," which was central to their study. This made the researchers feel defensive, and one of the researchers with little experience with schools felt particularly vulnerable (see Rossman et al., 1988, as reported in Marshall and Rossman, 1995, pp. 63–64). However, they did not give up. A second meeting was held with the teachers' union, and a third with the whole teaching staff. After this meeting the teachers voted to agree to participate in the study even though they had been initially suspicious. Thus, by being persistent and not allowing themselves to be undermined by the challenges made to their study, Rossman and her research colleagues succeeded.

However, the initial acceptance of a field researcher does not mean that the researcher will be unchallenged over the course of the study. Rossman found that in the course of her high school study she needed to continually renew her efforts at managing her relationship with the principal and the senior administrators of the school, especially after she had moved in closer to study the teachers and classrooms. Suspicions seemed to arise at the higher levels of the organization the nearer she got to examining the classrooms. However, her dilemma was that the closer she seemed to be to the principal, the more questionable her position became to the teachers, and she feared losing their trust; conversely, the more aligned she was with the teachers, the more concerned was the principal. Since her access to the school depended ultimately on the permission of the principal, Rossman made sure that she checked into the main office each day to report where she would be (see Marshall and Rossman, 1995, pp. 67–68).

Collecting Information

In psychological terms, observations define the reactions of the sensory apparatus to what a person sees, smells, hears, feels, (and tastes?). But how does one collect these sensory images? The field worker must use a system that will help the memory retain these images. By itself, the human memory is hardly a perfect system. Much of the material we think we have committed to memory cannot be recalled. Psychologists have shown that laying new experiences over old memories tends to bury the old memories. For this reason, it is important that field researchers record what they see before engaging in other activities. The box suggests that data can also be drawn from events that do not occur (or are not reported), that is, from *negative evidence*.

In the Field. What is observed in the field can be recorded in many ways. Tape recorders, video cameras, still cameras and note taking are all excellent tools. Tape recorders can be used if the people being observed approve of them. It is never advis-

LOOKING FOR NEGATIVE EVIDENCE IN THE FIELD

Lewis and Lewis warn that much of what is important in understanding a field setting may be lost or distorted if *negative evidence* is not considered. Negative evidence includes "(1) the non-occurrence of events, (2) an occurrence that is not reacted to or not reported . . . (3) [an occurrence which is reported] . . . in its raw form [but is} distorted in its interpretation or withheld from analysis and report" (Lewis and Lewis, 1980, p. 555). An example of this would be in the study of supposedly powerful elites. When there is no evidence of the intervention of the elite on a specific issue, this may suggest that the elite is not powerful. However, it might "reflect conscious agreement on non-intervention" (Lewis and Lewis, 1980, p. 548). Field researchers also may ignore very interesting aspects of a field because they are not sensitized to recognize them. For instance, Zablocki (1971), in his study of a commune in the 1960s, overlooked the sexism and sex-segregated work situations in the commune environment (Lewis and Lewis, 1980, p. 552). What Lewis and Lewis are suggesting is that what is *not* happening in a field may be an important clue to what is really happening.

Source: George H. Lewis and Jonathan F. Lewis, "The Dog in the Night-time: Negative Evidence in Social Research, " *British Journal of Sociology,* **31**:544–558, 1980.

able (and usually illegal) to record conversations with participants if they are unaware of your taping. In certain situations, taping may be perfectly acceptable; in others, it may not be. It is best to consult with those in the field about this method.

Cameras may also record field situations. Video cameras can offer an excellent means of capturing both sounds and scenes in a field setting (see the discussion of visual sociology below). Still cameras may also set down views of the field. Those in the field may not object to cameras as long as they do not wish to remain anonymous. Photographs may also help the researcher remember people and how things looked on a specific day.

Whose point of view to present?   In writing field notes, the researcher needs to decide in which voice the notes should be presented. Should they be written in the first person, that is, in the voice of the researcher? Emerson, Fretz, and Shaw (1995, pp. 53–55) suggest that writing in the first person is particularly useful for capturing the experiences of a researcher, especially when the researcher is a member of the group that is being studied. Moreover, first-person writing allows the researcher to both describe experiences as a participant and reflect on those experiences as a researcher.

Writing in the third person allows the notes to include the activities of the researcher as a participant observer (Emerson et al., 1995, p. 55). First-person asides may be included within those notes, often by bracketing them and referring to the self as "I." Some researchers like to use a "focused third-person" description in which the perspective of a specific person in the field is followed. It's as if the researcher were attempting to see through the eyes of a specific person in the field, viewing the scenes as that person does, trying to develop the outlook of the other person. Or field notes may switch the focus among a few participants: Emerson et al. (1995, p. 57) offer a supermarket checkout line as an example in which notes might first be written from the perspective of a customer waiting in line and then from the perspective of the checker, the customer being checked out, or the person bagging the groceries. this would require the researcher to fully consider the range of perspectives in this small social situation.

Ethnographers sometimes take an all-knowing perspective in their field notes, what Emerson and his colleagues call an "omniscient point of view" (1995, p. 58). Since the notes are written as if by someone "on high" who is seeing it all, this perspective allows the researcher to range across all the participants in the field, from one place to an-

other, and across time periods. However, such a point of view combines what the researcher has learned as a participant with observations and information from others. This makes it more difficult to unravel competing interpretations. Thus, many field researchers with symbolic-interactionist perspectives and those who hope to empower participants in the field do not support the use of this all-knowing voice (Emerson, et al., 1995, p. 59). Of course, researchers may employ different voices in their field notes at different points, but it is important that they be sensitive to how the voice of the writing may alter the development of subsequent interpretations of the field.

Jotting field notes.   Note taking is the backbone of collecting field data. It can be done in different ways. Taking notes in the field itself will depend on the field and on the role of the researcher. If you are a participant in a field, it is much more difficult to take notes because it will not be a part of your participating role but part of your role as an observer. If you are a full observer, note taking may make you very conspicuous. What, those in the field may wonder, is this person writing down? Thus, while some situations may lend themselves to unobtrusive note taking, in most cases detailed notes will have to be written after one has left the field. In the field, notes will consist largely of casual jottings whose primary purpose is to arouse your memory later when you are writing more detailed notes. Thus, casual jottings should concentrate on material that will serve to spark your memory once you have left the field. The memory "sparkers" may include

1. The cast of characters in the field during the observation time.
2. Certain details of the physical scene which appear unusual.
3. Verbatim comments that seem critical for describing the situation observed or for capturing the central meaning of what was happening.
4. Incongruent aspects of the scene. In this case you may write yourself questions: Why did something occur? What was X trying to ac-

complish by doing what he or she did? What did Y mean by saying that? Why wasn't Z in the field today?

These memory sparkers should help you add detail and substance when writing up your fuller notes. They should also help you remember significant moments in the field. Box 8-1 presents ideas on jotting notes in the field.

After Leaving the Field.   Most field researchers write notes after returning home or the next morning. The general rule is that as much time will need to be spent writing what you have seen as

was spent in the field itself. Naturally, this will vary depending on what was occurring in the field. (The more complex and/or significant the occurrence, the more notes are required to describe or explain it.) It is critical that these detailed notes be prepared within 24 hours of the field observation. Writing the notes may be time-consuming, but without them your ability to write a final report or a paper may be jeopardized.

It is good to take down the notes separately under different headings. For this purpose, sheets of paper or index cards may be used, depending on the type of filing system you set up. It is useful to have multiple copies of the notes so that they may

BOX 8-1

PARTICIPATING-IN-ORDER-TO-WRITE: JOTTING FIELD NOTES IN THE FIELD

In a very thoughtful book on the writing of ethnographic field notes, Emerson, Fretz, and Shaw (1995, pp. 17–38) indicate that field researchers generally fall into two camps in terms of whether they are committed to taking down notes during their time in the field or think that such an activity might weaken their immersion in what they are studying. Those whose fieldwork is based on "participating-in-order-to-write" find that their research purpose lies in "the interconnections between writing, participating, and observing as a means of understanding another way of life" (1995, p. 19).

Jottings in the field begin with "headnotes" (p. 19) and then may proceed to the jottings of key words or phrases (p. 20). In terms of materials for note taking, some prefer small notebooks, whereas others find notebooks intrusive and instead use folded sheets of paper. Often researchers develop shorthand ways of taking notes that may be meaningless to others. The worry about when to write notes is often present. Because the researcher often requires the collaborative support of others in the field, it is necessary to gain permission during the course of the fieldwork for taking notes on specific matters, and the researcher always needs to remember that those in

the field have the right not to reveal issues (p. 21). There is some disagreement among field researchers, about how specific the researcher needs to be about his or her intentions: Some believe that field notes are mainly for the researcher and therefore cannot harm those in the field. (These moral issues will be dealt with more fully in Chapter 14 on the ethics and politics of research.)

If the researcher plans to take notes directly during the fieldwork, he or she should start these open jottings early in the field experience (p. 22) so that those in the field will become more comfortable with this practice. However, the researcher needs to be careful that these open jottings do not strain relations with others in the field or distract the researcher from important events in the field (p. 23). Where to write field notes can also be a problem. These places range from "hidden places" to just pulling out the notepad and writing anywhere. It may be easier for a novice in the field to casually take jottings than it is for someone who is more well known. As Emerson and his colleagues state: "It is a defining moment in field relations when an ethnographer takes out a pad and begins to write down what people are saying and doing in the presence of those very people" (1995, p. 25).

be filed under different headings. You can achieve this by photocopying your notes. There are now a number of software programs which can help you sort out and organize qualitative notes (see chapter 11 for specific suggestions of software for qualitative analyses).

If you have access to a computer, putting your notes in a word processing system file is the most convenient system possible. You can move the notes around, copy them and use parts of them directly in your final report by transferring them from the note file to the report file.

Types of Note Materials. Lofland (1971) suggests five types of materials which should be included in your thorough notes.

Running descriptions. As Lofland describes *running descriptions,* they include "events, people, things heard and overheard, conversations among people, conversations with people" (p. 105). Every time a new person enters the scene or a different scene is encountered, new notes should be taken. Drawing maps can help preserve a more exact setting of the scene observed. Lofland stresses that these running descriptions should be *concrete;* that is, they should be filled with specific details, devoid of imputation (X was trying to get Y to . . .). Rather, the notes should try to include the *raw* actions as they occur. Also, the observer should make distinctions in the notes themselves as to how exact they are, whether they are verbatim quotations from conversations (perhaps these should be in quotation marks), inexact quotations (perhaps in single quotation marks), or merely reworded comments which are not precisely what was said (left without any marks) (Lofland, 1971, p. 105).

Recalled material that had been forgotten. As you move along in a field project, one day's observations may help you recall earlier incidents. This recalled material should be put into each day's notes but should be clearly labeled as *recalls* of earlier material.

Ideas that interpret the meaning of a situation. Lofland suggests that any notes which offer an analysis of the situation should be set off in square brackets so that when you go back to them, you will be able to differentiate what you have interpreted about a situation from the raw description of what took place (1971, p. 106). Of course, it is valuable to put your interpretations into your notes as you write them. Early interpretations may vary from those made weeks after an observation. Since you may forget your early interpretations as you forget your actual observations, put into your notes your ideas of what you think is happening in the field.

Lofland suggests that analytic ideas are usually of three different types: They address the central ideas of the project; they concern a major sub-area of the study; or they are very small ideas that may add some detail to the final report (Lofland, 1971, p. 106). These analytic themes throughout the field notes will guide you in developing your arguments and setting your position in the final report. Remember, every study has to find something. It has to make some case or state some position. It cannot be only a series of isolated facts. The more analytic your ideas in your notes are, the stronger your case will be when you get it all together.

Personal impressions and feelings. These impressions are the subjective reactions of the observer. They may be emotional states that you go through while making the observations or very personal reactions to a situation (for example, you felt that someone you observed had been mistreated). Again, you must label these personal impressions as such so that you will be able to separate these reactions from other types of notes.

Notes for additional information. The observer may make special notes as a reminder to take an extra look at something, to speak to someone about something, etc. These reminders may be interspersed throughout the notes but should be gathered up at the end of each note-taking session to guide the next observation period (Lofland, 1971, p. 107).

The Uses of Visual Data

Photographs accompanying sociological studies were used quite widely in the early years of sociology in America, but following this early period, visual imagery largely disappeared from sociological studies. In quantitative research, the use of visual data has its origins in the work of documentary photographers and the ethnographic work of anthropologists, such as Gregory Bateson and Margaret Mead's study of Bali (Stasz, 1979, p. 119). The documentary approach used by social scientists, especially anthropologists, is richer in theoretical interpretation than journalistic documentary photography. "The strength of such a film rests not only on its visual appeal, although this is of critical importance, but also on the clarity and insight of its basic propositions" (Curry and Clarke, 1977, p. 16).

Some research problems easily lend themselves to incorporating visual material; others lend themselves to this less easily. Visual images (pictures) can offer direct referents, and they can show relationships. It is in showing social relationships that "visual thinking becomes an important part of the research process" (Curry and Clarke, 1977, p. 20). The visual language of the photographic images, if separated from a written narrative, can be controlled by the researcher if the symbols and artifacts that make up the images are carefully ordered or presented in sequence so that they create a visual narrative.

Still and video cameras create visual images that enable a researcher to return to the original data, rather than depend on recollections (that is why they are popular in field settings), and they help in the defining of sequences. Howard Becker (1974) has argued that a visual image should help bridge the gap between a concept and its behavioral indicator. Finally, the meaning of visual images (theorizing about images) can advance the theoretical study of society. For example, Cloninger (1974) studied differences in the content, style of depiction, and use of background environments of the photographs by male and female photographers.

Proponents of visual methods contend that photographs and film provide a necessary component of the techniques of the social researcher. If you plan to carry out a field study, you should seriously consider the use of such visual methods.

DECIDING IF QUALITATIVE RESEARCH IS APPROPRIATE FOR YOUR TOPIC

Consider your topic carefully and ask yourself whether a study of a natural environment based on observations, interviewing, and/or written documents will give you the material you need. As was suggested in Chapter 1, some social researchers think that field studies are mainly desirable for the study of problems that are not yet well formulated—a method appropriate for underdeveloped research problems. Others choose this method as the only true way to study human behavior and society unimpeded by the artificial techniques that characterize other methods. I also stated that personal qualities of the researcher may determine which method to choose. Especially in fieldwork, a person may need to have (or develop) a certain ability to establish rapport with others, to enter into the worlds of others without imposing too much of the self on the research.

If you think that qualitative research might be the best way to approach your research problem, you must then consider how to carry it out. If it is a field study, you will need to prepare for the field; you may need help in gaining entry to the field. Careful consideration should be made of how you will record the information. (Will you use tape recorders, a camera, a video camera, a pencil and pad?) Most of all, remember that even though fieldwork is a "natural" method, with few formal techniques, this does not mean that the researcher can proceed without plans. Even though your preparations are not of use in the field and even though you may need to devise some new ways of doing things on the spot, it is better to have entered the field well prepared.

REVIEW NOTES

- Qualitative research includes a range of types of research methods, all of which present their findings in words, not numbers.
- Field studies require researchers to gather data directly in real social environments through observation, interviewing, or other types of data collection.
- Ethnographies are a form of field studies, the primary research method of anthropologists, in which the processes of observing in the field and data collection are integral to the purpose of the studies, which is to describe cultures.
- Action research engages the subjects of study into the research effort with the aim of achieving practical outcomes.
- Participatory action research (PAR) uses collaborative research strategies with community and group members to raise their consciousness and overcome negative social conditions.
- Grounded theory research involves a process of generating insights from data so that theoretical ideas are derived inductively from those data. Then, by sequentially gathering more data and trying to confirm these theoretical ideas with the new data, the researcher develops stronger theories that are grounded in the data.
- Phenomenological sociological research aims at describing the commonsense social world of everyday experience; it is associated with forms of research methods which seek to establish meaning or understanding (*verstehen*) from the point of view of the participants in a social environment.
- Ethnomethodology is a phenomenological form of qualitative research which tries to uncover the rules of ordinary human interaction by examining small-scale interactions to see how actors build shared understandings.
- Observation in qualitative studies focuses on people in social settings, pays attention to details, needs to be placed in social and historical context, seeks to capture the processual and dynamic quality of social action, and should not be overly predetermined.
- Participant observation is the most common role for a qualitative researcher who engages at some level in the social field being studied while making observations.
- Qualitative interviewing is a guided conversation which needs to be focused on themes but should be as natural as possible. Learning the interviewee understands the meaning of ideas and their place in her or his life world is the aim of interviewing.
- Standpoint theory requires researchers to construct their own standpoints from their lived experiences (often from autobiographical material) to uncover the meaning of the social world as it is experienced by those who will be studied.
- Types of things to observe in the field include the general setting, people and their relationships, actions and activities, verbal behavior, psychological stances, histories, and physical objects.
- Triangulation involves a researcher gathering data from multiple sources, using different types of methods, to address the questions at hand from different points of view. It can be used to test sources of information against each other to help determine which explanations are accurate, and it also may be used to establish validity.
- Negotiating entry to the field requires qualitative researchers to identify themselves and clarify how they may be useful in and not disruptive to the social environment. Researchers need to be persistent in their efforts and maintain support from those who control access.
- Field notes may be written in the first person, allowing the researcher to describe his or her experiences as a participant and then comment on them as an observer; in the third person, allowing researchers to include their activities in the field, focus on a specific person's perspective, or switch perspectives; or from an omniscient point of view that facilitates trying to see it all but may make it more difficult to unravel competing interpretations.
- Field notes may include running description, recalled material that had been forgotten, ideas

that interpret and examine the meaning of a situation, and personal impressions and feelings.

• Visual data from still photographs or video films can enhance the techniques of a qualitative researcher and may help bridge gaps between concepts and related behavioral indicators.

KEY TERMS

action research
anthropology
audit trail
ethnography
ethnomethodology
field studies
grounded theory research
intersubjectivity
member check
negative evidence
participant observation
participatory action research (PAR)
phenomenological research
running descriptions
qualitative research
standpoint theory
triangulation
verstehen

STUDY EXERCISES

1. Suppose you are training students to go out and do fieldwork. You decide to give them a short list of do's and don'ts. Make up such a list.
2. Think about Barrie Thorne carrying out her fieldwork at the elementary schools. Give examples of the types of *subjects* she would have covered in her notes. Write up a hypothetical field note from her playground observations in the first person (as if you had been Thorne).

RECOMMENDED READINGS

1. Ball, Michael S., and Gregory W. H. Smith: *Analyzing Visual Data,* Sage, Thousand Oaks, CA, 1992. A small volume on how to use still photographs as social data.
2. Denzin, Norman K.: *Interpretive Ethnography: Ethnographic Practices for the 21st Century,* Sage, Thousand Oaks, CA, 1997. This prominent qualitative researcher argues that the norms of journalism and social science can be merged in the forms of the postmodern, multinational interpretive ethnography developing in America.
3. Fetterman, David M.: *Ethnography: Step by Step,* Sage, Thousand Oaks, CA, 1989. An anthropologist's guide to carrying out field studies, from practical advice on equipment to conceptual ordering of the research cycle.
4. Lofland, John: *Analyzing Social Settings: A Guide to Qualitative Observation and Analysis,* Wadsworth, Belmont, CA, 1971, One of the most widely used and respected books on qualitative analysis and observation methods.
5. Marshall, Catherine, and Gretchen B. Rossman: *Designing Qualitative Research,* 2nd ed., Sage, Thousand Oaks, CA, 1995. A very useful guide for qualitative research with many vignettes from the educational fields studied by the authors as well as other researchers.
 6. Maxwell, Joseph A.: *Qualitative Research Design: An Interactive Approach,* Sage, Thousand Oaks, CA, 1996. Offers models for research and excellent sections on developing research questions and validity in qualitative research.
7. Rubin, Herbert J., and Irene S. Rubin: *Qualitative Interviewing: The Art of Hearing Data,* Sage, Thousand Oaks, CA, 1995. Very directive advice on how to keep on target, choose interviewees, build conversational partnerships and structure qualitative interviews.
 8. Strauss, Anselm, and Juliet Corbin: *Basics of Qualitative Research: Grounded Theory Procedures and Techniques,* Sage, Thousand Oaks, CA, 1990. How to make sense of all the data collected in a field study; how to create clear, theoretically sound formulations.

Methods of Analyzing Available Data

INTRODUCTION

This chapter presents a number of different methods of studying data that are already available. Available data can be found in two general ways. In some cases, data merely exist in one form or another but have not been drawn together by anyone. In this situation, the researcher must first decide which data to use for the study. Such data may be in the form of printed materials, visual or recorded materials, or artifacts that are of interest to the researcher. Historical research generally depends on written sources, though oral history based on interview data is being used increasingly as historical data. Content analyses are often based on written materials, though artifacts also may be studied. Or researchers may use or develop novel ways to measure things unobtrusively (amount and type of garbage, for example), which could facilitate studying certain subjects. Your first challenge as a researcher of available data is to find some type of data which can address your research problem and to use those data to answer the questions you wish to ask. This implies that you look for available data once you already have a research question defined. In other cases, data that have been collected for one set of analyses are made available to other researchers for new projects. Such formally available data may be in raw form, so that the second researcher can carry out an analysis (that is, a secondary analysis on a dataset prepared by another researcher), or in statistical form, in which case the researcher can reanalyze these existing statistics.

The use of available data for carrying out social research projects is therefore different from the methods described in the preceding three chapters—methods by which the researcher creates and collects new data. What is different between finding available data to analyze and creating and collecting your own is the point of time in the research process when the researcher and the data meet. In an experiment, survey, or field study, the initial research effort is to produce or create the data. In almost all cases (the exception may be a field study), the research questions are clearly formulated before the data are collected. When available data are used, naturally this order is reversed: the data have been collected or are available ready to be processed before you, the researcher, come along to pose a research question.

Studies in which you have collected your own data and those in which you use already collected data reach the same point at the research stage of data processing and analysis. One thing that may occur to you is that using already available data should be easier and quicker than collecting your own. In theory this should be the case, since such studies avoid the data collection process. However, the process of finding a body of data relevant to your research problem may be a slow one, and a more difficult and time-consuming effort is often required to code and process the data for your specific purposes. Since they were collected for different purposes, these data must be reconceptualized and manipulated so that they specifically address your concerns. Above all, they must not be used inappropriately. That is, issues of validity and reliability become a central concern in studies on already collected data. The researcher must understand the data well and not use them in ways which ignore or subvert their meaning.

Many types of social research are based on the analysis of available data. This chapter presents five different methods not commonly grouped together. They have been gathered together here because each one depends on the use of available data.

THE ART AND SCIENCE OF ANALYZING AVAILABLE DATA

Creative Aspects

It takes a creative idea to link a research problem to a set of available data. Generally, the researcher has a problem in mind, and then ingenuity is required to conceive of, and find, an available source of data to address the problem. The way the data are handled also may be quite creative. Schemes for selecting specific objects to study, coding the data, and ferreting out patterns within the data—all demand an eye for the unique and unusual.

Appreciation is also a central feature of analyzing available data. You must be able to appreciate the qualities of the data. In historical research, documents and artifacts from the past must be appropriately valued in order to be understood. Appreciating the strengths of an earlier survey (for secondary analysis) or a collection of pamphlets on a particular theme (for content analysis) demands a level of understanding which can take into account the qualities of the materials. Content analyses examine not only the manifest content of the material analyzed (such as words) but also the latent content (the underlying, implicit meaning of a body of content). This analysis of latent content requires sensitivity to the range of meanings a particular body of content presents. In the case of the content of mass media material (such as television programs), a researcher not only needs to analyze the latent and manifest content of the material but also must consider the intentions (and the cultural values underlying those intentions) of those who have produced the content. Studying unobtrusive measures requires the ability to select such indicators to illuminate a problem of interest.

Linking your interests to a set of materials in which these interests can be furthered is also a creative process. One thing to consider in analyzing available data is whether you have a special expertise in or knowledge about some materials (knowledge of a foreign language, experience in an environment from which these data were drawn, a

hobby which has given you a store of information about a set of objects or an area of interest). Such special knowledge areas may be ones in which you will be able to be more creative.

Scientific Aspects

Analysis of available data also often requires scientific operations and norms. Where the rules and formal procedures of a scientific method are used (as would be common in many forms of secondary analysis, analysis of existing statistics, and even in content analysis), the scientific model will operate. Because secondary analyses begin with a body of data, they are often used in very sophisticated state-of-the-art types of analyses. Sociological research studies in the major journals using the most modern and advanced analytic methods are often based on already collected datasets.

In some studies, inductive explanations may be drawn from the data by examining the patterns among factors and the possible reasons for observed changed. An inductive approach would often guide an analysis based on unobtrusive measures. Deductive analyses also can be carried out on already collected sets of data; in such cases, a hypothesis is posed and data are found and analyzed in order to test it.

In an analysis of existing statistics, for example, suppose the hypothesis is that raising the legal drinking age will reduce automobile fatalities. Data on auto fatalities could be compared from states with different drinking ages to see whether there is a relationship between these two factors.

The empirical foundation of a social-scientific study has already been laid once the data are collected. You must take care to understand how and why this was done in the original study, for whatever weaknesses occurred in the original study will continue as weaknesses in your own study. Conversely, the strengths will remain as strengths. The scientific method also depends on rules of rationality. Here the purposefulness and logic of your approach will foster the scientific credibility of the project.

QUANTITATIVE AND QUALITATIVE METHODS FOR ANALYZING AVAILABLE DATA

The three earlier chapters on experiments, survey research, and qualitative methods presented ways in which researchers can design studies which involve their own data collection. This chapter focuses on various methods for analyzing data which have already been collected. The data themselves help determine whether the forms of analysis will be quantitative, qualitative, or both. For example, one form of data to be described below are aggregated statistical data. These are data that have been prepared by data-gathering organizations such as the Census Bureau. For a researcher to use these data as the basis of a study would demand that quantitative analysis techniques be applied to these data. By contrast, many researchers use written documents as their data sources. In this case, either quantitative or qualitative techniques can be used. For example, if one is studying the minutes of meetings held by a community organization, one could count the number of times particular issues arise or the number of people who speak about an issue or one could read the minutes to try to understand the issues being studied and the values which underlie the expression of those issues, which are qualitative techniques. This is also the case when one uses mass media content such as television programs, advertisements, movies, and the lyrics of popular music. In all these cases, researchers may use quantitative or qualitative methods to analyze these forms of data.

We will begin with content analysis, which can employ either qualitative or quantitative techniques. Then we will examine historical research, which more often uses qualitative forms of analysis but also can employ quantitative methods. Next we will examine how unobtrusive measures can serve as the data for a study employing quantitative analyses. Secondary analyses generally refer to studies that take already collected datasets (often based on survey data) as the basis for new analyses, generally employing quantitative techniques. Finally, we will describe the analysis of existing statistical data, which requires quantitative techniques to be reanalyzed.

CONTENT ANALYSIS

Some problems can best be addressed through *content analysis*—an analysis of the content of communication. In a review of the varying definitions of content analysis, Ole Holsti (1969, pp. 3–5) found three common requirements. First, content analysis is *objective:* it "stipulates that each step in the research process must be carried out on the basis of explicitly formulated rules and procedures." The researcher needs to develop objective categories for coding the data, which represent objective decisions about this content, not the researcher's subjective ways of seeing the material. Replication tests for objectivity. Would another researcher set up similar procedures, criteria for data selection, and means of interpretation in order to analyze the body of communication for the same research problem?

The second requirement is that content analysis must be *systematic.* According to Holsti, "the inclusion and exclusion of content or categories is done according to consistently applied rules" (1969, p. 4). This means that content which fails to support the researcher's hypotheses must not be left out; categories for data coding must be applied consistently. As Holsti contends, these two qualities (objectivity and systematic application) are necessary but not sufficient to define content analysis, for they could also define indexes and other bibliographical techniques. Holsti's third point is that content analysis must possess *generality,* which "requires that the findings must have theoretical relevance" (1969, p. 5). The goal of content analysis is never just description; rather, the analyzed content must be related to some other factor or factors about the documents, the persons stating the content, the intended audience, or the times in which the content was produced.

In one of the earlier definitions of content analysis, Bernard Berelson stressed that it was a technique "for the objective, systematic, and quantitative description of the manifest content of communication" (1954, p. 489). While quantitative analysis is generally a primary objective in content analysis, it is not necessary to count the frequency of certain attributes in some document. Holsti suggests that studying the presence or absence of an attribute allows for a "contingency analysis" (1969, pp. 7–8). Or documents might be categorized in their totality by major themes.

Berelson's definition also focused on the content being *manifest*—in other words, stressing that what was said or written or shown was what would be studied. Here Holsti (1969, pp. 13–14) contends that in the coding stage of the research, the manifest material is all that the researcher can appropriately consider. However, at the interpretative stage, latent meanings in the data may well be drawn out, though the researcher must be careful to corroborate interpretations concerning the values, motives, and personality characteristics of the communicators.

One of the best ways to get a sense of this method is by considering examples of how it has been used. Since this method analyzes culturally created work, it tends to select "content" that is either "popular" and/or influential or culturally valued. By selecting popular works, the researcher can infer that such works affect, in some ways, large numbers of people; by selecting influential or culturally valued works, the researcher can assume that they represent important aspects of the culture under study.

Content analysis can be undertaken to test a hypothesis or assumption. Thus the content must be representative of some universe for which a population can be defined and a sample can be drawn. The content analyses offered below use both quantitative and qualitative methods and range from sociology textbooks, to legal briefs submitted to the Supreme Court, to dramatic prime-time television programs, to advice columns in magazines. In each study we will consider the problem posed, the methods of analyzing the content, the sample drawn, and the kinds of findings produced from the analysis.

FOUR EXAMPLES OF CONTENT ANALYSES

Treatment of Race, Class, and Gender in Introductory Sociology Texts

In a content analysis of a sample of mainstream introductory sociology textbooks, Ferree and Hall (1996) found that race, social class, and gender are analyzed at different levels within sociology (class at the societal "macro" level, race at the group "meso" level, and gender at the individual "micro" level). What we want to consider here is the type of method these authors used to do this study. They began with a sample of introductory sociology textbooks published between 1982 and 1988, which had appeared in *Books in Print* (a compendium of all books currently in print) under the headings "Sociology" or "Society." From the 35 introductory sociology texts listed, they selected 24 which had full chapters or distinct sections of chapters on race, class, and gender. In most cases, these chapters were presented in a section of the text entitled "Inequality" or "Social Inequality."

The authors carried out a content analysis of these 24 texts by examining the text writing itself, the index citations in the back of a book, and the choice of illustrations. Their analysis required them to determine approximately how much of the treatment of gender (or race or class) in a text was based on discussing gender socialization (a micro-level analysis) and how much was devoted to cross-societal, cross-national, or cross-cultural data (a macro-level analysis). In the presentation of material on race, the texts often addressed group processes (stressing positive associations between members of groups or intergroup conflict), which they considered to be a meso-level analysis. Then the authors use a quantitative approach to count up the numbers of citations or chapters or parts of chapters on a particular topic.

Table 9-1 presents frequency distributions of the coverage of "socialization" in chapters on race, class, and gender in the 24 textbooks. Note that the authors use index citations for race, class, and gender to see how far these topics are associated

TABLE 9-1

**FREQUENCY DISTRIBUTION OF COVERAGE OF SOCIALIZATION
IN CHAPTERS ON CLASS, RACE, AND GENDER IN 24 INTRODUCTORY
SOCIOLOGY TEXTBOOKS, 1988**

Measure of Coverage	Total	Chapter		
		Class	Race	Gender
Index citations associating class, race, or gender with socialization	96	26	6	64
Refer reader to inequality section	54	2	4	48
Refer reader to other topics[a]	42	24	2	16
Pictures labeled as about socialization in class, race, or gender chapters[b]	18	0	4	14
Books with text devoted to socialization in class, race, or gender chapters				
One page or more	—	0	0	18
Less than one page	—	0	3	2
No text	—	24	21	4

[a]Of the 42 referrals to other topics, 33 referred the reader to socialization, 1 to work, 6 to education, and 2 to social change.

[b]Pictures not labeled as being about socialization, especially in the gender chapters, also carry learning themes.

Source: Adapted from Ferree, Myra Marx, and Elaine J. Hall: "Rethinking Stratification from a Feminist Perspective: Gender, Race, and Class in Mainstream Textbooks," *American Sociological Review* 61, pp. 929–50, 1996.

with socialization compared with other types of topics. They also examine what the book's illustrations portray and the amount of coverage (number of pages) on socialization in the race, class, and gender chapter(s). From all these indicators, Ferree and Hall (1996, p. 939) see that socialization is overwhelmingly used as the major explanatory theme in discussing gender compared with race and class.

Note that this content analysis, like many others, uses both quantitative and qualitative methods. Its sampling method would be considered a nonprobability purposive sample. The counting of citations in the index, of pages devoted to a topic, and of pictures depicting certain images as well as the aggregation of these counts and their presentation in tables clearly constitutes a quantitative technique.

Keep in mind that the authors use largely quantitative methods when they examine the index citations: How many citations are there to this or that? How many referrals are there to such and such topics? Although they might have used more quantitative techniques in examining the text chapters themselves, such as counting the number of times the word *socialization* was used in the text material, instead they use more qualitative methods of reading the content of the material to see whether it is devoted to the coverage of a topic such as socialization.

Finally, we should note that this study of the treatment of race, class, and gender in sociology textbooks appeared as the lead article in the most prestigious journal in sociology (the *American Sociological Review*). Thus, content analysis clearly can be a powerful way to understand a body of content. Because college textbooks diffuse information so widely, they influence the thinking of college-educated people. Because introductory texts introduce students to a discipline, the materials they offer also tend to define how students understand that discipline. Thus, content analysis of the coverage of topics and the meaning of that coverage in chapters in textbooks can be a useful way to study how knowledge is constructed.

Violence on Television

One controversial subject of social research over the past 30 years has been violence on television and whether this prevalent phenomenon is related to aggressive behavior. To do such research, investigators must study the content of television programs to search for the presence and degree of violence in them. One of the best-known researchers in this hotly contested field is George Gerbner of the Annenberg School of Communication at the University of Pennsylvania. Gerbner's analyses are based on content analyses of television programs.

The programs are videotaped, and then coders analyze the programs, searching for a number of qualities. *Prevalence* is the incidence of violence in any program (P). The abbreviation %P is the percentage of programs with violence. *Rate* is the number of "violent episodes" occurring in each program (R/P) and each hour (R/H). *Role* is a measure of characters as "violent" (that is, committing violence) or "victims" (subjected to violence); "killers" or "killed" (1978, p. 181).

From these data, two scores are produced: the *program score,* based on prevalence and rate of violence, and the *character score,* based on the role measures. The *violence index* is then determined by the sum of the *program score* and the *character score.* This explanation has not been as detailed as it would need to be for you to comprehend it fully; the purpose here is to give you some idea of what can be done in a content analysis of television programs. (For more detailed descriptions, see Gerbner et al., 1978, 1980.)

Since 1967, when Gerbner and his colleagues began presenting their Violence Index, showing which types of programs, time slots, and networks feature the most violent shows, the controversy about how violence on TV is measured and what its effects are has increased. For example, Gerbner codes violence as "the overt expression of physical force (with or without a weapon, against self or others) compelling action against one's will on pain of being hurt and/or killed or threatened to be so victimized as part of the plot" (1980, p. 11). This leaves out simple threats, abusive language, and gestures that have no clear violent consequences. However, it includes "natural" and "accidental" violence and violence in comedy or fantasy shows. Some researchers have criticized the inclusion of violence in comedy or fantasy as well as natural and accidental violence in studies of TV violence (Wurtzel and Lometti, 1984), though Gerbner and his colleagues defend their method (Chaffee, Gerbner, et al., 1984).

Box 9-1 offers a content analysis of violence and sex in advertisements for television programs; this is another way to use content analysis to study the media.

Legal Briefs Submitted to the Supreme Court

In a study of the relationship of the content of legal briefs to the decision-making process of the Supreme Court, Bannan (1984) wanted to show that justices were affected not solely by their ideological positions but also by the amount and range of legal and other types of evidence brought to bear in specific cases. She contrasted the legal briefs for the petitioners with the briefs for the respondents in 37 cases brought before the Supreme Court over the "right of counsel to the indigent"—a right guaranteed by the Sixth Amendment to the U.S. Constitution. The petitioners in every case were very poor individuals who had been pleading the illegality of a decision of a lower court on the grounds that they had not been given counsel (that is, they had not been

BOX 9-1

ANALYZING THE SEX AND VIOLENCE CONTENT OF ADVERTISEMENTS IN *TV GUIDE*

In a content analysis of the words and images used in advertisements for television programs in *TV Guide,* Williams counted overt visual portrayals and verbal referents to physical violence and sexual behavior. First he selected a sample of issues of *TV Guide* from 1980 to 1985; then he defined the range of verbal referents ("Jessica plays cat and mouse with devious killer!" or "Blackmail in a sex clinic . . . ladies expose their sex lives to uncover vicious criminal") and visual presentations (characters pointing guns or individuals dressed in swimwear, lingerie, and other revealing clothing) for violence and sex. TV ads also were coded for program type, time slot, network, and size of ad. The analysis related qualities of the advertisements to the ratings of the programs and found "that sex and violence do have a positive impact on a program's rating" (1989, p. 973).

Source: Gilbert A. Williams, "Enticing Viewers: Sex and Violence in *TV Guide* Program Advertisements," *Journalism Quarterly,* **66**: 970–973, 1989.

provided with the services of a lawyer). In short, Bannan had selected a sample of Supreme Court cases on the basis of the type of constitutional right being challenged.

For each case, the number of *assertions* (arguments in favor of the legal position) and the number of *supports* for these assertions were estimated. In addition, the "content" of those supports was coded according to its source (official authorities such as constitutions and statutes, unofficial authorities such as social science surveys and law journal articles). From this a cumulative score was derived for the petitioner and for the respondent. Bannan sought to measure both the quantity and the range of the types of supporting evidence offered to test the expectation that the legal brief

with the superior "cumulative score" would "win" the Supreme Court decision. This proved to be the case in 33 of the 37 cases.

Marital Advice Columns

In a content analysis involving both qualitative and quantitative strategies, Cancian and Gordon (1988) examined how advice to married women on love and anger had changed across the first eight decades of this century. For their sample, they chose three magazines: two which are specifically targeted to women—*Ladies' Home Journal* and *McCall's*—and a third which has a broad general readership—*Reader's Digest.* The articles they selected were ones that were primarily directed to married women, offering them advice on overcoming disappointment and loneliness and recommending how they should feel about their husbands and behave toward them (1988, p. 312). The authors recognized that the readers of such magazines were most likely middle-class women and that by the 1970s, when more women's magazines began to focus on the increasing numbers of working women, the women who read these magazines might have been more traditional and conservative in their views.

Their qualitative analyses began by identifying ways in which the magazines "socialized" their readers into the correct emotional state. These included the use of vocabulary (for example, how *love* and *anger* were defined), scenarios (often of couples in loving or angry situations), norms (either ideal or working norms), sanctions (for breaking norms), management techniques, and justifying ideologies (1988, p. 314). Then the authors compared articles from different decades (1920s, 1940s, 1960s). This enabled them to consider changes across time in normative behavior (in the expressions of both anger and love). Moreover, they found that what had been considered gender-appropriate for women (being self-sacrificing and sweet) changed over time so that women were advised to be more self-actualizing (1988, p. 322).

Note that these qualitative techniques develop categories, frameworks, and definitions under which the contents of the articles are sorted and grouped. The focus in this qualitative analysis is on *ideas* of love and anger in marriages, not on cross-magazine comparisons or how the articles were structured within or among the magazines. But they did employ chronological comparisons. It was this focus on changes across the decades that led them into their quantitative analyses of the same materials.

For the quantitative analysis, Cancian and Gordon (1988, pp. 324–330) identified six categories of advice about the emotional content of the marriage relationship. For example, Category 1 was whether love was identified with compromise and self-sacrifice or with self-expression and fulfillment. The former was considered to be "traditional" advice, and the latter "modern" advice. Then 16 articles were randomly selected from each of the eight decades studied, and on the basis of the dominant themes of the advice offered, the articles were grouped under the six categories (this can be seen in Table 9-2). What we can denote from this table is that over time advice to married women generally swung from traditional to modern (though the 1920s were a more modern decade than the 1930s, 1940s, or 1950s). Through both the qualitative and the quantitative analyses, Cancian and Gordon (1988) were able to examine how the experience of marriage and the emotions surrounding it changed for wives from suppressing anger and being self-sacrificing to emphasizing the expression of feelings and challenging traditional gender roles across the first eight decades of the twentieth century (1988, p. 337).

COMPONENTS OF A CONTENT ANALYSIS

Selection of the Content and the Topic

In a content analysis, the selection of the topic must be closely coordinated with the selection of the content to be analyzed. It is desirable to begin with a specific research question and then select a body of material in which that question can be pursued. There should be some logic to the choice of the content to be studied. Often that logic is obvious: one clear way to study violence on television is to examine the contents of television programming. In other cases, a researcher may select a body of material to study among a number that might have been equally useful.

Sometimes the content seems to create its own research finding, such as family portraits which show changes in portrait positions that seem to indicate social changes in family positions. Working on the content may refine the research topic as it develops.

Sampling from the Body of Content

When the volume of material available for the study is great, it will be necessary to sample content for the analysis. Of course, the sample design must provide for representativeness. Methods of organizing the content according to some characteristics (for example, by year of publication) might be utilized to create a stratified sample. Once the sampling units are considered equivalent (for example, in the case of a set of documents, each is as desirable to bring into the sample as any other), the use of a random number table or systematic sampling methods would achieve a representative sample. (Review the sampling strategies in Chapter 5.)

Uncovering the Meaning of the Content

The usual strategy in content analysis is to "describe the attributes of messages, without reference to either the intentions of the sender (encoding process) or the effect of the message upon those to whom it is directed (decoding process)" (Holsti, 1969, p. 27). Often the researcher compares documents generated from a single source. The researcher may focus on two or more variables, looking for them in one or

TABLE 9-2

TRENDS IN U.S. MAGAZINE ARTICLES ON MARRIAGE, 1900–1979: NUMBER OF ARTICLES SUPPORTING TRADITIONAL (T) VERSUS MODERN (M) THEMES[a]

Traditional	Modern	1900–1909 T	M	1910–1919 T	M	1920–1929 T	M	1930–1939 T	M	1940–1949 T	M	1950–1959 T	M	1960–1969 T	M	1970–1979 T	M
Nature of love																	
(1.) Love means self-sacrifice, compromise.	Love means self-expression, individuality.	7	1	4	3	5	1	7	2	10	0	11	0	0	7	5	2
(2.) Romance is immature, routine is good.	Passion and impulse, fun and novelty are important.	3	1			3		7	1	5	2	4	5	4		7	
(3.) Sex not important.	Sex is important.	0	0	0	0	0	5	1	4	0	5	0	9	1	4	0	9
Expressing anger																	
(4.) Avoid anger, disagreements.	Express anger, disagreements.	1	1	1	0	3	2	6	2	4	0	6	3	4	4	4	9
(5.) Avoid conflict, keep up a front.	Communicate openly, confront problems.	1	2	2	0	3	2	5	3	4	0	4	6	4	8	3	10
Gender																	
(6.) Traditional female role.	Nontraditional.	10	7	14	4	8	10	11	7	8	9	13	5	8	10	6	13
Percentage of modern themes[b]		35		33		51		34		34		42		55		70	

[a] Sixteen articles were analyzed per decade.

[b] Percentage of modern themes equals the sum of modern themes across all six categories, divided by the number of modern plus traditional themes.

Source: Cancian, Francesca M., and Steven L. Gordon: "Changing Emotional Norms in Marriage: Love and Anger in U.S. Women's Magazines." *Gender & Society* **2**: 308–342, 1988.

more documents. He or she may use a deductive approach to test hypotheses. A set of documents can also be the basis for an inductive examination. For example, Holsti suggests that the coverage of foreign news in a set of newspapers could be analyzed to develop an index of foreign news coverage, which could then serve as a standard against which to study a particular newspaper (1969, p. 31). Finally, a researcher might use a standard developed by experts in evaluating the content of a set of documents or messages. For example, a group of physicians could set up standards for reporting on a certain disease, say, AIDS. Then a set of radio broadcasts on AIDS could be analyzed in terms of these standards.

Developing a Scheme to Code the Content

There are as many ways to process the content and break it down and recombine it into categories of meaning as there are researchers to devise them. However coding is devised, it is important to have the coders adequately trained. Each must understand what needs to be looked for and how it is to be recorded. Each must share with every other coder a common understanding of what the content consists of. This issue of reliability is of critical concern in content analyses. The examples given offer a number of the types of qualities of such codes.

Frequency.   One commonly used way to sort out the content of material is to count certain patterns which recur in the content. This was the case in the television violence study, where incidents of violence of various types were recorded and cumulated.

Amount.   Closely related to the frequency of appearance is the amount of each content piece which contains a particular quality. This may be measured in time (for television) and in space (for written material).

Presence or Absence of a Quality.   Another way to study the content of a communication source is to look for specific qualities to see how far they are present or absent in each work examined. In a family portrait study, it was important to determine whether the father had a dominant position in the painting.

Typology.   Another common feature of content analyses is sorting the contents by types. In the women's magazine analysis types of marital themes were looked for.

Origin or Source.   Sometimes the object is to establish who or what is responsible for a particular aspect of the content. In the Supreme Court study, the sources of support given for an assertion were categorized and recorded.

Degree of Intensity.   Content also may be differentiated by how strongly certain elements are present. For example, sexual explicitness in films could be measured in this way.

Analyzing the Coded Content

Once you have coded the content, you need to relate it to your research question. Tables and graphs often are used to present the aggregated patterns in the data. The interpretation of what these patterns mean is the essence of content analysis. If that cannot be done effectively, all one has is a description of material. The social significance of the study must be inferred from the patterns developed. Remember, however, that the ways in which you sort the content will also determine what you have to analyze. Thus, there is a back-and-forth strategy between devising the coding schemes and figuring out what findings you will produce with the various schemes. What may seem like very fruitful coding strategies may not lead to interesting findings with your body of content. You may then need to alter the coding schemes to characterize evidence that seems to be interesting. Remember that as in all data analyses, you need variation to have important findings. Ideas for analytic approaches and the types of tables and graphs which might best exemplify your data can be borrowed from others, or you can use an idea seen in one study and then elaborate on it yourself.

Issues of Validity and Reliability

Content analysis also needs to be subjected to considerations of whether the method devised is valid and reliable. To increase validity, a careful balance between the content being studied and the questions being asked needs to be considered. Does the content address the problem being studied? Will the coding scheme devised for the content fairly extract the meaning from the content data? This need to get at the specific contents that interest the researcher often requires complex coding and analysis.

Because of the complexity of the coding schemes, the reliability between different coders may not be high. Even a single coder may have trouble remaining consistent in coding data with a complex coding plan. This is a major challenge in content analysis: to devise ways of coding content that are reliable (that would lead to similar results if carried out at different times and by different coders) and to select and use content in ways that are valid (that produce analyses of content that correspondingly address the study's subject).

DECIDING IF CONTENT ANALYSIS IS APPROPRIATE FOR YOUR TOPIC

Content analysis might be the best method for you to use if your problem can be addressed by a study of patterns in various forms of communication. Studies using content analysis often seek to understand cultural values and broad social perspectives as portrayed in the media. The method also allows for studies with varying time dimensions by examining a form of media over a selected time span. At times you may have access to

a fascinating collection of material. Your college library or another institution in your immediate area may have an extensive collection of comic books, the complete series of a certain magazine, school textbooks in a particular field, films by a specific director, or the collected letters of a famous person. Such a source may prompt you to create a study in which one of these resources may be used. However, keep in mind that content analysis needs a theoretical framework. It can be an excellent method for testing hypotheses or inductively developing standards.

Content analysis almost always requires developing a somewhat ingenious means of sorting and coding the content to be studied. While coding will be discussed in greater depth in Chapter 11, the ability to handle detailed material carefully and systematically is essential for content analysis.

Content analysis as a method is perhaps the most distant from field research. Rather than going out into a social field to find data, the researcher defines a body of communication as the "social field" and looks within that set of material for descriptive qualities that can be quantified. Thus, content analysis lacks the spontaneity and unplanned qualities of field research. Instead it is a heavily planned method in which the researcher carefully organizes and orchestrates how the data will be treated. Because content analysis uses available forms of communication, it does not intrude on a social environment as is characteristic of field research. It is unobtrusive. The next section will examine other unobtrusive measures.

In many ways, the work of content analysts is also similar to that of historians. In both cases, written materials are usually of central concern. What is specific to content analysis is that quantitative aspects of the communication are central and the historical chronology of the period is not; in history, by contrast, interpretation of the deeper meaning of written materials and artifacts is generally sought in relation to the historical period in which they occurred. We will examine historical research before discussing unobtrusive measures.

HISTORICAL STUDIES

All studies of extant (that is, already collected) data are historical to some degree, because they are based on evidence from and about the past. Historical research, however, is not merely defined as studying anything from the past. It also implies certain methods and points of view that historians bring to the study of material from the past. This section will offer a few general considerations about the historical method and present two examples of historical studies of varying types.

History usually refers simply to an account of the past of human societies. Since that is such a vast subject that it can never be recounted, what history consists of is the study of what "can be known . . . [to the historian] . . . through the surviving record." It is what the late historian Louis Gottschalk referred to as *history as record*. This he differentiated from "the whole history of the past (which has been called *history as actuality*)" (1950, p. 45).

"The process of critically examining and analyzing the records and survivals of the past is . . . called *historical method*. The imaginative reconstruction of the past from the data derived by that process is called *historiography* (the writing of history)" (Gottschalk, 1950, p. 48). Historical writing always involves a *re-creation* of the past, not a *creation;* Gottschalk stresses, "These limits distinguish history from fiction, poetry, drama, and fantasy" (1950, p. 49). It is this blending of the study of written records with an interpretation of these materials in the light of other evidence and with the historian's own imagination that produces history.

Let me add at this point that there is currently great interest in *oral history,* that is, history based on verbal accounts instead of written records. It is considered especially useful in the study of historical crises of great magnitude and cultural traditions that seem to be disappearing where the likelihood of finding adequate written records is not considered high. An example would be oral material from the survivors of World War II concentration camps, recollections of black Americans of what their ancestors related to them about life under slavery, or the experiences of various ethnic communities in the United States.

Written records are nevertheless the central sources of data for historians. These sources are generally differentiated into two categories: *primary sources,* which are the records of eyewitnesses to events, and *secondary sources,* which are written materials which describe and/or interpret a past event either close to the time when it occurred or in later years. Naturally, historians are particularly fond of primary sources because such materials seem to be more accurate and less biased. Yet Gottschalk warns that all historical sources, whether primary or secondary, are written from a particular point of view and therefore organize the past according to certain principles. What the historian must do is take those materials and try to "get as close an approximation to the truth about the past as constant correction of the mental images will allow, at the same time recognizing that that truth has in fact eluded him forever" (Gottschalk, 1950, p. 47). "In short, the historian's aim is *verisimilitude* with regard to a perished past" (1950, p. 47).

Historical work thus generally centers on the study of written materials. These may be *archival material,* such as records, letters, diaries, and handwritten manuscripts, or printed books, pamphlets, and periodicals. Thus the historian must go to where these materials are, namely, the library, the archives, the museums, the government records office—wherever there are materials relevant to the historian's topic.

For this reason, historical research generally starts with searching for relevant sources and reading very broadly. Some historians go directly to the archives to search for the surviving records pertinent to their subjects; others read widely in secondary sources about the periods under study. One historian related to me that he had been told as a graduate student to go to a large research library and read everything, every written thing in that library, on his general subject. Of course, this is exaggerated advice. Historians cannot read everything in a field, and they do not wait until they have read everything to define a problem. However, it is certainly true that historians would tend to read more widely and deeply about a general topic than might other social researchers. This is at least in part because they tend to be *contextualists;* that is, they try to relate the phenomena they are studying to as many aspects of social life as possible.

Consider the differences between the historical method and that of other types of social research we have so far presented. The historical approach is somewhat like the approach of field researchers in that its object is usually not to isolate a narrow research topic, a hypothesis to test. Instead the historian tends to put together a multiplicity of contexts, to search for a whole set of reasons why an event occurred. Like field researchers, historians move into a field in search of a richer description of the historical era, the social environment, or the material examined. Rather than observing and interviewing the inhabitants of the field, however, the historian must read about this field. One of the objects of this reading of materials from the past is to determine the chronology of events, to understand how the chronological order of events has affected later events.

TWO HISTORICAL RESEARCH PROJECTS

The examples of research described here are wide-ranging studies that were chosen deliberately to show you the very different ways in which historical material can be used in social research. In terms of focus, a historical study can be very broad and address an entire society or social institution or can be narrow and study a selective set of people or events of interest. The former focus would take a *macro-level* historical view, and the latter a *micro-level* one. The evidence used to prepare the study may be drawn from a wide range of

written or visual materials or may consist of a more limited set of documents chosen specifically to address the issue of the study. The presentation of the material in a historical study may be written up (presented qualitatively) or may include quantitative data.

The purpose of a historical study can be largely descriptive, aiming to understand a development in a particular period of time and in a particular culture, or it can be explanatory, trying to test and prove (or disprove) widely held assumptions. Some social researchers and theorists have been interested in employing historical materials to examine what might be called the "meaning" of historical ideas, that is, how memories of historical people and events affect subsequent events. This type of research on the role of memory in the cultural system of a society can be used to study the impact of certain historical ideas at particular points in time.

Here we will briefly describe two different studies, each of which uses historical material to accomplish very different types of research objectives. Jo Burr Margadant's (1990) study of the earliest graduates of the first teacher's training college for women secondary school teachers in France in the late nineteenth century examines the collective experience of these women as students and teachers and in terms of their private lives and their impact on the teaching profession and more generally on the role of women in French society. Using historical material for a very different kind of analysis, Barry Schwartz (1996) studies how the memory of Abraham Lincoln was used during World War II as a way to explore the role of selected memories in the cultural system. The aim in this section is to show how historical evidence can be useful in studies that have very different objectives, both descriptive and explanatory, and to give you an idea of the novel ways in which historical material can be selected and used to develop interpretations and analyses of great interest. One of these studies was carried out by a historian (Margadant), and the other by a sociologist (Schwartz).

France's First Women Secondary School Teachers

One of the ways to understand the dramatic changes that have occurred in women's social roles is to look back at key events that opened opportunities for women in certain professions. This is what Jo Burr Margadant (1990) set out to do in her historical study of the first classes of graduates of France's first college that specifically trained women to teach in secondary schools (*lycées*). This school, the *Ecole Normale Supérieure* at Sèvres, brought women to prepare for the highly prestigious career of a lycée teacher. The graduates, called '*Sévriennes*,' had a certain status as a result of having been educated at one of the *grands écoles* (the great schools which in France have more prestige than do the universities). What Margadant wanted to do in this study was to see what happened to these women in terms of their careers, their personal lives, and the impact they had on the changing role of women in France.

What sorts of evidence did she use? Basically she employed the biographical evidence that exists on the first ten years of graduates from this school. Her sample was based on the 213 *Sévriennes* who entered the teacher training college between its founding in 1881 and 1890 and subsequently taught for at least one year in a girls' secondary school. There were dossiers on these young women in France's National Archives. Moreover, there was more evidence in the archives of the school itself and in those of the alumni association of that institution. She also looked at records of national professional examinations, the curricula of girls' secondary schools, reports on the conditions of those schools, salary scales of teachers, and other documents. One very interesting set of primary sources consisted of publications (mainly articles) that women graduates wrote for journals on the education of young women.

These primary sources refer to actual documents developed at the time of the events being studied. Historians prefer to use primary sources for any contemporary material written at the time

of the events of interest and secondary sources for subsequent scholarship. Naturally Margadant used secondary sources as well, that is, other published studies and books that addressed issues of interest to her study.

Margadant also gathered quantitative data from the *Sévriennes'* dossiers and was able to compare them with data for men from the most famous normal school for men, the *École Normal Supérieure,* and from the male population of working adults. For example, Table 9-3 addresses a very sociological theme: What were the social origins of the first generation of *Sévriennes*? Note that this table indicates that most came from a higher (bourgeois) or middle-level (white-collar) background, though the social origins of the women *Sévriennes* was not as high as those of the male *Normaliens.*

Supplementing her quantitative data with qualitative biographical material that enabled her to gain knowledge about both the women's public and private lives, Margadant was able to recognize that the types of professional relationships and work environments these highly educated women teachers sought paralleled the values of their middle-class families. Moreover, she found that this highly educated group of women came to support broader public roles for all women even as the type of curriculum and education they had received and supported over time was challenged by coeducation and the application of the curriculum for boys to all secondary students.

The Memory of Abraham Lincoln during World War II

While the Margadant study posed sociological questions and carried out sociological research about the past, Barry Schwartz's study shows the way in which the past can provide a framework for the present. He uses the concept of the "social frame of memory" to understand how far the role of memory was used to shore up American cultural beliefs in the rightness of World War II.

TABLE 9-3

SOCIAL ORIGINS OF *SÉVRIENNES* AND *NORMALIENS*, 1880S (IN PERCENT)

Profession of Father	Approximate Active Male Population (1872)	*Sévriennes* (1881–1890) N = 173	*Normaliens* (1880–1889) N = 352
Businessmen	9.2	8.1	17.5
Higher officials	1.0	1.2	5.0
Liberal professions	0.8	9.8	12.5
Commissioned officers	0.2	4.6	2.0
Universitaires	0.1	9.8	16.5
Total bourgeoisie	11.3	33.5	53.5
Other teaching corps	0.5	9.2	8.0
All white collar	4.5	22.5	15.0
Middle, lower officials		9.8	
Other white collar		12.7	
Artisans, shopkeepers	6.7	13.9	7.0
Total *classes moyennes*	11.7	45.6	30.0
Noncommissioned officers	1.1	7.5	—
Skilled labor	19.9	8.1	—
Unskilled labor	6.7	0.0	—
Farmers	35.0	5.2	—
Agricultural workers	14.3	0.0	—
Total *classes populaires*	77.0	20.8	16.5[a]

[a]Percentages here and hereafter are all rounded off to the nearest tenth of 1 percent, which explains why the sums do not always total 100 percent.

Source: Adapted from Margadant, Jo Burr. *Madame le Professeur: Women Educators in the Third Republic,* Princeton University Press, Princeton, N.J., Table 2.1, p. 51, 1990.

What he means by this social frame of memory is that the past is not just the past; rather, the past is an important element in the present. This means that memory structures experience as it occurs. Schwartz tries to study this phenomenon in his work on the importance of the memory of Abraham Lincoln during World War II.

Such an approach is sociological because it is about collective representations, that is, the images members of a society share in ways that give them a common identity. It is also historical, since history is a way of thinking about the present by relating it to events and experiences in the past. This happens in individual lives, but it also happens when individuals try to make sense of what events in the past brought them to where they are currently. Collectivities do this as well. Take, for example, the collective choice to fight a war. That choice is given meaning by a collective representation of the past. People have to feel that what they are doing as a nation in the present moment has meaning in terms of what the nation has done previously.

Keying is the way in which events in the present are connected to events in the past that are collectively understood to be particularly meaningful (primary events). Schwartz gathered and examined images of Lincoln produced by artists, writers, film directors, poets, politicians, and others during the years of World War II (1941–1945). Moreover, he analyzed the content of written material, songs, illustrations, political pieces, and propaganda (which are qualitative data) as well as quantitative polling data from surveys to show the proportions of Americans who supported various aspects of the war. One example of keying was to compare the death of Franklin Roosevelt in April 1945 (before the end of World War II) with the assassination of Abraham Lincoln, which occurred before the end of the Civil War (1996, p. 911).

The memory of Lincoln played a symbolic role during World War II in many ways. There were parallels drawn between Roosevelt's New Deal and Lincoln's emancipation of the slaves. Popular songs made comparisons, in some cases suggesting that Lincoln and Roosevelt had come from similar social classes (though Roosevelt had come from a very advantaged social background whereas Lincoln had had the simplest of origins). Using a quantitative indicator, Schwartz finds that *The New York Times* published 214 articles on Lincoln between 1940 and 1944, while it published only 36 articles on Lincoln between 1990 and 1994; the *Congressional Record* had 131 entries on Lincoln in the early 1940s, compared with only 26 entries in the early 1990s (1996, p. 913).

Despite the fact that there were historical similarities and continuities between World War I and World War II, World War I was not the event which gave World War II its deepest meaning. In part this was because many Americans considered U.S. participation in World War I to have been a mistake, but more basically it was because the most profound images of personal and collective sacrifice to the ideal of democracy were derived from the Civil War, which Americans understood as a second moral refounding of the nation itself.

Schwartz concludes that the historical memories of Lincoln were used by the Roosevelt administration as a way to try to legitimize U.S. participation in the war (p. 914) as well as to orient the public to the recognition that the war might be long and costly in terms of lives (pp. 914–915).

Lincoln's memory also was used to clarify the goals of the war to the citizenry, whose appreciation of what was being fought for was weak (pp. 915–916). Finally, these memories were used to inspire the citizens to fight and to console them for the many losses and casualties that resulted from the war (p. 917). Schwartz concludes that Lincoln, with his presidency covering the great struggle and many disappointments of the Civil War, "was the perfect symbolic code for World War II" (p. 920).

COMPONENTS OF HISTORICAL RESEARCH

Defining a Problem of Study from the Past

If the problem you select involves understanding more clearly an event, an institution, a city, a person, or an earlier period, you will carry out a historical study. The topic will need to be defined in terms of the types of written materials and other resources (artifacts, individuals to interview) available to you. Part of the historical research may be to determine what materials are available on your topic. In other instances, a set of available materials may trigger the study in the first place, and the specific topic may therefore be more narrowly defined once you know what materials you plan to use.

Establishing and Collecting Sources of Evidence

Whatever the period of time selected, historical research generally requires an appreciation not only of the specific topic but also of the period in which it occurred. For this reason, historians generally read widely in secondary sources, including other histories of the periods they are studying, to increase their familiarity with a period. Good university and college libraries tend to have a great deal of secondary source material on modern historical periods in America and Europe. Your library is also likely to have materials on earlier periods and nonwestern societies. For extensive materials on a subject, however, you may need to go to a large research library or a library with extensive holdings on a specific subject. In short, libraries are the obvious place to find secondary sources. Keep in mind that historical work on a specific topic continues to be done. For example, if one selects the history of slavery in the United States, historical interpretations of this institution written while slavery was still legal in the United States, after its abolition, and continuing up to the present time are available.

Consider also the primary sources. There were accounts of slaves in the form of diaries, letters, etc. (though because most slaves were illiterate, most could not write). Thus the written records of slaves tend to be from somewhat unusual slaves—those who had been taught to read and write or who had run away. There were also written accounts by those who held slaves (mistresses' diaries) as well as records of the slave trade and records of the slaves on particular plantations: their numbers, their roles, their births, their deaths. Various forms of unwritten records—stories, songs, and tales passed down—form the basis of oral historical material on slavery in America. Finally, artifacts bearing witness to certain practices still exist.

No researcher can examine all the material available. How to select the best sources is important for historical work. You need in some sense to draw up a sample of sources that you feel would represent what you must look at in order to generalize more widely. Since in historical research the full "population" of what is available can never be known, the sample of materials examined must always be a purposive one. What it represents and what it fails to represent should be considered.

Developing Means to Quantify Evidence

Some historical studies include data that may be quantified, such as marriage records. When this is the case, the presentation of the quantifiable data often is made in tables. Usually the forms of quantitative analysis need to be quite simple in historical studies because the data often include many missing elements and the determination of what population the data represent is usually very difficult to make.

Historical Writing

The quality of writing in historical work is of great importance. Ideas and materials must be *synthesized* into a historical narrative that is rich in content and clear in meaning. This is not to say that writing style is irrelevant in other forms of social research. But surveys and experiments, for example, have a kind of formal structure that must be followed, which helps organize the form of written presentation. In historical work, the structure of the study usually is set out less precisely; instead, the work builds on and develops out of varied types of sources.

Issues of Validity and Reliability in Historical Studies

There can be serious challenges to the validity of documents. Recall that a few years past a supposed diary of Hitler turned up; it was examined by historians and deemed authentic (in short, it had face validity), but later it was determined to be a hoax. Historians must be attentive to the authenticity of the documents and written records they use. Not only may documents and written records be false, they may be highly biased. Historical research must consider historical materials in a broad enough context so that a fair re-creation can be made.

Historians often study subjects that have previously been studied by others. However, a complete replication is virtually impossible to do. Because historical research involves so much choice along the way as to what to look at and what to ignore and because there is so strong a need to synthesize the material and put it into a framework, one historian cannot replicate another historian's research design. However, it is very common for subjects of historical interest to be studied over and over again. In each case, the later researchers are expected to be fully conversant with the work of the earlier historians. Thus, while reliability cannot be tested as in an experiment, historical research (both the selection and the interpretation of historical material) should be done and documented with great care so that another historian could build another study upon it.

DECIDING IF HISTORICAL RESEARCH IS APPROPRIATE FOR YOUR TOPIC

If you are studying a topic from the past or are beginning in a much earlier era and tracing the course of events or developments over time, you will need to use historical methods. Remember that looking at historical material is not the same as looking at current material. You need a strong foundation of knowledge about the period in which the material was written in order to understand the material itself. If you are planning to look at records from the nineteenth century, you should first read broadly about the subject you are studying in that century. What this means is that a great deal of concern must be centered on getting yourself grounded in the field you are studying. You also must make sure you can get the materials you need. Historians often have to travel to where the actual written materials are available (a library or an archive). Social researchers surely should not avoid historical research. If the subject you want to study is from the past, you will need to become a historian.

UNOBTRUSIVE MEASURES

In 1966, a book entitled *Unobtrusive Measures: Nonreactive Research in the Social Sciences* was published. Its authors—Eugene Webb, Donald T. Campbell, Richard D. Schwartz, and Lee

Sechrest—were social psychologists whose stated goal was "not to replace the interview but to supplement and cross-validate it with measures that do not require the cooperation of a respondent and that do not themselves contaminate the response" (1966, p. 2). Earlier (in the chapter on survey research) we discussed the problems of gaining the cooperation of respondents and keeping them committed to completing questionnaires and interviews. In discussing experimental studies, I addressed the problems of demand characteristics (where the subjects in an experiment are affected by what they think the experimenter wants from them) and the Hawthorne effect (where the occurrence of an experiment, even if it offers what would seem to be a meaningless or negative experimental stimulus, may itself produce an experimental effect). In field studies too the researcher needs to consider carefully how her or his role in the field may alter the actual field environment being studied.

The study of *unobtrusive measures* was devised to avoid such problems. As Webb and his colleagues stressed in their influential book, this approach developed as a supplementary method that would add to a study and help validate its findings. Another reason for the development of unobtrusive measures as a method was to avoid certain ethical issues. To study a subject unobtrusively is to avoid infringing on anyone else's privacy. As will be explained in Chapter 14, many research strategies encroach on private aspects of the lives of individuals.

In 1979, one of the authors of the original volume, Lee Sechrest, edited a volume on unobtrusive measurement in which updated studies were described. The editor noted that although the original book by Webb and his colleagues had been very widely read, the actual use of unobtrusive measurement by social researchers was not great. In what follows, the most influential type of unobtrusive measures delineated in the 1966 volume will be discussed.

TYPES OF UNOBTRUSIVE MEASURES

Webb and his associates defined three broad categories of unobtrusive measures: physical traces, archives, and observations. Here we will consider only the study of *physical traces* as representing a unique form of research method which researchers may be able to include in a project.

Physical Traces

Measures of erosion and accretion are certainly the most familiar types of unobtrusive measures. The initial example for an *erosion measure* was a study of the popularity of various exhibits at Chicago's Museum of Science and Industry. Rather than survey visitors or even observe the size of crowds around various exhibits, the researchers studied the wear and tear on the vinyl tiles surrounding various exhibits. They found, for example, that the tiles around the chick-hatching exhibit wore out very quickly (they needed to be replaced about every six weeks) (Webb et al., 1966, p. 36).

Other erosion examples include the wear on library books (as a measure of their popularity). Obviously, a researcher could determine a book's popularity by checking the library records to see how frequently it had been taken out. In this case, study of the erosion of books would be a way to cross-validate the popularity of the book and suggest that the book was being held and read, not just taken out and left on a shelf. It is also a way to study the use of reference works which are not checked out of libraries (Webb et al., 1966, pp. 37–38).

The most commonly studied *accretion measure,* that is, a measure of something that has been laid down or built up, is garbage. Consumer behavior (such as the use of diet foods) has been analyzed by studying garbage. For example, the weight, volume, and nature of the food consumed can be determined by this method (Rathje, 1979, p. 77). Analyzing garbage in this way is unobtrusive because it has no effect on the producers of

the garbage. Other commonly studied accretion measures are graffiti and household possessions.

Webb and his colleagues (1966) also differentiate between *natural* erosion or accretion measures and *controlled* measures. Natural measures are those which occur without any interference by the researcher (all the measures described above would be of this type). Examples of *controlled erosion measures* offered by Webb et al. include a before-and-after measure of the wear on children's shoes and having children wear special wristwatches to record their level of activity (1966, p. 43). *Controlled accretion measures* would include such researcher-intrusive strategies as were used in a study of how carefully advertisements were read in a magazine. In one study, small glue spots were used which would not stick together again once the pages were opened (Webb et al., 1966, pp. 44–45). By this means it was possible to tell whether readers had looked at various ads. In short, controlled erosion and accretion measures involve some form of pretest-posttest design or manipulated act by the researcher.

Issues of Validity and Reliability

The primary purpose of unobtrusive measures is to serve as a supplementary, not a primary, source of data. To the degree that unobtrusive measures offer additional means for supporting (or refuting) conclusions drawn from other forms of data, they increase the validity of a study. Recall that there are two forms of validity: internal and external. To the degree that data based on unobtrusive measures from the same subject of study add to other forms of evidence, they help establish the internal validity of a study. In other words, they provide additional evidence that what was found actually exists.

But unobtrusive measures can also add to the external validity of a study by providing additional evidence that may make the findings from one situation applicable to other situations. In short, unobtrusive measures may help increase the generalizability of a study's findings.

DECIDING IF UNOBTRUSIVE MEASURES ARE APPROPRIATE FOR YOUR TOPIC

If you are carrying out a study using records or other archival resources or if you plan an observational study in which you will in no way participate in the field or be known to those in the field, you will be using unobtrusive measures. The unfamiliar types of research suggested by this method are the erosion and accretion measures. If such measures can be devised and used in a project you plan, they may strengthen your research effort. Erosion and accretion measures tend to be novel and often easy to utilize, but they may not be easy to devise.

One might make the case that a study based on unobtrusive measures is a good choice for someone who is shy, since the researcher will not need to confront the subjects being studied. However, it takes a good deal of creative effort to devise such measures and an equal amount of systematic effort to measure them accurately and precisely. This is why it is not a good method for the casual researcher. Think about your topic carefully before deciding whether it can be studied unobtrusively.

SECONDARY ANALYSIS

Secondary analysis, as was stated before, is not a specific method per se; it simply means a new analysis of data collected for another purpose. Hakim defines it as "any further analysis of an existing dataset which presents interpretations, conclusions, or knowledge additional to, or different from, those presented in the first report" (1982, p. 1). Generally, it refers to using already collected survey data to study problems different from those addressed by the original researcher(s). Another reason for carrying out a secondary analysis may be to use already available survey data in the study of a research method. If one applies different methodological techniques to the same dataset, for example, much may be learned about a statistical technique.

For your purposes, you should consider secondary analysis if you want to use a dataset larger than what you could collect yourself. When you look for a dataset, you must hold clearly in mind what the essential needs of your study are. Does the survey you are considering have questions that address your needs? Is the sample of the survey adequate for your purposes? Will it allow you to generalize to the population you are aiming to consider?

In short, a set of already collected data offers you a "menu" from which you can pick out what you want to study—that is, you can create your secondary analysis. You must be sure that your project can be served by that menu and that you like what's on the menu. The menu metaphor also implies that until you've ordered and tasted the items ordered, you will not be precisely sure how much you like them. Naturally, you look carefully over a questionnaire before you decide to use the data generated from it, but often not until you start to work with data do you fully appreciate exactly how effective they will or will not be for your purposes. You also will need to consider the costs of purchasing the dataset and running the necessary computer analyses.

"One advantage of secondary analysis is that it forces the researcher to think more closely about the theoretical aims and substantive issues of the study rather than the practical and methodological problems of collecting new data" (Hakim, 1982, p. 16). This may be one of the reasons why it has become such a widely reputed method.

An Example of a Secondary Analysis

A colleague of mine at DePaul, Joyce Sween, and I received a federal grant in the late 1970s to study the potentially disruptive effects of childbearing and child rearing on women's career outcomes. The plan was to carry out a secondary analysis of a longitudinal dataset based on a national survey of college graduates of 1961 who were followed up five times across the 1960s until 1968. The longitudinal design would enable us to examine career activities and attitudes both before and after childbearing and to compare them across time. A sample of college graduates was attractive to us because we wanted to examine a group that included some women who would be sufficiently trained for the work force and hold sufficiently high career aspirations for the effects of childbearing on their careers to be of possible consequence to them. (For a paper from this analysis, see Baker and Sween, 1982.)

Acquiring the dataset was relatively easy. For a modest price, we purchased a data tape from the National Opinion Research Center (NORC), which had collected the dataset. It came with a large and complex codebook and a computer printout of the frequencies of responses to every item on the tape. It took some time to familiarize ourselves with this tape and select all the variables we needed to carry out our intended analysis.

We began, as is often the case, by considering a fairly wide range of variables. However, it is necessary in a secondary analysis to avoid carrying out what is termed a "fishing expedition," where the researcher "fishes" for one variable after another. To narrow our choice of variables, we considered which ones were the best measures of concepts that interested us (which ones had greater face validity). We also prepared many cross-tabulations of potentially interesting independent variables with our dependent variable (career status attainment) to decide which seemed to have the strongest relationships to higher attainment.

We also had to carry out a good deal of data manipulation (to be discussed in more detail in Chapter 11). To consider carefully how childbearing affected work patterns and attitudes, we had to develop new measures indicating the patterns of work activity, childbearing, returning to work, etc., which characterized the early adult years of young women. These patterns could then be compared to women with earlier or later first births, and to those with higher or lower career aspirations.

In a study such as this, the effort to collect these complex and very detailed data had already been completed by a professional survey research center whose standards for carrying out surveys were very widely respected. Not only would we have been unable to finance such a national survey ourselves, as only two sociologists we would not have been able to carry it out on our own. We spent the greatest amount of time creating new variables from old, selecting the variables for the final analyses, and then analyzing the results.

This is the virtue of secondary analysis. Most of the effort can be placed at the analytic stage rather than at the data-gathering stage. Remember, however, that you can transform variables only so far; you cannot make up data that are not there.

Using Longitudinal Datasets

In the opening section I mentioned that one factor that distinguishes the analysis of already collected data from studies where the researcher collects new data is time. When data are already available (that is, when they are extant), they represent a period of time prior to the efforts to carry out the new analysis. Some very interesting longitudinal survey datasets were collected in the past, and some excellent datasets are being collected in the present. Here I will first present a brief discussion of how Glen Elder (1974) undertook a reanalysis of a set of data initially collected in 1931. Then I will examine how a cross-generational longitudinal study has enabled Roberts and Bengston (1996) to study the effects of emotional closeness on self-esteem.

Children of the Great Depression.   To study the effects of economic factors on family relations across generations, Elder (1974) utilized a longitudinal dataset, the Oakland Growth Study. This panel of data was developed by the Institute of Human Development at the University of California at Berkeley. It began in 1931 as an extensive study of 167 children who were in the fifth and sixth grades of five different primary schools in one section of Oakland, California. These children were closely followed, using interviews and questionnaires, from 1932 to 1939. In the 1940s, data collection was continued in 1941 and again in 1948. Another follow-up was carried out during the period 1953–1954, yet another was done in 1957, and the final contact was made in 1964. Thus these longitudinal data covered a time period of 31 years.

By modern standards, the sample was not a very good one. In many secondary analyses, one of the major attractions of this method is that the quality of the sampling is superior to that which many researchers could afford to do. In Elder's case, however, the attraction of the Oakland Growth Study was the historical length of the dataset and the richness of data on intergenerational family matters. The original sample of 84 boys and 83 girls were all white, children of native-born Americans, and only slightly higher in social class than a more representative sample of Oakland residents from the same period.

The early data collection efforts were deep and broad. They included interviews with mothers and questionnaires administered to the pupils. In the 1930s, families were visited yearly and a log was kept on each member of the sample. Child-rearing practices, family relationships, and the activities of the children with friends were solicited. As the respondents moved into junior and senior high school, questionnaires on social and emotional behavior were administered on seven different occasions. In addition, the Strong Vocational Interest blank which measured occupational interests was used in one survey. Ratings of the family in terms of the closeness of the subject to each parent and the evaluation of the parents by the subject were made using a set of judges.

The follow-up surveys and interviews in the 1950s and 1960s produced a sample of 76 women and 69 men. For these individuals, life histories could be developed on the basis of occupational and family histories across the decades. In these later studies, subjects were given physical examinations, psychiatric assessments, and numerous personality tests. This gave Elder some insight into the mental health of the subjects and its relation to childhood conditions.

Working with old and complex data such as these presents many problems of validity. Whenever possible, Elder searched for multiple indicators, especially to use as dependent variables. Indexes were often formed so that multiple measures would reduce the possible errors that single measures might contain.

Elder also made use of other studies from the 1930s with which to compare his findings. Here the need to have some grounding in historical material from the period covered is important. Elder's interest, however, remained with the individual and the family across time. Let me offer you one among the many interesting findings of this study. Elder differentiated his sample between those who grew up in deprived families (those in which the breadwinner was unemployed) during the Depression and those who did not. In doing so, he found support for the hypothesis that "family life acquired value through exposure to conditions which made rewarding, secure relationships difficult to achieve and therefore scarce" (1974, p. 226). That is to say, those who had grown up in deprived families in the 1930s had a stronger preference for family activities in the 1950s and 1960s compared to nonfamily activities such as career, leisure, and community than did those whose families had not been deprived in the 1930s. This finding was especially true for women.

Affective Ties to Parents and Self-Esteem.   In a study based on a longitudinal panel study of survey data collected over a 20-year period, Roberts and Bengtson (1996) examine how the emotional closeness youths feel toward their parents affects their level of self-esteem 20 years later. This study was based on a very interesting dataset, the University of Southern California Longitudinal Study of Generations (LSG), a multiwave panel survey which has followed more than 200 families across three or four generations since 1971 (this was described in Box 3-4).

Recall that the original sample had been drawn from a population of the members of an early health maintenance organization (HMO) founded in the Los Angeles area. An early screening questionnaire had been sent to male members of the HMO age 55, requesting participation from those in families that had at least one grandparent, a parent, and a grandchild. The same family members were resurveyed in each wave, and the spouses and additional children of the original respondents were added. The resulting sample is largely white, working class to middle class, and somewhat above the average in terms of educational level.

The three waves of the survey used in this particular analysis were carried out first in 1971 (when the youths in the study were between ages 16 and 26), then 17 years later in 1988, and finally in 1991 (when the same respondents wcrc ages 36 to 46). Fifty-one percent of the original respondents were retained in the 20-year follow-up, with attrition being somewhat higher for men, those who were younger in 1971, and those from lower-income families. By the 1991 wave, there were 1,528 members in the sample.

Secondary analyses of longitudinal datasets on families (such as the LSG) allow researchers to study the effects of one generation of a family on a later one (a generational analysis), see the effects of recent historical periods on family members of different age cohorts (youths, young adults, the middle-aged, the elderly), and understand how certain social and psychological factors change across a life span and over historical time periods. What Roberts and Bengtson (1996) found was that strong affective ties between youths and their parents between the teenage years and young adulthood were related to higher levels of self-esteem in later years.

COMPONENTS OF A SECONDARY ANALYSIS

In theory, you should always know what you want to study before getting your data. In fact, secondary analysis often begins with finding a dataset you think is especially exciting or rich and then devising a problem which can be studied using those data. Here we will examine the components in the "proper" order, but remember that in practice the data may be chosen before the problem is set.

Selection of a Topic

A topic for a secondary analysis may be very ambitious. It may be one that only a large national (or even cross-national) dataset could address. Once you have posed a hypothesis or a research question, the operationalization must be carefully constructed. What control variables will be critical? Must the dependent variable be measured in a particular way? Usually there is some latitude in your design, and so if you find a relevant dataset that does not have every feature you want, you can adapt your study slightly to conform to what is available. In secondary analysis, you need to focus precisely on your topic to select an appropriate dataset.

Search for Available Data

In Chapter 3, a general discussion of where you might find available data was offered. A researcher with access to a computer can study a vast array of research topics, using datasets from well-designed surveys based on carefully constructed samples. Major survey research centers at universities and government agencies usually can carry out data collection procedures much more rigorously and thoroughly than a lone researcher can. The institution at which you are studying may be affiliated with a social science data archive that stores datasets and makes them available to users for a reasonable charge. Your institution may have its own data archive, or it may be affiliated with a group of universities which hold a collection of data tapes. Many datasets are now on-line.

The largest and best-known social science data archive, the Inter-University Consortium for Political and Social Research (ICPSR) at the University of Michigan, has thousands of machine-readable data files. These include surveys that have been collected by American centers such as the *General Social Survey (GSS)*, which was described in Chapter 3; the numerous datasets collected by the Census Bureau; and data from foreign sources. Any institution of higher education which includes social scientists can join ICPSR and have access to vast holdings of datasets. Box 9-2 describes a number of the most widely used databases available from ICPSR.

There are social science data archives in other countries as well (Kiecolt and Nathan, 1985, pp. 79–80). In Britain, the Social Science Research Council (SSRC) Data Archive at the University of Essex stores hundreds of datasets to which a user can gain access by filling out a very

simple application. You can check the SSRC's holdings by examining the *Guide to the Survey Archives Social Science Data Holdings and Allied Services*. The SSRC can also help you gain access to international datasets.

Public opinion data are held by the Louis Harris Center (at the University of North Carolina, Chapel Hill Social Science Data Library) and the Roper Center for Public Opinion Research (at the Institute for Social Inquiry at the University of Connecticut). The *Directory of Louis Harris Public Opinion Machine-Readable Data* describes the various surveys covering a wide array of social and political topics. Researchers looking for data on a specific topic can ask the Harris Center to conduct computer searches on the basis of key-words. The

BOX 9-2

MAJOR DATASETS IN THE UNITED STATES

SURVEYS OF NATIONAL SAMPLES ON BROAD-RANGING TOPICS

1. The *General Social Survey (GSS)* has been conducted by the National Opinion Research Center (NORC) yearly since 1972. It samples a national cross-section of noninstitutionalized English-speaking persons 18 years of age and older. In some years, special subsamples have been surveyed (such as black Americans). The *GSS* has measured attitudes toward controversial issues, such as abortion and civil liberties, over more than two decades, allowing for trend studies. In addition, measures are collected yearly on work and job satisfaction, personal happiness, family relations, and characteristics of the sample subjects, such as age at first marriage, number of children, and educational, marital, and military histories. (See Davis and Smith's *User's Guide,* in the Recommended Readings.)

2. Data collected by the Census Bureau are available in many forms at state data centers. The Public Use Microdata Samples (PUMS) offer different types of representative samples of the decennial census; some of the

census questions have been asked annually since 1910. The Current Population Survey (CPS) surveys a national sample of Americans monthly on labor force activity, with background data on marital, fertility, educational, and immunization histories.

SURVEYS OF NATIONAL SAMPLES ON FOCUSED TOPICS

1. Work and income: The National Longitudinal Surveys (NLS), carried out by the joint efforts of the Department of Labor and Ohio State University, provide a rich data source on labor market experience. The NLS surveys have covered panels of young women and men (ages 14 to 24), women ages 30 to 44, and men ages 49 to 59. Respondents were interviewed in 1966 and were reinterviewed over a period of 15 years. A new survey of young Americans was begun in the late 1970s and has been followed up.

   The Panel Study of Income Dynamics (PSID) conducted at the Institute for Social Research at the University of Michigan has surveyed low-income families, heads of households, and wives of male household heads.

Roper Center, the world's largest public opinion data archive, has data tapes from television and newspaper polls as well as the Gallup polls (conducted by the American Institute for Public Opinion), the Harris polls, and surveys from NORC and other survey centers. There are numerous reference guides to the Roper Center holdings, such as the *Roper Center American Collection*, which describes the center's U.S. holdings, and *Data Acquisitions*, which is published biannually.

Data archive centers usually can prepare the type of machine-readable tapes or disks you request for your specific computer system. Codebooks for the surveys are always available. Constructed indexes and scales prepared from the data are often included. Many centers prepare bibliographies of published studies and unpublished reports based on particular datasets. Some data archives will prepare datasets on request based on specific subsamples or statistical tables. The price of datasets is generally quite reasonable. To justify the public expense of data collection funded by the government, there is often an explicit agreement that the data must be accessible to others. Many datasets can now be "downloaded" direclty from the Internet.

Re-creation of the Data

Once you have acquired a dataset, you must make it meet your research objectives. This requires a few steps. First, you must search out the variables you think you need. Second, you must study them

Data are available on family units and individuals. (See the *User's Guide* in the Recommended Readings.)

2. Health: The National Center for Health Statistics (NCHS) prepares a catalog of public use data on health. The National Health Interview Survey (NHIS) focuses on specific systems of the body in order to identify diseases, as well as on other health topics, such as smoking. The National Health and Nutrition Examination Survey (NHANES) gains its data through physical and laboratory examinations and survey questions. A primary focus is nutrition.

3. Education: The National Center of Education Statistics of the U.S. Department of Education offers a number of datasets. These are the National Longitudinal Study of the High School Class of 1972 and *High School and Beyond*, a longitudinal survey of students who were high school sophomores and seniors in 1980. One of the most recent panel datasets is the National Educational Longitudinal Study of 1988 (NELS:88), which was based on an initial cohort of 25,000 eighth-graders attending 1,000 public and private schools in the United States in 1988. The

same students have been resurveyed in 1990, 1992 (when those who had stayed in school would have graduated from high school), 1994, and 1997. This extraordinary dataset includes a range of fascinating features: data from students, dropouts, parents, teachers, and the schools the pupils attended can be integrated; supplementary data on geographic, demographic, and subgroup populations are also linked to the data. NELS:88 also can be linked to the two above mentioned educational surveys from the 1970s and 1980s.

4. Politics: The Center for Political Studies and the Survey Research Center of the University of Michigan's Institute for Social Research have been carrying out election surveys since 1948. This American National Election Study assesses political and social attitudes, including appraisals of domestic and foreign policy, reactions to social groups, the mass media, social-psychological predispositions, and voting behavior and party identification. Data from panel studies have been gathered in certain years, as well as extensive cross-sectional data. These data are also available through ICPSR.

carefully. If you have the frequency counts on each variable, this will intensify your knowledge of them. (If, for example, a large proportion said "don't know" to a specific question, this is a factor which will be important in deciding whether to use the item and how to use it.) Third, you must select a set of variables which will fully address the needs of your study but will not overwhelm you. (The typical mistake is to take on too many variables and get bogged down in too many analyses.)

As a secondary analyst, you can re-create many of the data to suit your needs. But you must always be careful not to use the data for a purpose for which they are inappropriate. (You cannot turn a sow's ear into a silk purse, as the proverb goes.) If you create your own indexes and scales, you should take care to give them valid names.

You may also decide to use only subsets of the sample (only the males, only those over age 21, only those born in the southeastern United States, etc.). If you do this, you will need to reconsider the sample design to see what effects your selection will have on the quality of the sample. You will need to consider how representative the subsample of the population was from which it was drawn.

Analyzing the Data and Comparing Results

The major effort of such a study is to analyze the data. Chapters 12 and 13 will explain analytic techniques. Your secondary analysis of a dataset becomes a part of the corpus of analyses of that data. Survey research centers often develop bibliographies of the studies carried out and the publications prepared using a specific dataset. You may want to compare your efforts to those of others who have used the data and inform the survey center of your project.

Issues of Validity and Reliability

In selecting a dataset for a secondary analysis, the issue of validity should be your primary criterion. You must be strongly convinced that the data mea-

sure what they purport to measure and that these measures in fact are ones that are appropriate for the variables you need for your project. To meet these objectives, the following qualifications should be considered in selecting a dataset: (1) the quality of the data-gathering organization, (2) the purpose of the original researchers, and (3) the extent to which the dataset contains indicators that will enable you to test your research problem, in particular, what will be used for the dependent variable and the primary independent variables.

Because these data have already been analyzed, many questions about their validity have already been addressed. If scales and indexes have been created, validity and reliability tests (described in Chapter 4) may already have been carried out. Examinations of how variables of interest to you were related to other variables in already prepared analyses from the dataset should help you see whether the variable seems to be measuring what you would expect it to measure.

Secondary analyses based on highly professional data-gathering techniques often contain measures of higher validity and reliability than a single researcher would be apt to prepare. Because the data have to be analyzed again, the issues of reliability and validity are also raised again. In the selection of such data, the researcher examines and challenges the validity of indicators within the study. These additional efforts to reappraise the data will offer greater information on their value.

DECIDING IF SECONDARY ANALYSIS IS APPROPRIATE FOR YOUR TOPIC

For many social researchers, secondary analysis is *the* preferred method. Some social researchers (and professors who teach social research methods) believe that beginning researchers should be encouraged to carry out secondary analyses because of the quality of the data that can be used. Of course, a lot of data will never be fully analyzed by the original researchers. A large survey contains so many variables that many researchers working on many different problems are required to analyze all the material.

If you have a problem that needs to be addressed with a large body of data and you know of a dataset which contains relevant material for your study, you should consider secondary analysis. Of course, your adviser may want you to collect your own data (for a class project, a master's thesis, or a doctoral dissertation), and there is much to be learned by doing so. But it is worth bearing in mind that there are so many available datasets still not fully analyzed that it is sensible to consider examining already collected survey data before setting out to do your own data collection. Let me add that even if you want to carry out your own survey, it often makes sense to begin by examining and analyzing earlier survey data that may address the same problem. Finally, every project has its time span and effort span; secondary analysis concentrates that effort on the analysis stage of research by abbreviating the need for data collection and manipulation.

THE ANALYSIS OF EXISTING STATISTICS

The analysis of *existing statistics*—that is, statistical data that have already been prepared and reported— is similar to secondary analyses in that the data already have been collected but rather than providing the second researcher with raw data to be analyzed, the researcher using existing statistics has "created" data. This is both an advantage and a disadvantage. Existing statistics generally report on large aggregate datasets which might be very time-consuming and difficult for a researcher to prepare on his or her own. Such statistics often are drawn from the census or other very large-scale data-gathering operations. As such, the use of these statistics offers high-quality evidence to a researcher. However, since these statistics are already analyzed, it often is not possible for the second researcher to alter them to suit the new study. Instead, they must often be used as they appear.

One widely used type of study on the analysis of existing statistics is the social indicators study.

This will be discussed in Chapter 10 on evaluation research. Here I would like to give you a few examples of how aggregated data have been used by others and suggest how you might use them as the basis of a study or as supporting data in a study.

The wealth of data regularly collected by the government and by other bodies and published in the form of statistics allows for a great range of potential analyses. This form of analysis is used mainly to compare rates of major social factors between large conglomerates, such as nations (for example, rates dealing with health, crime, prosperity), or to compare changes over time using the same indicators as a form of trend analysis. Government planning and decision making may depend on these forms of analysis, and various branches of the U.S. government prepare these forms of statistics regularly.

A Research Project Based on Existing Statistics

How Arrest Rates Relate to Change in Income Inequality and Educational Attainment.   In an analysis of existing statistics, LaFree and Drass (1996) relate four types of available sets of statistical data to the question of why crime rates have increased over a period of time in which great strides in educational attainment and high economic growth were achieved. They hypothesize that the income inequality within racial groups that followed the dramatic increase in educational attainment and economic growth may have been a major factor in this increase in crime.

What types of existing statistics did they use? They used aggregated datasets collected regularly over time (times-series data) by various branches of the federal government. For the arrest rates, they looked at the annual datasets of African-American and white homicide, burglary, and robbery arrest rates between 1957 and 1990. These statistics come from the Uniform Crime Report (UCR). The measures of intraracial income inequality were drawn from family income ranges prepared by the

U.S. Bureau of the Census. For the educational attainment measures, they use median years of education for African-American and white men age 25 and over (also from the Census Bureau). The measures of economic well-being are based on six different indicators: three from the U.S. Bureau of the Census—(1) median family income, (2) median income of males 14 years and older, and (3) median income of males in the full-time year-round labor force—and two from the U.S. Bureau of Labor Statistics—(5) male unemployment and (6) percentage of males not in the labor force.

In addition, LaFree and Drass (1996) controlled for four other factors which they thought might affect the relationships in the major model. These factors included the inflation rate measured by the consumer price index (from the Census Bureau); the relative size of the youth age cohort (ages 14 to 29) in the population of African-Americans and whites (from the Census Bureau); and a measure of criminal opportunity as measured by decreased supervision in the home because both parents work or because a parent lives alone or with unrelated persons (based on measuring female labor force participation in husband-present households and non-husband-present households and dividing that by the number of total households). Finally, they considered the incarceration rate (from the U.S. Bureau of Justice Statistics) and "lagged" its effect on the arrest rates (this means that the incarceration rate in 1985 was related to the arrest rate in 1986) thereby controlling the number of subjects who were available to be arrested.

Using various multivariate statistical techniques which examine many variables at once, LaFree and Drass were able to show that the degree of income inequality within a racial group (such as African-Americans or whites) increased between 1957 and 1990 and that this variable was one of the most highly related to increasing crime rates. Since increased educational attainment and economic well-being are related to income inequality, this seems to explain why these two factors are highly correlated with increased crime rates. It is interesting that for whites both income

inequality and the negative effects of economic well-being were related to increased crime rates, while for African-Americans only the income inequality factor was significantly related. This appears to support the theory of Cloward and Ohlin (1960) that it is the relative perception of deprivation rather than absolute measures of deprivation which are more related to crime (LaFree and Drass, 1996, p. 629).

Using Existing Statistics

As a researcher, you may want to incorporate *aggregate data* into your studies or use sets of aggregate data as the basis of a new analysis. Let me give you an example of how I used current data on the status of American women. In the summer of 1983, I was preparing to attend the Australia/New Zealand Sociological Meetings in Melbourne. I had offered to give a paper on my current research, but the organizer said he preferred that I give a more general talk on the status of American women after the defeat of the Equal Rights Amendment (ERA). Such a paper would, like most papers, require a theoretical argument and some evidence. In terms of data, I needed to show how the conditions of American women had changed from before 1973 (when the ERA was first passed by Congress) until 1982, when the time to gain the necessary two-thirds support of the states for ratification had run out. Since the ERA broadly addressed the social role of women, I needed aggregate statistical evidence on how the role of women had changed in the United States during that precise period of time.

Such data are widely available. The U.S. Bureau of Labor Statistics regularly publishes aggregate data describing the work status of women. These data are presented in relation to other factors, such as marital status, presence of children, educational attainment, age, and race. Many of the tables compare the labor force participation rates, unemployment rates, income, or other work measures across a period of years so that changes over time can be seen. The Bureau publishes monthly reports, compiles special reports, and contributes data to various other statistical abstracts, and so these materials are readily available in most libraries. Because I wanted the most recent data possible, I went directly to the office of the Bureau of Labor Statistics in Chicago (where I then lived). Most of the existing statistical data I used came from this bureau.

The remaining statistical data I needed, such as marital status, childbearing, and head-of-household information, came largely from *Current Population Reports* from the U.S. Census Bureau. Data on the estimated number of legal abortions were available in the Census Bureau's *Statistical Abstract of the United States* and had been gathered by a private institute. With these data I was able to write a section in my paper entitled "A Statistical Portrait of American Women in the 1980s." While the ERA is no longer a pressing issue, existing statistics on women's (and men's) work and family patterns are still available.

COMPONENTS OF AN ANALYSIS OF EXISTING STATISTICS

Determining the Problem

Many research problems require large sets of aggregate data in order to be addressed. Any question that concerns a national trend about a social phenomenon requires such data. Has there been an increase in drug addiction in the United States? Are there more automobile accident fatalities in states where the drinking age is lower? Has cycling become a more popular sport among adults? Questions such as these may be of interest to various bodies. Data on drug addiction may interest social welfare workers, law enforcement agencies, and health planners. Politicians and policymakers are concerned with the drinking-driving relationship, as are the liquor and automobile industries. Cycling trends are of interest to bicycle manufacturers, sporting goods stores, and people and organizations that offer services or support physical fitness. Note that existing statistics from aggregate data may be used to evaluate changes that have occurred (they

may be the basis of an evaluation research project as we shall refer to it in Chapter 10), but they may also merely monitor change or stability.

If you have a problem which might be addressed by an aggregate data source, you must carefully consider the types of statistical evidence that could speak to it. Remember how I used data on changes in employment rates, employment rates in relation to marriage and childbearing, and fertility rates and income data to show that women's employment patterns had altered radically over the preceding 20 years. You may be able to strengthen your analysis by incorporating already available statistics into your study.

Treating the Data

Since aggregate data are established against a defined base, it is often impossible to disaggregate them. For example, if you find the rates of home ownership over the past 50 years, you cannot arbitrarily break those data down between the sexes, if this has not already been done. What you can often do is compare information from datasets based on smaller aggregates, say, states or cities. This would allow you, for example, to compare factors such as unemployment rates and rates of home ownership for the 10 largest American cities. Remember that there may be many types of measures that could represent the same social indicator. Try to select the one that is the best measure of the concept you are trying to explore. Don't just take the first thing you find.

One of the primary problems that may occur in analyzing existing statistics is to imply that these findings based on aggregate data can be applied to individuals or subgroups within the dataset. Suppose you are using statistics on teenage pregnancies in the United States and note that there are higher rates in the northeastern states than in the west. Suppose you also note that there are higher proportions of racial minority groups in the northeastern states. From this you might want to draw the conclusion that teenage pregnancies are higher in one section of the country because pregnant teenagers are more likely to be members of racial minority groups. However, you could be committing an *ecological fallacy* by extending conclusions based on group data to individuals. It could be that the white teenagers in the northeast have higher rates than those in the west, while the rate for minority teenagers shows no difference between the areas or is lower. Recall the discussion of the ecological fallacy in Chapter 3 when units of analysis were discussed. In any study of existing statistics, the units of analysis are an aggregate group. It is very important to have a clear sense of what that group is and make inferences from the statistical data only about the group itself.

Referencing Data

The sources of these data must always be referenced and understood. Careful notation of the dates of the data presented, the population base, and the exact type of measurement of the indicator must be clearly recognized. Be sure to take down exactly where a data source came from. You may want to photocopy the table so that you have the source. Often you need to return to the data or find some supporting evidence. By looking widely and then photocopying the tables you desire, you will be able to select the best presentations for your study.

Issues of Validity and Reliability

One could argue that a good reason for using available statistics is that many of the validity and reliability issues have been handled very well. The measurement of indicators in existing statistics is usually based on widely used and accepted means for such measurement. For example, crime rates and unemployment rates are measures that have been developed, critiqued, and redeveloped over many years. There is a great deal of consensus on the way to measure such variables. However, there is still a high degree of error in such statistics because of the way in which the measurements are carried out and their degree of completeness. In crime statistics, for instance, there are problems stemming from unreported crime and differential

arrests of persons of different social class origins. These problems can undermine the reliability of the data. It is important for the researcher to be aware of such problems: the researcher must not uncritically accept the weight of statistical evidence as fact.

To increase validity in using existing statistics, researchers should try to find more than one measure of a finding. Replicating evidence is a good way to increase confidence that the finding is real. It is also important that the researcher find evidence that actually tests her or his theoretical notions. This requires, of course, that there be a logical relationship between the statistics that are used and the hypothesis posed (or research question asked). Remember that studies which use existing statistics that were compiled and presented in order to offer an aggregate picture must be selected and handled carefully when they are being related to another purpose. You must examine the original purpose for which the data were collected to be certain that you are not distorting or falsifying them.

DECIDING IF THE ANALYSIS OF EXISTING STATISTICS IS APPROPRIATE FOR YOUR TOPIC

Since it is generally a very economical way to carry out research, the use of existing statistics should be given serious consideration. Because census data and other large-scale data cannot be developed by individual researchers, these sources offer valuable assets to all those who are trying to study society. In short, using existing statistics has many advantages. The hard work of data collection and preparation of statistical analyses has already been done for you. What you need to determine is whether the evidence you need has been prepared, where it is available, and how it can be presented in your study. Relating such statistics to your research problems may not be easy. You need to use the statistics appropriately, you must be sensitive to the errors they might contain, and you must discuss them in terms of the units of analysis they represent.

As I have suggested for beginning researchers, existing statistics may best be used for supplementary data in a study. They can serve as an excellent reference for a researcher who wants to gain an overall sense of a field of evidence. In some areas of social research, such as criminology, existing statistics are central. It is probably a good idea, once you have defined a problem, to consider carefully whether there are existing statistics that might be used to study or supplement your research efforts.

USING MULTIPLE METHODS TO STRENGTHEN A RESEARCH DESIGN

This chapter has presented five different types of research methods which use already existing data. Chapters 6 to 8 offered three primary ways to design studies that generate their own data. It is highly advantageous to use *multiple methods* to address any problem. Anderson used interviewing, written material, participant observation, and analyses of written material to develop the comprehensive body of material he used to write his community study of Philadelphia. In many research projects primary research designs involve generating original data, but the projects could be strengthened by also carrying out a content analysis of documents, a secondary analysis of already existing survey data or statistics, or a study of some unobtrusive measures.

In Chapter 8 it was suggested that field research can be strengthened by using the tactic of triangulation to measure phenomena. In other words, multiple measures, both qualitative and quantitative, more effectively zero in on the meaning of a piece of evidence. However, Brewer and Hunter (1989) suggest that the multimethod approach be applied to all stages of the research design. They stress that the multimethod strategy is "to attack a research problem with an arsenal of methods that have nonoverlapping weaknesses in addition to their complementary strengths" (1989, p. 17). They note the advantage of using more than one major research method (field work, survey re-

search, experimentation, or the analysis of existing data) is that the researcher can more thoroughly test the theories underlying the research. Repeating investigations can strengthen (or undermine) a theory; using more than one method to investigate a problem also offers the advantage of an added investigation and employs the corrective features that one method may have over another (1989, p. 48). Another argument strengthening the case for multiple methods is that often the ideal method for studying a problem cannot be employed for strategic, ethical, or economic reasons. In such cases, using multiple methods may better help approximate the ideal method, create realistic alternatives and generalizable evidence, and avoid researcher bias (1989, pp. 52–53).

PROBLEMS TO CONFRONT IN ANALYZING AVAILABLE DATA

In this chapter, five different methods of social research have been presented. These methods not only share the use of already collected data but also require certain common efforts on the part of the researcher regardless of the method. In the first place, the researcher must consider why the data were collected. This issue was raised most directly in historical research, where the data may seem the most obscure. However, it is necessary whenever already collected data are examined that the researcher clearly address the question of why they were collected in the first place: what was the motivation of the person(s) who collected the data?

This is true because all forms of analyzing available data demand a careful consideration of the assumptions underlying the data themselves. Without a consideration of this kind, it will be impossible for you to use the data effectively or know the limits beyond which they cannot be used. In the case of current survey data, you should ask yourself what to make of all the questions. You must not accept the data as given and valuable just because they are available. You must look at them with fresh eyes and try to see them as they are in regard to their strengths and flaws. For content analyses, this task of considering the underlying assumptions must be done before one selects the content to be analyzed. Once the content is selected, these latent concerns give way to a study of the more manifest meaning of the content. In historical research, the examination of the underlying assumptions is often the essence of the historical effort. Finally, in the analysis of existing statistics, you need to consider whether the assumptions of those who built the indicators and set out the statistical findings seem justified.

REVIEW NOTES

- Content analysis is a research technique used to describe in an objective, systematic, and quantified manner the content of a body of communication.
- Ways to describe the content of communication materials include determining (1) frequencies, (2) amount of specific types of content, (3) presence or absence of a quality, (4) typologies and sorting by types, (5) origins or sources, and (6) degree of intensity.
- Content analyses generally require developing a complex means of sorting and coding data in a careful and systematic manner.
- The historical method involves critically examining and analyzing records and other surviving materials from the past.
- History may take for its subject broad, macro-level historical topics, or it may focus on a specific event or person with a micro-level historical approach.
- Unobtrusive measures refer to studies of physical traces, archives, and observations without participation.
- The study of physical traces includes examining the unintentional erosion of products (wear and tear) and the accretion (laying down or building up) of objects of human origin (such as garbage and graffiti).
- The primary aim of unobtrusive measures in a study is to serve as a supplementary source of data.

- Unobtrusive measures avoid errors generated both by the subjects being studied and by the researcher interacting with the subjects.
- Secondary analyses involve carrying out additional analyses beyond those made by the original researcher on already collected data. In sociological journals, secondary analyses are one of the most common forms of research published.
- In selecting a dataset for a secondary analysis, you should consider the quality of the data-gathering organization, the purpose of the original researchers, and whether the primary indicators you need are measured in those data.
- The analysis of existing statistics is a way to study the relationship of different trends in American society, in other societies, and in aggregate bodies within a society.
- The use of multiple methods in a social research project can strengthen its design.

KEY TERMS

accretion measures
aggregate data
archival research
content analysis
contextuality
erosion measures
existing statistics
historiography
history as actuality
history as record
keying
manifest content
multiple methods
oral history
physical traces
primary sources
secondary analysis
secondary sources
unobtrusive measures
verisimilitude

STUDY EXERCISES

1. Give a one-sentence description of each of the five different methods of analyzing available data given in this chapter.

2. Consider the following social issues that emerged in the 1990s.
   a. The crisis in the delivery and cost of health care in the United States
   b. Efforts to dismantle affirmative action
   c. The reappearance of strikes among workers in labor unions

   Either design a study using one of the analyses of available data methods for one of these issues *or* select an appropriate method from the five discussed in this chapter for each of the three issues and defend your choice of method in each case.

RECOMMENDED READINGS

1. Brewer, John, and Albert Hunter: *Multimethod Research: A Synthesis of Styles,* Sage, Newbury Park, CA, 1989. This book makes a strong case for the use of multiple methods in social research projects, addressing its advantages in orienting research and theory to each other.
2. Davis, James A., and Tom W. Smith: *The NORC General Social Survey: A User's Guide,* Sage, Newbury Park, CA, 1991. This guide makes this dataset very accessible.
3. Gottschalk, Louis: *Understanding History: A Primer of Historical Method,* Knopf, New York, 1950. This is an old but very careful and considered discussion of the methods of historical research.
4. Hakim, Catherine: *Secondary Analysis in Social Research: A Guide to Data Sources and Methods with Examples,* Allen & Unwin, London, 1982. A thoughtful introduction to and appraisal of secondary analyses, with extensive suggestions for data sources.
5. Hill, Martin S.: *The Panel Study of Income Dynamics: A User's Guide,* Sage, Newbury Park, CA, 1991. This less detailed guide presents a clear overview of the survey design and content and data preparation and quality.
6. Holsti, Ole R.: *Content Analysis for the Social Sciences and the Humanities,* Addison-Wesley, Reading, MA, 1969. A classic overview of the method.
7. Kiecolt, K. Jill, and Laura E. Nathan: *Secondary Analysis of Survey Data,* Sage, Newbury Park, CA, 1985. This little volume has an excellent compilation of sources for locating datasets as well as research strategies for using existing survey data.
8. Krippendorff, Klaus: *Content Analysis: An Introduction to Its Methodology,* Sage, Beverly Hills, CA, 1980. Written by a professor of communications, this volume covers the conceptualization and design of content analyses as well as analytic techniques (unitizing, sampling, recording, developing constructs) and issues of reliability and validity.
9. Webb, Eugene J., Donald T. Campbell, Richard D. Schwartz, and Lee Sechrest: *Unobtrusive Measures: Nonreactive Research in the Social Sciences,* Rand McNally, Chicago, 1966. This is the central work in the study of unobtrusive measurement. It includes many fertile suggestions for measures.

Evaluation Research, Case Studies, and Other Forms of Applied Research

INTRODUCTION

*I*t is not easy to decide what to cover in a chapter on applied research and evaluation research because the range of types of research carried out under these categories is vast and can employ very different sorts of research methods. *Evaluation research* is not really a different method of doing research; rather, it is research done for a specific purpose: to evaluate some social activity, usually a social program, which has been set up to address and ameliorate a social problem. *Applied social research* refers to any type of research whose findings will be applied to assist, help, change, or enhance a social program or effort. The methods used in applied social research and evaluation research can include any of those described in earlier chapters, including both quantitative and qualitative approaches.

Case studies simply refer to any type of research effort in which the focus is on a single organization, institution, program, event, decision, policy, or group which serves as the case being studied, though sometimes a study comparing a few different cases can form the basis of a *multiple case study*. A *needs assessment* is carried out to determine the types and sources of problems (or needs) that are confronted in a social program or activity so that the organization sponsoring the program can set priorities and make decisions about how those needs should be addressed. *Action research* refers to various types of applied research in which the "subjects" are actively engaged in the research process and the object of the research is to bring about a practical outcome (an action). In this way action research involves a collaboration between the researchers and the organization or program being studied. Case studies, needs assessments, and action research are forms of research that often characterize applied social research and/or evaluation research projects.

We will cover a lot of ground in this chapter; to hold the central core that runs through most of these different types of applied efforts, I will describe the processes of two applied research projects which colleagues of mine at California State University at San Marcos have been carrying out. The first project, under the direction of Sheldon Zhang, is an evaluation of a boot camp for juvenile offenders in Los Angeles County. The second is a study of the cultural competency of a counseling agency under the direction of my colleague Darlene Piña. The second project can be characterized as a *needs assessment;* it is also an example of *action research,* and it is a *case study* of a single agency. From these two examples we will develop more generally the components and designs of evaluation research, needs assessments, action research, and case studies. Finally, we will conclude by briefly considering social indicators research, which has been widely used at the national and international levels to describe (and often evaluate) social problems, issues, and institutions (such as crime, health, schools, and economic factors) as well as to measure community indicators.

AN EVALUATION OF A DRUG TREATMENT BOOT CAMP

Since the early 1980s, certain communities have established boot camps for juvenile offenders who have been convicted of nonviolent crimes. Both politicians and criminal justice practitioners had come to believe that such military-style environments might help "shock" youths into conforming with the norms of society. Boot camps of this type were military-type operations in which the youths would be under the orders of drill sergeants (who were actually probationary staff members) and would be divided into platoons and made to go through the exercises and training typical of military recruits. This regimentation of the military style of discipline as a form of incarceration was an example of "shock incarceration."

Los Angeles County was one of the areas which instituted such camps. The Los Angeles boot camp was a 24-week experience which differed from conventional camps in terms of its military-style atmosphere and training and was followed by a special 10-week aftercare plan which the graduates were strongly encouraged to attend. During the 24-week camp experience, a 15-week drug education program was offered by chemical dependency treatment professionals. In the aftercare program, which emphasized education and vocational and employment assistance, graduates were provided with close supervision, personal counseling, and coordinated services from other community agencies. Another special feature of this program was that parents were carefully integrated into the camp experience and the aftercare component.

My colleague Sheldon Zhang designed an evaluation research study to examine the effects of the Los Angeles boot camp experience. Naturally, his first effort was to examine all the existing evaluation studies of boot camps to determine what was already known about the effects of boot camps, what methods of data collection seemed the most effective, and how to design his study so that it could make a unique contribution to the field. What he designed can be considered a very good example of an evaluation study. Zhang's central objective was to get information on the effectiveness of military-style boot camps as forms of incarceration for youths convicted of serious (though nonviolent) crimes. He wanted to learn how far the boot camp experience would reduce recidivism and help drug users. In addition, he hoped to be able to delineate the qualities and characteristics of successful boot camp graduates.

Zhang's boot camp evaluation had three substudies within it. The first was a *boot camp cohort study* in which an entering group of 120 boot camp members would be interviewed in the first couple of days after they had entered the camp and then would be followed up for six months after they had left the camp. Note that this study has no comparative group of youths who did not have the

boot camp experience. The second substudy was a *comparative postcamp interview study* in which 100 graduates of the boot camp were interviewed one year after leaving the camp and were compared with a group of 100 youths who had gone through a conventional (non-military-style) camp. This postcamp substudy had the advantage of including a comparative (control) group that had not gone through the boot camp experience; however, it did not have any precamp (time 1) measures. The third study was to be based on official record data. It would collect data from the records on 400 graduates of boot camps and compare their recidivism rates and other relevant data to those of a comparison sample of 400 graduates of conventional camps. This would be a *comparative official records study*.

One of the ways in which Zhang's evaluation study would differ from other evaluations of boot camp programs was that two of the substudies would gather self-report data from the members and graduates directly rather than basing recidivism measures purely on official records. (Recall that in Chapter 1, when we discussed Hirschi's classic study of the causes of delinquency, one of the qualities of that study was that the measure of delinquency was based on self-reports.) Since the perpetrators of most criminal activity are not apprehended, official records in no way measure the true degree of such behavior.

One of the major challenges of the comparative postcamp study was to get a matched comparative sample of boot camp graduates and conventional camp graduates. This was the strategy Zhang used. Among the 2,000 graduates of the Los Angeles boot camps, 400 of the earliest graduates who had no prior camp experience (they had not attended another camp at any point in time) were selected. They then were matched with 400 graduates from conventional camps. Only graduates who were males between the ages of 16 and 18 when they went to the camps, had had no prior camp incarceration experience, and had been held for nonviolent and nonsexual offenses were selected from both types of camps. Moreover, graduates from the two camps were matched in terms of the length of time since they had left the camp and their racial and ethnic characteristics. Three ethnic groups were compared: whites, Hispanics, and African-Americans. From those meeting these qualifications, 100 recent boot camp graduates and 100 comparison subjects would be drawn randomly into the study.

The Design of the Boot Camp Cohort Study

Let me describe here in greater detail the plans for the first substudy: the boot camp cohort study. The primary objective of this study was to see what factors would relate to recidivism within a certain period of time after incarceration in a military-style boot camp. The 120 new boot camp recruits would include all the new referrals taken into the boot camp during a five-week period (there were roughly 20 to 25 new recruits each week). Using telephone interviewing as the major form of data collection, interviewers called boot camp entrants within a few days of their arrival at the camp. Six months after graduating from the boot camp, the respondents were reinterviewed, and these questions were asked again to provide pre- and postmeasures.

The interviews measured a number of factors, including (1) measures of self-esteem involving how a respondent related to others, to his family, and to school, (2) a set of items measuring attitudes toward authority, (3) gang activities, (4) drug use, (5) measures of school work and progress, and (6) a self-report delinquency measure. The self-report delinquency measure would be based on 30 items from the International Self-Report Delinquency questionnaire (ISDR), which had been developed by an international team of criminologists from 15 western countries and had been piloted on a sample of detained Los Angeles juvenile offenders which had supported the validity and applicability of its use (Junger-Tas and associates, 1994). The ISDR included measures on the types and frequency of delinquent acts committed during a time period as well as the circumstances of those incidents.

An additional objective of this study was to measure the long-term effects of the drug treatment program offered in the camp. While Zhang could not set up a classical experimental design in which the subjects would be randomly placed in treatment or nontreatment groups, this boot camp cohort study planned to follow a cohort of camp graduates who had been pretested for drug use for a period of six months after leaving the camp in order to measure changes in their drug use. This pre- and posttest longitudinal design with a cohort that had gone through the drug treatment efforts of the camp would be a way to try to determine whether the drug treatment programs had had any ameliorative effects. Again, these measures would be based on self-reports.

Another objective of the study would be to measure the graduates' abilities to integrate and reintegrate themselves into various roles in the community and to examine the role of parents' involvement in fostering a successful return of the boot camp graduates. Lastly, the study would carefully distinguish the characteristics of those graduates who were successful at not recidivating, which might help in better understanding for whom the boot camp experience was most likely to be effective.

FOUR OTHER CLASSIC EXAMPLES OF EVALUATION PROJECTS

To expose you to a broader range of types of research which fall under the heading of evaluation research, I will here describe four different types of evaluation research projects. These four types exemplify commonly used forms of evaluations: an *ex post facto (after-only) experimental design,* in this case applied to the study of a federally funded preschool program; a *cost-benefit analysis,* here applied to mental health treatment covered by Medicaid in a single state; a *community impact assessment* addressed to the potential effects of busing in a particular city; and a *time-series analysis,* using aggregate existing crime data to analyze the effects of a federal gun control act.

An Ongoing Program Evaluation: Head Start

The Head Start program was a federal program initiated in 1965 to offer preschool education to disadvantaged children to help them perform more effectively in school. Numerous evaluations of this program were carried out, but the one that had the greatest effect on social policy-making was the large study developed by the Westinghouse Learning Corporation at Ohio University. The final report of this evaluation, *The Impact of Head Start,* which appeared in 1969, concluded that Head Start had produced only a marginally positive effect on the long-range cognitive abilities (reading readiness and IQ) of the children who had attended full-year Head Start programs and virtually no effect on those who had attended only summer programs. The researchers also concluded that the long-term effects of the program on affective outcomes (such as improved self-esteem and school behavior) were virtually nonexistent.

How had the evaluators reached those conclusions? Since they had been selected as the researchers to study a program which had been in existence for four years, it was not possible for them to assign the children by means of randomization to participate in the program (the experimentals) or not to participate (the controls). Instead, they were obliged to evaluate the effects of the program on those who had already completed their participation and compare those effects with the performance of a group of children who might have participated (in that they shared similar characteristics with those who had participated) but in fact had not done so. (This would be a *nonequivalent control group,* as explained in Chapter 6). Furthermore, the focus was on the long-term effects of Head Start, since children who had already experienced the program and were now in the first, second, or third grade were to be studied. This meant that pretesting was not possible; rather, the experiment would have an *after-only,* or *ex post facto,* design.

Simply described, the researchers selected geographic regions in which Head Start programs had been set up. They then defined two subpopulations of children: those who had attended a Head Start program and those with similar characteristics who had not. From these subpopulations, a sample of attenders was selected (serving as the experimental group), and a sample of nonattenders was drawn from those children who matched the experimental subjects best regarding a number of specific variables (race, sex, socioeconomic status) and whether the child had subsequently attended kindergarten.

Once the samples were selected, data were collected from a number of sources, including interview material from parents, grade school teachers' observations of a child's behavior, and various tests of a child's cognitive abilities and affective qualities. Since Head Start children from across the United States were studied, this project was large and demanding. There were efforts to systematize the data collection procedures by means of careful training of the data collectors.

The analyses of the data were complex and varied. The basic objective of these analyses was to determine whether the experimentals (those who had attended Head Start) performed better than the controls (those who had not attended Head Start) on cognitive and affective factors. As was stated above, the evaluators found modest gains for the experimentals on cognitive factors among those who had attended full-year programs. These gains were greater for black children and for those attending programs in the southeastern United States. (Later analyses of these data, however, challenged these interpretations.)

A Cost-Benefit Analysis: Mental Health Care

The influence of economics has been widely felt in evaluation research. As the support for funding expensive social programs came under greater pressure in the 1970s and 1980s, cost-benefit analyses became a much more popular design for social program evaluation. Very simply, a cost-benefit analysis seeks to assess whether the benefit of a program or social strategy is worth the cost. There can be serious problems with measuring costs and benefits which may not make this approach viable for many types of studies. Naturally, it is most feasible to carry out such a study when the costs of the implementation of what is being studied can be measured in terms of dollars (such measurement is often but not always the case). It is also useful if the benefits can be measured in terms of dollars as well. When this is difficult, proxy measures must be developed to operationalize the benefits.

A cost-benefit analysis of mental health care services provided to the poor in Massachusetts under Medicaid used a comparative model according to which Medicaid recipients were compared to non-Medicaid recipients who also sought mental health services (Davenport and Nuttall, 1979). The Massachusetts Department of Public Welfare was trying to determine which of its varied services was most cost-effective, that is, which of the services produced the greatest positive effect for the lowest cost. First the researchers needed to determine the range of services offered, the costs of the various treatments, and their benefits. The range of services was great, though there were some controls on their variation by policies governing different forms of care. For example, the researchers determined the cost of therapy sessions with various types of mental health personnel both in clinical settings where a range of mental health care professionals offer therapy and in nonclinical settings where only physicians can offer therapy (Davenport and Nuttall, 1979, p. 177).

This first aspect of the evaluation study was simply to describe the range in costs of the various services available and relate them to the services offered (the benefits). These benefits were measured in terms of length of treatment, type of diagnoses, and use of medication. Note that the first of these categories, length of treatment, could easily be translated into dollars, while the other two could not.

The second aspect of the evaluation examined the impact changes in state policies had had on the delivery and cost of services. For example, psychiatrists' fees had been cut. Within six months this led to a drop in reimbursements (amounts paid to doctors) but an increase in claims (more patients were seen). After a year, the reimbursements increased and the number of claims decreased. In another six months the first pattern reappeared. This suggested that the cut in psychiatrists' fees did not bring about the desired drop in the program's costs. Rather, the cut in fees brought about different types of effects (more patients were seen in clinics where the fees were higher; there were some cases of fraud in which psychiatrists used less trained personnel for the therapy sessions but billed the state the psychiatrist-level fees) (1979, p. 179). This second aspect of the evaluation design required an analysis of existing records as part of the design. Box 10-1 on page 306 describes the policy implications of a cost-benefit evaluation of long-term care programs.

A Community Impact Assessment: A School Busing Program

The cost-benefit model for evaluation research assumes that containing costs while trying to maximize benefits is in everyone's interest. This suggests that individuals consider each situation from a *utilitarian* point of view and decide where their benefits lie. Allen and Sears (1979, p. 172) suggest that socialization theory would offer a different view of how people orient themselves to particular social situations. In this view, individuals are affected by values and attitudes which are adopted in childhood and are resistant to change.

Controversial social policies, such as busing to achieve racial integration, require community support. One form of evaluation research, *community impact assessment,* can be used to try to determine what effect a new policy might have on a community. Impact assessment studies often are based on surveys where the attitudes of those who might be affected by a program are gathered and related to other characteristics of the respondents.

BOX 10-1

THE POLICY IMPLICATIONS OF COST-BENEFIT STUDIES

In an experimental study of the cost-effectiveness of community-based health services in Georgia for a sample of low-income (eligible for Medicaid) elderly, Skellie, Mobley, and Coan found that although the experimental group that received the community-based care spent fewer days in nursing homes and lived longer, its care (both Medicaid and Medicare expenses) cost more than that of the control group.

But when the experiment focused only on clients who were more at risk for entering a nursing home (those who were less able to care for themselves), their care cost less than that of the control group. Hence, the authors stress that in studies of cost-effectiveness of alternative health services, it is critical that the target population be screened so that those most in need of the services have access to them. It is when they are provided to this most needy group that such alternative services will be most cost-effective.

Data from F. Albert Skellie, G. Melton Mobley, and Ruth E. Coan, "Cost Effectiveness of Community-Based Long-Term Care: Current Findings of Georgia's Alternative Health Services Project," *American Journal of Public Health*, **72**:353–358, 1982.

For example, in a telephone survey of the attitudes of a random sample of Los Angeles residents, Allen and Sears (1979) found that opposition to busing (the dependent variable) was much more strongly related to racial intolerance and political conservatism than to the respondent's specific self-interest. The researchers thus challenged the notion that individuals respond to social policies on the basis of rational considerations of what they have to gain or lose (1979, p. 175).

A Time-Series Analysis: The Effects of Gun Legislation

Laws are forms of social policies which carry punishments if they are infringed. The problem with some laws is that they are difficult to enforce; in such cases there is always the fear that if they are widely abused and ignored, contempt for the law will grow. In 1968, responding in particular to the assassination of Robert Kennedy, Congress enacted the Gun Control Act. Its object was to control the use of handguns by outlawing the importation of firearms except for sporting purposes, restrict interstate traffic in firearms and ammunition, and forbid certain categories of persons from using them.

What Zimring (1976) set out to evaluate was whether in fact the Gun Control Act had reduced the use of handguns in violent crimes. How could one measure the effects of the law itself? One way to examine the impact of the legislation would be to look at indicators of what should have changed as a result of the new legislation. One indicator Zimring used was the number of guns imported into the United States. He was able to show a sharp increase in the importation of handguns into the United States from 1964 to 1968, followed after 1968 by a drop in handgun imports, which remained quite steady from 1969 to 1973. Since the new law is the independent variable in this study, measures of its short-term specific effects (reduction in gun importation) validate the claim that the law brought about some of its expected consequences.

To study the long-term effects of this legislative initiative requires a focus on what a reduction in handguns might lead to: a reduction in criminal acts related to the use of guns. Zimring could examine this by using the years before and after the legislation as a measure of the effect of the legislation. Then, using a *time-series analysis* of aggregate data from the law enforcement agencies, Zimring examined whether there was a shift in the amount of crime related to handguns after the legislation. (Refer to Chapter 6 for a discussion of time-series analysis as a form of quasi-experimental design.) To compare the short-term and long-term effects of this law, Zimring drew up graphs to show the proportion of crime related to handguns and how it changed after the introduction of the Gun Control Act. (It should be noted that firearm assaults include those related both to handguns and to other types of guns, though about 80 percent of the firearms used in assaults are handguns.)

The proportion of crimes (homicides and assaults) carried out with handguns peaked shortly after the legislation was enacted and then leveled off (though it continued to rise very slowly). Zimring offers various suggestions for why the law was not more effective. One factor was that it actually led to the use of other types of weapons ("Saturday night specials"), which came to replace some of the illegal types of guns.

COMPONENTS OF AN EVALUATION RESEARCH PROJECT

Clarify the Purpose

Evaluation research usually is carried out at the request of someone else (who also covers the cost). It is that someone who must define the purpose of the research. However, the decision makers who are requesting the study may not have defined their purpose clearly. Your first job as an evaluator is to help them do this. Only then can you begin your study.

Carol Weiss (1972, p. 12) suggests a number of reasons why an evaluation may be sought. First, it may be required to fulfill a contract or grant commitment (many publically funded programs must include an *evaluation component*). Second, the evaluation may be a kind of delaying tactic or a way to shift responsibility or get favorable publicity for the program (Weiss, 1972, p. 11). In other words, the people requesting the evaluation may be interested in having it done not to find out how effective their program is but instead to use the evaluation effort to alter the political situation in the organization. These ulterior motives can deeply affect a researcher's ability to clarify the purpose of an evaluation.

One good way to get at the purpose is to consider for whom the study is being done. Weiss suggests seven potential utilizers of the results (1972, p. 18): (1) a funding organization, (2) a national agency, (3) a local agency, (4) the project directors, (5) the staff of the project, (6) the program's clients, and (7) researchers and other learned individuals who may use the findings of this project to further research in other studies. Note, for example, that if the primary users are the staff, the *inputs* to the program (what is being offered) may need to be closely considered; if the clients are the primary users, the *outputs* of the program may be the primary focus of the evaluation.

One commonly used means for differentiating types of evaluations is that developed first by Scriven (1967) to evaluate educational programs—that is, to differentiate between *formative evaluations,* which set out to study a program in process and where the information will be "plowed back" into the program to reform it as it is being administered, and *summative evaluations,* which summarize the effects of a program after it is completed. What this distinction does is focus the attention of the evaluator on different aspects of the program being evaluated, set a timing perspective on the evaluation, and determine how firm and conclusive the findings of the evaluation can be.

In a formative evaluation, the focus is on the dynamic process of the program itself: it is the study of an ongoing system of social interaction. The time dimension in a formative evaluation is the present. Final conclusions cannot be drawn about the effectiveness of the program; rather, the evaluation must make proposals directed toward improving the ongoing operation of the program (or possibly aborting it). In a summative evaluation, the focus is on the program as a completed entity. The time frame is the past. Conclusions can be drawn. Here the purpose of the conclusions may be to advise others about the effectiveness of this particular program, to suggest its weaknesses and problems as well as its strengths and accomplishments.

Establish the Dependent Variable

As in most types of social research, the evaluator needs to hone in on precisely what he or she will be looking for. What should the program have accomplished? What were its ends, its goals? In the Head Start evaluation, the dependent variables were cognitive abilities and affective qualities. The expected variation was that those who had attended Head Start would have made greater gains in cognitive (intellectual) and affective (emotional) readiness than those who had not. In the mental health care study, the dependent variable was based on the services offered (measured in terms of number of visits, types of diagnoses, etc.). In the community impact study, the dependent variable was opposition to busing (or its converse, support for busing). In the gun legislation evaluation, there were a number of dependent variables: the number of crimes committed with handguns, the number of handguns imported, etc.

Weiss warns that the choice of the evaluation goals, the dependent variable(s) in the study, should be considered in the light of their practicality, to whom they are important, and whether they are short-term or long-term goals (1972, pp. 30–31). Selecting an impractical dependent variable may make the results of the evaluation of little use. Considering who will use the findings and, among those who will use it, who the most important users are likely to be is a way of addressing the political implications of evaluation research. If the program directors need information on what to do at the present time, short-term goals are critical. All these considerations require that the researcher work out the final goals, the dependent variables, with those who will be using the evaluation (Weiss, 1972, p. 31).

These dependent variables will generally be the outputs of the program (in an impact assessment study they would be the likely impact of a supposed new policy). Although they are rarely easy to define, they may be even more difficult to operationalize. Note that in the mental health study, what would seem to be the true output is improving the mental health of the patients. Since

this is so difficult to ascertain, the output indicators become measures of the services themselves (which supposedly are indicators of improved mental health). In Lawmann's survey of sexual behavior, the dependent variables were types and frequency of sexual activity. In the busing impact study, the dependent variable was based on a five-item scale of opposition to busing.

If the dependent variable is unreliable, if its validity is doubtful, this may throw the whole evaluation into doubt. For this reason, it is critical to be careful in conceptualizing the dependent variable and developing a means of measuring it. Weiss (1972, pp. 34–39) offers some suggestions for developing the outcome indicators (the dependent variables in the evaluation). If the outcomes are attitudes, it may be wise to consider using already developed attitudinal scales which have been tried out in other studies. The track record of such measures will include evidence on the range of probable responses, the likelihood that persons will change their responses easily (an issue of reliability), and the question of whether the measures are actually related to other factors that would seem probable (an issue of validity). Another way to strengthen the measurement of outcomes is to develop multiple measures. As Weiss states, "By the use of a number of measures, each contributing a different facet of information, we can limit the effect of irrelevancies and develop a more rounded and truer picture of program outcomes" (1972, p. 36). When the true goals of what is being evaluated will be realized only in the future, it is difficult to select indicators for measuring the outcome. Weiss suggests that in such cases only proximate measures can be developed (1972, pp. 37–38). Such measures should represent intermediate goals, outcomes which seem to be propitious for the long-term goal.

Determine the Independent Variables

Independent variables are the inputs to the program being studied. In most evaluation studies, what is being evaluated (the social intervention program, for example) is itself the independent variable. In experimental design studies, where a program is being evaluated, being "in the program" is the primary independent variable (this would be true of the Head Start experiment). In such a case, operationalization is easy: the experimental group is in the program, the control group is not. Even in studies where membership serves as the major independent variable, other qualities and characteristics of the program may be included as input variables.

In some evaluations, other types of independent variables are used. In the opposition-to-busing evaluation, the independent variables included measures of the self-interest of Los Angeles residents as well as measures of general attitudes toward racial toleration and political conservatism (Allen and Sears, 1979, p. 173). In the mental health evaluation, personal characteristics of the patients (age, sex, race), the location of their treatment (clinical or nonclinical), and their ability to pay (Medicaid or private patients) were related to the dependent variables of length of treatment, di-

agnosis, and types of therapy received (Davenport and Nuttall, 1979, p. 178). Box 10-2 offers Weiss's suggestions for developing input measures for an evaluation research design.

Set Up the Research Design

Once you have clarified your dependent and independent variables, you are ready to lay out the design of your study. In an experiment, you need to determine what type of control group will be necessary (and what type is feasible). Should it be a group which is not exposed to the program or a group exposed to a variant of the program? Do you need to be worried about Hawthorne effects? (If so, you may need two control groups, one exposed to some type of program but not the one you are studying and the other not exposed to any program.) Are there other characteristics of the experimental or control groups that need to be controlled?

BOX 10-2

SUGGESTED INPUT MEASURES FOR AN EVALUATION PROJECT

Among possible input measures of the program to be evaluated, Weiss includes the following: (1) *purpose* of the program, (2) *principles* of the program, (3) *methods* used in the program, (4) *staffing* of the program, (5) *persons served* by the program, (6) *length of service* provided by the program, (7) *location* of the program, (8) *size* of the program, (9) under whose *auspices* the program is being offered, and (10) *management* of the program (1972, p. 46).

Weiss goes on to suggest that if persons are being put through the program and the effect of the program on those persons is of primary interest, characteristics of the clients themselves can be considered input variables. She proposes the following 11 factors to be measured regarding the persons being served by the program: (1) age, (2) sex, (3) socioeconomic status, (4) race, (5) length of residence in the community, (6) attitude toward the program, (7) motiva-

tion for participating in the program, (8) aspirations relevant to the general objectives of the program, (9) expectations of what they hope to achieve as a result of participating in the program, (10) attitude of other family members about the program, and (11) degree of support from other family members concerning the hoped-for outcomes of participating in the program (pp. 46–47).

Finally, Weiss cautions that the comprehensiveness of these lists should not encourage you to go out and measure everything. Analyzing data is time-consuming and demanding. If you have too many variables, you may get submerged in the details and find it difficult to concentrate on what is of central significance.

Source: Carol H. Weiss, *Evaluation Research*, Prentice Hall, Englewood Cliffs, NJ, 1972.

If randomization in the assignment of subjects to groups is feasible (which it often is not), it should be done. The statistical test you will be likely to use to compare the experimental group to the control group can be used appropriately only if there has been randomization in assignment. For an experiment, you need to consider whether a pretest is possible. Remember that the point of a pretest is to determine a baseline against which the effects of the program (the independent variable) can be compared. In many experimental designs for evaluation, a pretest cannot be carried out before the experiment. In the Berkowitz and Geen experiment on the effects of mass media violence, you may recall from Chapter 6, there were preexperiment measurements of the mood of the subjects against which postexperiment measurements of moods could be compared.

Specify the Control Variables

If you are carrying out a survey, you will need to consider variables both antecedent to the independent variable and intervening between the independent and dependent variables which may affect the direct relationship between the input and output variables. Drawing a diagram of the potential relationships between all the variables is a good way to try out all the possible design strategies.

A part of the design will be to specify all other factors which you think may affect the evaluation of the program or event to be studied. Can you measure these factors effectively? You may want both to test whether these other factors make a difference to the outcome measures (does sex or race make a difference?) and to control for these other factors by excluding them or making them equivalent between comparison groups. In the evaluation of a social program, you may need to consider situational factors which characterize the environment but are not of primary concern in your study. Might they affect the results? Can they be controlled?

Ethical Implications and Political Impact

Evaluations using experiments where some people are exposed and others are not exposed to a social program may raise many questions of fairness. Are the people who need the program getting it? In many cases, assignment based on randomization to experimental and control groups cannot be carried out for ethical reasons. In this case (recall from Chapter 6) various types of quasi-experimental designs may be used. Furthermore, the use of records, interviewing techniques, and the treatment of subjects in the study may all raise ethical considerations which need to be addressed carefully in designing the evaluation.

Most evaluations have some political impact on those who will use the findings. If you suggest that changes be made, some will come to a defense of the program and try to have your study ignored. Conversely, others may take up your findings to fight their own causes, which may in some cases be ones that your study would not advocate. Box 10-3 describes ways in which evaluations can be resisted. Most people do not like to be evaluated, and so you must be prepared to face efforts to contain your research in the beginning and to bury the findings once the study is done. The better the evaluator understands the political situation of the program or agency being evaluated, the better she or he will be able to consider ways of carrying out the evaluation.

The other common drawback with the use of the findings is that they may not be used at all. As Weiss aptly puts it, those who do the evaluations are often academics who may lack appreciation of the mundane considerations that those being evaluated want to know. The evaluator may try to ferret out the most profound and academically interesting findings from the study and ignore many practical aspects of the study which would be of greater interest (and possibly greater use) to the program staff (1972, p. 111). The staff may also need more specific conclusions and suggestions than the evaluator feels confident to make (Weiss,

BOX 10-3

**WAYS PROGRAM EVALUATION
MAY BE RESISTED**

Posavac and Carey suggest eight forms of resistance to program evaluation studies that must be considered in the planning stage of the study so that the researchers will be ready to address opposition. These problems include (1) program directors' expectations that the evaluation will show a "slam-bang" effect, which may make them unreceptive to negative or weak findings, (2) fear that the evaluation of the program will inhibit innovative changes, (3) fear of program termination, (4) fear of information abuse, (5) fear that the subjective benefits of the program will be ignored after the arrival of quantitative data, (6) fear that evaluation costs drain resources, (7) fear of loss of control over the program, and (8) fear that the evaluation will have little impact.

Source: Emil J. Posavec and Raymond G. Carey, *Program Evaluation: Methods and Case Studies,* 3d ed., Prentice Hall, Englewood Cliffs, NJ, 1989, pp. 39–42.

1972, p. 111), but without the specific recommendations, the evaluation report may be ignored. The agency may have no one able to fully understand the research findings in the evaluation study (no one who has had a good research methods course). For this reason, the evaluator may need not only to do the evaluation but also to *sell* the results to those for whom it was done (Weiss, 1972, p. 113).

DESIGNING AN EVALUATION RESEARCH PROJECT

The types of designs for evaluation research can be loosely grouped as *experimental* designs and *nonexperimental* designs. Whichever type your study follows, considerations of the time frame of the study and the types of subjects to be studied are important. The design must be considered in terms of its validity: is the *real* effect going to be measured?

Experimental Designs

Chapter 6 offered a comprehensive overview of the types and qualities of experimental designs. Here we will discuss how to determine whether what you are trying to evaluate can be studied by an experimental design. Remember that for a true experiment you need randomization of the subjects between experimental and control groups. Some experiments are able to randomly assign subjects to the experimental and control groups; the Head Start evaluation carried out by the Westinghouse research organization was not. If the experiment is set up before the program begins, the evaluation can be preprogramed. In such a case, the experimental design would be set up and built into the intervention program itself. In the Head Start evaluation, the study was retrospective; the experimental subjects had experienced the program two to five years before the evaluation was made. In this case, a comparison group of subjects to serve as controls had to be developed. This meant that the Head Start evaluation was an ex post facto, or after-only, design with a comparison group. (Strictly speaking, then, the Head Start evaluation would not qualify either as a quasi-experimental design, in which data from before the program might be used to study the program effects in a time-series fashion, or as a nonequivalent control group design, in which preprogram measures were available.)

With a true experimental or a quasi-experimental design, selection of subjects and controls before exposure to the program is needed. Usually preprogram indicators are needed (though sometimes they may be available to be measured after the evaluation has begun; for example, prior school grades or earlier test scores might be available for that purpose).

Nonexperimental Designs

Nonexperimental designs include experimental design studies which fail to meet the criteria for experiments as well as other types of designs. Examples would be surveys which assess the effects of a program or the potential impact of a proposed policy, the analysis of available data related to the imposition of a new law or social practice, and a cost-benefit analysis of the relationship between the inputs and outcomes of a program. In these cases, both the *time dimension* and the *basis for comparison* need to be fully considered.

The Time Dimension. Every evaluation study has a primary focus in terms of time. It may focus on the past (the Head Start project), the future (the busing impact study), or the present (the mental health cost-benefit study). Whatever the primary focus, some concern about the relevance of the past needs to be taken into account. In surveys, information about background characteristics is often needed, frequently in terms of family origin (social class, ethnicity, number of parents present, employment status of parents, number of siblings) or other demographic factors, such as sex, race, and size and location of hometown (urban, suburban, rural). The validity of retrospective measures must always be questioned. While nearly everyone can indicate the hometown and other basic characteristics of family origin, many cannot fully recall attitudes that may have been held in the past or reactions to experiences that have been undergone.

Projections about the future must also be cautiously weighed. First, there must be a very careful operationalization of variables to measure projections about the future. (For example, in the literature on career aspirations among youth, there is a clear distinction between aspirations, which indicate hopes, and expectations, which imply plans and more realistic appraisals. In addition, there is variation in the degree of commitment—a measure of motivation—to future hopes and plans.) Sec-

ond, evaluation projects which conclude with recommendations must focus on the future. But to project suggestions for the future requires not only that you consider what the likely fate of the program you are studying will be but also that you consider the social and political context in which this program will operate.

A Comparative Baseline. Evaluation studies need some form of comparative basis for determining whether what is being evaluated is a success or a failure. This is a major reason why experimental designs are popular for evaluations, since the control group offers a solid comparative baseline in such designs. (You must remember of course that only control groups in which the members have been assigned to the group by randomization offer a true experimental basis of comparison.)

Other types of nonexperimental studies tend to use comparative bases as well. The comparisons are usually between the subjects' experiences: an example from the evaluations we have cited was being on Medicaid or not. Comparisons may also be made in time, from before and after what is being evaluated: the gun control act study was of this kind. Most time-series studies, in fact, use as their primary comparative base a before-and-after comparison in measuring trends thought to be affected by the input being studied.

Probably the weakest example of a comparative base was the community impact opposition-to-busing study: here comparisons could be made only on the basis of certain characteristics of the sample (such as having or not having school-age children, which would presumably affect level of interest in the issue). Other background characteristics of subjects, such as age and educational attainment, are also often used for comparative purposes; for example, the busing evaluation found that the age and education of the residents were related to their attitudes. These factors were then used comparatively to assess differences in the potential impact of busing.

Will Your Design Lead to the Real Effect That Must Be Evaluated?

Let's say you have set out the components of the study and put them into a research design, paying appropriate attention to the time frame of the study and the comparisons which you will be able to make. It is now the moment to review your design and consider seriously whether it will accomplish what you need to do and evaluate what you need to evaluate.

A good way to review this question is to think again about precisely who the persons or organizations are, the effects on whom you are trying to measure. Weiss (1972, pp. 39–42) delineates four possible *primary recipients* of the effects of what you are trying to evaluate: the persons to be served, the agencies or organizations offering the services, larger systems (such as public education or mental health), and the general public. Let's consider an evaluation study we have described in terms of who is primarily affected. The boot camp quasi-experiment focused its primary attention on those persons who had been consigned to boot camps (the persons being treated). The mental health study in Massachusetts had as the primary recipient the mental health agencies in that state—how effectively (in terms of cost) services were provided, in which types of settings, and with which types of personnel.

The Zhang evaluation of the Los Angeles boot camps was also directed both to the needs of Los Angeles County and to the criminal justice research community.

Finally, the community impact assessment study of opposition to busing and the gun control act evaluation were both examples of trying to measure effects on the general public. In the busing study, the public is any community which might be ordered to set up a system of busing to achieve racial integration of the schools. The gun control act evaluation also specified the public (that is, anyone who might become the victim of a crime committed with the use of a handgun) as the primary recipient. Once you have decided who or

what is being primarily affected in your study, you should go through every aspect of your research design to be sure that what you are planning to do will produce the type of evidence needed to measure how strong the effect is.

ASSESSING CULTURAL COMPETENCY IN A COMMUNITY COUNSELING CENTER

The project was launched when Darlene Piña, a sociologist, met with the administrators of a community counseling agency which offered different types of counseling and resource information to families in the greater San Diego County area. For ease of reference and to maintain the confidentiality of the agency, we will call this agency the Center for Family Counseling (CFC). The motivation for the meeting arose from both Piña's desire to set up a collaborative research project with a community service agency so that she could introduce our first set of master's degree students to applied research and because the agency felt that it needed to work on its "cultural competency" given the characteristics and needs of its clients. What will be related here is the planning process for the study, the characteristics of the research design, and the way in which this effort exemplifies a needs assessment, an action research project, and a case study. Since the use of focus groups was the primary means of data collection, we will examine them carefully.

The Planning Process

At the first meeting Darlene Piña had with administrators at the agency, they informed her that they had a need to better understand and improve the "cultural competency" of their organization. Given the cultural diversity of the population in Southern California, in which Latinos and Latinas make up a sizable proportion of the population, some of the staff members at CFC were bilingual and some of the programs offered by CFC were designed specifically for Latino and Latina clients and were held in Spanish. However, there was some concern on the part of the agency that its efforts to serve the diverse cultural needs of the community were not fully successful and needed to be improved. There was also a sense of separation between the Latino staff and the non-Latino staff.

Because the agency took in a number of graduate student interns each year and offered them a preparatory workshop, Piña was asked to offer a half-day workshop on "cultural competency" for these incoming student interns. This type of public presentation helped establish her credentials and expertise at the agency and served as a good way for her to begin to build a relationship with the agency before the initiation of the research project. Clearly, it is essential for applied researchers to form positive relationships with the agencies and organizations they study.

The next and very critical step was to meet with the agency's manager most responsible for the research and development (R&D) aspects of the agency. In the case of CFC, this was the director of research and development. He laid out to Piña how the agency had defined cultural competency and provided her with literature on the issue and with the ten goals of the agency (which included trying to improve its "cultural competency").

It was at the meeting with this director that Piña developed the basic plan for the project which would be carried out. Once the plan was formed, she was asked to bring it to the executive committee of the agency with the R&D director. Once their clearance was gained, the executive committee determined the three-member subcommittee which would help Piña set up the final research design. It was this subcommittee that helped with the selection of the three subprograms that would be studied. Piña then met with the managers of those three programs to learn about the issues they faced so that she could begin to figure out how she would select a sample of their staff members and clients for the study. Clearly, Piña's research was to involve agency staff and clients as integral parts of the project. In

so doing, it was an example of *action research* (see Box 10-4).

Were All the Administrators at CFC Enthusiastic about the Proposed Study?   Clearly not. Piña's experiences here were like those of many who have gone into the field to study social agencies. At the most positive end, one of the program directors was truly enthusiastic about the project. This person made himself available to Piña, returned her phone calls, and invited her to speak to his staff, in short, opened doors for her. At the other end, some of the program directors at CFC were skeptical about the project and the topic and expressed cynicism that such a study could have any positive effects. Their reactions to Piña included not returning telephone calls, being unavailable to her, and generally treating the project very pessimistically. In the middle, some of CFC staff members seemed lukewarm about the project. An example was a director with a largely Latina staff who herself seemed not to understand "cultural competency." However, she returned calls and was not overly negative about Piña's efforts.

What can a researcher do to work with staff members who don't really want the project being proposed? Piña tried to present her project as one that would be for the organization. She presented herself as a collaborator with the agency; she tried to align her own schedule so that she could be available to the agency according to its time schedules. When talking to the most negative program director, Piña tried to "sell" her study as being important for the clients and as a way to make the work of the staff easier. She asked a lot of questions and took notes on what the program director stated. In no way did she want to pose as an expert from the university who might expose them; instead, she presented herself as working for them.

Meanwhile, Piña needed to figure out how to bring the graduate students from Cal State San Marcos into the project as coresearchers. The students who were first drawn into the project were enrolled in a seminar on community and family Piña was offering in this first term of our newly

BOX 10-4

ACTION RESEARCH

Action research is community-based research in which those who are being studied (the subjects) participate actively in the design and execution of the study (the research process). The objective of action research is to enhance the lives and social communities of individuals by helping them figure out what strategies might be effective in confronting the issues and problems they face. This style of research is very much a response to widespread criticism of social research (by feminists, postmodern theorists, etc.) that stated that the results of most community studies were not helpful to those being studied because the research that led to the results had been developed by experts outside the community, was imposed on the community, and was therefore not responsive to or inclusive of the needs and realities of the community members.

Action research seeks to remedy these problems by converting the role of the researcher into that of a facilitator. As Stringer (1996) defines it, community-based action research stems from the efforts of researchers to approach their studies of communities (which are often evaluations) in "a more democratic, empowering, and humanizing" (p. 9) way. Thus the researcher tries to engage the subjects in the research process by having those who would be studied become part of the research team in designing, carrying out, and interpreting the meaning of the results of the study. In this way, not only is the research inclusive and fair to those being studied by taking their perspectives in full account, the results of the research should be liberating and help enhance their lives (p. 10).

This means that community-based action research is collaborative by encouraging people to study their own community problems as they conceive them, interpret the meaning of those problems by using the most advanced methods to analyze their situations, and then devise ways to deal with and address their problems

(Stringer, 1996, p. 15). Stringer sees action research as a set of interacting spirals in which observation, thinking, and acting keep building on each other and encouraging more observations, more interpretations, and new forms of actions (1996, p. 17). He stresses that the types of relationships researchers and community members build need to be based on equality and should avoid conflicts and attempt to resolve conflicts through cooperation and sensitivity to the perspectives of others so that harmony can be achieved (1996, p. 26).

Action research needs to have an organizational base; it has to be steered by appropriate operating principles which will make possible the providing of support and the monitoring of the research process so that the action team can reach decisions (Stringer, 1996, p. 129). A very nonhierarchical organizational model is proposed, with one facilitator and three teams led by team coordinators whose roles might be very different within the different teams. The teams should be self-managing and should set out their own agendas and objectives. The research facilitator should encourage teams to interact with each other regularly so that they can share ideas and strengthen the overall sense of community (Stringer, 1996, p. 133). Stringer suggests that facilitators use inclusive forms of expression (*we*, not *you/they*), and maximize openness in decision making, trying to keep everyone informed and "in the loop," and that facilitators and team coordinators encourage team members to be reflective and not offer critical or judgmental opinions but instead advise and assist, providing information that can keep the members committed to and encouraged about the research (1996, pp. 134–137). Finally, once a research project is complete, the research team should take the occasion to celebrate its achievements, which will further continuing community-based efforts (1996, pp. 140–141).

Source: Ernest T. Stringer: *Action Research: A Handbook for Practitioners,* Sage, Thousand Oaks, CA, 1996.

established master's degree program in sociological practice. The design of our graduate program would require most of the students to carry out a field placement in a human services organization and on the basis of that experience set up and carry out an applied research project in that field. Thus the research project Piña was about to initiate at CFC would be an excellent training ground for meeting the objectives of our new graduate program because it would offer graduate students first hand experience in an applied social research project.

The Research Design for Studying Cultural Competency at CFC

The definition of the problem to be studied had been set by the agency itself; it wanted to better understand and address the degree to which it had the "cultural competency" to serve its clients effectively. In her meeting with the director of R&D, it became clear to Piña that the director was familiar with the literature on cultural competency. Piña suggested that a good method to use for coming to understand what both the clients and the staff thought about the cultural competency of CFC could be determined by carrying out *focus groups* (see Chapter 7).

Because the aim of the research was to assess the needs of the agency to improve its cultural competency, this would be an exploratory needs assessment. In short, it was unclear what the current level of cultural competency was at CFC; whether the staff, the administrators, and the clients agreed on what that level of competency was; and what factors were considered relevant to understanding this issue. Thus, all the players (both clients and staff) needed to be heard. The R&D director strongly believed that the clients should be interviewed first.

From this information and from the literature on this topic, Piña prepared a research proposal, which she took to the executive committee. Such a proposal also could have been used to seek outside funding. Out of the meeting with the executive committee, a planning subcommittee was formed to assist in the preparation of the study. It included the R&D director; the director of clinical services, who was a psychologist; and the assistant executive director of the agency. With the help of this subcommittee, decisions were made about which programs within the agency would be studied, how the sampling would be done, what kinds of issues the focus groups would address, and how the clients and staff would be invited or requested to participate in the study.

Setting Up the Focus Groups

The first challenge was to figure out a good way to invite (entice) clients to attend the focus group. Piña and two of the graduate students went to the last night session of one of the programs to be studied: a parenting class. They explained the objectives of their study, passed out flyers explaining the study, and offered a $15 incentive to participate in a focus group interview. Then they went to another program group. In all, five focus groups with clients would be carried out, two in English and three in Spanish. Because of the large number of Latino and Latina clients, Piña included a number of Latina graduate students as participants in the focus groups.

To invite the staff to participate in the staff focus groups, Piña went to a staff meeting. In addition, letters were sent out to staff members with times and dates requesting that the staff RSVP. Through this process three staff focus groups were carried out; a fourth had to be canceled when too few staff members showed up for it. Finally, one focus group was set up for managers, who were sent letters that were followed up by telephone calls.

Developing the Focus Group Questions.   Piña worked with her students, taking ideas both from the meetings she had had with the staff at CFC and from readings on cultural competency to prepare the questions for the focus groups. Box 10-5 presents the questions used in the client focus groups,

BOX 10-5

CLIENT FOCUS GROUP QUESTIONS

1. Think back to when you first started coming to CFC.
   - What did you expect it to be like?
   - What did you expect from the counselors/teachers?
2. Where are you from, and how long have you lived in this area?
   - What do you look for in a counselor/teacher?
3. In what ways has CFC met your expectations and not met your expectations?
4. What has happened at CFC that has been the most helpful and least helpful?
   - In what ways was this helpful? (meaningful, useful, relevant, validating, responsive)
   - In what ways was this not helpful? (not meaningful, useful, or relevant, stereotyping, stigmatizing, disrespectful)
5. How do you know when your counselors/teachers understand you?
   - Give examples of when a counselor/teacher can really relate to your experiences.

- How much is the counselor aware of cultural considerations? (problems of immigration, citizenship, your values, etc.)
- Can you tell us about a time when you felt misunderstood by your counselor/teacher?
- Can you tell us about a time when you felt respected by your counselor/teacher?

6. How comfortable does your counselor seem in working with you?
   - How does your counselor react when you speak Spanish?
   - How does your counselor react to the way you talk, dress, ask questions?
   - Does this depend on whether the counselor/teacher is the same ethnicity as (or a different ethnicity from) you?
   - What would you like your counselors/teachers to know about you?
7. What changes or suggestions would you like to recommend to CFC?

and Box 10-6 presents the questions used in the staff focus groups.

First let's consider the client questions. Clients were asked to consider different time frames (when they first came to CFC compared to the present); they were asked to consider their range of reactions to the services offered by CFC, from those which were most helpful to those which were least helpful. (Note the tendency to try to get the participants to make comparisons by asking for their reactions at the extremes: the most helpful and the least helpful.)

The questions explored cultural understanding by asking clients to appraise whether the staff at CFC understood various aspects of their cultural situations. They probed for the types of misunderstandings that had occurred and, conversely, for times when the client had felt respected. Then they

explored the clients' perspectives on how comfortable the CFC staff was with them. Lastly, they asked for recommendations for change.

For the staff focus groups they developed questions about how the staff members defined cultural competency and what they understood it entailed and asked for examples of how culturally competent (or incompetent) behaviors and attitudes arose in concrete situations. They also requested the types of information the staff members might need to better understand and serve their clients. They also tried to probe critical incidents, for example, when a staff member was surprised at, confused by, or unclear about some aspect of a client's cultural background.

They also probed how far the staff members could see a fit (or a lack of fit) between the information they offered clients and the clients' experience.

BOX 10-6

STAFF FOCUS GROUP QUESTIONS

1. Where are you from, and how long have you lived in this area? How long have you been a staff member of CFC? What programs have you worked in?

2. In your opinion, what is *cultural competency*? Create a vision of cultural competency in action. What does it look like?

3. What specific *knowledge* would help you meet your clients' needs? What would you like to know about your clients?

CULTURAL CONSIDERATIONS

4. Describe the times when you have felt curious (surprised) (unclear) about or confused by the behavior of clients from a cultural background different from your own.

5. Can you tell us about times when cultural differences got in the way and times when they helped the situation?

6. How can you tell when the information you present to your clients fits their experience and does not fit their experience? (relevant, useful, meaningful)

7. What skills are needed to handle a situation in a culturally appropriate manner? What do you think is the *most helpful* and the *least helpful* in cross-cultural relationships?

8. When *dealing with differences*, how do you "walk in someone else's shoes"? (relate, understand, respect)

9. How do you find *similarities* between yourself and your diverse clients?

10. What changes or *suggestions* would you like to recommend to CFC?

Asking the staff to delineate which skills were the most and the least useful in promoting cross-cultural relations led to the question of what it meant for them to "walk in someone else's shoes." This was followed by asking the staff members to find similarities between themselves and their clients. Note here how the questions move from the more impersonal—how well their information fit the needs and interests of the clients—to the more personal—whether the staff could "walk in someone else's shoes," that is, how close the staff felt to the client population. The focus group with the staff ended by requesting suggestions for changes the agency might make.

How the Focus Groups Were Carried Out. Each focus group had a moderator and a comoderator. A group consisted of four to eight participants. Piña was the moderator of the three-client focus groups that were carried out in English, and one of the Latina students, Maria, who had been born and raised in Mexico, carried out the two Spanish-speaking interviews. Piña moderated the three staff and the one managers' focus groups. Various students served as comoderators of the different client focus groups.

The focus groups were held in a room at the center that had an oblong table. The moderator would sit in the middle of a side of the table, and the comoderator would sit at one end with a tape recorder. The comoderator would make sure the taping was going effectively and occasionally would take notes as well. Piña and Maria (who moderated the Spanish-speaking focus groups) struggled with how much structure they should impose on the group discussions. Should they ask a set of questions in order, or should they let the discussion move in a more unstructured way? In the beginning they tended to follow the more structured approach, but over time they came to feel that a more unstructured approach led to richer, more in-depth, and more "natural" discussions. This included the telling of stories which were often infused with layers of meaning.

NEEDS ASSESSMENTS

The CFC study was a needs assessment in that its objective was to assess the degree to which the CFC needed to improve its competency in dealing with clients and problems that stemmed from a different culture, resulted from cross-cultural misunderstandings, or created cultural barriers. According to Witkin and Altschuld (1995), a needs assessment (NA) involves setting up procedures that enable an organization to identify needs so that it can set priorities and make decisions that bridge the gap between a current condition and a more desired future state (1995, p. 4). This was clearly the kind of effort Darlene Piña and her students were engaged in with the counseling family center.

Note that the CFC study followed a systematic approach by gathering data through established procedures (focus groups). The data from these group interviews were used to develop a report with recommendations setting priorities and suggesting possible solutions that might determine how resources would be allocated. The object of the study had been to lead to improvements. All these qualities of the CFC study are qualities of a needs assessment.

An obvious question to pose is how you can do a needs assessment if you don't know what the needs of an agency are. For this reason, Witkin and Altshuld propose that needs assessments be done in three phases: the preassessment, the main assessment, and the postassessment (1995, pp. 14–15). As was true in the CFC assessment, in the preassessment phase of the CFC study, first Piña had to explore with the members of the agency what their primary needs were. Preassessment involves the identification of major concerns from an exploratory effort in which the purpose and focus of the study are determined. While preassessment is a planning phase, plans cannot be drawn up without thinking all the way through to the desired outcomes for the assessment. In terms of a general research model which we earlier discussed, the preassessment period is the time when the research design of the NA is devel-

oped. The researcher needs to decide what data will be collected and from which sources and how the data are likely to be used.

The functions of the preassessment phase, as Witkin and Altschuld contend (1995, p. 25), are to set up the assessment groups and define obligations or to devise a plan for carrying out the assessment (which may require doing some preliminary investigative work) and get approval for it. Since this may involve political efforts, these factors need to be thought through. Usually a needs assessment project is run by a needs assessment committee (NAC). This committee would include the researcher and also representatives of those in the organization who have a major stake in the assessment. Hence, it is good to have a broadly based NAC, though too large a committee may prove unwieldy. Witkin and Altschuld propose that a NAC may have 20 to 25 people, though a core of 8 to 12 people would do most of the work (1995, p. 28). Recall that Piña had just four members, including herself, in her committee.

It is strongly advised that for a fairly large NA a written memorandum of agreement (sometimes called a memorandum of understanding, or MOU) be prepared. The MOU clarifies in writing what is being proposed, what the roles and responsibilities of the researchers are, and the dates for completion of the project and a budget (Witkin and Altschuld, 1995, p. 28). Because an NA takes place in a specific time frame, it is important that the researcher (and the NAC) consider both the prior history of the agency and the typical time frame in which the agency (or organization) generally operates. Some agencies (or institutions, such as schools) set cycles or terms in which certain types of activities occur. The preassessment phase needs to plan for these cycles.

The main assessment phase is when the data are collected. In the CFC assessment, this would be the period when the focus group interviews were carried out. As the data are being collected, however, planning for the assessment continues. Here the issue of determining the scope of the NA is crucial. If the scope is very wide, so many data may be gathered that the needs will become obscured. Conversely, if the scope is not wide enough, some very important sources of evidence of needs may be ignored. Perhaps more data are needed. Perhaps the types of data being collected are not fully adequate for the outcomes. It is always essential to keep in mind why the NA is being carried out, who the findings are primarily for, and how the findings may be used. Moreover, as the delineation of needs comes into clearer focus through the process of data gathering, a reexamination and reevaluation of the needs developed in the preassessment can be carried out and a prioritizing of the major needs can be undertaken. One alternative is to decide to carry out a subsystem NA in a special area that has been highlighted as having special needs.

The political issues arising in an NA may arise during the main assessment. For this reason, it is often argued that the NAC should include persons with differing points of view so that the political issues will be addressed. However, too much political debate can stymie the research effort, and so it is good to have planning supporters who are flexible and open-minded. Witkin and Altschuld (1995, p. 37) suggest that an evaluation be set in place as a part of the NA. If the NA will be a long-term project, a formative evaluation which monitors progress on the NA as it is being carried out can be helpful. Much of this can be an informal process in which the members of the NAC discuss the progress of the project or other groups in the agency may be asked to participate in evaluating the NA.

The needs come to be defined as "an initial state (what is) and a desired target state (what should be)" (Witkind and Altschuld, 1995, p. 41). Needs often may be designated at three levels: level 1, which are needs of the clients; level 2, which are needs of the service providers; and level 3, which are resources of the broader system (if the agency or institution is part of a larger structure) or the wider community within which the agency operates. The researcher must consider where causal factors reside (at which level) or whether they are generated by factors beyond the

clients, providers, or even the community. Don't forget that there may be large-scale causal factors (such as environmental factors) that are largely beyond the agency's ability to affect.

Note that a wide range of methods can be used for NA. The CFC NA used focus group interviewing, which is a way of gathering data from a group. Witkind and Altschuld (1995) mention two other types of group methods to gather data: the community forum, in which the members of a community are summoned to come to a "town hall" meeting to address an urgent issue, and the nominal group technique (NGT). In a community forum, it is often good to get a variety of interests represented, though one pitfall of a community meeting can be seen when one or two very outspoken people dominate the proceedings. Sometimes a short questionnaire is presented at the beginning of the meeting to focus the group's attention on the issues at hand.

The setting for a community meeting has become familiar to us, since presidential candidates in the 1990s have made use of such gatherings frequently. A theaterlike setting focuses the group on the leader; microphones are needed with a group of 50 or more. It may be necessary to limit speaking times. The leader needs to keep the discussion orderly and moving along, encouraging as much participation as possible and summarizing as the meeting proceeds. Such meetings generally are taped, and usually there are other recorders taking notes which may address aspects of the meeting which are not caught on the tape. Immediately after the session, the leader and the recorders and other assistants should debrief and discuss the outcomes so that they do not lose the meaning of the event. It is desirable that a written summary of the meeting be sent to all the group members, thanking them for their participation (Witkind and Altschuld, 1995, pp. 161–166).

A *nominal group technique* (NGT) is a group in name only, not necessarily in practice. This means that for much of the group session, verbal interaction among the members will not be the primary activity. The object is to identify problems and consider possible causes and consequences of actions. NGTs often are used when it is important to gather information from subordinates and superiors who may be uncomfortable expressing their views together. The leader of an NGT is often a person external to the agency. Once NGT members are selected and invited to attend the meeting, the leader needs to explain the structure of the session.

Often there are silent work activities in which group members are asked to write out ideas; these are silent brainstorming sessions. This may be followed by a "circle-in-the-round" discussion asking for ideas, beginning first with the most positive ones. These ideas should be written on a board. As the ideas are generated, the group may be asked to take straw votes. This procedure of listing ideas and voting should go on until no more ideas are generated. During the circle-in-the-round period, the leader should seek clarification on ideas that are unclear. Then each member either rank-orders the ideas as to their importance or selects his or her top three choices or allocates some set of points among the ideas. Then there is a break in which the scores are tallied and the results are presented to the group for discussion. At this point, the discussion within the group is more like group interaction in a regular group. Again, written summaries of the results should be sent to the group members. There may be various NGTs in a needs assessment, and ideas from the various groups may be circulated among the groups (Witkind and Altschuld, 1995, pp. 167–171).

Finally, the postassessment phase occurs. This is the time when the recommendations are prepared and disseminated. Now the needs must be fully prioritized, alternative solutions must be considered, and plans for implementation must be determined. Usually a plan of action needs to be implemented so that solutions to problems can be advanced. The researchers normally prepare a report for the agency being studied which concludes with recommendations. The report is distributed, and its ideas are disseminated through meetings and other types of oral briefings.

CASE STUDIES

The CFC assessment was also a case study, since it focused on a single agency. We will consider here in detail the nature of case studies.

A Definition

A case study is not a specific method of social research. Though field studies of specific organizations or social groups or environments are case studies, so are many program evaluations, which often use preexperimental or quasi-experimental designs. Thus a *case study* is a research strategy which focuses on a single organization, institution, event, decision, policy, or group (or possibly a multiple set). Both studies described earlier in this chapter were also case studies. Sheldon Zhang's evaluation of Los Angeles boot camps was, in fact, a case study of the boot camps of a single (though very large) county; his research purpose was to evaluate the effectiveness of this form of incarceration as it had been designed and set into place by Los Angeles County. Darlene Piña's study of the cultural competency of CFC was a case study of a counseling agency. Her primary purpose was to assess the needs of this agency in terms of its "competency" in handling multicultural and intercultural relations.

Zhang's method was quasi-experimental; data was collected through telephone interviews and from official records. Piña's qualitative study drew its data from focus groups and other interviews with the staff and clients of CFC.

As Robert Yin (1989, p. 17) proposes, case studies are appropriate when the research question to be addressed asks *how* and/or *why*. This means that a case study often seeks an explanation, as an experiment might. Case studies may be largely exploratory, or they may be descriptive. But often the reason to study a particular case is to try to figure out why a certain situation prevails or how an organization or group has succeeded. Evaluations of programs and organizations are explanatory in their purpose and are a form of case study research.

When the phenomenon to be explained happened in the more distant past, the best method of study may be historical research. Some historical materials may be used when the question addresses a contemporary case, but many of the data will be collected not from accumulated evidence from the past (records, documents, other written sources) but by the researcher through observation, interviewing, and contemporary written materials. Within this contemporary time frame, a study of a single event, group, or organization is considered a case study. Experimental designs are generally inappropriate in a case study because the researcher cannot control the course of action and the types of behaviors which will occur.

Yin (1989, p. 23) defines a case study as an empirical study which (1) "investigates a contemporary phenomenon within its real-life context; when (2) the boundaries between phenomenon and context are not clearly evident; and in which (3) multiple sources of evidence are used." In other words, a case study examines a current phenomenon in its real-life situation, using whichever research strategies are necessary to address the problem at hand.

Designing a Case Study

The first effort, as always, is to set up the research question. Let's take an example. Suppose the elementary schools in your city or town are considered inadequate in many ways; however, Jones School, in the poorest part of town, is widely considered very successful. This could well be a subject for a case study. Clearly the research question would be of the *why* and *how* variety. *Why* is Jones School successful even though it has the same inadequate funding, the same source of teachers, and the same ill-prepared students as the other, less successful schools? *How* does the school manage to get such positive results (test scores, positive attitudes about the school, etc.) when the same problems seem to undermine the efforts of its sister schools? The final research question might be more focused: it could be on a specific reading program in the school, on the decision-making strategy employed in the school, or on how decisions are implemented.

Yin suggests that the researcher develop propositions linking the research question to specific things that will be carefully examined in the study. One proposition could be that Jones School is successful because the teachers and administrators have identified ways to meet certain objectives (i.e., improving reading scores), and a second proposition could be that they have perfected a means to work together to achieve those goals. This proposes that the leadership of the school is effective in defining, stating, and getting the teachers to support specific objectives, and it proposes that the teachers and administrators work successfully together to achieve their goals.

Yin argues (1989, p. 31) that the way the research question is set up will define the actual units of analysis in the study. In the Jones School study, the units of analysis depend on the exact nature of the research question. In a study focused on a specific program or programs, the unit of analysis is a program. In a study directed at how decisions are made, the units of analysis are decisions. In a study of how decisions are implemented in the school to reach results, the unit of analysis is the implementation process.

Next the researcher must collect data that address the propositions. As Yin states (1989, p. 33), this is no easy matter. In a formal experiment, subjects are assigned to treatment conditions which connect the hypotheses to the data. However, in a real-life case study, this type of control cannot be gained. How can the researcher know whether the data to be gathered will really address the proposition? Suppose the Jones School study focuses on the implementation of a strategy to teach reading. The researcher might select several types of information that zero in on how the strategy was implemented (qualities of training sessions for teachers, incentives for teachers to undertake training and implement the strategy, how teachers presented new techniques in class). A researcher who could study various training sessions with different leaders or watch different teachers incorporating this new method in their classes might detect patterns in which the implementation seemed to be more effective and might relate these patterns to specific training sessions, specific teaching styles, etc.

This ability to *link the data collected to the propositions* set out for the study is related to the final component needed in a case study research design: the setting of criteria to determine the findings of the study (Yin, 1989, p. 35). In the Jones School study, the criteria would need to differentiate levels of effectiveness of implementation.

Case Study Theory Building

The first step in theory building is setting up propositions to link the data to be collected with the research question. A theory offers a provisional explanation of why certain factors might lead to certain results. In the Jones School study, one theory might be that reading scores improved most when the teachers were given certain incentives for implementing the new program. A rival theory could state that the success was due to a change in the administrative structure of the school, giving teachers more authority and autonomy.

One case being studied is not representative of a sample of similar cases; thus it cannot be the basis for statistical generalizations. However, as Yin contends, the case study allows for "analytic generalizations in which a previously developed theory is used as a template with which to compare the empirical results of the case study" (1989, p. 38). Such generalizations strengthen the explanatory power of the study. Classic case studies in the literature have often enabled researchers studying cases in very different places and at different times to find similar processes and similar explanations operating.

Issues of Reliability and Validity

If another researcher studied this case with the same research question, would the results be the same? Researchers need to design their studies so that the audience will be able to follow exactly what happened. Could another researcher read the case study through its various steps, think through the logic of how to link the propositions to the data, repeat the research effort, and reach the same conclusions? To strengthen the replicability of a case study, the researcher must carefully document each step in research design and data collection in a *case study protocol,* described below.

Three types of validity issues arise in a case study. *External validity,* as described in Chapter 6, addresses whether the findings of a study can be generalized to another example. Again, as Yin argues, the issue is not to analogize to some broader population, for a case study is not based on a sample. Rather, as in an experiment, we need to be able to test the external validity of the study through replication. For example, if another school used the Jones School's incentive strategy, would it achieve similar results?

The problem of establishing *internal validity* arises when a case study seeks to explain a phenomenon. In such a study a spurious unmeasured factor, rather than the proposed cause, might actually account for the result. A case study, unlike an experiment, does not allow the researcher to even attempt to reduce extraneous factors. But he or she can carefully consider all the possible unmeasured factors and then infer what effects such factors might have.

Yin particularly stresses the need to address the problem of *construct validity* (1989, pp. 41–42): does the operationalized measure of the effect of the study actually measure what the researcher states that it measures? Many case studies examine "change" in the organization, group, or whatever case is being studied; the issue is whether the measure or measures of change actually reflect the kinds of alterations the study is focused on and whether the types of changes studied closely relate to the original objectives of the study. Yin strongly advises that a case study researcher get multiple sources of evidence and/or try to establish a chain of evidence so that one can pick out the steps that lead to a final effect.

Case Studies as a Method for Evaluating Programs

Organizations and agencies that receive funding from the government to implement programs are generally required to evaluate the effectiveness of these efforts. Thus evaluation research has become a growing industry. In most cases, researchers study the outcomes or processes of specific programs rather than setting up comparative research designs. Thus much evaluation research is in fact based on the study of single cases. In their comprehensive text on program evaluation, Posavec and Carey (1989) use five case studies to exemplify the methods of evaluation research. Box 10-7 describes these exemplary forms of using case studies as the research design for evaluations.

Developing a Protocol for the Case Study

As was suggested above, a *protocol* is the major way of establishing the reliability of a case study. A protocol is a written plan, based on a comprehensive outline, of how the study will be carried out. Yin suggests (1989, pp. 70–80) that the protocol have the following sections: (1) an overview of the entire project, which includes its objectives, and the readings that are relevant to it, (2) a description of field procedures, including forms of access, relevant credentials if needed, sources of information, and various reminders of how to operate in the field, (3) the questions to be answered in the study, which will guide the data collection and suggest sources of information for answering the questions, and (4) the guide for preparing the final case study report. This written protocol guides the entire research effort, and at the end of the project it becomes an additional document in the final report.

Qualities of Effective Data Collection for a Case Study

Yin stresses three general goals that researchers must strive for in collecting data in a case study (1989, pp. 95–103). First, they must seek *multiple*

sources of evidence, such as data from surveys, interviews, focus groups, documents, and other official records.

Second, Yin stresses that a case study researcher must develop a *case study database* separate from the report of the case study. The data, or evidentiary, base in a case study is parallel to the computerized dataset of aggregated responses to the questions in a survey. In survey research, as described in Chapter 7, this dataset is fully separate from the written research report or paper that is the end product of the research. Similarly, in a case study, the database must be a separate set of materials. It may include aggregated answers to survey questions (if the case study utilized a survey), responses to specific interviews, notes from observations, case study documents, and tabular materials. In addition, Yin advises that the case study database contain *narratives.*

A case study researcher, using the narrative technique, composes open-ended answers to the questions in the protocol. As Yin states,

> each answer represents an attempt to integrate the available evidence and to converge upon the facts of the matter or their tentative interpretation. The process is actually an analytic one and is an integral part of the case study analysis (*1989, p. 101*).

Yin compares the preparation of these answers to completing a take-home exam in a graduate course, in which certain types of evidence are linked and related to the issues in the study and citations to other related work are included.

Third, Yin stresses the need to maintain a *chain of evidence.* He compares this strategy to that of a criminological investigation where all the facts need to be gathered, their relevance to the case assessed, and the logical links between facts and other forms of evidence carefully connected and addressed to the problem at hand. The reader of a case study should be able to track the course of the research backward to where the researcher began and figure out the logical steps in the development of the research project (1989, p. 102).

BOX 10-7

EXAMPLES OF CASE STUDIES AS PROGRAM EVALUATIONS

Posavec and Carey offer five exemplary case studies to explain the methods of program evaluation. The following brief descriptions of these cases show the range of ways in which the case study approach serves the needs of evaluation.

CASE 1: REDUCE STRESS OF EMPLOYEES IN A BURN UNIT OF A COUNTY GENERAL HOSPITAL

The evaluation was designed to assess the problems in the work environment, provide feedback to the staff, plan and institute changes, and then reassess the work environment. The intervention strategy consisted of a set of eight group meetings led by a psychiatrist. The study focused on several dimensions of the work environment, including relationships, goal orientation of employees, and system maintenance and change (clarity of expectations, use of rules to control behavior, level of innovation encouraged, and pleasantness of physical setting).

CASE 2: ALCOHOL EDUCATION PROGRAM AT A STATE UNIVERSITY

An advertising campaign was instituted to try to affect students' attitudes toward drinking. The project focused on two attitude themes: could students resist peer pressure to drink heavily and would students stop their friends from driving while drunk? The campaign used a variety of carefully timed media efforts (posters, ads in newspapers, a call-in radio show, and information booths) over a 10-week period, and the researchers interviewed students during the intervention to measure their awareness of the themes. In the last two weeks the researchers mailed a survey to find out whether the media effort had been effective.

CASE 3: UNAUTHORIZED ABSENCES AMONG MARINES

The experimental design randomly divided eight battalions into control and treatment groups. The treatment groups were exposed to varying versions of the intervention program, which involved setting objectives, monitoring absence rates, clarifying and communicating commanders' policies, monitoring command actions, providing rewards, and training field commanders in the goals of the absence prevention program.

CASE 4: A COST-BENEFIT ANALYSIS OF TITLE XX FUNDING FOR FAMILY PLANNING SERVICES IN TEXAS

This study was carried out in 1981 to determine the effectiveness of the program and relate it to the costs. The outcome of the study was the prevention of unwanted births, but it is difficult to measure what does not occur. The researchers developed a surrogate measure based on the difference between the expected number of births in the population being studied and the observed number of births. In this study, the family planning services themselves are the "intervention." The costs of these services could then be related to the welfare costs saved by the state for the births that were averted. The type of contraception used by each woman studied was the only other data used. The research determined a benefit rate in terms of dollars saved.

CASE 5: FAMILY PRACTICE RESIDENCY PROGRAM

In this university evaluation, no intervention took place. Instead, a careful study of the program included an analysis of documents; in addition, key faculty members described and explained the program's goals, a small number of residents were closely observed over a three-day period, and all the residents were interviewed. The areas deemed most in need of improvement were those in which there was the greatest discrepancy between the program's goals and the residents' experiences. These areas were comprehensiveness and continuity of care, formal teaching sessions, and the quality of clinical teaching and training.

Source: Emil J. Posavec and Raymond G. Carey, *Program Evaluation: Methods and Case Studies,* 3d ed., Prentice Hall, Englewood Cliffs, NJ, 1989, pp. 289–320.

When Is the Case Study Method Most Appropriate?

Case studies have often been wrongly considered easy to carry out. Like other types of research, they require forethought, careful planning, data collection, analysis, and final preparation for reporting. While they focus on a single social environment or institution, the strategies involved are as comprehensive as those in other research methods. Case studies are often the bases of doctoral dissertations. More and more, studies of the degree of success of new policies require multiple case studies. Effective case studies serve as classic exemplars of how social research can be done. They may reach theoretical conclusions which have widespread and long-range implications both politically and in terms of theoretical developments in a field.

SOCIAL INDICATORS

Definition and Origins of Social Indicators

What are *social indicators?* Quite simply, they are measures of aggregate social conditions that are of interest to a society because they offer a way to evaluate the overall state of that society. As explained by the federal government,

> A social indicator . . . may be defined to be a statistic of direct normative interest which facilitates concise, comprehensive and balanced judgments about the condition of major aspects of a society (*U.S. Department of Health, Education and Welfare, 1969, p. 97*).

For example, the "average life expectancy at birth" given in years is a social indicator of the "health" of a society. It is reported as a mathematical average (a descriptive summary statistic). Such statistics generally are presented comparatively across a number of years so that *trends* can be noted.

Undoubtedly, the health of a nation is of social concern, and average life expectancy is an indicator of the state of this health. This indicator is nor-mative in that it suggests how various rules and values of the society (pertaining to health care, hygiene, health education, and public health issues) are affecting the state of health of the nation. The social indicator must be measured accurately and must be a simple enough statistic, based on sufficiently fair evidence, that many people will both understand and trust what it supposedly represents.

In the 1960s, interest was generated in the United States in having available a range of easily understood social indicators that would enable policymakers and others to make better decisions about social conditions in America. The early conception of which social indicators to develop, as laid out by the then U.S. Department of Health, Education and Welfare, stressed the *positive output* qualities of the definition. For this conception, a social indicator was "a direct measure of welfare and is subject to the interpretation that if it changes in the 'right' direction, while other things remain equal, things have gotten better, people better off" (Carley, 1981, p. 22). This definition emphasized two factors: that the *outputs* of a social system were critical and that they should be measured in terms of *positive accomplishments,* the betterment of persons, and social welfare (Carley, 1981, p. 23).

Others challenged the normative, or positive, stress on the definition since what was currently a positive social good might become a negative social evil later on (an example here might be the rate of population increase). Social indicators were closely allied to various forms of policy analysis. If the health of poor Americans was getting better, did this indicate the success of the Medicaid program? In other cases, an analysis of social indicators might suggest areas in which new policies need to be formulated so that new programs and funding might ameliorate social ills.

The Use of Social Indicators

The analysis of social indicators is a form of evaluation that encompasses all of society. It is based on analyzing aggregate data and presenting tables, graphs, and discussions which show social trends over time. The social indicators generally are based on an aggregate unit of analysis such as a city or a country. The actual data usually are measured in terms of that aggregate unit, though they may be based on data from surveys of individuals which are then aggregated. *Objective social indicators* refer to measures of some actual occurrences (completion of high school, family income); *subjective social indicators* refer to the attitudes and perceptions of individuals about special social conditions (for example, job satisfaction or a sense of well-being). Social indicator analyses often combine both objective and subjective indicators.

Most studies using social indicators present sets of tables and graphs. However, this is not always the case. Box 10-8 describes how John Naisbitt used social indicators in writing what became a very popular book, *Megatrends* (1982). This book was followed by *Megatrends 2000* (Naisbitt and Aburdene, 1990), which projects trends for the 1990s.

BOX 10-8

MEGATRENDS FOR THE 1980S AND 1990S

In 1982, John Naisbitt published *Megatrends*, which delineated 10 major trends, based on a form of social indicators analysis (a term he does not use), that would guide the 1980s. He projected the following trends for the 1980s:

1. The United States is moving from an economy based on industry to one based on "creating and distributing information."
2. High technology is being introduced side by side with a greater stress on self-help and personal growth (what Naisbitt calls "high touch").
3. The United States is now part of a world economy rather than being a self-sufficient national economy.
4. Planning is being based on longer-term considerations.
5. Innovation in the governance of cities and organizations has a high priority.
6. Greater reliance on individuals and less dependence on institutions are being stressed.
7. Representative democracy is being affected by the mass media and their ability to provide instantaneous information.
8. Hierarchical structures are being replaced with more informal networks (especially in business).
9. Population has shifted to the sun belt.
10. A wider and wider range of options are being offered to Americans in terms of consumer goods and lifestyle choices.

In *Megatrends 2000*, Naisbitt and Aburdene set out 10 new trends they project will influence the 1990s:

1. A booming global economy
2. A renaissance in the arts
3. The emergence of free-market socialism
4. Global lifestyles and cultural nationalism
5. The privatization of the welfare state
6. The rise of the Pacific Rim
7. The decade of women in leadership
8. The age of biology
9. The religious revival of the New Millennium
10. The triumph of the individual

The sources of evidence supporting these new projected trends are detailed in footnotes, many of which refer to newspaper and popular magazine articles. Note that the trends for the 1990s are often merely catchphrases ("the decade of women in leadership," "the age of biology"). What evidence could show at the end of the 1990s that these trends had not occurred? Or are these propositions so general and nonspecific that they cannot be disproved?

There will be many "trend" lists of this type as the new century starts.

Material from John Naisbitt, *Megatrends: Ten New Directions Transforming Our Lives*, Warner, NY, 1982, p. 13; John Naisbitt and Patricia Aburdene, *Megatrends 2000*, Morrow, NY, 1990, p. 13.

One of the uses of social indicators is to provide a rich source of information on a nation. In the United States, the first effort to present social indicators for the country was *Social Indicators, 1973* (Office of Management and Budget, 1973), which contained numerous tables and graphs on various aspects of American social life. A second, even larger volume appeared later: *Social Indicators, 1976* (U.S. Department of Commerce, 1977). During the late 1960s and throughout the 1970s, there was a vigorous growth in research on social indicators for both national and international measures. However, with the closing of the Center for Coordination of Research on Social Indicators in Washington, D.C., in 1983, there was a reduction in government support for such widespread statistical reporting (Andrews, 1986, p. xi). At the international level, the Organization for Economic Cooperation and Development (OECD) in Paris also reduced its statistical reporting activities. Other international organizations are currently providing comparative indicators: the World Watch Institute develops yearly State of the World reports (see Brown, 1991), and the World Bank presents economic data for the countries of the world on a yearly basis that is computerized as well as in print (see World Bank, 1991).

Social Indicators as a Form of Evaluation Research

Social indicators research is large-scale evaluation research. It generally is based on data aggregated on a country as a whole, though it may be based on smaller units. Its purposes are for social reporting so that governments can recognize the strengths and weaknesses of social factors in society. It also may serve as a means for evaluating how certain social policies or programs (say, Medicare or national student loans) are affecting the social conditions of large numbers of individuals in a society.

Social indicators data can be used by other researchers as background or as comparative data for their own studies. If you are doing a small-scale evaluation of an organization, you might compare, for example, indicators of overpreparation for the job among employees of different sexes and racial groups with national data. As stated in Chapter 9 on the analysis of existing statistics, it is always very important to be careful that you understand how the indicator is measured, report carefully the group on which it is aggregated, and avoid the ecological fallacy of imputing trends seen in aggregate groups to individuals or subgroups within those larger groups (see Chapter 3 for a discussion of the ecological fallacy).

DECIDING IF EVALUATION RESEARCH, CASE STUDIES, OR OTHER FORMS OF APPLIED SOCIAL RESEARCH ARE APPROPRIATE FOR YOUR TOPIC

If you are carrying out a research project requested by an organization to study its operations, you will be involved in evaluating that agency. Since most evaluation research is funded by the agencies seeking the evaluation, it is not difficult to decide in such instances whether evaluation research is the appropriate purpose of the study.

You may, however, carry out many types of evaluations without the funding of an outside source. You might design your own community impact assessment. You might use existing data sources over a period of years to try to carry out a time-series analysis of the effects of a major social change on a set of indicators. You also may be able to study a small program, for example, a new writing course at your college or the effects of a new student activity at your college. In cases like these, you will be able to build a much more effective design if you are able to collect data from students or from those offering the services (faculty or staff) at different points in time: before the program is offered, during the program, and after it is over (or after the individuals you are studying have completed the program). You will also want to consider comparing those who participated in the program with those who did not. You should recall Darlene Piña's assessment of the "cultural competency" of a family counseling center set up to assess the needs of the agency by including the clients and staff in the center in designing and carrying out the study. In this way her research project was a form of community-based action research. Given that its focus was a single agency, it was a case study whose aims were largely exploratory.

While applied research must be undertaken with great care, a student researcher can initiate an applied study very successfully (even one that has required that compromises be made in the design) as long as he or she understands the quality of the study that has been attempted and is sufficiently humble in presenting what may be partial or only tentative results.

REVIEW NOTES

- Evaluation research is not a separate type of research method but research carried out for the purpose of evaluating a social program, law, or activity.
- Evaluations of social programs may begin before the initiation of the program (preprogram) or during the course of the program (ongoing evaluation).
- Cost-benefit analyses seek to assess whether the benefit of a program or social strategy is worth the cost. It may be difficult to measure costs and benefits. It is easier if the measurement of both costs and benefits can be operationalized in terms of dollars.
- Community impact assessment studies can determine what effect a new policy might have on a community.
- One way to examine the impact of new legislation is to compare indicators that should be affected by the law from before to after its enactment, using a time-series analysis design.
- Evaluation projects may be directed to many different audiences: funding agencies; local, state, or national agencies; project directors or staff; program clients; and the research community.

- Formative evaluations set out to study programs in process and feed the findings of an evaluation back into the program; in contrast, summative evaluations summarize the major effects of a program once it has been completed.
- Ways of strengthening the reliability and validity of the dependent variable in an evaluation project include using an already developed measure or multiple measures.
- In evaluations of social programs, participation or nonparticipation in the program is usually the independent variable.
- Possible input measures include the purposes, principles, methods, staff, clients, location, length of service, size, and management of the program as well as under whose auspices the program is being offered.
- The findings of evaluation studies may be "contained" or "buried." Evaluation research is often underutilized because it lacks practicality and specific recommendations.
- Evaluation studies need a comparative baseline for determining the success or failure of what is being evaluated.
- Action research is community-based and involves those being studied, who participate actively in the design and execution of the study. The aim of action research is to help community members study problems so that they become empowered to address them.
- A needs assessment (NA) sets up procedures that enable organizations to identify needs, set priorities, and make decisions that help address those needs.
- Case studies investigate current phenomena in real-life settings, using various research methods. Program evaluations are often case studies.
- Social indicators are measures of aggregate social conditions of social interest.

KEY TERMS

action research
applied research
case study protocol

community impact assessment
cost-benefit analysis
ex post facto design (after-only)
formative evaluation
needs assessment (NA)
nominal group technique (NGT)
nonequivalent control group
ongoing program evaluation
preprogram evaluation
social indicators
summative evaluation

STUDY EXERCISES

You have been hired by North High School to design an evaluation study of its college counseling program.

1. Your first step is to consider the purposes of the program. How would you go about doing this?
2. Having determined the purpose of the counseling program, define one or more measurable outputs of the college counseling program. Be sure they would serve as measures of the effectiveness of the program.
3. Now define the inputs to the program that you would want to study in relation to the outputs.

RECOMMENDED READINGS

1. Carley, Michael: *Social Measurement and Social Indicators: Issues of Policy and Theory,* Allen & Unwin, Boston, 1983. Social indicators, as measures used to monitor social change, have been developed in various countries. However, there is a general lack of agreement about what constitutes measures of social indicators. The most typical examples are measures from the health field.

2. Love, Arnold J.: *Internal Evaluation: Building Organizations from Within,* Sage, Newbury Park, CA, 1991. Organizations are increasingly taking the initiative in self-evaluation. This resource book can help in the development of studies evaluating goal achievement, effectiveness, and efficiency in an organization.
3. Nas, Tevfik F.: *Cost-Benefit Analysis: Theory and Application,* Sage, Thousand Oaks, CA, 1996. This work provides a systematic overview of the design and implementation of cost-benefit studies with examples of how they are used in evaluations of the environment and health care.
4. Posavec, Emil J., and Raymond G. Carey: *Program Evaluation: Methods and Case Studies,* 3d ed., Prentice Hall, Englewood Cliffs, NJ, 1989. This thorough and thoughtful text overviews program evaluation, covering program planning and monitoring, evaluations of outcomes, applications of findings, and case studies.
5. Rossi, Peter H., and Howard E. Freeman: *Evaluation: A Systematic Approach,* 5th ed., Sage, Thousand Oaks, CA, 1993. This is a comprehensive text on evaluations, including quasi-experimental impact assessments and full-coverage programs.
6. Stringer, Ernest T.: *Action Research: A Handbook for Practitioners,* Sage, Thousand Oaks, CA, 1996. This is a useful guide to carrying out community-based action research with many practical suggestions.
7. Witkin, Belle Ruth, and James W. Altschuld: *Planning and Conducting Needs Assessments,* Sage, Thousand Oaks, CA, 1995. This book offers very practical suggestions for carrying out a three-phase needs assessment with methods for conducting the assessment such as the use of the critical incident technique.
8. Yin, Robert K.: *Case Study Research: Design and Methods,* Sage, Newbury Park, CA, 1989. A comprehensive guide on how to design, conduct, and analyze a case study.

PART FOUR

The Analysis
of Social Research Data

In this final section of the text we shall discuss various ways of analyzing data. Remember that the primary reason for designing a study and collecting the data is to enable you to establish and present your findings. This requires careful analysis of your data. You begin by carefully setting out and cataloging everything you have collected. Then you must figure out what you have found. This analysis can be done in a number of ways and will vary depending on whether the data are quantitative or qualitative. The data may be rearranged so that those parts of the data which are similar are grouped together. This is normally what is done in survey analysis, where variables from each of the cases are aggregated across all the cases. In a qualitative field study, where notes have been taken, the analysis may be considered a sifting process in which the relevant materials are sorted out and other material is discarded. Whatever the type of data, the object of a data analysis is to turn the amorphous heap of evidence into firmer, more solid findings. These more condensed data, which you have decided to focus on, then need to be interpreted.

You must examine the findings in terms of the hypotheses or research questions which you originally posed. How far does the evidence support your hypothesis? Are there answers in the analyzed data to the research questions you posed? Data analysis may seem a bit like a game in which the strategy is to see whether the evidence fits the case. You look for the strengths in the analyzed data: the clearest patterns among the variables, the strongest association between particular variables. Then you try to make the best case for what you have found. However, in the analysis of social data, the evidence may *not* fit the case. In such a circumstance you must report that you have not found support (or have only weak support) for your hypothesis. Remember, having evidence to reject a hypothesis is often as interesting as having evidence to support it.

Chapter 11 serves as an introduction to the ways to analyze qualitative and quantitative data. Data preparation will naturally vary, depending on the types of data you have. In the chapter, I concentrate first on *qualitative* data and how they can be prepared and presented and then on *quantifiable* data which are generally analyzed with the help of a computer. I will also describe various computer programs that help in analyzing qualitative data. To analyze your data on a computer, you must prepare them to be transferred to a computer through procedures such as coding. Since there are many different types of computer systems, the chapter offers only general guidelines regarding what needs to be done to computerize your data. In short, Chapter 11 offers sound principles of data handling which should be considered by all researchers, whatever their plans for analysis.

Chapter 12 offers an example of data analyses which will be referred to in all the following data analysis chapters. It is from a data analysis prepared specifically for this text: an analysis of a small survey on recycling attitudes and behaviors which my students carried out in a research methods class at Cal State at San Marcos. The data analysis presented addresses an important but fairly simple and straightforward research hypothesis. The chapter includes presentations of univariate tables, the most elementary form of tables, and two-variable (bivariate) tables, showing how these tables are prepared and how they may be interpreted, as well as three-variable (trivariate) analyses and the elaboration model of analysis, which is a classic means of interpreting trivariate tables.

Chapter 13 describes some elementary social statistics and shows when and where to use them, offering examples from the dataset presented in Chapter 12. Some of the students using this text may already have had a course in statistics. For students with a background in statistics, Chapter 13 can serve as a refresher course in the uses of a few regularly employed statistical tests in social research. For students without any previous background in statistics, Chapter 13 offers some very basic guidelines for the use of statistics in social research and suggests which statistical tests might be good to use with different types of variables and analyses. Like any human endeavor, social research can have negative as well as positive consequences. For example, certain types of social research may require a degree of manipulation and deception of subjects which may raise serious ethical questions. In Chapter 14, these ethical concerns are addressed, including how ethics is applied in program evaluations. Chapter 15 concludes Part Four with a discussion of the steps to be followed in preparing and presenting a final research report.

Ways of Analyzing Qualitative and Quantitative Data

INTRODUCTION

*T*he data you have collected, regardless of your method, will be in the form of *raw data*—that is, data that have not yet been processed in any way. Your first step in analyzing the data will be to prepare these data for the types of analyses you plan to carry out. If you are doing a field study, the major form of analysis may involve organizing your notes to address your primary research question and then writing up those notes in a paper. In this type of analysis, there may be no information to convert into quantifiable categories. We will begin by describing methods used to prepare data for qualitative analyses, including ways to condense, display, and interpret such data.

Then we will turn to a quantitative analysis. Here the initial information gathered (the raw data) must be converted into numerical equivalents for the purposes of quantitative analyses and (possibly) statistical testing. We will discuss how to turn potentially quantifiable raw data into numbers which will represent the range of meanings—the variation—in the raw data themselves. Such a procedure is necessary in order to prepare tables, charts, and graphs that will *describe* the data precisely and to *explain* how far the data support your hypotheses. If you plan to test your hypotheses statistically, measures to determine the *strength of relationships* may be established. If your data have been drawn from a probability sample, other statistical tests will allow you to make inferences from the sample to the population from which it was drawn. Analyzing qualitative data requires a consideration of the nature of this type of data. In this chapter we will address how qualitative data are condensed, how they are displayed, how conclusions from them can be drawn and findings can be tested in qualitative analyses, and what types of computer programs are available to assist in the analysis of qualitative data.

Quantitative data preparation will be explained in three stages. The first stage, in which the raw data are coded into numbers, is the *coding stage*. The second stage, *establishing a computerized data file* involves transferring the data to a computer. Here the method for developing a computer data file will vary with the typed computer being used and the software program selected. (There are now so many different types of computer systems and software programs that it is not possible to give you specific instructions on how to use your system. Enough general information will be provided, however, to show what you will need to do to set up a data file if you have access to one of the more commonly available software programs.) The third stage involves *cleaning the data* once they are on the computer. This means that you need to check the accuracy of the data after they have been entered into the computer, since errors can be introduced at every stage of data handling.

SETTING UP QUALITATIVE ANALYSES

Qualitative data usually come in the form of field notes and also may include notes from interviews; written records, including reports, articles, minutes, and memos as well as the recorded observations of the researcher; and photographs, graphics, and other pictorial representations. Figuring out a way to systematically organize and handle these data is a great challenge. We will begin by considering the characteristics of qualitative data that must be considered in designing an analytic strategy.

Characteristics of Qualitative Data

One of the most frequently cited descriptions of qualitative data states that such data are naturalistic (Miles and Huberman, 1994). What this means is that these data generally result from observations taken over a fairly long period, often in the very ordinary environments which characterize the homes, workplaces, and public settings in which people normally conduct their lives. When the research is ethnographic in character, its aim is to capture a holistic sense of the environment being studied. Thus, it does not aim toward precise details or quantitative accuracy but toward representing a whole social space. Recall from Chapter 8 that the objective of qualitative research is often to gain a deep understanding, *verstehen,* of a social situation, which takes account of the perspectives of those being observed. The challenge to the researcher is to figure out what themes, which central ideas, help tie all the material together and make sense of it in a way that those who are insiders to the situation would recognize as their own. Finally, qualitative analysis is generally written in words, sometimes with pictorial additions but less frequently with numbers (Miles and Huberman, 1994, pp. 5–7).

There are three major tasks which the qualitative researcher must accomplish. First the data need to be condensed. This requires choosing which information to keep and which to discard and determining how to combine notes without stripping away the meaning and significance of the subject. The second effort requires figuring out ways to present the information so that it will be vivid and vital to the readers; this may require visual displays of diagrams, matrices, and charts which help organize and lay out the data clearly. The second task is one of data display. Finally, the data have to be interpreted so that conclusions can be drawn which the researcher can establish as valid and convincing.

Condensing the Data

Condensing the data requires processing the body of notes in such a manner that the central themes and meanings can be ascertained and pulled together. Emerson, Fretz, and Shaw (1995) suggest that this requires a number of analytic writing steps. They delineate a number of types of writing

and note-taking strategies to capture and give meaning to field notes. In the first instance, as part of the actual taking down of notes while researchers are in the field, Emerson and colleagues suggest that researchers write *asides,* which are "brief, analytic writing that succinctly clarify, explain, interpret, or raise questions about some specific happening or process described in a field-note" (Emerson, Fretz, and Shaw, 1995, p. 101). These personal reactions to events that occur help the researcher recall impressions as they were formed. These reactions may include the researchers' reactions to the "lived sense" of the social environment (ibid.).

A more extensive reaction to a social situation may call forth a *written commentary.* These commentaries often present exactly what the researcher was doing in the field during the field observation and may link one observation to an earlier one and make suggestions for later research efforts (Emerson, Fretz, and Shaw, 1995, pp. 102–103). Finally, at the end of a field observation day, researchers often take down *in-process memos* which include plans for later analyses, reactions to how the events observed that day may help explain earlier observations, and practical issues of what types of methods to employ subsequently (Emerson, Fretz, and Shaw, 1995, pp. 103–105). These in-process memos try to establish a point of view that an outside audience might have so that the observations are explained in a way that gives meaning to those who have not been observers. However, since taking these forms of "in-the-field" analytic notes can limit the time a researcher has to take descriptive field notes, Emerson and colleagues warn researchers to pay close attention to the allocation of time spent on asides, commentaries, and in-process memos (1995, p. 105).

Most of the coding and memoing will occur as part of the postobservation analysis of the field notes. The first phase of such an analysis requires the researcher to read all the field notes in depth "to identify, and formulate, any and all ideas, themes, or issues they suggest; this is referred to as *open coding* (Emerson, Fretz, and Shaw, 1995,

p. 143). It is important that the reading of the field notes be done very carefully in the way that would occur if the notes had been taken down by someone other than the researcher. The open codes can be jotted down in the margins or collected on separate sheets that have been linked to the notes; if the researcher is using a software program to organize field notes, they can be included in the comments section of the program (if such a section exists).

Researchers should not be stuck with only the initial categories they thought would organize their observations, but instead should be open to new ways to categorize and organize their ideas. Naturally, the same observation may be coded in different ways, depending on the focus of the researchers. For example, Emerson and colleagues suggest that in the study of a household the same set of notes may be coded in terms of economic factors and the division of labor or may be examined in terms of the invisible work the woman is carrying out (Emerson, Fretz, and Shaw, 1995, pp. 151–152).

When one examines notes from a very complex and deeply developed observation, theoretical ideas may emerge. This indicates the formation of explanations and interpretations emerging from the meaning of the situation. Writing these theoretical ideas and models is what Emerson and colleagues call *memoing* (Emerson, Fretz, and Shaw, 1995, pp. 155–156). Such memos may take ideas from a number of different observations and may analyze the connections and implications across observations. From the memos, researchers should be able to develop *themes* which stand out and form the core ideas of the observation. When the themes have been set out, the notes can be reviewed again to see how the various sections fit under the themes (Emerson, Fretz, and Shaw, 1995, pp. 157–160).

Once the themes are developed, the researcher can go through the notes again, doing very *focused coding*. Such coding often leads to subcodes of the original open codes. Focused coding enables the researcher "to recognize a pattern in what initially

looks like a mass of confusing data" (Emerson, Fretz, and Shaw, 1995, p. 161). Finally, the researcher, having developed open coding, memos, themes, and focused coding, is ready to combine and build up analyses with *integrative memos*. These integration efforts are drawn from different observations, relations between themes, and the progression of ideas toward a more holistic and meaningful discussion of the social world that has been observed (Emerson, Fretz, and Shaw, 1995, pp. 162–166). Many of these strategies for condensing data can be facilitated by the use of computer software programs for qualitative research. Box 11–1 describes some of the qualities of these programs.

Different Coding Schemes. For initial coding in the field, it is often useful to look for a coding structure. Strauss (1987) describes a four-part coding structure which includes (1) conditions, (2) interactions among actors, (3) strategies and tactics, and (4) consequences. Conditions often are laid out in sentences that include the words *because* and *since*. Consequences may appear in sentences that include *as a result of* and *because of* (see Miles and Huberman, 1994, pp. 59–61). Lofland (1971) developed a scheme for coding that included six categories running from narrow-level (micro) acts or activities, to meanings, participation, and more macro-level relationships and settings. Bogdan and Biklen (1992) have a 10-part coding scheme which lays out (1) setting and context, (2) definitions of the situation (how the actors define the situation they are in), (3) perspectives (shared ways of thinking), (4) ways of thinking about people and objects (this is more specific than perspectives), (5) the process of how events flow, which indicates transitions, changes, and sequencing, (6) activities (regularly occurring events), (7) events (specific activities), (8) strategies (how people get things done), (9) relationships and social structure (such as friendships and coalitions), and (10) methods (issues about the process of the research).

BOX 11-1

COMPUTER SOFTWARE PROGRAMS FOR QUALITATIVE ANALYSES

Naturally, the type of computer you have and the type of dataset you have gathered will affect your choice of a software program. Some qualitative software programs have been designed for the Macintosh, and others for DOS, UNIX, or mainframe computers. You need to consider whether your data are drawn from numerous types of sources, whether you are doing a comparative or a single-case study, and whether your notes have been taken in a free-form writing style or are more organized, coded, and fixed. If the data contain different types of information on the same subject (interviews, written records, visual materials), you will need a way to link these elements. Finally, it is important to consider how large your dataset is.

Some software programs basically search for words or combinations of words; these programs are generally referred to as *word retrievers*. Then there are *text base managers*, which may require the data entry to be set up into records and fields and can include quantitative as well as qualitative data. Qualitative researchers have created software programs which group and combine bunches of data so that patterns can be established. Programs such as NUDIST and HyperQual (for the Macintosh) and ATLAS/ti and the Ethnograph for a DOS system can code sets of information and then retrieve those coded sets. NUDIST and ATLAS/ti also can link different codes, building ordered classification systems which enable a researcher to develop and test theories. ATLAS/ti also enables a researcher to develop graphic network models. Because of the fast pace of software development and change, you have to keep looking for the newest programs available.

Source: Miles and Weitzman, Sage, Thousand Oaks, CA, 1994, pp. 311–317.

Contact and Document Summaries.   Miles and Huberman (1994) suggest that summary sheets should be prepared to cover the observational experiences of contacting a person (a contact summary) or reading through documents and records (document summaries). Figure 11–1 presents an example of a contact summary form involving a school principal. Note that the basic information of who attended and when the meeting occurred are at the top. Then the researcher goes over the notes from the meeting, and the most significant points are laid out and categorized under themes or aspects. For example, we see that there are two points that refer to the teaching STAFF, two that refer to POWER DISTRIBUTION, and two that relate to emotional responses (RESISTANCE and STEREOTYPING). At the left the researcher takes down the field note page numbers on which the points occurred.

Figure 11–2 presents a document summary form of a school weekly news sheet that reports on activities and issues in two schools. Note that the content of the newsletter is included on the sheet, along with the significance of the document and basic identifying information. These types of summaries can help a field researcher keep track of major forms of input.

Displaying the Data

A qualitative researcher also needs to use inventive ways to display her or his data. Texts consisting of words are the most common form, but often the written text needs to be highlighted with diagrams, matrices, and other figurative models to elaborate the ideas that are being developed. The relationship between display and analysis moves from summarizing to analyzing in order to make

CONTACT SUMMARY FORM

Type of contact:	Mtg. <u>Principals</u>	<u>Ken's office</u>	<u>4/2/96</u>	SITE: <u>Westgate</u>
	Who, what group	place	date	Coder <u>MM</u>
	Phone _____	_____	_____	Date coded <u>4/18/76</u>
	With whom, by whom	place	date	
	Inf. Int. _____	_____	_____	
	With whom, by whom	place	date	

1. Pick out the most salient points in the contact. Number in order on this sheet and note page number on which point appears. Number point in text of write-up. Attach theme or aspect to each point in CAPITALS. Invent themes where no existing ones apply and asterisk those. Comment may also be included in double parentheses.

PAGE	SALIENT POINTS	THEMES/ASPECTS
1	1. Staff decisions have to be made by April 30.	STAFF
1	2. Teachers will have to go out of their present grade-level assignments when they transfer.	STAFF/RESOURCE MANAGEMENT
2	3. Teachers vary in their willingness to integrate special ed kids into their classrooms—some teachers are "a pain in the elbow."	*RESISTANCE
2	4. Ken points out that tentative teacher assignment lists were leaked from the previous meeting (implicitly deplores this).	INTERNAL COMMUNICATION
2	5. Ken says, "Teachers act as if they had the right to decide who should be transferred." (would make outcry)	POWER DISTRIBUTION
2	6. Tacit/explicit decision: "It's our decision to make." (voiced by Ken, agreed with by Ed)	POWER DISTRIBUTION/ CONFLICT MANAGEMENT
2	7. Principals and Ken, John, and Walter agree that Ms. Epstein is a "bitch."	*STEREOTYPING
2	8. Ken decides not to tell teachers ahead of time (now) about transfers ("because then we'd have a fait accompli").	PLAN FOR PLANNING/TIME MANAGEMENT

Source: M. B. Miles and A. M. Huberman, *Qualitative Data Analysis,* 2nd ed. Sage, Thousand Oaks, CA, 1994, p.54.

FIGURE 11-1
Contact summary form for a school principal

sense in setting up a display. In the next cycle, the display sets out themes, patterns, and clusters which are then analyzed so that comparisons and contrasts can be drawn and displayed. In the third cycle the displayed patterns are examined to determine relationships which are analyzed in terms of how they might be integrated and elaborated. Such integrated analyses also can be displayed graphically or figuratively. In the final cycle, these displays may lead to explanations, which may then lead to ideas for reanalyses (Miles and Huberman, 1994, p. 101). In short, writing up the analysis is the way that it is thought through; working out how to diagram it or present it figuratively helps make sense of what has been written and then leads back to analysis.

Partially Ordered Displays. When a project is in its early stages, attempting to explore a subject, Miles and Huberman suggest that a partially ordered display may be preferable to develop. One form of this would be the context chart, which may use key players in the context being studied, to be laid out in separate boxes that are then linked to each other by plus (+) or minus (−) signs. Moreover, within each box, signs may be used to designate certain positions of the players. For example, if one is studying a new innovation in an organization, an "I" may be placed within each box to designate whether the individual supports the innovation and another sign might be used to indicate whether each person is highly influential in terms of supporting the innovation (Miles and Huberman, 1994, pp. 102–104).

<u>DOCUMENT SUMMARY FORM</u>   Site: Carson _____
Document: 2 _____
Date received or picked up: Feb. 13 _____
Date: Feb. 13 _____

Name or description of document:

  The Buffalo (weekly sheet)

Event or contact, if any, with which document is associated:

  Paul's explanation of the admin.
  team's functioning

Significance or importance of document:

  Gives schedule for all events in the district for the week.
  Enables coordination, knits two schools together.

Brief summary of contents:

  Schedule of everything from freshman girls' basketball to "Secret Pals Week" in the elementary school.

  Also includes "Did you know" items on the IPA program (apparently integrating the *IPA News*).

  And a description of how admin. team works: who is on team, what regular meetings deal with, gives working philosophy (e.g., "We establish personal goals and monitor progress," "We coordinate effort, K-12, and all programs," "We agree on staff selection"). Concluding comment: "It is our system of personnel management."

  Also alludes to the 26 OPERATIONAL GUIDELINES (Document 16)

  (I'll guess that the admin. explanation does not appear every week—need to check this.)

IF DOCUMENT IS CENTRAL OR CRUCIAL TO A PARTICULAR CONTACT

(e.g., a meeting agenda, newspaper clipping discussed in an interview), make a copy and include with write-up. Otherwise, put in document file.

Source: M. B. Miles and A. M. Huberman, *Qualitative Data Analysis,* 2nd ed. Sage, Thousand Oaks, CA, 1994, p.55.

FIGURE 11-2
Document summary form for weekly school newsletter

Another form of partially ordered display is a checklist matrix. These matrices may be set up in a broad range of ways. Figure 11–3 shows a matrix prepared for a study of how well a school was prepared for an innovative new practice. Note that the left-hand column lays out the individual role players in the school. The users include teachers, teachers' aides, and the strongest supporters of the innovation—the prime movers. Then there are two sets of factors (psychosocial conditions and the implementation plan) which need to be coordinated with the players. Rather than merely checking which factors fit with each player, the researcher might use brief words to describe the level of presence or support that each player has with each factor. The same set of ideas might be displayed with the conditions laid out as the left-hand vertical column and the individuals displayed across the top of the matrix.

Time-Ordered Display. Another way to set up matrices is to base them on time order. In this strategy, time periods are set up across the top of the matrix and then subdivisions of what is being studied (for example, in a study of schools ranging from the state level, to the district, to the local area, to a specific school) may be set out in the left-hand column. A different method of displaying time is with a flowchart in which events are boxed and, using arrows and placement, are set up to show what happened first, second, and so on. Still another method for showing time order is to set up a matrix of critical incidents and then display them with sequential time periods so that one can see how events followed each other. Figure 11–4 presents a decision modeling display which shows alternative directions that might be followed depending on the decision taken. This also is a time-ordered display, since each decision depends on the prior one.

		PSYCHOSOCIAL CONDITIONS						IMPLEMENTATION PLAN			
		Relevant Prior Experience	Commitment	Understanding	Skills	School Admin. Support	Central Admin. Support	Materials	Front-End Training	Ongoing In-Service	Planning, Coordination Time	Etc.
Users	1											
	2											
Building Administrator (principal)	1											
	2											
Central Office Administrator	1											
	2											
Other Central Office Staff												

Source: M. B. Miles and A. M. Huberman, *Qualitative Data Analysis,* 2nd ed. Sage, Thousand Oaks, CA, 1994, p.108.

FIGURE 11–3

Checklist matrix on how well a school was prepared for an innovative program

Role-Ordered Matrix.   In a role-ordered matrix, significant role players in the study form the heading for either the rows or the columns and their most important characteristics and reactions to what is being studied are cross-referenced. Returning again to a school example, specific teachers who have been at the school for different periods of time might be selected to represent different role perspectives, along with department chairs, the principal, and the central office. They then could be cross-referenced with their reactions to a new school initiative or program. One also might develop a role-by-time matrix (Miles and Huberman, 1994, pp. 122–127).

Cognitive Maps.   Cognitive maps set out one person's views on an issue. The map might portray the process of *how* a change has occurred or *what* has occurred, laying out the various components of the situation. These maps must be accompanied by descriptive accounts of how the map is to be read (Miles and Huberman, 1994, pp. 134–137).

Effects Matrix.   Effect matrices relate outcomes to initial objectives and also the perspectives of various role players in the situation. Using plus and minus signs, Figure 11–5 looks at three levels of outcomes: direct effects, metaeffects (large scale), and side effects. Here we see that there are complex matrices in which the effects of an environmental program in a high school are examined in terms of program objectives as they were originally projected and as seen by those who used the program and the administration in relation to the program's effects on pupils, staff members, the community, and the organization of the school (as seen only by the administrators). This matrix enables one to compare the extent of positive and negative effects, direct effects, large-scale metaeffects, and unintended side effects with effects on different role players and the community. Thus, one figure presents a whole body of findings (Miles and Huberman, 1994, pp. 139–140).

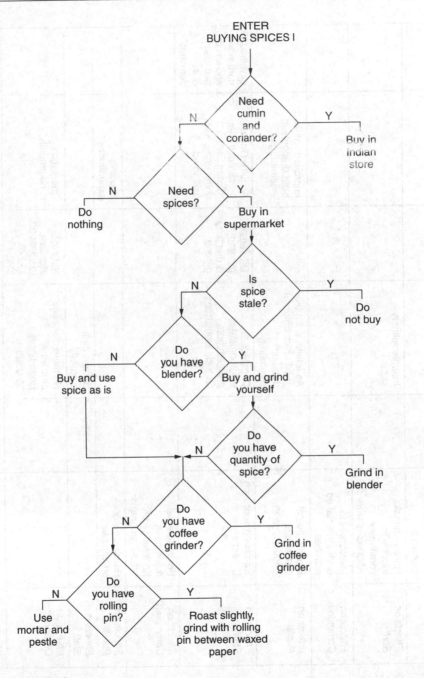

FIGURE 11-4

Decision modeling: time-ordered sequence
Source: O. Werner and G. M. Schoepfle, *Systematic Fieldwork:* Vol 2, *Ethnographic Analysis and Data Management,* Sage, Newbury Park, CA, 1987, as reproduced in Miles and Huberman, *Qualitative Data Analysis,* 2nd ed. Sage, Thousand Oaks, CA, 1994, p. 118.

		DIRECT EFFECTS +	DIRECT EFFECTS —	METAEFFECTS +	METAEFFECTS —	SIDE EFFECTS +	SIDE EFFECTS —
PROGRAM OBJECTIVES	*Effects on Pupils*	Plan and conduct environmental tasks Awareness of environmental problems					
	Effects on Staff	Hands-on tasks Work with community After-class work		Interdisciplinary skills			
	Effects on Community	Investment in environmental ed. activities					
SEEN BY USERS	*Effects on Pupils*	Environmental awareness Hands-on-work		As adults, will make good environmental decisions in community		Improved values Kept dropouts in + self-images	
	Effects on Staff	Hands-on approach Looser style		Completes environmental program here Outside workshops	Off-campus program is dumping ground	Acquired more off-campus sites "Expert" in community. Kept user in ed.	Crystallized hard work and low pay because of its demands*
	Effects on Community	Environmental awareness Knowledge of school programs					
SEEN BY ADMIN'RS	*Effects on Pupils*	Hands-on work off-campus				Success experiences	
	Effects on Staff			Utilizes their creativity			
	Effects on Organization			No more discipline problems Rounds out program	Not cost-effective to transport 14 kids to site	Orientation to community	
	Effects on Community						

Underscoring indicates that claim was made strongly by one person or by more than one respondent.
*Inference made by researcher.
Source: M. B. Miles and A. M. Huberman, *Qualitative Data Analysis,* 2nd ed. Sage, Thousand Oaks, CA, 1994, p.140.

FIGURE 11–5
Effects matrix: direct, meta-, and side effects of a program

Developing and Testing Conclusions

Miles and Huberman (1994) suggest 13 strategies for drawing conclusions from qualitative data. First, they stress that the researcher needs to look for patterns and themes (p. 246). Second, they encourage researchers to examine how far the findings are plausible. If they seem plausible, the researcher should look for further evidence to substantiate them (p. 246). Third, they encourage researchers to cluster ideas and look for overlaps. One might cluster behaviors or acts, actors, processes, settings, or sites (Miles and Huberman, 1994, p. 249). The fourth strategy is to develop metaphors in which two concepts are compared, using only the comparative qualities in each and ignoring what is not comparable. Many qualitative researchers use some form of counting to help them draw conclusions from their findings—this is the fifth strategy. A sixth strategy would be to make comparisons or contrasts between cases, outcomes, or the effects of time (Miles and Huberman, 1994, p. 254). Seventh, qualitative researchers might help themselves draw conclusions by partitioning variables through coding and reconceptualizing. This should be done early in a study so that the acuity of meaning can be heightened (pp. 254–255). An eighth strategy is to generalize from a set of particulars. Ninth, a researcher might look for factors that draw together clusters of previously disparate items. This strategy stems from the analytic method of factor analysis, in which abstract, hypothetical factors are determined through a statistical examination of commonalities between measures. The tenth strategy is to determine the relations between variables and use the strength of those relationships to draw conclusions. The eleventh and twelfth strategies will be presented in Chapter 12 on quantitative analysis as the search for intervening variables and the attempts to build logical chains of findings (pp. 259–260). Finally, once conclusions are drawn, the researcher needs to move toward developing complex concepts which generalize and build on each other (form constructs) and from

there toward proposing and developing theoretical ideas (pp. 261–262).

LINKING QUALITATIVE AND QUANTITATIVE DATA

In social research, there are strong differences of opinion about whether quantitative or qualitative data are more important to collect and analyze. However, many researchers would make the case that research designs which incorporate both quantitative and qualitative data and link them together are highly desirable. Such multilevel analyses have the advantage of triangulation, which enables a researcher to try to corroborate the findings from one type of data analysis with the evidence from another type. Moreover, having both types of data can deepen or intensify the findings noted in a quantitative study with qualitative data or lend certain strengths to qualitative evidence by enriching it with some quantitative detail. Third, using a different form of data may enable a researcher to follow up on new and unexpected ideas that have sprung up in the course of the study (Miles and Huberman, 1994, p. 41).

A researcher might combine quantitative and qualitative data from the very beginning of a study. Or a researcher might do fieldwork between the waves (data collection points) of a longitudinal quantitative study (such as a survey). Some researchers do qualitative observational research or in-depth interviewing and focus groups before designing a survey and/or may follow a survey with the collection and analysis of qualitative data to enrich the evidence found in the survey analysis. Qualitative research also might bridge two types of quantitative data collections (perhaps one a survey and the second an experiment). Miles and Huberman (1994) suggest that in many qualitative studies, some quantifying may be helpful. They call this establishing the "quantizing level" (p. 42). An example might be observing the interaction between professionals and clients; one might count how many times a professional interrupts a client (Miles and Huberman, p. 42).

Research designs that initially set out to collect both quantitative and qualitative data may be particularly effective in testing competing theoretical models. A study of the elderly by Wilson and Bolland (1992) involving services to the elderly in a community began with the collection of the number of referrals and types of activities offered by different agencies, after which community leaders were selected on the basis of nominations from the organizations. The leaders of the organizations who were determined to be the most central were then interviewed. The analyses based on both the quantitative and the qualitative results were considered jointly to determine which of the explanatory models was most fully supported by the evidence.

SETTING UP QUANTITATIVE ANALYSES

The most common form of quantitative analysis which sociologists carry out is the survey (see Chapter 7). In many cases students design a questionnaire to be distributed and completed. At other times students prepare an interview schedule and carry out face-to-face interviews. We will begin by giving general suggestions for preparing data from a survey for computer entry. Once we have done this, we will describe the recycling survey which was carried out as a telephone interview and will supply the data for the analyses that will be presented in Chapters 12 and 13.

COMMITMENT TO CARE

Careful attention to the methods and procedures of data preparation described in this chapter is vital to your study. Whatever your form of data, unless you handle the data with great care and try to minimize and rectify the errors that occur at each step of your preparation (as they almost always do), your results may be seriously jeopardized. The data preparation phase of your study is not simply "busy work" that anyone can do. It may be true that anyone could do it, but it is not true that anyone could do it *right*. If you have assistants helping

you code or transfer your data, you must nevertheless stay in command of the situation and check their efforts at every stage. There is no reason to suppose that your assistants will deliberately make errors, but you must assume that their knowledge of the study (however much you have explained it to them) and their personal commitment to its outcome will never be as great as your own.

The fanciest computer program, the largest research grant, and the cleverest statistical routines cannot convert messy, dirty, sloppy data into valid results. Thus, the issue of care in data handling is another area where the validity of a study can be challenged. There is a well-known saying about computer analyses: "Garbage in, garbage out." This means that if the data you enter into the computer are full of errors—if, for example, what is supposed to be the measure of "attitude toward income inequality between the sexes" for the fifteenth case in the sample is mistakenly entered into the computer as the measure of "attitude toward nuclear disarmament"—once the variable of income equality attitude is computed, the mistaken fifteenth case will have distorted the finding. Further, if there are many such errors, the measure of income equality attitude may no longer represent that attitude.

In such an instance, all your efforts at designing the variables so that they would truly get at the concepts you are trying to measure and all your efforts at gathering the data so that the respondents would comprehend the questions and answer them with understanding can be for naught. If errors are added into the data, when they are put on the computer, the data will be spoiled. Thus, "garbage in, garbage out": If you put bad data into a computer, no matter what is done to them in the computer, you will get bad analyses out of the computer. So think carefully about the suggestions offered in this chapter in relation to your study. Some of the precautions and suggested procedures may not be necessary in your particular study, but a consideration of the reasons for each will help clarify what you must be sure to do and what you must be sure to avoid in the handling and preparation of your dataset. Remember, your data are the most precious resource in your research project, so *treat them with care!*

DEVISING A CODING SYSTEM
General Principles to Follow

Coding the data involves taking the information—the raw data—you have and putting it into a form which can be quantified for analysis. There are a number of principles to keep in mind in organizing a coding system. *The first principle is that coding must resolve issues of definition and ambiguity so that the codes can be applied consistently. This requires making decisions on the basis of how best to code responses to the variables to maintain the meaning of the concept which your variable represents.* These decisions can be made on the basis of theoretical and empirical criteria.

In considering these issues in coding, you might look back to the material presented in Chapter 4 on conceptualization and operationalization. Operationalizing a variable is not completed once you have developed a survey question with its categories. If you recode that question once the data are collected (if you combine categories or rename these combined categories, the criteria used to carry out these changes will alter the initial operationalization and thereby change the relationship between the concept and the measured variable. That is why you must do this data handling and coding thoughtfully and deliberately.

Theoretical criteria test whether the scale (or set) of attributes making up the types of variation in a variable has been fairly carried over to a set of numerical codes which accurately represent the range of meaning you wanted to measure in the variable. Such criteria test for the *validity* of the variable. *Empirical criteria* test how far the results from measuring the variable seem to represent reasonable and expected outcomes; in other words, they help you determine how far the respondents understood what was being asked of them and how far they shared the meaning you gave to the question. The essential concern here is whether the respondents would be likely to respond to the item in a consistent fashion, that is, whether you can reasonably expect them to respond to the same question in the same way if they were asked again. In deciding this, you are testing for the item's *reliability*. Note that one difference between the use of theoretical criteria and the use of empirical criteria in making decisions about coding is that theoretical criteria can be applied before data collection begins through the use of precoding (to be described below). Empirical criteria, by contrast, may be fully established only after the data are gathered and certain patterns evident in the responses can guide coding decisions.

From a theoretical point of view, you must assign codes that represent the range of meaning you want a variable to have. This range must be sensitive to the types of variation possible. Are the responses to the question actual numbers that can be worked with mathematically (such as income, age, number of children)? Do the responses represent an ordering which should be carried over into the coding pattern (attitudes with which respondents can "strongly agree," "somewhat agree," etc.)? Or are the responses merely categories which have no ordered relationship to one another but are merely different from one another (religious affiliation, race, sex)? In this latter case, it may make no difference which category is given the highest number, what order the categories are in, or what number codes are actually given.

For example, there are theoretical considerations inherent in coding "don't know" responses that can be solved only by thinking through what exactly you meant by offering "don't know" as a response (assuming it was one) or what you had planned to do when respondents gave "don't know" responses even though they were not offered. For attitudinal items, "don't know" would seem to be a valid response meaning *no settled opinion;* for information about personal background and history, it could mean *a failure of memory* (e.g., educational attainment of one's father) or *lack of access to the information* (e.g., one's blood type). In each case, you should give

consideration to the intended meaning of the question before deciding how to code the variable.

From an empirical point of view, you want to code the data in a way that preserves the full variation given by the respondents, but you may also feel justified in combining certain types of responses in certain cases. Remember that the *second general principle of coding is to preserve as much as possible of the actual meaning of the responses and the variation presented in the data.* This can be understood by reference to an example from open-ended questions. With open-ended items, you may plan on the prospective answers, but final coding decisions must wait until the data are collected. This after-the-fact type of coding is based on what the empirical results came out to be.

Suppose you have asked people to list their favorite pastimes. You might have decided on prearranged categories for (1) sports, both competitive and individual, (2) films, plays, concerts, (3) reading, listening to music, watching television, (4) homemaking activities—gourmet cooking, needlepoint, gardening, and so on, (5) hobbies, collections. What do you do, however, when a respondent cites "washing the dog" or "shopping"? Should you start a new category for "pets"? (Is washing the dog a hobby? Is shopping a homemaking activity?) These are situations where you have to decide how much of the original information you want to preserve. The usual strategy is to code all the data to avoid discarding any information or collapsing any categories in the course of coding. Instead, it is preferable to leave the process of reducing and recoding the data to a later time. This will give you more options in regard to how you might use the variables as you proceed with the analyses.

The third general rule is to plan your coding system as far as possible at the time you design your data collection instrument. Theoretical issues in coding should be considered carefully if you are designing a questionnaire and coding guides can be included on the instrument (see the discussion below). *Fourth, the coding system should help re-*

duce the number of times the data must be handled, for every time they are handled, additional mistakes may be added. For this reason, coding systems should be clear and precise. *To serve as a guide to the coding system and a record of all the coding decisions made, a codebook should be prepared and updating procedures should be arranged—this is the fifth rule of good coding procedures.* This codebook will be needed not only to guide you in the coding but to refresh your memory as to what a variable really measures as you carry out your analyses. Some data analysis software programs set up code books for you.

Prestudy Coding

As was stated above, it is a good idea to have your coding system planned out at the time you are designing your study. If questionnaires are to be used, it is best that they include coding information on the actual instrument. This greatly simplifies and speeds up the data transfer procedure itself. If the coding appears on the questionnaires, the person entering the data into the computer is able to transfer the information directly from questionnaires to the data entry mechanism for the computer. If it does not, the coding must be written either on the questionnaires or on the coding sheets.

In large studies, coding is often done by persons other than the study designer. When this is the case, as was mentioned earlier, the chances of error are increased since an outside coder is less likely to understand the coding system or the intended meaning of a question than is the questionnaire designer. Therefore, if you plan to have others help you code your data, you should plan to give them as much assistance as possible, and a precoded questionnaire should help increase accuracy during coding.

Codebook Preparation

A precoded questionnaire may serve as a guide to carrying out the coding procedure, but it will not remind you of the decisions you made in setting up the codes as you did and it will not include the variables you "constructed" subsequent to the data collection. For these reasons, you might want to prepare (and update) a *codebook*.

Defining the Purposes of a Codebook. A codebook is, first of all, a *notation* of what you have decided to call your variables (and the attributes within the variables) and how these names correspond to what was measured by the variable. Second, a codebook is a *guide* to where each variable can be found (by its name in the computer file or wherever, depending on how your data will be processed). Finally, a codebook is a *record of the decisions* you reached in determining how to set up the variable. Ambiguities in the question, differences in the definitions a question might suggest, must be resolved through coding, and these decisions should be systematically recorded in your codebook so that you remember your rationale for treating a variable in the particular manner you chose to handle it.

Setting Up a Codebook. A codebook catalogs each variable first by its formal name and then by the name by which it will be referred to in the computer program. Then it gives the numerical code for each of the values, or attributes, of the variable (for an athletic participation variable, I = "have not participated," etc.). In addition, a codebook might note the position on the computer file where the variable can be found; this is called its *computer entry form*. Some codebooks (particularly for datasets which have been prepared for secondary analyses) include the actual number of respondents whose answers were coded under each of the code numbers. The various parts of the coding information will be broken down into the following components, which are typical of many codebooks.

Components of Codebook Entries. The data to be entered for each variable in a codebook should be consistent from one case to the next. The following are the typical types of information which should be given for each variable in the codebook.

Formal name. Every variable should be given a formal name which will identify what it measures. For example, if the variable is sex, this is such an obvious name that it needs no further elaboration in the codebook. Social class, however, may be too inexplicit to be used as a formal name. It may be better to specify the type of socioeconomic measuring instrument used in the formal name (for example, "Respondent's current socioeconomic status—Duncan Scale," described in Chapter 4) might be the formal name given. In selecting a variable to use in a secondary analysis, we would need to give it a name and record the name in the codebook we would devise.

Computer name. Here there are two common conventions. One is simply to number the variables. A common method is to label them Q1, Q2a, and Q2b to refer to questions on the questionnaire. This is the way the variable is to be identified by the computer and by the researcher as well. Or, if sex is the first variable entered in the computer file, it might be given the name VAR1 (variable 1) or it might be given a *mnemonic:* a word or set of letters used to recall some specific thing. SEX is a name which is so short that it can serve as its own mnemonic. Thus, the second convention is to give the variable a word name.

Value labels for the attributes of a variable. Value labels are the actual codes for the various categories (or scale numbers) of a variable. The number of digits depends on the range of the attributes. For single digit variables, 8 is often used for "don't know" and 9 for a missing value. Frequency distributions may serve as an additional codebook in which the codes given to the categories (or attributes) of the variable are presented.

A variable with an ordinal scale set of responses should be coded in order: for example

1 = "strongly agree," 2 = "agree," 3 = "undecided," 4 = "disagree," 5 = "strongly disagree." For a variable with responses representing actual numbers, the codes can be the responses themselves. For example, in the case of age, the categories can simply be the actual number of years the person has lived. (Naturally, you would not need to write in the codebook 1 = "1," 23 = "23," etc.) When the numbers are a continuous series with fractional amounts, such as weight, the coded numbers will have to be rounded in a systematic and consistent manner.

Case numbers.   As every variable in a study is given a variable name, ever respondent to a study is usually given a case number. The primary reasons for doing this are to keep your responses systematic and to make checking for errors (cleaning) easier. If the respondents have filled out questionnaires, the case numbers might be written in on the top of each questionnaire (from, for example, 001 to 250). Then these numbers should be entered into the computer as if they were a variable in the study. Thus the codebook might include the variable ID, which could be described for a sample of 250 as a three-digit code from 001 to 250.

Creating a Flexible Codebook.   In preparing your own codebook, consider using a looseleaf folder that holds 3 × 5-inch index cards with punched holes. Each card can record a different variable. You can then sort the cards in different ways and may insert a card for any new variable (which may often be created from recoding or combining other variables) next to the card for the original variable on which it was based. Such a codebook therefore gives you a lot of flexibility for adding to and rearranging your variables. Nowadays many data analysis software programs will create a codebook for the researcher once the data have been entered.

Cross-referencing.   One of the helpful techniques you might incorporate into your codebook

is to cross-reference variables. For example, from the name of the city, suburb, or rural area in which respondents reside, you might create a new variable entitled urban/suburban/rural. This means that you would have one variable with the name of each place coded and a second variable with only three categories: urban, suburban, and rural. In such a case, when new versions (or constructed variables) of earlier variables have been created, you should cross-reference these variables in the codebook. You also might want to refer to variables that are identical but were collected at different times (SES measures taken in different years) and variables that measure very similar qualities (number of years of schooling completed, highest degree attained).

Noting reasons for coding decisions.   As was mentioned above, it is important to remember why you coded variables as you did. Don't trust memory alone. Brief notes included with the code for the variable are much more reliable.

Coding Open-Ended Questions.   There are three possible strategies for coding open-ended questions. One is to develop in advance the set of categories you think will cover exhaustively all the possible responses to the question, give those categories codes, and then classify the answers according to these codes. For many types of questions, you can precode all such responses. For example, you might decide to code responses to a question about occupation into the categories "white collar" and "blue collar." Remember that you must also include the category "other" for occupations which you might not be able to fit into either of the first two categories. (By some definitions, of course, all occupations could be placed in one of these two categories.) Finally, for respondents who failed to give an answer to the question, you would need a "no response" category.

One problem that may rise with the strategy of coding open-ended questions in advance is that some categories may not have any responses falling into them. If that is so, they are *irrelevant* categories. To minimize this possibility, it may be helpful to try out the open-ended questions in a pretest to see which coding categories should be used and which should be left out.

Another form of precoding is to separate the possible responses to a single question into different variables. Let's say you have asked respondents to list their favorite sports. You might have a study where the major sport which interests you is swimming. In this case you might want to look at each sport mentioned, coding the answer as follows: 1 = "swimming, mentioned," 0 = "swimming not mentioned," 9 = "no answer." Then if baseball is mentioned, it will form another variable, etc. In this case, none of the information would be lost, but a single question would form the basis of a number of variables.

The third common strategy is to develop a set of categories on the basis of the responses themselves. This postsurvey technique is particularly suitable for questions which might generate many different types of answers which you cannot fully predict in advance. For example, suppose you ask people, with an open-ended question, why they voted for a particular political candidate. Since you are unsure of the range of reasons the respondents might give, you must begin by looking at the responses and making a list of the types of responses given—the respondent likes the candidate's economic position, approach to foreign policy, social policy, personality, and so on. In listing the types of responses in this way, you will in effect be categorizing them. This means that you must decide on the number and kinds of categories you need.

Take the area of social policy, for example. Do you need only one category for liking the candidate's stand on any type of social policy, or would it be better to have separate categories for the candidate's position on issues such as abortion, Medicare, social welfare, or whatever? Here the choice you make must depend on what you hope to be able to analyze. If you want to be able to compare respondents who support candidates who are pro-choice or pro-life, for example, you had better categorize abortion positions separately. If you think that this social issue will need to be considered only in terms of a broader social issues category, however, you should feel comfortable with collapsing this category and combining it and other social issues responses into a single category.

You may be concerned that at the coding stage you will not know exactly what forms of analyses you plan to carry out. In fact, that is often the case. In such situations, it is a good rule to use *more* categories rather than fewer. It is always possible to collapse categories which are not needed (or which contain too few cases) into other available categories once the data have been coded. Finally, once open-ended questions have been coded, the principles used for doing the coding should be entered in the codebook.

Coding Missing Data.   There are always some data missing in a study. In a questionnaire, respondents may not choose to answer every question, may inadvertently skip questions, or may think that certain questions are not relevant to them. Moreover, answers may be given that are inappropriate to the question: for an open-ended question, an answer may make no sense in terms of answering the question; for a forced-choice question, instructions may not have been followed appropriately (e.g., where "Circle the single best answer" has *three* answers circled). In other cases, open-ended responses may be illegible.

For the purposes of coding, you must still code these responses in some way. Here is where "no response," "not relevant," or some other type of no-meaningful-data-available-for-this-case-on-this-variable response may need to be used. As stated above, the convention is to code "no response" as a 9. If you can make distinctions between "no response" and "not relevant" and these distinctions seem important to you for the study, you should give them different codes. Often a questionnaire will include a "don't know" category for respondents to select; this is conventionally coded as an 8. If you are using two-digit codes, the 9 would be 99 and the 8 would be 98.

In analyzing the variables, missing data often are excluded from the analyses. Most computer programs for analyzing data offer easy means to specify data as missing when you have coded them clearly as such. One of the main reasons you want to keep information on missing data is to assess its prevalence within the sample. If a variable has too much missing information, it may not be worthwhile to use in your analysis. If you are comparing the responses of two or more subgroups, you must be concerned that one group does not have a much higher proportion of missing data on a specific variable of interest than another. Knowledge of missing data will be important for you in your analyses, and so you must be sure to code it fully and accurately in the coding procedure.

Using a Blank Questionnaire as a Codebook.   It may not be wise to use a blank questionnaire as the sole form of a codebook, because it does not have the space to incorporate all the decisions you have made or to include constructed variables or those derived from sources other than the questionnaire. But if the data were drawn from questionnaires, it will probably be useful to *code* a blank questionnaire to accompany your codebook as you carry out the coding. The coded questionnaire form will serve as a guide.

Types of Coding Strategies

Typical questions usually offer one of five types of response categories. The first type involves answers (often to attitudinal questions) with a set of ordinal scale responses, such as "strongly agree," "agree," "disagree," "strongly disagree." The second offers answers which are dichotomies; a yes-or-no response is an example, as well as answers that measure whether a quality is present. "Do you play tennis? Yes/No" is equivalent to "Which of the following sports do you engage in? Tennis, Swimming, Boxing, etc." In the latter case, each sport would be the basis of a different dichotomized variable such that those who checked "tennis" would be coded 1 = "plays tennis," 0 = "does not play tennis."

The third type of response category offers answers which are a set of categories that have no specific order (such as your religion—Catholic, Protestant, Jewish—which have no logical order). The fourth involves questions which can be answered directly by a number (income, age, number of children). The fifth type of question allows open-ended responses, which must be coded one by one on the basis of the content of the answers and which can then be reconverted into numerical categories.

Spot-Checking for Errors

Since coding involves a number of different types of shifts, there is a great potential for error. Most cleaning of data for computer entry is done after the data have been entered into the computer. However, I suggest that you do a spot check of your data before transferring them to the computer. You may discover that one or two questions were particularly susceptible to miscoding. If you can find any patterns in the noted errors, you will have a chance to correct them before transferring the data to a computer-readable form.

If the number of cases in the study is very large, your coding may be done by a team of people rather than only by you, the primary investigator. In this case, there may be even more chances for error or lack of comparability in the coding done by different coders. Intercoder reliability can be checked by testing how far different coders classify the same data in the same way. This will require monitoring coders over the course of the coding procedures.

ESTABLISHING A COMPUTERIZED DATA FILE

If you are putting your data on a computer in order to produce tables and statistical tests, you will most likely do so with the aid of a computer software program. Recall that the computer equipment itself is referred to as *hardware*. The data will be entered into the computer to form the basis of a *raw data file*. If you are planning to use a software program to process the data, you will need to enter this computer program into the computer, access it, and link your dataset to that program.

Computer Software for Quantitative Data Analysis

The instructions, or commands, that tell the computer what to do are the *software* of the computer. Software consists of computer programs, which may be developed by an individual computer user (or *programmer*) for a specific task (using one of the computer languages which can be understood by the computer) or, more commonly, already prepared for the use of social researchers.

In Chapters 12 and 13, computer output from a dataset using the Statistical Package for the Social Sciences (SPSS Windows version 7.5) software program will be presented. This may not be the computer program you will be using. Whatever you use, we will try here to explain some of the procedures that software programs of this type can carry out for you. If you are planning to use this version of SPSS, there is an elementary description of how to run certain subprograms within this program in Appendix C. Tables produced by this program will accompany the description of analytic techniques and statistical tests in the following chapters on the analysis of data. Moreover, these tables are not very different from ones you would produce if you used a different software program.

Once your data have been read into the computer and form the basis of a raw data file, you probably will want to process this raw data with a computer software program, very likely a software

program specifically designed for social research analyses. Such a program will have the necessary subprograms to produce the quantitative tables you want and generate the statistical tests required for your study. If you know computer programming, you may not want to use such a program, since you will be able to write your own programs to produce tables and compute statistical tests. Most individuals who do social research, however, do not have (and do not need to have) the programming skills to do this. The software programs available to social researchers are so comprehensive in terms of what they are capable of doing yet so relatively easy to use that few programmers could carry out the tasks more effectively or efficiently.

A software program such as SPSS enables you to use its simplified commands in requesting what you want from the computer to produce the tables, graphs, and statistical tests you need for your analysis. Such a program is a combination of a cookbook and a translator. As a cookbook, the program tells you what ingredients are needed to produce the quantitative analyses you want. Also like a cookbook, the program manual can actually suggest different recipes—different types of quantitative analyses and statistical tests that might be useful for specific types of data. In short, it can give you a taste of what each subprogram might offer that will help you in making choices about which subprograms to run.

As a translator, the software program is an intermediary between you and the computer. The program allows you to make your requests in terms of simple statements. In short, you don't need to know a computer language to be able to run a program such as SPSS. Instead, relatively simple command statements are translated into a computer language by the software program.

Setting Up an Initial Computer Run

A computer *run* involves having the computer carry out the tasks that have been requested, in other words, getting the computer to do its work.

The product of this work is referred to as a *job*. Once the computer run is complete, your job will be done. Setting up an initial run requires coordinating three things: (1) your raw data, (2) the computer software program, and (3) the computer system you are using. You must first access (or call forth) the computer software program on your computer system. The commands you use to link the software program to your computer system will vary from one type of computer to another and from one computer location (or *installation*) to another. You must ask at your computer installation for assistance in accessing your data and selecting the best software program for your purposes.

Once the data and software are accessed, the data must be transformed from a *raw input data* file to a *system file*. This system file will contain both the data you plan to use (from the raw data file) and all the necessary commands (from the computer software program) needed by the computer to recognize the data accurately and process it effectively so that statistical analyses can be carried out. In such a file, every variable is named, its position in the data file is shown, and the range of codes to be used for every attribute is given. This system file will also be the file you access each time you want to run another computer job.

For purposes of analyses, the object of your initial computer runs will be to "see what the variables look like." This means that you want to know how many cases can be described by each of the attributes of a variable (if the variable was sex, for example, that would mean how many cases are males and how many are females; if the variable was a math test score, you would want to know how many people attained each possible score on the test).

In addition to knowing how many males and how many females there are in your sample, for example, you would then want to know what proportion of the sample was male and what proportion was female. This could be produced by determining the percentage of males and females in the sample. Tables which give you this information are referred to as frequency distributions, since

they indicate how the sample is distributed across the range of possible attributes of the variable. For the math test score, which is numerical and can be treated as a number scale, you might prefer to know the mean score and the standard deviation, which would tell you the nature of the distribution of scores.

Cleaning the Computerized Variables

Once you have taken a look at the data, your first step is to clean up variables which look messy or inaccurate. For example, if your cases refer to high school students and for the variable of age you find a case with an age of 75, what effect will such a strange response have on your findings? Let's say you plan to use student age as a variable in your analyses. The means and standard deviations which are often used for computational purposes would be distorted by even one case in such a high category.

If you conclude that a mistake has been made in the data, there are a number of possible ways to clean up this variable. In the example given, you might want to look back to the original data (the questionnaires, let's say) to see if there was a 75-year-old subject. You might decide to recode the age variable into age categories, enabling you to combine that case with the highest category, say, 25 and older. Another choice would be to convert that case to a *missing value* so that it would not distort your findings.

If you find a large number of cases falling into strange categories, you need to go back to check the variable at earlier stages. To check on what was actually entered into the computer as a part of your raw data file, you should examine your file information (or file info) listing. Going back further will require you to check whatever you used to enter data into the computer. If you entered it into a terminal, the file information listing would have what you entered. To check back even further, you should go back to the original questionnaires, interview schedules, or whatever were the original forms on which the information was put.

This can be time-consuming and discouraging, but it is essential to clean up your variables before you try to use them in statistical analyses. Often you will be able to find a source of error quite quickly. If you cannot find it or if you cannot change it once it is found, you might consider not using that variable in the analyses (or at least not using it in the most important parts of your analysis).

DATA MANIPULATION PRIOR TO ANALYSIS
Handling Missing Data

Whatever program you are using, there will be methods for handling missing data. The computer must be told which cases to identify (or flag) as missing on each variable so that they can be excluded from the analyses. You often do not want to exclude a case entirely from consideration in a study if only a few variables are missing; instead, you want those variables included which have actual responses and those variables flagged as missing which have no responses. In the language of the software programs, this is called *pairwise deletion* of missing data. You may, conversely, choose to exclude a case from an analysis if there is missing data on any variable being considered for that analysis; this is referred to as *listwise deletion* of missing data. As was mentioned before, 9, 98, and 99 are the code numbers conventionally used to designate missing values. Once a value is designated as missing, it will be kept out of the analyses, though the number of cases missing on that variable will be reported on the tables.

Some computer programs allow you to have a mean number entered to replace a missing response. This means that individuals who skipped a question are assigned the average response for the whole sample as their response. This helps maintain the number of cases (the *case base*) for each analysis, but it gives cases responses they did not offer. Don't forget that the treatment of missing data could affect the validity and reliability of a variable. If there are too many missing cases, the aggregate response may not really rep-

resent the views of the sample. If the variable with the missing data is being analyzed in relation to another variable, this relationship may also be distorted if there are many missing cases on one of the variables.

Recoding Variables

One of the most common manipulation procedures you will use in setting up your variables for analyses is recoding. The purpose of recoding is generally to reduce the number of categories in a variable to a number more manageable for numerical analysis. If you plan to examine the relationships between two or more variables (a subject to be discussed in Chapter 12), you may want to reduce the number of categories in a variable so that you can see whether the cross effects of two variables on each other indicate strong or weak trends. Once you have recoded a variable, however, the original set of categories will be permanently altered. To avoid this, it is usually better to create a new variable from the old one, keeping the old one with the original set of categories and having the new one represent the recoded set of categories.

There are two main principles to consider in deciding how to recode a variable. Either it makes sense *theoretically* (i.e., a recoded variable will better represent the meaning of the variable you want in your study—an example here would be deciding to combine all the members of racial minorities in your study into one group because you have decided that the distinction between white and nonwhite is the only one you are interested in), or it makes sense *empirically* (i.e., you will use the way the respondents answered the question in deciding how to regroup the variable—an example here would be to decide to combine all the minority groups once you have examined the data, since each minority group is too small in number to be analyzed on its own).

Let me offer a few other examples. Suppose you are doing a study on attitudes toward the federally supported Medicare program. Since people can qualify for Medicare at age 65 and since you think people's attitudes are likely to vary according to whether they do or do not qualify for the program, it might make sense to recode the variable age of respondent into two variables: younger than 65 and 65 and older. This would be a theoretical reason for the recoding, since your decision to recode the variable was based on ideas that you held about how the variable would be best used to support your research question or hypothesis.

Take another example: Suppose you are studying unemployment and know the region of the country in which each respondent lives. You might want to combine those living in the northeast and midwest into one group, those living in the southeast and southwest (the sun belt) into another group, and those in the far west, Great Plains, and northwest into a third group. Your rationale here would be that the unemployment rate is different in these sections of the country. Both of these examples offer explanations for recoding based on what you already know and think about the subject of your study, and they make sense because they should help test your hypothesis and highlight and clarify your findings. In these cases, the recoding has been carried out for theoretical reasons.

However, let's say that in a study of fifth-graders' school achievement the variable to be recoded is a math aptitude score. Now, for many types of analyses which would use the average score as the primary unit for analysis, there would be no need to recode. If, however, you want to know what proportion of students who come from varying racial background or whose families are at different social class levels did very well or not too well on the test, one procedure would be to calculate the average scores for each of the subgroups of interest. Another way, however, would be to split the data according to *percentiles* (representing ten groups of 10 percent each), *quintiles* (representing five groups of 20 percent each), or *quartiles* (representing four groups of 25 percent each).

Let's say you decided to use quartiles. You would want to rank the scores from the highest to the lowest. Then you would start at one end of the range of scores and form the quartile groups at the points at which each successive 25 percent of the cases had been accounted for. In this way, the 25 percent of the students with the highest scores would be the top quartile, the next 25 percent would be the second quartile, the next lower 25 percent would be the third quartile, and the lowest 25 percent would be the bottom quartile. Now, rather than having a variable with (say) 50 or more categories based on the actual math test score, you have a new variable with 4 categories based on the math scores ranked in descending order and then grouped into quartiles. In this case you have taken the aggregate findings of the data (the empirical evidence) and used them as the basis for recoding the variable.

Data Preparation in Social Research

The procedures described in this chapter may not have seemed to you to have been very important or challenging. Yet such efforts are at the core of what makes social research scientific. Recall in Chapter 2 that one of the characteristics of scientific research is that it must be systematic, that the language used must be careful and precise so that observations can be accurately recorded and aggregated, one with another. The quantification of data fosters this objective. By turning numerous responses into the same codes which can be analyzed by computers, the systematization of observations is achieved. Although a study in which quantitative data have been systematically prepared for analysis will not necessarily make a contribution to the social sciences, an unsystematic study where the data have been haphazardly treated has no chance of adding to the cumulative knowledge of the social sciences. Careful data preparation is one of the cornerstones of scientific research.

CONSTRUCTING THE RECYCLING SURVEY

The recycling survey was designed by students in my Social Research Method class in the spring of 1997 at California State University at San Marcos. We would carry it out as a telephone survey in our CATI (computer-assisted telephone interviewing) lab, which is a part of the Social and Behavioral Research Institute (SBRI) on our campus. Box 11–2 presents the recycling survey.

Let's look over this survey. Because the survey was to be carried out over the telephone, the text the interviewers were to read began with an introduction. Note that this introduction presents the student interviewer and indicates where she or he is calling from and then gives a rationale for the survey and indicates the topic the survey will address. The interviewee is then told how much time the survey will take (actually, it took somewhat less than seven minutes). This is followed by three statements that address ethical issues: the voluntary nature of the survey, the confidentiality of the responses, and how the interview might be monitored.

Consider Q1 (that is, Question 1). This asks the respondents to quantify the amount of their refuse that they recycle (from 0 to 100 percent). Here the codes are open, and the interviewer types in whatever percentage number the respondent gives. Note that code 108 is to be entered for "don't know" responses and code 109 is used for those who refuse to answer. This will produce a numerical scale. Q2 sets up an ordinal variable that measures what types of products the respondent recycles: there are nine versions of this question which cover the range of products (from glass to green waste) which typically are recycled. The response choices are based on an ordinal scale of frequency that includes "almost all of the time," "most of the time," "some of the time," and "almost never."

Q3 presents six reasons why a person may recycle. These include two economic reasons, two social approval reasons, an environmental reason, and a psychological reason. For the response categories, levels of importance are to be indicated on a four-point ordinal scale from "very important," to "important," to "not important," to "not at all important."

There are six demographic questions which can be used in the analysis to characterize and differentiate the respondents. These questions include qualities of the household: number of residents, number of children, and type of dwelling. Then there are two questions on provisions for recycling at home. Finally, there are four background questions, which include number of years living in North County San Diego, year born (age), educational attainment, and household income. There were two other variables that could be connected to each case that had been provided with the registered voters' sample: sex and political party affiliation.

Carrying Out the Recycling Survey

Note that for all the questions in Box 11–2, the responses are numbered so that the numbered codes can be entered into the computer program by the interviewer as the questions are answered. Let's picture this CATI lab. Interviewers, who were students in the Social Research Methods class, would sit in front of a computer monitor. First the screen would show a name to be called, along with a telephone number. The student would dial the number and ask for the person to be interviewed. From there the interviewer would move to a response screen to indicate whether the party could be reached and, if not, whether a future call should be made. If a future call was indicated, the name of the person was returned to the sample, to be selected either at a specific time which had been designated or at a later time.

The CATI screens are very easy to read. They are split horizontally, with the top half of the screen having the questions the interviewer is to

BOX 11-2

THE RECYCLING SURVEY

INTRO:

Hello, my name is_____ and I'm calling from Cal State University San Marcos. My Sociology class is collecting local opinions on issues related to trash and waste disposal from North County residents like yourself.

The Survey takes about 7 to 8 minutes. I need to let you know that your participation is voluntary, that all of your answers will be kept confidential, and that this call may be monitored for quality control purposes.

First of all, I'd like to ask you a few questions about the way you dispose of trash and waste items around your home.

Q1. If you had to estimate the percentage of your waste items that you dispose via recycling, where 0% would be recycling nothing and 100% would be recycling everything, what would you say your percentage would be?

_____%
[108 = DON'T KNOW; 109 = REFUSED]

Q2. Let's talk a bit about recycling. I'm going to read to you a list of types of items that can be recycled. I'd like for you to think about how often you recycle these types of items. For each type of item, please tell whether you recycle them **almost all of the time, most of the time, some of the time** or **almost never.**

The first item is:

Q2a. Glass. Would you say
  1. Almost all of the time
  2. Most of the time
  3. Some of the time
  4. Almost never
  8. DON'T KNOW
  9. REFUSED
Q2b. Aluminum Cans. [Would you say]
Q2c. Newspaper. [Would you say]
Q2d. Mixed paper other than newspaper. [Would you say]
Q2e. Cardboard. [Would you say]

Q2f. Plastic containers. [Would you say]
Q2g. Tin cans. [Would you say]
Q2h. Hazardous materials such as motor oil, paint and toxic substances. [Would you say]
Q2i. Green waste or yard waste. [Would you say]
Q3. People have told us a lot of different reasons why they do or do not recycle. I'd like you to tell me how important some of these reasons are for you. As I read each of the following statements, please tell me whether they are
  1. Very important
  2. Important
  3. Not important
  4. Not at all important
  8. DON'T KNOW
  9. REFUSED
to you in deciding whether or not to recycle.
Q3a. I recycle to make money for myself.
Q3b. I recycle to donate money to charitable or civic groups.
Q3c. My neighbors would disapprove if I didn't recycle.
Q3d. I recycle to be a good example for children.
Q3e. Recycling helps protect the environment.
Q3f. I recycle because it makes me feel good.

Now I have just a few more questions about yourself and your household...

DEM1. Besides yourself, how many other people live in your household?_____ (NUMBER)
DEM2. How many of those people are children under the age of 18?_____ (NUMBER)
DEM3. How would you describe the type of dwelling you live in? Would it be a
  1. Single-family home
  2. Apartment, townhouse or condominium
  3. Mobile home, or
  4. Something else?
  8. DON'T KNOW
  9. REFUSED

Q5. Do you have separate recycling bins, cans or dumpsters at your home or apartment to aid in recycling?

1. YES

0. NO

Q6. [IF YES ON Q5] Were these containers provided by your city, trash company or landlord, or did you purchase them yourself?

1. PROVIDED BY OTHERS

2. PURCHASED MYSELF

3. BOTH 1&2

DEM4. How long have your lived in North County San Diego?_____ (YEARS)

DEM5. In what year were you born?_____ (YEAR)

DEM6. Which of the following categories best describe the highest grade of school or year of college that you have completed?

1. 8 grades or less

2. Some high school

3. High school diploma

4. Some college

5. 2 year college degree

6. 4 year college degree

7. Graduate school or degree

8. REFUSED

DEM7. And please stop me when I reach the category that best describes your total annual household income before taxes? Would it be...

1. Less than $15,000

2. 15 to under $25,000

3. 25 to under $35,000

4. 35 to under $50,000

5. 50 to under $60,000

6. 60 to under $75,000

7. 75 to under $99,999

8. $100,000 and above

99. REFUSED

98. DON'T KNOW

QCOMMENT. And finally, are there any other thoughts that you have about waste disposal and recycling that you would like to mention, either things that you like or things that you dislike?

Thank you for your time and patience, and thanks for participating!

state (written out in regular small letters and capitals) and with a one-color background, say, red, and the bottom of the screen having a contrasting background color, say, blue, and including the response choices written in all-capital letters. The interviewer asks the question from the red screen and then offers the response categories from the blue screen and punches in the number of the response the respondent gives.

Over a two-week period with each student volunteering to be a telephone interviewer for one four-hour block of time (mostly evenings and weekends), the 27 students in the spring 1997 class carried out 272 successful interviews (approximately 10 interviews per student) with registered voters in North County San Diego. This small survey could be undertaken with a telephone interviewing design, with written questionnaires, or through face-to-face interviews. The results of the recycling survey we carried out at Cal State at San Marcos will serve as the data set to be analyzed in Chapters 12 and 13.

REVIEW NOTES

- Qualitative data analysis generally is carried out through observation and interviewing over a long period of time in ordinary environments: these data are naturalistic.
- The qualitative researcher must condense data, display it, and reach and test conclusions.
- The analysis of field notes can be facilitated if the qualitative researcher prepares asides, written commentaries, in-process memos, open coding, memoing, developed themes, focused coding, and integrative memos.

- Computer software programs for analyzing qualitative data include programs that are word retrievers, text base managers, and programs which can group and cluster sets of information.
- Contact summary forms should be filled out for completed interviews; document summary forms should be completed for written records.
- Qualitative data can be displayed in partially ordered displays, time-ordered displays, role-ordered matrices, cognitive maps, and effects matrices.
- Combining qualitative and quantitative data in the same research project is often a highly desirable strategy.
- Data preparation must be carried out with great care.
- Coding requires the solving of ambiguous issues in the definition of variables.
- Coding should try to preserve the actual meaning and range of variation in the variable.
- Precoded questionnaires facilitate later coding and data transfer.
- Codebooks serve as systems of notation for variables and records of coding decisions. Codebooks should be flexible and should allow for cross-referencing.
- Initial computer runs allow you to check and clean variables, label missing cases, and recode variables to facilitate later analyses.

KEY TERMS

codebook
cognitive maps
contact summary form
document summary form
effects matrix
focused coding
memoing
missing data
open coding
qualitative data
quantitative data
recoding variables
role-ordered display
time-ordered display

STUDY EXERCISES

1. Considering Barrie Thorne's ethnographic observation study of children at play from Chapter 1, what strategies might she have used to condense her field notes?
2. Reviewing Arlie Hochschild's interview study of two-career couples with pre-school-age children from Chapter 1, what types of displays might she have used for the data she collected?
3. Suppose you had a study with three variables: race, tobacco use, and parents' tobacco use. Prepare a codebook for these three variables, creating for each one all the information you would need to include to have a useful and comprehensive codebook.
4. Suppose you ask an open-ended question of a group of college students: "What is your college major?" You end up with a very wide range of responses and decide to recode them to reduce the number of categories. Describe one rule for recoding the variable college major that you might follow for combining categories based on theoretical groups and another rule you might follow based on empirical grounds.

RECOMMENDED READINGS

1. Emerson Robert M., Rachel I. Fretz, and Linda L. Shaw: *Writing Ethnographic Fieldnotes,* University of Chicago Press, Chicago, 1995. This volume is rich in detailed ideas for taking down, organizing, and searching out the meaning of field notes.
2. Miles, Matthew B., and A. Michael Huberman: *Qualitative Data Analysis,* 2nd ed., Sage, Thousand Oaks, CA, 1994. This very comprehensive source-book is filled with suggestions for carrying out innovative and creative qualitative analyses.
3. Riley, Matilda White: *Sociological Research: A Case Approach,* Harcourt Brace, New York, 1963. This classic text, widely available in libraries, combines selections from a wide range of studies and shows how the analyses were developed for those studies.

CHAPTER 12

Univariate, Bivariate, and Trivariate Analyses

INTRODUCTION

*T*o give you a model for analyzing quantitative data, I have prepared a set of analyses from the recycling survey that was introduced in Chapter 11 to take you through the necessary steps. Beginning with a simple hypothesis, we will carefully go through all the steps for testing this hypothesis. Then we will present a few other hypotheses and show how they can be tested using various types of data analyses. We will use the same recycling survey in Chapter 13 when we present the statistics that would accompany these analyses.

Data analysis in the social science can take many forms. Now that computers and software data analysis programs have made it relatively easy to carry out very complex analyses, one can find a wide range of types of analyses in academic social science journals. Understanding the meaning of these analyses is not easy, but most research done for public consumption (as evaluation research, as a study carried out for an agency or organization, as the results of a study to be published in a newspaper or popular magazine) generally presents very simple tables, charts, or graphs which can be readily understood by a wide sector of the public. Thus there is a dilemma. On the one hand, academic social science research depends on complex, sophisticated multivariate analyses—that means analyses with multiple variables—while on the other hand, the public for which much social research is produced cannot and will not master the complexities of multivariate data analysis.

As a student, you will want to begin by learning how to carry out data analyzes that are relatively simple, clear, and logical. You will need to know how to set up computer tables, charts, and graphs to enhance your research report. The analyses in this chapter present tables prepared using the SPSS version 7.5 software program. Reproductions of the computer screens from these analyses carried out using this program are presented in Appendix C. If you want to examine these screens as we go through the tables in this chapter, turn back to that appendix.

We will begin first with the most primary ingredient in quantitative analysis: single variables. We will look at each variable in the analysis we are designing, one at a time. These one-variable tables are called *univariate* tables. After we have looked carefully at the distribution of each variable, we will construct and analyze two-variable, or *bivariate,* tables, and progress to *trivariate* (three variables) analyses. In Chapter 13 we will present information on regression analysis, which is a multivariate technique.

TRYING OUT A DATA ANALYSIS OF OUR OWN

Having described the recycling survey in Chapter 11, we will use the data collected in that survey to build a set of analyses. Recall that in Chapters 1 and 2 we saw that one way to test a hypothesis is to select variables to represent each of the factors in the hypothesis and then set up a table to relate (to cross-tabulate or cross-classify) those variables to one another. For example, Hirschi chose self-reported delinquent acts to represent delinquency, his dependent variable, and intimacy of communication with one's father to represent attachment, one of his independent variables. Then, by examining the relationship between these factors—by preparing a cross tabulation of delinquency by attachment—he could see to what extent those who were more attached to their fathers reported delinquent acts compared with those who were less attached. This type of cross-tabular analysis is one of the most common and widely used forms of data analysis in the social sciences, and it is the kind of analysis we will use in the following presentation.

Who Recycles?

Defining the Research Problem. To move speedily into our data analysis, I will sketch the background of the problem to be studied very briefly. Naturally, you would need to do more to substantiate a rationale for a study, but I am going to skip over most of that effort here and move directly to an analytic model. Suppose we hypothesize that people who place very high importance on the attitude that "recycling makes them feel good" are more likely to recycle than are those who place less importance on this attitude. What this suggests is that carrying out the activities of recycling gives people a sense that they are being good citizens, are sensitive to environmental issues, and are responsible to the broader commonweal—hence, they feel good about themselves. Our theoretical foundations are based on a hypothesis of egotism: those who think that recycling will enhance their image of themselves are more likely to do it. (A psychologist friend of mine suggested that one could also propose that recycling makes them feel good because it helps them avoid guilt.)

In addition, our analysis here will propose that a person's age may affect both that person's attitude toward recycling and that person's propensity to do it. Older people tend to have more free time (because many of them are retired and are no longer raising families) than younger people and may be longer-term residents of communities and thus more committed to improving their communities; involvement in the environmental concerns of the community may "make them feel good." Therefore, we would expect to find a difference between older and younger people in terms of whether those who believe that recycling makes them feel good will be more likely to recycle. Finally, we will consider gender. Because of the

broader role women typically play in home management, we expect that women who may gain greater gratification from being good community members by recycling tend to recycle more than would women who place less emphasis on feeling good about recycling. Moreover, we expect that women would hold this attitude more strongly than men would.

Setting up the Analytic Model. Hypothesizing that the importance of feeling good about recycling increases the amount of waste people recycle, we set up our basic research model as shown in Figure 12-1. That figure states that the independent variable—the attitude that "recycling makes me feel good"—may be related to the dependent variable—amount of waste recycled. What we will try to see is whether those who hold this attitude are more likely to recycle more of their waste items. In Figure 12-1, you can see that we are predicting that believing that this attitude is important will be related to higher levels of recycling. Thus, having the attitude that "recycling makes me feel good" serves as the independent variable (IV) in this analysis and amount recycled serves as the dependent variable (DV).

Selecting the variables. Our model has four variables in it.

1. *Amount recycled.* This variable is Q1 from the recycling survey in Chapter 11. It was based on an estimated percentage of waste that is recycled: from 0 to 100 percent. For cross-tabular analyses, it will require recoding into categories. In terms of its level of measurement, Q1 was a ratio variable, but once it is recoded, it will be reduced to an ordinal variable.

FIGURE 12-1
Hypothesized relationship between the importance of the reason for recycling—"recycling makes me feel good"—and the amount of waste recycled.

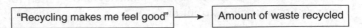

2. *"Recycling makes me feel good."* This variable was Q3f in the recycling survey, one of a set of possible reasons for recycling. The original variable had four values: 1 = very important, 2 = important, 3 = not important, 4 = not at all important, which form an ordinal variable.

3. *Age.* Age is a variable that will need to be constructed from DEM5: year born. Because the sample was drawn from a sampling frame of registered voters, the youngest members of the sample would be 18, the minimum age to register to vote. Again, once the variable was constructed, it would need to be recoded into categories for cross-tabular analyses. In this case, age would be a ratio variable, but when it is recoded, it will become an ordinal variable.

4. *Sex.* This variable is GENDER. It has two categories: male and female. In terms of measurement level, sex was clearly a nominal variable.

UNIVARIATE ANALYSES

The first step in seeing what your data look like is to examine each variable separately. This can be accomplished by getting the distributions of each variable one by one. As was stated above, such single-variable analyses are called *univariate* analyses, that is, analyses based on one variable. Frequency distributions are one type of univariate analysis. Another type that examines the central tendencies of each variable (such as mean, mode, and median; the standard deviation; and the range of responses with the minimum and maximum values) can be used when the variable is numerical, that is, when it is based on an interval or ratio scale. Because two of the variables in this analysis were originally measured at the ratio level (amount recycled and age), we can look at both types of univariate measures: those indicating central tendency and range and frequency distributions.

Frequency Distributions and Measures of Central Tendency for Numerical Variables

The simplest way to see how data are distributed is to examine a frequency distribution of the variable. This will give you the number of cases which fall into each of the attributes of the variable. If the variable is a categorical variable (e.g., sex), the frequency distribution will give you the number and the related percent of the total who fall into each of the categories (male and female). When the variable is a numerical variable (either at the interval or at the ratio level of measurement), it is important to examine measures of central tendency (mean, median, and mode) and the range in responses as well as the frequency distribution.

These are the most basic types of information you can produce about a numerical variable. They will provide you with a foundation for understanding a particular variable and help you decide how to use it in later analyses. These basic univariate tables will help you see what the computer "thinks" your variable looks like and tell you whether you need to do additional "cleaning" activities (setting up or changing missing values or recoding) to make the variable more usable for your analyses.

As was mentioned in Chapter 11, the recycling survey was prepared in our Social and Behavioral Research Institute (SBRI) at California State University, San Marcos, and the data were entered into an SPSS system file. Reproductions of many of the SPSS version 7.5 computer command screens that were used to produce the tables and charts in both this chapter and in Chapter 13 can be found in Appendix C.

The Variable *AGE*. Now let's look at the way we developed the variable AGE. First, we needed to construct this variable from responses to the question QDEM5: In what year were you born? _____ (YEAR). Let's first look at the frequency distribution for QDEM5: year of birth. Table 12-1 gives that distribution. The values in that table refer to

TABLE 12-1

FREQUENCY DISTRIBUTION FOR QDEM5: YEAR OF BIRTH

		Frequency	Percent	Valid Percent	Cumulative Percent
Valid	1	1	.4	.4	.4
	6	1	.4	.4	.7
	8	1	.4	.4	1.1
	9	1	.4	.4	1.5
	11	3	1.1	1.1	2.6
	12	1	.4	.4	3.0
	13	3	1.1	1.1	4.1
	14	4	1.5	1.5	5.5
	15	3	1.1	1.1	6.6
	16	1	.4	.4	7.0
	17	3	1.1	1.1	8.1
	18	3	1.1	1.1	9.2
	19	1	.4	.4	9.6
	20	5	1.8	1.8	11.4
	21	8	2.9	3.0	14.4
	22	1	.4	.4	14.8
	23	5	1.8	1.8	16.6
	24	3	1.1	1.1	17.7
	25	5	1.8	1.8	19.6
	26	2	.7	.7	20.3
	27	5	1.8	1.8	22.1
	28	2	.7	.7	22.9
	29	6	2.2	2.2	25.1
	30	2	.7	.7	25.8
	31	4	1.5	1.5	27.3
	32	3	1.1	1.1	28.4
	33	3	1.1	1.1	29.5
	34	2	.7	.7	30.3
	35	2	.7	.7	31.0
	36	3	1.1	1.1	32.1
	37	2	.7	.7	32.8
	38	3	1.1	1.1	33.9
	39	2	.7	.7	34.7
	41	5	1.8	1.8	36.5
	42	7	2.6	2.6	39.1
	43	5	1.8	1.8	41.0
	44	2	.7	.7	41.7
	45	2	.7	.7	42.4
	46	10	3.7	3.7	46.1
	47	9	3.3	3.3	49.4
	48	3	1.1	1.1	50.6
	49	7	2.6	2.6	53.1
	50	5	1.8	1.8	55.0
	51	4	1.5	1.5	56.5
	52	2	.7	.7	57.2
	53	7	2.6	2.6	59.8

(continued.)

TABLE 12-1—(Continued)

	Frequency	Valid Percent	Cumulative Percent	Percent
54	4	1.5	1.5	61.3
55	3	1.1	1.1	62.4
56	6	2.2	2.2	64.6
57	8	2.9	3.0	67.5
58	3	1.1	1.1	68.6
59	8	2.9	3.0	71.6
60	10	3.7	3.7	75.3
61	8	2.9	3.0	78.2
62	5	1.8	1.8	80.1
63	4	1.5	1.5	81.5
64	5	1.8	1.8	83.4
65	2	.7	.7	84.1
66	4	1.5	1.5	85.6
67	1	.4	.4	86.0
68	6	2.2	2.2	88.2
69	1	.4	.4	88.6
70	4	1.5	1.5	90.0
71	4	1.5	1.5	91.5
72	6	2.2	2.2	93.7
73	2	.7	.7	94.5
74	5	1.8	1.8	96.3
75	3	1.1	1.1	97.4
76	4	1.5	1.5	98.9
77	2	.7	.7	99.6
78	1	.4	.4	100.0
Total	271	99.6	100.0	
Missing 99				
Refused	1	.4		
Total	1	.4		
Total	272	100.0		

the last two digits of the year in which each respondent was born, and so value 1 means that one person was born in 1901. Note that the years in which the largest groups of respondents were born were 1946 (in which 10 individuals were born) and 1960 (in which another 10 were born).

As you can see, the most recent year in which any respondent was born was 1978. Since the sample was obtained in fall 1996 before the November 1996 election, those who were 18 had to have been born in 1978 (1996 – 18 = 1978). This subtraction exercise provides the logic we will use to construct the variable age. To do this, we will use the Compute command in SPSS, which en-

ables us to create new variables from old ones by using mathematical formulas. What we did here was give the new (target) variable the name AGE and then subtract the year born from 96.[1]

Table 12-2 presents the frequency distribution and accompanying statistics for AGE. As you can see, the values (or ages) now range from 18 to 95.

---

[1]If you are wondering why we didn't use 97 rather than 96, since the recycling survey was collected in April 1997, it was because we decided that since there were still nine months remaining in 1997 and only 3 months had been concluded, most members of the sample would not yet have had their birthdays in 1997 and been a year older. However, some would have.

TABLE 12-2

FREQUENCY DISTRIBUTION FOR AGE: AGE OF RESPONDENT

		Frequency	Percent	Valid Percent	Cumulative Percent
Valid	18	1	.4	.4	.4
	19	2	.7	.7	1.1
	20	4	1.5	1.5	2.6
	21	3	1.1	1.1	3.7
	22	5	1.8	1.8	5.5
	23	2	.7	.7	6.3
	24	6	2.2	2.2	8.5
	25	4	1.5	1.5	10.0
	26	4	1.5	1.5	11.4
	27	1	.4	.4	11.8
	28	6	2.2	2.2	14.0
	29	1	.4	.4	14.4
	30	4	1.5	1.5	15.9
	31	2	.7	.7	16.6
	32	5	1.8	1.8	18.5
	33	4	1.5	1.5	19.9
	34	5	1.8	1.8	21.8
	35	8	2.9	3.0	24.7
	36	10	3.7	3.7	28.4
	37	8	2.9	3.0	31.4
	38	3	1.1	1.1	32.5
	39	8	2.9	3.0	35.4
	40	6	2.2	2.2	37.6
	41	3	1.1	1.1	38.7
	42	4	1.5	1.5	40.2
	43	7	2.6	2.6	42.8
	44	2	.7	.7	43.5
	45	4	1.5	1.5	45.0
	46	5	1.8	1.8	46.9
	47	7	2.6	2.6	49.4
	48	3	1.1	1.1	50.6
	49	9	3.3	3.3	53.9
	50	10	3.7	3.7	57.6
	51	2	.7	.7	58.3
	52	2	.7	.7	59.0
	53	5	1.8	1.8	60.9
	54	7	2.6	2.6	63.5
	55	5	1.8	1.8	65.3
	57	2	.7	.7	66.1
	58	3	1.1	1.1	67.2
	59	2	.7	.7	67.9
	60	3	1.1	1.1	69.0
	61	2	.7	.7	69.7
	62	2	.7	.7	70.5
	63	3	1.1	1.1	71.6
	64	3	1.1	1.1	72.7

(continued.)

TABLE 12-2—(Continued)

	Frequency	Valid Percent	Cumulative Percent	Percent
65	4	1.5	1.5	74.2
66	2	.7	.7	74.9
67	6	2.2	2.2	77.1
68	2	.7	.7	77.9
69	5	1.8	1.8	79.7
70	2	.7	.7	80.4
71	5	1.8	1.8	82.3
72	3	1.1	1.1	83.4
73	5	1.8	1.8	85.2
74	1	.4	.4	85.6
75	8	2.9	3.0	88.6
76	5	1.8	1.8	90.4
77	1	.4	.4	90.8
78	3	1.1	1.1	91.9
79	3	1.1	1.1	93.0
80	1	.4	.4	93.4
81	3	1.1	1.1	94.5
82	4	1.5	1.5	95.9
83	3	1.1	1.1	97.0
84	1	.4	.4	97.4
85	3	1.1	1.1	98.5
87	1	.4	.4	98.9
88	1	.4.	.4	99.3
90	1	.4	.4	99.6
95	1	.4	.4	100.0
Total	271	99.6	100.0	
Missing System Missing	1	.4		
Total	1	.4		
Total	272	100.0		

Statistics

	N						
	Valid	Missing	Mean	Median	Mode	Standard Deviation	Range
AGE: age of respondent	271	1	50.06	48.00	36ª	18.68	77

ªMultiple modes exist. The lowest value is shown.

The modal ages are 36 (those born in 1960) and 50 (those born in 1946), which we saw in the QDEM5 table (both of these years occurred during the period called the baby boom). If we look at the accompanying measures of central tendency, we see that the mean = 50.06, the median = 48, and the mode = 36 (in fact, it is both 36 *and* 50). The standard deviation is 18.68, the minimum value was 18, and the maximum was 95, giving a range of 77. In short, there is a very broad range of ages, and the largest group of respondents consisted of those born between 1946 (age 50 in 1996) and

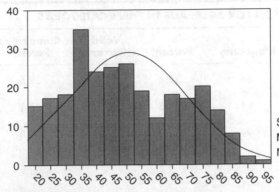

Age of Survey Respondents in Years

Standard deviation = 18.68
Mean = 50
N = 271.00

FIGURE 12-2
Histogram: age of survey respondents in years.

1960 (age 36 in 1996) representing members of the baby boom generation which spans the period from 1946 to 1964.

Figure 12-2 presents a histogram of AGE that shows the highest proportions of respondents in the range of 30 to 50, though with a very broad spread up to age 95. Recall that a histogram is a chart for numerical continuous variables, as was explained earlier in Chapter 4. Note that because the respondents were all registered voters, the lowest point, age 18, has a sizable number of respondents; thus, the shape of the histogram does not gradually diminish in the way it does at the upper age limits.

Now we are ready to recode AGE into a categorical, ordinal variable to be used for cross-tabular analyses. By looking at the frequency distribution for AGE and examining the "Cumulative Percent" column, we can break the distribution into thirds. The youngest group would go from the youngest age (18) up to the 32.5 percent point: age 38. The middle-aged group would go from age 39 up to the 66.1 percent point: age 57. The highest-age group would then be those age 58 to 95. This prepares a second version of the variable for "age" which we call AGER; it has been divided into three ordered categories. Now we are ready to produce a frequency distribution for AGER. If this seems very laborious, let me state that once you get accustomed to using the SPSS program (or whatever program you are using), the handling of variables

(defining them, labeling them, recoding them) will go very rapidly.

Table 12-3 presents the frequency distribution for AGER, the age of respondents in three categories. Note that because we broke down the distribution into thirds, if we look under "Valid Percent," we see that the percentage of respondents who are 18 to 8 (32.5 percent) is nearly identical to the percentage who are between 39 and 57 (33.6 percent) and also those age 58 to 95 (33.9 percent). This means that we have built a recode on empirical evidence—what we have called "young" are those who are in the lowest third of the age distribution of this sample; those who are in the middle-aged group are the middle third of this sample, and those who are old represent the oldest third of the respondents.

The Variable Percent of Waste Recycled.
Table 12-4 presents the frequency distribution for Q1: percent of waste recycled. Given that the respondents could choose any percent from 0 to 100 percent and that people could naturally only make rough estimates, it is not surprising to find a very wide range of replies. The mean of 52.88 percent indicates that the average North County resident recycled just over half his or her waste. The median of 50 and the mode of 50 give similar indications that the central tendency in this distribution was to recycle about half one's waste items.

TABLE 12-3

FREQUENCY DISTRIBUTION FOR AGER: AGE IN THREE CATEGORIES

		Frequency	Percent	Valid Percent	Cumulative Percent
Valid	1. 18–38 (young)	88	32.4	32.5	32.5
	2. 39–57 (middle)	91	33.5	33.6	66.1
	3. 58–95 (old)	92	33.8	33.9	100.0
	Total	271	99.6	100.0	
Missing	System missing	1	.4		
	Total	1	.4		
Total		272	100.0		

Figure 12-3 presents the histogram for percent of waste recycled. Note the number of high points in the graph mostly toward the upper end of the scale. The histogram shows quite an uneven distribution. This graph with the measures of central tendency (mean, median, and mode) and the frequency distribution show us a lot about how the sample responded to this question.

If we use the "Cumulative Percent" column to break the responses on percent of waste recycled into three roughly equal-size groups (in other words, trichotomize the responses), we see that 33.7 percent of the respondents recycled 35 percent or less of their waste, the middle third of the respondents recycled between 36 and 74 percent of their waste, and the highest third of the recyclers recycled 75 percent or more of their waste. Using a recode statement, we can break the variable Q1 into three categories, renaming it Q1R. Table 12-5 presents the frequency distribution for Q1R: percent of waste recycled in three categories. Note we have made the highest recyclers (75 percent or more of their waste recycled) into Category 1. We have set this up in this way so that Q1R can serve as the dependent variable for our bivariate analysis (this will be explained fur-

ther below). Note as well that we are not able to break the distribution so precisely into thirds (as we did for AGER), as the responses clump at points which force a large group into one category or another. Thus the highest third of recyclers include 37.5 percent of respondents, the middle third only 28.8 percent, and the lowest third 33.7 percent.

Frequency Distributions for Categorical Variables

The Variable Q3f: Importance of Attitude: "Recycling Makes Me Feel Good."   The other two variables in our analysis are not numerical variables: Q3f: "Recycling Makes Me Feel Good" is an attitudinal variable based on an ordinal scale of responses, and Gender is a nominal variable with two categories. The distribution of Q3F: Reason for Recycling: Makes Me Feel Good is shown in Table 12-6. Nearly two-fifths (39.3 percent) of the respondents gave this as a "very important" reason, and more than a third listed it as "important." Also, 15 percent of the respondents stated that it was "not" important, while another 9.9 percent stated that it was "not at all important."

TABLE 12-4

FREQUENCY DISTRIBUTION FOR Q1: PERCENTAGE OF WASTE RECYCLED

		Frequency	Percent	Valid Percent	Cumulative Percent
Valid	Recycles 0 nothing	11	4.0	4.1	4.1
	3	1	.4	.4	4.5
	5	3	1.1	1.1	5.6
	6	1	.4	.4	6.0
	7	1	.4	.4	6.4
	10	20	7.4	7.5	13.9
	11	1	.4	.4	14.2
	15	5	1.8	1.9	16.1
	20	21	7.7	7.9	24.0
	25	6	2.2	2.2	26.2
	30	13	4.8	4.9	31.1
	33	1	.4	.4	31.5
	35	6	2.2	2.2	33.7
	40	17	6.3	6.4	40.1
	45	3	1.1	1.1	41.2
	48	1	.4	.4	41.6
	50	34	12.5	12.7	54.3
	60	12	4.4	4.5	58.8
	65	4	1.5	1.5	60.3
	68	1	.4	.4	60.7
	70	4	1.5	1.5	62.2
	74	1	.4	.4	62.5
	75	33	12.1	12.4	74.9
	80	16	5.9	6.0	80.9
	85	3	1.1	1.1	82.0
	90	14	5.1	5.2	87.3
	95	7	2.6	2.6	89.9
	98	1	.4	.4	90.3
	Recycles 100 everything	26	9.6	9.7	100.0
	Total	267	98.2	100.0	
Missing	108 Don't know	5	1.8		
	Total	5	1.8		
Total		272	100.0		

Statistics

	N		Mean	Median	Mode	Standard Deviation	Range
	Valid	Missing					
Q1: percentage of waste recycled	267	5	52.88	50.00	50	30.99	100

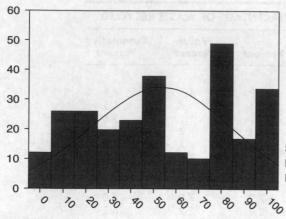

FIGURE 12-3
Histogram: percentage of waste recycled.

TABLE 12-5

**FREQUENCY DISTRIBUTION FOR Q1R: PERCENT
RECYCLED TRICHOTOMIZED**

		Frequency	Percent	Valid Percent	Cumulative Percent
Valid	1. 75–100%	100	36.8	37.5	37.5
	2. 36–74%	77	28.3	28.8	66.3
	3. 0–35%	90	33.1	33.7	100.0
	Total	267	98.2	100.0	
Missing	System missing	5	1.8		
	Total	5	1.8		
Total		272	100.0		

TABLE 12-6

**FREQUENCY DISTRIBUTION FOR Q3F: MAKES ME FEEL
GOOD REASON FOR RECYCLING**

		Frequency	Percent	Valid Percent	Cumulative Percent
Valid	1. Very important	107	39.3	39.3	39.3
	2. Important	97	35.7	35.7	75.0
	3. Not important	41	15.1	15.1	90.1
	4. Not at all important	27	9.9	9.9	100.0
	Total	272	100.0	100.0	
Total		272	100.0		

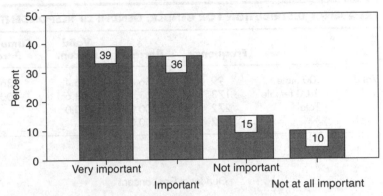

FIGURE 12-4
Bar chart: "Recycling makes me feel good," percentage.

TABLE 12-7

FREQUENCY DISTRIBUTION FOR Q3F2: RECYCLING MAKES ME FEEL GOOD: HOW IMPORTANT?

		Frequency	Percent	Valid Percent	Cumulative Percent
Valid	1. Very important	107	39.3	39.3	39.3
	2. Important	97	35.7	35.7	75.0
	3. Not important	68	25.0	25.0	100.0
	Total	272	100.0	100.0	
Total		272	100.0		

Figure 12-4 presents the bar chart for the distribution on the attitude "Recycling Makes Me Feel Good." In developing bar charts for these types of analyses, it is better to have the vertical axis present percents rather than raw numbers because this provides a common base for comparison. What one can see from this bar chart is that if the two negative categories were combined, there would be roughly equal-sized percentages in a three-category version of this variable. Table 12-7 shows the frequency distribution of Q3FR. Now the "not important" and "not at all important" categories combined to equal 25 percent.

The Variable Gender. Table 12-8 presents the frequency distribution for gender. This indicates that 64 percent of the respondents were women

and 36 percent were men. Figure 12-5 presents this distribution in a bar chart. Now one can see the more than two-thirds to less than one-third split between women and men quite explicitly.

Statistics for Univariate Analyses

There are a number of statistical techniques for describing the distribution of a single variable, which will be fully explained in Chapter 13. The type of statistics that can be employed meaningfully will depend on the *level of measurement* of the variable in question. For variables measured on a numerical scale, a broad array of statistical measures can be used to describe the central point of a distribution, the range of responses, and the frequency of each response. For variables measured with categories

TABLE 12-8

FREQUENCY DISTRIBUTION FOR GENDER: GENDER OF RESPONDENT

		Frequency	Percent	Valid Percent	Cumulative Percent
Valid	.00 male	99	36.4	36.4	36.4
	1.00 female	173	63.6	63.6	100.0
	Total	272	100.0	100.0	
Total		272	100.0		

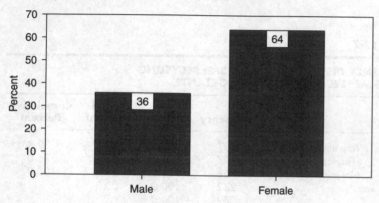

FIGURE 12-5
Bar chart: gender of respondent, percentage.

that form a nominal or ordinal scale—such as most of the variables in our recycling survey—fewer statistics apply. Now that you have learned how to produce univariate tables, we will turn to the discussion of bivariate tables. These tables will be needed to test our hypothesis regarding amount of waste recycled.

BIVARIATE ANALYSES

A Note on Terminology

Bivariate tables based on percentage distributions of one variable in relation to another can be referred to by a number of terms. Computer programs generally refer to them as *cross tabulations.* These are tables in which the categories of one variable are crossed with the categories of another variable to form a matrix type of table. Another

way of referring to these tables is to call them *cross-classification tables,* suggesting that one variable is being sorted in terms of the categories (or classification system) of the other variable. Finally, the term *contingency tables* also is widely used. This term stresses the relationship between the variables being studied, because the table shows how contingent (or dependent) one variable is on another.

Bivariate Tables for the Recycling Survey

By cross-tabulating different pairs of our variables in our study of recycling, we will see how the variables are related to one another. Three types of bivariate relationships interest us. First, we want to see whether believing that recycling makes you

TABLE 12-9

PERCENT RECYCLED BY IMPORTANCE OF "RECYCLING MAKES ME FEEL GOOD"

Q1R Percent Recycled Trichotomized * Q3F2 Recycling Makes Me Feel Good: How Important? Cross-Tabulation

			Q3F2 Recycling Makes Me Feel Good: How Important?			
			1. Very Important	2. Important	3. Not Important	Total
Q1R% recycled trichotomized	1. 75–100%	Count	59	30	11	100
		% within Q3F2 Recycling Makes Me Feel Good: How Important?	56.2%	31.6%	16.4%	37.5%
	2. 36–74%	Count	23	34	20	77
		% within Q3F2 Recycling Makes Me Feel Good: How Important?	21.9%	35.8%	29.9%	28.8%
	3. 0–35%	Count	23	31	36	90
		% within Q3F2 Recycling Makes Me Feel Good: How Important?	21.9%	32.6%	53,7%	33.7%
Total		Count	105	95	67	267
		% within Q3F2 Recycling Makes Me Feel Good: How Important?	100,0%	100.0%	100.0%	100.0%

feel good is directly related to increased levels of recycling (the association representing our major hypothesis). Second, we want to see whether age relates to recycling (an alternative hypothesis). Third, we want to examine whether there are important differences in the recycling behavior of women and men.

Is a Major Reason for Recycling That It Makes You Feel Good?   To examine this, we need to set up a cross tabulation between the amount recycled (the dependent variable) and the importance of this reason (the independent variable). We will place the dependent variable at the left-hand side of the table to serve as the row variable and the independent variable at the top to serve as the column variable. (This can be requested from the SPSS version 7.5 program.)

Cross-Tab Table Formats.   Table 12-9 is a computer-prepared table showing the relationship between the dependent and independent variables.

In Table 12-9, first examine the table setup. Note that the highest level of recycling is the first member of the set of categories (coded as 1), as is the highest level of importance that recycling makes you feel good. Since the hypothesis states that those who attach the highest importance that recycling makes them feel good will recycle more, the measures of each of these highest qualities are coded as 1, and the categories meet in the upper left-hand cell of the table. (A *cell* in a table is a position where two categories meet. Thus, Table 12-9 has nine cells.)

At the bottom of each column are the column base numbers on which the percentages are computed; these are referred to as *marginals*. For each of these columns, the percentage of each category of the dependent variable (the row variable) appears in each cell. The percentages in the cells of the table can be totaled down each of the columns to 100 percent. The computer table also includes a total row percentage, that is, the proportion of all cases in the table which are in that row. (Do you know what number would serve as the base for these row percents? It is the total table number, 267, which is at the base of the row totals.)

Understanding the table. Looking at Table 12-9, note that the differences in the column marginals are fairly large (with over 100 cases in the "Very Important" column and fewer than 70 cases in the "Not Important" column). Yet percentaging allows you to compare these different columns by making each of them equivalent to 100. Again, we will follow the principle of "percentage down, read across" and compare the column distributions across each category of the independent variable.

Over 55 percent of those believing that recycling made them feel good was "very important" recycled more than 75 percent of their waste; this was 25 percentage points higher than those who believed it was "important" and 50 percentage points higher than those who believed it was "not important." In the middle row, you see that the distribution narrows so that more similar proportions of the different belief groups recycled between 36 and 74 percent of their waste. Looking at the bottom row, those who recycled the least, we see that the distribution widens again, but in a converse manner to the top row. More than twice as many of those believing recycling made them feel good was not important recycled a third or less of their waste.

There is a steady increase in the proportion recycling more waste among those holding the reason to be more important. These steadily increasing (or decreasing) percentages across a table between two variables show *monotonicity*. This means that higher levels of the independent variable are related incrementally to higher (or lower) levels of the dependent variable. (Of course, we would hope to find steady increases in the expected direction of how the independent variable relates to the dependent variable, but we might find opposing evidence of a monotonic relationship. This search for patterns in the distributions (steady increases or steady decreases) would be a primary aim of the analysis of tables.

In some cases, it might also be useful to consider the differences between specific percentages in the first and last columns. Such high-low percentage differences are referred to as *epsilons*. In Table 12-9, there is a 39.8 percentage-point difference between the "very important" and "not important" belief groups for recycling 75 percent or more of their waste. Note that in the middle row, there is only an 8 percentage-point difference. But in the bottom row, the epsilon is 31.8 percentage points, closer in size to the epsilon in the top row, though the cell location of the highest percentages is reversed. In short, an epsilon represents the differences between the percentages falling into extreme cells of a table.

We can conclude from Table 12-9 that there is a relationship between believing that recycling makes you feel good and recycling a large amount of your waste. But actually how important relative to other possible factors is this belief in affecting how much people recycle? How would the age and gender of the respondents affect recycling behaviors? The next sets of tables will examine this.

How Age and Gender Relate to the Attitude "Recycling Makes Me Feel Good." Since the next two tables will examine the independent variable in terms of the groups to which the respondents belong, the tables serve as subgroup comparisons. The primary object of subgroup comparisons is to describe the differences between groups. Our object here will be to analyze whether some types of respondents are more likely to place greater importance on the attitude "Recycling Makes Me Feel Good" than are others.

TABLE 12-10

IMPORTANCE OF "RECYCLING MAKES ME FEEL GOOD" BY AGE

Q3F2: Recycling Makes Me Feel Good: How Important? * AGER: Age in Three Categories Cross-Tabulation

			AGER: Age in Three Categories			
			1. 18–38 (Young)	2. 39–57 (Middle)	3. 58–95 (Old)	Total
Q3F2 Recycling Makes Me Feel Good: How Important?	1. Very important	Count	29	33	44	106
		% within AGER: Age in 3 categories	33.0%	36.3%	47.8%	39.1%
	2. Important	Count	42	27	28	97
		% within AGER: Age in 3 categories	47.7%	29.7%	30.4%	35.8%
	3. Not important	Count	17	31	20	68
		% within AGER: Age in 3 categories	19.3%	34.1%	21.7%	25.1%
Total		Count	88	91	92	271
		% within AGER: Age in 3 categories	100.0%	100.0%	100.0%	100.0%

Table 12-10 reports the cross tabulation for AGER with the attitude, and Table 12-11 reports the cross tabulation for GENDER. In Table 12-10 we see a strong relationship between being older (age 58 to 95) and rating the reason for recycling that it makes you feel good as very important. We find an 11-point difference in favor of the older group compared to the middle-aged group and nearly a 15-point difference in favor of the older compared to the youngest group. Clearly, the distribution of the age groups in attaching importance to this attitude about recycling varies. Since AGER ranges from low to high, it establishes order, and therefore we can analyze Table 12-10 in terms of monotonicity. When we compare the importance of this attitude "recycling makes me feel good" across the three age groups, we see distinctive differences. The oldest respondents were more likely to place high importance on this attitude, and the middle-aged were more likely than the younger to place high importance on it. There is a clear ordering between the groups such that believing that this attitude is very important rises with each older age group. This is evidence of monotonicity in the relationship between age and placing importance on the attitude "recycling makes me feel good."

Table 12-11 reports the cross tabulation for GENDER. We see a strong relationship between being female and believing that "Recycling Makes Me Feel Good" is very important. More than twice the percentage of women than men find it very important (48.6 percent to 23.2); that is more than a 25-point difference in favor of the women. Clearly, women were much more likely to offer this as a reason for recycling than were men.

TABLE 12-11

IMPORTANCE OF "RECYCLING MAKES ME FEEL GOOD" BY GENDER

Q3F2: Recycling Makes Me Feel Good: How Important? * GENDER: Gender of Respondent Cross-Tabulation

			GENDER: Gender of Respondent		
			.00 Male	1.00 Female	Total
Q3F2 Recycling Makes Me Feel Good: How important?	1. Very important	Count	23	84	107
		% within GENDER: Gender of respondent	23.2%	48.6%	39.3%
	2. Important	Count	40	57	97
		% within GENDER: Gender of respondent	40.4%	32.9%	35.7%
	3. Not important	Count	36	32	68
		% within GENDER: Gender of respondent	36.4%	18.5%	25.0%
Total		Count	99	173	272
		% within GENDER: Gender of respondent	100.0%	100.0%	100.0%

For our research problem, what is now important is to consider how far these two background characteristics affect the relationship of the attitude to the recycling behavior. To examine this requires setting up trivariate tables. Before we do this, however, let us recapitulate the meaning of bivariate tables.

The Nature of Bivariate Relationships

A two-variable table tells you how one variable is related to another. It does not show whether one variable *determines* or *causes* the other, since other factors currently being ignored in the two-variable association may help explain the relationship between the two being studied. However, it is useful to begin by first trying to understand the relationship between two variables. The best way to start is to consider the *direction of the relationship*.

What you want to look for is the extent to which variation in one variable relates to variation in another. Are the cases that are categorized as high on one variable also high on the other? Or are they low on the other? If the first case is true (high is related to high, low is related to low), there is a *positive*, or *direct, association* (relationship) between the two variables. If the second case is true and those high on one variable tend to be low on the other, there is a *negative*, or *inverse, association* (relationship). In either case, the relationship would be considered *linear* in that as the values of one variable go up, the values of the other also go up (a positive association) or down (a negative association). (Looking for the direction of the relationship between two variables requires that the categories of each variable have some order. However, if one of the variables, such as sex, is measured at the nominal level and therefore has no implied order, this concept of the direction of the relationship does not apply.)

Positive and Negative Associations. Whether a positive or negative association is considered strong or weak depends on your hypotheses about the type of relationship you expected to find. In Chapter 13, statistical tests will be presented to test the strength of the relationship between variables. However, even a statistically weak relationship may be considered important, depending on what you had expected the relationship to be according to your theory or hypotheses.

In many tables, the pattern of relationship is less evident (*high* may be related to high, medium, *and* low; *low* may be related to low, medium, *and* high). In such an instance, the relationship is less clear-cut. If one variable is related to both high and low values of a second variable, the relationship is not linear but *curvilinear.* (Chapter 13 will show graphic examples of these.) One way to determine whether a table is positive or negative is to see whether more cases appear in the cells that cross the table diagonally. If the high categories have been coded as 1 for the computer and are in the upper left-hand corner, the positive diagonal will go from the upper left-hand corner to the lower right-hand corner. Conversely, if the high categories are given the higher number codes, the highest code will appear above the upper right-hand cell, and the positive diagonal will go from the upper right-hand corner to the lower left-hand corner. Our discussion assumes that tables are set up where the high categories are coded as 1 and the positive diagonal runs from the upper left-hand corner to the lower right-hand corner.

If in a table you find more cases in the cells forming the positive diagonal even though the cases are widely dispersed, this may be evidence of a *weak positive association* between the variables. If there are fairly large percentages along the negative diagonal even though the cases are widely scattered across the cells, the relationship would be called a *weak negative* one. Eventually, you must learn to read a table so quickly and carefully that you can *see* by its appearance whether the associations are positive or negative. With experience, you will be able to do this with ease.

As was mentioned above, how you set up your bivariate table may well determine whether the relationship you find will be positive or negative. If you expect (or hypothesize) that women are more likely to recycle, you should set up the table so that they will be given the code of 1 (and will be placed in the table in the upper left-hand cell). Likewise, high levels of recycling should be given a 1. This causes the hypothesized association of gender (female) and high amounts of recycling to converge in the upper left-hand cell of the table. Programs such as SPSS allow you easily to recode the categories in your variables before carrying out your computer runs. This will enable you to set up your variables to test the hypothesis you want to test. Recall that in Table 12-8, recycling had been recoded to make "75 percent or more" category 1, and the recycling makes me feel good reason had been set up so that "very important" was category 1. We found that the larger percentages were in the upper left-hand and lower right-hand cells (along the positive diagonal).

Bivariate tables also can be analyzed in terms of the *strength of association* (or strength of relationship) between the two variables. Statistical tests indicate the degree of strength of the association. Chapter 13 presents statistical tests for the bivariate analyses presented in this chapter as well as correlation statistics appropriate for variables measured on numerical scales. Statistical material is in a separate chapter so that students with varying exposure to statistics can concentrate on this subject if they need more background.

The Issue of Spuriousness. Even when you find a strong relationship between two variables, you cannot be certain that the one caused the other. A number of other phenomena may explain the relationship between the two variables being considered. One such explanation could be that the relationship between the two variables being examined has in fact come about because of a third, unexamined variable. When this happens, the relationship between the two variables is said to be *spurious;* it is in fact caused by an unseen third variable. To test whether two-variable relationships are spurious requires moving from the analysis of two-variable relationships to the analysis of three-variable relationships.

TRIVARIATE ANALYSES

Adding a third variable to an analysis can make an enormous difference. As was stated earlier, this third variable may be referred to as a *control variable*. This implies that you plan to examine a two-variable relationship, *controlling* for the possible effects of a third variable by looking at the two-variable relationship under each condition of the third, or control, variable. (Your purpose here may be to check for possible spuriousness between the dependent and independent variables.) The third variable in an analysis is also often referred to as a *test variable,* meaning that the analysis will test for the effects of the third variable on the two-variable association. The terms *test variable* and *control variable* can be used interchangeably.

A number of different terms are used to differentiate bivariate from trivariate tables (and bivariate from trivariate relationships). Sometimes the bivariate relationship is called the *original relationship* and the trivariate relationship is called a *partial relationship.* This means that each partial table represents only part of the sample presented in the original table and that the sample has been divided among all the partial tables. For example, if the original table related attitude toward recycling to amount recycled and if a third variable, sex, were then used to "partial" the original relationship, there would be two partial tables, one relating the attitude to amount recycled for men and the other relating the same two variables for women.

Bivariate tables can also be referred to as *zero-order tables,* meaning that they are at the lowest or most basic level, and trivariate tables can be labeled *first-order tables,* which means that they are raised up to the next higher level. In this case, you

could also have second-order, third-order, or higher-order tables where the zero-order table is subdivided (broken down, or partialed) first by one test variable, then the first-order tables are broken down by a second test variable, etc.

Trivariate Tables for the Recycling Survey

In this section, we will examine our original relationship of reason for recycling to amount recycled, controlling for two test variables. What this does is separate the dataset into the categories of the test variable and then cross-tabulate the two original variables.

How the Control Variables Might Affect the Original Relationship between the Attitude "Recycling Makes Me Feel Good" and Amount of Waste Recycled.   When the variables from the recycling survey were selected, two variables were included as possible factors which might change the relationship between the independent variable, reason for recycling, and the dependent variable, amount recycled. These two control variables were age and gender.

Figure 12-6 diagrams the predicted effects of age and gender on the relationship of the independent variable to the dependent variable. Because we predict that the effect of the independent variable on the dependent variable will vary under each condition of the control variable, we are expecting the control variable to interact in the original relationship between the independent and dependent variables. This is called an *interaction effect.* In terms of the interaction effect of genders, we expect that the independent variable will be positively related to the dependent variable for both males and females but that the relationship should be stronger for females. In terms of the interaction effect of age, we predict that the relationship between the independent and dependent variables will be stronger for those who are older.

Predicted Effects with Gender as the Control Variable

GENDER: MALE

GENDER: FEMALE

Predicted Effects with Age as the Control Variable

AGE: YOUNG (18–37)

Reason for recycling: "Makes me feel good" → Amount recycled

AGE: MIDDLE (38–57)

Reason for recycling: "Makes me feel good" –?→ Amount recycled

AGE: OLD (58–95)

Reason for recycling: "Makes me feel good" → Amount recycled

FIGURE 12-6
Hypothesized relationship between reason for recycling and amount recycled, showing interaction effects of age and gender.

What Happens to the Original Relationship between Amount Recycled and Reason for Recycling When Gender Is Controlled?   Table 12-12 presents these partial tables. Let's first look at the top part of the table, which is for males. Compare the total number of cases (to the far right under "Total"), which is 98, to the total number for the sample, which we recall is 272. Where are the other cases? They are in the table at the bottom for females (total = 169). Since 98 + 169 = 267, this

indicates that there are five missing cases in a table which combines data for those by Q1R, Q3F2, and GENDER.

This table is read in precisely the same way as a bivariate table. The difference is that you want to compare this table for males to the one for females. If you compare the distribution of amount recycled across the importance of the attitude groups and then contrast those differences in distributions for males and females, you can see that the distributions show little difference between the males and the females. This suggests that gender did not affect the bivariate relationship much.

Now we should consider the percentage differences (or epsilons) between those who felt the attitude was "very important" and those who felt it was "not important" and compare these epsilons between the sexes. In the table for males, there is a 42.6-percentage-point difference in the importance of the attitude for those who recycle 75 percent or more, while in the table for females, the percentage-point difference is slightly lower (36.7 percent). If we compare epsilons for the lowest-level recyclers (those who recycle 35 percent or less), we see that the difference between the sexes is also very low (34.8 percent – 61.1 percent = –26.3-percentage-point difference for males) and females (18.3 percent – 45.2 percent = –26.9-percentage-point difference for females). If we consider monotonicity, we find that reducing the level of importance of the attitude that "recycling makes me feel good" is related in a stepwise fashion to smaller proportions of high-level recyclers among both males and females.

What Happens to the Original Relationship between Amount Recycled and Reason for Recycling When Age is Controlled?   Table 12-13 presents the partial tables for age groups. Note that the total number of respondents in each of the subtables is nearly the same ($N = 88$ for the young, 90 for the middle-aged, and 88 for the old). This is the case because the variable AGER was broken into three equivalent-size groups. Examining the

TABLE 12-12

PERCENT RECYCLED BY IMPORTANCE OF "RECYCLING MAKES ME FEEL GOOD" BY GENDER

Q1R Percent Recycled Trichotomized * Q3F2 Recycling Makes Me Feel Good: How Important? * GENDER: Gender of Respondent Cross-Tabulation

GENDER: Gender of Respondent				Q3F2: Recycling Makes Me Feel Good: How Important?			
				1. Very Important	2. Important	3. Not Important	Total
.00 Male	Q1R % recycled trichotomized	1. 75–100 %	Count	13	9	5	27
			% within Q3F2 Recycling Makes Me Feel Good: How Important?	56.5%	23.1%	13.9%	27.6%
		2. 36–74%	Count	2	12	9	23
			% within Q3F2 Recycling Makes Me Feel Good: How Important?	8.7%	30.8%	25.0%	23.5%
		3. 0–35%	Count	8	18	22	48
			% within Q3F2 Recycling Makes Me Feel Good: How Important?	34.8%	46.2%	61.1%	49.0%
	Total		Count	23	39	36	98
			% within Q3F2 Recycling Makes Me Feel Good: How Important?	100.0%	100.0%	100.0%	100.0%
1.00 Female	Q1R % recycled trichotomized	1. 75–100%	Count	46	21	6	73
			% within Q3F2 Recycling Makes Me Feel Good: How Important?	56.1%	37.5%	19.4%	43.2%
		2. 36–74%	Count	21	22	11	54
			% within Q3F2 Recycling Makes Me Feel Good: How Important?	25.6%	39.3%	35.5%	32.0%
		3. 0–35%	Count	15	13	14	42
			% within Q3F2 Recycling Makes Me Feel Good: How Important?	18.3%	23.2%	45.2%	24.9%
	Total		Count	82	56	31	169
			% within Q3F2 Recycling Makes Me Feel Good: How Important?	100.0%	100.0%	100.0%	100.0%

TABLE 12-13

PERCENT RECYCLED BY IMPORTANCE OF "RECYCLING MAKES ME FEEL GOOD" BY AGE

Q1R Percent Recycled Trichotomized * Q3F2: Recycling Makes Me Feel Good: how Important? * AGER Age in Three Categories Cross-Tabulation

AGER: Age in Three Categories				Q3F2: Recycling Makes Me Feel Good: How Important?			
				1. Very Important	2. Important	3. Not Important	Total
1. 18–38 (young)	Q1R % recycled trichotomized	1. 75–100%	Count	15	9	2	26
			% within Q3F2 Recycling Makes Me Feel Good: How Important?	51.7%	21.4%	11.8%	29.5%
		2. 36–74%	Count	4	15	5	24
			% within Q3F2: Recycling Makes Me Feel Good: How Important?	13.8%	35.7%	29.4%	27.3%
		3. 0–35%	Count	10	18	10	38
			% within Q3F2: Recycling Makes Me Feel Good: How Important?	34.5%	42.9%	58.8%	43.2%
	Total		Count	29	42	17	88
			% within Q3F2: Recycling Makes Me Feel Good: How Important?	100.0%	100.0%	100.0%	100.0%
2. 39–57 (middle)	Q1R % recycled trichotomized	1. 75–100%	Count	14	5	3	22
			% within Q3F2: Recycling Makes Me Feel Good: How Important?	43.8%	18.5%	9.7%	24.4%
		2. 36–74%	Count	12	13	8	33
			% within Q3F2: Recycling Makes Me Feel Good: How Important?	37.5%	48.1%	25.8%	36.7%
		3. 0–35%	Count	6	9	20	35
			% within Q3F2: Recycling Makes Me Feel Good: How Important?	18.8%	33.3%	64.5%	38.9%
	Total		Count	32	27	31	90
			% within Q3F2: Recycling Makes Me Feel Good: How Important?	100.0%	100.0%	100.0%	100.0%

(continued.)

TABLE 12-13—CONTINUED.

| AGER:
Age in Three
Categories | | | | Q3F2: Recycling Makes Me Feel Good: How Important? | | | |
				1. Very Important	2. Important	3. Not Important	Total
3. 58–95 (old)	Q1R % recycled trichotomized	1. 75–100%	Count	30	16	6	52
			% within Q3F2: Recycling Makes Me Feel Good: How Important?	69.8%	61.5%	31.6%	59.1%
		2. 36–74%	Count	7	6	7	20
			% within Q3F2: Recycling Makes Me Feel Good: How Important?	16.3%	23.1%	36.8%	22.7%
		3. 0–35%	Count	6	4	6	16
			% within Q3F2: Recycling Makes Me Feel Good: How Important?	14.0%	15.4%	31.6%	18.2%
	Total		Count	43	26	19	88
			% within Q3F2: Recycling Makes Me Feel Good: How Important?	100.0%	100.0%	100.0%	100.0%

distribution of the percentages across the rows indicates that for every age group (in this study, the young are from 18 to 38, the middle-aged from 39 to 57, and the old from 58 to 95) there is a strong association between believing that recycling makes me feel good is very important and recycling a large amount of one's waste.

If we consider the epsilons for the top rows of the three subtables, we note very little difference among the three age groups (39.9-percentage-point difference for the young, 34.1-percentage-point difference for the middle-aged, and 38.2-percentage-point difference for the old). However, if we examine the epsilons in the bottom row of each subtable—that is, for those who recycle 35 percent or less of their waste—we see that there is a very large negative epsilon for the middle-aged (–45.7-percentage-point difference) and much smaller epsilons for the young (–24.3-percentage-

point difference) and especially for the old (–17.6-percentage-point difference). What we might want to think about is that for the middle-aged group who are among the baby boomers, rejecting the attitude that recycling makes them feel good closely relates to their behavior of not recycling much. Among the older respondents, even those who reject the attitude often recycle. Note again that there is monotonicity present in each of the subtables, indicating a stepwise decline in the percentages across the attitude groups.

Condensing Trivariate Tables

One of the objects of data analysis is to compress data—to restrict as much as possible the amount of data it is necessary to present in order to make one's point—while at the same time maximizing the amount of information each table can give.

TABLE 12-14

CONDENSED TRIVARIATE TABLE OF RECYCLING 75 PERCENT OR MORE OF WASTE BY AGE: IMPORTANCE OF REASON FOR RECYCLING

Age	Importance of Reason for Recycling: "Recycling Makes Me Feel Good:		
	Very Important	Important	Not Important
18–37	51.7 (29)	21.4 (42)	11.8 (17)
38–57	43.8 (32)	18.5 (27)	9.7 (31)
58–95	69.8 (43)	61.5 (26)	31.6 (19)

For trivariate tables, this can often be done by presenting one category of the dependent variable in a table that cross-tabulates the independent variable with the test variable. Let's take the set of trivariate tables for age and show how much of the information from the three tables can be condensed into one.

Suppose we are primarily interested in finding out which is more highly associated with recycling the greatest amount of waste. Specifically, this means we want to compare proportions of respondents with particular combinations of ages and reasons for recycling. How can we show this in one table? Look at Table 12-14. This table presents the percentage of high-level recyclers among those with certain combinations of ages and importance levels of reasons for recycling. Since the proportions of those who recycled at lower levels are not presented, the columns in Table 12-14 do not add up to 100 percent.

Here we see that feeling good about recycling actually is more important for recycling among younger respondents (40 percent more of those who find the reason very important recycle a lot than those who think it is not important) as compared to the oldest or middle-aged groups.

If a condensed table is prepared from variables with two categories, then it is easy for the reader to determine what the rest of the table would look like (by merely subtracting the percents shown in the table from 100 percent). In the example given, however, where the dependent variable has three

categories, the original tables cannot be reconstructed from the condensed table; nevertheless, the condensed table reports on the most important category of the dependent variable (for an ordered variable, this might be the highest category) and indicates more succinctly the effects of the independent and control variables.

ELABORATION

A third variable may alter the relationship between dependent and independent variables in a number of different ways. Certain types of outcomes that can occur after the entry of a third variable into a bivariate relationship have come to serve as exemplary models for social analyses. These effects were studied first by Samuel Stouffer, a well-known social researcher whose studies of the U.S. Army were very influential in the development of social research after World War II (Stouffer, 1949). Stouffer's ideas were formulated and disseminated more widely by Paul Lazarsfeld, Patricia Kendall, Robert Merton, and others at the Bureau of Applied Research at Columbia University (see Kendall and Lazarsfeld, 1950). Perhaps the most widely used work applying the principles of elaboration to cross-tabular analysis has been Rosenberg's *The Logic of Survey Analysis* (1968).

These analytic models have been so influential in social science analyses that they are often referred to as the *elaboration paradigm*. For our purposes, what is important about elaboration is that it is a way to try to explain what happens to two-variable relationships under the conditions of a third (test) variable. We will examine the different forms of the elaboration model by using in certain instances the trivariate tables we have already discussed and in other instances some hypothetical results that might have occurred.

There are two factors to consider in an elaboration. The first is whether the third variable logically comes in a time sequence *before* the independent variable (in which case it is *antecedent*) or whether it occurs *between* the independent and dependent variables (in which case it is *intervening*). Figure 12-7 shows trivariate models with antecedent and intervening test variables as well as applications of these models where the variables from our recycling survey have been fit into the models.

The second consideration comes into play once the partial tables are formed. When the third variable is introduced, the relationships between the independent and dependent variables under the various conditions of the test variables may either remain the same as in the original table or change. If the relationships between the dependent and independent variables remain largely the same in the partial tables, they represent a *replication*. If the relationships between the dependent and independent variables weaken in the partial tables and the test variable is antecedent to the independent variable, the original relationship has been explained and is therefore considered *spurious*. (In this case, the antecedent variable would be an extraneous variable producing the spurious relationship.) Using the terms of the elaboration paradigm, such an occurrence is referred to as an *explanation;* i.e., the original relationship has been explained by an extraneous factor.

If the original relationship weakens but the test variable was intervening between the independent and dependent variables, the intervening factor has largely destroyed the original relationship. This form of elaboration would be called an *interpretation*. This generally means that both the

independent and the dependent variables were related to the intervening variable, which is also the case in an explanation. Thus, when the sample is divided into the different categories "of the test variables, the partial relationships between the original variables will vanish" (Kendall and Lazarsfeld, 1950). In short, when the intervening test variable is used to stratify the sample, it serves largely to wipe out the relationship between the original two variables.

Finally, if the two partial relationships show different trends in comparison to the original relationship such that one partial relationship is stronger than the original relationship and the other is weaker, the results are referred to as a *specification*. What this implies is that under one condition of the test variable the relationship between the dependent and independent variables strengthened, while under another condition of the test variable it weakened or largely disappeared. In other words, the third variable *specified* the condition in which the original relationship is the strongest. Recall that this is also referred to as an *interaction effect*.

Using Gender as the Test Variable

Now we will try out our own elaboration analysis by returning to the recycling study to reexamine a trivariate analysis to see what the partial relationships showed about the original relationship between the importance of a reason for recycling and the level of recycling behavior. To do this, we will begin by carefully going through every step of a three-variable relationship, thinking through what we can learn at each step. Our example will use gender as the test variable.

Recycling Behavior: "Importance of Recycling Makes Me Feel Good" and Gender. We will return to our trivariate analysis of Table 12-12, which cross-tabulates for males and females. This is the diagram we saw above in Figure 12-7. Clearly, sex is empirically antecedent to both

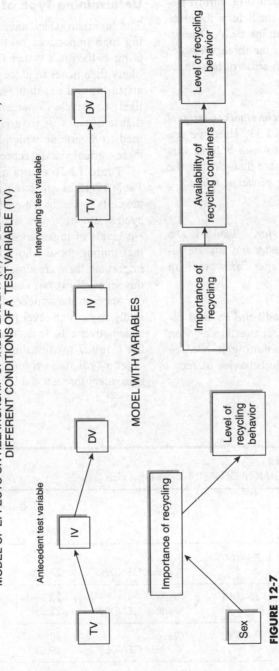

FIGURE 12-7
Trivariate models with antecedent and intervening test variables.

variables in its time of designation (at birth). Before reexamining this table in the light of the elaboration model, let us first examine each of the bivariate relationships between the three variables in order to develop a thorough sense of how these variables relate to one another.

Gender: Importance of "recycling makes me feel good." Reconsider Table 12-11. Here we see that the proportion of females who believe this reason is very important is more than double the proportion of males. In short, gender is related to having this reason for recycling.

Gender and recycling behavior. Table 12-15 presents the association of gender and amount recycled. Here we see advantages for women in amount recycled.

"Recycling makes me feel good" and amount recycled. This is the original relationship as seen earlier in Table 12-9. Reexamining it, we see again how the attitude and the behavior of recycling are strongly associated.

Determining Type of Elaboration

The bivariate tables have indicated (1) that placing high importance on the attitude fosters recycling behavior, (2) that females are much more likely than males to place high importance on this attitude, and (3) that females are much more likely to recycle 75 percent or more of their waste than are males. A trivariate table must be examined to determine which type of elaboration the three-variable model represents.

Table 12-16 offers a condensed version of Table 12-12 in which the percentages presented in the cells represent the proportion of high-level recyclers among males and females holding different levels of importance for the attitudes. We see that among those who think the attitude is very important, there are almost *no* differences between the sexes. However, among those not placing importance on the attitude, female are slightly more likely to be high-level recyclers. Since the difference between the sexes is so slight, this means that the original relationship has been replicated. In other words, the original relationship is roughly equivalent for men and for women.

TABLE 12-15

PERCENT RECYCLED BY GENDER

Q1R: Amount Recycled Recode * GENDER GENDER * Cross-Tabulation

| | | | Gender | | |
			0. Male	1. Female	Total
Q1R: amount recycled recode	1. 75–100%	Count	27	73	100
		% within GENDER	27.6%	43.2%	37.5%
	2. 36–74%	Count	23	54	77
		% within GENDER	23.5%	32.0%	28.8%
	3. 0–35%	Count	48	42	90
		% within GENDER	49.0%	24.9%	33.7%
Total		Count	98	169	267
		% within GENDER	100.0%	100.0%	100.0%

Using Age as the Test Variable

If we go back and examine how age affected the relationship between the dependent and independent variables (Table 12-13), we can see that those who consider the attitude "very important" are more likely to be major recyclers in every age group, that for the older group there is not much difference in the percentage recycling 75 percent or more who consider the attitude "important," and that nearly a third of the members of the older group who consider the attitude "not important" also recycle 75 percent or more of their waste. Comparing this pattern to those of the young and middle-aged groups, we see that for them there is a much greater drop in the percentages of strong recyclers among those who see the attitude as "important" or "not important."

This indicates that when we examine the original relationship under the different conditions of a third variable—age—we learn that it is different for the older group compared with the middle-aged and younger groups. In terms of elaboration, when the relationships vary under conditions of the test variable, we have a *specification*. Note that the specification would be even stronger if for one of the age groups the pattern of percentages had been reversed (such that those who thought the attitude was "not important" were more likely to be strong recyclers).

Specification as a form of elaboration differs from other types of elaboration because it uses the test variable to examine under what conditions the original relationship is reinforced. As Rosenberg states, "The object of this procedure is clarification—clarification of the true value of the relationship" (1968, p. 131). Here, rather than finding that the association between the original two variables disappears (or weakens) in the partial tables, you look for which attribute of the test variable *strengthens* the original association. You know you have found an example of specification when one of the partial tables (representing one condition of the test variable) increases the relationship between the independent and dependent variables, while the other partial table (representing another condition of the test variable) weakens the original relationship. What you are doing is *specifying* the conditions where the relationship is strong. For this type of elaboration, the test variable may be either antecedent to the independent variable or intervening between the independent and dependent variables.

Explanation

This form of elaboration raises the issue of spuriousness, which we discussed earlier. The aim is to see whether the original relationship between the two variables can be explained by the effects of an

TABLE 12-16

CONDENSED TRIVARIATE TABLE OF AMOUNT RECYCLED BY IMPORTANCE OF "RECYCLING MAKES ME FEEL GOOD" BY GENDER

(Percent Recycling 75 Percent or More of Their Waste)

Gender	Importance of "Recycling Makes Me Feel Good"		
	Very Important	**Important**	**Not Important**
Male	56.5	23.1	13.9
	(23)	(39)	(36)
Female	56.1	37.5	19.4
	(82)	(56)	(31)

antecedent variable to which both variables are related. If such an effect can be established, it will mean that the antecedent test variable really explains why an association between the first two variables occurred. Given such findings, the original relationship would be considered spurious, because it would have been fully accounted for by the introduction of the test variable. The test variables of sex and age are characteristics of the respondents that *precede* the formation of attitudes about recycling. They represent antecedent test variables. Thus, in the case in which the relationship between the attitude and the recycling behavior was reduced for both sexes, this means that what was first seen in the original relationship really occurred because of the unexamined influence of sex differences.

Interpretation

As was stated above, when the test variable is intervening and the partial relationships again largely or completely disappear, this is referred to as an interpretation. Hyman (1955) described interpretation as trying to determine "the process through which the assumed cause is related to what we take to be its effect" (p. 276). What this means is that we need to examine the intervening period between the time at which the independent variable had its effect and the time at which the dependent variable occurred. If we can select a factor that took place in the interim which might have altered the effect of the independent variable on the dependent variable, we would be able to interpret the original relationship. Figure 12-8, a diagram comparing *interpretation* to *explanation,* was first offered by Kendall and Lazarsfeld (1950).

In explanation, the test variable is antecedent to the *xy* relationship and affects each variable separately. In interpretation, the test variable is intervening between the *xy* relationship.

If the time sequence between the independent variable and the test variable were unclear (that is, if you were not sure whether the test variable was

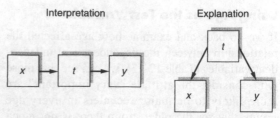

FIGURE 12-8

Effects of a test variable (*t*) on the relationship between an independent variable (*x*) and a dependent variable (*y*). [Patricia L. Kendall and Paul F. Lazarsfeld, "Problems of Survey Analysis," in Robert K. Merton (ed.), Continuities in Social Research, Free Press, Glencoe, IL, 1950, p. 157.]

intervening or antecedent), it would be impossible to distinguish between interpretation and explanation. If the test variable intervenes between the independent and dependent variables, the test variable has *interpreted* the meaning of the original relationship.

Suppressor and Distorter Variables

When an original relationship shows no clear association between the variables, this generally tends to dissuade the researcher from pursuing any further possible meaning in the relationship. However, numerous researchers have found that in some instances a zero-order association which is weak may become much stronger in the first-order tables when certain test variables are introduced. Rosenberg (1968) coined the terms *suppressor* and *distorter* control variables to account for the appearance of strong associations in the partial tables when the original table had shown only a very weak relationship.

Suppressor Variables. One of the studies considered by Rosenberg had been conducted by Middleton (1963), who had hypothesized that black Americans would be more "alienated" than white Americans because their subordinate social status was a "disabling condition." For most of his measures of alienation, that is precisely what Middle-

TABLE 12-17

SOCIAL CLASS AND ATTITUDE TOWARD CIVIL RIGHTS BY RACE[a]

Civil Rights Score	Middle Class	Working Class
High	30%	45%
Low	70	55
Total percent	100%	100%
Number	(120)	(120)

	African-Americans		White Americans	
Civil Rights Score	Middle Class	Working Class	Middle Class	Working Class
High	70%	50%	30%	20%
Low	30	50	70	80%
Total percent	100%	100%	100%	100%
Number	(20)	(100)	(100)	(20)

[a]Hypothetical.

Source: Adapted from Morris Rosenberg, *The Logic of Survey Analysis,* Basic Books, New York, 1968, pp. 94–95.

ton found. On the factor of "cultural estrangement," though, there was virtually no difference between white and black people. He discovered, however, that when education was entered as a test variable, white people among both the lower and the higher educational groups appeared to have higher cultural estrangement.

Thus the important differences between the races in their degree of cultural estrangement had been suppressed by the variable of education. Because the factor of education in the original table was ignored, the relationship of race to cultural estrangement was *suppressed*. Once the partial associations were examined for the various educational groups, it was clear that race had an important effect on a sense of cultural estrangement.

In short, if you have a zero-order table which shows a very weak relationship, there may still be an important relationship between the two variables that is being suppressed by a third unexamined variable. In this case, finding that important third variable and examining its influence through trivariate analyses may help uncover the original relationship.

Distorter Variables. In certain instances, an original table of moderate strength may reverse itself to show the opposite relationship. Rosenberg gives the example of examining social class and attitudes toward civil rights. In Table 12-17, the original relationship between class and support of civil rights indicated that the working classes were slightly stronger supporters of civil rights than were the middle classes (45 percent of the working-class respondents compared to 30 percent of the middle-class respondents had high civil rights scores). However, when the test variable of race was used to partial the original relationship, the opposite was found in the partial relationships: the middle classes appeared to be stronger supporters. This was especially true among the African-Americans (there was a 40 percent difference in the proportion of high scorers among the middle-class compared to the working-class African-American respondents but only a 10 percent difference in the proportion of high scorers among middle-class compared to working-class white respondents).

How can you account for the change in and strengthening of the relationship between social class and civil rights scores in the partial relationship tables? In this instance, race (which was the test variable) would have been *distorting* the original relationship between social class and civil rights attitudes such that when it was entered as a test variable and the sample was subdivided into African-Americans and white Americans, a much stronger and different association between class and civil rights support appeared for the black respondents and a weaker, though changed, relationship appeared for the white respondents. This is to say that in the partial tables it was the middle classes who had the larger proportions of high civil rights scores, while the working classes had the smaller proportions. Race, the test variable, had been a *distorter variable* in the original relationship.

Elaboration: What Does It Tell Us?

The reason why an understanding of the elaboration model is useful is that it makes you think carefully about (1) the temporal order of your variables and (2) the types of associations produced by your variables. In short, it is a way to push toward a causal explanation. Naturally, there may be more than a third variable affecting a relationship (to study this possibility you need to employ multivariate techniques). Here I merely want to stress that understanding how a third variable may alter or replicate the original association noted will strengthen your logical abilities in discovering the interdependencies among variables.

REVIEW NOTES

- Data analyses aim to test the hypotheses or research questions posed in a study.
- Tables prepared to present the evidence need to be set up in such a way that the hypothetical relationship being studied can be examined easily. Careful attention must be given to forms of table presentation to facilitate an understanding of the evidence. Data analysis begins after the problem has been defined, an analytic model has been set up, the data have been secured, an appropriate

sample (or subsample) has been selected, and the variables to be examined have been chosen.
- Univariate tables, those based on one variable, are the most elementary form of tables. One of the most common forms of univariate tables is a frequency distribution which shows the percentage breakdowns of the categories of a variable.
- Most quantitative data analyses are now carried out by computers, which can produce a great range of formats. However, for presentation in a paper or report, the researcher may change computer-generated tables so that they present more complete labels and exclude unnecessary information.
- Bivariate tables reveal the relationship of two variables to each other. They are also referred to as cross tabulations, cross classifications, and contingency tables.
- Bivariate tables allow for the testing of two-variable hypotheses.
- Table formats should facilitate the examination of the expected (hypothesized) relationship and should be presented in a consistent fashion throughout a study.
- Bivariate tables generally are set up so that the dependent variable is the row variable and appears to the left of the table; the independent variable is the column variable and appears at the top of the table. Then the table is *percentaged down* (the separate categories of the independent variable form the bases on which percentages of the dependent variable are given) and *read across* (so that the distributions on the dependent variable are compared across the subgroups of the independent variable).
- Positive associations are those in which the data show that those with high responses to the dependent variable have high responses to the independent variable and those with low responses to the independent variable have low responses to the dependent variable. Negative associations occur where high responses on one variable are matched with low responses on the other. Positive associations generally support the hypothesis. These directional associations cannot be determined if the variables are nominal.

- Evidence of a strong relationship between variables may be caused by the unexamined effects of a third variable. When this is the case, the relationship is termed spurious.
- Trivariate analyses include a third variable which serves as a control or test variable for the hypothesis.
- Trivariate tables may be called first-order tables in contrast to zero-order bivariate tables. Trivariate relationships also may be referred to as partial relationships in contrast to the original relationship of the bivariate table.
- Condensed trivariate tables can be made by presenting the percentage of one category of the dependent variable in a cross tabulation of the independent and test variables.
- The elaboration paradigm offers explanatory models for trivariate analyses. When a third variable causes no change in the bivariate relationship, it represents a replication. When the original relationship weakens after the introduction of the test variable, it represents an explanation (if the test variable is antecedent to the independent variable) or an interpretation (if the test variable is intervening between the independent and dependent variables). If the partial relationships are stronger than the original relationship under certain conditions of the test variable but weaker under other conditions, this represents a specification.
- When a weak original relationship becomes stronger in the partial relationship, this may be the result of the test variable serving as a suppressor variable. When a partial relationship reverses the association noted in the original relationship, this may be caused by a test variable serving as a distorter variable.

KEY TERMS

antecedent variable
bivariate table
cell
condensed trivariate table
contingency table
control variable
cross classification
cross tabulation
distorter variable
elaboration paradigm
epsilon
explanation
first-order table
interaction effect
interpretation
intervening variable
marginals
monotonicity
negative association (inverse)
original relationship
partial relationship
positive association (direct)
replication
specification
spurious relationship
subgroup comparison
suppressor variable
test variable
trivariate table
univariate analysis
univariate table
zero-order table

STUDY EXERCISES

1. In the following five examples, indicate what form of elaboration (replication, explanation, interpretation, or specification) has been discovered.
   a. The negative relationship between knowledge of a foreign language and educational attainment disappears when the variable of whether English is spoken in the home is controlled.
   b. The relationship between the purchase of fluoride or nonfluoride toothpaste and the number of cavities of buyers disappears when the control variable of frequency of brushing is examined.

c. The relationship between juvenile delinquency and whether the juveniles' mothers work strengthens if the mother-child relationship is negative and weakens if the mother-child relationship is positive.

d. The association between the number of swimming medals won by suburban high schools compared to urban high schools weakens when one controls for the presence of a swimming pool in a school.

e. The relationship between high expectations of parents for their children's achievement in mathematics and the children's mathematical achievement noted in Japan occurs in the United States as well among children whose parents hold high expectations.

2. Consider the hypothesis "Catholics are more likely to support tax credits for private education than are non-Catholics."

a. Set up a bivariate table to test this hypothesis.

b. Now add the control variable of presence of school-aged children. Set up the trivariate tables that would be needed to test for the effects of the control variable.

Note: Be sure to set these tables up so that the dependent variable is the row variable and the independent variable is the column variable. Also arrange the categories so that the hypothesized effect is being tested in the upper left-hand cell.

RECOMMENDED READINGS

1. Caplovitz, David: *The Stages of Social Research,* Wiley, New York, 1983. There are very good chapters on bivariate and multivariate analyses with further development of the elaboration model.

2. Frost, Peter J., and Ralph E. Stablein: *Doing Exemplary Research,* Sage, Newbury Park, CA, 1992. A collection of researchers' reflections on how they thought through and carried out their research analyses.

3. Merton, Robert K., and Paul F. Lazarsfeld: *Continuities in Social Research,* Free Press, Glencoe, IL, 1950. An old, but widely available, classic reader on data analysis in the testing of hypotheses. The Chapter "Problems of Survey Analysis" by Kendall and Lazarsfeld gives excellent examples of the elaboration model.

4. Rosenberg, Morris: *The Logic of Survey Analysis,* Basic Books, New York, 1968. This comprehensive and clearly written exposition of survey analysis offers perhaps the best coverage of the elaboration model.

CHAPTER 13

Elementary Statistics for Social Research

INTRODUCTION

*S*tatistics are needed in social research to improve our ability to describe and interpret the meaning of large amounts of information. If you have information on only one item or a few subjects, you probably can give an adequate description in words, citing central characteristics and qualities. Naturally, you may be wrong in your description of even one case, but you have the resources in terms of language to carry out the task. When you have information on 10,000 cases, it becomes much more difficult to describe this information in words. *Descriptive statistics* are tools which can enable you to describe large bodies of data in a summary fashion. The most common forms of descriptive statistics describe the central tendencies and variability of a set of data.

When your findings are from a probability sample, summary descriptions, or *statistics,* of the findings may be used to estimate the corresponding population parameters by using certain assumptions about the distribution of the underlying population. Statistical procedures that allow you to *infer* from what you found in a representative sample to the whole population are called *inferential statistics.* Such statistics can be used to test hypotheses about the relationships that may exist within a population under study. Simply speaking, this is done by asking whether the patterns actually found in the sample data would differ from those in the population from which the data were drawn. Another branch of inferential statistics is estimation of the population parameters based on representative samples. As was described in Chapter 5 (which discusses the normal curve and confidence intervals), a mean from a sample can be used to estimate the confidence interval in which the population mean would occur.

The main purpose of this chapter is to suggest statistical tests that would be helpful in some of the types of research projects described in this text. The purpose is to help you become a useful "consumer" of statistics. For those of you who have taken statistics courses, most of these statistics will be familiar and the material in this chapter can serve as a refresher session. For those of you without a prior course, this chapter will offer an introductory overview of certain statistical techniques commonly used in elementary social analyses. We also will raise issues that surround the use of statistics, such as what options are available, what the numbers mean in relation to the study, and what assumptions are being made in the use of a particular test. When the mathematics are easy to understand, the statistical formulas will be given to help you get a clearer sense of what a statistic is actually representing. In other cases, statistical tests will be described unaccompanied by their formulas, which you can examine in an introductory statistics text if you wish.

USING AND MISUSING STATISTICS

Some statistical techniques that are useful in the analysis of data generated by the research methods explained in his text will be presented in this chapter. By applying a few commonly used statistical tests to the cross-tabular analyses we have developed in our recycling survey we can see how statistical tests can enhance our understanding of the data we have.

Nowadays, almost all statistics that are produced are generated from a computer. Thus, what we present in this chapter will be statistical tests produced by the statistical computer package program SPSS version 7.5, which we have been using. Statistics not only are easy to use but also are easy to misuse. Computer programs generate tables and accompanying statistical tests so readily that there is often a tendency to have the computer turn out a lot of statistics whether or not your sampling design and the data you have collected are appropriate to these statistical tests.

All of us as researchers would like to be able to say that our findings are "statistically significant." In many situations the samples we draw, the kinds of data we have, and the measurement of our variables prevent us from being able to use certain types of statistical tests or require us to interpret the tests in a particular fashion. This concern for the appropriateness of statistics will be a central theme in this chapter. Remember that a computer program (usually) cannot decide which types of statistics are appropriate for your study. *You* must make those decisions.

We begin by presenting a brief overview of certain statistics; then we will return to the recycling survey to see what statistical tests might be used to describe our data and test our hypotheses. Finally, we will examine a few other commonly applied statistical tests to see with what types of data they could be used profitably.

OVERVIEW OF STATISTICAL CONCEPTS AND MEASUREMENT

Measurement (described in Chapter 4) and sampling (described in Chapter 5) are central to the discussion of statistics. Measurement theory and sampling theory are two of the major branches of statistics. We will need to recall some of the information from those chapters as we lay out some of the central concepts and forms of measurement in statistics. Since this discussion will include only a few hand calculations of statistical tests, you may want to refer to an introductory statistics text for more detail.

Measures of Central Tendency

Recall from Chapter 4 that there are two types of measurement: categorical and numerical. Categorical measurement may involve categories that are merely characterized by *distinctiveness,* in which case the measurement scale is referred to as a *nominal* scale, or the categories may be both distinctive and ordered, in which case the measure-

ment is referred to as an *ordinal* scale. Numerical scales may be based on a true number scale with a meaningful zero point (such as age or weight) or may only imply equal intervals between numbers but have no true zero point (characteristic of psychological tests, IQ scores, and Fahrenheit and Celsius scales). The former types of scales are called *ratio* scales; the latter type, *interval* scales.

Numerical scales (both interval and ratio) may be used for *discrete* variables, that is, those which can take only whole numbers as values (such as number of children), or they may be used with *continuous* variables, that is, those which can be defined over intervals that have no breaks between all the possible values of the variable. In other words, a continuous variable can assume a countably infinite number of values (for example, time, height, weight). Furthermore, you can measure a continuous variable with a high level of accuracy (in decimals), depending on the type of measuring instrument you use.

There are three measures of central tendency. The *mean* represents the arithmetic average. If we add together every number representing each case in the sample (or population) and then divide this sum by the number of cases, the resulting arithmetic mean describes the center of the distribution. For this reason, cases at the extremely high end of the distribution or at the extremely low end will disproportionately influence the mean. In addition, if the cases are unevenly distributed so that, for example, a large proportion of them are at one end, the distribution will be highly *skewed.*

Skew refers to an asymmetrical distribution of the data such that the data are not evenly spread around the central point. Thus, when you consider the *skewness* of the distribution of data, you are looking for the degree to which the data are symmetrically distributed in relation to their central point. When data are highly skewed, the mean will naturally be affected, and it will not serve as effectively as a measure of central tendency. In such an event, the *median,* which represents the center-most position in an ordered series of cases and largely ignores the skew of the distribution, may

TABLE 13-1

DATA DISTRIBUTION FOR THE MEAN
Family income (N = 12)

Unordered Data	Income Values ($)
Case 1	10,000
Case 2	12,000
Case 3	15,000
Case 4	24,000
Case 5	20,000
Case 6	8,000
Case 7	12,000
Case 8	10,000
Case 9	14,000
Case 10	21,000
Case 11	12,000
Case 12	18,000

Summed total: 176,000
Number of cases: 12
$\bar{x}$ = summed total ÷ number of cases
$\bar{x}$ = $176,000/12 = $14,667

TABLE 13-2

DATA DISTRIBUTION FOR MEDIAN AND MODE
Family Income (N = 12)

Ordered Data	Income Values ($)
Case 6	8,000
Case 1	10,000
Case 8	10,000
Case 2	12,000
Case 7	12,000
Case 11	12,000
Case 9	14,000
Case 3	15,000
Case 12	18,000
Case 5	20,000
Case 10	21,000
Case 4	24,000

Median = midpoint
= (Case 11 + Case 9) ÷ 2
= ($12,000 + $14,000) ÷ 2
= $13,000
Mode = most popular value
= Cases 2, 7, 11
= $12,000

be the right choice as a measure of central tendency. The *mode* represents the most popular value (or position) in the distribution, the one representing the largest number of cases. Thus the mode is not sensitive to the spread of the distribution. Deciding which measure of central tendency to use also will depend on the type of question you are interested in answering.

Let's say the variable you are studying is the yearly income of the parents of a sample of 12 high school students, rounded off to the nearest thousand dollars. It is possible to compute the *mean* income by adding up all the incomes given by the respondents and dividing this number by the number in the sample. No specific order is required to compute a mean. However, the cases must be ordered to determine the median. An ordered list facilitates the determination of the mode as well (in order to see how many cases share the same value). Tables 13-1 and 13-2 show, comparatively, the distributions of a set of cases for income data for ascertaining the mean, the median, and the mode.

The Mean.   The *mean* is a very useful statistic when a variable is based on a number scale, such as weight or income. As was stated above, if the scale of numbers is not fairly evenly distributed, the mean will not be a good indicator of the central tendency of the distribution. In deciding whether to use a mean, consider carefully whether the variable you want to analyze is based on a type of measurement that can be represented by an arithmetic mean. (Remember that a nominal variable should not be represented by a mean.) If a mean is an appropriate descriptive statistic for the variable you are studying, you also may want to include information on the *dispersion* (or variation) of scores around the mean (this was described in Chapter 5). Ways to describe the range of scores (the most common being the *standard deviation*) will be described below.

The Median. In contrast to the mean's sensitivity to the whole range of values, the *median* reflects only the centermost case (or cases). The purpose of the median is to describe that case which falls exactly in the center of the range divided by 2. The median is often preferable to the mean, where the distribution is skewed. In such a case, the centermost case—that is, the median—will represent the central tendency of the distribution better than the mean will. If the distribution contains an odd number of cases, the centermost case will be easy to select as the median. (If there were 11 cases, the median would be the sixth, with 5 cases on either side.) In the example given, where there are an even number of cases (12), it would be easily computed as halfway between Case 11 and Case 9. Figure 13-1 depicts the median's position.

The median is somewhat more difficult to compute when you have grouped data, such as data distributed among income groups of below $10,000, $10,000 to $13,000, $13,001 to $16,000, etc. When data are grouped, each category represents a range of values. The median number for the range falls somewhere within the interval which contains the centermost value (median). There is a formula that will help you estimate where in the centermost group (let's say between $16,001 and $19,000) the actual median would fall.[1]

The Mode. The mode is the most easily determined measure of central tendency. It is merely the

value which occurs most frequently in the full range of values. In Table 13-2, the mode was $12,000 because three cases were represented by that amount.

Measures of Variation

When you compute a mean, you have estimated a central position representative of all the data in your sample. What you have not done is consider how these data are distributed, how widely or narrowly they are dispersed, and how much variation there is across all the cases in the sample. Consider the average weight of students in a college class. Let's say you know that the average is 140 pounds. What you would not know was whether most of the students weighed close to the 140-pound mark, or whether they ranged from a very low weight to a very high weight, or whether the distribution was skewed (i.e., whether there were many weights above 140, with a few low ones keeping the average at 140). Measures of variation, or dispersion, which were described in Chapter 5, will again be briefly examined (see p. 142).

Recall that *variance* is a way of measuring how far different units which have been used to establish a mean vary from the mean. The principle is that you take the difference between every measure and the average measure, square these differences, sum them, and then divide this sum by the number of measures considered. More commonly, the square root of the variance, called the standard deviation, is considered.

Assuming a sufficient number of cases, you could plot distributions on a graph in which the vertical axis would indicate the number of individuals with the measure (the frequency) and the horizontal axis would show the scale of the variable ranging from the lowest to the highest. Then, if you plotted all these by placing dots on the graph appropriately and if you connected the points on the graph, you would be likely to find a curved shape which was highest (had the most cases) around the point of the mean and then fell off as it moved away from the mean. This would resemble

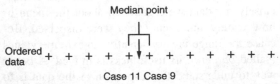

Median point

Ordered data

Case 11   Case 9

FIGURE 13-1
Establishing the median from the data in Table 13-2.

[1]Statistics texts generally show methods for computing a median from grouped data.

the bell-shaped curve, the *normal curve* described in Chapter 5. Recall that the more values you had, the greater the likelihood was that the curve would come nearer to resembling the bell shape. However, you should remember that the bell-shaped curve does not occur in every distribution.

Distributions may, for example, have more than one high point. This might be true (for example) for the variable of length of college terms: for those on a semester system, the high point would be 15 weeks, with variations from 13 to 16, while for those on a quarter system, 10 weeks would be the high point, with variation from 8 to 11 weeks. When this is the case, the distribution is referred to as a bimodal distribution.

When variables are categorical, such as religion, line graphs generally are not used, though bar graphs and pie charts are appropriate. In either type of graph, percentages of the total characterized by a certain category are represented proportionately. More often, categorical variables are presented as *frequency distributions,* in which the percentages are given for each category of the variable. We have already examined many frequency distributions in Chapter 12. Table 12-1 is an example of a frequency distribution.

The Standard Deviation. Recall from Chapter 5 that the standard deviation is the square root of the variance, that is, the mean of the squared difference between the values of each case in the distribution and the value of the mean. What the standard deviation tells you is how much *dispersion* (or spread) there is in the distribution of values in a sample: 68 percent of the cases fall within one standard deviation above and below the mean, 95 percent fall within two standard deviations, and more than 99 percent of the cases fall within three standard deviations above and below the mean. If you assume that the population from which the sample was drawn had a normal distribution, you can apply the standardized normal distribution, the *normal curve,* to your sample and thus determine the range within which the population mean probably would fall.

The *standardized normal distribution,* the normal curve, has been very influential in the development of statistics. As we saw in Chapter 5, the normal curve is used to represent the sampling distribution of means from all possible samples of the same sample size drawn from a population. In most cases, of course, only one sample has been drawn. The standardized normal distribution has a mean of 0 and a standard deviation of 1. What is so useful about the normal curve is that it indicates the proportion of the values that will fall between the mean and so any standard deviations away from the mean. These standard deviation end points can serve as *confidence levels,* and the set of all values between the confidence limits, the *confidence intervals,* serve to indicate the range within which the mean of the population would be enclosed.

Range. Various other measures are even easier to compute and can give you an indication of the dispersion of the frequencies. One of the simplest is the *range.* This is simply the distance between the highest and lowest points in a set of cases. Returning to the example of the range of weights among students in a class, if the lightest person in your class was 89 pounds and the heaviest person was 220 pounds, the range could be determined by subtracting 89 from 220, giving 131 pounds. In this example, the *maximum value* would be 220, and the *minimum value* 89. Knowing the maximum, the minimum, the range, and the mean would tell you quite a lot about the variation of the distribution. What these statistics would not tell you is how closely the data were gathered about the mean or how widely and evenly they were dispersed. Because the range is very sensitive to extreme values (called *outliers*), its usefulness is limited. A better way to understand the dispersion of the data is to use the standard deviation. In addition, there are measures of dispersion which determine the degree of skewness (or tilt) of the distribution.[2]

---

[2]Consult a statistics text for other measures of dispersion.

DESCRIBING RELATIONSHIPS BETWEEN VARIABLES

The choice of which statistical test to employ depends on the level of measurement of the variables. Recall that when the variables are categorical, the data represent the number of counts in each category (the number of Catholics, Protestants, and Jews related to the number of voters and nonvoters) rather than a set of values on a numerical scale (for example, age and IQ score). When both variables are ratio or interval measures (such as age and IQ score), correlations (such as Pearson's *r*) can be used; when the variables are nominal or ordinal (religion and voting status), you can use other measures of association between the variables.

What will follow is a brief discussion of some of the more common types of statistical measures of association. In the cases where the statistical formulas are very simple to comprehend, these formulas will be reviewed; where the formulas are more complex, they will not be presented. In any case, it would be useful to refer to an introductory statistical text to examine the mathematics of these measures.

MEASURES OF ASSOCIATION

A number of different statistical tests can be used to determine the strength, and sometimes the direction, of an association between variables. As was stated above, the choice of tests to use depends on the level of measurement of the variables being considered. In some cases, it also depends on the number of categories in the variables being associated. The statistical tests suggested here are not the only ones available. By consulting a statistics text (a number of texts are listed in the Recommended Readings section at the end of this chapter), you will find other measures of association appropriate for variables with different levels of measurement.

Lambda (λ)

This easy-to-compute statistic is appropriate for nominal-level variables. It is based on the princi-

ple of being able to reduce the proportion of errors in the prediction of one variable by knowing the distribution of another. This principle of *proportionate reduction of error (PRE)* means that you are trying to assess whether knowing the distribution of the dependent variable in relation to the categories of the independent variable would enable you to reduce the errors in predicting the distribution of the dependent variable compared with predicting the variable distribution without any knowledge of the independent variable. Because this statistic is based on a simple formula, it will be presented and explained in Box 13-1, using the relationship of sex to participation in high school athletics as the example.

Lambda ranges from 0 to 1. If lambda were 0, there would be no reduction in error in predicting the distribution of the dependent variable if we know the distribution of the dependent variable cross-classified with the independent variable. Conversely, if lambda were 1, your knowledge of the independent variable would allow you to predict accurately the dependent variable without making any errors. In the example (Table 13-3), a lambda of .164 indicates that something is gained (in terms of predicting the dependent variable) by knowing the distributions of the independent variable but that you are still unable, by knowing only the sex distribution, to reduce all the errors in the prediction of participation in athletics.

Yule's Q

This statistic is an appropriate measure of association for 2×2 tables. It is simply computed on the basis of the cross products of the cells of the table. Consider a 2×2 table in the following way:

Dependent Variable	Independent Variable	
	Present	**Absent**
Present	*a*	*b*
Absent	*c*	*d*

BOX 13-1

COMPUTING A LAMBDA

TABLE 13-3

PARTICIPATION IN HIGH SCHOOL ATHLETICS BY SEX

Participation in High School Athletics	Sex		Row Total
	Female	Male	
Have participated actively	2,632	4,384	7,016
Have not participated	5,758	3,234	8,992
Column total	8,390	7,618	16,008

If you had to predict whether a particular student was active in athletics and all the information you had was the distribution on the dependent variable (participation in athletics) which is portrayed in the row totals, you would make more accurate judgments by predicting that students *have not* participated than by predicting that they *have*. In other words, if you predicted that students have not participated, you would make only 7,016 errors (compared to 8,992 errors if you had predicted that they have participated).

However, if you could make your predictions knowing as well the distributions of participation for males and females separately, for males you would predict they have participated actively and would make 3,234 errors; for females you would predict they have not participated and would make 2,632 errors. Knowing the distribution of participation by sex produces 5,866 errors (3,234 + 2,632), while knowing the distribution of only the dependent variable led to 7,016 errors. Thus the additional knowledge of the distribution of the independent variable (IV) reduced the errors by 1,150 (7,016 − 5,866). Lambda then equals 1,150 *fewer errors* divided by the 7,016 *total errors* [knowing only the distribution on the dependent variable (DV)].

The formula for lambda is

$$\frac{\text{Number of } fewer \text{ errors knowing distribution of the DV within categories of the IV}}{\text{Number of errors knowing only DV distribution}}$$

In this example $1,150 \div 7,016 = .164$.

The formula for this statistic is

$$Q = \frac{ad - bc}{ad + bc}$$

In cross-classifications where there are more cases in which both the independent variable and the dependent variable are present (cell *a*) or both variables are absent (cell *d*), the product of the major diagonal (*ad*) will be greater than the product of the minor diagonal (*bc*). In this event Q will be positive, indicating a positive association between the independent and dependent variables. Conversely, in cross-classifications where there are more cases in which the dependent variable is present but the independent variable is absent (cell *b*) or in which the independent variable is present but the dependent variable is absent (cell *c*), the product of the *bc* diagonal will be greater than the product of the *ad* diagonal. In this event, Q will be negative. This is referred to as the *direction* of the association. If one of the cells has a 0, the Q will equal 1. If either cell *a* or cell *d* is 0, the Q will be −1; if either cell *b* or cell *c* is 0, the

Q will be +1. In the case of nominal variables where the two categories indicate no order, the direction of the Q may well be ambiguous (Davis, 1971, p. 49), but the magnitude of the Q may be used on its own.

Conventions for Setting Up 2 × 2 Tables. As you might recognize from the distribution of the four cells in a 2 × 2 table, if you set up your table so that the larger cell frequencies appear in the a and d cells, you will have a positive relationship; conversely, if the b and c cells have the larger frequencies, the Q will be negative. Your object is not to try to get a positive relationship but to test what you would *predict* to be the stronger relationship in the a and d cells. What you should do is set up your table so that the a cell in the upper left-hand corner will contain the combination of variable categories which you are interested in studying, which will test your hypothesis, or which you think will be associated more strongly. Then if it is the case that the ad diagonal is greater, the positive sign will confirm your prediction. However, if it is not the case (that is, if the b and c cells are greater), the negative sign will challenge your hypothesis.

Let me add that this way of setting up tables is merely a convention; sometimes the a cell is in the upper right-hand corner. The important thing is not to get confused when you see a cross tabulation or when you set up your own. If you are preparing your own tables, be consistent in how you set them up so that you know which diagonal you are expecting to be greater. If you are reading tables created by others, be sure to look carefully to see how they have set up the tables before you try to interpret the meaning of a positive or negative sign. Table 13-4 gives two examples of the use of Q, one with ordinal variables and the other with nominal variables.

Describing the direction and magnitude of a Q. James Davis (1971) offers a summary set of conventions for describing the strength and direction of Yule's Q. These statements, presented in the box, should help you formulate your findings in words. Using Davis's terms to describe the examples in Table 13-4, you would state the following.

In the first example, it would be accurate to say

There is a substantial positive association between believing that being very successful in one's line of work is very important and believing that making lots of money is very important.

For the second example, the following statement would be appropriate:

There is a substantial association between sex and type of English course taken. Males are more likely to take composition.

These statements make clear the strength of the association and also describe its direction.

Goodman and Kruskal's Gamma (γ)

This is an extended version of Q that is appropriate for tables larger than 2 × 2 when variables are ordinal in measurement. It will produce a statistic between −1 and +1. In this measure, the cross products must be extended to take into account every cell in the table. The sums of these cross products then become the terms in the gamma formula. Box 13-2 explains how it is computed.

DAVIS'S CONVENTIONS FOR DESCRIBING YULE'S Q

Value of Q	Appropriate Phrase[a]
+.70 or higher	A very strong positive association
+.50 to +.69	A substantial positive association
+.30 to +.49	A moderate positive association
+.10 to +.29	A low positive association
+.01 to +.09	A negligible positive association
.00	No association
−.01 to −.09	A negligible negative association
−.10 to −.29	A low negative association
−.30 to −.49	A moderate negative association
−.50 to −.69	A substantial negative association
−.70 or lower	A very strong negative association

[a]*Correlation* and *relationship* are synonyms for *association*.

Source: James A. Davis, *Elementary Survey Analysis*, Prentice-Hall, Englewood Cliffs, N.J., 1971, p. 49.

TABLE 13-4

COMPUTING YULE'S Q

For Ordinal Variables[a]: Importance of Money by Success

	Being Successful in My Line of Work	
Having Lots of Money	**Very Important**	**Somewhat or Not Important**
Very important	75	50
Somewhat or not important	25	50

$$Q = \frac{(75)(50) - (50)(25)}{(75)(50) + (50)(25)}$$

$$= \frac{3,700 - 1,250}{3,750 + 1,250}$$

$$= \frac{2,500}{5,000}$$

$$Q = +.50$$

For Nominal Variables[a]: English Course by Sex

	Sex	
Type of English Course Taken in College	**Male**	**Female**
Literature	40	75
Composition	60	25

$$Q = \frac{(40)(25) - (75)(60)}{(40)(25) + (75)(60)}$$

$$= \frac{1,000 - 4,500}{1,000 + 4,500}$$

$$= \frac{-3,500}{5,500}$$

$$Q = -.64$$

[a]Hypothetical data.

BOX 13-2

COMPUTING A GAMMA

MODEL FOR A 3 × 3 TABLE

Independent Variable

Dependent Variable	High	Middle	Low
High	a	b	c
Middle	d	e	f
Low	g	h	i

In this table, the encircled set of cells (*aefhi*) takes the role that cells *a* and *d* played in the calculation of Q. For gamma, you multiply each cell by the elements to the right and under it (those on the positive diagonal) after eliminating its row and column, and then you add all these up:

Positive diagonal combinations = $a (e + f + h + i)$
$+ b (f + i) + d (h + i) + e (i)$

Then you consider the set of cells which will take the role of the *b* cell in the calculation of Q. You multiply each cell by the elements to the left and under it (those on the negative diagonal) after eliminating the values in the same row and column:

Negative diagonal combinations
$= c (d + e + g + h) + b (d + g) + f (g h) + e (g)$

In other words, gamma is an extension of Q in which the *ad* product is based on the sum of all the positive diagonal combinations and the *bc* product is based on the sum of all the negative diagonal combinations. As for Q, once the combinations are determined, the numerator is based on subtracting the negative combinations from the positive; the denominator is based on the sum of the positive and negative combinations. Thus the formula for gamma is:

$$\text{Gamma} = \frac{\left(\begin{array}{c}\text{Positive diagonal}\\\text{combinations}\end{array}\right) - \left(\begin{array}{c}\text{negative diagonal}\\\text{combinations}\end{array}\right)}{\left(\begin{array}{c}\text{Positive diagonal}\\\text{combinations}\end{array}\right) + \left(\begin{array}{c}\text{negative diagonal}\\\text{combinations}\end{array}\right)}$$

where the *positive* diagonal combinations replace the *ad* pair of the Q formula and the *negative* diagonal combinations replace the *bc* pair from the Q formula.

Pearson's r

This statistic is referred to as a *product-moment correlation coefficient* or, more commonly, as a linear *correlation coefficient*. It can be used to determine both the strength and the direction of a linear relationship between two interval-scale variables. There is also a way to calculate the *statistical significance* of the *r* (not presented here) which tests whether the linear relationship between two variables measured by *r* exists in the population.[3] *Pearson*'s *r* is a test of the null hypothesis that there is no linear correlation in the population

(that $r = 0$). This statistic is commonly used in educational and psychological research where test scores are being correlated. For this reason, correlations were discussed in Chapter 4, when reliability and validity were described.

To use Pearson's *r*, a number of conditions must be satisfied. First, as was already mentioned, both of the variables should be interval or ratio variables such that it is meaningful to determine their mean. (It should be noted that researchers often use *r* with ordinal-level variable as well.) Second, it must be assumed that the relationship between these variables is *linear*, such that an increase in one variable will show a corresponding increase in the other (or a decrease in one will be paired with a decrease in the other) or an increase

---

[3]There are tests for the statistical significance of lambda and gamma as well.

in one variable will be matched by a decrease in the other. This means that *r* tests for the *direction of a relationship.* The size of the *r* will indicate how strongly a pattern of variation (or change) in one variable is matched by change in another variable. Thus, *r* also tests for the *strength of relationship* between two variables.

For example, it would be assumed that students who achieve higher American College Test (ACT) scores (or SAT scores) would also have higher grades in high school. What this means is that you expect a positive linear relationship between ACT scores and high school grade-point average (GPA) or, conversely, that students who have achieved lower ACT scores would be expected to have lower grades. The matching of high with high and low with low would produce a positive linear relationship. If the high school measure were absentee rates from school instead of GPA, we would expect that lower absentee rates would be matched with higher ACT scores and that higher absentee rates would be matched with lower ACT scores. This matching of high scores on one variable with low scores on another produces a negative linear association. Finally, you must have an adequate sample size to meet the assumptions for carrying out a correlation coefficient. As a rough guide, a sample size of 30 is usually acceptable.

A correlation coefficient can best be understood by examining the relationship of two variables on a *scattergram.* If you had only a single variable and wanted to make the best prediction of an individual case, your best prediction (or guess) would be the mean for the variable. However, if you had a second variable and knew the values on the second variable for every value on the first variable, you would have the information to make a scattergram and determine Pearson's *r.* Figure 13-2 presents a hypothetical scattergram of high school GPA with ACT scores. At a glance, you can see that the higher the high school GPA (the *x* value, the independent variable), the higher the ACT score (the *y* value, the dependent variable). Figure 13-2 clearly indicates that there is a linear

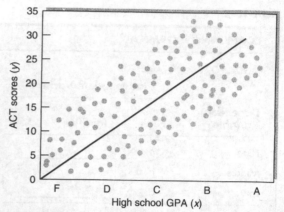

FIGURE 13-2
Scattergram of *x* and *y*.

relationship between high school grades and ACT scores and that this relationship is *positive* such that the higher the high school GPA, the higher the ACT score.

To understand this actual scattergram better, we need to consider the ideal relationships we would like to find if the variables were perfectly related and then compare them with the relationships we are likely to find in the real world. Figure 13-2 shows a positive relationship between *x* and *y*. However, it is not a perfect relationship such that in every case a higher GPA is related to a higher ACT score. If there were a perfect correspondence between the two variables, the relationship would look like Figure 13-3, in which all scores would fall on the positive diagonal line. This is called a *direct,* or *positive, relationship.* In this case *r* would equal +1. If, conversely, for every increase in high school GPA there was a related decrease in ACT score, there would be a perfect negative (or inverse) relationship between grades and college aptitude tests, and *r* would equal −1. This *inverse,* or *negative, relationship* is depicted in Figure 13-4. (Note that it would be very unlikely to find a negative relationship between GPA and ACT scores; it would be quite likely to find a negative relationship between high school absenteeism and ACT scores.) Figures 13-3

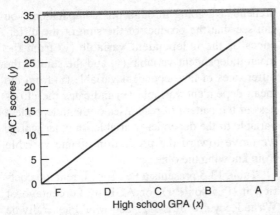

FIGURE 13-3
Direct relationship between x and y.

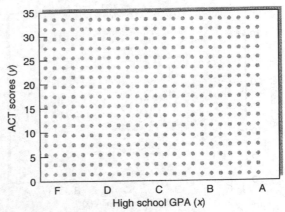

FIGURE 13-5
No relationship between x and y.

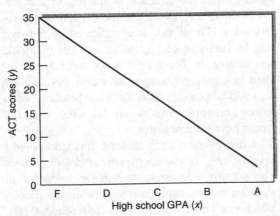

FIGURE 13-4
Inverse relationship of x and y.

and 13-4 both show ideal linear relationships. As we saw in Figure 13-2, in real instances, there is almost always a wide scatter of points representing the position on the graph where the measure on one variable meets the measure on the other. However, if there is a general tendency for an increase in one variable to be related to an increase (or decrease) in the other variable, the relationship will be considered linear.

There might also be a case where every value of the ACT occurred with equal frequency for every value of the GPA. This would mean that r would equal 0 and could have been produced from the scattergram in Figure 13-5. In such a distribution, the observation points are scattered in such an overall pattern that there appears to be no way to draw a diagonal line that would reduce the distance of the points to the line (or that would best fit the scatter of points; such a line is called the *best-fit line*). In this case, a horizontal (or vertical) line would be the best-fit line. This would indicate no linear association between x and y. Note that in this case it would be impossible to predict an ACT score on the basis of the high school GPA. In figure 13-2, if you knew a respondent's GPA, depicting the best-fit line relationship of GPA to ACT would enable you to predict the ACT score. We will turn to this topic in the following section on linear regression.

Finally, Figure 13-6 shows points clustered in a curved shape which represent a *curvilinear relationship*. This would mean that those with the high-level and low-level grades in high school had the lowest ACT scores and that those with the middle-level grades had the highest ACT scores. While a curvilinear relationship is unlikely to occur for these two measures, there are variables that are likely to produce curvilinear relationships. An example might be the relationship between fer-

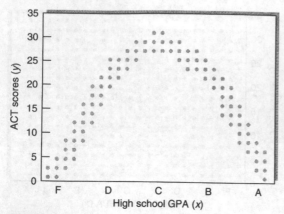

FIGURE 13-6
Curvilinear relationship between *x* and *y*.

tility rate and income. It has sometimes been shown that those with the highest and lowest incomes have the highest fertility, while those with middle-level incomes have the lowest fertility. In this case the curvilinear relationship would be the opposite of the one in Figure 13-6: it would be U-shaped with the high points on the two ends and the low point in the middle. Recall that one of the assumptions of *r* was that the relationship would be linear. Pearson's *r* cannot be used with variables that relate to one another in a curvilinear manner; there are, however, other statistics, such as *eta*, which can be employed when the relationship is curvilinear.

The best-fit line you draw to come closest to all the points on the scattergram uses the principle of least squares. The line represents one in which the *sum of the squared differences between the points on the graph and the line is the smallest possible*. It is important for you to understand that the *r* represents the degree of scatter around the line or the systematic explained variance that remains once the best-fit line between the variables is established. Thus *r* indicates how good the best-fit line is for predicting one variable from another. Box 13-3 describes the formula and the mathematical procedures required to calculate Pearson's *r*. While it is tedious to compute an *r* by hand, the mathematical procedures are fairly easy to com-

prehend. By going through this computation, you can see that the product of the sum of the differences of the independent variable (y) from the mean independent variable ($\bar{y}$) and the sum of the differences of the dependent variable (x) from the mean dependent variable ($\bar{x}$) indicates the closeness of the pattern of responses of the independent variable to the dependent variable. In other words, we move toward the prediction of one variable from knowing the other.

Table 13-5 presents a Pearson correlation coefficient (Pearson's *r*) for AGE by Percentage of Waste Recycled. It is .277 and would generally be rounded to .28. This means that there is a moderate relationship between being older and recycling more. Remember that the correlation coefficient signifies both the direction of the relationship between the two variables and the strength of the relationship. The direction is indicated by the sign (but be sure you keep in mind how each variable was coded). In Table 13-5, since older age is related to higher percentages of waste recycled, the sign will be positive. Had older age been related to lower percentages of waste recycled, the sign would have been negative.

Often Pearson's r is squared. It is then called *r squared* (r^2), or the *coefficient of determination*. This statistic, *r squared*, denotes the proportion of variation in one variable (the dependent variable) which can be explained by the independent variable. The *r squared* gives the amount of variance explained by the linear model. By subtracting r^2 from 1 ($1-r^2$), you estimate the degree of error remaining. In Table 13-5, *r squared* would be .076 or .08. This means that only eight percent of the variance in the amount of waste recycled can be predicted from someone's age.

This seems to be a low correlation. If only eight percent of the variance is explained, then 92 percent remains unexplained. However, depending on your expectations, your hypothesis, and the other factors you think may be affecting the relationship, will help you to decide how to describe the correlation coefficient. For the correlation between percent recycled and age, you have little evi-

BOX 13-3

COMPUTING A PEARSON'S *r*

The formula[a] for *r* is

$$r = \frac{\sum (x - \bar{x})(y - \bar{y})}{\sqrt{[\sum (x - \bar{x})^2][\sum (y - \bar{y})^2]}}$$

where x = the independent variable scores
    $\bar{x}$ = the mean independent variable score
    y = the dependent variable scores
    $\bar{y}$ = the mean dependent variable score

Thus *r* is calculated as the sum (Σ) of the difference of each independent variable score from the mean independent variable score times the sum of the difference of each dependent variable score from the mean dependent variable score—this is the numerator—divided by the square root of the product of these same differences $(x - \bar{x})$ and $(y - \bar{y})$ which have been squared.

    Use GPA and ACT scores as an example and follow steps 1 to 11.

1. Calculate the mean GPA and the mean ACT score.
2. Subtract every GPA (from every respondent in the study) from the mean GPA to determine the $x - \bar{x}$ difference.
3. Sum these differences.

4. Subtract every ACT score (from every respondent in the study) from the mean ACT to determine the $y - \bar{y}$ difference.
5. Sum these differences.
6. Multiply the sum of the $x - \bar{x}$ differences (step 3) by the sum of the $y - \bar{y}$ differences (step 5).

Now you have calculated the numerator.

7. Square the sum of the $x - \bar{x}$ differences (square the results of step 3).
8. Square the sum of the $y - \bar{y}$ differences (square the results of step 5).
9. Multiply the squared results of step 7 and step 8.
10. Take the square root of the product created in step 9.

Now you have calculated the denominator.

11. Divide the numerator by the denominator to calculate *r*.

[a]This is the mean deviation method, which is the traditional method for computing *r*. Social scientists often use more simplified methods, such as the raw score method, which can be examined in any statistics text (see Elifson, Runyan, and Haber, 1990).

dence that the variance in the percent recycled has been partially explained by the age of the person doing the recycling. If you were trying to decide what would be good predictors of recycling, you might examine the correlation coefficients from a number of different variables (though they need to be variables that are numerical in their scale). In this way, you would be using *r squared* to select relevant predictor variables. For such purposes, consideration of the *r squared* helps you to better understand your observations. It assists you in understanding the empirical nature of the study.

REGRESSION ANALYSES

Linear Regression

We noted that Pearson's *r*, the correlation coefficient, indicates the amount of variance that remains once the best-fit line has been established. The *linear regression* equation expresses the relationship of the two variables *x* and *y*. Let's start with a simple example. Suppose the independent variable, *x,* is hours worked per day and the dependent variable, *y,* is work hours per week. Now it is easy to set up the equation *y* = 5*x*.

TABLE 13-5

PEARSON CORRELATION OF AGE AND PERCENTAGE OF WASTE RECYCLED

		AGE	Percentage of Waste Recycled
Pearson Correlation	AGE	1.000	.277**
	Percentage of Waste Recycled	.277**	1.000
Sig. (2-tailed)	AGE		.000
	Percentage of Waste Recycled	.000	
N	AGE	271	266
	Percentage of Waste Recycled	266	267

**Correlation is significant at the 0.01 level (2-tailed).

Table 13-6 presents the work hour data for seven employees. If the weekly hours were on the y axis of a graph and the daily hours were on the x axis, you would easily see that the line drawn to connect dots representing each worker's weekly and daily hours (the *best-fit line*) would be a straight line.

If you can recall from your algebra courses, the formula for a straight line is

$$\hat{y} = a + bx$$

in which x and y represent the independent and dependent variables whose values change from case to case, b represents the slope of the best-fit line that relates y to x, and a equals the value of y when x is zero (this is called the y intercept). In the example given, $y = 0$; therefore, $a = 0$ and the linear regression equation is

$$y = 0 + 5x \quad \text{or} \quad y = 5x$$

TABLE 13-6

DAILY AND WEEKLY WORK HOURS OF A GROUP OF WORKERS

Worker	Weekly Hours (y)	Daily Hours (x)
Mary	42.5	8.5
Fred	37.5	7.5
Susan	40.0	8.0
Karen	45.0	9.0
Jack	40.0	8.0
Homer	35.0	7.0
Sarah	32.5	6.5

For most pairs of variables, the y intercept has a nonzero value, either above zero (a positive y intercept) or below zero (a negative y intercept). The slope (b) refers to the amount of change in y expected from a change in x (or the ratio of the change in y to the change in x). If you know the values of a and b for a series of data on x and y, for a new case in which you have data for the independent variable (x), you can predict the value of y. In our simple example, $a = 0$ and $b = 5$. If a new employee, Sam, works four hours per day, we can predict his weekly hours:

$$y = 0 + 5(4)$$
$$y = 20$$

Multiple Regression

This widely used statistical technique is based on an extension of the linear regression model. In this case, instead of using one independent variable to predict a dependent variable, we use a number of independent variables (x_1, x_2, x_3 . . .). This means that a one-dimensional line cannot be fitted to the many x's with the y; instead, a three-dimensional best-fit model needs to be established. This is precisely what multiple regression analysis tries to do. The equation for a multiple regression with three independent variables is

$$\hat{y} = a + b_1x_1 + b_2x_2 + b_3x_3$$

where $\hat{y}$ = the dependent variable's predicted value

a = the y *intercept*

b_1 = the slope of the first independent variable

b_2 = the slope of the second independent variable

b_3 = the slope of the third independent variable

x_1 = the value of the first independent variable

x_2 = the value of the second independent variable

x_3 = the value of the third independent variable

The slope of b_1 indicates the change in the dependent variable y accounted for by an increase of one unit in x_1 if x_2 and x_3 are held constant; b_2 represents the change in y accounted for by one unit of change in x_2 if x_1 and x_3 are held constant. This suggests that the larger the b, the more its related x (the independent variable) helps predict y (the dependent variable).

The b value generally is referred to as the *regression weight,* the *beta weight,* or just the b. The larger this number, the greater the weight of the variable in question in predicting the dependent variable. Hence, one of the purposes of most regression analyses is to determine which independent variables have the highest weights associated with them (in other words, which independent variables lend more to the prediction of the dependent variables or, more simply, which independent variables are better predictors of the dependent variable).

In addition, a researcher often wants to know how much all the independent variables taken together can predict the dependent variable. This requires computing a multiple correlation coefficient similar to Pearson's r for two variables, which is reported as R. Squaring this multiple correlation coefficient—R^2, or the *coefficient of multiple determinants*—produces a more useful measure. It indicates the percentage of variance in the dependent variable that has been explained jointly by the independent variables.

Because multiple regression is a complex mathematical procedure, such analyses are nearly always carried out by computer. For our purposes, we will conclude this discussion by presenting a regression analysis that Peter Rossi offered in his study on homelessness in Chicago (1989). This example shows how the b values for a set of independent variables can increase one's understanding of an independent variable. One of Rossi's aims was to determine what factors favored individuals spending nights on the streets instead of in some form of alternative shelter.[4]

Table 13-7 presents these findings. The dependent variable (y) is reported in the title: "Percentage of Nights Spent on Streets." The independent variables are the 11 characteristics of the homeless listed in the left-hand column. The table presents b (that is, the regression coefficients or beta weights) for each of the independent variables, the intercept (or a value), the R^2 (or coefficient of multiple determination), and the N (or number of cases) on which the data are reported.

Let's begin by looking at the list of characteristics. Note that all but two are at the interval or ratio level of measurement—"female" and "white" have been treated as dichotomous (or dummy) variables, with the presence of the characteristic given a 1 and the absence of the characteristic given a 0. As was described in Chapter 4, *dummy variables* are two category variables in which the presence of an attribute is coded as a 1 and its absence is coded as a 0. This means that any variable, whatever its measurement level, can be converted into a dummy variable. Categorical variables, set up so that the presence of a characteristic = 1 and its absence = 0, often are used in regression analyses. Looking a the b column, you

---

[4]Rossi's book, addressed to a broad range of educated readers, presents only one regression analysis; all other data presentations are given in percentages.

TABLE 13-7

PERCENTAGE OF NIGHTS SPENT ON STREETS REGRESSED ON CHARACTERISTICS OF THE HOMELESS
(Winter 1986 Only)

Characteristics	b
"Shabby and unkempt" interviewer rating[a]	.077‡
"Incoherent and confused" interviewer rating	.071†
Detoxification, mental hospital, or both [b]	−.075*
Depression scale	.014†
Psychotic symptoms scale	.000
Criminal justice experiences scale	−.029
Age (years)	.001
Female	−.100*
White	.045
Log of time homeless	.008
Worked sometime last month	−.006
Intercept	.021
R^2	.18‡
N	335

Note: Dependent variable is percentage of past seven days spent on streets or in public places.

[a]Number of negative ratings made by interviewer of respondent's appearance, neatness, dress, and cleanliness.

[b]Count of mental hospitalizations and having been in a detoxification center.

*$p < .05$; †$p < .01$; ‡$p < .001$

Source: Peter H. Rossi, *Down and Out in America: The Origins of Homelessness,* University of Chicago Press, Chicago, 1989, p. 104.

see that some of the values have negative signs, meaning that a decrease in that independent variable was related to an increase in the dependent variable. Some, with asterisks, report the statistical significance of the beta weights. Note that the larger the *b* is—the closer the number is to ±1— the more likely it is to be significant, though other factors, such as the order in which the independent variables are entered in the equation, also affect the likelihood that the weight is significant. The significance levels reported at the bottom of Table 13-7 refer to *p* as the probability that the population value is equal to zero.

We see that the best predictors of spending nights on the streets during a Chicago winter were a shabby appearance, incoherent behavior, and evidence of depression. Surprisingly, the less time the individual had spent in a mental hospital or detoxification center, the more likely that person was to spend nights on the streets. Finally, the negative sign for "female" indicates that being male was predictive of spending more nights on the street (−.100 means that females spent 10 percent fewer nights and males 10 percent more nights on the streets). The variables without asterisks added some weight to the prediction of spending nights on the streets, but not to a significant degree.

The R^2 of .18 was significant, meaning that 18 percent of the variance in the percentage of nights on the streets was explained by the 11 independent variables in the regression equation. Rossi concludes that "those who consistently use the streets and public places are most likely to fit one of the stereotypes of the homeless as disreputable in appearance, incoherent in speech, and demoralized and depressed" (1989, p. 104). Rossi surmises that such individuals may feel more negative toward shelters, perhaps in response to rules of behavior which the shelters claim to enforce.

INFERENTIAL STATISTICS

While descriptive statistics are used to describe the association between variables as well as the distributions of single variables, inferential statistics are used to infer whether the relationships among the variables in the sample would be likely to recur in other samples drawn from the same population, that is, that they did not occur only as a result of chance. You may never know exactly what the true values of the population characteristics (that is, the *parameters*) are on the basis of data drawn from a sample representative of that population. However, you can use the rules of probability in selecting a sample that will allow you to make inferences from evidence on your sample to the probable characteristics in the population with some degree of confidence.

To do this, you use hypothesis tests. What you will do is test the null hypothesis, which is based on a logical assumption that there is no relationship (no association) between the two variables being studied in the population. Inferential statistics enable you to test this assumption. In other words, you are testing whether the relationship between the variables in the sample is sufficiently strong to warrant rejecting the null hypothesis that in the population the variables are independent of each other. This means that the relationship found in the sample is unlikely to have occurred by chance or, to put it another way, that the kind of relationship which might occur if only chance were operating would be highly unlikely to reappear if you were to select other samples from the population.

Statistical Significance of r

You might want to use r (described above) to make a claim for the statistical significance of a relationship you have found. Again, it must be restated that for statistical significance to be determined, the assumptions for computing the r must be met. The probability that the size of the correlation coefficient which occurred in your sample happened by chance and that a correlation of similar magnitude or a more extreme one would be likely to be found if many other samples were drawn from the same population is the significance level of the test, sometimes called the P value. You are testing whether the magnitude of the r found in your sample could have occurred as a result of chance, assuming the null hypothesis that in the population from which you drew your sample, $r = 0$. (In the case of the population, the r should be written with the Greek letter rho—P.) When the sample size is very small, the probability that the r occurred by chance increases. Therefore, it may be unwise to suggest that a correlation coefficient from a small sample is statistically significant even if its value is quite large. Keep in mind that when a correlation is deemed to be statistically significant, this means that the r value in

your sample is sufficiently large to infer that the null hypothesis (that the correlation in the population is 0) should be rejected.

It is generally accepted that an r of .10 is weak, while an r of .70 is strong. (However, with a large sample size, even a weak correlation can be statistically significant.) Between .10 and .70 is where most correlation coefficients occur in the social sciences. As Simon and Burstein (1985, p. 325) suggest, in a field such as economics, where time-series analyses of aggregate measures are examined (such as economic indicators), the correlations are high because the variables move together. By contrast, in educational psychology, where the data represent cross-sectional measures of student ability or achievement in relation to educational programs or qualities of schooling, there is so much that is unaccounted for that correlations tend to be low. This reinforces the need to take into account the type of data you have and the time dimension the data represent when your are deciding whether a correlation is strong or weak.

The Chi-Square (χ^2) Test

This is one of the most widely used tests for statistical significance in the social sciences when the variables under study are nominal or ordinal in measurement. The chi-square simply tests whether there is any variation in the data different from mere chance variation. It tells you whether you can safely assume that there is some relationship (between the variables being studied) in the population from which your sample was drawn.

More formally, the *chi-square* (χ^2) test is called a *test of independence*. It tests whether the row classifications (of the dependent variable) are related to, or affected by, different levels of the column classifications (the independent variable). It does not measure the strength of the relationship between the variables but instead measures whether there is a significant relationship at all, whether the variation differs from chance.

Consider this example. Let's assume you were studying the association of political conservatism and sex. If there were 40 percent males and 60 percent females in the sample and you assume no association between the variables, 40 percent of the conservatives would be male and 60 percent would be female. These would be the *expected values,* assuming independence between the variables.

Box 13-4 shows how to compute χ^2. To determine the cell frequencies for the expected values in Table 13-8, you would merely take 40 percent of the total (65) and put that figure (26) in cell *a* (as seen in the parentheses). Cell *b* would then be the other 60 percent of the 65. Similarly, you would take 40 percent of the 35 to determine the *c* cell; the remaining 60 percent would be the *d* cell. These are the *expected frequencies.* Then you compare these expected frequencies to the actual observations, the *observed frequencies,* to determine how different they are. The chi-square tests how far the expected values deviate from the observed values.

To determine whether the chi-square is significant, you must compare your statistic to a table of critical values of chi-square (see Appendix B).

You need one other number besides the computer chi-square to determine its significance. This number is the *degrees-of-freedom* figure in the table. To compute the degrees of freedom (*df*) in a chi-square table, you take the number of rows minus 1 times the number of columns minus 1: $df = (r - 1)(c - 1)$. In Table 13-8, this would be $(2 - 1)(2 - 1) = 1$.

Turning to the chi-square table in Appendix B, we find that with 1 degree of freedom, a chi-square of 14.9 would occur in fewer than 1 sample in 100 if there was no association between the variables (that is, if the null hypothesis was true and the finding was merely due to chance). In fact, 14.9 is much greater than the needed χ^2 of 6.635 for the .01 level. We can therefore reject the null hypothesis and state that the hypothesis is statistically significant at greater than the .01 level ($p < .01$). This means that if 100 different samples were drawn from the population, in (at most) 1 of them the χ^2 would be larger than 6.635 if there was no relationship between these variables in the population.

Statistical and Substantive Significance

Statistical significance tells us the degree of risk being taken in assuming that there is a systematic pattern or finding within the population. Statistical significance does not mean the same thing as strength of relationship. Even if, as in the example shown in Table 13-8, you prove statistical significance, showing that there is a statistically significant relationship between the two variables, this does not mean that one variable causes another or explains its behavior. Note as well that chi-square is always positive; it does not measure the direction of a relationship. It only means that when the two variables are present, they occur in certain patterns.

If the sample is based on individuals, this indicates that certain individuals will be more likely to be characterized by certain combinations of characteristics than they would if the characteristics were distributed solely by chance. A significant chi-square does not make such patterns necessarily interesting or theoretically significant. However, if no statistical significance is shown, perhaps you should not bother to explore the association more fully.

Statistical tests cannot establish the substance or meaningfulness of your findings. This requires a consideration of other matters: whether your findings meet the expectations set by the theory (here you would want to examine the size of your findings in the light of your hypotheses) and what relevance your findings have to other research in the field.

COMPUTERS AND STATISTICS

Although this chapter has shown you how to compute a number of statistical tests by hand (or with the help of a small calculator), most statistics computed today (and most of those you will be likely to compute) are produced by a computer. Naturally, you must tell the computer what you want, and therefore you must know what you want. Remember, a computer will compute anything you

BOX 13-4

COMPUTING A CHI-SQUARE (χ^2)

TABLE 13-8

POLITICAL CONSERVATISM AND SEX[a]

Expected Frequencies

Political Conservatism	Sex		Total
	Male	**Female**	
Conservative	a (26)	b (39)	65
Not conservative	c (14)	d (21)	35
Total	40	60	100

Observed Frequencies

Political Conservatism	Sex		Total
	Male	**Female**	
Conservative	35	30	65
Not conservative	5	30	35
Total	40	60	100

[a]Hypothetical data.

You can readily see by comparing the two parts of Table 13-8 that there are fairly large differences between the expected and observed frequencies. On the basis of this information, a χ^2 can be computed. The formula is

$$\chi^2 = \Sigma \ \frac{(\text{Observed frequencies} - \text{expected frequencies})^2}{\text{Expected frequences}}$$

For the example given,

$$\chi^2 = \frac{(35-26)^2}{26} + \frac{(30-39)^2}{39} + \frac{(5-14)^2}{14} + \frac{(30-21)^2}{21}$$

$$= \frac{9^2}{26} + \frac{(-9)^2}{39} + \frac{(-9)^2}{14} + \frac{9^2}{21}$$

$$= \frac{81}{26} + \frac{81}{39} + \frac{81}{14} + \frac{81}{21}$$

$$= 3.1 + 2.1 + 5.8 + 3.9$$

$$= 14.9$$

ask it to compute, but it won't decide whether it makes sense to do so. It will compute a χ^2 for data from a nonprobability sample. It will compute an r for nominal variables or a lambda for interval variables. You must know what to ask for in order to have the computer assist your analysis rather than let the computer simply grind out numerous statistical tests that are inappropriate for your data and your sample. The object of this chapter has been to help you understand what is appropriate and necessary to particular types of studies.

You can get statistical advice from many sources. If you have taken statistics courses, peruse your texts. Many excellent statistics books are comprehensible to those with only a basic knowledge of arithmetic. A number of titles are suggested at the end of this chapter. Your instructor will also have suggestions regarding which statistics would be appropriate for your study. Although many types of statistical tests have not been presented here, those shown in this chapter are particularly popular in social science analyses of survey data and cross-classification tables. We will conclude this discussion of statistics by returning to our recycling survey to see how we might have used some of these statistics to further our understanding of those data.

STATISTICAL TESTS IN THE RECYCLING SURVEY

We will return to our study of the effects of the importance of feeling good about recycling to see how statistical tests can be applied to these data. Let's reexamine the primary bivariate table relating importance of feeling good and amount recycled (Table 12-9). The table is offered again in this chapter as Table 13-9, but now incudes the gamma statistic prepared by the computer when the data were run. We noted in Chapter 12 that the data supported the conclusions that there was a strong trend showing that importance of feeling good about recycling was strongly related to recycling more than 75 percent of one's waste.

The Gamma.   In order to test the strength of this association between the importance of feeling good and the amount recycled, we will use a measure of association appropriate for variables measured at the ordinal level: the gamma. As was shown in the previous section, gamma is computed on the basis of products of positive diagonal cells minus negative diagonal cells, divided by the sum of these cross products.

Figuratively, gamma determines (1) how far the data cluster along the diagonals or (conversely) how widely dispersed they are across all the cells and (2) whether the data lie more along the positive diagonal than along the negative diagonal. If the data are more concentrated along the diagonals and in the cells beneath the diagonals, the gamma will be larger. If the values are greater along the positive diagonal, the gamma will have a positive sign; if the values are greater along the negative diagonal, the gamma will have a negative sign. Note that in Table 13-9, the gamma is .444 (or rounded to .44) and the sign is positive. This is a moderate-size gamma. Therefore, it could be said that there is a *moderate positive association* between the importance of feeling good about recycling and the amount recycled.

If we consider a trivariate table of the relationship of feeling good about recycling and amount recycled by sex (Table 12-13, shown here as Table 13-10), we can compare gammas for two bivariate tables of the "feeling good" attitude by recycling for both sexes. We see that the gamma for the males is .391 and the gamma for the females is .391. Comparing these gammas to the tables themselves, we can easily see that the differences in the rows between the high and low values (the epsilons) were slightly greater for the men than for the women but that the positive diagonal cells and the negative diagonal cells are very similar. In other words, there is a moderate positive association between the level of importance of feeling good about recycling and the amount recycled for both men and women.

TABLE 13-9

Q1R PERCENT RECYCLED TRICHOTOMIZED * Q3F2: RECYCLING MAKES FEEL GOOD: HOW IMPORTANT? CROSS TABULATION

			Q3F2 Recycling Makes Feel Good: How Important?			
			1. Very Important	2. Important	3. Not Important	Total
Q1R % recycled trichotomized	1. 75–100%	Count	59	30	11	100
		% within Q3F2: Recycling Makes Feel Good: How Important?	56.2%	31.6%	16.4%	37.5%
	2. 36–74%	Count	23	34	20	77
		% within Q3F2: Recycling Makes Feel Good: How Important?	21.9%	35.8%	29.9%	28.8%
	3. 0–35%	Count	23	31	36	90
		% within Q3F2: Recycling Makes Feel Good: How Important?	21.9%	32.6%	53.7%	33.7%
Total		Count	105	95	67	267
		% within Q3F2: Recycling Makes Feel Good: How Important?	100.0%	100.0%	100.0%	100.0%

Symmetric Measures

		Value	Asymp. Std. Error[a]	Approx. T[b]	Approx. Sig.
Ordinal by ordinal	Gamma	.444	.071	5.884	.000
Number of valid cases		267			

[a]Not assuming the null hypothesis.
[b]Using the asymptotic standard error assuming the null hypothesis.

We can also take the trivariate table of the same relationship, controlling this time for age (which was Table 12-12 and is here shown as Table 13-11). What we find here is a moderate positive gamma among the youngest respondents (.37) and the oldest respondent (.38) and substan-tial positive association for the middle ages (.56). This indicates that feeling that recycling makes you feel good is more highly associated with actu-ally recycling for the middle-aged.

The gamma from both of these sets of trivari-ate tables can be used to apply to the elaboration

TABLE 13-10

Q1R PERCENT RECYCLED TRICHOTOMIZED * Q3F2 RECYCLING MAKES FEEL GOOD: HOW IMPORTANT? *GENDER: GENDER OF RESPONDENT CROSS TABULATION

GENDER: Gender of Respondent				Q3F2 Recycling Makes Feel Good: How Important?			
				1. Very Important	2. Important	3. Not Important	Total
.00 Male	Q1R % recycled trichotomized	1. 75–100 %	Count	13	9	5	27
			% within Q3F2 Recycling Makes Feel Good: How Important?	56.5%	23.1%	13.9%	27.6%
		2. 36–74%	Count	2	12	9	23
			% within Q3F2 Recycling Makes Feel Food: How Important?	8.7%	30.8%	25.0%	23.5%
		3. 0–35%	Count	8	18	22	48
			% within Q3F2 Recycling Makes Feel Good: How Important?	34.8%	46.2%	61.1%	49.0%
	Total		Count	23	39	36	98
			% within Q3F2 Recycling Makes Feel Good: How Important?	100.0%	100.0%	100.0%	100.0%
1.00 Female	Q1R % recycled trichotomized	1. 75–100%	Count	46	21	6	73
			% within Q3F2 Recycling Makes Feel Good: How Important?	56.1%	37.5%	19.4%	43.2%
		2. 36–74%	Count	21	22	11	54
			% within Q3F2 Recycling Makes Feel Good: How Important?	25.6%	39.3%	35.5%	32.0%
		3. 0–35%	Count	15	13	14	42
			% within Q3F2 Recycling Makes Feel Good: How Important?	18.3%	23.2%	45.2%	24.9%
	Total		Count	82	56	31	169
			% within Q3F2 Recycling Makes Feel Good: How Important?	100.0%	100.0%	100.0%	100.0%

GENDER: Gender of Respondent			Value	Asymp. Std. Error[a]	Approx. T[b]	Approx. Sig.
.00 Male	Ordinal by ordinal	Gamma	.391	.130	2.812	.005
	Number of valid cases		98			
1.00 Female	Ordinal by ordinal	Gamma	.391	.096	3.822	.000
	Number of valid cases		169			

[a]Not assuming the null hypothesis.
[b]Using the asymptotic standard error assuming the null hypothesis.

TABLE 13-11

Q1R PERCENT RECYCLED TRICHOTOMIZED * Q3F2: RECYCLING MAKES FEEL GOOD: HOW IMPORTANT? AGER: AGE IN THREE CATEGORIES CROSS-TABULATION

AGER Age in Three Categories				Q3F2 Recycling Makes Feel Good: How Important			
				1. Very Important	2. Important	3. Not Important	Total
1. 18–38 (young)	Q1R % recycled trichotomized	1. 75–100%	Count	15	9	2	26
			% within Q3F2: Recycling Makes Feel Good: How Important?	51.7%	21.4%	11.8%	29.5%
		2. 36–74%	Count	4	15	5	24
			% within Q3F2: Recycling Makes Feel Good: How Important?	13.8%	35.7%	29.4%	27.3%
		3. 0–35%	Count	10	18	10	38
			% within Q3F2: Recycling Makes Feel Good: How Important?	34.5%	42.9%	58.8%	43.2%
	Total		Count	29	42	17	88
			% within Q3F2: Recycling Makes Feel Good: How Important?	100.0%	100.0%	100.0%	100.0%
2. 39–57 (middle)	Q1R % recycled trichotomized	1. 75–100%	Count	14	5	3	22
			% within Q3F2: Recycling Makes Feel Good: How Important?	43.8%	18.5%	9.7%	24.4%
		2. 36–74%	Count	12	13	8	33
			% within Q3F2: Recycling Makes Feel Good: How Important?	37.5%	48.1%	25.8%	36.7%

(Continued)

		3. 0–35%	Count	6	9	20	35
			% within Q3F2: Recycling Makes Feel Good: How Important?	18.8%	33.3%	64.5%	38.9%
	Total		Count	32	27	31	90
			% within Q3F2: Recycling Makes Feel Good: How Important?	100.0%	100.0%	100.0%	100.0%
3. 58–95 (old)	Q1R % recycled trichotomized	1. 75–100%	Count	30	16	6	52
			% within Q3F2: Recycling Makes Feel Good: How Important?	69.8%	61.5%	31.6%	59.1%
		2. 36–74%	Count	7	6	7	20
			% within Q3F2: Recycling Makes Feel Good: How Important?	16.3%	23.1%	36.8%	22.7%
		3. 0–35%	Count	6	4	6	16
			% within Q3F2: Recycling Makes Feel Good: How Important?	14.0%	15.4%	31.6%	18.2%
	Total		Count	43	26	19	88
			% within Q3F2: Recycling Makes Feel Good: How Important?	100.0%	100.0%	100.0%	100.0%

Symmetric Measures

AGER Age in Three Categories			Value	Asymp. Std. Error[a]	Approx. T[b]	Approx. Sig.
1. 18–38 (young)	Ordinal by ordinal	Gamma	.373	.139	2.549	.011
	Number of valid cases		88			
2. 39–57 (middle)	Ordinal by ordinal	Gamma	.560	.110	4.580	.000
	Number of valid cases		90			
3. 58–95 (old)	Ordinal by ordinal	Gamma	.379	.140	2.487	.013
	Number of valid cases		88			

[a]Not assuming the null hypothesis.
[b]Using the asymptotic standard error assuming the null hypothesis.

model. In the case of the test variable of sex, note that the gammas (.39) are very similar to the bivariate gamma of .44. This is basically a case of replication. And contrasting the gamma from the bivariate table with the gammas from the trivariate tables facilitates determining what type of elaboration is evident.

In the case where age was the test variable, the gammas split more fully. For the youngest and oldest, the gamma is fairly close (though lower) to the bivariate gamma (.37 and .38 compared to .44 for the bivariate). However, for the middle-aged there is a rise in the gamma to .56. This signifies a specification in which the egotistical reason for recycling as a response to making one feel good is greater for those between ages 39 and 57. This generational difference may represent another quality of the baby boom cohort (the 38- to 57-year-olds are in this group), who may seek greater social approval for their behaviors.

Regression Analysis. Recall from earlier in this chapter that a linear regression presents the association of a set of predictor variables (x_1, x_2, x_3, . . . = set of variables that may predict the dependent variable) to a dependent variable (y). For the recycling survey, the dependent variable (Q1) is amount recycled and the predictor variables are the importance of feeling good about recycling (Q3FR), AGE, and GENDER. Because regression analysis (similar to Pearson's r) requires that variables be measured at the interval or ratio level—in other words, they must be numerical variables—we needed to convert the two numerical variables (Q1: amount recycled and AGE) back into their original ratio levels (Q1: 0 to 100 percent of waste recycled and age: 18 to 95 years). Gender was converted into a dummy variable (1 = female, 0 = male). The importance of feeling good about recycling also was converted into a dummy variable (the new variable Q3FR had 1 = importance of feeling good, 0 = no importance).

Once all the variables have been converted, they are entered into the regression analysis. Note that we are presenting the simplest type of regression analysis, in which all three of the predictor variables are entered into the equation simultaneously.

Table 13-12 gives the output from the SPSS version 7.5 program for regression. We will briefly describe some of these findings. Note on the top table that the three predictor variables AGE, Q3FR, and GENDER were all entered. Under that we see the summary table. The R Square reported in the summary table is a multiple correlation coefficient which has been squared. This statistic indicates that the degree of variation in the amount recycled has been accounted for by these three variables jointly. R Square = .163 indicated that 16 percent of the variance in the amount of waste recycled has been accounted for by these three variables.

Examining the same statistics we looked at for the Rossi study of homelessness earlier in this chapter, we want to turn to the coefficients in the lowest table. We need to examine the unstandardized B weights, in which the variables are in their actual units as measured, and the Beta weights, which are the standardized weights in which all the variables have been converted to a standardized measure so that they can be fairly compared. What the B weights show is how much of an increase in the amount recycled can be accounted for by the addition of each independent variable. Note that for the addition of AGE, there is an increase of 0.4 percent in the amount recycled for every year of the respondent's age. For GENDER, we see that women (who were measured as "1") recycled 9 percent more than did men and that those who held that recycling makes them feel good was very important or important recycled 16 percent more of their waste than did those who felt that this was not important.

If we consider the Beta weights in which all the measuring units have been standardized so that the three independent variables can be compared, we see that the largest Beta weights is for AGE (.259), the second highest is for Q3FR (.231), and the lowest is for GENDER. Note, however, that all three Betas are significant so that a sizable degree

TABLE 13-12

REGRESSION: PERCENT OF AMOUNT OF WASTE RECYCLED REGRESSED ON AGE, IMPORTANCE OF RECYCLING MAKES ME FEEL GOOD, AND GENDER

Variables Entered/Removed[a]

Model	Variables Entered	Variables Removed	Method
1	AGE: Age of Respondent, Q3RF: Recycling feels good -2 categories, GENDER: Gender of Respondent[b]		Enter

[a]Dependent variable: Q1 percentage of waste recycled.

[b]All requested variables entered.

Model Summary

Model	R	R^2	Adjusted R^2	Standard Error of the Estimate
1	.404[a]	.163	.153	28.47

[a]Predictors: (constant), AGE, age of respondent; Q3FR, recycling feels good −2 categories; GENDER, gender of respondent.

ANOVA[a]

Model		Sum of Squares	df	Mean Square	F	Sig.
1	Regression	41318.124	3	13772.708	16.998	.000[b]
	Residual	212289.50	262	810.265		
	Total	253607.62	265			

[a]Dependent variable: Q1 percentage of waste recycled.

[b]Predictors: (constant), AGE, age of respondent; Q3FR, recycling feels good −2 categories; GENDER, gender of respondent.

Coefficients[a]

Model		Unstandardized Coefficients		Standardized Coefficients		
		B	Std. Error	Beta	t	Sig.
1	(Constant)	13.566	5.926		2.289	.023
	Q3FR: Recycling makes me feel good	16.403	4.106	.231	3.995	.000
	GENDER: Gender of Respondent	9.035	3.708	.141	2.436	.015
	AGE: Age of Respondent	.432	.095	.259	4.573	.000

[a]Dependent variable: Q1, percentage of waste recycled.

of variation in the equation is explained by each of the independent predictor variables, though AGE contributes the most. What we see here is whether particular variables continue to make a difference in determining variation in the independent variable when these variables are considered as one of a group of predictor variables. In short, we have seen that age matters the most but that all three of the independent variables make significant contributions to our understanding of why people differ in terms of the amount they recycle.

The Chi-Square.   The other type of statistical test you might want to apply to these tables concerns hypothesis testing. We have been hypothesizing that the importance of feeling good about recycling is related to recycling larger amounts of waste. But how can we know that the findings in our tables did not occur merely by chance?

To test this hypothesis statistically, we need to test the *no association,* or *null hypothesis:* that there is no association between the attitude that recycling makes one feel good and amount recycled. Such a *hypothesis of indifference* predicts that there is no likelihood that the values we found in this sample would be similar to those found in another sample—that the finding in this sample was merely the result of chance. Recall from above that the chi-square is affected by the size of the sample. With the recycling survey, which has a fairly small sample size, we would find that fairly large differences between the expected and observed frequency tables are required for the chi-square to be significant.

Table 13-13 presents the chi-square tests for the importance of feeling good about recycling and amount recycled; the $\chi^2 = 34.34$ with a significance level of 0.000. That means that in no more than 1 in 1,000 times would a table such as this have occurred in a sample drawn from a population in which there was no association between these two variables. This is equivalent to saying that in only 1 in 1,000 times would the result be due to sampling error. This presupposes that if numerous samples were drawn from the population of North County

residents, the probability of obtaining a chi-square of this size (if there was no relationship in the population) would be less than .0001. Such a table is therefore considered statistically significant at greater than .00001 (we will give the significance level as $p < .01$). Note that the chi-squares for the associations by gender ($\chi^2 = 14.88$, sig. .005 and 16.38, sig. .003) are significant. For the age groups ($\chi^2 = 12.11$, sig. .017 for the youngest, $\chi^2 = 18.79$, sig. .001 for the middle-aged), the oldest cohort has a chi-square that does not reach the significance level of .05 ($\chi^2 = 8.15$, sig. .0086).

Now let's examine two variables that we would not expect to be related. Table 13-14 presents a cross tabulation from a large national survey of being or not being a twin with sex. Here the chi-square test would be testing the null hypothesis that there is no association between being a twin and sex designation, which is what we would logically expect. Table 13-14 shows that the chi-square for that association is very low (.83) and is not significant (.36). This means that the probability of this table occurring by chance would be 36 times in 100. In this case, the null hypothesis must be accepted and we must conclude that sex and being a twin are independent of each other and therefore that the relationship in this table between being a twin and sex designation could well have occurred by chance.

Choosing and Using Statistics

This chapter has provided some introductory material on the nature of statistics and a brief overview of a few statistical tests commonly used in social research. As in the use of anything, the way to be a good consumer is to both understand your needs and understand what options are available to meet your needs. Statistics can help you summarize information on a lot of data; they can enable you to determine the strength of association between variables. In addition, for data which have been collected from a probability sample, statistics may be used for hypothesis testing to examine the assumption that the relationships found

TABLE 13-13

CHI-SQUARE TESTS: Q1R BY Q3F2

	Value	df	Asymp. Sig. (2-sided)
Pearson Chi-Square	34.341[a]	4	.000
Likelihood Ratio	34.631	4	.000
Linear-by-Linear Association	29.887	1	.000
Number of Valid Cases	267		

[a]0 cells (0%) have an expected count less than 5. The minimum expected count is 19.32.

Chi-Square Tests: Q1R by Q3F2 by GENDER

GENDER: Gender of Respondent		Value	df	Asymp. Sig. (2-sided)
.00 Male	Pearson Chi-Square	14.881[a]	4	.005
	Likelihood Ratio	14.430	4	.006
	Linear-by-Linear Association	8.869	1	.003
	Number of Valid Cases	98		
1.00 Female	Pearson Chi-Square	16.381[b]	4	.003
	Likelihood Ratio	16.335	4	.003
	Linear-by-Linear Association	13.837	1	.000
	Number of Valid Cases	169		

[a]0 cells (.0%) have an expected count less than 5. The minimum expected count is 5.40.
[b]0 cells (.0%) have an expected count less than 5. The minimum expected count is 7.70.

Chi-Square Tests: Q1R by Q3F2 by AGER

AGER: Age in Three Categories		Value	df	Asymp. Sig. (2-sided)
1. 18–38 (Young)	Pearson Chi-Square	12.114[a]	4	.017
	Likelihood Ratio	12.138	4	.016
	Linear-by-Linear Association	6.736	1	.009
	Number of Valid Cases	88		
2. 39–57 (Middle)	Pearson Chi-Square	18.793[b]	4	.001
	Likelihood Ratio	18.684	4	.001
	Linear-by-Linear Association	16.206	1	.000
	Number of Valid Cases	90		
3. 58–95 (Old)	Pearson Chi-Square	8.154[c]	4	.086
	Likelihood Ratio	8.132	4	.087
	Linear-by-Linear Association	5.923	1	.015
	Number of Valid Cases	88		

[a]One cell (11.1%) has an expected count less than 5. The minimum expected count is 4.64.
[b]No cells (.0%) have an expected count less than 5. The minimum expected count is 6.60.
[c]Three cells (33.3%) have an expected count less than 5. The minimum expected count is 3.45.

TABLE 13-14

BEING A TWIN BY SEX
With Presentation of Chi Square

"Are You a Twin?"	Sex	
	Female	Male
Yes	2.57%	2.35%
	(230)	(188)
No	97.43%	97.65%
	(8,706)	(7,828)
	100.00%	100.00%
	(8,936)	(8,016)

$x^2 = .83$; $df = 1$; $p < .36$ (not significant)

in your sample was not merely the result of chance and therefore that the variables are dependent on one another.

This chapter should have helped you select the statistics that are appropriate for your study and given you some guidance on what these statistical tests do and what they signify about your data. The material presented here is only a beginning, however. Your instructor, other statistics texts, and various computer package programs are all good sources to tap for other ideas in the selection and use of statistics.

REVIEW NOTES

- Descriptive statistics are tools that summarily describe large bodies of data.
- Inferential statistics are based on comparisons of summary descriptions (or statistics) from a probability sample to expected distributions in the population. Such tests allow one to make inferences from the evidence in the sample to the unseen evidence in the population.
- The mean, median, and mode are measures of central tendency. The mean is the arithmetic average of a distribution of values; the median is the centermost position in ordered data; the mode is the most popular value in a distribution.
- The standard deviation is a measure of dispersion. It is based on the sum of the squared dif-

ferences between the separate values of each case and the mean.
- The standardized normal distribution, or normal curve, is a model representing the variability in a population. It has a mean of 0 and a standard deviation of 1. It allows one to establish confidence limits between the mean and one or more standard deviations above or below the mean. The confidence intervals, between the limits, establish the range of the values that would need to be considered to account for the true population mean.
- Lambda is a measure of association appropriate for nominal variables.
- Yule's Q is an appropriate measure of association for 2×2 tables. Gamma is an extension of Q that is appropriate as a measure of association for ordinal variables.
- Pearson's r (Pearson's product-moment correlation, more commonly referred to as a correlation coefficient) is an appropriate measure of the strength and direction of relationships between interval-scale variables. The R^2 (R Square) denotes the proportion of variance in the dependent variable that can be explained by the independent variable.
- Multiple regression is a statistical technique for predicting a dependent variable using a best-fit model from a number of independent variables.
- The chi-square (χ^2) test is an inferential statistic testing the null hypothesis of independence between two variables.
- Most statistical tests are now calculated by computers, but the researcher must select the appropriate statistics to be presented with a particular table.

KEY TERMS

best-fit line
chi-square (χ^2)
confidence intervals
confidence levels
curvilinear relationship
degrees of freedom
descriptive statistics
dispersion

dummy variable
frequency distribution
gamma (γ)
inferential statistics
lambda (λ)
linear regression
linear relationship
mean
median
mode
multiple regression
negative (inverse) relationship
normal curve
null hypothesis
parameters
Pearson's r (correlation coefficient)
positive (direct) relationship
proportionate reduction of error (PRE)
R-Square (R^2) (coefficient of determination)
range
scattergram
skew
standard deviation
statistical significance
statistics
strength of relationship
variance
Yule's Q

STUDY EXERCISES

1. State which of the descriptive statistics described in this chapter (Q, gamma, lambda, or Pearson's r) would be appropriate to use to test the strength of relationship between the following variables:
   a. IQ score by age
   b. Has life insurance (does not have life insurance) by sex
   c. Race by religion
   d. Satisfaction with job by type of job (from professional to unskilled)
2. Consider the following table, based on a sample of 50 college students at Eatwell University, set up to examine the (exciting) hypothesis: "Students in the Arts and Sciences College are more likely to eat in the cafeteria than are students in the Business College." (The table contains the raw numbers.)

Eat in college Cafeteria	College	
	Arts and Science	Business
Yes	7	19
No	18	6

a. Fill in the column percents and the marginals (the row and column totals).
b. Compute a lambda for this table. Write a one-sentence analysis of the meaning of the results.
c. Compute a Q for this table. Write a one-sentence analysis of the meaning of the results.

RECOMMENDED READINGS

1. Davis, James A.: *Elementary Survey Analysis,* Prentice-Hall, Englewood Cliffs, N.J., 1971. This very helpful small volume sets up the cross-classification tables and explains how they are interpreted. Offers a very clear explanation of Yule's Q.
2. Elifson, Kirk W., Richard P. Runyon, and Audrey Haber: *Fundamentals of Social Statistics,* 2d ed., McGraw-Hill, New York, 1990. A clear, easy-to-understand statistics text which includes all the statistics most commonly used by social researchers. This text covers all the relevant mathematical formulas as well as offering a review of basic mathematical operations.
3. Frankfort-Nachmias, Chara: *Social Statistics for a Diverse Society,* Pine Forge, Thousand Oaks, Calif., 1997. This book links statistics with current social issues.
4. Johnson, Allan: *Social Statistics without Tears,* McGraw-Hill, New York, 1977. This text aims to help students understand how statistics are used and what they mean as they are presented in social research studies.

The Ethics of Social Research

INTRODUCTION

$\mathcal{S}$ocial research sometimes is criticized for being unethical, and charges such as these demand a serious assessment of the abuses that can occur in this field. Of course, it is easier to attack than to defend practices. Further, it is important to remember that the right to carry out research is a form of freedom of thought and expression, one of the basic rights of citizens. Yet in exercising the right to carry out research, social researchers must be careful to weigh other rights which are equally important and may be subverted or come into conflict with one another in the course of a research project—the right to privacy as opposed to the right of the public to be informed about the activities of public agencies and officials, for example.

Social researchers, moreover, want more than the right to practice their profession. They demand to be taken seriously. They want their work to be understood as contributing to the advancement of knowledge and social progress, and they would like their actions to be free from attacks based on ethical objections. They cannot expect this to occur without paying attention to the challenges posed by abuses of social research.

THE ABUSES OF SOCIAL RESEARCH

Since social research can have as its subject any facet of the study of human society and behavior, a social research project may lead to abuses in various ways. By delving into the social experiences of individuals, groups, or organizations, social researchers may threaten or harm those they are studying. For this reason, there has been widespread insistence in the past decade that social researchers consider, before carrying out a research project, all the aspects of their research which may raise ethical questions.

For students who have not yet done social research, such a discussion may seem overly cautious and premature. As a student, you will probably carry out a study in which the subjects are at little, if any, risk. Or you may reanalyze already collected data in a study in which you are yet a further distance from the subjects. In this book, however, the emphasis is on the doing of research, and as a modern, up-to-date beginning researcher, you must be prepared to consider all the possible ethical issues raised by your study that the most experienced social researcher would be required to consider. Furthermore, in the 1990s social researchers must consider the ethical aspects of their studies and decide whether their research plans need to be altered or radically changed to meet ethical standards before they proceed with their projects.

The following sections address (1) the primary types of abuses, (2) the ethical considerations required to avoid research abuses, (3) ethical issues encountered in program evaluations, and (4) specific guidelines offered by professional associations to curtail abuses.

Primary Areas of Possible Abuse in Social Research

You may be familiar with certain studies in sociology in which very private behavior, such as homosexual encounters or nude bathing, has been observed. You may even have been asked to participate in a survey, as I was as an undergraduate, and reveal very personal information about your life. You may have wondered whether such research is legitimate. In the context of the survey on sexual experience in which I was asked to participate, I wondered whether I should give information honestly. Questions ran through my mind: "Should I answer the questions at all? Why is this person doing the survey? Do I risk any harm to myself by cooperating with this request?"

Perhaps this is all new ground to you. If so, you will find some of the most important types of abuses described here, and examples of studies that have been subject to charges of abuse will be detailed. The object is not to point a finger of blame at specific researchers, for where abuse has been charged, there have always been counterarguments supporting some aspects of the method of research which would justify the possibly abusive activity. However, I do want to sensitize you to some of the primary concerns different types of research methods pose, and in order to do that, it is necessary to give some examples of studies that have raised ethical questions. Whether you think the charges are fair will ultimately be your decision.

Three types of research procedures may raise ethical concerns: covert research, which usually entails some forms of deception; studies in which there is coercion of subjects to participate in certain ethically questionable practices as a part of a study; and research that is considered an invasion of privacy.

Covert Research. In principle, any area of social life, any group of individuals, is open to study by a sociologically imaginative researcher. However, there are social institutions whose activities are considered so important that social scientists have wanted to uncover more fully the nature of social interaction and influence in such environments, even in institutions where open study would clearly affect their proper functioning. (A jury, with its special emphasis on the closed and confidential character of the jurors' deliberations, is a very good example of an institution like this.) It is with an interest in studying such social phenomena that social scientists have undertaken covert methods of observation. *Covert research* involves carrying out research without the knowledge or consent of those being studied; it may involve the researcher misrepresenting his or her role as a researcher in order to enter the environment to be studied as an actual participant.

Kai Erikson has argued "that it is unethical for a sociologist to deliberately misrepresent his identity for the purpose of entering a private domain to which he is not eligible; and, second, that it is unethical for a sociologist to deliberately misrepresent the character of the research in which he is engaged" (1967, p. 373). The first concern is relevant to field studies where researchers have entered environments as full participants. The second is also implied in convert participant observation studies but may apply as well to surveys or especially to experiments. Here are some examples of studies about which issues of the legitimacy of covert research have been raised.

On the psychiatric ward. Covert research often takes the form of giving false information to or about subjects to deceive them into believing something for the purpose of studying their reactions. In a study of mental hospital wards, for example, Rosenhan and seven other researchers posing as patients entered mental hospitals in various parts of the United States (1982). Each pretend patient called the hospital for an appointment and arrived with the same story of having had a hallucination of hearing voices that were "empty," "hollow," and like a "thud." False names and employment statuses were also given. Beyond these deceptive pieces of information, all other details of the pseudopatient's life and experiences were truthfully given, including the quality of interpersonal relationships with family, attitudes, and desires. All eight were admitted to psychiatric wards with a primary diagnosis of "schizophrenia." In each case, while one or two senior members of the hospital staff knew the real identity and purpose of the pseudopatient, the staff of the ward did not. In every case the ward staff gave the same treatment to the pseudopatient as was given to the other patients, and in no instance did a staff member uncover the sanity of the pseudopatient (though fellow patients often questioned their insanity).

In this covert role, Rosenhan and the other pseudopatients were able to carefully observe the behaviors on the psychiatric ward: the frequency of interaction between the staff and patients and the quality of care and compassion for the patients. By this means, Rosenhan determined the high degree of powerlessness of the patients and the depersonalized manner in which the staff related to them:

> A nurse unbuttoned her uniform to adjust her brassiere in the presence of an entire ward of viewing men. One did not have the sense that she was being seductive. Rather she didn't notice us (Rosenhan, 1982, p. 33).

The staff's inability to recognize sanity attested to the "stickiness of psychodiagnostic labels: (Rosenhan, 1982, p. 22). Once the pseudopatients were labeled as "schizophrenic," there was nothing they could do "to overcome the tag" (1982, p. 22).

Could this finding have been established without the use of covert methods? Were the rights of the mental hospital staff infringed on by the covert activities of the researchers? Did the entry of the pseudopatients into the world of the mental ward alter the environment in such a way that an accurate observation of its workings could not be made? These were the questions Rosenhan and his fellow researchers were obliged to address by their critics.

In the classroom.   In their study of psychiatric wards, Rosenhan and his associates misrepresented their identity as researchers and offered false information regarding their mental state. In other cases, covert research has not misrepresented the identity of the researchers as such but has involved their offering a false account of their projects. An example of this type of study is the one carried out by Robert Rosenthal and Lenore Jacobson (1968) in a grade school in Massachusetts. The researchers wanted to test the theory of how a self-fulfilling prophecy might operate in a classroom, particularly in relation to minority students. They falsely described a standard but unfa-

miliar IQ test as the Test of Inflected Acquisition, a test that could supposedly determine which pupils might be expected "to bloom" within the next academic year. Under this pretext, the test was administered to students throughout the school in the spring of the school year.

The following autumn, the teachers were given a short list of names of pupils in their current classes who had supposedly received scores on the Test of Inflected Acquisition that indicated their propensity to bloom. The names on the lists were in fact selected purely at random and bore no relation to abilities measured in the test. Furthermore, the test was not a measurement of potential to bloom, for such a measure does not exist and educational psychologists have no evidence that such a propensity even exists.

Was this deception harmful to the teachers who received the false lists? Was it harmful to the pupils whose names were randomly left off the lists, implying that they would *not* be bloomers? Rosenthal and Jacobson's finding that such a false prophecy actually raised the test scores of the pupils on the list above the expected gains when they were retested the following year led the researchers to conclude that the teachers had unknowingly helped the listed pupils fulfill the false prophecy of intellectual growth. If teachers could be influenced to alter pupils' behaviors by slips of papers with names on them from a research team, how much more might they be influenced by deeply held prejudices and assumptions about how certain types of students might perform?

This study prompted not only charges of ethical questionability but also the charge that the contrivance of the study distorted whatever processes might have been occurring in the classroom. How could the researchers even isolate the influence of the list of names? Was the cost of deceiving teachers worth the benefit of studying a prophecy which might have been largely meaningless to the teachers? Those who saw the study's findings as very problematic thought the benefits were clearly not worth the costs. Others disagreed.

On the jury.   In the 1950s, with the full approval of the judge and lawyers, hidden microphones were placed in a jury room in Wichita, Kansas, as a means of studying jury deliberations. The jurors, however, were not informed that their discussions were being recorded. The social scientists and law professors who were carrying out this research were interested in the human behavior of jurors as they interacted during their deliberations. They believed that such knowledge would lead to a greater understanding of the legal system. The researchers also took extreme precautions to hide the identities of the jurors and handle the tapes with care. However, once this research became known, a Senate subcommittee held public hearings on the ethics of taping juries, and this led to the passage of a law forbidding the recordings of the deliberations of juries. (For a detailed presentation of the differing positions in this case, see Katz, 1972). While jury proceedings are essential to our system of public justice and the precise nature of their operation is therefore a matter of considerable potential interest, can it be said that this interest is more important than maintaining the principle of absolute confidentiality regarding jury deliberations? The forced termination of this project implied that it is not.

Summary.   In the mental hospital study, the role of the researcher was covert and deceptive; in the classroom study, the teachers were deceived about the significance of test scores; in the jury study, the jurors were deceived not by telling them a falsehood but by withholding from them the information that they were being taped during their deliberations. In none of these studies did the researcher foresee any major harm to the subjects. Moreover, in all three cases the presumed benefits of greater and closer understanding of socially important contexts (mental hospital wards, classrooms, jury deliberations) seemed to outweigh any potential costs to those being covertly studied. Critical discussion of these and similar studies has raised concerns about the "costs" of covert re-

search. Some would point out that there is no clear penalty for doing covert research and that many such studies (including a number of the above) have been considered classic research efforts. Others have concluded that such research should be avoided.

Coercion of Subjects.   Another major procedural technique that raises ethical questions in social research is the coercion (either explicit or implicit) of subjects to participate in a specific study, to engage in behaviors that might lead to psychological or physical harm. Subjects who are in some ways "captive," such as prisoners, children, and mental patients, may not be able to withhold compliance from an authority figure who asks them to cooperate. Such helpless subjects may believe, whether or not they are so informed, that favors may be granted to them in return for compliance. In other cases, even where subjects are not in a powerless position vis-à-vis the researcher, they may nevertheless be pressed to participate in a research project or comply with the researcher's requests during a study. Subjects are often persuaded that the benefits of the study (for society as a whole, for the researcher's career, for some group) far outweigh any inconvenience to themselves or other subjects as individuals.

Stanley Milgram's research on obedience (Milgram, 1965) will be described here as a classic example of a study that has raised questions about the ethical problem of coercion of subjects. Out of the experience of the Holocaust in Germany and other atrocities of World War II, there grew the belief that many, if not most, people would obey orders given by a superior to carry out atrocities against innocent people. Furthermore, they would justify these actions on the grounds that they had been ordered to carry them out, thereby refusing to accept personal responsibility for their actions. Evidence from the history of the atrocities of Nazi Germany suggested that it was not difficult to get people to follow orders of any kind. Milgram's study of obedience was set up to test this notion. If individuals could be easily made to harm others as a result of complying with authority, could this be tested in an experimental situation?

Milgram brought adult men from various backgrounds to a laboratory setting where they were asked to participate in an experiment on learning. Each subject drew lots with a "confederate" researcher posing as another subject for the study to see who would be the "pupil" and who would be the "teacher." The true subject always drew the teacher assignment. The teacher was placed in front of a control panel and told to read word pairs to the pupil. If the pupil made an error, the teacher was instructed to administer an electric shock by turning on switches on the control panel that graduated from "Low" to "Danger—Severe Shock." At the same time, the pupil was taken into the next room and strapped into a chair where electrode devices were attached to the wrists.

The teacher would begin reading the word pairs. Each time the pupil made an error, a light on the control panel would light up: the teacher was then expected to administer the shock, beginning at the "Low" level and gradually progressing toward the level of "Danger—Severe Shock." The confederate pupil always carried out the same set of behaviors, including screaming for mercy, begging for the experiment to end, kicking the wall, and finally making no sound at all. All these reactions were of course faked by the confederate pupil. The electric control panel was merely a piece of scenery. However, the subject acting as the teacher did not know this.

In the first experimental setting Milgram established, two-thirds of the subjects carried out the instructions of the researcher to shock the pupil when he was wrong and continued doing so through all the levels of shock up to the highest. A much smaller proportion, 12 percent, refused to administer any more shocks once the pupil began kicking the wall. When the experiment was over, the subjects were told that they had in fact not been administering real shocks, and they were given an explanation of the true purpose of the study. Some subjects stated that they had actually felt the pain themselves, some experienced a high degree of tension after the experiment, and a few had uncontrollable seizures.

Covert methods had been used in this study to disguise the identity of the pupil and conceal the purpose of the study; more important, subjects had been successfully coerced, in many cases without much pressure, into "harming" an innocent person. The ethical issue raised by this experiment included the morality of duping a subject and then persuading him or her to comply with an experimenter's wishes even when the possible price of such compliance was harm to the psychological well-being of the subject. Of course, all the subjects had to do to protect themselves from the negative feeling many of them experienced was to refuse to go on with the experiment. Milgram argued that the knowledge gained had been worth the costs to the subjects, which, though temporarily painful, had no lasting effects. Others disagreed.

Invasion of Privacy.   At some level, every study with human subjects can be considered as invading someone's privacy. Yet certain areas of life are generally regarded as more private than others. In the United States, the question "Where were you born?" is rarely considered an invasion of privacy, yet if this were asked of an illegal alien, it might be a threatening question. The question "Are you a homosexual?" would widely be considered as addressing a private matter, not something a person would expound on to a stranger. Yet such behavior became the subject of a study that has been widely viewed as raising ethical concerns. In the mid-1960s Laud Humphreys became a covert observer of male homosexual liaisons in men's public rest rooms (1970). Since such encounters are illegal as well as illicit yet are carried on in public places, the consenting pair depend on a third person acting both as a voyeur and as a guard to warn them if others are approaching. Humphreys took on this role (called a "watchqueen" in the lingo of the homosexual world) and observed the pattern of homosexual activity in this context.

In addition, Humphreys noted the license plate numbers of the men he observed. With this information and the cooperation of the police, who gave him access to license registers (though without knowledge of his purpose), he was able to ferret out the names and addresses of most of the individuals observed. Then, as part of another study on general health issues in which he was involved, he disguised himself and went to interview these men, among others, on matters relating to their health, careers, and families. In this way, he discovered the very "normal" and wide-ranging backgrounds of the men he had observed in the rest rooms.

While the identities of the men were never made known and Humphreys believed that none had recognized him from his earlier role as a watchqueen, one can ask whether social scientists should practice such deception in order to observe very private behavior of this type. Was this not ethically dubious conduct (both as a threat to the privacy of the individuals and as a questionable activity in itself) for a scientist to be engaged in? Defenders of the study argued that though the behavior observed was private in nature, it had occurred in a public place. Moreover, the researcher had taken on the watchqueen role and carried out the services such a person would regularly carry out if he were not a sociologist without any intention of harming those he observed by divulging their names.

But even if it were legitimate to observe this private behavior in a public arena, was it acceptable to copy the license numbers with the intent of determining the identity of the participants observed? This is clearly the type of data that could *not* have been gathered with the consent of the participants. Further, Humphreys could not have remained an overt outsider and also be permitted to observe the encounters. Was the benefit of learning about the backgrounds of those who engage in casual homosexual encounters worth the risk (however unrealized) of potentially exposing these men's private behavior?

Matters such as the nature of sexual behavior, religious beliefs, attitudes toward minority groups, and the sources and amount of one's income are frequently considered private and rarely detailed to casual acquaintances (though there are great variations among people of different social statuses and life stages in regard to their propensity to divulge such information). A college professor might easily ask how much an undergraduate earned on a part-time job (this might be considered an expression of the professor's concern for the student's economic well-being). However, an undergraduate asking how much a professor earned as a part-time consultant would not be construed in the same light. Rather, it would appear as intrusive and not the business of an undergraduate. Why is this so? Because the status of the professor vis-à-vis the student is such that the income that a professor might be able to earn because of his or her special expertise must remain unknown, part of the mystique of the person of knowledge. Requesting this information would imply a lack of deference toward the professor on the part of the student, and intrusion on the professor's private domain.

Tampering with Results and Plagiarism.   Ethical issues also arise in the reporting of social research. Cases have come to light in which the handling of scientific data has been questioned. In the well-known research on IQ and heredity, Cyril Burt's evidence on the correlation between IQ scores of identical twins reared apart compared to identical twins reared together had been used by numerous other researchers as the foundation for arguing that hereditary factors are more important than environmental ones in determining intelligence. After Burt's death, other psychologists looking at Burt's evidence more carefully came to question it. Burt had first reported on 21 pairs of twins reared separately in 1955; in 1958, he had published evidence on over 30 pairs of twins separately reared; and in 1966, he had located 53 pairs of identical twins reared apart. What was peculiar was that in every case the correlation he found between the IQ scores of the twins was .771. Yet it would be highly improbable statistically to arrive at the same correlation (Chapter 13 explained correlations) using different sets of data. There were a few other strange factors about Burt's material. One was that he gave very little other information about the twins he had studied (their sex, their age when tested) or the type of IQ test he had given them. In addition, some of his work was coauthored by two women, Margaret Howard and J. Conway, who did not seem to exist.

Sir Cyril Burt was a famous and prominent British psychologist. Why would he have tampered with results? Two possible explanations were offered. The friendlier explanation was that Burt, as he grew older, became careless and inattentive to details. Perhaps the correlations were misprints, or perhaps he had merely carried over the findings from earlier studies to the newer ones. Were the unknown collaborators pseudonyms for Burt himself? The "less friendly" view was that Burt's work was a fraud. As Leon Kamin, the psychologist who first detected the peculiarities of Burt's work, proclaimed: "[The evidence on the IQ scores of twins] was a fraud linked to policy from the word go. The data were cooked in order

for him to arrive at the conclusions he wanted" (Wade, 1976, pp. 916). Box 14-1 describes a famous scientific misconduct case which gained widespread attention.

The desire to have the evidence match the preconceived hypotheses and notions of the researcher is naturally strong. In some cases, the career of the scientist may seem in jeopardy unless the results turn out as he or she expected. Researchers may feel pressured by the agencies that fund their research to produce "exciting" findings. That is how people become established as scientists. Yet no other unethical activity threatens the sciences as much as this. If scientists commit fraud, if they flagrantly disregard the scientific ethos discussed in Chapter 2, not only will the public lose confidence in the value of science, the institution of science may suffer serious damage itself: "Because intentional creation of error is so antithetical to the aims of science, effects (of fraud) may be beyond loss of confidence to a sense of disorientation and despair" (Weinstein, 1979, p. 648).

Closely related to altering the results is the incorporation of someone else's work into one's

BOX 14-1

WERE THE DATA FRAUDULENT OR NOT?

In one of the most celebrated and controversial cases in which a scientist was accused of committing scientific fraud, Dr. Thereza Imanishi-Kari, an immunologist who was a researcher at the Massachusetts Institute of Technology, was charged in the late 1980s with publishing a paper that included faked data. What made the case so prominent is that the paper had been coauthored by the Nobel Prize winner David Baltimore, who initially launched a national campaign to clear his coauthor's name.

Because the research had received federal financing, the case was turned over for review to the Office of Research Integrity, part of the National Institutes of Health, which concluded that

there was little evidence to support the claim of fraud. However, the House of Representatives Committee on Energy and Commerce under its chair, John Dingell, then got involved in the case. They brought in the Secret Service to examine the notebooks in which Dr. Imanishi-Kari had reported her data, and this led to charges that the notes had been written over, different inks had been used, and pages had been pasted together. With this new evidence in hand, the Office of Research Integrity charged her with falsification and fabrication.

Data from *The New York Times*, November 27, 1994, p. 15.

own without proper acknowledgment. This is the act of *plagiarism,* which occurs infrequently in the writings of social researchers. It is also an unethical activity observed among some students. Students' reasons for plagiarizing are usually different from those of social researchers. In the case of students, the action is usually a shortcut to meeting the requirements for a course without actually doing the required assignment. Students often do not realize that using other people's work (their writing, their ideas, their point of view) without acknowledging that they are doing so destroys their integrity as students and undermines the trust that must be at the basis of the relationship between students and teachers. If a researcher is suspected of using someone else's material without citation or of cheating in the collection or presentation of data, that person's career can be irreparably damaged.

The Right to Privacy vs. the Public's Right to Know

By focusing on the protection of individual rights, are we confining social research to the study of those who have nothing to hide or those who lack the power to refuse to be studied? Consider how journalists operate. Their primary value is the public's right to know. They have secured their right to research for information on people in public positions and public organizations. The courts have decided that those who serve the public may be subjected to greater scrutiny than others. The Watergate story was uncovered by the press. By using unnamed informants and other tactics to get at the story, reporters made those in power accountable. Galliher (1980, p. 303) warns that the study of those in power should not be left solely to journalists, for "social science offers a unique type of interpretation of events not usually found in . . . American journalism."

Yet powerful individuals and institutions have means of warding off the intrusion of those seeking to study them. Corporations protect their privacy carefully, and to uncover information in a corporation requires that the social researcher provide a needed service to the organization and establish trust among those with whom he or she deals. Studies of corporations can be successful if the researcher is able to establish a relationship of trust with a number of individuals in the organization who can serve as major informants and supporters. It has more often been the case that social researchers have studied those with lower status than themselves rather than higher. Indigent and poorly educated people do not have the resources or knowledge, the lawyers, or the "I'm too busy" excuses to fend off social researchers.

Whatever the status of the person or group under investigation, if there is potential harm to the right of privacy of those being studied, that harm must be considered in relation to the right to know. As Cassell (1978) puts it, the risk of doing research must be weighed in relation to the benefits. In research involving deception, both those being studied and the researcher confront risks. The research project itself may be threatened if the subjects suspect that they are being deceived. In field studies, subjects may also face emotional risks in their relation to the researcher: if the researcher has developed "friendships" among those being studied, his or her departure may be painful for the subjects. However, benefits may be gained by the subjects in a study. Cassell suggests that there may be material benefits (help, money), intellectual benefits (an opportunity to understand more about one's social circumstances), and emotional benefits (the pleasure of talking to someone interested in one's social world, one's attitudes and opinions) (1978, pp. 137–139).

Please keep in mind as you read this discussion of ways to reduce abuses in social research that this concern should not result in choosing to carry out studies only on "safe" subjects (that is, on those with little power). In addition, you should treat all your subjects fairly and uniformly regardless of their status.

Means for Ensuring the Protection of Subjects

In survey research, there are various approaches to ensuring the protection of the respondents. Questionnaires often elicit information regarding attitudes toward minority groups, religious beliefs and behaviors, levels of income, and sexual activities (commonly requested in population studies). Survey researchers have long recognized that such questions may deter some respondents from completing the instrument. Yet, depending on the objectives of the survey research, such information may be vital. Remember that information on specific individuals is not the goal. It is the aggregate data representing the entire sample that interests the researcher. What John Doe earned last year is of little interest, but the median income of employed males in the United States is of substantial interest.

Most potential respondents would not be concerned about having information about their income (or even their sexual activity) used to help establish a norm for a larger group. But how can their privacy be guaranteed? Three principles can be used to help establish such privacy: anonymity, confidentiality, and informed consent.

Anonymity. Granting information to someone who promises that you will remain completely anonymous is the maximum assurance you can receive that your privacy will not be invaded. Anonymity implies that no one, not even the researcher, could connect your name with the information about you. Thus *anonymity* is an assurance that subjects' identities will not be disclosed in any way. How can this be done?

If questionnaires are mailed to respondents who return them without any form of code or identifying information on them, they are completely anonymous. (This assumes, of course, that the respondent's handwriting cannot be identified by the researcher because the researcher is not familiar with it or because machine-readable forms rather than handwritten replies are used.) Yet if a questionnaire remains completely anonymous, the re-

searcher will be unable to determine who has and who has not answered; therefore, no follow-up surveys can be sent and no patterns of nonresponse can be established. Thus, while anonymity in survey research can be achieved, it usually is given only in certain circumstances, such as when questionnaires are administered in groups. Instead, researchers prefer in most cases to offer confidentiality as the safeguard for the protection of subjects.

Confidentiality. *Confidentiality* is a promise to keep the identities of the subjects known only to the researcher and perhaps selected members of his or her staff and to minimize in any available way the possible exposure of a subject's identity. This is often done through the use of code numbers on surveys or pseudonyms for persons and places that might be identifiable. Sometimes the code lists and their corresponding names are held at locations distant from the site of the research, and access to this list is strictly limited to the researcher alone. Also, a list of code numbers may be destroyed when it is no longer needed.

In field research, interviews, and experimental studies where subjects have been directly seen by the researcher, confidentiality can again be guaranteed by procedures to store the data on subjects under codes and fictitious names. In some field studies where confidentiality has been promised, the resulting published studies may nevertheless make it possible for subjects and others to identify specific people and places in the study. Such a situation developed after the publication of Arthur Vidich and Joseph Bensman's study of a small town, *Small Town in Mass Society,* in 1960. Some of the principal individuals in the study were quite easily identifiable to members of their community. This was a case in which confidentiality has been promised but not maintained. While names and obvious identifying characteristics had been altered, roles and situations made it quite easy for subjects to be identified by others. Thus when you conduct a study, you may want to warn participants that although confidentiality is the goal, under certain conditions the identities of certain

per...   Such a
wa...   ...onsent
stat...

Inf...   ...ole
issu...   ...pri-
vac...   ...ner the subject
has...   ...rch in which he
or s...   ...*ned consent* is
achi...   ...hat the study is,
und...   ...confidentiality in
the...   ...bjectives of the
stud...   ...Under such conditions...   ...vacy is lifted and
the p...   ...d. In such a case,
partic...   ...is crucial here is
that...   ...d. First, the re-
searc...   ...irate and complete...   ...urpose of the
study...   ...in it. In a
mail...   ...espond
and c...   ...he same
time...   ...that they
need...   ...ie quality of
volun...   ...gnized by the
subjec...

Se...   ...o presupposes
that th...   ...erstanding what
he or...   ...ias been given a
clear e...   ...College students,
adults...   ..., and many others
may w...   ...the nature and purpose o...   ...t. Others may not.
In thes...   ...ist be taken to explain t...   ...nsible fashion. (In
the cas...   ...iformed consent is
often s...   ...As was mentioned
above, ...nd less power are
often les...   ...be studied. They
may not...   ...of the informed
consent...   ...nk they have no
option b...   ...a higher-status,
educate...   ...the social researcher...   ...too emphati-
cally the potential danger or inconveniences of the

study. The social researcher cannot tell a person that he or she is incapable of understanding whether to participate. The only sensible course of action seems to be to develop an informed consent statement appropriate for the intended audience.

ETHICAL CONSIDERATIONS

The ethical considerations raised in this chapter can be reduced to a simple question: Whose rights are more sacred, those of the scientist, those of individuals or institutions who may be studied by scientists, or those of the public to learn from the research? In this section, these rights will be compared.

The Scientific Right to Study Any Subject of Interest

The right of social scientists to study whatever they deem to be of scientific interest is fundamental in a free society. This right, however, carries with it the responsibility that the research conform to scientific rules and that these rules include the protection of human subjects. We will here consider both the importance of maintaining high standards in carrying out research and the need for full disclosure.

Use of High Technical Standards. Anything may be a possible subject of study, but topics must be studied in accordance with the highest technical standards of the methods available to the researcher to obtain the necessary data. To maintain high technical standards, researchers must be familiar with both the range of types of research already available on a given topic and the methods used to study this topic. They must know which studies have been most successful in gaining the desired information, and they must understand precisely the procedures by which these studies have been carried out.

A researcher with technically high standards not only knows how to do what he or she is doing but can be critical of his or her own method. In other words, a researcher must consider the possible alternative ways of carrying out the study in order to appreciate the advantages and disadvantages of the method chosen. In this text, acceptable standards for each method will be detailed. However, no formal set of procedures can ever cover all the possible contingencies that may arise in setting up a research project. There will always be situations where the researcher will need to exercise discretion in implementing any method. It is precisely within this area of discretion that ethical considerations may arise.

Full Disclosure.   Science requires that all evidence generated and analyzed be made available to the relevant scientific community. This means that all aspects of a research project must be open for the inspection and understanding of others. In cases where confidentiality has been guaranteed, this somewhat reduces the full measure of disclosure. Usually, however, the information that is guaranteed to be confidential (names and addresses of subjects) is without scientific interest anyway.

Full disclosure of methods and findings requires that negative and insignificant as well as positive findings be presented. The objective must be to make the procedures and findings of a study fully enough available to the reader that he or she could replicate the study. In Chapter 2, in the discussion of the scientists who studied the evidence from the Apollo missions, it was suggested that this scientific norm often was not followed and that secrecy and lack of full disclosure were characteristic of much scientific activity. Thus it would seem that while full disclosure is an ideal of scientific researchers and that social researchers should aim to disclose whatever they find, this goal is not always characteristic of scientific research as it is practiced. Beginning researchers should design and carry out their research with the intention of making all their research available. In this regard, it is important to keep careful records of all the steps in a research project so that you are later able to disclose it fully.

The Rights of Human Subjects

Human subjects have the right not to be physically or psychologically abused. They have the right of privacy and protection of their reputations. While the right to protection from physical abuse seems self-evident, the case for the protection of privacy is more complex. A substantial case can be made for the rights of privacy of individuals. However, this concern can lead to practices which are overly cautious. Now that the institutions in which most scientists do their work require that all research on human subjects be approved by an *institutional review board* and all grants received from the government must also go through such an appraisal, there is fear that the concern to protect the rights of individuals may have turned into an obsession with privacy, precluding many important areas of research. Again, as in so many of these ethical areas, there are trade-offs. The ethical issues arise in cases where these choices need to be made.

Whose Rights?   Many would contend that the rights of individuals to privacy and freedom from harassment and harm supersede the rights of scientists to seek knowledge. They therefore preclude the practice of covert research in which the researcher deceives subjects by misrepresenting his or her role. They preclude experiments that coerce subjects to react in ways that may be detrimental to their sense of well-being. Further, they preclude research that invades areas of individuals' lives that are part of their private domain, unless, of course, the individual freely and knowingly gives up this right. [For an eloquent defense of the individual's right to privacy, see Shils (1982).]

As was stated above, however, some people are "more equal" than others. Social scientists should not limit their research only to those who are unable or unconcerned to protect their interests (real or perceived). There are many important aspects of social life in which the participants may resist being studied for various reasons, and the researcher will need to think seriously about the research strategies that may be available to counter such resistance. There may be instances in which it is necessary to study individuals without their explicit permission in order to secure the public's right to know. Perhaps the best middle ground is to try to gain access to "difficult-to-enter" organizations and situations by serving in a role different from that of a researcher.

Unfortunately, there are real losses to social research when all research that may require covert activity, coercion, or invasion of privacy is barred. The studies, such as Rosenhan's study of the treatment of mental institution patients and Milgram's classic study of obedience, offered keen insights into important institutions and forms of human behavior that might not have been gleaned by another method. Covert research methods have enabled researchers to study socially undesirable behaviors. Some would argue that without such techniques, the investigation of what Erving Goffman (1959) called "backstage" human interaction is seriously constrained.

Some social scientists have devised ways of studying the problems and topic in which they are interested that have avoided the potential abuse of deception. For example, in studies in which research done by a covert insider may seem to offer the only practical means of gathering data, the researcher should consider the alternative possibilities: (1) acting as overt outsider, frankly stating one's role as a researcher (as Rubinstein, 1973, did in his study of the Philadelphia police force) or (2) acting in the role of covert outsider, as Cohen and Taylor (1972) did in serving as lecturers for prisoners' courses as a way of observing prison life (see Bulmer, 1982, for a discussion). Neither of these roles requires that the researcher pose as an individual he or she is not. Instead, one either accepts the overt role of the researcher (many claim, with Rubinstein, 1973, that doing so makes little difference to insiders once their trust has been gained) or takes on another valid role as an outsider that is compatible with the conduct of the research as a secondary activity.

The Importance of Trust

Since social science is an interactive human activity, meaning that it requires the scientist to act in relation to other human beings, it creates its own behavioral by-products. This chapter has pointed out that some of these by-products may be or appear to be unethical. The accumulation of too many of these negative by-products could make it difficult for social researchers to continue their activities. The work of social scientists, like that of any other professionals whose work involves human subjects, depends ultimately on the trust of those with whom it deals. One covert researcher might be able to collect data surreptitiously on a specific group, but will the public evidence of this foreclose or limit the research possibilities of later researchers?

It is better that each researcher establish a level of trust among participants necessary in whatever social environment is being studied such that those being studied understand that their rights are being protected and find their participation in the study beneficial. Most individuals are fascinated with their own lives, with their own social memberships and social environments. To share this knowledge with an interested and sympathetic outsider whom they have come to trust is for many people a rewarding experience.

It may not be possible for you to establish the trust necessary to study every topic you find interesting, but you should select an environment for your research that allows you to be forthright about who you are, what you are up to, and why someone should view involvement in your study as beneficial. In addition to being less problematic or painful for your subjects, such a study will be easier for you in the long run as well.

ETHICAL ISSUES IN THE EVALUATION OF PROGRAMS

Because program evaluators appraise the efforts of those who develop and deliver programs, complex ethical considerations are raised in setting up and carrying out evaluations. Evaluators not only serve as consultants to a program or agency but also design research to evaluate programs. In this capacity, they administer the evaluation itself. They then serve in the role of collectors of data, which may involve interviewing, focus groups, and other data collection techniques in which employees and clients probably will be asked to participate. Hence, the evaluator comes to know the range of problems and perspectives of various members of the organization which may be at odds with each other. Moreover, the evaluator needs to analyze and report on her or his findings. Therefore, throughout the process, the evaluator shapes, guides, and finalizes the ultimate evaluation.

Newman and Brown (1996) present five ethical principles (drawn from the work of Kitchener, 1984) which they stress must guide the activities of the evaluator. These include respecting autonomy, doing no harm, benefiting others, being just, and being faithful (pp. 38-50). Autonomy is needed by the evaluator, but she or he is also obligated to respect the autonomy of those being studied. For this reason, the rule of autonomy signifies the importance of obtaining informed consent from those being studied and providing full disclosure of information. Autonomy also raises the issue of competence. Researchers cannot claim autonomy in areas in which they lack the appropriate skills.

Nonmalficence, or doing no harm, is an obvious ethical rule. To avoid physical or psychological harm, evaluators sometimes may either do something or avoid doing something which may cause harm. Evaluations are very often stressful to those being evaluated; care must be taken that the consequences of recommendations and evaluations will be seriously considered. Evaluators need to consider the possible political and social effects a possible action may bring forth. It is important that the evaluators practice "due care" to lessen the chance of doing harm.

Conversely, evaluators should try to do good by benefiting others. An evaluator should try to avoid any loss or damage to the clients, the employees, or any other stakeholders in the evaluation. An example of this occurs when an evaluator finds that there are few short-term results after being in the program for a fairly short period but the literature suggests that such programs need to be experienced longer to have results. It would then be good for the evaluator to include a fully developed section on how longer exposure to the program appears to be necessary to produce significant effects (Newman and Brown, 1996, p. 44).

The principle of justice means that everyone should be afforded the response he or she deserves regardless of race, class, or gender. The evaluator needs to take into consideration "distributive justice," which signifies the "appropriate distribution or nondistribution of social benefits and burdens" (Newman and Brown, 1996, p. 47). The principles under which benefits should be distributed are controversial: they include distributing equally or by need, effort, contribution, or merit.

The final principle is fidelity, which covers loyalty, honesty, and keeping promises (Newman and Brown, 1996, p. 49). The evaluator needs to take care in making promises so that he or she can keep them. It is important that the expectations of the agency be made as explicit as possible in the contract with the evaluator; however, there are always some implicit expectations which the evaluator needs to gauge and carefully consider. Not neglecting clients is also an important aspect of loyalty to the evaluation process.

Studies of the types of ethical violations which are most common in evaluations have noted that the most serious violations entail promising confidentiality when it cannot be maintained, serving as an evaluator when one lacks the competence to do the research, altering the questions the organization wants addressed so that the data generated can be analyzed in a way which the evaluator favors, and not consulting with the staff of the organization when the evaluator makes decisions (Newman and Brown, 1996, pp. 79–86).

To make decisions about ethical issues, the evaluator needs to be sensitive to his or her own intuition about what may or may not seem right. Newman and Brown suggest that one issue might be whether the evaluator is being accompanied too closely (p. 101); another might be that the evaluator has a personal friend among the staff members (p. 103). In cases which present a dilemma to the evaluator, the issue arises whether the evaluator should withdraw from the evaluation or whether there is some way to address the ethical issue. The evaluator needs to consider whether there is a specific ethical code that is being violated (consider Box 14-2 which reproduces sections of the Code of Ethics of the American Sociological Association). If no specific rule or code is being violated, the evaluator should consider the five principles that were listed above (autonomy, not doing harm, doing good, justice, and fidelity). The evaluator's personal values must also be considered. Finally, an evaluator needs to consider taking action to redress the ethical problem.

Once a full consideration of the impact of the action has been undertaken which would include consultation with colleagues in the organization and the evaluation team, a plan to address the ethical issue can be devised and carried out (Newman and Brown, 1996, pp. 101–109).

GUIDELINES

Many colleges and universities have institutional review boards which set ethical guidelines for research carried out in and by members of an institution; they also evaluate research proposals to ensure that the rights of human subjects are protected. These boards may review student projects as well as faculty-initiated research. One of the primary responsibilities of a professional association is to proctor the activities of its members so that they are not accused of acting in disreputable ways detrimental to the profession. In short, professional associations try to monitor the behaviors (read, reduce the misbehavior) of their members to protect or enhance their profession in the public eye. Social scientists have never been as fully in the public limelight as, say, doctors, yet their misbehaviors have often brought them to public attention more than have their accomplishments. For this reason, the establishment and maintenance of public trust is now a more pressing concern among social scientists than it was before.

Numerous professional associations have revised their codes of ethics to address the major moral concerns of their disciplines. Box 14-2 presents a number of sections of the revised Code of Ethics on the practice of sociology approved by the membership of the American Sociological Association in 1997.

SOCIAL RESEARCH ABUSES RECONSIDERED

This chapter has raised issues of central concern to the social sciences. It has presented points of view on the ethical issues confronting social research. Clearly, it is not the purpose of social research to trample on the rights of individuals, and this chapter has tried to make you think seriously about those rights. However, it has also raised the issue of the accountability of people in public positions and the need for those doing social research not to shy away from studies of the powerful, who have much greater means of maintaining their privacy.

Some social scientists feel a moral need to reveal how power is exercised in order to maintain privilege and the status quo. If they cannot gain access to the organizations where power is held, they feel morally justified in gaining information through whatever means are available. In cases such as that, where a researcher seeks to study individuals or organizations that resist being studied or will not willingly consent to being studied, the risk-benefit dilemma becomes most acute. Does the value to be gained from the study (either the advancement of knowledge in the discipline or for practical reasons) outweigh the risk to the subjects, the relationship of

BOX 14-2

SECTIONS OF THE 1997 REVISED CODE OF ETHICS OF THE AMERICAN SOCIOLOGICAL ASSOCIATION

PREAMBLE

This Code of Ethics articulates a common set of values upon which sociologists build their professional and scientific work. The Code is intended to provide both the general principles and the rules to cover professional situations encountered by sociologists. It has as its primary goal the welfare and protection of the individuals and groups with whom sociologists work. It is the individual responsibility of each sociologist to aspire to the highest possible standards of conduct in research, teaching, practice, and service.

The development of a dynamic set of ethical standards for a sociologist's work-related conduct requires a personal commitment to a lifelong effort to act ethically; to encourage ethical behavior by students, supervisors, supervisees, employers, employees, and colleagues; and to consult with others as needed concerning ethical problems. Each sociologist supplements, but does not violate, the values and rules specified in the Code of Ethics based on guidance drawn from personal values, culture, and experience.

GENERAL PRINCIPLES

The following General Principles are aspirational and serve as a guide for sociologists in determining ethical courses of action in various contexts. They exemplify the highest ideals of professional conduct.

Principle A: Professional Competence

Sociologists strive to maintain the highest levels of competence in their work; they recognize the limitations of their expertise; and they undertake only those tasks for which they are qualified by education, training, or experience. They recognize the need for ongoing education in order to remain professionally competent; and they utilize the appropriate scientific, professional, technical, and administrative resources needed to ensure competence in their professional activities. They consult with other professionals when necessary for the benefit of their students, research participants, and clients.

Principle B: Integrity

Sociologists are honest, fair, and respectful of others in their professional activities—in research, teaching, practice, and service. Sociologists do not knowingly act in ways that jeopardize either their own or others' professional welfare. Sociologists conduct their affairs in ways that inspire trust and confidence; they do not knowingly make statements that are false, misleading, or deceptive.

Principle C: Professional and Scientific Responsibility

Sociologists adhere to the highest scientific and professional standards and accept responsibility for their work. Sociologists understand that they form a community and show respect for other sociologists even when they disagree on theoretical, methodological, or personal approaches to professional activities. Sociologists value the public trust in sociology and are concerned about their ethical behavior and that of other sociologists that might compromise that trust. While endeavoring always to be collegial, sociologists must never let the desire to be collegial outweigh their shared responsibility for ethical behavior. When appropriate, they consult with colleagues in order to prevent or avoid unethical conduct.

Principle D: Respect for People's Rights, Dignity, and Diversity

Sociologists respect the rights, dignity, and worth of all people. They strive to eliminate bias in their professional activities, and they do not tolerate any forms of discrimination based on age; gender; race; ethnicity; national origin; religion; sexual orientation; disability; health conditions; or marital, domestic, or parental status. They are sensitive to cultural, individual, and role differences in serving, teaching, and studying groups of people with distinctive characteristics. In all of their work-related activities, sociologists acknowledge the rights of others to hold values, attitudes, and opinions that differ from their own.

Principle E: Social Responsibility

Sociologists are aware of their professional and scientific responsibility to the communities and societies in which they live and work. They apply and make public their knowledge in order to contribute to the public good. When undertaking research, they strive to advance the science of sociology and to serve the public good.

ETHICAL STANDARDS

1. Professional and Scientific Standards

Sociologists adhere to the highest possible technical standards that are reasonable and responsible in their research, teaching, practice, and service activities. They rely on scientifically and professionally derived knowledge; act with honesty and integrity; and avoid untrue, deceptive, or undocumented statements in undertaking work-related functions or activities.

2. Competence

(a) Sociologists conduct research, teach, practice, and provide service only within the boundaries of their competence, based on their education, training, supervised experience, or appropriate professional experience.

(b) Sociologists conduct research, teach, practice, and provide service in new areas or involving new techniques only after they have taken reasonable steps to ensure the competence of their work in these areas.

(c) Sociologists who engage in research, teaching, practice, or service maintain awareness of current scientific and professional information in their fields of activity, and undertake continuing efforts to maintain competence in the skills they use.

(d) Sociologists refrain from undertaking an activity when their personal circumstances may interfere with their professional work or lead to harm for a student, supervisee, human subject, client, colleague, or other person to whom they have a scientific, teaching, consulting, or other professional obligation.

11. Confidentiality

Sociologists have an obligation to ensure that confidential information is protected. They do so to ensure the integrity of research and the open communication with research participants and to protect sensitive information obtained in research, teaching, practice, and service. When gathering confidential information, sociologists should take into account the long-term uses of the information, including its potential placement in public archives or the examination of the information by other researchers or practitioners.

11.01 Maintaining Confidentiality

(a) Sociologists take reasonable precautions to protect the confidentiality rights of research participants, students, employees, clients, or others.

(b) Confidential information provided by research participants, students, employees, clients, or others is treated as such by sociologists even if there is no legal protection or privilege to do so. Sociologists have an obligation to protect confidential information, and not allow information gained in confidence from being used in ways that would unfairly compromise research participants, students, employees, clients, or others.

(c) Information provided under an understanding of confidentiality is treated as such even after the death of those providing that information.

(d) Sociologists maintain the integrity of confidential deliberations, activities, or roles, including, where applicable, that of professional committees, review panels, or advisory groups (e.g., the ASA Committee on Professional Ethics).

(e) Sociologists, to the extent possible, protect the confidentiality of student records, performance data, and personal information, whether verbal or written, given in the context of academic consultation, supervision, or advising.

(f) The obligation to maintain confidentiality extends to members of research or training teams and collaborating organizations who have access to the information. To ensure that access to confidential information is restricted, it is the responsibility of researchers, administrators, and principal investigators to instruct staff to take the steps necessary to protect confidentiality.

(g) When using private information about individuals collected by other persons or institutions, sociologists protect the confidentiality of individually identifiable information. Information is private when an individual can reasonably expect that the information will not be made public with personal identifiers (e.g., medical or employment records).

11.02 *Limits of Confidentiality*

(a) Sociologists inform themselves fully about all laws and rules which may limit or alter guarantees of confidentiality. They determine their ability to guarantee absolute confidentiality and, as appropriate, inform research participants, students, employees, clients, or others of any limitations to this guarantee at the outset consistent with ethical standards set forth in 11.02(b).

(b) Sociologists may confront unanticipated circumstances where they become aware of information that is clearly health- or life-threatening to research participants, students, employees, clients, or others. In these cases, sociologists balance the importance of guarantees of confidentiality with other principles in this Code of Ethics, standards of conduct, and applicable law.

(c) Confidentiality is not required with respect to observations in public places, activities conducted in public, or other settings where no rules of privacy are provided by law or custom. Similarly, confidentiality is not required in the case of information available from public records.

11.03 *Discussing Confidentiality and Its Limits*

(a) When sociologists establish a scientific or professional relationship with persons, they discuss (1) the relevant limitations on confidentiality, and (2) the foreseeable uses of the information generated through their professional work.

(b) Unless it is not feasible or is counterproductive, the discussion of confidentiality occurs at the outset of the relationship and thereafter as new circumstances may warrant.

11.04 *Anticipation of Possible Uses of Information*

(a) When research requires maintaining personal identifiers in data bases or systems of records, sociologists delete such identifiers before the information is made publicly available.

(b) When confidential information concerning research participants, clients, or other recipients

of service is entered into databases or systems of records available to persons without the prior consent of the relevant parties, sociologists protect anonymity by not including personal identifiers or by employing other techniques that mask or control disclosure of individual identities.

(c) When deletion of personal identifiers is not feasible, sociologists take reasonable steps to determine that appropriate consent of personally-identifiable individuals has been obtained before they transfer such data to others or review such data collected by others.

11.05 *Electronic Transmission of Confidential Information*

Sociologists use extreme care in delivering or transferring any confidential data, information, or communication over public computer networks. Sociologists are attentive to the problems of maintaining confidentiality and control over sensitive material and data when use of technological innovations, such as public computer networks, may open their professional and scientific communication to unauthorized persons.

11.06 *Anonymity of Sources*

(a) Sociologists do not disclose in their writings, lectures, or other public media confidential, personally identifiable information concerning their research participants, students, individual or organizational clients, or other recipients of their service which is obtained during the course of their work, unless consent from individuals or their legal representatives has been obtained.

(b) When confidential information is used in scientific and professional presentations, sociologists disguise the identity of research participants, students, individual or organizational clients, or other recipients of their service.

11.07 *Minimizing Intrusions on Privacy*

(a) To minimize intrusions on privacy, sociologists include in written and oral reports, consultations, and public communications only information germane to the purpose for which the communication is made. (b) Sociologists discuss confidential information or evaluative data concerning research participants, students, supervisees, employees, and individual or organizational clients only for appropriate scientific or professional purposes and only with persons clearly concerned with such matters.

11.08 Preservation of Confidential Information

(a) Sociologists take reasonable steps to ensure that records, data, or information are preserved in a confidential manner consistent with the requirements of this Code of Ethics, recognizing that ownership of records, data, or information may also be governed by law or institutional principles.

(b) Sociologists plan so that confidentiality of records, data, or information is protected in the event of the sociologist's death, incapacity, or withdrawal from the position or practice.

(c) When sociologists transfer confidential records, data, or information to other persons or organizations, they obtain assurances that the recipients of the records, data, or information will employ measures to protect confidentiality at least equal to those originally pledged.

12. Informed Consent

Informed consent is a basic ethical tenet of scientific research on human populations. Sociologists do not involve a human being as a subject in research without the informed consent of the subject or the subject's legally authorized representative, except as otherwise specified in this Code. Sociologists recognize the possibility of undue influence or subtle pressures on subjects that may derive from researchers' expertise or authority, and they take this into account in designing informed consent procedures.

12.01 Scope of Informed Consent

(a) Sociologists conducting research obtain consent from research participants or their legally authorized representatives (1) when data are collected from research participants through any form of communication, interaction, or intervention; or (2) when behavior of research participants occurs in a private context where an individual can reasonably expect that no observation or reporting is taking place.

(b) Despite the paramount importance of consent, sociologists may seek waivers of this standard when (1) the research involves no more than minimal risk for research participants, and (2) the research could not practicably be carried out were informed consent to be required. Sociologists recognize that waivers of consent require approval from institutional review boards or, in the absence of such boards, from another authoritative body with expertise on the ethics of research. Under such circumstances, the confidentiality of any personally identifiable information must be maintained unless otherwise set forth in 11.02(b).

(c) Sociologists may conduct research in public places or use publicly available information about individuals (e.g., naturalistic observations in public places, analysis of public records, or archival research) without obtaining consent. If, under such circumstances, sociologists have any doubt whatsoever about the need for informed consent, they consult with institutional review boards or, in the absence of such boards, with another authoritative body with expertise on the ethics of research before proceeding with such research.

(d) In undertaking research with vulnerable populations (e.g., youth, recent immigrant populations, the mentally ill), sociologists take special care to ensure that the voluntary nature of the research is understood and that consent is not coerced. In all other respects, sociologists adhere to the principles set forth in 12.01(a)–(c).

(e) Sociologists are familiar with and conform to applicable state and federal regulations and, where applicable, institutional review board requirements for obtaining informed consent for research.

12.02 Informed Consent Process

(a) When informed consent is required, sociologists enter into an agreement with research participants or their legal representatives that clarifies the nature of the research and the responsibilities of the investigator prior to conducting the research.

(b) When informed consent is required, sociologists use language that is understandable to and respectful of research participants or their legal representatives.

(c) When informed consent is required, sociologists provide research participants or their legal representatives with the opportunity to ask questions about any aspect of the research, at any time during or after their participation in the research.

(d) When informed consent is required, sociologists inform research participants or their legal representatives of the nature of the research; they indicate to participants that their participation or continued participation is voluntary; they inform participants of significant factors that may be expected to influence their willingness to participate (e.g., possible risks and benefits of their participation); and they explain other aspects of the research and respond to questions from prospective participants. Also, if relevant, sociologists explain that refusal to participate or withdrawal from participation in the research involves no penalty, and they explain any foreseeable consequences of declining or withdrawing. Sociologists explicitly discuss confidentiality and, if applicable, the extent to which confidentiality may be limited as set forth in 11.02(b).

(e) When informed consent is required, sociologists keep records regarding said consent. They recognize that consent is a process that involves oral and/or written consent.

(f) Sociologists honor all commitments they have made to research participants as part of the informed consent process except where unanticipated circumstances demand otherwise as set forth in 11.02(b).

12.03 Informed Consent of Students and Subordinates

When undertaking research at their own institutions or organizations with research participants who are students or subordinates, sociologists take special care to protect the prospective subjects from adverse consequences of declining or withdrawing from participation.

12.04 Informed Consent with Children

(a) In undertaking research with children, sociologists obtain the consent of children to participate, to the extent that they are capable of providing such consent, except under circumstances where consent may not be required as set forth in 12.01(b).

(b) In undertaking research with children, sociologists obtain the consent of a parent or a legally authorized guardian. Sociologists may seek waivers of parental or guardian consent when (1) the research involves no more than minimal risk for the research participants, and (2) the research could not practicably be carried out were consent to be required, or (3) the consent of a parent or guardian is not a reasonable requirement to protect the child (e.g., neglected or abused children).

(c) Sociologists recognize that waivers of consent from a child and a parent or guardian require approval from institutional review boards or, in the absence of such boards, from another authoritative body with expertise on the ethics of research. Under such circumstances, the confidentiality of any personally identifiable information must be maintained unless otherwise set forth in 11.02(b).

12.05 Use of Deception in Research

(a) Sociologists do not use deceptive techniques (1) unless they have determined that their use will not be harmful to research participants; is justified by the study's prospective scientific, educational, or applied value; and that equally effective alternative procedures that do not use deception are not feasible, and (2) unless they have obtained the approval of institutional review boards or, in the absence of such boards, with another authoritative body with expertise on the ethics of research.

(b) Sociologists never deceive research participants about significant aspects of the research that would affect their willingness to participate, such as physical risks, discomfort, or unpleasant emotional experiences.

(c) When deception is an integral feature of the design and conduct of research, sociologists attempt to correct any misconception that research participants may have no later than at the conclusion of the research.

(d) On rare occasions, sociologists may need to conceal their identity in order to undertake research that could not practicably be carried out were they to be known as researchers. Under such circumstances, sociologists undertake the research if it involves no more than minimal risk for the research participants and if they have obtained approval to proceed in this manner from an institutional review board or, in the absence of such boards, from another authoritative body with expertise on the ethics of research. Under such circumstances, confidentiality must be maintained unless otherwise set forth in 11.02(b).

12.06 Use of Recording Technology

Sociologists obtain informed consent from research participants, students, employees, clients, or others prior to videotaping, filming, or recording them in any form, unless these activities involve simply naturalistic observations in public places and it is not anticipated that the recording will be used in a manner that could cause personal identification or harm.

13. Research Planning, Implementation, and Dissemination

Sociologists have an obligation to promote the integrity of research and to ensure that they comply with the ethical tenets of science in the planning, implementation, and dissemination of research. They do so in order to advance knowledge, to minimize the possibility that results will be misleading, and to protect the rights of research participants.

13.01 Planning and Implementation

(a) In planning and implementing research, sociologists minimize the possibility that results will be misleading.

(b) Sociologists take steps to implement protections for the rights and welfare of research participants and other persons affected by the research.

(c) In their research, sociologists do not encourage activities or themselves behave in ways that are health- or life-threatening to research participants or others.

(d) In planning and implementing research, sociologists consult those with expertise concerning any special population under investigation or likely to be affected.

(e) In planning and implementing research, sociologists consider its ethical acceptability as set forth in the Code of Ethics. If the best ethical practice is unclear, sociologists consult with institutional review boards or, in the absence of such review processes, with another authoritative body with expertise on the ethics of research.

(f) Sociologists are responsible for the ethical conduct of research conducted by them or by others under their supervision or authority.

13.02 Unanticipated Research Opportunities

If during the course of teaching, practice, service, or non-professional activities, sociologists determine that they wish to undertake research that was not previously anticipated, they make known their intentions and take steps to ensure that the research can be undertaken consonant with ethical principles, especially those relating to confidentiality and informed consent. Under such circumstances, sociologists seek the approval of institutional review boards or, in the absence of such review processes, another authoritative body with expertise on the ethics of research.

13.03 Offering Inducements for Research Participants

Sociologists do not offer excessive or inappropriate financial or other inducements to obtain the participation of research participants, particularly when it might coerce participation. Sociologists may provide incentives to the extent that resources are available and appropriate.

13.04 Reporting on Research

(a) Sociologists disseminate their research findings except where unanticipated circumstances (e.g., the health of the researcher) or proprietary agreements with employers, contractors, or clients preclude such dissemination.

(b) Sociologists do not fabricate data or falsify results in their publications or presentations.

(c) In presenting their work, sociologists report their findings fully and do not omit relevant data. They report results whether they support or contradict the expected outcomes.

(d) Sociologists take particular care to state all relevant qualifications on the findings and interpretation of their research. Sociologists also disclose underlying assumptions, theories, methods, measures, and research designs that might bear upon findings and interpretations of their work.

(e) Consistent with the spirit of full disclosure of methods and analyses, once findings are publicly disseminated, sociologists permit their open assessment and verification by other responsible researchers with appropriate safeguards, where applicable, to protect the anonymity of research participants.

(f) If sociologists discover significant errors in their publication or presentation of data, they take reasonable steps to correct such errors in a correction, a retraction, published errata, or other public fora as appropriate.

(g) Sociologists report sources of financial support in their written papers and note any special relations to any sponsor. In special circumstances, sociologists may withhold the names of specific sponsors if they provide an adequate and full description of the nature and interest of the sponsor.

(h) Sociologists take special care to report accurately the results of others' scholarship by using correct information and citations when presenting the work of others in publications, teaching, practice, and service settings.

13.05 Data Sharing

(a) Sociologists share data and pertinent documentation as a regular practice. Sociologists make their data available after completion of the project or its major publications, except where proprietary agreements with employers, contractors, or clients preclude such accessibility or when it is impossible to share data and protect the confidentiality of the data or the anonymity of research participants (e.g., raw field notes or detailed information from ethnographic interviews).

(b) Sociologists anticipate data sharing as an integral part of a research plan whenever data sharing is feasible.

(c) Sociologists share data in a form that is consonant with research participants' interests and protect the confidentiality of the information they have been given. They maintain the confidentiality of data, whether legally required or not; remove personal identifiers before data are shared; and if necessary use other disclosure avoidance techniques.

(d) Sociologists who do not otherwise place data in public archives keep data available and retain documentation relating to the research for a reasonable period of time after publication or dissemination of results.

(e) Sociologists may ask persons who request their data for further analysis to bear the associated incremental costs, if necessary.

(f) Sociologists who use data from others for further analyses explicitly acknowledge the contribution of the initial researchers.

14. Plagiarism

(a) In publications, presentations, teaching, practice, and service, sociologists explicitly identify, credit, and reference the author when they take data or material verbatim from another person's written work, whether it is published, unpublished, or electronically available.

(b) In their publications, presentations, teaching, practice, and service, sociologists provide acknowledgment of and reference to the use of others' work, even if the work is not quoted verbatim or paraphrased, and they do not present others' work as their own whether it is published, unpublished, or electronically available.

15. Authorship Credit

(a) Sociologists take responsibility and credit, including authorship credit, only for work they have actually performed or to which they have contributed.

(b) Sociologists ensure that principal authorship and other publication credits are based on the relative scientific or professional contributions of the individuals involved, regardless of their status. In claiming or determining the ordering of authorship, sociologists seek to reflect accurately the contributions of main participants in the research and writing process.

(c) A student is usually listed as principal author on any multiple authored publication that substantially derives from the student's dissertation or thesis.

20. Adherence to the Code of Ethics

Sociologists have an obligation to confront, address, and attempt to resolve ethical issues according to this Code of Ethics.

20.01 *Familiarity with the Code of Ethics*

Sociologists have an obligation to be familiar with this Code of Ethics, other applicable ethics codes, and their application to sociologists' work. Lack of awareness or misunderstanding of an ethical standard is not, in itself, a defense to a charge of unethical conduct.

20.02 *Confronting Ethical Issues*

(a) When sociologists are uncertain whether a particular situation or course of action would violate the Code of Ethics, they consult with other sociologists knowledgeable about ethical issues, with ASA's Committee on Professional Ethics, or with other organizational entities such as institutional review boards.

(b) When sociologists take actions or are confronted with choices where there is a conflict between ethical standards enunciated in the Code of Ethics and laws or legal requirements, they make known their commitment to the Code and take steps to resolve the conflict in a responsible manner by consulting with colleagues, professional organizations, or the ASA's Committee on Professional Ethics.

20.03 *Fair Treatment of Parties in Ethical Disputes*

(a) Sociologists do not discriminate against a person on the basis of his or her having made an ethical complaint.

(b) Sociologists do not discriminate against a person based on his or her having been the subject of an ethical complaint. This does not preclude taking action based upon the outcome of an ethical complaint.

20.04 *Reporting Ethical Violations of Others*

When sociologists have substantial reason to believe that there may have been an ethical violation by another sociologist, they attempt to resolve the issue by bringing it to the attention of that individual if an informal resolution appears appropriate or possible, or they seek advice about whether or how to proceed based on this belief, assuming that such activity does not violate any confidentiality rights. Such action might include referral to ASA's Committee on Professional Ethics.

20.05 *Cooperating with Ethics Committees*

Sociologists cooperate in ethics investigations, proceedings, and resulting requirements of the American Sociological Association. In doing so, they make reasonable efforts to resolve any issues of confidentiality. Failure to cooperate may be an ethics violation.

20.06 *Improper Complaints*

Sociologists do not file or encourage the filing of ethics complaints that are frivolous and are intended to harm the alleged violator rather than to protect the integrity of the discipline and the public.

---

the social researcher to subjects, the maintenance of trust between the field of social research and the society it seeks to study? Social researchers should not veer away from a subject simply because they think it may raise some ethical issues or difficulties. But it is important to make sure that you think through those issues and difficulties thoroughly before you proceed. Social researchers need not be so timid and deferential that any challenge to their plans sends them running. Instead, if it is your project, talk to others about it: your professors, the review board at your institution, those whose opinions you value.

Think through the uses of the study; consider the potential abuses. Then decide whether the value of the study is worth the risks. Research demands not only caution but courage as well.

REVIEW NOTES

• The three types of research procedures that raise ethical concerns are covert research methods, research which involves coercion of subjects, and research procedures that may be considered an invasion of privacy.

- Unethical practices that may arise in the reporting of social research constitute tampering with results and plagiarism.
- In the study of persons in public positions and public organizations, the right of privacy must be balanced against the public's right to know.
- Measures for ensuring the protection of subjects in a research study are anonymity, confidentiality, and informed consent.
- Many institutions and professional associations that sponsor research have drawn up guidelines to follow in ensuring the rights of human subjects.
- Evaluators of programs should observe the following ethical principles: respect autonomy, do no harm, benefit others, be just, and be faithful.

KEY TERMS

anonymity
coercion of subjects
confidentiality
covert research
full disclosure
informed consent
institutional review board
invasion of privacy
plagiarism
rights of human subjects
tampering with results

STUDY EXERCISES

1. Which of the studies mentioned in this chapter as being "charged" with abuses seems to you to bear the greatest ethical problems? Why did you make this choice?

2. Considering Zhang's evaluation of the Los Angeles boot camps (Chapter 10), how might the five ethical practices suggested by Newman and Brown (1996) apply to this study?

RECOMMENDED READINGS

1. Bulmer, Martin (ed.): *Social Research Ethics,* Macmillan, London, 1982. This collection of essays includes both appraisals of covert participation observation studies and considerations of the ethical issues raised (invasion of privacy, academic freedom, restrictions on research).

2. Kimmel, Allan J.: *Ethics and Values in Applied Social Research,* Sage, Thousand Oaks, Calif., 1998. This volume addresses the value issues confronted in doing research for organizations and agencies. A useful guide.

3. Lewis, George H.: *Fist-Fights in the Kitchen: Manners and Methods in Social Research,* Goodyear, Pacific Palisades, Calif., 1975. This very lively reader includes considerations of ethical issues in experiments, the rights of subjects, and Irving Louis Horowitz's exposé of the government-sponsored Project Camelot.

4. Newman, Dianna L., and Robert D. Brown: *Applied Ethics for Program Evaluation,* Sage, Thousand Oaks, Calif., 1996. Using examples from actual evaluation projects, this volume examines how and why researchers need to follow ethical principles in making decisions about designing and carrying out their evaluations.

5. Sieber, Joan E.: *Planning Ethically Responsible Research: A Guide for Social Science Students,* Sage, Thousand Oaks Calif., 1992. This useful volume explains how to prepare a protocol for an institutional review board and how to handle issues of confidentiality, privacy, deception, and consent.

Presenting the Research Results

INTRODUCTION

This chapter offers an overview of the various ways in which social research is presented to others. Social research has a social purpose, a function. But if it is not disseminated, or shown to others, it can not play a social role.

Naturally, there are very different publics for social research. You may be writing a research project paper for an undergraduate methods course, in which case your immediate audience will be your professor. You may be writing a research paper to be presented to an audience at a professional meeting or published in an academic journal. If you are funded by a grant, you may be writing a final report for the funding agency to tell it what you have found. Social research projects also may serve as the basis of a book. All the surveys and qualitative studies detailed in Chapter 1 were finally developed into books. Often a research project is disseminated in several ways: as a paper presented at a professional meeting, in one or more published articles, and possibly also as a book.

The usual way of disseminating social research is through a research report. Whether it is written for a course paper or for an academic journal or conference, the general form of such a research paper is roughly the same. The principles for organizing such a research report will form the major section of this chapter.

FORMS FOR DISSEMINATING SOCIAL RESEARCH

When to Decide on the Form

Research projects vary in their purpose. If you are carrying out your project for a course, you know that it will culminate in a project paper that will be handed in to the course instructor. If you are doing an evaluation research project for a particular agency, you know that you must prepare a report of your findings for the agency. If you have a research grant, you are obliged to prepare a final report for the granting agency. These types of projects have preresearch writing commitments. In such a case, the manner in which the project will be disseminated should guide the design of the project throughout. In Chapter 3, the outline for the research proposal was similar to an outline for the final research report.

Sometimes research projects are begun without a clear idea of what the form of dissemination will be. This can lead to problems if, after finally deciding what the form of dissemination should be, you discover that your research data do not enable you to produce it. The flexibility of your project in terms of how many types of disseminated products it might lead to will depend on the size and focus of the project.

If you do a very tight little experiment with a small sample which tests a single hypothesis, you may be able to write only a single article to address its findings. If, however, you engage in a large longitudinal study on which all the data are not yet collected, your writings from that one research effort may be numerous and go on for years. Such a comprehensive survey can be analyzed from so many different perspectives, since it contains so many different variables which can be manipulated in so many different ways, that it is not likely that a single researcher can exhaust all the research analyses possible in that study. This is why such datasets become the bases for secondary analyses (as discussed in Chapter 9).

When you are working with a large dataset, with numerous experiments, or with a complex content analysis, you must decide at some point precisely which subtopic within the larger project you plan to write about and what material from all that is available can be used to address it. In other words, with a large project, which probably will form the basis of a number of disseminated writings and presentations, you may not in the beginning have specified all the writing you plan from it; they may evolve over time. The problem with this type of planning is that often you may not have exactly the data you require to address each new idea for a paper. Then you will need to operate as a secondary analyst would—being willing to substitute a less perfect measure for a concept than you might have chosen if you had planned this particular paper before collecting the data.

BASIC INGREDIENTS NEEDED FOR A RESEARCH REPORT

If you look back to Chapter 3 on the 11 steps of a research project, you will see that we have reached the eleventh step. Before you write your research project, you must assemble four basic ingredients which come from different steps of the research effort:

1. *A clear topic.* Your topic must be precisely worked out in written form. It cannot be simply "Delinquency," "Prejudice," or "Problems of Hispanic Children in Schools." All these titles are too vague and unspecified. The topic must be posed in the form of a research question or a hypothesis.

2. *A review of other relevant evidence.* The background literature may well have been gathered together when the research was designed. It is likely that you will need to round out your review by going through the most recent journal articles relevant to your topic which have appeared since you began and by carefully considering whether the topic on which you are writing requires evidence from areas which you had not examined previously.

3. *A research design.* The research design is the model which controls your project. In most cases, this design will have been formally worked out during the planning (or *proposal* writing) stage of your study. During the course of the research itself, the design may have undergone some changes. To write up the final project, you must clarify the precise model you worked from. If the study is being

written for a class project paper, it may make sense to describe how the research design evolved over the course of the study; if it is being written for a more formal presentation or publication, the final research design will be the one to present. A research design is primarily the model you propose to use to analyze the data, but it also must include the plans for measuring the major variables and collecting the data. In many cases, analytic designs can be best presented with diagrams, where variables are laid out with lines and arrows pointing out their relationship to one another.

4. *Analyzed data.* The findings of your study reside in the analyzed data. Writing a report or paper on the data is often the very way in which the analyses are produced. Some researchers take notes on each table when it is examined; other merely select tables to discuss as they write the analysis.

From Research Project to Research Report

In addition to the four basic ingredients of the paper, you will need introductory, connective, and explanatory material to form the research project into a logical whole. The most critical explanatory material is the information on the methods used. This can include discussions of the form of data collection, the instruments used, the nature of the sample, and issues of conceptualization and measurement. The *structuring* ingredients vary with the type of dissemination you are doing.

Types of Research Reports

Research Papers for Courses.   These papers should include comprehensive discussions and evidence of the methods used. Since such papers often are completed to fulfill the requirements of a methods course, you must make it very clear to the instructor that you understand every one of the methodological steps which were taken to carry out the project. In my experience, students seem to have two problems in this regard. First, they often skip crucial steps by jumping over a procedure that was crucial to the study but may have been forgotten once subsequent steps were completed (a good example here might be the pretest). You should therefore keep a clear record of the steps in your research as you go along. Second, students often become too detailed about certain aspects of the research effort, describing them in so much depth that the discussion becomes repetitive and redundant (a good example here would be the coding).

Research papers for classes often require that the instruments for data collection, the raw data, frequencies for all variables, or other sorts of evidence of the data be presented in an appendix.

Presentation Before a Professional Audience. These papers often have a greatly reduced discussion of the methods used. Such papers usually must be highly focused to address a subtopic of the central research topic. The discussion of others' relevant research findings may be reduced to those bearing most directly on your findings. Presented papers emphasize the findings section since this is what will interest the audience most. In addition, such papers need to draw sharp conclusions to make sure the audience remembers what has been said. Not every study produces decisive findings, but you can often draw interesting conclusions even from a study with inconclusive findings. Your research also may have raised stimulating questions: What was the probable cause of the inconclusiveness? What type of future research project might be able to produce more conclusive evidence on this topic?

Publication in Professional Journals. Such papers require the ability to write concisely. Because printing costs are high and journals tend to have page limits, the art of writing for journals lies in being able to describe what is essential about your study in a very few words. The reader is often given references to help locate more explicit evidence (from the author, from a research organiza-

tion, from another publication on the same research). Extensive appendices are rare, though sometimes certain elaborations of critical aspects of the methodological approach (e.g., how an index which served as the dependent variable was formed) are added. Because a published article becomes a part of the literature on this research subject, greater care must be taken to make certain that the evidence presented is without error, the implications of the findings are the most rational and cogent that can be produced, and the background literature supporting the project is the most relevant and current.

Papers Prepared for the Mass Media. The findings of many research projects are made available to the public through the mass media. Usually this occurs at a second stage, after the research was first disseminated through another form (such as being presented at a professional meeting or appearing in a book). Sometimes the reports of such research are very brief and may be written by reporters on the basis of reading or hearing your paper. A journalist may telephone you to discuss the evidence.

You also may prepare a written piece or article for a mass-media form. Here the details of your methods cannot be given, though the most central facts (the size of your sample, the types of individuals sampled) will be needed. What is often left out entirely is the background literature, how the concepts were measured, and how the data were collected. There is a tendency to report the findings as bold facts with the only qualification being some general information on the sample. When you prepare such material yourself, be sure to include the most critical information the reader will need in order to apply your findings. If your measure of work orientation could be translated as "commitment" but not as "job satisfaction," make certain that it is described accurately. If your finding is that the nursing homes you studied were deficient in some manner, make certain that the types of homes you actually observed are described quite explicitly. If there are any strong reservations hanging over your findings—let's say you have grounds for doubting that your control group was comparable to the experimental group so that the findings you have presented may not be completely fair—put them in. The public is rarely turned off by reservations that are stated simply and directly. You cannot overload a piece for the mass media with qualifications and reservations, but the most central ones may be slipped in without overburdening it.

If you are writing for a nontechnical audience, you will need to drop all the jargon used in the field. Phrases such as "random sample," "control group," and "participant observer," which may be understood by anyone with an undergraduate course in research methods, probably will mean nothing to most readers of a newspaper. All these phrases can be described as a "fair representation of the voters of James County," a control group as a "comparable group who were not given the treatment," and a participant observer as "one who visits an organization both to collect information for a study and to offer consultation to the management." Note that these phrases tend to be longer, which explains why technical jargon is often developed.

Finally, if you are preparing a piece for dissemination in the mass media, you may need to consider what it is about your study that would be most fascinating to a lay audience. You may have a finding which is relatively minor in terms of your overall study but should form the basis of your piece because it addresses an issue of wide public interest. For example, if in addition to the topic of your primary research you have interesting data on the attitudes of Catholics toward abortion or those of the elderly toward changes in taxing social security, these additional data may well appeal to the public.

Dissemination in Book Form.   A book is a much more ambitious form of dissemination. Books based on social research studies often follow the general outlines of a research article,

which will be given below, but sometimes they vary quite substantially from such an article. If the book will contain quantitative data in tables, it will be necessary to explain the methods used early in the manuscript. However, if the book is based on a field study, the methods may be left for the end and may appear only in an appendix. In such a field study the goal is to try to get the writing to "flow" in a manner somewhat like a novel; complex explanations of methodological techniques should not impede this objective.

Books are also written for different audiences. Most books based on social research studies are intended for other researchers, faculty members, students, and members of the public who have a particular interest in the subject matter. However, sometimes a social research project forms the basis of a book which will have an even wider audience. The wider the audience you hope to address, the less you should emphasize your methodological techniques. These details may be cited in notes or references so that professionally interested readers may consult them if they wish. The wider the audience you hope to address, the more explicitly and simply you need to state your findings. The wider the audience you hope to address, the more you must relate your finding to issues of current relevance to the general public. This is why social research is often written to address current social policy issues. The public is rarely interested simply in whether you have supported or refuted some other researcher, a hypothesis, or an abstract theory.

Commissioned Research Reports.   These reports may be prepared because you are fulfilling the obligations of a grant or a contract or because you are preparing a report for an agency or organization which hired you to carry out a study for purposes of evaluation or to formulate policy. In such cases there is nearly always an earlier proposal which was prepared to secure the grant. Your primary obligation is to give the agency what you promised. Often this is all you give the agency, all that is really wanted. But agencies do not want just data. They also want analyses that back up the data. Sometimes you may offer analyses that diverge from the original directives of the proposal because you feel certain that these new directions are relevant to the needs and interests of the granting agency. When you do this, you should make it clear that what you are analyzing was not proposed earlier.

If the project is being carried out for an organization so that its managers can make decisions on the basis of it, you should offer your policy suggestions at the end of the report (this was discussed in Chapter 10 on evaluation research). Don't feel that it is presumptuous to do so because you are not an employee of the organization. You are only doing what you were paid to do. You may well have some hesitations about your policy suggestions, in which case you should simply state them. Be bold about your suggestions, however. It is always better to be explicit and forceful while maintaining some reservations than to be so timid and wishy-washy that it is impossible for those receiving the report to know precisely what you have concluded.

Multiple Dissemination Modes

As was stated earlier, any research project can produce a great variety of written materials for different audiences and in different formats. What is necessary for each piece of writing is that the relevant audience be considered and the proper format be used. Once an initial writeup of a project has been prepared for one purpose, others can be devised which take up different aspects of the findings or address different audiences. Whoever the audience and whatever the subject, it is necessary to cast the problem for the paper is such a way that the attention of the audience is caught. That's why you must know what audience you are writing for.

Papers for courses, journals, and presentations often address problems which diverge from the initial ideas that fostered the project in the first place. As findings are discovered, the original research problem may be recast to lead up to newly

discovered, interesting findings. This does not mean that finding that your initial hypothesis was not supported by the data means that you should bury this evidence. Scientific research should not ignore disproving hypotheses. In some cases, your initial hypothesis may be of such interest and importance that people will want to know that it was disproved. Often, however, the hypothesis may not be a matter of wide interest, and to base a paper on showing that it was disproved may make little sense. Such an exercise may be appropriate for a course paper but would not meet the requirements of having sufficient interest for a professional audience.

Any research project may produce numerous written papers. First you must write the paper that meets your primary commitment. Once this is done, you can consider how else to disseminate it. Some of the papers you write from a piece of research may be ones that were never considered in the early design stages of the project.

CASTING THE PROBLEM OF THE PAPER

Every paper needs a primary focus, usually a specific problem. Naturally, problems may vary enormously. The late David Caplovitz suggested that most quantitative research projects have one of the following three foci: a dependent variable, an independent variable, or a special group (1983, pp. 391-398). In a *dependent variable study,* the problem is to understand why, how, and under what conditions the dependent variable occurred. In survey research projects, the object may be to determine the other variables which are most strongly related to or predictive of the attribute of the dependent variable in which you are interested. Let me emphasize this point. Suppose you are studying why students drop out of college or the self-concepts of male and female first-graders. In each case, you are focusing primarily on one end of the variable. In the dropout study, your interest is in why students leave college, not in why they stay (which is the other end of the variable). In the self-concept study, you would be interested in high, positive levels of self-esteem (or if it were a longitudinal study, you might be interested in positive changes in self-concept) more that in average or low levels. Naturally, you could just as easily be interested in why students stay in college or maintain a low self-concept. The important thing is that you know what end of the variable interests you so that your study focuses clearly on that end.

Dependent variable studies are often easy to diagram. The dependent variable generally comes at the end of a number of other possibly contributing factors. One truism which is often stated (but is still worth repeating) is that the more clearly defined and easier to understand the dependent variable is, the better able the researcher is to keep the project on a clear course. When I was a graduate student, I knew a young man who was studying why students dropped out of college. He surveyed a sample of first-year students, and at the beginning of the next academic year he was able to determine which ones had dropped out. This was a precise dependent variable. (A student had or had not dropped out.) The focus of the study was very sharp. In contrast, my study on the weakening of authoritarianism was much more difficult to handle. How far did students need to move on the Autonomy Scale before I considered their authoritarianism to have weakened? Furthermore, the very concept of authoritarianism (or autonomy) was much fuzzier to begin with. When you design your study, ask yourself if you have a clear, precise dependent variable as your focus. It will facilitate and clarify your analyses and help keep you on a sure path to your conclusions.

An *independent variable study* tends to compare one social context to another. The experiment in which domestic violence offenders were arrested that is described in Chapter 1 and many of the evaluation research projects discussed in Chapter 10 were focused on an independent variable. While such studies examine the outcome or effects of such social action programs (arresting offenders, Head Start programs, a federal law, or

whatever), the primary interest is in the program or social enactment itself. Did it bring about the desired effect? Did it have any effect? Often in an evaluation program there may be variation built into the independent variable itself. (In the arresting offenders experiment treatment given to the offenders was randomly administered). Here the interest is in determining which form of the treatment seemed to be the most effective. Those who commission the evaluation want to know whether a treatment or a social program works and, if it does, how does it affect measurable outcomes?

Finally, Caplovitz identified the type of study which focuses on a *special population.* This is typical of anthropological studies of primitive tribes and studies of a particular group of people, such as the homosexuals of Humphreys's (1970) research described in Chapter 14. In these studies there is no control group with which the special group is being contrasted. Usually these studies are very descriptive; they try to give a complex view of the group in question.

ORGANIZING A STUDENT RESEARCH PROJECT PAPER

Whatever the central focus of your project, you will do best to set up an outline of the sections you plan to include in your paper. The following seven-point outline should be applicable to nearly all types of research methods approaches. You might want to refer back at this point to the 11 steps of a research project described in Chapter 3. These steps will be collapsed into the seven parts of the research paper.

I. General Statement of the Research Problem

This will serve as the introduction to the paper. You must state clearly and concisely what your problem is, what the general issue is that the study will address. This will cover step 1 of the research project: *defining the research topic.* You will want to write this first, but you are likely to return to it once the analyses have been written to make some changes it it. Remember that while you went into this project with a firm (let's hope) research problem in mind so that you might have written this general statement before you collected your data, the research problem may well have altered somewhat over the course of your project.

This is where the type of focus your study has—whether it centers on a search for the determinants of a dependent variable, an appraisal of a program or condition serving as the independent variable, or a special group—will be addressed. Sometimes students are confused about exactly what they are studying. One might say, "I'm studying people who voted for Bob Dole." Yet note that this could imply many different types of studies. Is the student studying the characteristics of those who voted for Dole in contrast to those who did not? Or is the student studying why Dole supporters voted for him? The general problem must be stated in such a way that the design of the study, the data collection, and the analyses make logical sense as a way to address that problem. The section defines the purpose of the study, the reason why you are carrying it out. If it is to explore, describe, or explain a problem, this must be stated in the beginning of the study.

II. Background of the Problem

Research problems do not fall ready-made from outer space. They grow from the ideas and findings of earlier studies, earlier observations of what we are studying. Therefore, you must present these earlier findings. This is the background literature, or review of the literature, section which covers step 2 of the research project: *finding out what is known about the topic.* Finding the most central and important studies which have laid the groundwork for your study is not a simple task. Naturally you must understand clearly what your primary focus is. If you are writing a dependent variable study, you will need to have reviewed research by others on the same variable.

Other studies on your topic may be numerous. In selecting which ones to include in your review, consider the following points:

1. How similar to your study is the other one in terms of the variables studied, the types of samples used, and the theoretical positions put forth?
2. How recent is the study? All thing considered, a more recent study is more useful to you if it has been well done, because it should have taken into account earlier studies. This stems from the cumulative nature of science.
3. Are the researchers who carried out the study important authorities on the subject? This is the issue of reputation. As in all fields, social research has its stars. Certain researchers have an eminence and an established reputation which make their research more prominent than the work of lesser-known social researchers. This is a somewhat complex issue. The fact that someone does not have a famous reputation does not mean that his or her work is not good. Another problem for a student is that you may be much less familiar with who is and who is not prominent in any given area. If you look through enough studies on your topic, however, you will find that certain researchers are cited repeatedly. These are surely the more prominent ones. You cannot be certain, however, that every citation is a good one. The only way to determine the quality of the reference is to examine the study itself and weigh it according to the canons of the research techniques you have learned. You probably will want to address the work of the most central researchers in the field whatever else you do, but do not neglect the work of other scholars that you think is important for your purposes.

There are also a number of *don'ts* for a literature review:

- *Don't* use articles from the mass media as if they were social research articles. Although you may get some statistical material or ideas from newspapers or popular magazines, you do not want to base your study on the writings of journalists. Theirs is a different field, a different way of collecting and presenting material.

- *Don't* include a study in your literature review simply because it addresses a topic similar to your own. Be critical. If you haven't learned anything of interest concerning your research project by reading an article, don't use it.
- *Don't* simply use the abstract of an article or transfer the abstract into your paper almost verbatim. Read the article, searching for the parts which are most relevant to your study, and then report on this material. You will need to say a few general things about each study you report on, such as the general problem being studied and the type of sample used. Otherwise, use from an article the precise points you need; these points are rarely found in an abstract.
- *Don't* automatically assume that if a piece of research studies a concept with the same name as the one you study, these concepts are directly comparable. Remember that how the concept has been operationalized and measured in each case may be so different that you are really dealing with two concepts that bear the same label but have very little else in common. Be sure to explain how central concepts in the research which you are comparing to your study were measured in the study under review.

In writing the literature review, keep it well organized. Often such a review will have a number of subheadings that indicate the various subareas of the study which are being addressed. For example, in writing an article on work orientation in women, my former colleague Judith Bootcheck and I (Baker and Bootcheck, 1985) divided the literature review section into two major parts:

1. *The Changing Conception of Women's Work Orientation.* This section addressed the various conceptions of women's work attitudes which came to bear on what we termed *work orientation,* including earlier-developed concepts of *career aspirations, career expectations, career commitment, career salience,* and *taste for employment.* The object of this section was to lay the groundwork for our use and operationalization of the concept of work orientation. It was the part of the literature review that focused on our dependent variable.

2. *Work Orientation in Women: Factors Related to Change.* This section addressed the various independent variables in the study. The subsections included (1) higher education, career preparation, and training, (2) marriage, motherhood, and singlehood, (3) sex-role ideology, and (4) characteristics of family of origin (mother's employment and social status). Under each of these sections, we reported on studies in which these factors were related to some quality of women's work orientation.

Literature review sections should be full of good, relevant material explained clearly and concisely. Remember that you are reporting on other work only because it will bear on your study. For this reason, literature review sections usually cannot be written until your analyses have been carried out so that you are certain what the variables of central import in your study are. However, many researchers prepare a preliminary draft of the literature review section after doing a search of the literature at the beginning of the project.

III. Design of the Study

This is where the formal statement of your specific research question or hypothesis is made. Generally you draw on ideas that were introduced first in Section I on the general statement and developed in Section II on the background literature. Your paper should build in Sections I and II with a kind of crescendo to this Section III, where the problem you will be addressing in this paper is explicitly laid out.

It should be clear in most cases from the research question or hypothesis what type of study focus you have, what your primary dependent and independent variables will be. In some cases, diagrams of the research model are presented. The major concepts should be defined theoretically and explained operationally. This undertaking accomplishes step 3 of the research project: *clarifying concepts and their measurement.* The exact measurement of the central variables may not be presented until the analysis section, but a description of the operationalized variables and the research instruments which measured them should be offered. If you are addressing or testing a specific theory, this theory should be laid out and associated with your study objectives here in this section. Remember, this is where it should be made clear whether the study was deductive (hypothesis testing) or inductive.

IV. How the Data Were Obtained

This is the section of your paper that tells the reader *how* you did the study. It is the central methods section. There are always two primary aspects to the design: what you did to get the data (data collection) and from whom you got the data (the sample).

Data Collection Methods.   The research method used to gather your data needs to be described carefully. In this section you must report how you *established an appropriate data collection method,* which was step 4 in your research project. No aspect of your method should be ignored in preparing this section, though some aspects may need to be mentioned only very briefly. The section also should include the type of instrument used. The general issues of operationalization, reliability, and validity should be highlighted in this discussion. Thus this section of the written paper also describes step 5 of the research project: *the design of the research instruments,* which includes the *operationalized concepts.* The exact measurement of the central variables may not be presented until the

analysis section, but a description of operationalized variables should be offered. The section should describe the conditions under which the data were collected, the identity of the data collectors, the training of the data collectors, the type of pretesting done, and some evaluation of the data collection procedures so that any weaknesses may be considered in appraising the evidence.

How the Sample Was Designed.   A detailed but concise description of the sample studied must be given. This was step 6 in our research project: *selecting a sample of subjects to study.* If you developed your own sample, you must compare your final sample to the one you hoped to obtain. Remember to offer a definition of the population from which the sample was drawn. Don't make your sample sound better than it is. If you have collected your own data using a purposive sample, there is nothing wrong with that. Be forthright about what you have; this will strengthen, not weaken, your study. Sometimes tables are presented that summarize basic characteristics of the sample, such as sex distribution, work status, educational status, age, race, or other factors which are central to your study.

Ethical Issues.   It is usually in the data collection and sample selection phases that ethical issues arise. Were the respondents deceived in any way? Was the role of the researcher covert? Did the data collection procedures or specific questions invade the privacy of others? How far had your subjects given an *informed consent* to their participation in the study? There may be reasons to use some forms of deception or convert research activities, but you should know and state explicitly the ethical issues raised and how you tried to deal with them. You should explain how the confidentiality or anonymity of your subjects was preserved, if indeed it was. Addressing the ethical issues of your research will cover step 7 of your research proposal: *the purpose, value, and ethics of the study.* This section has covered the outcome of step 8 in the research project; *data collection.* Remember that for a survey research project it is essential to report the *response rate*. The results of pretesting and refining the data collection procedures should be addressed if they affected the final data obtained.

V. Analysis of Data

This is the heart of the paper. Yet without the introductory materials in the earlier section, the reasons for the analysis and an understanding of what the data represent could not be reached. Don't just report "the facts." Remember that all facts must be interpreted, and it is the choice of interpretations (as well as the choice of facts) that will form the basis of the analysis. To analyze the data, you first had to accomplish step 9 of the research project: *processing the data*. However, these procedures are rarely elaborated in a paper, though they may be referred to in a methodological footnote or appendix. The written analyses cover step 10 of the research project: *analyzing the data*.

In quantitative studies, this section has the tables in it. These tables must be carefully planned so that they show the reader what he or she needs to be shown to understand a table. Tables must be well labeled and must be presented in a format which is conventionally used for that type of data. By looking at the presentation of other tables in studies similar to your own, you will develop a sense of how your tables should look. Remember that there are many different ways of presenting a cross tabulation; some styles are used more often in certain types of journals. But however they are set up, they must be readily accessible to others.

Quantitative studies often begin with a summary table that offers some basic evidence on the frequency of the dependent variable in relation to one or more other central factors in the study. Such a table may be a series of different frequency distributions strung together; in such a case, not all categories of each independent variable need to be presented. Tables then move across the analysis, trying to address all the theoretical issues raised by the research problem. When multivariate analyses

are used, such tables are often the last in a paper, since they serve to tie together all the tables that were presented earlier.

In a field study, the analysis section offers the findings of the study in relation to the problem you set out to study. Since there are no hard numerical "facts" to substantiate your position, you must present your findings in such a convincing manner that they are seen as fulfilling your research concerns.

Analysis sections need to be highly focused. Beware of a tendency to report every finding, to move from one point to the next without a clear sense of which findings are more important and more central to the purpose of your study. Don't let the analysis get out of hand: you must keep it in control by addressing *only* what is relevant to your research concern. Many of your findings, let's say from a survey, should not be reported. I am not urging you to throw out findings that seem insignificant but instead to be strict with yourself in deciding what is really important for your presentation and what is not.

If you are writing a course research paper testing a hypothesis and your evidence does not support it, report that. Negative findings can be as interesting as positive ones. It is difficult, however, to write a paper on a nonexistent finding. It can be done. But it is also fair, and widely practiced, to reexamine your data for other, potentially more interesting analyses.

VI. Discussion

Once you have presented your findings, you need to discuss them in more general terms, relating them back to what your expectations were when you designed the study. In other words, the discussion should relate the empirical findings back to the theory. This covers step 11 in the research project: *presenting the results*. Thus, if a hypothesis is not proved, is the time to speculate on why this might be the case. Did the study address (or even challenge) a paradigm in the social sciences? Here you may relate your major findings to those of others mentioned in the review of literature section. Did you corroborate their findings? Did your analyses offer different dimensions that now need to be considered in the discussion of this research topic? Make clear what is important, even memorable, about this study. Is there any method or finding of your research that might be profitably used by other researchers?

VII. Conclusions and Summary

What did this research project prove? Was the program evaluated effectively? What brought about change in the dependent variable? What was the central meaning of the environment studied in the field? What was the significance of the content analyzed? These are the questions you must ask yourself and answer for your reader in the conclusion of your paper. What in your study might be considered worthwhile and contributing to the field? Did your study address the changing nature of society? Did it have a dynamic quality in which institutions or individuals undergoing changes were examined? Were there implications in the findings of your study for current social policies or laws? Did your research lead to a deeper understanding of a social group, a condition, or an event? Such question, if appropriate, might be addressed in your conclusions. In addition, suggestions for future research might be offered.

A brief summary of the study may come at the end of the paper, or in some cases, as in journal articles, it may be abbreviated as an abstract at the beginning. The summary will touch on all seven sections: stating the general problem, possibly referring to an important earlier finding, describing the research design, data collection and sampling procedures, analyzing the data, giving the central findings, and making a brief conclusion.

JUST BEFORE YOU FINISH A RESEARCH PROJECT

When you are nearly at the end of writing your research project, stop and consider some of the important issues that were discussed earlier in this book. Did the study support the rationale for doing the study in the first place? Did the study make use of some experience of yours, some particular knowledge, so that you were able to capitalize on your strengths in the course of the research project? Often the quality of a research effort will represent a project which highlighted the strengths of its researcher. It often is the case, however, that a project may get bogged down in the areas of your weakness. It is in such situations that the research project itself becomes a teacher. You find that you learn what you need to learn for the project.

In such a sense, doing research is a form of education, growing, trying to use your strengths, and improving your abilities. You've done a "scientific" study based on explanatory models and with empirical evidence. You were forced to be creative in this study because you had to figure out how to measure, question, organize, and develop a new way of doing something. At the end of a course in research methods students often say, "Whew! I never thought I'd make it." when you've finished your project, ask yourself what you've gained in the course of carrying out a research project. You may conclude that what you have learned is among the most valuable sets of skills and knowledge you've been exposed to. Having thought about what you as a student or a young researcher may have learned from doing a research project, ask yourself what you have contributed by doing your social research. Maybe you have in some small (or not so small) way added to what we know about how our society works. Thanks for doing social research.

REVIEW NOTES

- The basic ingredients in writing a research report are a clear topic, a review of the relevant evidence, a research design, and the analyzed data.
- The degree of detail in discussing the methods used vary with the form of dissemination of the research project being prepared.
- Types of research papers that might be prepared include those written (1) to fulfill course re-

quirements, (2) to be presented to professional or academic audiences, (3) to publish in professional and academic journals, (4) for popular journals, magazines, newspapers, television, or other mass-media forms, (5) in the form of a book, or (6) as a commissioned research report.

- Caplovitz proposed that all quantitative research projects have one of three foci: a dependent variable, an independent variable, or a special group. In a dependent variable study, the aim is to understand why, how, and under what conditions the dependent variable occurred. In an independent variable study, one social context is compared to another. In a special population study, usually based on qualitative data, the primary aim is to develop a careful description of the special population.

- A seven-point outline for a student research report should have the following sections:
  1. A general statement of the problem
  2. Background to the problem based on a review of the related literature
  3. The research model and design of the study
  4. How the data were obtained, including the data collection procedure, the method and success of the sampling procedure, a consideration of ethical issues, and the results of the data collection
  5. An analysis of the data
  6. A discussion of the findings
  7. The conclusion and summary

KEY TERMS

dependent variable study
independent variable study
proposal
special population study

STUDY EXERCISE

1. If your assignment for this term has been to prepare a proposal for a project or to complete a project, briefly show what you would include under each of the seven points of the research outline.

RECOMMENDED READINGS

1. Becker, Howard S.: *Writing for Social Scientists: How to Start and Finish Your Thesis, Book, or Article,* University of Chicago Press, Chicago, 1986. An engaging book on writing for academic purposes. Becker relates many of his own experiences as a researcher, writer, and editor. The book offers fertile suggestions to facilitate writing and avoid the hangups (what to do if you can't say it just right, how to edit by ear). There is a good chapter by Pamela Richards on the need to take risks.

2. Fink, Arlene: *How to Report on Surveys,* Sage, Thousand Oaks, Calif., 1995. This work provides helpful information on how to prepare written and oral survey reports, including suggestions for overhead transparencies.

3. Richardson, Laurel: *Writing Strategies: Reaching Diverse Audiences,* Sage, Newbury Park, Calif., 1990. Covers science writing, literary devices, narrative, establishing authority, and discovering a collective story.

4. Strunk, William, Jr., and E. B. White: *The Elements of Style,* Macmillan New York, 1959. This is a classic work on writing that has been very influential among both academic and nonacademic writers.

5. Sociology Writing Group: *A Guide to Writing Sociology Papers,* 2nd ed., St Martin's Press, New York, 1991. This helpful volume was written by a group of teaching assistants, counselors, and writing tutors in the sociology and English departments at the University of California, Los Angeles. It is a practical guide to preparing a paper based on a textual analysis or on library, field, or quantitative research.

6. Van Wagenen, R. Keith: *Writing a Thesis: Substance and Style,* Prentice-Hall, Englewood Cliffs, N.J., 1991. How to write up research, particularly in the social and behavioral sciences, is the subject of this volume. Writing a research introduction, results from various types of statistical analyses, discussion sections, and suggestions for improving writing styles are addressed.

7. Wolcott, Harry F.: *Writing Up Qualitative Research,* Sage, Newbury Park, Calif., 1990. This readily accessible guide to writing up field studies has many thoughtful suggestions for students.

Using a Library for Social Research*

INTRODUCTION

*I*n Chapter 3 there is a discussion of how to use the library to enhance your knowledge about a research topic. To do this effectively, you must know the range of resources that are available to you and the best methods of accessing and utilizing those resources.

To begin, there are a number of very good overall guidebooks on how to use the library to help you carry out social research, including Pauline Bart and Linda Frankel: *The Student Sociologist's Handbook* (Random House, 1986) and Stephen H. Aby: *Sociology: A Guide to Reference and Information Sources* (Libraries Unlimited, 1987) as well as Nancy Herron: *The Social Sciences: A Cross-Disciplinary Guide to Selected Sources,* 2d ed. (Libraries Unlimited, Inc., 1996). These are useful guides covering a range of reference sources in social science disciplines as well as in the subject-oriented sociological fields. In a related area, Jeffrey G. Reed and Pam M. Baxter: *Library Use: A Handbook for Psychology* (American Psychological Association, 1992) and Frederick T. Leong and James T. Austin, eds.: *The Psychology Research Handbook: A Guide for Graduate Students and Research Assistants* (Sage Publications, 1996) cover similar resources with examples from the field of psychology. This appendix will cover some of the most important resources in the field and describe how to find and use them.

---

*Prepared by Jacqueline M. Borin, Reference and Electronic Resources Librarian, California State University San Marcos.

USING THE ONLINE CATALOG

The online (computer) catalog in a university or college library contains a listing of all the titles the library holds indexed by author, title, subject, and in many cases keywords (or words in the title). To find the correct subject heading for your topic, consult the Library of Congress Subject Headings (Library of Congress, Washington, D.C., 1992) located in the reference section of your library. If, for example, you were looking up the sexual behavior study from Chapter 1 in your college library, you probably would find it under subjects such as "Sexual Behavior Surveys" and "Sex—America." Similarly, if you looked under the subject heading "Juvenile Delinquency," you would have found Hirschi's *The Causes of Delinquency* (1969).

The field studies described in Chapter 1 were all the basis for books. If you do not know the author of a specific study in your area of interest, searching subject headings can be especially helpful. For example, Hochschild's book *The Second Shift* (1989) can be found under both "Dual-Career Families" and "Sex Role." Under what topics would you find Anderson's study of urban neighborhoods? Some possibilities are "Inner Cities—Pennsylvania—Philadelphia" and "Neighborhood—Pennsylvania—Philadelphia." These books also are cataloged under the author's name, but searching by subject will uncover other studies in the area you are interested in. Looking at current studies often can give you references to older classic studies.

Your library also may have access via computer to other libraries' online catalogs. Books that you have a citation for but cannot find in your library generally may be requested through an interlibrary loan.

FINDING RELEVANT PRINTED MATERIAL

Book Reviews

One way to find books related to your topic of interest is to read book reviews. Many journals in-

clude reviews of books within that journal's field. *Contemporary Sociology: A Journal of Reviews* is a sociological journal devoted solely to book reviews. Issues generally include more than a dozen review essays, around 100 shorter reviews divided into subject categories, and an extensive listing of recent publications. Here, for example, Arlie Hochschild's book was reviewed in a symposium at the front of the journal while Barrie Thorne's book was reviewed under the subject heading "Life Course: Stages and Institutions." Other sociological journals, such as the *American Journal of Sociology,* regularly include some book reviews. Book reviews in sociological journals can be located easily if your library has access to Sociofile (CD-Rom) by using the book title and the journal title as you search, for example, "Contemporary Sociology and Gender Play".

If your topic relates to psychology, check for book reviews in *Contemporary Psychology* (also accessible through PsychLit CD-Rom). For social work topics, book reviews can be found in *Social Work, Social Case Work,* and *Social Service Review.*

To find book reviews on topics of current popular interest, look for the *New York Review of Books* and the *New York Times Book Review,* a section of the Sunday *New York Times.* These national book reviews include social research books that have wide public interest as well as their usual fiction reviews. You also may be able to search these on CD-ROM or through a service such as Lexis/Nexis. Finally, both *Book Review Digest* and *Book Review Index* will tell you where to locate reviews of books from many different fields. *Book Review Digest* includes brief abstracts of the reviews.

Dissertations

As doctoral dissertations result from original research, they can be an important resource in the field of sociology. The advantage of looking at a dissertation which has been based on social research is that the method—how the study was done—is usually delineated in a lot of detail.

Dissertations may even refer to the problems encountered in trying to accomplish the aims of the study (rarely reported on in an article). Copies of most doctoral dissertations written in the United States are sent to *University Microfilms International* (UMI). UMI then microfilms the dissertation and lists it in *Dissertation Abstracts International* (DAI). UMI also sells copies of the dissertation.

DAI is published in three parts: Part A, The Humanities and Social Sciences; Part B, The Sciences and Engineering; and Part C, WorldWide. Parts A and B include references to about 35,000 dissertations produced each year at American, Canadian, and British universities. Part C includes dissertations from other countries. Dissertations are indexed under broad disciplines, and within that by subfields, so you want to check the keyword index to locate dissertations in your subject area. In larger academic libraries you will be able to search DAI online through a keyword search.

Copies of dissertations may be purchased from UMI, although this can be expensive. Some dissertations may be available through interlibrary loan, so check at your library. Some dissertations become published books and so you might want to check in the reference book *Books in Print* under the author's name to see if the author has published a book on the dissertation material. (Remember, the exact title of the dissertation may not be used for the title of the book; book titles tend to be shorter than dissertation titles!)

Bibliographies

There are bibliographies at many levels: The broadest are bibliographies of bibliographies, next are bibliographies of broad disciplines, and last and most narrowly focused are bibliographies of specific fields or subjects. Some bibliographies are annotated; that is, they offer a short abstract or description of each book. Others just give basic bibliographical information: author, title, publisher, publication place, and date. Check with a reference librarian about where to locate bibliographies in your specific field of interest.

Examples of General Bibliographies

Advanced Research Methodology: An Annotated Guide to Sources (R. Barker Bausell, Scarecrow, 1991)

London Bibliography of the Social Sciences (Mansell Information, 1931–)

NORC (National Opinion Research Center) Bibliography of Publications 1941–1991 (compiled by Patrick Bova and Michael Preston, NORC, 1991)

Public Opinion Polls and Survey Research: A Selective Annotated Bibliography of U.S. Guides and Studies from the 1980's (Graham R. Walden, Garland, 1990)

Women in Sociology: A Bio-Bibliographical Sourcebook (ed. by Mary Jo Deegan, Greenwood Press, 1991)

A World Bibliography of Bibliographies, 4th ed. (Theodore Besterman, Lausanne Societas Bibliographica, 1965). Supplement 1964–74 (Alice Toomey, 1977)

Dictionaries

Dictionaries are useful for defining terms and clarifying concepts.

Examples of Dictionaries

Blackwell Dictionary of Twentieth-Century Social Thought (Blackwell, 1993)

Blackwell Dictionary of Sociology: A User's Guide to Sociological Language (Allan G. Johnson, Blackwell, 1995)

Collins Dictionary of Sociology, 2d ed. (David Jary and Julia Jary, HarperCollins, 1995)

The Concise Oxford Dictionary of Sociology (ed. by Gordon Marshall, Oxford University Press, 1994)

A Critical Dictionary of Sociology (Raymond Boudon and Frances Bourricaud, University of Chicago Press, 1989)

Definitions in Sociology: Convergence, Conflict and Alternative Vocabularies (ed. by Vladislav A. Tomovic, Diliton Publications, 1979)

Dictionary of Personality and Social Psychology (MIT Press, 1986)

Dictionary of Polling: The Language of Contemporary Opinion Research (Michael L. Young, Greenwood Press, 1992)

Dictionary of Quotations in Sociology (Panos D. Bardis, Greenwood Press, 1985)

Dictionary of Statistical Terms, 5th ed. (International Statistical Institute, Wiley, 1990)

Dictionary of Statistics and Methodology: A Non-Technical Guide for the Social Sciences (W. Paul Vogt, Sage Publications, 1993)

Encyclopedias and Handbooks

Encyclopedias define a field's key concepts and provide information on the major leaders in that field. Handbooks and annual reviews contain edited collections of articles that provide an authoritative summary of a specific topic, including evaluations of theory and research. The essays address the most important subjects, methods, and problems which are currently being studied. When doing research, you want to consider both older studies in the field and current studies and annual reviews to bring you up to date on current concerns.

Examples of General Encyclopedias (look in your library catalog for subject specific encyclopedias, such as women's studies and criminology):

Encyclopedia of Sociology (ed. by E. F. Borgatta, Macmillan, 1992).

Encyclopedia of the Social Sciences (ed. by Edwin R. A. Seligman, Macmillan, 1930)

International Encyclopedia of the Social Sciences (David L. Sills, Macmillan, 1968).

International Encyclopedia of Sociology (ed. by Michael Mann, Continuum, 1984)

Social Science Encyclopedia, 2d ed. (ed. by Adam Kuper and Jessica Kuper, Routledge, 1996)

Examples of Handbooks

Analyzing Gender: A Handbook of Social Science Research (Beth B. Hess and Myra Marx Ferree, Sage Publications, 1987).

Approaches to Social Research, 2d ed. (Royce A. Singleton, Oxford University Press, 1993)

Child Abuse and Neglect: An Information and Reference Guide (Timothy J. Iverson and Marilyn Segal, Garland, 1990).

A Guide to Writing Sociology Papers, 4th ed. (Sociology Writing Group, UCLA, St. Martin's Press, 1998)

Handbook of Aging and the Social Sciences 7th ed. (Robert H. Binstock and Linda K. George, Academic Press, 1996).

Handbook of Clinical Sociology (ed. by Howard M. Rebach and John G. Bruhn, Plenum Press, 1991)

Handbook of Research Design and Social Measurement, 5th ed. (Delbert C. Miller, Sage, 1991)

Handbook of Social Psychology, 3rd ed. (ed. by Gardner Lindzey and Elliot Aronson, L. Erlbaum Associates, 1985).

Handbook of Sociology (ed. by Neil Smelser, Sage Publications, 1988)

International Handbook of Contemporary Developments in Sociology (ed. by Raj P. Mahan and Arthur S. Wilke, Greenwood Press, 1994)

Publishing Options: An Author's Guide to Journals, 3d ed. (American Sociological Association, 1992)

The Student Sociologist's Handbook, 3d ed. (Pauline Bart and Linda Frankel, Random House, 1986)

Guides to the Literature

Examples:

Social Science Reference Sources: A Practical Guide, 2d ed. (Tze-chung Li, Greenwood Press, 1990)

Social Sciences: A Cross-Disciplinary Guide to Selected Sources, 2d ed. (Nancy Herron, Libraries Unlimited, 1996)

Author's Guide to Journals in the Behavioral Sciences (Alvin Y. Wang, L. Erlbaum Associates, 1989)

Sources of Information in the Social Sciences, 3d ed. (William H. Webb, American Library Association, 1986)

Social Sciences: An International Bibliography of Serial Literature, 1830–1985 (Jan Wepsiec, Mansell, 1992)

Sociology: An International Bibliography of Serial Publications, 1880–1980 (Jan Wepsiec, Mansell, 1983)

World List of Social Science Periodicals, 8th ed. (UNESCO, 1991)

Statistics

Examples:

Compendium of Social Statistics and Indicators, 4th ed. (United Nations, 1988)

County and City Data Book (U.S. Bureau of the Census, 1949–)

Demographic Yearbook (United Nations, 1948–)

Hispanic Americans: A Statistical Sourcebook (ed. by Louise Hornor, Information Publications, 1995)

Historical Statistics of the United States: Colonial Times to 1970 (U.S. Bureau of the Census, 2 vols, Krause International, 1989)

Major U.S. Statistical Series: Definitions, Publications, Limitations (ed. by Jean Slemmons Stratford and Juri Stratford, ALA, 1992)

Social Indicators of Development (World Bank, Johns Hopkins University Press, 1994)

Statistical Handbook on Women in America, 2d ed. (ed. by Cynthia Taeuber, Oryx Press, 1996)

Statistical Record of Women Worldwide, 2d ed. (ed. by Linda Schmittroth, Gale Research, 1995)

USING INDEXES AND ABSTRACTS TO LOCATE JOURNAL ARTICLES

Most published sociological research appears in the form of journal articles. The best way to find articles relating to a topic that interests you is to look in one of the indexes listed below.

Indexes and Abstracts in the Social Sciences

Begin with the *Social Sciences Index* (New York, Wilson, 1974–), which was formerly called the *Social Sciences and Humanities Index* and before that the *International Index of Social Sciences and Humanities.* This index lists articles from social science journals under subject and author headings and is available in both print and CD-ROM.

Sociological Abstracts, or "Soc Abstracts," as it is often called, is a primary index for sociology and related disciplines. After locating an article in *Social Sciences Index,* you can turn to *Sociological Abstracts* to get a brief abstract of the article. You can also use it as a primary source for locating articles, as it includes articles from 1,200 scholarly journals. From 1986 on *Sociological Abstracts* has indexed articles according to the *Thesaurus of Sociological Indexing Terms,* which provides you with an alphabetical list of subject headings. The *Thesaurus* also uses historical notes to help you locate articles published before 1986. *Sociological Abstracts* is also available online and is available in CD-ROM as *Sociofile.*

If your topic is in the area of social psychology, you should look in *Psychological Abstracts.* It is indexed according to the subject headings in the *Thesaurus of Psychological Indexing Terms.* The online version of *Psychological Abstracts* is called PsychInfo, and the CD-ROM version is called **PsychLit.** For education topics check **ERIC** (Educational Resources Information Center), which is divided into two resources: (1) CIJE (*Current Index to Journals in Education*) and (2) RIE (*Resources in Education*). CIJE provides subject and author access to articles from approximately 800 journals in education and related disciplines. RIE is an index to published and unpublished curriculum guides, research reports, conference proceedings, and other types of documents collected by ERIC. Many libraries also carry the microfiche that RIE indexes, usually filed by the ERIC document number found in the index. Both RIE and CIJE contain brief abstracts of the cited articles and use the *Thesaurus of ERIC Descriptors* as a source of subject headings. Along with the print version, ERIC is available online, in CD-ROM, and over the Internet.

If you are looking for earlier material, examine *The Combined Retrospective Index Set to Journals in Sociology, 1895–1974* (CRIS), a six-volume set which indexes about 400,000 articles in 531 journals, primarily from the United States and the United Kingdom. It indexes many earlier journals not covered by other indexing services and includes English-language journals covering all periods and areas of sociology.

If your topic is in criminology, examine *Crime and Delinquency Abstracts;* if it has to do with studies on children, look at *Child Development Abstracts and Bibliography;* and if it concerns an area of social work, there is *Social Work Research and Abstracts,* which indexes almost all social work journals and offers short abstracts of articles.

If you are unable to locate an article you are seeking in the *Social Sciences Index* or *Sociological Abstracts,* try the *Public Affairs Information Service* (PAIS), which indexes (in addition to journal articles) government publications, pamphlets, and reports of agencies, or try *Human Resources Abstracts,* which includes many abstracts of unpublished reports on social action programs and governmental and community programs and printed materials. Other topical abstracts which might be of help include *Sage Family Studies Abstracts, Sage Race Relations Abstracts,* and *Sage Urban Studies Abstracts* as well as *Women's Studies Abstracts.*

Using a Citation Index

Once you have found an article that interests you, another way to expand your search and locate other relevant articles is to use a citation index. The citation index for the social sciences is *Social Sciences Citation Index* (SSCI), which your library may carry in either a paper or an electronic format. Citation indexes are based on the idea that published research in an area includes references to previously published papers which provide the basis for the new work. Therefore, if you can locate an important early article in the field, you should be able to identify later articles that cite that source. The SSCI provides complete coverage of approximately 1,400 journals, with selective coverage of a further 3,300 journals in the social sciences. It contains four main divisions: the Citation Index, the Source Index, the Corporate Index, and the Permuterm Subject Index.

To use the SSCI, first take an article of central interest to you and turn to the author of the article in the Citation Index to see where the author has been cited. The citations will be listed first by the journal containing the original article and then by the author of the article that cited yours. When you find the name of an author who cited your first author in a journal that may be relevant to your interests, turn to the Source Index to find the exact citation of that article (in this location, the affiliation of the author will be listed as well). Alternatively, if you do not have a specific article of interest to work from but do have a specific subject of interest, you can start at the Permuterm Subject Index, which indexes significant words (keywords) from articles. Under the subject of interest, there will be various subcategories of subjects, each with one or more authors cited. From these authors, turn back to the Source Index for a complete citation. SSCI takes some practice to use but offers a number of ways to locate articles in your area of interest.

If your library carries the CD-ROM version, your search will be easier. For example, in searching the 1996 SSCI CD-ROM, you could find at least 95 references that cite Arlie Hochchild's *The Second Shift,* including articles on "Supermoms of the Nineties" and " Mothers' Work Hours and Marital Quality." In doing the same search on Barrie Thorne's *Gender Play,* you could locate related references to "Shortchanging Boys and Girls" and "Gender Interaction and Delinquency." If your library does not carry SSCI, ask a reference librarian if he or she can direct you to a library that does.

Computer Searches

So far we have mentioned a number of tools that you can use to identify literature within your field. If you have a topic that combines several different concepts, this type of search can be time-consuming. If your search is complex, constructing it on a computer in a CD-ROM or online database will make your task much easier.

Because there are many CD-ROM and online databases available, there are also many different search techniques. Most libraries that have these

available will also have handouts or brochures on how to search the database, or you may ask a reference librarian. In beginning your search, you first need to choose a database relevant to your subject and then structure your search strategy so that you will obtain the most relevant citations and abstracts.

Databases

Below is a selected list of databases, some of which may be available in your library. Databases may be available on CD-ROM, online on services such as Dialog and BRS after Dark, or on the Internet. Some are available in all formats. If your library does not carry the CD-ROM or online version, check to see whether it carries a print version. Some libraries may have other online services available, for example, Lexis/Nexis (good for current events and newspaper articles) and CARL UnCover (a general index to about 18,000 journals across all disciplines). Check with a reference librarian to find out exactly what CD-ROM and online databases your library offers.

Once you have selected an appropriate database, take the following steps:

Database	Date	Notes
America: History and Life	1982+	History/culture, United States and Canada
Chicano Database	1967+	The Mexican-American experience
Child Abuse and Neglect	1965+	Mistreatment of children
Current Contents Search	1994+	Table of contents of research journals
Dissertation Abstracts	1861+	Over 1 million dissertation citations
Family Studies	1970+	Family science and human ecology
Historical Abstracts	1982+	Covers history from 1450 to the present
PAIS International	1972+	Public policy aspects of social science
PsychLit	1974+	International psychology journal articles
Social Work Abstracts Plus	1977+	Abstracts and citations of social work journals
Social Research Methods Database	1970+	Social science research methods
Social Science Abstracts Full Text	1984+	Includes full text of over 100 journals
Social Science Citation Index	1986+	Access to over 1700 social science journals
Social Sciences Index	1983+	Covers over 400 English-language journals
Sociofile	1974+	Worldwide abstracting of over 2,300 journals
Women's Studies on Disc	1989+	Broad range of issues in women's studies

1. State your topic concisely, e.g., "Arrest of Domestic Assault Suspects"
2. Write the major concepts in your topic, e.g., "Domestic Assault, Arrests"
3. Look up the major concepts in the thesaurus for your database; for example, the thesaurus for Sociofile is the *Thesaurus of Sociological Indexing Terms.*
4. Write down the terms from the thesaurus that define your topic. Using the above thesaurus, they would be "Family—Violence," "Spouse—Abuse," and "Assault and Arrests."
5. Write out your search statement using the connectors "and" and "or" between each subject, e.g., "Family—Violence" or Spouse—Abuse" and "Arrests."

Refining Your Search

If you do not retrieve enough articles, you may expand your search by eliminating one of your terms (e.g., eliminate "Family—Violence" from the above search). If you retrieve too many, you may narrow your search by adding another subject (e.g., "assault"), restricting yourself to a particular geographic area, or limiting yourself to articles published only during a certain time period (e.g., articles published after 1990).

Getting the Article

Once you have located a citation to a journal article you need, you will first need to see whether your library carries that journal. Either check your library's online catalog or ask a reference librarian if the library has a bound list of journals for you to look at. If your library does not carry the journal you need, you usually can order it through an interlibrary loan and it will be obtained from another library for you.

SEARCHING THE INTERNET

Most libraries now have Internet access available on many of the workstations in their reference areas, and many people can access the Internet directly from home to conduct searches for information. The World Wide Web offers a lot of resources, but not all are equally valuable or reliable. When looking for information on the Web, you should keep the following criteria in mind:

- Who authored the page or site? Is it original work? Is there contact information for the individual or group? Does the person list his or her qualifications? Check for links to a local home page or institution.
- What is the authority or expertise of the individual or group that created the site? Is any sort of bias evident? Is there a stated criterion for the inclusion of information.
- When was the page or site mounted? When was it last revised? How stable is the information?
- How comprehensive is the site? How are the links selected, and are they relevant or appropriate? How up-to-date and reliable are the links?

In addition, you can use review tools such as

- Excite Reviews
- Lycos Top 5%
- Magellan Internet Guide
- Webcrawler Best of the Net

While each of these uses specific criteria for its evaluations, the implementation of the evaluations may be subjective or biased.

SOCIAL SCIENCE INTERNET RESOURCES

Internet sites often change so if you do not find a particular site at the address listed on the next page, do a search for the site by using a search engine such as InfoSeek, Excite, or Yahoo. These sites are only a few of the many available. The sociology links sites following will lead you to many additional sites.

General Sites

Dead Sociologists Index http://diogenes. baylor.edu/WWWproviders/Larry Ridener/ DSS/Index.html

Internic Sociology Links http://www.internic. net/aldea/soc.html

Princeton Sociology Links http://www. princeton.edu/~sociolog/links.html

Society for Social Research (classical sociological theory, including excerpts from the classics) http://www.spc.uchicago.edu/ ssrl/PRELIMS/theory.html

Sociology (WWW Virtual Library) http:// www.w3.org/pub/DataSources/bySubject/ Sociology/Overview.html

Sociology Timeline from 1600 http:// www.wwu.edu/~Stephan/Schedule/302/ timeline.html

Western Connecticut State University: Sociology Internet Resources http://www.wcsu. ctstateu.edu/socialsci/socres.html

Social Science Information Gateway http:// sosig.esrc.bris.ac.uk/

SBER Sociology Program (National Science Foundation's Sociology program; supports research on problems of human social organization, demography, and processes of individual and institutional change; includes grant information and submission forms) http://www. nsf.gov/sbe/sber/sociol/start.htm

Associations, Institutes, and Centers

American Sociological Association http:// www.asanet.org/

ASA Style Guide http://www.asanet.org/ style.htm

ASA Code of Ethics http://www.asanet. org.asaethic.htm

Center for the Study of Group Processes http://www.uiowa.edu/~grpproc/

Institute for Social Research (ISR) (the nation's longest-standing laboratory for interdisciplinary research in the social sciences) http://www.isr.umich.edu/

ICPSR (located within the ISR, the Inter-University Consortium for Political and Social Research provides access to the world's largest archive of computerized social science data) http://www.icpsr.umich.edu

General Social Survey (GSS) http://www. icpsr.umich.edu/gss/

International Sociological Association http:// www.ucm.es/OTROS/isa/

Journals

American Journal of Sociology (includes tables of contents) http://www.journals. uchicago.edu/AJS

American Sociological Review http://www. pop.psu.edu/ASR/asr.htm

Annual Review of Sociology (includes abstracts of articles from the past 12 years) http:// www.annurev.org/soc/home.htm

Canadian Journal of Sociology (provides samples from the journal) http://gpu.srv. ualberta.ca/~cjscopy/cjs.html

Current Research in Social Psychology (a peer-reviewed electronic journal covering all aspects of social psychology) http://www. uiowa.edu/~grpproc/crisp/crisp.html

Public Culture (an interdisciplinary journal of cultural studies published three times per year by Duke University Press) http://www2. uchicago.edu/jnl-pub-cult/

Sociological Methodology (annual volume on methods of research in the social sciences) http://weber.u.washington.edu/~socmeth2/

Teaching Sociology (a quarterly publication of the American Sociological Association) http://www.lemoyne.edu/ts/tsmain.html

Abstracts

Child Development Abstracts and Bibliography http://www.journals.uchicago.edu/ CDAB/journal/

Sociological Abstracts http://www.socabs.org/

APPENDIX B

TABLE OF RANDOM NUMBERS

10 09 73 25 33	76 52 01 35 86	34 67 35 48 76	80 95 90 91 17	39 29 27 49 45
37 54 20 48 05	64 89 47 42 96	24 80 52 40 37	20 63 61 04 02	00 82 29 16 65
08 42 26 89 53	19 64 50 93 03	23 20 90 25 60	15 95 33 47 64	35 08 03 36 06
99 01 90 25 29	09 37 67 07 15	38 31 13 11 65	88 67 67 43 97	04 43 62 76 59
12 80 79 99 70	80 15 73 61 47	64 03 23 66 53	98 95 11 68 77	12 17 17 68 33
66 06 57 47 17	34 07 27 68 50	36 69 73 61 70	65 81 33 98 85	11 19 92 91 70
31 06 01 08 05	45 57 18 24 06	35 30 34 26 14	86 79 90 74 39	23 40 30 97 32
85 26 97 76 02	02 05 16 56 92	68 66 57 48 18	73 05 38 52 47	18 62 38 85 79
63 57 33 21 35	05 32 54 70 48	90 55 35 75 48	28 46 82 87 09	83 49 12 56 24
73 79 64 57 53	03 52 96 47 78	35 80 83 42 82	60 93 52 03 44	35 27 38 84 35
98 52 01 77 67	14 90 56 86 07	22 10 94 05 58	60 97 09 34 33	50 50 07 39 98
11 80 50 54 31	39 80 82 77 32	50 72 56 82 48	29 40 52 42 01	52 77 56 78 51
83 45 29 96 34	06 28 89 80 83	13 74 67 00 78	18 47 54 06 10	68 71 17 78 17
88 68 54 02 00	86 50 75 84 01	36 76 66 79 51	90 36 47 64 93	29 60 91 10 62
99 59 46 73 48	87 51 76 49 69	91 82 60 89 28	93 78 56 13 68	23 47 83 41 13
65 48 11 76 74	17 46 85 09 50	58 04 77 69 74	73 03 95 71 86	40 21 81 65 44
80 12 43 56 35	17 72 70 80 15	45 31 82 23 74	21 11 57 82 53	14 38 55 37 63
74 35 09 98 17	77 40 27 72 14	43 23 60 02 10	45 52 16 42 37	96 28 60 26 55
69 91 62 68 03	66 25 22 91 48	36 93 68 72 03	76 62 11 39 90	94 40 05 64 18
09 89 32 05 05	14 22 56 85 14	46 42 75 67 88	96 29 77 88 22	54 38 21 45 98
91 49 91 45 23	68 47 92 76 86	46 16 28 35 54	94 75 08 99 23	37 08 92 00 48
80 33 69 45 98	26 94 03 68 58	70 29 73 41 35	53 14 03 33 40	42 05 08 23 41
44 10 48 19 49	85 15 74 79 54	32 97 92 65 75	57 60 04 08 81	22 22 20 64 13
12 55 07 37 42	11 10 00 20 40	12 86 07 46 97	96 64 48 94 39	28 70 72 58 15
63 60 64 93 29	16 50 53 44 84	40 21 95 25 63	43 65 17 70 82	07 20 73 17 90
61 19 69 04 46	26 45 74 77 74	51 92 43 37 29	65 39 45 95 93	42 58 26 05 27
15 47 44 52 66	95 27 07 99 53	59 36 78 38 48	82 39 61 01 18	33 21 15 94 66
94 55 72 85 73	67 89 75 43 87	54 62 24 44 31	91 19 04 25 92	92 92 74 59 73
42 48 11 62 13	97 34 40 87 21	16 86 84 87 67	03 07 11 20 59	25 70 14 66 70
23 52 37 83 17	73 20 88 98 37	68 93 59 14 16	26 25 22 96 63	05 52 28 25 62
04 49 35 24 94	75 24 63 38 24	45 86 25 10 25	61 96 27 93 35	65 33 71 24 72
00 54 99 76 54	64 05 18 81 59	96 11 96 38 96	54 69 28 23 91	23 28 72 95 29
35 96 31 53 07	26 89 80 93 54	33 35 13 54 62	77 97 45 00 24	90 10 33 93 33
59 80 80 83 91	45 42 72 68 42	83 60 94 97 00	13 02 12 48 92	78 56 52 01 06
46 05 88 52 36	01 39 09 22 86	77 28 14 40 77	93 91 08 36 47	70 61 74 29 41
32 17 90 05 97	87 37 92 52 41	05 56 70 70 07	86 74 31 71 57	85 39 41 18 38
69 23 46 14 06	20 11 74 52 04	15 95 66 00 00	18 74 39 24 23	97 11 89 63 38
19 56 54 14 30	01 75 87 53 79	40 41 92 15 85	66 67 43 68 06	84 96 28 52 07
45 15 51 49 38	19 47 60 72 46	43 66 79 45 43	59 04 79 00 33	20 82 66 95 41
94 86 43 19 94	36 16 81 08 51	34 88 88 15 53	01 54 03 54 56	05 01 45 11 76

Source: The Rand Corporation, *A Million Random Digits*, Free Press, Glencoe, IL, 1955, pp. 1–3, with the kind permission of the publisher.

CHI-SQUARE DISTRIBUTION

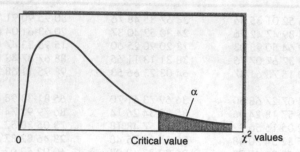

Degrees of Freedom (*df*)	Area in Shaded Right Tail (α)		
	.10	.05	.01
1	2.706	3.841	6.635
2	4.605	5.991	9.210
3	6.251	7.815	11.345
4	7.779	9.488	13.227
5	9.236	11.070	15.086
6	10.645	12.592	16.812
7	12.017	14.067	18.475
8	13.362	15.507	20.090
9	14.684	16.919	21.666
10	15.987	18.307	23.209
11	17.275	19.675	24.725
12	18.549	21.026	26.217
13	19.812	22.362	27.688
14	21.064	23.685	29.141
15	22.307	24.996	30.578
16	23.542	26.296	32.000
17	24.769	27.587	33.409
18	25.989	28.869	34.805
19	27.204	30.144	36.191
20	28.412	31.410	37.566
21	29.615	32.671	38.932
22	30.813	33.924	40.289
23	32.007	35.172	41.638
24	33.196	36.415	42.980
25	34.382	37.652	44.314
26	35.563	38.885	45.642
27	36.741	40.113	46.963
28	37.916	41.337	48.278
29	39.087	42.557	49.588
30	40.256	43.773	50.892

Example of how to use this table: In a chi-square distribution with 6 degrees of freedom (*df*), the area to the right of a critical value of 12.592—i.e., the α area—is .05.

Source: This table is abridged from Table IV of Sir Ronald A. Fisher and Frank Yates, *Statistical Tables for Biological, Agricultural and Medical Research*, 6th ed., Longman Group, Ltd., London (previously published by Oliver & Boyd, Ltd., Edinburgh), 1974. Reproduced with the permission of the authors and publishers.

Generating the Computer Tables in this Text Using SPSS for Windows 7.5

INTRODUCTION

This is not a comprehensive introduction to the use of the statistical social science software program SPSS for Windows 7.5. Rather this appendix will confine itself to describing what the computer steps would be and how the computer screens would look if you were preparing the quantitative analyses that have been presented in this text. SPSS is a software package that is vastly more comprehensive than the material to be covered here. If you plan to use this program, you will want to carefully examine the range of subprograms it comprises and the guides to using the program.

What is SPSS? SPSS, the Statistical Package for the Social Sciences, is one of the oldest software programs (developed and made available in the 1960s) that has been redeveloped and revised over three decades. It includes the range of data manipulation and statistical analysis procedures that are in use today. SPSS for Windows, version 7.5, is a currently available version of this program that can be used on personal computers. The tables it produces are set up in a way that is quite

different from the 6.1 version and earlier versions which preceded it. What this appendix offers is a visual presentation of what you would see on your computer screen if you were to try to generate the tables that appear in Chapters 12 and 13.

Let's begin with Figure AP-1. This shows you part of the matrix of data from the Recycling Survey that was entered into the computer from the telephone interviewing survey and then converted into a SPSS data file, which can be viewed here on the data editor (see top line of the screen: RECYCLE2 - SPSS Data Editor). Note first that down the left column numbers descend that present the case number, which is the respondent's number. These numbers would continue down to 272, which represents the total number of respondents in this survey. In the next column there is the heading @resnum that indicates the respondent's computer identification number. Moving across the top row, you see the variable names, the first being *q1*, which is the variable: *Amount of Waste Recycled* that was the primary dependent variable in the analyses presented in Chapters 12

FIGURE AP-1

RECYCLE2 - SPSS Data Editor

File Edit View Data Transform Statistics Graphs Utilities Window Help

1:@respnum   10000

	@respnum	q1	q2a	q2b	q2c	q2d	q2e	q2f	q2g	q2h	q2i	q3a	q3b	q3c	q3d	q3e	q3f	qdem1	qdem2
1	10000	10	1	1	1	1	1	1	4	4	4	4	4	1	1	1	4	1	0
2	10001	0										4	4	4	4	1	3	5	0
3	10002	0										4	4	4	1	1	1	0	2
4	10003	30	4	4	4	4	1	4	1	2	1	4	1	4	1	1	3	3	0
5	20000	70	4	4	4	4	4	3	3	4	4	3	3	3	2	1	2	1	2
6	20001	30	7	2	2	2	1	4	1	1	7	4	4	2	4	2	4	0	0
7	20002	100	4	4	4	4	4	4	4	4	4	4	2	8	1	1	2	2	1
8	20003	20	4	4	4	1	2	4	4	4	7	3	3	4	1	1	2	1	0
9	20004	68	4	4	4	3	4	4	4	4	4	4	2	4	4	2	4	0	0
10	20005	40	4	4	4	2	2	3	4	4	4	4	4	3	4	1	2	1	0
11	20006	40	3	4	4	3	4	4	4	4	8	4	3	4	1	1	2	1	0
12	20007	40	4	4	4	2	1	4	4	4	4	1	4	4	4	1	4	3	0
13	20008	25	4	4	4	1	2	4	4	4	4	2	3	3	3	2	1	1	0
14	20009	50	2	4	4	2	2	1	1	4	4	4	4	4	1	1	2	2	1
15	20010	50	3	4	3	3	1	2	4	1	4	2	3	3	3	2	2	1	1
16	50000	70	4	4	4	1	4	4	4	4	4	3	4	3	4	3	2	2	0
17	50001	50	4	4	1	1	1	1	4	1	4	3	4	3	4	1	2	0	1
18	50002	108	4	1	4	4	1	1	4	4	4	4	4	4	4	3	1	0	1
19	50003	100	4	4	4	4	4	4	4	7	4	4	4	4	4	1	1	1	0

SPSS Processor is ready

and 13. Next to that column is the column of data for q2a, and so on.

We can see that this matrix is composed of the variables spread out across the rows and the cases (that is, the respondents' answers to each variable question) going down the column. So case 1 recycled 10 percent of waste, case 2 recycled no waste, as did case 3. Case 7 recycled all of their waste (100 percent). Now note case 18, did this respondent recycle 108 percent of his/her waste? No, 108 is the response code given for respondents who answered "don't know" to this question. This code, as well as 109, which means that no answer was given, would need to be "flagged" as missing data so they would not be computed with the rest of the values.

Figure AP-2a presents the computer screens for the Frequencies windows and its accompanying Statistics selection window superimposed on the Data Editor. For this figure, first look at the Data Editor and note that we will examine the variable *"age."* Note the ages going down the column from 30 to case 9 who is a person of 75 years (this is all we can see on this screen). The small window in the upper-left is the Frequencies window from which the variable "age" has been moved over to the Variable(s) window in order to compute its percentage distributions. The lower-right-hand window is the Statistics window that accompanies the Frequencies program. We have asked that the Central Tendency statistics of Mean, Median, and Mode be generated and that the measures of Dispersion: Standard Deviation and Range be estimated. Please turn back to Table 12-2, in Chapter 12, which shows the frequency distribution with the accompanying statistics that SPSS generated following these commands. Note that at the bottom of the table, the requested statistics are presented.

Now, let's examine Figure AP-2b. This shows the same Frequencies window in the upper left-hand corner, but in the lower right-hand corner is the command window that generates Charts to accompany the frequency distributions. Given that "age" is a numerical variable measured at the ratio level, it is appropriate to generate a histogram. In that window, Histogram has been darkened and we have asked to have a normal curve superimposed on it. In Chapter 12, we can see the histogram for "age" presented as Figure 12-2.

Our next effort will be to manipulate the age variable so as to trichotomize (break into three equal parts) the data into age blocks that will contain roughly the same proportions of respondents in each. One way to know where these breaks would be is to examine the cumulative percentage column, the right column, in the frequency distribution (Table 12-2). We see that at age 38, 32.5 percent of the respondents are that age or younger. So those from ages 18 to 38 are in the youngest 1/3 of this sample. Next we move down the Cumulative Percent column to 66.1, which corresponds to age 57. Hence those between 39 and 57 are in the middle third of the age distribution. Finally the oldest third would be those aged 58 to 95.

Looking now to Figure AP-3, we see the Recode into Different Variables window. By recoding the variable "age" into a new variable, "ager," we will keep the old variable and make a new one. (We could have recoded into the same variable which would have wiped out the old version of "age" and turned it into the new version). I nearly always recode into a different variable because it opens more options. So Figure AP-3 illustrates in the upper-left corner the recode window with the variable list at the left and the variable "age" has been moved from the Numeric Variable to the Out Variable window. I then had to type in "ager" into the Output Variable window under Name and gave it a Label of "Age in 3 Categories." I then clicked on Old and New Values and this brought up the window which can be seen in the lower-right window. By examining the Old to New box on the right, you can see that I have already replaced the system or user-missing value (by darkening the circle under the Old Value) into the System-missing New Value and then clicking Add. Next I darkened the Range in the Old Value and

FIGURE AP-2a

FIGURE AP-2b

entered 18 through 38, put in the Value of 1 in the New Value and entered Add, and then repeated this effort for the age group 39 to 57, turning them into category 2. What you see on this screen is the entry of the oldest group (58 through 95) whose value in the new value will be 3 before the Add box has been clicked. Once this category has been added, the new variable "ager" will have been fully prepared.

Now if you turn to Figure AP-4, you can see on the Data Editor that the computer has inserted a new column for "ager" with values going from 1.00 to 3.00. If you double click on the top of the column in the box which says "ager," you will bring up the Define Variable window (in the upper left-hand corner). Let me add here that to get rid of the decimal points and the zeroes, you would click on Type and you could request to drop these features. What the lower-right window shows is what comes up if you click on Labels. For the new variable "ager," new value labels defining the three categories would need to be added. Recall that the Variable Label for "ager" was defined in the Recode window, but the value labels were not. To do this you move the cursor to Value and put in 1 and then under Value label type in 18 to 38 (Young) and click on Add and that value is put into the box; then note that we have done this for value 2. What the window shows is how we are entering Value 3 to be "58 to 95 (Old)." Once we click the Add box, and then the Continue box, this will be completed.

Figure AP-5 presents a Crosstabs window with its accompanying statistics window. These commands will create a bivariate table in which qlr (a three-way breakdown of the variable q1 measuring the amount of waste recycled which has been trichotomized similarly to the way "ager" was developed) is the dependent variable in the row position and q3f2, the attitude that recycling makes me feel good, is the independent variable in the column position. To move the appropriate variables in the Row and Column posi-

tion the arrow buttons can be used once the relevant variable has been highlighted in the variables list to the left. To the right is the Crosstabs: Statistics window that has been brought to the screen after clicking the Statistics button at the bottom of the Crosstabs window. Note that we have checked Chi-square and Gamma as the two statistical tests that we want carried out with this table. To see the table that was produced from Figures AP-5, turn to Table 12-9.

Now, move on to Figure AP-6, which presents the same Crosstabs window on the left, but this time a third variable has been entered under Layer 1 of 1. This means that the crosstab of qlr by q3f2 will now be prepared for each categorical group of "ager." On the right is the window that comes up when the Cells button is selected. Here we check the Column Percentages as we have set up our table to require the percentages of each attitude group in relation to the amount of waste recycled. This trivariate crosstab can be seen as Table 12-13 in which the crosstab of q1r by q3f2 is presented as three sub-tables for the three different age groups (Young, Middle, Old).

Figure AP-7 presents the simple window that can be called up to run a Pearson's r, the correlation coefficient. Recall from Chapter 13 that a correlation can only be run on numerically measured variables. So here we prepare Table 13-5, which is the correlation coefficient between q1, amount of waste recycled (from 0 to 100 percent) before it was recoded, and age (18 to 95), before that variable was recoded. Note that we check the box for a Pearson, a two-tailed test of significance, and we ask that the significant correlations be flagged.

Finally Figure AP-8 shows the window instructions to carry out a Linear Regression. Here we have entered q1 as the dependent variable and age, q3f (in its original four-category form) and gender and select the "Enter" method, which means that all three independent variables will be entered together. Table 13-12 presents the results of this linear regression analysis.

FIGURE AP-3

FIGURE AP–4

RECYCLE2 SPSS Data Editor

File Edit View Data Transform Statistics Graphs Utilities Window Help

1:ager

	q3ar	q3fr	ager2	educr	kidsr	gender	edu	q3f2	ager	val
1	2	1			2	.00	16.00	3	1.00	
2	2	0			2	1.00	13.00	3	1.00	
3	1	1	2		2	1.00	12.00	1	3.00	
4	1	1	2		1	1.00	12.00	3	2.00	
5	2	1	3		2	1.00	16.00	2	1.00	
6	1	1	3		2	.00	13.00	3	3.00	
7	2	1	3		1	1.00	14.00	2	1.00	
8	2	1	2		2	.00	13.00	2	2.00	
9	2	1	3		2	1.00	14.00	3	3.00	
10	2	1	1		2	.00	18.00	2	3.00	
11									2.00	
12									2.00	
13									1.00	
14									1.00	
15									1.00	
16									2.00	
17									1.00	
18									3.00	
19									3.00	

Define Variable

Variable Name: ager

Variable Description
Type: Numeric 8.2
Variable Label: Age in 3 Categories
Missing Values: None
Alignment: Right

Change Settings
Type...   Missing Values...
Labels..   Column Format...

OK   Cancel   Help

Define Labels: ager

Variable Label: Age in 3 Categories

Value Labels
Value: 3
Value Label: 58 to 95 (Old)

Add
Change
Remove

1.00 = "18 to 38 (Young)"
2.00 = "39 to 57 (Middle)"

Continue   Cancel   Help

SPSS Processor is ready

FIGURE AP-5

482

RECYCLE2 - SPSS Data Editor

File Edit View Data Transform Statistics Graphs Utilities Window Help

1:ager

qdem7	icgender	icparty	iccooper	icndrstd	zipcode	intertim	age	q3br	q3dr
5	1	3		1	92027	8	30	0	3
								0	0
								0	3
								3	3
								1	2
								0	0
								2	3
								1	3
								2	0
1				1	92026	4	68	0	0
1				1	92027	6	54	1	3
1				1	92025	5	42	0	0
1				1	92056	6	32	0	0
1				1	92056	6	36	1	1
1		2		2	92028	6	32	0	1
7	1	2	1	1	92057	5	47	1	3
2	2	1	1	1	92054	5	30	1	1
1	2	2	2	2	92027	15	62	0	0
6	2	1	1	1	92056	5	67	0	0

Crosstabs

qdem4
qdem5
qdem6
qdem7
icgender
icparty
iccooper
icndrstd
zipcode
intertim
age
q3br
q3dr
q3er
altruism
incomer
q3ar

Row(s):
q1r

Column(s):
q3f2

Previous Layer 1 of 1 Next

ager

Display clustered bar charts
Suppress tables

OK
Paste
Reset
Cancel
Help

Statistics...   Cells...   Format...

Crosstabs: Cell Display

Counts
☑ Observed
☐ Expected

Percentages
☐ Row
☑ Column
☐ Total

Residuals
☐ Unstandardized
☐ Standardized
☐ Adj. standardized

Continue
Cancel
Help

SPSS Processor is ready

FIGURE AP-7

RECYCLE2 - SPSS Data Editor

File Edit View Data Transform Statistics Graphs Utilities Window Help

1:ager

	qdem7	icgender	icparty	iccooper	icndrstd	zipcode	intertim	age	q3br	q3dr
1	5	1	3	1	1	92027	8	30	0	3
2	2	2	2	1	1	92084	6	22	0	0
3	1					2028	6	75	0	3
4	8					2082	6	41	3	3
5	7					2027	5	37	1	2
6	1					2054	7	76	0	0
7	4					2069	5	28	2	3
8	4					2008	5	53	1	3
9	99					2026	6	75	2	0
10	4					2026	4	68	0	1
11	3					2027	6	54	1	3
12	7					2025	5	42	0	1
13	7					2056	6	32	0	0
14	7					2056	6	36	1	1
15	98	1	3	1	2	92028	6	32	0	1
16	7	1	2	1	1	92057	5	47	1	3
17	2	2	1	1	1	92054	5	30	1	1
18	1	2	2	2	2	92027	15	62	0	0
19	6	2	1	1	1	92056	5	67	0	0

Bivariate Correlations

iccooper
icndrstd
zipcode
intertim
q3br
q3dr
q3er
altruism
q1r
incomer

Variables:
q1
age

OK
Paste
Reset
Cancel
Help

Options...

Correlation Coefficients
☑ Pearson ☐ Kendall's tau-b ☐ Spearman

Test of Significance
● Two-tailed ○ One-tailed

☑ Flag significant correlations

SPSS Processor is ready

483

FIGURE AP-8

RECYCLE2 - SPSS Data Editor

File Edit View Data Transform Statistics Graphs Utilities Window Help

1:ager

	qdem7	icgender	icparty	iccooper	icndrstd	zipcode	intertim	age	q3br	q3dr
1							8	30	0	3
2							6	22	0	0
3							6	75	0	3
4							6	41	3	3
5							5	37	1	2
6							7	76	0	0
7							5	28	2	3
8							5	53	1	3
9							6	75	2	0
10							4	68	0	0
11							6	54	1	3
12							5	42	0	0
13							6	32	0	0
14							6	36	1	1
15					92057		6	32	0	1
16	7		2	1	92054		5	47	1	3
17	2		1	1	92027		5	30	1	1
18	1	2	2	2	92056		15	62	0	0
19	6	2	1	1			5	67	0	0

Linear Regression

iccooper
icndrstd
zipcode
intertim
age
q3br
q3dr
q3er
altruism
q1r
incomer
q3ar
q3fr
ager2
educr
kidsr
gender
edu
q3f2
ager

Dependent:
q1

Block 1 of 1   Previous   Next

Independent(s):
age
q3fr
gender

Method: Enter

Selection Variable: Rule...

Case Labels:

WLS >>

Statistics... Plots... Save... Options...

OK
Paste
Reset
Cancel
Help

SPSS Processor is ready

484

REFERENCES

INTRODUCTION

Merton, Robert K.: "Notes on Problem-Finding in Sociology," in Robert K. Merton, Leonard Broom, and Leonard S. Cottrell, Jr. (eds.), *Sociology Today,* Basic Books, New York, 1959.

Mills, C. Wright: *The Sociological Imagination,* Oxford University Press, New York, 1959.

CHAPTER 1

Anderson, Elijah: *A Place on the Corner,* University of Chicago Press, Chicago, 1978.

_____: *Streetwise: Race, Class, and Change in an Urban Community,* University of Chicago Press, Chicago, 1990.

Darley, John M., and C. Daniel Batson: "'From Jerusalem to Jericho': A Study of Situational and Dispositional Variables in Helping Behavior," *Journal of Personality and Social Psychology,* **27**:100–108, 1973.

Darley, John M., and Bibb Latane: "Bystander Intervention in Emergencies: Diffusion of Responsibility," *Journal of Personality and Social Psychology,* **8**:377–383, 1968.

Gottfredson, Michael R., and Travis Hirschi: *A General Theory of Crime,* Stanford University Press, Stanford, CA, 1990.

Hirschi, Travis: *Causes of Delinquency,* University of California Press, Berkeley, Calif, 1969.

Hochschild, Arlie: *The Second Shift,* Avon, New York, 1989.

Junger-Tas, Josine. "The International Self-Report Delinquency Study: Some Methodological and Theoretical Issues," in J. Junger-Tas, G. T. Terlouw, and M. W. Klein (eds.), *Delinquent Behavior among Youngsters in the Western World,* Kugler Publishing, Amsterdam, 1994.

Latane, Bibb, and John M. Darley: "Group Inhibition of Bystander Intervention in Emergencies," *Journal of Personality and Social Psychology,* **10**:215–221, 1968.

Laumann, Edward O., John H. Gagnon, Robert T. Michael, and Stuart Michaels: *The Social Organization of Sexuality: Sexual Practices in the United States,* University of Chicago Press, Chicago, 1994.

Michael, Robert T., John H. Gagnon, Edward O. Laumann, and Gina Kolata: *Sex in America: A Definitive Survey,* Warner Books, New York, 1994.

Mullins, Nicholas C.: *Theories and Theory Groups in Contemporary American Sociology,* Harper & Row, New York, 1973.

Pate, Anthony M., and Edwin E. Hamilton: "Formal and Informal Deterrents to Domestic Violence: The Dade County Spouse Assault Experiment," *American Sociological Review,* **57**:691–708, 1992.

Sherman, Lawrence W., Richard A. Berk, and Patrol Officers of the Minneapolis Police Department *et al.*: "Deterrent Effect of Arrest for Domestic Assault," *American Sociological Review,* **49**:261–271, 1984.

Sherman, Lawrence W., Richard A. Berk, and Patrol Officers of the Minneapolis Police Department *et al.*: "Deterrent Effect of Arrest for Domestic Assault," *American Sociological Review,* **57**:680–690, 1992.

_____, Douglas A. Smith with Janell D. Schmidt, and Dennis P. Rogan: "Crime, Punishment, and Stake in Conformity: Legal and Informal Control of Domestic Violence," *American Sociological Review,* **57**:680–690, 1992.

Barrie Thorne: *Gender Play: Girls and Boys in School,* Rutgers University Press, New Brunswick, N.J., 1993.

_____, and Nancy Henley: "Language and Sex Difference in Dominance," in B. Thorne, C. Kramarae, and N. Henley, (eds.), *Language, Gender, and Society,* Newbury House, New York, 1983.

CHAPTER 2

Belenky, Mary; Blythe Clinchy; Nancy Goldberger; and Jill Tarule: *Women's Ways of Knowing: The Development of Self, Voice, and Mind,* Basic Books, New York, 1986.

Darley, John M., and C. Daniel Batson: "'From Jerusalem to Jericho': A Study of Situational and Dispositional Variables in Helping Behavior," *Journal of Personality and Social Psychology,* **27**:100–108, 1973.

Darley, John M., and Bibb Latane: "Bystander Intervention in Emergencies: Diffusion of Responsibility," *Journal of Personality and Social Psychology,* **8**:377–383, 1968.

Gottfredson, Michael R., and Travis Hirschi: *A General Theory of Crime,* Stanford University Press, Stanford, CA, 1990.

Grant, Linda, Kathryn Ward, and Xue Rong: "Is There an Association between Gender and Methods in Sociological Research?" *American Sociological Review,* **52**:856–862, 1987.

Harding, Sandra: "Is There a Feminist Method?" in S. Harding (ed.), *Feminism and Methodology: Social Science Issues,* Indiana University Press and Open University Press, Bloomington, IN, 1987.

Hirschi, Travis. *Causes of Delinquency,* University of California Press, Berkeley, CA, 1969.

Hochschild, Arlie: *The Second Shift,* Avon, New York, 1989.

Junger-Tas, Josine: "The International Self-Report Delinquency Study: Some Methodological and Theoretical Issues," in J. Junger-Tas; G. T. Terlouw; and M. W. Klein (eds.), *Delinquent Behavior among Youngsters in the Western World,* Kugler Publishing, Amsterdam, 1994.

Kuhn, Thomas S.: *The Structure of Scientific Revolutions,* 2d ed., University of Chicago Press, Chicago, 1970.

Latane, Bibb, and John M. Darley: "Group Inhibition of Bystander Intervention in Emergencies," *Journal of Personality and Social Psychology,* **10**:215–221, 1968.

McDonald, Lynn: *The Women Founders of the Social Sciences,* Carlton University Press, Ottawa, Canada, 1994.

Merton, Robert K.: *Social Theory and Social Structure,* 3d ed., Free Press, Glencoe, IL, 1968.

_____: *The Sociology of Science,* University of Chicago Press, Chicago, 1973.

Mitroff, Ian: "Norms and Counter-Norms in a Select Group of the Apollo Moon Scientists: A Case Study of the Ambivalence of Scientists," *American Sociological Review,* **39**:579–595, 1974.

Mulkay, Michael: *Science and the Sociology of Knowledge,* Allen and Unwin, London, 1979.

Newton-Smith, W. H.: *The Rationality of Science,* Routledge and Kegan Paul. Boston, 1981.

Popper, Karl: *The Logic of Scientific Discovery,* Harper and Row. New York. 1968.

Reinharz, Shulamit: *Feminist Methods in Social Research,* Oxford University Press, New York, 1992.

Rosenau, Pauline Marie: *Postmodernism and the Social Sciences,* Princeton University Press, Princeton, NJ, 1992.

Barrie Thorne: *Gender Play: Girls and Boys in School,* Rutgers University Press, New Brunswick, NJ, 1993.

Wallace, Walter: *The Logic of Science in Sociology,* Aldine, Chicago. 1971.

CHAPTER 3

Adorno, T. W., et al.: *The Authoritarian Personality,* Harper & Row, New York, 1950 (Norton, 1969).

Anderson, Elijah: *Streetwise: Race, Class, and Change in an Urban Community,* University of Chicago Press, Chicago, 1990.

Babbie, Earl: *The Practice of Social Research,* 7th ed., Wadsworth, Belmont, CA, 1995.

Cooper, Harris M.: *Integrating Research: A Guide for Literature Reviews,* 2d ed., Sage, Newbury Park, CA, 1989.

Heist, Paul, and George Yonge: *Omnibus Personality Inventory: Research Manual,* University of California, Center for the Study of Higher Education, Berkeley, CA, 1968.

Hirschi, Travis: *Causes of Delinquency,* University of California Press, Berkeley, CA, 1969.

Hochschild, Arlie: *The Second Shift,* Avon, New York, 1989.

Laumann, Edward O.; John H. Gagnon; Robert T. Michael; and Stuart Michaels: *The Social Organization of Sexuality: Sexual Practices in the United States,* University of Chicago Press, Chicago, 1994.

Macooby, Eleanor, and Carol Jacklin: *The Psychology of Sex Differences,* Stanford University Press, Stanford, CA. 1974.

Merton, Robert K.: "Notes on Problem-Finding in Sociology," in Robert K. Merton, Leonard Broom, and Leonard S. Cottrell, Jr. (eds.), *Sociology Today,* Basic Books, New York, 1959.

Michael, Robert T.; John H. Gagnon; Edward O. Laumann; and Gina Kolata: *Sex in America: A Definitive Survey,* Warner Books, New York, 1994.

Platt, Stephen: "Unemployment and Suicidal Behavior: A Review of the Literature," *Social Science Medicine,* 19:93–115, 1984.

Roberts, Robert E. L., and Vern L. Bengston: "Relationships with Parents, Self-Esteem, and Psychological Well-Being in Young Adulthood," *Social Psychology Quarterly,* 56:263–277, 1993.

Robinson, W. S.: "Ecological Correlations and the Behavior of Individuals," *American Sociological Review,* 15:351–357, 1950.

Simon, Julian L.: *Basic Research Methods in Social Science,* Random House. New York. 1969.

CHAPTER 4

Adorno, T. W., et al.: *The Authoritarian Personality,* Harper & Row, New York, 1950 (Norton, 1969).

Allen, Mary J., and Wendy M. Yen: *Introduction to Measurement Theory,* Wadsworth, Belmont, CA, 1979.

American Psychological Association, American Educational Research Association, and National Council on Measurement in Education: *Standards for Educational Tests,* American Psychological Association, Washington, 1974.

Anderson, T. W., and Stanley L. Sclove: *Introductory Statistical Analysis,* 2d ed., Houghton Mifflin, Boston, 1986.

Beere, C.A.: *Women and Women's Issues: A Handbook of Tests and Measures,* Jossey-Bass, San Francisco, 1979.

Bohrnstedt, George W.: "Measurement," in Peter H. Rossi, James D. Wright, and Andy B. Anderson (eds.), *Handbook of Survey Research,* Academic, New York, 1983.

Borgatta, Edgar F., and George W. Bohrnstedt: "Levels of Measurement: Once Over Again," *Sociological Methods and Research,* 9:147–160, 1980.

Bradburn, Norman M., and David Caplovitz: *Reports on Happiness,* Aldine, Chicago, 1965.

Brayfield, Arthur H., and Harold F. Rothe: "An Index of Job Satisfaction," *Journal of Applied Psychology,* 35:307–311, 1951.

Buros, O. K. (ed.): *Eighth Mental Measurement Yearbook,* Gryphon Press, Highland Park, NJ, 1978.

Carmines, E., and R. Zeller: *Reliability and Validity Assessment,* Sage, Beverly Hills, CA, 1979.

Chronbach, L. J., and P. E. Meehl: "Construct Validity in Psychological Tests," *Psychological Bulletin,* 52:281–302, 1955.

Department of Labor: *Dictionary of Occupational Titles,* 4th ed., Department of Labor, Washington, 1991.

Hodge, Robert W.; Paul M. Siegel; and Peter H. Rossi: "Occupational Prestige in the United States, 1925–63," *American Journal of Sociology,* 70:286–302, 1964.

Miller, Delbert C.: *Handbook of Research Design and Social Measurement,* 3rd ed., McKay, New York, 1977.

_____: 5th ed., 1991.

Nunnally, J. C.: *Psychometric Theory,* New York, McGraw-Hill, 1967.

Reiss, Albert J.: *Occupations and Social Status,* Free Press, Glencoe, IL, 1961.

Robinson, J. P.; R. Athanasiou; and K. B. Head: *Measures of Occupational Attitudes and Occupational Characteristics,* Survey Research Center, Ann Arbor, MI, 1969.

Robinson, J. P.; J. G. Rusk; and K. B. Head: *Measures of Political Attitudes,* Survey Research Center, Ann Arbor, MI, 1968.

Robinson, J. P., and P. R. Shaver: *Measures of Social Psychological Attitudes,* Survey Research Center, Ann Arbor, MI, 1969.

Shaw, M. E., and J. M. Wright: *Scales for the Measurement of Attitudes,* McGraw-Hill, New York, 1967.

Srole, Leo: "Social Integration and Certain Corollaries: An Exploratory Study," *American Sociological Review,* **21**:703–716, 1956.

Stevens, S. S.; "Mathematics, Measurement and Psychophysics," in S. S. Stevens (ed.), *Handbook of Experimental Psychology,* Wiley, New York, 1951.

Treiman, Donald J.: *Occupational Prestige in Comparative Perspective,* Academic Press, New York, 1977.

U.S. Bureau of the Census: *Statistical Abstract of 1992,* Washington, 1992.

U.S. Department of Commerce: *Social Indicators III, Selected Data on Social Conditions and Trends in the United States,* Bureau of the Census, Washington, 1980.

Zeller, Richard A., and Edward G. Carmines: *Measurement in the Social Sciences: The Link between Theory and Data,* Cambridge University Press, New York, 1980.

CHAPTER 5

Babbie, Earl: *The Practice of Social Research,* 6th ed., Wadsworth, Belmont, CA., 1992.

Davis, James A. and Tom W. Smith: *General Social Surveys, 1972–1988: Cumulative Codebook,* National Opinion Research Center, Chicago, 1990.

Frankfort-Nachmias, C. F., and D. Nachmias: *Research Methods in the Social Sciences,* 5th ed., St. Martin's Press, New York, 1996.

Hirschi, Travis: *Causes of Delinquency,* University of California Press, Berkeley, CA, 1969.

Hochschild, Arlie: *The Second Shift,* Avon, New York, 1989.

Kish, Leslie: *Survey Sampling,* Wiley, New York, 1965.

Kraemer, Helena Chmura, and Sue Thiemann: *How Many Subjects? Statistical Power Analysis in Research,* Sage, Newbury Park, CA, 1987.

Laumann, Edward O.; John H. Gagnon; Robert T. Michael; and Stuart Michaels: *The Social Organization of Sexuality: Sexual Practices in the United States,* University of Chicago Press, Chicago, 1994.

Rand Corporation: *A Million Random Digits with 100,000 Normal Deviates,* Free Press, New York, 1955.

Slonim, Morris J.: *Sampling,* Simon and Schuster, New York, 1966.

Sudman, Seymour: *Applied Sampling,* Academic Press, New York, 1976.

Williams, Bill: *A Sampler on Sampling,* Wiley, New York, 1978.

CHAPTER 6

Anderson, Barry F.: *The Psychology Experiment,* Brooks/Cole, Belmont, CA, 1971.

Baron, James N., and Philip C. Reiss: "Same Time, Next Year: Aggregate Analysis of the Mass Media and Violent Behavior," *American Sociological Review,* **50**:347–363, 1985.

Berkowitz, Leonard, and Joseph T. Alioto: 'The Meaning of an Observed Event as a Determinant of Its Aggressive Consequence," *Journal of Personality and Social Psychology,* **28**:206–217, 1973.

_____ and Russell G. Geen: "Film Violence and Cue Properties of Available Targets," *Journal of Personality and Social Psychology,* **3**:525–530, 1966.

_____ and _____: "Stimulus Qualities of the Target of Aggression," *Journal of Personality and Social Psychology,* **5**:364–368, 1967.

_____ and Edna Rawlings: "Effects of Film Violence on Inhibitions against Subsequent Aggression," *Journal of Abnormal and Social Psychology,* **66**:405–412, 1963.

Campbell, Donald T., and Julian C. Stanley: *Experimental and Quasi-Experimental Designs for Research*, Rand McNally, Chicago, 1963.

Cook, Thomas D., and Donald T. Campbell: *Quasi-Experimentation: Design and Analysis Issues for Field Settings,* Houghton Mifflin, Boston, 1979.

Darley, John M., and Bibb Latane: "Bystander Intervention in Emergencies: Diffusion of Responsibility," *Journal of Personality and Social Psychology,* **8**:377–383, 1968.

Latane, Bibb, and John M. Darley: "Group Inhibition of Bystander Intervention in Emergencies," *Journal of Personality and Social Psychology,* **10**:215–221, 1968.

Orenstein, Alan, and William R.F. Phillips: *Understanding Social Research: An Introduction,* Allyn and Bacon, Boston, 1978.

Orne, Martin T.: "On the Social Psychology Experiment: With Particular Reference to Demand Characteristics and Their Implications," in George H. Lewis (ed.), *Fist-Fights in the Kitchen,* Goodyear, Pacific Palisades, CA, 1975.

Pate, Anthony M., and Edwin E. Hamilton: "Formal and Informal Deterrents to Domestic Violence: The Dade County Spouse Assault Experiment," *American Sociological Review,* **57**:691–708, 1992.

Philips, David P.: "The Impact of Mass Media Violence on U.S. Homicides," *American Sociological Review,* **48**:560–568, 1983.

_____ and Kenneth A. Bollen: "Same Time, Last Year: Selective Data Dredging for Negative Findings," *American Sociological Review,* **50**:364–371, 1985.

Roethlisberger, F.J., and W. J. Dickson: *Management and the Worker,* Harvard University Press, Cambridge, MA, 1939.

Rosenthal, Robert, and Ralph L. Rosnow: *The Volunteer Subject,* Wiley, New York, 1975.

Sherman, Lawrence W.; Richard A. Berk; and Patrol Officers of the Minneapolis Police Department *et al.*: "Deterrent Effect of Arrest for Domestic Assault," *American Sociological Review,* **49**:261–271, 1984.

Wasserman, Ira M.: "The Effects of War and Alcohol Consumption Patterns on Suicide: United States, 1910–1933," *Social Forces,* **68**:513–530, 1989.

CHAPTER 7

Bradburn, Norman, and Seymour Sudman: *Improving Interview Method and Questionnaire Design,* Jossey-Bass. San Francisco, 1979.

Converse, Jean M., and Howard Schuman: *Conversations at Random: Survey Research as Interviewers See It,* Wiley, New York, 1974.

de Vaus, D. A.: *Surveys in Social Research,* Allen & Unwin, Boston, 1986.

Downs, Cal W.; G. Paul Smeyak; and Ernest Martin: *Professional Interviewing,* Harper & Row, New York, 1980.

Gallup, G.: "The Quintamensional Plan of Question Design," *Public Opinion Quarterly,* **11**:385, 1947.

Groves, Robert M., and Robert L. Kahn: *Surveys by Telephone: A National Comparison with Personal Interviews,* Academic Press, New York, 1979.

Hess, J. M.: "Group Interviewing," in R. L. Ring (ed.), *New Science of Planning,* American Marketing Association, Chicago, 1968.

Hirschi, Travis: *Causes of Delinquency,* University of California Press, Berkeley, CA, 1969.

Kish, Leslie: "A Procedure for Objective Respondent Selection within the Household," *Journal of the American Statistical Association,* **44**:380–387, 1949.

Klineberg, Steven: Houston Area Survey, Houston, 1983, unpublished survey.

Merton, Robert K., and Patricia L. Kendall: "The Focused Interview," *American Journal of Sociology,* **51**:541–557, 1946.

_____,; Marjorie Fiske; and Patricia L. Kendall: *The Focused interview: A Manual of Problems and Procedures,* 2nd ed., The Free Press, New York, 1990.

Riesman, David: "Some Observations on the Interviewing in the Teacher Apprehension Study," in Paul F. Lazarsfeld and Wagner Thielens, Jr. (eds.), *The Academic Mind: Social Scientists in a Time of Crisis,* Academic Press, New York, 1958.

Riley, Matilda White: *Sociological Research: A Case Approach,* Harcourt, Brace & World, New York, 1963.

Roth, Julius: "Hired Hand Research," *The American Sociologist,* **1**:190–96, 1966.

Stewart, David W., and Pren W. Shandasani: *Focus Groups: Theory and Practice,* Sage, Newbury Park, CA, 1990.

Suchman, Lucy, and Brigitte Jordan: "Validity and the Collaborative Construction of Meaning in Face-to- Face Surveys," in Judith M. Taner (ed.), *Questions about Questions: Inquiries into the Cognitive Bases of Surveys,* Russell Sage Foundation, New York, 1992.

Sudman, Seymour: "The Uses of Telephone Directories for Survey Sampling," *Journal of Marketing Research,* **10**:204–207, 1973.

_____ and Norman Bradburn: *Response Effects in Surveys,* Aldine, Chicago, 1974.

Wallace, Walter: *The Logic of Science in Sociology,* Aldine, Chicago, 1971.

Warwick, Donald P., and Charles A. Lininger: *The Sample Survey: Theory and Practice,* McGraw-Hill, New York, 1975.

Wheatley, K. L., and W. A. Flexner: "Dimensions That Make Focus Groups Work," *Marketing News,* **22**:16–17, 1988.

CHAPTER 8

Anderson, Elijah: *Streetwise: Race, Class, and Change in an Urban Community,* University of Chicago Press, Chicago, 1990.

Bales, Robert F.: *Interaction Process Analysis: A Method for the Study of Small Groups,* Addison-Wesley, Cambridge, MA, 1951.

_____: *SYMLOG Case Study Kit,* Free Press, New York, 1980.

Becker, Howard S.: "Photography and Sociology," *Studies in the Anthropology of Visual Communication,* **1**:3–26, 1974.

Cloninger, Sally J.: The Sexually Dimorphic Image: The Influence of Gender Difference on Imagemaking, unpublished dissertation, Ohio State University, 1974.

Clough, P. T.: *Feminist Thought: Desire, Power and Academic Discourse,* Blackwell, Cambridge, MA, 1994.

Cresswell, John W.: *Research Design: Qualitative and Quantitative Approaches,* Sage, Thousand Oaks, CA, 1994.

Curry, Timothy J., and Alfred C. Clarke: *Introducing Visual Sociology,* Kendall/Hunt, Dubuque, IA, 1977.

Denzin, Norman K.: *Interpretive Ethnography,* Sage, Thousand Oaks, CA, 1997.

Emerson, Robert M.; Rachel I. Fretz; and Linda L. Shaw: *Writing Ethnographic Fieldnotes,* University of Chicago Press, Chicago, 1995.

Fetterman, David M.: *Ethnography Step by Step,* Sage, Newbury Park, CA, 1989

Freeman, Derek: *Margaret Mead and Samoa: The Making and Unmaking of an Anthropological Myth,* Harvard University Press, Cambridge, MA, 1983.

Gold, Raymond L.: "Roles in Sociological Field Observations," in George J. McCall and J. L. Simmons (eds.), *Issues in Participant Observation,* Addison Wesley, Reading, MA, 1969.

Grant, L., and G. A. Fine: "Sociology Unleashed: Creative Directions in Classical Ethnography," in M. D. LeCompte, W. L. Millroy and J. Preissle (eds.), *The Handbook of Qualitative Research in Education,* Academic Press, New York, 1992.

Hochschild, Arlie: *The Second Shift,* Avon, New York, 1989.

Kvale, Steinar: *InterViews: An Introduction to Qualitative Research Interviewing,* Sage, Thousand Oaks, CA, 1996.

Lewis, George H. and Jonathan F. Lewis: "The Dog in the Nighttime: Negative Evidence in Social Research," *British Journal of Sociology,* **31**:544–558, 1980.

Lofland, John: *Analyzing Social Settings: A Guide to Qualitative Observation and Analysis,* Wadsworth, Belmont, CA, 1971.

Marshall, Eliot: "A Controversy on Samoa Comes of Age," *Science,* **219**:1042–1045, 1983.

Marshall, Catherine, and Gretchen B. Rossman: *Designing Qualitative Research,* 2nd ed., Sage, Thousand Oaks, CA, 1995.

Rossman, G. B.; H. D. Corbett; and W. A. Firestone.: Change and Effectiveness in Schools: A Cultural Perspective, SUNY Press, Albany, NY, 1988.

Rubin, H. J., and I. S. Rubin: *Qualitative Interviewing,* Sage, Thousand Oaks, CA, 1995.

Schwandt, Thomas A.: *Qualitative Inquiry: A Dictionary of Terms,* Sage, Thousand Oaks, CA, 1997.

Stasz, Clarice: "The Early History of Visual Sociology," in Jon Wagner (ed.), *Images of Information: Still Photography in the Social Sciences,* Sage, Beverly Hills, CA, 1979.

Suelzle, Marijean, and Lenore Borzak: "Stages of Fieldwork," in Lenore Borzak (ed.), *Field Study: A Sourcebook for Experimental Learning,* Sage, Beverly Hills, CA, 1981.

Wagner, Jon (ed.): *Images of Information: Still Photography in the Social Sciences,* Sage, Beverly Hills, CA, 1979a.

_____: "Avoiding Error," in Jon Wagner (ed.), *Images of Information: Still Photography in the Social Sciences,* Sage, Beverly Hills, CA, 1979b.

Wax, Rosalie H.: *Doing Fieldwork: Warnings and Advice,* University of Chicago Press, Chicago, 1971.

Whyte, William Foote: *Street Corner Society: The Social Structure of an Italian Slum,* University of Chicago Press, Chicago, 1943.

Withall, John: "Assessment of the Social-Emotional Climates Experienced by a Group of Seventh Graders as They Moved from Class to Class," *Educational and Psychological Measurement,* 12:440–452, 1952.

Zablocki, B.: *The Joyful Community,* Penguin, Baltimore, 1971.

CHAPTER 9

Baker, Therese L., and Joyce A. Sween: "Synchronizing Post-Graduate Career, Marriage, and Fertility," *Western Sociological Review,* 13: 69–86, 1982.

Bannan, Rosemary S.: "Briefing the Court: Dialectic as Methodological Perspective," *Journal of Contemporary Law,* 10:121–139, 1984.

Berelson, Bernard: "Content Analysis," in Gardner Lindzey (ed.), *Handbook of Social Psychology,* Addison-Wesley, Cambridge, MA, 1954.

Brewer, John, and Albert Hunter: *Multimethod Research: A Synthesis of Styles,* Sage, Newbury Park, CA, 1989.

Cancian, Francesca M., and Steven L. Gordon: "Changing Emotion Norms in Marriage: Love and Anger in U.S. Women's Magazines Since 1900," *Gender & Society,* 2:308–342, 1988.

Cantor, David, and Kenneth C. Land: "Unemployment and Crime Rates in the Post-World War II United States: A Theoretical and Empirical Analysis," *American Sociological Review,* 50:317–332, 1985.

Chaffee, Steven H.; George Gerber; et al.: "Defending the Indefensible," *Society,* 21:30–35, 1984.

Davis, James A., and Tom W. Smith: *The NORC General Social Survey: A User's Guide,* Sage, Newbury Park, CA, 1991.

Elder, Jr., Glen H.: *Children of the Great Depression,* University of Chicago Press, Chicago, 1974.

Ferree, Myra Marx, and Elaine J. Hall: "Gender, Race, and Class in Mainstream Textbooks," *American Sociological Review,* 61:929–950, 1996.

Gerbner, George, et al.: "Cultural Indicators: Violence Profile No. 9," *Journal of Communication,* 28:177–207, 1978.

_____ et al.: "The 'Mainstreaming' of America: Violence Profile No. 11," *Journal of Communication,* 30:10–29, 1980.

Gottschalk, Louis: *Understanding History,* Knopf, New York, 1950.

Hakim, Catherine: *Secondary Analysis in Social Research,* Allen and Unwin, London, 1982.

Holsti, Ole R.: *Content Analysis for the Social Sciences and the Humanities,* Addison-Wesley, Reading, MA, 1969.

Kiecolt, K. Jill, and Laura E. Nathan: *Secondary Analysis of Survey Data,* Sage University paper 53, Sage, Newbury Park, CA, 1985.

LaFree, Gary, and Kriss A. Drass: "Variables Affecting Arrest Rates of Blacks and Whites, 1957 to 1990," *American Sociological Review*, **61**:614–634, 1996.

Margadant, Jo Burr: *Madame le Professeur: Women Educators in the Third Republic*, Princeton University Press, Princeton, NJ, 1990.

Office of Management and Budget: *Social Indicators*, Government Printing Office, Washington, 1973.

Rathje, William, L.: "Trace Measures," in Lee Sechrest (ed.), *Unobtrusive Measurement Today*, Jossey- Bass, San Francisco, 1979.

Riccobono, J., et al.: *National Longitudinal Study: Base Year (1972) through Fourth Follow-up (1979), Data File Users Manual*, National Center for Education Statistics Research, Triangle Park, NC, 1981.

Roberts, Robert E. L., and Vern L. Bengston: "Affective Ties to Parents in Early Adulthood and Self-Esteem across 20 Years," *Social Psychology Quarterly*, **59**:96–106, 1996.

Schwartz, Barry: "Memory as a Cultural System: Abraham Lincoln in World War II, *American Sociological Review*, 61: 908-927, 1996.

Sechrest, Lee, and Melinda Phillips: "Unobtrusive Measures: An Overview," in Lee Sechrest (ed.), *Unobtrusive Measurement Today*, Jossey-Bass, San Francisco, 1979.

Social Science Research Council Survey Archive: *Guide to the Survey Archives Social Sciences Data Holdings and Allied Services*, University of Essex, Essex, (n.d.).

U.S. Bureau of the Census: *Current Population Reports*, Government Printing Office, Washington.

_____: *Statistical Abstract of the United States*, Government Printing Office, Washington, 1879–present.

U.S. Department of Justice: *Uniform Crime Reporting Handbook*, Federal Bureau of Investigation, Washington, 1980.

Webb, Eugene; Donald T. Campbell; Richard D. Schwartz; and Lee Sechrest: *Unobtrusive Measures: Nonreactive Research in the Social Sciences*, Rand McNally, Chicago, 1966.

Williams, Gilbert A.: "Enticing Viewers: Sex and Violence in *TV Guide* Program Advertisements," *Journalism Quarterly*, **66**:970–973, 1989.

Wurtzel, Alan, and Guy Lometti: "Researching Television Violence," *Society*, **21**:22–30, 1984.

CHAPTER 10

Allen, Jr., Harris M., and David O. Sears: "Against Them or for Me: Community Impact Evaluations," in Lois-Ellin Datta and Robert Perloff (eds.), *Improving Evaluations*, Sage, Beverly Hills, CA, 1979.

Andrews, Frank M. (ed.): *Research on the Quality of Life*, Survey Research Center, Institute for Social Research, University of Michigan, Ann Arbor, MI, 1986.

Carley, Michael: *Social Measurement and Social Indicators*, Allen and Unwin, London, 1981.

Davenport, Barbara C., and Ronald L. Nuttall: "Cost-Effective Medicaid Mental Health Policies: Design and Testing," in Lois-Ellin Datta and Robert Perloff (eds.), *Improving Evaluations*, Sage, Beverly Hills, CA,

Junger-Tas, Josine: "The International Self-Report Delinquency Study: Some Methodological and Theoretical Issues," in J. Junger-Tas; G. T. Terlouw; and M. W. Klein (eds.), *Delinquent Behavior among Youngsters in the Western World*, Kugler Publishing, Amsterdam, 1994.

Naisbitt, John: *Megatrends: Ten New Directions Transforming Our Lives*, Warner, New York, 1982.

_____ and Patricia Aburdene: *Megatrends 2000*, Morrow, New York, 1990.

Office of Management and Budget: *Social Indicators, 1973*, Government Printing Office, Washington, 1973.

Posavec, Emil J., and Raymond G. Carey: *Program Evaluation: Methods and Case Studies*, 3d ed., Prentice Hall, Englewood Cliffs, NJ, 1989.

Scriven, Michael: "The Methodology of Evaluation," in R. W. Tyler, R. M. Gagne, and M. Scriven (eds.), *Perspectives of Curriculum Evaluation*, Rand McNally, Skokie, IL 1967.

Skellie, F. Albert; G. Melton Mobley; and Ruth E. Coan: "Cost Effectiveness of Community-Based Long-Term Care: Current Findings of Georgia's Alternative Health Services Project," *American Journal of Public Health,* **72**:353–358, 1982.

Stringer, Ernest T.: *Action Research: A Handbook for Practioners,* Sage, Thousand Oaks, CA, 1996.

U.S. Department of Commerce: *Social Indicators, 1976,* Government Printing Office, Washington, 1977.

U.S. Department of Health, Education, and Welfare: *Toward a Social Report,* Government Printing Office, Washington, 1969.

Weiss, Carol H.: *Evaluation Research,* Prentice Hall, Englewood Cliffs, NJ, 1972.

Westinghouse Learning Corporation, Ohio University: *The Impact of Head Start: An Evaluation of the Effects of Head Start on Children's Cognitive and Affective Development,* U.S. Department of Commerce, Washington, 1969.

Witkin, Belle Ruth, and James W. Altschuld: *Planning and Conducting Needs Assessments: A Practical Guide,* Sage, Thousand Oaks, CA, 1995.

World Bank: *World Tables 1991,* The Johns Hopkins University Press, Baltimore, MD, 1991.

Yin, Robert K.: *Case Study Research: Design and Methods,* rev. ed., Sage, Newbury Park, CA, 1989.

Zimring, Franklin E.: "Firearms and Federal Law: The Gun Control Act of 1968," in Gene V. Glass (ed.), *Evaluation Studies Review Annual,* Sage, Beverly Hills, CA, 1976.

CHAPTER 11

Emerson, Robert M; Rachel I. Fretz; and Linda L. Shaw: *Writing Ethnographic Fieldnotes,* University of Chicago Press, Chicago, 1995.

Miles, Matthew B., and A. Michael Huberman: *Qualitative Data Analysis,* 2nd ed., Sage, Thousand Oaks, CA, 1994

_____, and Eben A. Weitzman: "Choosing Computer Programs for Qualitative Data Analysis, in Miles, Matthew B., and A. Michael Huberman: *Qualitative Data Analysis,* 2nd ed., Appendix, Sage, Thousand Oaks, CA, 1994.

Werner, O., and G. M. Schoepfle: *Systematic Fieldwork: Vol. 2. Ethnographic Analysis and Data Management,* Sage, Newbury Park, CA, 1987.

CHAPTER 12

Hyman, Herbert: *Survey Design and Analysis,* Free Press, Glencoe, IL, 1955.

Kendall, Patricia L., and Paul F. Lazarsfeld: "Problems of Survey Analysis," in Robert K. Merton (ed.), *Continuities in Social Research,* Free Press, Glencoe, IL, 1950.

Middleton, Russell: "Alienation, Race, and Education," *American Sociological Review,* **28**:973–976, 1963.

Rosenberg, Morris: *The Logic of Survey Analysis,* Basic Books, New York, 1968.

Stouffer, Samuel A., et al.: *The American Soldier,* Princeton University Press, Princeton, NJ, 1949.

CHAPTER 13

Davis, James A.: *Elementary Survey Analysis,* Prentice Hall, Englewood Cliffs, NJ, 1971.

Elifson, Kirk W.; Richard P. Runyon; and Audrey Haber: *Fundamentals of Social Statistics,* 2d ed., McGraw-Hill, New York, 1990.

Rossi, Peter H.: *Down and Out in America: The Origins of Homelessness,* University of Chicago Press, Chicago, 1989.

Simon, Julian L., and Paul Burstein: *Basic Research Methods in Social Science,* 3d ed, Random House, New York, 1985.

CHAPTER 14

American Sociological Association: Code of Ethics, Washington, DC, 1997.

Bulmer, Martin: "The Merits and Demerits of Covert Participant Observation." in Martin Bulmer (ed.), *Social Research Ethics,* Macmillan, London, 1982.

Cassell, Joan: "Risk and Benefit to Subjects of Fieldwork." *The American Sociologist,* **13**:134–143, 1978.

Cohen, S., and L. Taylor: *Psychological Survival: The Effects of Long-Term Imprisonment.* Penguin, Harmondsworth. Middlesex, England, 1972.

Erikson, Kai T.: "A Comment on Disguised Observation in Sociology." *Social Problems,* **14**:367–373,1967.

Galliher, John: "Social Scientists' Ethical Responsibilities to Superordinates: Looking Upward Meekly," *Social Problems,* **27**:298–308, 1980.

Goffman, Erving: *The Presentation of Self in Everyday Life,* Doubleday, New York, 1959.

Humphreys, Laud: *Tearoom Trade,* Aldine, Chicago, 1970.

Katz, Jay: *Experimentation with Human Beings,* Sage, New York, 1972.

Milgram, Stanley: "Some Conditions of Obedience and Disobedience to Authority," *Human Relations,* **18**:57–75, 1965.

Newman, Dianna L., and Robert D. Brown: *Applied Ethics for Program Evaluation,* Sage, Thousand Oaks, CA, 1996.

Rosenhan, D.L.: "On Being Sane in Insane Places," in Martin Bulmer (ed.), *Social Research Ethics,* Macmillan, London, 1982.

Rosenthal, Robert, and Lenore F. Jacobson: *Pygmalion in the Classroom,* Holt, New York, 1968.

Rubinstein, J.: *City Police,* Farrar, Straus & Giroux, New York, 1973.

Shils, Edward "Social Inquiry and the Autonomy of the Individual," in Martin Bulmer (ed.), *Social Research Ethics,* Macmillan, London, 1982.

Vidich, Arthur J., and Joseph Bensman: *Small Town in Mass Society,* Anchor, New York, 1960.

Wade, Nicholas: "I.Q. and Heredity: Suspicion of Fraud Beclouds Classic Experiment," *Science,* **194**:916–919, 1976.

Weinstein, Deena: "Fraud in Science," *Social Science Quarterly,* **59**639–652, 1979.

CHAPTER 15

Baker, Therese L., and Judith A. Bootcheck: "The Relationship of Marital Status and Career Preparation to Changing Work Orientations of Young Women: A Longitudinal Study," in A. Kerckhoff (ed.), *Research in Sociology of Education and Socialization,* vol. 5, 1985.

Caplovitz, David: *The Stages of Social Research,* Wiley, New York, 1983.

Humphreys, Laud: *Tearoom Trade,* Aldine, Chicago, 1970.

accretion measures *Unobtrusive measures* of accumulated *physical traces* of social behavior (e.g., garbage, graffiti).

action research Research directed towards social change which can involve the subjects being studied so as to improve their outcomes. See *participatory action research.*

aggregate data Data on large numbers of subjects showing a common characteristic. *Existing statistics* are a source of aggregate data.

anonymity Assurance that subjects' identities will not be disclosed in any way.

antecedent variable A third variable in a trivariate analysis that logically comes in a time sequence before the independent variable.

anthropology A discipline focusing on the nature of human culture in which field research is the primary method of study.

applied research Research for which one of the primary rationales is that the study may have some practical use.

archival research A method of studying organizations or societies, based on the collected records they have produced.

attrition The loss of members of a sample, usually as a result of their refusal to respond or the researcher's inability to contact them.

audit trail An organized effort by a third party in a qualitative study to go over the way in which the collected materials have been organized so as to make sense of the qualitative data collected. The process of auditing can establish whether the procedures have been dependable.

bar graph A graph on which categories of a variable are presented on the horizontal axis and their frequencies are presented on the vertical axis. The height of each bar represents the frequencies of each attribute of a variable. The bars have gaps between them on the scale. See *histogram* and *frequency polygon.*

best-fit line The line that would best reduce its distance to all points in a *scattergram.*

bivariate table A two-variable table.

case studies Observational studies of a single environment (an organization, a neighborhood, a public place). Field research is often based on a single case study.

case study protocol A written plan based on a comprehensive outline of how the case study will be carried out. It should include an overview of the entire project, the field procedures, questions to be answered in the study, and a guide for preparing the final report.

categorical variables Variables made up of sets of categories that do not represent a numerical measure. See *mutually exclusive categories* and *exhaustive categories.*

cell In a cross-classification table, the position where two categories meet. In a 2×3 bivariate table, there will be six cells.

chi-square (χ^2) An inferential statistic testing the *null hypothesis* of independence between two variables.

classical experiment A *true experiment* in which a pretest is given to both the experimental and control groups, the experimental group is "treated" with the independent variable, and both groups are given the posttest.

classical test theory The theory that if a test (or measure) is repeated over and over again, errors will tend to cancel each other out over time. See *random measurement error.*

closed-ended question Questions in a questionnaire that force the respondent to select from a list of possible responses (often called forced-choice question).

codebook A list of variables showing where they can be found and what decisions were made in setting up and recoding them.

coercion of subjects Forcing subjects to participate in a study which may be inconvenient or detrimental to them. Subjects may be in a "captive" situation (prisoners) or unable to defend their interests (children).

cognitive map A graphic depiction of how one person in a qualitative study views an issue, showing the process of a change or what occurred in various parts of the situation.

cohort studies Studies based on a longitudinal study design in which the subjects are grouped by their ages for comparative purposes. The groups are sometimes referred to as generations.

community impact assessment   Evaluation research that tries to determine how a policy might affect a community.

computer-assisted telephone interviewing (CATI)   An interviewing technique in which the interviewer uses a computer to select telephone numbers, reads the interview questions off the screen, and enters the responses.

concurrent validity   A form of *criterion-related validity* in which the criterion to test the validity of the variable is measured at the same time as the variable itself.

condensed trivariate table   A three-variable table in which the percentage of one category of the dependent variable is presented in a cross tabulation of the independent and test variables.

confidence intervals   The range of values within which a population parameter (e.g., the mean of the population) would be expected to fall on a *normal curve*.

confidence levels   Probability estimates that a population parameter would fall within a particular confidence interval.

confidentiality   A promise to restrict knowledge of the identities of research subjects to the researcher and staff members.

conflict theory   An explanation of human society as the result of struggle between social classes (Karl Marx) and/or status groups (Max Weber). Open conflict might break out or be contained through forces of social control.

constant   A measure that shows no variation.

construct validity   A form of validity testing in which hypotheses generated from a concept are tested, and the results of these tests are correlated with the original concept.

contact summary form   Summary form detailing the experience of contacting a person for a meeting or interview. Form details the major points covered in the meeting.

content analysis   A research technique that describes in an objective, systematic, and quantified manner the content of a body of communication.

content validity   The most basic form of validity testing in which the measure of a concept is examined in light of its meaning. See *face validity* and *sampling validity*.

contextuality   Trying to relate historical phenomena to as many aspects of social life as possible so as to understand and not distort the past.

contingency question   Question in a survey that depends on the responses to earlier questions or which has questions dependent on it.

contingency table   A table that cross-tabulates two variables. Also called a *cross classification* or *cross tabulation*.

continuous variables   Variables measured on a numerical scale which has an infinite number of points.

control group   The comparison group in an experiment who are not exposed to the experimental treatment.

control variable   The third variable in a trivariate analysis. The relationship between the dependent and independent variables is examined under each condition of the control variable. See *test variable*.

convenience sample   A nonprobability sample composed of subjects available and willing to participate.

cost-benefit analysis   An assessment of whether the benefits of a program or social strategy are worth the costs.

covert research   Carrying out research without the knowledge or consent of those being studied or by misrepresenting the role of the researcher.

criterion-related validity   A test of validity in which a variable under examination is correlated with another variable to which it should logically be related. (For example, college grades could be a criterion for testing the validity of college entrance examination scores.)

criterion variable   This is another name for a *dependent variable*. It is the criterion measure for determining whether the *predictor variable* brought about its expected effect.

cross-classification   A table that cross-tabulates two variables.

cross-sectional   Data gathered at one point in time.

cross tabulation   A table that presents one variable classified by another. A *cross-classification,* or *contingency, table*.

curvilinear relationship   A curved *best-fit line* indicating that an increase in the value of one variable is not related to an increase in the value of another.

deductive method   A method in which hypotheses are logically derived from theories.

degrees of freedom (*df*)   In a chi-square table, *df* are determined by the formula $(r - 1)(c - 1)$ in which r = number of rows in the table and c = number of columns. The *df* is then used in conjunction with the computed *chi-square* statistic to determine significance level using a chi-square table.

demand characteristics Inadvertent cues conveying the experimental hypothesis to subjects in such a way that they may try to cooperate in validating the experimental hypothesis. This undermines the *internal validity* of the experiment.

dependent variable The variable in an experiment or survey that is affected, or subject to being affected, by the independent variable.

dependent variable study A study that investigates why, how, and under what conditions change in a dependent variable occurred.

descriptive statistics Summary numerical descriptions of large bodies of data, most commonly stating the central tendencies and variability of given variables or the relationship between variables.

dimensions In conceptualization and measurement, dimensions refer to the different qualities of a concept. Indicators to measure each dimension are sought. A concept may have one (unidimensional) or more (multidimensional) dimensions. See *indicators*.

discrete variables Variables measured on a numerical scale in which each point on the scale represents a whole number.

dispersion The degree of variation of scores around the mean. This is measured by the *standard deviation*.

disproportionate sampling A sampling design which deliberately increases the sample size of some subgroups (for example, minority groups) so that there will be a sufficiently large number of subgroup members in the study for the purposes of analysis. See *weighting*.

distorter variable A third variable that reverses a relationship originally observed between two other variables. Controlling this third variable eliminates the distortion seen in the original relationship.

document summary form Summary form detailing documents and written records forming a part of a qualitative research project. Includes a summary of the contents and the importance of the document for the study.

double-blind experiment The practice in true experiments of having neither the subjects nor the experimenter know which subjects are in the experimental or control groups.

dross numbers These are telephone numbers that for one reason or another do not lead to households. In telephone surveys, the ratio of good to dross numbers is about one to five.

dummy variable A two-category variable, in which "1" represents the presence of an attribute and "0" represents its absence. In any statistical analysis in which variables based on numerical scales are required (such as regression analysis), categorical variables can be converted into dummy variables.

ecological fallacy Using evidence from a group level of analysis to reach conclusions about individuals.

effects matrix A graphic presentation relating outcomes to objectives in a qualitative analysis which may include various perspectives of different role players in the situation.

elaboration paradigm An exemplary model to explain certain types of outcomes that can occur with the entry of a third variable into a bivariate relationship. The outcomes are called replications, explanations, interpretations, or specifications.

elements The individual *units* composing a sample, usually individual persons.

empirical Based on observable evidence.

empirical generalizations Formed out of observations in the research process; the search for regularities. See *scientific model*.

EPSEM (equal probability of selection method) Probability sampling in which every unit in the population has an equal chance of being selected into the sample. See *probability sample*.

epsilon High-low percentage differences between the first and last columns in a *cross tabulation*.

erosion measures Unobtrusive measures of wear or use.

ethnography The observational description of a people or some other social unit.

evaluation research Research to measure the effectiveness of a social program or institution.

exhaustive categories Categories that cover all the potential range of variation in a variable.

existing statistics Created statistical data that are available to researchers for analysis.

experiment A research method that seeks to isolate the effects of an independent variable on a dependent variable under strictly controlled conditions.

experimental group The group in an experiment that is exposed to the experimental treatment. See *control group*.

experimental mortality Loss of subjects in an experiment over time. This is a potential cause of *internal validity* problems.

explanation In the elaboration paradigm when a test variable is antecedent in time to both the independent and dependent variables, if the bivariate relationship weakens under every condition of the test variable, it can be claimed that the test variable has explained the relationship of the independent to the dependent variables. See *elaboration paradigm*.

ex post facto design   An after-only evaluation research design where pretesting is not possible.

external validity   The generalizability of an experiment to other settings, other treatments, other subjects.

face-to-face interview   A method of administering a survey in which an interviewer questions an interviewee using a structured set of questions. See *interview schedule*.

face validity   A form of *content validity;* a careful consideration and examination of the measurement instrument is made in order to determine whether the instrument is measuring what it purports to measure (sometimes called armchair validity).

factorial design   The design of an experiment in which more than one independent variable is being measured.

feminist theory   As applied to the practice of social research, feminist theory attests to women's contributions to a range of types of research, questions whether some research methods are biased against women, and seeks an improvement in the development and practice of research methods which are favorable to the study of women.

field experiment   An experiment taking place in a real-world environment, where it is more difficult to impose controls.

field research   A research method based on careful observation of behavior in a natural social environment.

first-order table   Another name for a trivariate table in which one variable is cross-referenced by two other variables indicating a higher level analysis. See *zero-order table, trivariate table*.

focus group   A small group of individuals drawn together to express views on a specific set of questions in a group environment. This method may serve a number of functions in social research: as a starting point for developing a survey, to recognize potential problems in a research design, or to interpret evidence.

focused coding   After open coding when themes in the fieldnotes have been formulated, another pass through the notes can identify patterns and lead to narrower subcodes of the original open codes.

follow-up procedures   The methods of following up nonrespondents to mail questionnaires to increase *response rate*. Methods include sending postcard reminders, sending second questionnaires and requests, and telephoning to solicit cooperation or to get the responses over the telephone.

formative evaluation   An evaluation of a program in process, information from which will be used to reform or improve the program. See *summative evaluation*.

frequency distribution   The distribution of cases across the categories of a variable, presented in numbers and percentages.

frequency polygon   A graph, representing the same data from numerical variables as a histogram, which substitutes the midpoints of each histogram bar with dots which are then connected with lines to indicate the shape of the distribution. See *histogram* and *bar graph*.

full disclosure   The practice of making all evidence generated and analyzed in the course of scientific research available to the relevant scientific community. This means that negative and insignificant findings should be presented as well as positive findings.

gamma (γ)   An extension of the statistic *Yule's Q*, appropriate for ordinal variables.

grounded theory research   Research aimed at building theories through an inductive process, starting with data collection and moving from forming generalizations to developing theories and then returning to the data to verify the theories.

Hawthorne effect   When subjects in an experiment produce the expected experimental effect without being exposed to the experimental treatment (they are affected by merely being in the experiment itself). A Hawthorne control group, exposed to a meaningless treatment, is often added in an experiment.

hired-hand research   Hired research assistants (often interviewers) may not hold the same dedication to carrying out a research project as designed, but may cut corners and not follow the rules for collecting and handling data. To avoid this, researchers should tie hired research assistants closely into the research project to increase their commitment to it.

histogram   A graph depicting the frequency distribution of a numerical variable with bars which have at their centermost point the value being presented. The edge of each bar is halfway to the next value and touches the next bar. See *frequency polygon* and *bar graph*.

historiography   The writing of history, which involves the imaginative reconstruction of the past from the surviving data.

history as actuality   The whole history of the past including what can never be fully known.

history as record   The study of what can be known of the past through the surviving record.

hypotheses   Conditional statements, relating the expected effects of one variable on another, that can be subject to testing.

independent variable   The variable, in an experiment or survey, that exercises an effect on a *dependent variable.*

independent variable study   A study in which one social group or context is compared to another.

index   A composite measure developed to represent different components of a concept.

indicators   Observable phenomena that can be used to measure dimensions of a concept.

inductive method   Reasoning from particular cases to more general theories.

inferences   In probability theory, the object is to be able to make accurate guesses (or inferences) from evidence gathered on a relatively small probability sample to a much larger population. See *inferential statistics* and *probability sample.*

inferential statistics   Statistics that allow a researcher to draw conclusions regarding the general population from the findings of a representative sample drawn from that population.

informed consent   This is achieved when subjects in a research study comprehend its objectives, understand their level of *confidentiality,* and agree to cooperate.

institutional review board   Committees in institutions where scientific research is being carried out who review the research methods to be sure that the rights of human (or animal) subjects are being protected.

interaction effect   The tendency for a third variable to interact with the independent variable, thereby altering the relationship of the independent variable to the dependent variable. This means that the relationship between the independent and dependent variable will vary under different conditions of the third variable.

internal validity   The extent to which an experiment actually has caused what it appeared to cause.

interpretation   In the elaboration paradigm when a test variable is intervening in time between the independent and dependent variables, if the bivariate relationship weakens, it can be claimed that the test variable has interpreted the relationship of the independent to the dependent variables. See *elaboration paradigm.*

intersubjectivity   The shared perceptions of individual observers. The greater the intersubjectivity, the greater the validity and reliability of the observations.

intervening variable   A third variable in a trivariate study that logically falls in a time sequence between the independent and dependent variables.

interview schedule   A set of questions with guided instructions for an interviewer to use in carrying out an interview.

invasion of privacy   A possible abuse in social research, in which rights of privacy have been ignored. Must be weighted in relation to the public's right to know. See *informed consent.*

judgmental sample   A *nonprobability sample* composed of subjects judged to be relevant to the needs of the study.

keying   Ways in which events in the present are linked to particularly meaningful (primary) events in the past.

laboratory experiment   An experiment taking place in a laboratory setting, where it is possible to maintain a large number of controls.

lambda (λ)   A statistical measure of association appropriate for nominal variables.

levels of measurement   There are four commonly defined levels for measuring variables: *nominal,* for distinct categories with no order; *ordinal,* for ordered categories; *interval,* for numerical scales with mathematically defined intervals between points on the scale, but no true zero point; and *ratio,* for numerical scales with mathematically defined intervals and a true zero point.

linear regression   A statistical analysis which represents the best-fit line between two variables. See *best-fit line* and *linear relationship.*

linear relationship   Indicated by a diagonal *best-fit line* in a *scattergram,* a linear relationship shows that an increase (or decrease) in one variable is related to an increase (or decrease) in the other.

longitudinal designs   Studies based on longitudinal data include *trend studies,* in which data are compared across time points on different subjects; *cohort studies,* in which data on subjects from the same age cohort are compared at different points in time; and *panel studies,* in which the same subjects are compared across time points.

mail survey   A survey consisting of a self-administered questionnaire, instructions, and a request for participation sent out through the mail to a selected sample. See *questionnaire*.

manifest content   In content analyses the actual content of material such as words as compared to the latent content which has implicit meaning.

marginals   The row totals that appear to the right of a *cross tabulation* and the column totals that appear at the bottom of each column. They are the base numbers on which the percentages in each cell of the table are calculated.

matching   An experimental procedure in which subjects to be placed in the experimental group are matched with subjects possessing similar characteristics in the control group. This is not equivalent to *randomization in assignment to groups* required for *true experimental designs*.

matrix questions   Sets of questions in a questionnaire that use the same set of response categories.

maturation   A potential cause of internal validity problems in an experiment, due to the subjects getting older between the pre- and posttests, becoming more experienced, more (or less) intelligent, or physically strong.

mean   The arithmetic average determined by adding up the quantities of each unit in a distribution and then dividing by the number of units.

measurement   A process in which numbers are assigned according to rules of correspondence between definitions and observations.

measurement error   Error which is unavoidably introduced into measurement in the process of observing a phenomenon. An observed measure (or score) is therefore based on the true score plus or minus the error. In social research this error may necessarily be great because of the crudity of the instruments used in measuring social phenomena.

median   A measure of central tendency that represents the midpoint in a distribution of ordered data.

member check   Others in a qualitative study are asked to corroborate the findings. This may serve to confirm the findings.

memoing   Forming theoretical explanations and interpretations from fieldnotes. Ideas may be drawn by seeking connection from various observations.

missing data   Computer analyses of data must employ some method to handle missing evidence by flagging cases in which data are absent. For analyzing the data, those cases which have missing data on a variable being examined may be deleted only for those parts of the analysis in which that variable is examined (pairwise deletion) or may be totally deleted from the analysis (listwise deletion).

mode   A measure of central tendency that represents the most frequent value in a distribution.

monotonicity   Steady increases (or decreases) across the cells of a cross tabulation, indicating that an increase (or decrease) in the independent variable is related to an increase (or decrease) in the dependent variable.

multiple methods   Using more than one research method, each with different strengths, to better approximate an ideal method and to create more generalizable evidence so as to better test the theories underlying the research.

multiple regression   A statistical analysis which extends the linear regression model, relating one dependent variable to more than one independent variable. The influence of each independent variable can be computed separately, holding constant the influence of all other independent variables; the relative weights of each independent variable can then be determined. The combined effects of all the independent variables on the dependent variable can also be determined. See *linear regression*.

multistage cluster sampling   A form of *probability sampling* in which clusters are selected first and then members of the clusters are selected at a second stage.

multistage probability sampling   Sampling done in a series of stages beginning with heterogeneous clusters (such as organizations or geographical areas) and later stages in which members of the larger clusters are selected. In every stage, random methods of selection must be employed. See *multistage cluster sampling*.

mutually exclusive categories   Categories of variable that must be distinct from one another.

natural experiment   An experiment that has not been brought about by the efforts of the experimenter, but has naturally occurred in the real world, and is being selected out for study by the experimenter.

needs assessment (NA)   A form of research carried out to determine the types and sources of problems (or needs) being confronted in a social program or activity so that priorities can be set and decisions made to address needs.

negative evidence   In a field study, the nonoccurrence of expected events, an occurrence which is not reacted to, or one which is distorted in its interpretation or withheld from analysis.

negative (inverse) association   A type of relationship between two variables in which cases that are *low* on one variable are *high* on the other. See *positive (direct) association.*

nominal definition   Specifying the meaning and components of a concept in order to study it more rigorously. See *operational definition, real definition.*

nominal group technique (NGT)   A technique used to gather information for a needs assessment from people who might not be comfortable presenting it in a regular group session. The leader is generally drawn from outside the organization. Some meeting formats may be used such as silent brainstorming and circle-in-the-round techniques in which ideas are generated and rank-ordered.

nonequivalent control group   A control group which was not selected on the basis of random assignment. Usually created as a rough comparison group to participants in a social intervention program being evaluated. See *ex post facto design.*

nonprobability sample   A sample based on a method for selecting nonprobability sample subjects that is not based on the rules of probability.

nonsampling error   Mistakes in the data due to errors such as those caused by respondents' misunderstandings, the interviewer's incorrect entries, or faulty transcribing of the data by coders. See *sampling error.*

normal curve   A frequency curve with a characteristic bell-shaped form. The distributions of continuous variables approach this curve as samples are repeated or as sample sizes increase.

null hypothesis   A logical assumption that there is no relationship between the two variables being studied in the population. This assumption can be tested with *inferential statistics.*

numerical variables   Variables measured on a numerical scale.

observation   The primary work of science. In social research, various methods are used to facilitate observation for its measurement, recording, and analysis.

ongoing evaluation   Evaluation research carried out over the course of a social intervention program to assess its progress while in operation. See *preprogram evaluation.*

open coding   Post-observation in-depth reading of fieldnotes in order to formulate and identify ideas and themes.

open-ended question   Question in a questionnaire that allows the respondent to answer in his or her own words.

operational definition   Specifying ways to measure a concept once it has been fully theoretically defined. See *real definition, nominal definition.*

operationalization   The process of figuring out how to measure *concepts* using empirical evidence.

oral history   History based on verbal accounts instead of written records.

original relationship   The bivariate relationship representing the base-level association between a dependent variable and an independent variable. See *partial relationship* and *bivariate table.*

panel studies   Based on a longitudinal study design in which the same group of respondents is followed up over time for comparative purposes.

paradigm   The set of presuppositions on which scientific activity is built; the body of theories, ideas, models, test cases, and values shared by a scientific community; and the specific scientific accomplishments (exemplars) that influence future scientific activity.

parameters   The true values of population characteristics, which may only be inferred from the descriptions of these values in a sample.

partial relationship   The relationship of two variables for the partial group category of a third variable.

participatory action research (PAR)   A form of action research carried out in communities or organizations that are trying to overcome negative or oppressive conditions. See *action research.*

participant observation   A method of doing *field research* in which the researcher participates in a role in the field (for example, as a consultant) at the same time as the field observations are being collected.

Pearson's r   Referred to also as a *correlation coefficient* or more formally as *Pearson's product-moment correlation;* it is a statistical measure of the strength and direction of relationships between interval scale variables.

phenomenological research   Research aimed at describing the social world more validly. Includes research emphasizing interaction, its symbolic importance, and attempts to uncover the rules which govern human interaction, referred to as ethnomethodology. See *symbolic interaction theory, verstehen.*

physical traces   *Unobtrusive measures* which include the examination of unintentional erosion and accretion of products of human origin or endeavor.

plagiarism   The incorporation of the work of one person into the presentation of work of another, without citing the source.

population The collection of all elements (either known or unknown) from which a sample is drawn. In a *probability sample,* the population consists of the *elements* in the *sampling frame.*

positive (direct) association A type of relationship between two variables in which cases that are *high* on one variable tend to be *high* on the other, and cases that are *low* on one variable tend to be *low* on the other. See *negative (inverse) association.*

positivist One who strives to accumulate facts as the sole means of establishing explanations.

posttest In an experiment, measuring the effect of the experimental treatment. The results are often compared to a *pretest.*

postmodern theory Rejects scientific model, focuses on individual cases and interpreting the contradictory narratives (discourses) that shape their meaning. One form, deconstructionism, claims that the world can not be apprehended outside of language which is always ambiguous and changing.

posttest-only control group design A more streamlined *true experimental design* in which neither the experimental nor the control group is subject to a pretest and both are administered a posttest.

predictive validity A form of criterion-related validity in which the measure being examined is correlated with a criterion which the measure should predict. See the example given in *criterion-related validity.*

predictor variable Another name for the *independent variable;* it is the variable on which a prediction can be based. See *criterion variable.*

preexperimental designs These are experimental designs that do not meet all the criteria for a true experiment. They include the one-shot case study, the one-group pretest-posttest design, and the static-group comparison.

preprogram evaluation Evaluation research initiated before a social intervention program is established to anticipate possible effects of the program. See *ongoing evaluation.*

pretest A base-line measure in an experiment that can be compared with the postexperimental treatment test, the *posttest.*

pretesting A strongly recommended procedure in survey research in which the instrument is given to trial subjects.

primary sampling unit In a sample to be drawn in more than one stage, the primary sampling units are the groups specified (*strata* or *clusters*) to be drawn

first, the *secondary sampling unit,* the units to be drawn second, etc.

primary sources Written materials historians use based on records of eyewitnesses to events.

probability proportionate to size (PPS) sampling A selection method used in cluster sampling to select strata within clusters that are proportionate to their size.

probability sample A sample designed according to the rules of probability, which allows a determination of how likely the members of the sample are to be representative of the population from which they were drawn.

proportionate reduction of error (PRE) A ratio of the number of prediction errors when the researcher has no information about the independent variable to the prediction errors when the researcher has information about the independent variable. See *lambda.*

proposal See *research proposal.*

purposive sample A form of *nonprobability sample* in which the subjects selected seem to meet the proposed needs of the study.

qualitative data Data collected from a qualitative research project generally from notes from observations, the reading of written materials, or from interviews. Such data are not generally summarized by numbers or analyzed with statistics.

qualitative research Research designs that are naturalistic and open. Often based on observation in a real-life field and/or intensive interviewing and analysis of written documents. See *action research, case studies, field research, grounded theory, phenomenological research.*

quantitative data Data from quantitative research which is aggregated from multiple cases, computerized, and subject to numerical summarizations and statistical analyses.

quantitative research Research designs such as surveys and experiments in which the findings can be reduced to numerical summaries. See *experiment, survey research.*

quasi-experimental designs Experimental designs where some experimental conditions required for a true experiment (often the *randomization in assignment* of subjects to groups) cannot be carried out. See *regression discontinuity* and *time-series experiment.*

questionnaire A written set of questions used to survey respondents. See *mail survey.*

quota sample A form of nonprobability sample in which subsamples are selected from clearly defined groups.

random-digit dialing (RDD) A computerized method of selecting telephone numbers randomly for a telephone survey.

random measurement error Measurement errors incurred in the process of observing phenomena. Because some of the errors will be higher than the true measure and some lower, over an infinite number of repeated measures such errors would cancel one another out. See *classical test theory.*

random numbers Sets of randomly determined numbers generated from a computer program or from a published random number list. See *simple random sampling (SRS).*

randomization in assignment to groups Procedures for placing subjects randomly in the experimental or control group in a true experiment.

range The distance between the highest and lowest point (the minimum and maximum value) in a distribution of cases.

real definition Philosophical effort to capture the ultimate or essential nature of an actual phenomenon. See *nominal definition, operational definition.*

recoding variables One of the most common forms of manipulating variables on a computer so as to reduce (or increase) the number of codes by combining, resorting, or re-ordering the categories of a variable.

reductionism The tendency to reduce complex social phenomena to a single cause. A common example is psychological reductionism, which uses individual personality traits to explain the behavior of groups.

regression discontinuity A *quasi-experimental design* usually set up to study the effects of a program or treatment on a group that needs and gets it, as compared with a group that does not.

regularities Repeated patterns seen in data.

reliability The degree to which a measurement procedure produces similar outcomes when it is repeated. Tests for reliability include measures of stability (test-retest reliability) and measures of equivalence.

replication The repeating of a research design in order to test whether the same findings can be generated. The precision of experiments enables them to be replicated.

research proposal The written plan to guide a research project.

response In an experiment, the effect that is produced by the experimental stimulus. Equivalent to the *dependent variable.*

response rate The proportion of the sample that returns questionnaires. Response rates for mail questionnaires can be increased by using *follow-up procedures.*

response set The tendency in answering a survey to give the same responses to different questions. This can be reduced by switching the positive and negative direction of the response choices.

rights of human subjects The right of subjects of research to be protected from physical or psychological abuse and to be helped to maintain their privacy and their good reputations.

role-ordered display Graphic presentation in which role players and their characteristics and reactions to a situation are cross-referenced in a matrix.

r squared (r^2) Also called the *coefficient of determination.* The square of *Pearson's r.* It denotes the proportion of variance in the dependent variable that can be explained by the independent variable (or the amount of *variance* explained by the linear model).

running descriptions These are types of field notes that include concrete descriptions of events, people, statements, and conversations seen and heard in the field.

sample A set of selected subjects for study drawn according to some principles of sampling.

sampling distribution mean This is the distribution of means from repeated samples from the same population. The greater the number of samples drawn, the more closely this distribution approximates a normal curve.

sampling error In a *probability sample,* this is the variability of a mean of the sample from the mean of the population. See *nonsampling error.*

sampling frame A list of all the *elements* in a population from which a *probability sample* may be drawn.

sampling interval Needs to be defined for systematic sampling. Is equal to the population size divided by the desired size of the sample. See *systematic sampling.*

sampling ratio The proportion of the members of the population that will be selected. Is equal to the sample size divided by the population size.

sampling validity A form of testing for the *content validity* of the measure of a concept by looking to see if the measure includes a fair representation (or sample) of the various domains of meaning within the concept.

scale A composite measure of a concept, based on some aspect of the *intensity structure* of the interrelationships between items in the scale.

scattergram A graph on which the values of one variable measured on the vertical axis have been plotted in relationship to the values on the other variable on the horizontal axis. See *best-fit line*.

scientific ethos   Norms or institutional imperatives governing the behavior of scientists which protect the integrity of the scientific enterprise. Merton defined four primary norms: universalism, communism, disinterestedness, and organized skepticism.

scientific model   Includes theories and observations, generalizations, and specifications. See *deductive method* and *inductive method*.

secondary analysis   A research method in which data from an earlier study (often a survey) are used as the basis for a new study.

sampling ratio   The proportion of the members of the population that will be selected. Is equal to the sample size divided by the population size.

secondary sampling unit   In a sample to be drawn in more than one stage, the secondary sampling units (strata or clusters) to be drawn second. See *primary sampling unit*.

secondary sources   Written materials which describe or interpret some past event either close to the time it occurred or in later years.

serendipity factor   A term used to describe the unanticipated ways in which tests of hypotheses from one theory can sometimes lead to the development of quite unrelated theories.

simple random sampling (SRS)   A method of *probability sampling* in which *elements* in a *sampling frame* are numbered and then drawn into the sample if they match the *random numbers* selected from a random number list.

skew   Assymetry in the distribution of data, or the degree to which the distribution is not evenly spread around the central point.

snowball sample   A form of nonprobability sample in which the researcher selects a few subjects who possess the qualities being studied, then asks these subjects to generate the names of others, who are in turn asked to generate names of others.

social desirability   The tendency of respondents to respond to potentially threatening (sensitive) questions in such a way as to make themselves look better.

social indicators   Measures of aggregate social conditions that are of interest to a society as a way of evaluating the overall state of that society.

Solomon four-group design   The most comprehensive type of *true experimental design* in which both experimental and control groups are pretested and posttested.

special population study   A study (usually based on qualitative data) the primary aim of which is to develop a careful description of a special population.

specification   In the elaboration paradigm when a test variable specifies the conditions in which the bivariate relationship strengthens and weakens, the test variable has specified the relationship of the independent to the dependent variables. See *elaboration paradigm*.

sponsorship   Financial or official support for research often received from organizations, agencies, or foundations. It is important to make this sponsorship known in the cover letter of a questionnaire or in an interview.

spurious relationship   A strong relationship between two variables that disappears when the relationship is examined under the controlled conditions of a third variable. This means that the unseen influence of the third variable caused the original strong relationship between the dependent and independent variables.

standard deviation   The square root of the variance; this commonly used measure indicates the degree of *dispersion* of all the values in a distribution from the mean value.

standard error (SE)   A statistical measure indicating how closely the mean from one sample represents its population mean. It is the standard deviation of the sampling distribution mean.

standpoint theory   Rejects the perspective that a researcher can stand outside a subject and study it value-free without biases. Instead researchers need to develop their own standpoints from their own lived experience.

statistical regression   The tendency in an experiment for those scoring at the extremes in the pretest to move to more middle-range scores on the posttest. This occurs because the extreme scores are more subject to error than the middle-range scores. It can cause a problem of *internal validity* in an experiment because the greater change in the scores of the extreme scorers may be falsely registered as an effect of the experimental treatment.

statistical significance   The likelihood that the magnitude of the statistical association shown in a sample would be found consistently if repeated samples were drawn from the same population. In other words, the likelihood that the association observed is not the result of chance or error.

statistics   Tools allowing summary descriptions of large bodies of data. When data are from probability samples, statistics can be used to estimate corresponding population parameters. See *descriptive statistics* and *inferential statistics*.

stimulus   In an experiment this is the *independent variable,* designed to bring about a *response.*

strata   The homogeneous groups selected from which a *stratified sample* will be drawn.

stratified sample   A form of probability sampling in which a *sampling frame* is divided into one or more *strata* (sex, grade) from which the sample is drawn using simple random or systematic sampling strategies.

strength of relationship   The degree of relationship between the two variables in a bivariate analysis.

structural-functionalism   A theory emphasizing how societies develop norms to hold themselves together which form how the society is structured (e.g., its division of labor) and its cultural practices (e.g., its religion).

subgroup comparisons   When the independent variable represents a group to which the subjects belong, the object of the analysis can be a comparison of the differences in the dependent variable between the subgroups.

summative evaluation   A type of evaluation which summarizes the effects of a program after it is completed. See *formative evaluation.*

suppressor variable   A third variable that strengthens an originally observed weak relationship between two other variables. Controlling this third variable eliminates the suppression.

survey research   A research method that analyzes the responses of a defined sample to a set of questions measuring attitudes and behaviors.

symbolic interaction theory   Focuses on everyday life and how individuals derive meaning from their social interaction with others and with cultural symbols.

systematic sampling   A form of probability sampling in which every *n*th element is selected into the sample, following a random start.

tampering with results   An abuse in scientific research in which results may be altered or fabricated, often to have the evidence match preestablished hypotheses.

telephone survey   A survey administered over the telephone, requiring somewhat different techniques from a mail survey or a face-to-face interview. See *computer-assisted telephone interviewing (CATI)* and *random-digit dialing (RDD).*

test variable   The third variable in a trivariate analysis. A variable under whose conditions the strength of the relationship between the dependent and independent variables can be tested. See *control variable.*

theories   Proposed explanations for a set of coordinated occurrences or relationships.

time-ordered display   A graphic presentation in which time periods are cross-referenced with subjects of study, or critical events in a matrix or flow charts can be developed.

time-series experiment   A quasi-experimental design used when there is a large set of already collected data indicating rates over time. The experimenter examines the effects of an event (e.g., a new law) occurring at some point in time and studies changes in the rates before and after the event.

trend studies   Based on longitudinal study design in which similar data collected in different years (and from different subjects) are compared.

triangulation   Drawing together multiple types of evidence gathered from different sources using different methods of data collection.

trivariate table   A three-variable table.

true experimental designs   These are designs organized in such a way as to meet the criterion for an experiment (that an independent variable be related to change in a dependent variable) and at the same time to address most successfully the potential problems of invalidity. They include the *classical experiment,* the *Solomon four-group design,* and the *posttest-only control group design.*

unit   This is another term for the *elements* in a sample.

units of analysis   The social entities whose characteristics are the focus of study. In social research these may include individuals, groups, programs, organizations and institutions, larger communities (nations), or cultural artifacts.

univariate analysis   Analyses of single variables, such as frequency distributions or analyses of central tendencies, such as mean, median, or mode.

unobtrusive measures   The study of physical traces, archives, and observations without participation, generally used as supplementary sources of data in a research project.

validity   Tests for determining whether a measure is measuring the concept which the researchers think is being measured. See *content validity, criterion-related validity,* and *construct validity.*

variable   A measure on which differences in response can be established.

variance   A way of measuring how far different units which have been used to establish a mean vary from the mean. See *standard deviation*.

verisimilitude   The historian's objective to get as close to approximating the truth as the records and other archival information will allow.

verstehen   The understanding of social action, the objective of field research.

visual sociology   This term refers to a branch of sociology in which social action is studied by photographing or filming social environments and the people who inhabit them.

weighting   A method used in probability sampling to give adequate emphasis to subgroups of disproportionate size or to cancel out the effects of differential response rates.

Yule's Q   A statistical measure of association appropriate for 2×2 cross-classification tables.

zero-order table   Another term for a bivariate table indicating that one variable is being cross-referenced with only one other variable at the lowest or most basic level. See *first-order table, bivariate table*.

INDEX